HOSEA

VOLUME 24

THE ANCHOR BIBLE is a fresh approach to the world's greatest classic. Its object is to make the Bible accessible to the modern reader; its method is to arrive at the meaning of biblical literature through exact translation and extended exposition, and to reconstruct the ancient setting of the biblical story, as well as the circumstances of its transcription and the characteristics of its transcribers.

THE ANCHOR BIBLE is a project of international and interfaith scope: Protestant, Catholic, and Jewish scholars from many countries contribute individual volumes. The project is not sponsored by any ecclesiastical organization and is not intended to reflect any particular theological doctrine. Prepared under our joint supervision, THE ANCHOR BIBLE is an effort to make available all the significant historical and linguistic knowledge which bears on the interpretation of the biblical record.

THE ANCHOR BIBLE is aimed at the general reader with no special formal training in biblical studies, yet, it is written with the most exacting standards of scholarship, reflecting the highest technical accomplishment.

This project marks the beginning of a new era of co-operation among scholars in biblical research, thus forming a common body of knowledge to be shared by all.

William Foxwell Albright
David Noel Freedman
GENERAL EDITORS

THE ANCHOR BIBLE

HOSEA

A New Translation
with
Introduction and Commentary

Francis I. Andersen
and
David Noel Freedman

DOUBLEDAY & COMPANY, INC.
GARDEN CITY, NEW YORK
1980

Library of Congress Cataloging in Publication Data

Bible. O.T. Hosea. English. Andersen-Freedman. 1980.
Hosea, a new translation with introduction and
commentary.

(The Anchor Bible; v. 24)
Bibliography: p. 79.
Includes index.
1. Bible. O.T. Hosea—Commentaries.
I. Andersen, Francis I., 1925– II. Freedman,
David Noel, 1922– III. Title. IV. Series:
Anchor Bible; v. 24.
BS192.2.A1 1964.G3 vol. 24 [BS1565.3] 220.7′7s [224′.6′077]
ISBN: 0-385-00768-X
Library of Congress Catalog Card Number 73–9008

To the Memory
of our teacher
William Foxwell Albright

PREFACE

This is the first of five volumes on the Book of the Twelve Prophets and with the companion, second volume of the group, on Amos and Micah, has been underway for a decade. Andersen will write two further volumes with six further minor prophets: Joel, Obadiah, and Jonah in the first; and, in the second, Nahum, Habakkuk, and Zephaniah. Carol and Eric Meyers of Duke University are preparing a commentary on Haggai, Zechariah, and Malachi.

We began work on these volumes while we were members of the Graduate Theological Union at Berkeley, Andersen serving on the faculty of the Church Divinity School of the Pacific and Freedman on the faculty of San Francisco Theological Seminary. We continued to collaborate by correspondence and during periods of study at the Albright Institute of Archaeological Research (AIAR) in Jerusalem, and at The University of Michigan in Ann Arbor. We acknowledge the support of these institutions, and of Macquarie University, where Andersen now teaches; the Australian Institute of Archaeology for aid to Andersen; and the American Council of Learned Societies, for aid to Freedman.

Scholarly succor has been abundant. Freedman has several times discussed Hosea with the members of the Biblical Colloquium, whom he thanks; and Andersen has profited from collaboration with Dean Forbes, of Palo Alto, California, in computer studies of the Hebrew Bible. Leona Running, of Andrews University in Berrien Springs, Michigan, typed the manuscript with the competence only a Semitist could bring to bear. M. O'Connor, of Doubleday and The University of Michigan, edited the manuscript and made an honest effort not to be hedged in with thornbushes and walled in with a wall (Hos 2:8).

FRANCIS I. ANDERSEN
North Ryde, New South Wales
DAVID NOEL FREEDMAN
Ann Arbor, Michigan

St. Andrew's Day, 1978

CONTENTS

PART II. HOSEA'S PROPHECIES

LIST OF ILLUSTRATIONS

ABBREVIATIONS

ASV	*American Standard Version*
B.C.E.	Before the Common Era
BH³	*Biblia Hebraica*³
BHS	*Biblia Hebraica Stuttgartensia*
BJ	*Bible de Jérusalem*
c(c)	chapter(s)
cg	common gender
C.E.	Common Era
conj.	conjunction
f	feminine gender
JB	*Jerusalem Bible*
KJV	*Authorized Version*
LXX	Septuagint
LXXᴸ	Lucianic recension
LXXᴮ	Vaticanus
m	masculine gender
MT	Masoretic Text
n	note
NAB	*New American Bible*
NEB	*New English Bible*
neg.	negative
pl	plural
1QapGn	*The Genesis Apocryphon of Qumran Cave I* (Fitzmyer 1971)
1QH	*The Psalms* (*Hodayot*) *of Qumran Cave I* (Mansoor 1961)
RSV	*Revised Standard Version*
RV	*Revised Version*
s	singular
Sam	Samaritan Pentateuch
*	unattested form (not used on citation forms)

HOSEA
A Translation

PART I. HOSEA'S MARRIAGE

I. *Title and Hosea's Wife and the Naming and Renaming of the Children (1:1–2:3)*

1:1 Title

1 ¹The word of Yahweh which came to Hosea ben-Beeri in the era of Uzziah, Jotham, Ahaz, Hezekiah, the kings of Judah, and the era of Jeroboam ben-Joash, the king of Israel.

1:2–2:3 Hosea's wife and the naming and renaming of the children

1:2 The divine imperative

²At the beginning, when Yahweh spoke with Hosea, then Yahweh said to Hosea: "Go, take for yourself a promiscuous wife and children of promiscuity, for the land has been promiscuous away from Yahweh."

3–5 Jezreel

³So he went and took as his wife Gomer bat-Diblaim; then she conceived and bore him a son. ⁴Yahweh said to him, "Call his name Jezreel: for in a little while I shall surely punish the dynasty of Jehu for the blood shed at Jezreel, and I shall put an end to its rule over the state of Israel. ⁵It will happen on that day that I will break Israel's bow in the Jezreel Valley."

6–7 Lo-Ruhama

⁶Then she conceived again and bore a daughter. He said to him, "Call her name Lo-Ruhama, because I — as Yahweh their God — never again shall I show pity for the state of Israel, or forgive them at all; ⁷nor for the state of Judah will I show pity, or save them. I will not save them from bow and sword and weapons of war, from horses and horsemen."

8–9 Lo-Ammi

⁸When she had weaned Lo-Ruhama, she conceived and bore a son. ⁹He said, "Call his name Lo-Ammi, for you are not my people, and I am not Ehyeh to you."

2:1–3 The great day of Jezreel: the restoration of Israel and the reversal of names

2 ¹Then it will happen that the number of the Israelites will be like the sands of the sea, which cannot be measured and cannot be counted. And it will happen in the place where it was said to them, "You are not my people," it will be said to them, "(You are) children of the Living God." ²The Judahites and the Israelites will gather themselves together, and they will appoint for themselves one head, and they will come up from the land. How great is the day, O Jezreel — ³you will say to your brothers, Ammi, and to your sisters, Ruhama.

II. *Defection and Retribution: Reconciliation and Renewal*
(2:4–25)

Desertion and discipline

   The dissolute behavior of the wife
4   "Argue with your mother, argue
         — for she is not my wife
         and I am not her husband —
      so that she remove her promiscuity from her face
      and her adultery from between her breasts
5   lest I strip her naked,
            and set her out as on the day of her birth,
         lest I treat her as in the wilderness,
            and deal with her as in the arid land
            by killing her with thirst."
6   To her children I shall not show pity
         because they are children of promiscuity.
7   Indeed, their mother was promiscuous,
         the one who conceived them behaved shamefully
         for she said, "Let me go after my lovers
            who provide me with my bread and my water,

> my wool and my flax,
> my oil and my liquor."

The hoped-for repentance

8   Therefore, behold, I will hedge in your way with thornbushes,
> and I will wall (her) in with its wall,
> so that she cannot find her pathways.

9   When she pursues her lovers,
> she will not overtake them.
When she seeks them,
> she will not find (them).
Then she may say,
> "Let me go and return to my first husband,
> because it was better for me then than it is now."

The punishment and consequences

10   As for her, she didn't know
that it was I who provided her
with grain and must and oil,
that I lavished silver upon her,
and gold which they made into a Baal.

11   Therefore I will reverse myself
and take back my grain in its time
and my must in its season;
and I will rescue my wool and my flax
to uncover her nakedness.

12   Now I will expose her lewdness in the sight of her lovers
but no one will rescue her from my power.

13   I shall put an end to all her merriment—
her annual, monthly and weekly celebrations—
all her assemblies.

14   I shall lay waste her vines and her fig trees.
Those of whom she said,
> "They are my wages, which my lovers paid me,"
> I shall consign them to the jungle,
> and wild animals of the countryside will devour them.

15   So shall I punish her for the time of the Baals
to whom she burns incense

when she decked herself with nose ring and necklace
and went after her lovers — but me she forgot.
Oracle of Yahweh.

Renewal and restoration

The new exodus

16   Therefore, behold, I am going to entice her.
I will lead her through the wilderness
and speak intimately to her.

17   Then I will assign to her there her vineyards
and the Valley of Achor as a doorway of hope.
May she respond there as in the time of her youth,
as on the day she came up from the land of Egypt.

The end of Baal worship

18   It will happen on that day — Oracle of Yahweh —
you will call me Ishi
and you will never again call me Baali.

19   I shall remove the names of the Baals from her mouth;
never again will they be mentioned by their names.

Covenant and betrothal

20   I shall make for them a covenant on that day
with the wild animals of the countryside
and with the birds of the sky
and the reptiles of the ground.
Bow and sword and weapons of war
I shall destroy from the land.
I shall make them lie down in safety.

21   I shall betroth you to me forever.
I shall betroth you to me
with righteousness and with justice,
and with mercy and with pity.

22   I shall betroth you to me in faithfulness.
Then you shall know Yahweh.

Consummation: the great chorus

23   It will happen on that day
I will respond — Oracle of Yahweh —

> I will respond to the skies
> and they will indeed respond to the earth.

24   The earth will respond to the grain and must and oil
> and they themselves will respond to Jezreel.

25   Then I shall sow her to me in the land
> and I will have pity on Lo-Ruhama
> and I will say to Lo-Ammi, "You are my people,"
> and he will say, "My God."

III. *Hosea and the Woman* (3:1–5)

The recovery of Hosea's wife

3 ¹Then Yahweh said to me once more: "Go love the woman who is beloved of another and an adulteress, just as Yahweh loves the Israelites, although they are turning to other gods and are lovers of raisin cakes." ²So I procured her for myself with fifteen shekels of silver, and a homer of barley, and a letek of barley. ³Then I said to her: "For many days you will wait for me. You will not be promiscuous and you shall not belong to a man. Then indeed I will be yours."

Israel: repentance and restoration

⁴For many days the Israelites will wait, without king and without prince, without sacrifices and without cult pillars, without ephod and teraphim. ⁵Afterwards, the Israelites will return and seek Yahweh their God and David their king. And they will come trembling to Yahweh and his goodness at the end of the age.

PART II: HOSEA'S PROPHECIES

THE STATE OF THE NATION

IV. *Preface* (4:1–3)

Hosea addresses all Israel

4:1a Hear the word of Yahweh, Israelites.

  1b Indeed Yahweh has a dispute with the inhabitants of the land
      For there is no integrity and no mercy and no knowledge of
          God in the land.

  2a Swearing, lying, murdering, stealing, committing adultery,

  2b They break out — blood everywhere — and they strike down.

  3a Therefore the land dries up
      and all its inhabitants are enfeebled.

  3b Along with the wild animals and birds of the sky and even
        fish of the sea, they are swept away.

V. *Priest and People* (4:4–19)

A chief priest rebukes Hosea

4:4a Let no one dispute,
        let no one debate.

Hosea replies. The word of Yahweh to the priest

  4b My contention is indeed with you, priest.

  5a You will stumble by day
        and the prophet will stumble with you by night

  5b   and I will ruin your mother.

  6a My people are ruined for lack of the knowledge.
      Because you have rejected the knowledge,
        I will reject you from being priest to me.

  6b You have forgotten your God's instruction —
        I will forget your children.

The actions of the chief priest's children

7a   As they grew proud, so they sinned against me.

7b   Their Glory they exchanged for Ignominy.

8a   The sin-offering of my people they devour

8b   and toward their iniquity-offering they lift their throats.

Yahweh's principle

9a   It shall be: Like the people, like the priest.

9b   I shall punish each for his conduct,
      I shall requite each for his deeds.

The chief priest's children's fate

10a   They have eaten, but will not be satisfied.
      They have been promiscuous, but will not increase.

The actions of the chief priest

10b   For they have deserted Yahweh.

11a   He holds to promiscuity through wine.

11b   Through must he takes away my people's heart.

12a   He makes inquiry of his Wood
      And his Staff reports to him.

12b   By a promiscuous spirit he has led them astray.
     They act promiscuously in defiance of their God.

The actions of the chief priest's children
      Male

13a   On mountain tops they make sacrifice
      and on high peaks they burn incense.
      Female

13b   Under oaks, poplars, and terebinths, whose shade is good,
     Because your daughters are promiscuous
      and your daughters-in-law commit adultery

14a   I will punish your daughters because they are promiscuous
      and your daughters-in-law because they commit adultery.
      Male

14b   They segregate themselves with sacred prostitutes
      and make sacrifices with sacred prostitutes.
     A people without discernment will be ruined.

Oaths and actions forbidden the people
The forbidden oaths

15a   "You, Israel, are not a prostitute."
"Let Judah not be held guilty."
The prohibitions

15b   Don't go to Gilgal.
Don't go up to Beth Awen.
Don't swear "As Yahweh lives!"

The results of the chief priest's action: Israel and Ephraim in apostasy

16a   Indeed like a rebellious cow
    Israel has rebelled.

16b   Now Yahweh will shepherd them.
  Like lambs in a wide pasture

17a   Ephraim has been joined to idols.

17b   He has abandoned them for himself.

18a   He has turned aside from their drunkenness.

The actions of the chief priest's children

18b   They have been promiscuous,
    they have made love continually.
He has constrained the Ignominy, with its shields,

19a   her lustful spirit, with its wings.

19b   They have behaved shamefully at their altars.

VI. *The Leaders' Profanity* (5:1–7)

An address to the leaders

5:1a   Hear this, priests!
    Pay attention, house of Israel!
    House of the king, give heed!

1b   This verdict applies to you.
    You have become a trap for Mizpah
      and a net spread on Tabor.

2a   The rebels are deep in slaughter.

2b   I am a chastisement to them all.

The effects of their sins

3a I know you, Ephraim.
   Israel cannot hide from me.
3b Now you, Ephraim, have been promiscuous.
   You, Israel, are defiled.

A description of the leaders

4a Their deeds do not permit them to return to their God.
4b A promiscuous spirit is in their midst
   and Yahweh they do not know.

Further effects of their sins

5a Israel's pride will testify against it.
5b Israel and Ephraim will stumble in their iniquity.
   Judah will stumble with them.
6a With their flocks and herds they will go to seek Yahweh.
6b But they will not find him. He has withdrawn from them.
7a Against Yahweh they have been traitorous.
   They have engendered foreign children.
7b Now he will eat their property at the New Moon.

VII. *The Nation's Politics* (5:8–11)

The alarums of war

5:8a Blow horns in Gibeah,
        trumpets in Ramah!
8b Rouse alarms in Beth Awen:
   "We are behind you, Benjamin!"

The background of the war and its effects

9a Ephraim, you will be a desolation on the day of accusation.
9b Among the tribes of Israel I have made that known
   with certainty.
10a The princes of Judah are like those who move boundary
    stones.
10b Over them I will pour my fury like the waters of the flood.
11a Ephraim will be oppressed. He will be crushed in judgment.
11b He has persistently gone off after Filth.

VIII. *Assyria and Yahweh's Sentence* (5:12–15)

Yahweh as the vermin of the people's open sores

5:12a   I am like larvae in Ephraim
12b   and like decay in the house of Judah.
13a   Ephraim saw his wound
                and Judah his oozing infection.
           Ephraim went to Assyria
                and (Judah) sent to the Great King.
13b   But he cannot heal you,
                and he cannot cure the infection of either of you.

Yahweh as the ravisher of his people

14a   I am like a lion for Ephraim
                and like a young lion for the house of Judah.
14b   I, yes I, will rip them to pieces.
           I will go and carry them off.
           No one will rescue them.
15a   I will go and return to my lair.
15b   When they realize they are guilty
           they will seek my favor.
           When they are distressed
           They will search hard for me.

IX. *Israel's Repentance* (6:1–3)

The people speak

6:1a   Come, let us return to Yahweh.
1b   Although he tore us apart, he will heal us.
                Although he smashed us, he will bandage us.
2a   He will revive us after two days,
                and on the third day he will raise us up.
2b   We will live in his presence so that we know him.
3a   We will pursue knowledge of Yahweh.
           His utterance is as certain as sunrise.
3b   He will come like rain for us.
                Like spring rain he will water the earth.

X. *Yahweh's Sentence* (6:4–6)

Yahweh speaks

6:4a How shall I deal with you, Ephraim?
   How shall I deal with you, Judah?

 4b Your mercy passes away like a morning cloud,
   and like early dew it passes away.

 5a That is why I hacked them with my prophets;
   I killed them with the words of my mouth.

 5b My judgment goes forth like the sun.

 6a For I desire mercy rather than sacrifice

 6b   and the knowledge of God rather than offerings.

XI. *The Priests' Crimes* (6:7 – 7:2)

Priestly crime in open country

6:7a They, as at Adam, broke the covenant;

 7b   there they practiced deception against me.

 8a In Gilead is the city of evildoers,

 8b   a deceitful city, because of bloodshed.

 9a Those who lay in wait, bands of men,
   gangs of priests,

 9b Committed murder on the Shechem road.
   They have perpetrated enormities.

National defilement

 10a In the house of Israel I have seen disgusting things.

 10b There Ephraim has promiscuity,
   Israel is defiled.

 11a Judah also—he set a harvest for you.

 11b When I restore the fortunes of my people,

7:1a   when I bring healing to Israel,
   Then Ephraim's iniquity will be uncovered
   and Samaria's wicked acts.
   They have manufactured an idol.

Priestly crime in the city

 1b A gang of thieves will come.
   A gang of thieves will mug (people) in the streets.

2a They do not speak honestly
>   but all their wickedness I have remembered.
2b Now their deeds surround them.
>   They are right in front of me.

XII. *Domestic Policies* (7:3–7)

A priestly attack on the court

7:3a In their wickedness they made the king rejoice,
3b   and in their wily schemes, the princes.
4a All of them are adulterers;
>   they are like a burning oven.
4b The baker ceases to be alert,
>   to knead the dough until it's leavened.
5a By day they made our king ill,
>   the princes, with poisoned wine.
5b He stretched out his hand with scoffers.
6a When they drew near,
>   their heart was like an oven.
>   During their ambush all night long
6b   their baker slept until morning.
>   It was burning like a blazing flame.
7a All of them became heated like an oven.
>   Then they devoured their judges.
7b   All their kings fell down.
>   Not one of them calls on me.

XIII. *International Politics* (7:8–16)

Ephraim: raw food, rotten food

7:8a Ephraim—he is mixed up with the nations.
8b   Ephraim has become an unturned cake.
9a Foreigners have eaten away his strength,
>   but he has not realized it.
9b Mold is sprinkled upon him,
>   but he has not realized it.
10a The pride of Israel will testify against him.
10b They have not returned to Yahweh their God.
>   They have not sought him in all this.

Ephraim: a dumb dove
11a   Ephraim became like a silly brainless dove.
11b   They called to Egypt,
            they went to Assyria.
12a   As they have certainly gone to Assyria —
            I will spread my net over them.
12b   Like birds of the skies I will bring them down.
         So I will chastise them according to report of their treaties.

Ephraim wanders from Yahweh
13a   Woe to them, for they have wandered away from me.
         Destruction to them, for they have rebelled against me.
13b   Yet I was the one who redeemed them.
            They were the ones who told lies about me.
14a   They did not cry out to me from their hearts.
         They did not shriek from their beds.
14b   For grain and must they lacerate themselves.
            They have departed from me.

Ephraim turns to a no-god
15a   I was the one who trained them;
            I strengthened their arms;
15b   But they plotted evil against me.
16a   They turned to a no-god.
            They became like a slack bow.
16b   Their princes fell by the sword —
         out of the rage of the tongue of the One who mocked them —
         in the land of Egypt.

THE SPIRITUAL HISTORY OF ISRAEL

XIV. *The Calf of Samaria* (8:1–8)

Mutual rejection
8:1a   Like a horn to the mouth!
            Like an eagle over Yahweh's house!
   1b   Because they transgressed my covenant
            and rebelled against my instruction,
   2a   Although they cried out to me,

2b   "God of Israel, we know you!"
3a   The Good One rejects Israel.
3b   As an enemy he will pursue him.

Errors of politics and religion
4a   They made kings, but not from me.
       They made princes, but I did not acknowledge them.
4b   With their silver and gold they made
       idols for themselves.
  So that it will be cut off
5a   he rejects the calf of Samaria —
  My anger is kindled against them.
5b   How long will they be unable to be clean? —
6a   even from Israel.
  As for it, an artisan made it
6b   and it is no god.
  The calf of Samaria will become fragments.

An agricultural curse and a pseudo-sorites
7a   They will sow when it is windy,
       They will reap in a whirlwind.
7b   If it grows, there will be no sproutage on it.
       It will not make meal.
  But if it does make (meal), foreigners will swallow it.
8a   Israel has been swallowed.
8b   Now they have become among the nations
       like a jar that gives no enjoyment.

XV. *Alliances* (8:9–14)

Making alliances and the economic demands
8:9a   Indeed, they have gone up to Assyria. . . .
       Ephraim is a wild ass wandering off alone.
 9b   They have hired lovers.
10a   Indeed, they have hired them among the nations.
       Even now, I will assemble them.
10b   They were contorted in pain a little while ago
       Kings and princes, on account of the tribute.

The religious demands

11a Indeed, Ephraim has behaved arrogantly—

11b He had altars for sin offerings,

12a So I wrote against him altars for sin offerings.

—With arrogance against my instruction.

12b They are considered pagans.

13a Sacrifices of my loved ones they sacrificed.

They ate flesh.

Yahweh does not accept them.

13b Now he keeps track of their iniquity.

He will punish their sins.

. . . They have returned to Egypt.

Closing

14a Israel forgot its maker.

He built palaces.

Judah multiplied them, in fortified cities.

14b So I will send fire into its cities

and it will devour its fortifications.

XVI. *Desolation and Prophecy* (9:1–9)

Promiscuity, starvation, defilement

9:1a Don't rejoice, Israel.

Don't exult like the peoples.

For you have been promiscuous away from your God.

1b You made love for a fee by every threshing floor.

2a Grain—

From threshing floor and wine vat Yahweh will not
nourish them.

2b — and must Yahweh will cause to fail from it.

3a They will not reside in Yahweh's land.

3b Ephraim will return to Egypt.

In Assyria they will eat unclean food.

Deprivation, pollution, isolation

4a They will not pour out their wine as a libation for
Yahweh,

and they will not bring their sacrifices to him.

Indeed, the food of idols is theirs.
All who eat it become unclean.

4b　Indeed, their food was for their life's preservation.
He will not enter Yahweh's house.

5a　How will you celebrate the festival day,

5b　　　Yahweh's assembly day?

Devastation, dispossession, visitation

6a　For behold, they flee from the devastation —
　　　Egypt will collect them.
　　　Memphis will bury them.

6b　— with the best of their silver things.
　　　Weeds will dispossess them,
　　　thorns, from their tents.

7a　The days of visitation have come.
　　　The days of recompense have come.

Prophecy, hostility, memory

7b　Let Israel know —
　　(They say) "The prophet is a fool,
　　　　the man of the Spirit is insane,
　　　　because your iniquity is great,
　　　　and your hostility is great."

8a　The prophet is a watchman of Ephraim with my God,

8b　　　a trap set on all his paths,
　　　hostility in the house of his god.

9a　— that they have deeply defiled themselves
　　　as in the days of Gibeah.

9b　He will remember their iniquity.
　　　He will punish their sins.

XVII. *Baal Peor and Gilgal* (9:10–17)

Past and present

9:10a　O Israel, like grapes
　　　　I found in the wilderness
　　　　I discovered your forebears
　　　like a fig tree's best yield in its first season.

10b　They came to Baal Peor.

They dedicated themselves to Shame.
They became disgusting like the one who loved them.
11a   O Ephraim, like a bird their Glory will fly away.

Curse and indictment
11b   No childbirth. No gestation. No conception.
12a   Even if they raise children,
     I will bereave them before maturity.
12b   Yes! Woe to them also, when I turn from them.
13a   I saw Ephraim as in that place, by the Rival —
     [a fig tree] planted in a meadow
13b   —Ephraim indeed brought his children to the Slayer.

The prophet's prayer
14a   Give them, Yahweh! What will you give?
14b   Give them miscarrying wombs and dry breasts!

Curse and indictment
15a   Because of all their evil in Gilgal
     indeed there I came to hate them.
Because of the wickedness of their deeds,
     I will expel them from my house.
     I will never love them again.
     All their princes are rebels.
16a   Ephraim is smitten.
     Their root has dried up.
     They will never produce fruit.
16b   Yet even if they do have children
     I will murder the darlings of their womb.

The prophet's prediction and the final curse
17a   My God will cast them off
     because they did not obey him.
17b   They will be wanderers among the nations.

XVIII. *Misattribution and Misuse* (10:1–8)

Yahweh's gifts are misunderstood
10:1a   He made Israel, the vine, luxuriant.
     He made it yield fruit for himself.

1b   The more Yahweh multiplied his fruit
          the more Israel multiplied at their altars.
      The richer Yahweh made his land
          the more generous they were to the pillars.

Yahweh is repudiated

2a   Their heart became false.
          Now let them be guilty.
2b   He will wreck their altars,
          he will devastate their pillars.
3a   Now they say,
          "We do not acknowledge a (divine) king.
3b   Indeed, we do not fear Yahweh.
          The (divine) king can do nothing to us."

Yahweh's covenant is violated

4a   They uttered promises.
          They swore falsely.
          They made a covenant.
4b   Judgment flourished like poisonous weeds
          on the furrows of the field.

The false god will go into exile

5a   About the heifers of Beth Awen they are excited
          and about the Resident of Samaria.
5b   His people will indeed mourn over him,
          his idol-priests, over him.
      They will be in agony over His Glory
          because he has gone into exile from it.
6a   He will be brought to Assyria,
          a present for the Great King.

The false god will fail its followers

6b   Ephraim will receive shame.
          Israel will be ashamed of his image.
7a   The king of Samaria has been destroyed,
7b   divine wrath over the waters.
8a   The high places of Awen shall be destroyed,
          the Sin of Israel.

He makes thorns and thistles grow around their altars.
8b   They will say to the mountains, "Cover us!"
        to the hills, "Fall on us!"

XIX. *Gibeah and Beth Arbel* (10:9–15)

Gibeah: war

10:9a   Since the days of Gibeah, you have sinned, Israel.
9b   There they stood —
        Indeed, war overtook them in Gibeah.
                        — beside the Wicked Ones.
10a   When I came, I chastened them.
10b   Armies assembled against them,
                when I chastened them for their double iniquity.

Fieldwork: farming

11a   Ephraim, whom I love, is a heifer trained to thresh.
        I placed upon her neck a fine yoke.
11b   I harnessed Ephraim.
            Let Judah plow.
            Let Jacob harrow for himself.
12a   Sow for yourselves for the sake of righteousness.
            Reap for the sake of mercy.
            Break up for yourselves virgin soil.

Trust and mistrust: farming

12b   It is time to seek Yahweh
                until he comes and rains righteousness for you.
13a   You have plowed iniquity
            Lawlessness you have reaped.
            You have eaten the fruit of lies.

Beth Arbel: war

13b   For you trusted in your power
                and in the large numbers of your crack troops.
14a   Tumult shall rise up from your army.
                All your fortresses will be devastated,
                the way Shalman devastated Beth Arbel.
14b   On the day of war, mothers were dashed to pulp beside
            children.

15a   So may he do to you in Bethel because of your wicked
          wickedness.
15b   When the sun rose, the king of Israel was utterly ruined.

XX. *Childhood and Consummation* (11:1–11)

Childhood: out of slavery in Egypt
11:1a   When Israel was a youth, I loved him.
  1b   From Egypt, I called him "My child."
  2a   They called to them.
          They departed from me.
  2b   They sacrificed to Baals.
          They burned incense to images.
  3a   I was a guide for Ephraim.
          I took from his arms the bonds of men.
  3b   They did not acknowledge that I had healed them,
  4a   That I had drawn them with cords of love on their jaws,
  4b   That I treated them like those who remove the yoke.
          I heeded (his plea) and made (him) prevail.

Consummation: back to slavery in Egypt and Assyria
  5a   He will surely return to the land of Egypt,
          his own king, to Assyria,
  5b   because they refused to return to me.
  6a   The sword will damage his cities.
          It will finish off his strong men.
  6b   It will consume their schemers.
  7a   My people are bent on turning from me.
  7b   They did not call on him as the Supreme God.
          He did not exalt him as the Only One.
  8a   How can I give you up, Ephraim?
          How can I relinquish you, Israel?
      How can I make you like Admah?
          How can I deal with you like Zeboiim?
  8b   My mind is turning over inside me.
          My emotions are agitated all together.
  9a   I will certainly act out my burning anger.
          I will certainly come back to destroy Ephraim.

9b For I am a god and not a human.

> I, the Holy One, will certainly come into the midst of
> your city.

10a Behind Yahweh they will walk.

> Like a lion he will roar.

10b Indeed he himself will roar.

> The children will come trembling from the west.

11a They will come trembling like a bird from Egypt,

> like a dove from the land of Assyria.

11b I will settle them on their estates.

> Oracle of Yahweh.

RETROSPECT AND PROSPECT

XXI. *Jacob-Israel in History and Prophecy* (12:1–15)

Parents and children: Bethel, Egypt, and Assyria

12:1a Ephraim has surrounded me with deception,

> the House of Israel with treachery.

1b Judah still wanders with the holy gods.

> He is faithful to the holy gods.

2a Ephraim shepherds in the wind.

> He pursues in the east wind.
>
> All day he multiplies lies and destruction.

2b They made a covenant with Assyria.

> Oil is conveyed to Egypt.

3a Yahweh has a dispute with Judah.

3b He will certainly punish Jacob for his ways.

> For his deeds he will requite him.

4a In the womb he grabbed his brother's heel.

4b In his vigor he contended with God.

5a He contended with God.

> He overcame the angel.

He wept and implored him.

5b At Bethel he met him.

> There he spoke to him.

6a Yahweh is God of the Armies.

6b Yahweh is his name.

Children and parents: wealth, prophecy, and idolatry

7a   You should return to your God.

7b   Keep loyalty and judgment.
> Wait for your God continually.

8a   Canaan: in his hands are treacherous scales.

8b   He even defrauds an ally.

9a   Ephraim said, "How rich have I become!
> I have acquired wealth for myself!

9b   None of my crimes will ever catch up with me,
> my iniquity which I have wrongfully committed."

10a   I am Yahweh your God, from the land of Egypt.

10b   I will make you live once more in tents,
> as in the days of the Tabernacle.

11a   I speak through the prophets.
> I make visions numerous.

11b   Through the prophets I create parables.

12a   They were in Gilead with idols,
> indeed, with false gods in Gilgal.
They sacrificed to bulls.

12b   Their altars were indeed like stone heaps
> beside furrows of the fields.

13a   Jacob fled to the land of Aram.

13b   Israel worked for one wife.
> For another wife he kept sheep.

14a   By one prophet Yahweh brought Israel up from Egypt.

14b   By another prophet he was watched.

15a   Ephraim has caused bitter provocation.

15b   He will hold him responsible for his murders.
> His Lord will return his disgrace upon him.

XXII. *The End of Ephraim* (13:1 – 14:1)

The sin of idolatry and human sacrifice

13:1a   Truly He had spoken terrifyingly against Ephraim.
> He had lifted up (his voice) against Israel.

1b   He became guilty at Baal and died.

2a   Now they continue to sin.
They made a cast image for themselves.
From their silver they made images
> according to their skill.

2b The whole thing is the work of artisans.
   Those who sacrifice people speak to them.
      They kiss the calves.
3a Therefore they will be like morning mist
      and like dew that goes away early,
3b Like chaff that is whirled from a threshing floor
      and like smoke from a chimney.

The origins of the sin
4a I am Yahweh your God, from the land of Egypt.
4b You have never known any god but me.
      There is no deliverer except me.
5a I knew you in the desert,
5b   in the land of drought.
6a When I fed them they became self-satisfied.
      When they were self-satisfied, their heart became
         arrogant.
6b Therefore they forgot me.

The punishment for the sin
7a I will be to them like a lion.
7b   Like a leopard by the road I will watch.
8a I will fall upon them like a bereaved she-bear.
      I will rip the lining of their heart.
8b I will devour them there like a lion,
      like wild animals that tear them apart.

The inevitability of the punishment
9a I will destroy you, Israel,
9b   for (you rebelled) against me, against your helper.
10a Where is your king, who would bring you victory,
      in all your cities, where are your judges
10b Of whom you said,
      "Give me a king and princes"?
11a I gave you a king in my anger.
11b   I took him away in my wrath.

The avoidance of the inevitability
12a Ephraim's iniquity is wrapped up.
12b   His sin is hidden away.

13a The pangs of a woman in childbirth came for him.
     He was an unwise child.

13b At the time when children are born, he would not have
     survived.

14a From the grasp of Sheol I ransomed them.
     From Death I redeemed them.

14b Where are your plagues, O Death?
     Where are your ravages, O Sheol?
     The cause of sorrow is hidden from my eyes.

15a He became the wild one among his brothers.

The punishment for the sin

15b The east wind, Yahweh's wind, comes.
     It rises from the wilderness.
     His spring will dry up.
       His fountain will become dry ground.
     He shall plunder the treasure,
     all the attractive objects.

14:1a Samaria has become guilty,
     for she rebelled against her God.

1b They will fall by the sword.
     Their infants will be smashed.
     His pregnant women will be torn open.

XXIII. *Return, Renunciation, and Restoration* (14:2–10)

The people are implored to address Yahweh

14:2a Return, O Israel, to Yahweh your God,
   2b   although you have stumbled in your iniquity.

3a Bring vows with you.
     Return to Yahweh.

3b Say to him: "You will forgive all iniquity—
     accept all that is good.
     Let us pay in full the promises we have made.

4a Assyria will not rescue us.
     We will not ride on horses.

4b We will never again say 'Our god' to the work of our
     hands.
     —for the orphan is pitied by you."

Yahweh's reply is sketched out

5a I will heal their apostasy,
          I will love them generously,
5b for my anger has turned back from him.
6a I will be like the dew for Israel.
6b He will prosper like the crocus
          and will strike his roots like the Lebanon crocus.
7a His suckers will spread everywhere.
7b His Glory will be like the olive tree
          and his fragrance like the Lebanon olive.
8a Once again those who live in his shadow will flourish.
          Like grain they will prosper.
8b Like the vine is his remembrance
          and the wine of Lebanon.
9a Ephraim, I won't deal with idols any more.
          I have answered and have watched him.
9b I am like a luxuriant fir tree.
          Your fruit is obtained from me. .

Coda

10a Whoever is wise
          let him understand these things.
      Whoever is intelligent
          let him learn them.
10b The paths of Yahweh are upright.
      The righteous will walk in them.
          Sinners will stumble in them.

INTRODUCTION

THE EIGHTH CENTURY B.C.E.

The eighth century was pivotal in the history of both Israel and Judah. During the first half, both nations attained pinnacles of political power and economic wealth reminiscent of the halcyon days of the United Monarchy. Jeroboam II in the north and Uzziah (Azariah) in the south achieved successes of a major order against traditional enemies, expanded national borders, and exercised influence and leadership beyond their own territories. As foreign successes increased domestic prosperity and sense of security, people could be forgiven for believing that the golden age of Israel's empire had returned and that the sister kingdoms had entered upon an era of unsurpassed well-being. According to popular and prevailing theological norms there was a permanent correlation between divine favor and prosperous existence. Whether one argued from cause to effect, or backwards from outcome to input, the conclusion was the same: the elect people of God were enjoying the just rewards of their faithful behavior, or looked at the other way, the benefits bestowed upon Israel and Judah, the blessings which rained down on them from a benevolent heaven, were adequate proof not only of divine favor but of Israel's moral merit.

Whatever we may think of the reasoning and its tendency to become circular, there were other factors in the picture which tended to undermine the rosy dream of eternal bliss, notably the unstable international scene with its shifting balance of forces and consequent unpredictable future. Thus in their relationships with their neighbors, Israel and Judah were never able to maintain continuous dominance or control. As in the period of the Judges, temporary and provisional superiority kept shifting so that each nation enjoyed periods of hegemony mingled with those of subordination and its attendant ills. In the period immediately preceding the military successes of Jeroboam II, Israel had only begun to recover from decades of harassment and oppression by the Arameans. It was only a question of time before one or another of the hostile neighbors not only reasserted its independence but exercised some measure of suzerainty over the high-flying Yahwistic nations. An even larger and darker shadow hung over the smaller nations of the Near East. On either side of Syria-Palestine were the great powers, Egypt and Assyria, temporarily immobilized by internal and external problems of their own, but each under geopolitical necessity to try to win control of its territory, the apparent key to total conquest and long-range administration of the known world. Although briefly disabled, both powers were ready to try again as in times past. Here was a threat which could only be ignored by the naive or piously confident. Prophetic voices could already be heard focusing on the foreign powers (especially Assyria) as the instruments of divine judgment and executioners of the nation states which stood in their way, including the two which belonged to Yahweh.

Contacts between the Israelites and the two world powers extended over the whole history of the people, and the nations formed by them, from the time of the escape from Egypt around 1200 B.C.E. until the destruction of the northern kingdom and the suppression of the southern kingdom in the eighth century, and the ultimate collapse of Judah at the beginning of the sixth century under repeated blows administered alternately by the Egyptians and the Babylonian successors of the Assyrians. In the earlier period the Egyptian threat was the more serious; after Shishak's devastating raid through the territories of both kingdoms during the reigns of Rehoboam and Jeroboam I, there was little stirring from that quarter, as Egypt drifted into external passivity. Action picked up in the north and by the middle of the ninth century, the rising Assyrian power had begun its march westward to the Mediterranean. Both the great northern kings of the mid-ninth century, Ahab and Jehu, had been confronted by Shalmaneser III. Ahab joined forces with Aramean and other city states and fought off the Assyrian armies at least once, in 853, at the battle of Qarqar. Jehu laid down his arms and paid heavy tribute to keep his nation alive (and himself on the throne) in 841; he is depicted kissing the ground before the Great King in Shalmaneser's Basalt Obelisk. Then there was a lull of nearly a century while the Assyrians attended to other regions and regrouped their forces, with sporadic forays in the west but no concerted and continuing effort to overwhelm the region. The accession of Tiglath Pileser III (745–727), also known as Pul(u), changed all that. He launched what was to be the final assault; his successors Sargon II and Esarhaddon completed the conquest of Syria-Palestine, and eventually Egypt. During this period Israel first sought the aid of the Assyrians by accepting vassal status (Menahem paid tribute to Pul in the 740's, *ANET* 283); subsequent efforts at independence were ruthlessly suppressed, and the nation was progressively dismembered and formed into Assyrian provinces; the process ended in the siege and destruction of Samaria, the capital city, in 722 and the conversion of the remaining enclave of Israel (i.e. Ephraim) into the Assyrian province of Samerina.

The Assyrian tide engulfed Philistia and Judah as well, so that by 701, early in the reign of Sennacherib (704–681), only Jerusalem and a small area around it remained independent, though under brutal siege. Destruction was avoided only through payment of a huge indemnity by Hezekiah.

The prophetic literature of the eighth century (including the four prophetic books specifically associated with this period: Hosea, Amos,

First Isaiah, Micah) focuses attention on the circumstances leading up to and culminating in the destruction of the northern kingdom and the near-devastation and narrow escape of the southern kingdom. The chrono-logical limits are defined by the introductory rubrics of these books, which list the Judahite kings in whose reigns the prophets uttered their oracles and the events transpired, from Uzziah (Azariah) to Hezekiah (roughly 790–690); only Jeroboam II is listed for the north (roughly 790–750). Narrowing the range in the several cases is more difficult, and allowance must always be made for editorial and supplemental material of a later date.

For Amos and Hosea the point of initiation is the reign of Jeroboam II, explicitly in the case of the former, and almost as clearly in the case of the latter. It is a common assumption that the oracles of both these prophets originate in the later years of this king and continue from that point. With respect to Amos the picture is fairly constant, with the exception of a few passages, and a single short period would suffice for the major oracles preserved in the book, perhaps the decade preceding the death of the king (ca. 760–750). In any event the historical pattern of the oracles fits this period well: Israel in the midst of hostile neighbors, quarreling, fighting, winning and losing, but with all of the nations threatened by an unnamed but obviously menacing power from the northeast. Not until Tiglath Pileser III ascended the throne a few years later (745) and regrouped and redirected the forces of Assyria toward the west did the shadows form a distinct shape and the identity of the enemy become clear.

At the same time, the internal conditions described by the two prophets reflect both the prosperity and grandeur introduced by the eminently suc-cessful Jeroboam II, and the poverty and injustice which were concurrent with the other features. While the prophets emphasize different aspects of the body politic, they agree on the diagnosis proferred by another prophet, Isaiah, for the south: the whole head is sick, the whole body is diseased. Furthermore the northern prophets' attacks on the ruling house date their words to the period before its collapse with the deaths of Jeroboam and his son Zechariah, at least in part. We may therefore associate both sets of oracles with the period between roughly 760 and 750. For Amos that may suffice since there is overall homogeneity in the book; for Hosea it is only a starting point, as both the rubric and the contents make clear.

While the oracles against the house of Jehu must precede the end of the dynasty, subsequent references to a sequence of illegitimate kings (Hos 8:4) and to what is probably the assassination of one of them (Hos 7:3–7) point to the chaotic period following the decease of the powerful and long-lived Jeroboam, who reigned for forty-one years. Within a year of his death at least three other kings sat on the throne of Israel, an *annus mirabilis* like 69 c.e. in the Roman empire. This seems most likely to be the point of reference in Hosea (cf. 13:11), although a similar revolving-door pattern recurred some years later: with the death of Menahem, we have a rapid succession of rulers, including his son Pekahiah, assassinated after two years by Pekah, who was in turn assassinated by Hoshea, the last king of Israel. It is not easy to choose between the periods and circumstances, especially because Hosea, unlike Amos, is loath to name names, and is tantalizingly obscure about details. It is possible that the book spans both periods during which kings came and went in dizzying rotation and profusion, each successor having no legitimate claim to such authority, either by birth or by divine choice and prophetic designation. In view of other circumstances, however, we believe that the main period of the prophecies of Hosea is the earlier one, and that the unauthorized sequence of kings around 750 is the subject of Hosea's alarmed and disgusted attack on the politico-ecclesiastical establishment. While he does mention Egypt and Assyria distinctly and frequently, unlike Amos (who is chary about the foe from the east), they are in the wings and Assyria especially does not yet play the active and violent role which it did in the events of the 730's, when Tiglath Pileser III overran much of the northern kingdom and tore loose huge chunks of the coast, Galilee, and Gilead. The picture rather is that of Israel seeking protection and aid against one or more neighbors (including Judah, an aggressor in the days of its dynamic and imperious monarch Uzziah), a condition fulfilled in the reign of Menahem ben-Gadi, who, like Jehu long before, paid heavy tribute and protection money to the Assyrian king.

The circumstances described in c 5 of Hosea, which involve a military struggle between Judah and Benjamin, have been linked with the Syro-Ephraimitic war (of 735–733) by no less an authority than Alt (1919), and many, perhaps most, scholars have been influenced by his weighty views on the subject. Nevertheless, the connection seems tenuous to us, especially because the attack is initiated by Judah against Benjamin, and not the other way around, which would seem necessary if the Syro-Ephraimitic war against Judah were in view. A hypothetical case must then be made; we prefer to place such an attack in the heyday of the great and aggressive Uzziah, who also conquered Philistia and subjugated Edom in his reign, rather than at a time when Judah was weak and nearly helpless (as the debate in Isaiah 7 shows — there is no thought of a Judahite invasion of the north then). At a time when the monarchy in Israel was in convulsions, and kings were rotating in and out of office, the country was riven by feuding rivals for the throne, and perhaps already divided into two political entities by the Jordan River (Ephraim on the west and Gilead = Israel on the east), the opportunity to split off Benjamin from Ephraim (or Israel) would be eagerly sought and promptly acted on by King Uzziah. After all, according to tradition, Benjamin had gone with Judah at the time of the great split after the death of Solomon and we may be sure that Judah never willingly relinquished that claim. The death of Jeroboam II, a strong king, not only triggered the ambition of internal adventurers such as Shallum, who slew Zechariah, the rightful king, and Menahem, who slew Shallum, but stirred the irredentism of Judah, which could hardly be expected to overlook an opportunity to dismember a sister kingdom—especially if prophets both north and south provided some moral justification for the more acceptably Yahwistic south, or at least ample charges against the hopelessly delinquent north. The main historical picture in the Book of Hosea fits the circumstances of the north beginning with the last years of Jeroboam, focusing on the transition year of the four kings. The central contents of the Book of Hosea and the principal ministry of the prophet would seem to fit best into the decade roughly from 750–740 or perhaps the more loosely defined period 755/50–745/40, during which the first great crises of the northern kingdom occurred. From these there was a temporary apparent recovery, but the march to ruin was irreversible, as the prophets had insisted almost from the start and as events proved. The initial division of the kingdom may have occurred during that appalling year (if, as some have suggested, Pekah also became king of the east when Menahem seized power in the west), to be followed rapidly, once Assyria had been invited to be suzerain, by dismemberment (Galilee and Gilead in 733) and then absorption into the empire with the capture of Samaria (in 722).

Pinpointing historical occasions in the Book of Hosea is a frustrating task—since the prophetic utterances are masterfully obscure (whether deliberately or not, and whether they might have been more intelligible to contemporaries than they are to us, at a far remove in time and place, or not), and tantalizingly allusive. It is a fact that while Hosea speaks about specific persons in high places and attacks them mercilessly and directly, he never names them. Given the large list of possible candidates, actual identification can never be certain, although the effort to narrow the range and to clarify the picture is a worthy one. Fortunately, some help is available from other biblical texts (e.g. Kings and Chronicles and prophets such as Isaiah, Amos, perhaps Micah) and extra-biblical sources, especially the Assyrian records.

Before proceeding with historical identifications, however, it may be well to say a few words about chronology. Considerable progress has been made in recent decades in the reconstruction of the chronology of this period of the two kingdoms within the framework of Near Eastern history. In general the summary statement Freedman (1965b) made some years ago holds true: for this period the variation among the major chronologies rarely exceeds ten years, and most often is less than that. The margin of error is similarly negligible, and if we strike a balance between extremes we will be close to the actual dates. While proponents and opponents of each system in particular, and all systems generally, deplore such indiscriminate blending, each of the various systems has both strong and weak points, and in spite of claims to the contrary none is really faultless. For our purposes, which are to explain and expound the oracles of Hosea, and place them reasonably in their appropriate historical setting, approximation is not only sufficient but, in the present state of our knowledge, a necessity. Precision would be not only presumptuous but erroneous or misleading.

Jeroboam II reigned from about 790 to 750, and was succeeded by his son Zechariah, who reigned only six months before being assassinated by Shallum. The latter in turn was put to death after a reign of one month by Menahem, who then reigned ten years, until about 740. He was succeeded by his son Pekahiah, who reigned for two years and was assassinated by Pekah. Pekah reigned for some time before being assassinated in turn by Hoshea. It is generally agreed that Hoshea came to the throne in 732, and continued in office until 724/23 when he was deposed, shortly before the capture of Samaria by the Assyrians, and the demise of the northern kingdom.

The only serious difficulty in this reconstruction concerns Pekah, who is credited with a twenty-year reign in the Bible (II Kings 15:27), but for whom a much smaller span of time is available between Pekahiah and Hoshea, especially in light of Assyrian synchronisms. There are various explanations, but Thiele's (1965) best accounts for the biblical evidence. It grows from the supposition that Pekah claimed as his all the years from the last legitimate king, Zechariah, excluding Menahem and Pekahiah (and no doubt Shallum). Thiele is not the first advocate of this view (see p. 124 for earlier forms of the proposal), but he is certainly the most thorough (pp. 73–140, esp. 124–126, summarized in de Vries 1962). It is important to note that Thiele's explanation of overlapping reigns was developed to account for the chronological data. Its historical plausibility is supported by other material. The core proposal is that Pekah had *de facto* control of the land of Gilead, east of the Jordan, while Menahem and Pekahiah were restricted largely to Ephraim and the capital city Samaria, west of the Jordan. This is suggested by the clear assertion of the biblical record that Pekah's seizure of power was supported by Gileadite forces (II Kings 15:25). According to this scenario, Pekah set up an independent capital in Gilead (perhaps at Ramoth-Gilead) during the upheavals after Jeroboam II's death and ruled there, posing a continual threat to Menahem in Samaria. This pressure eventually led Menahem to appeal to Tiglath Pileser for aid, polarizing the anti-Assyria sentiment gathering around Rezin of Damascus, and involving Jotham of Judah. The

Assyrian intervention was evidently enough to guarantee Menahem's position. After his death, Pekah, it is supposed, submitted himself (and presumably Transjordan) to Menahem's son Pekahiah in an effort to lure him into the anti-Assyrian league. Whether because these efforts failed or out of a quest for greater glory, Pekah after a two-year lapse killed his king, who had installed him as the leading military official of the larger realm. The stimulus for this may have been the death of Uzziah, which left Jotham sole ruler of Judah.

The geopolitical lines involved are traditional. Menahem's homeland would be Ephraim, the later Assyrian province of Samaria; and Pekah's Gilead, Assyrian Gal'aza. The remaining areas of Israel, the coastal region (Assyrian Du'ru) and the Galilee-Jezreel area (Assyrian Magido = Megiddo), may well have gone with Pekah, as in the Assyrian conquest all regions except for the heartland were taken together.

We may have indirect attestation of this transfer of power from the Samaria Ostraca, a homogeneous group of tax receipts from this period. Shea (1977, 1978) has explained the diversity in dating some ostraca to years 8 and 9 (in Hebrew words) and others to year 15 (in Egyptian hieratic numerals) by linking the first group to Menahem and the second to Pekah, in Samaria after Pekahiah's assassination. The recipients of the texts were royal officers and it is instructive to note that no officers from the ostraca of years 8–9 appear on the year 15 ostraca: "One may . . . speculate that those officials who served under Menahem may have suffered the same fate as Pekahiah when their replacements were installed" (Shea 1977:25).

By the mid-730's, all the political factors noted had been rearranged in the constellation of the Syro-Ephraimitic War, which is in the background of the early preaching of Isaiah. As suggested earlier, that war is outside the scope of Hosea's oracles.

We can place Hosea's active ministry and the major contents of the book which bears his name in the latter years of Jeroboam II (Hosea's family life and the origins of his calling may go back a decade or more before that) and in the years of turmoil that followed Jeroboam's death, a time of desperate international negotiations, with Assyria but also with Egypt, to salvage the faltering kingdom. That could bring us to the end of the house of Menahem, but hardly much beyond that. The dismemberment of the kingdom of Israel by Tiglath Pileser III seems to be still in the future; certainly the fall of Samaria is not yet in the picture. We can speak, then, of the period from 760 to about 735 as the larger framework, with most of the action centered in the period from 755 to 740. Greater precision is hardly feasible.

There are several references or allusions to kings in the Book of Hosea:

the royal house (5:1); an assassination plot(?) (7:3–7); the revolving door (8:4); impending doom (10:7,15 — more than one king was murdered in Samaria); the divine rage (13:10–11). The association of priest and prophet in c 4 is especially intriguing in light of the links with the royal house (c 5). Thanks to help provided by Amos on the one hand and II Kings on the other, we can propose labels for some of these anonymous "heroes." The dominant king is probably Jeroboam II, whose notable achievements, including military and diplomatic success abroad, and security, stability, and prosperity at home, brought on him a blistering attack by Amos and apparently Hosea for a long list of crimes against God and people. Fundamental and unforgivable covenant violation is asserted by both prophets, Amos emphasizing the gap between covenant requirements in the social and economic spheres and the realities in the kingdom of Israel (cf. Amos 2:6–15 and passim), while Hosea speaks even more vehemently about religious commitments and cult practices, charging the establishment with nothing less than idolatry, apostasy, and cultic enormities including sexual promiscuity and human sacrifice.

According to Amos, the ecclesiastical leader and co-conspirator against God was Amaziah, priest of Bethel, and this may be the man Hosea attacks with even greater vehemence as "The Priest" in c 4. When it comes to the latter's colleague and fellow stumbler, "The Prophet," help may be provided by the account in II Kings of the reign of Jeroboam II. In the eyes of the historian, Jeroboam was better than most of the northern kings, and Israel was the recipient of divine grace during his reign. The evidence for this was the restoration of borders and the general prosperity and stability which came to Israel after the disastrous Aramean wars of earlier decades. In these accomplishments Jeroboam was aided and abetted, encouraged and admonished by a court prophet, Jonah ben-Amittai, (II Kings 14:25), otherwise known to us only through the story about him contained in the Book of Jonah. While he is taken to be an authentic prophet of Yahweh (and doubtless was so regarded not only by the king but by many in Israel), it would be understandable that a prophet like Hosea would take a different and much dimmer view of such a man and even more of such a message. If for Hosea the doom of the house of Jehu had come, and it was necessary to pronounce the judgment of God against it, as was true also for Amos, then the opposing encouragement and authorization provided by an official prophet would precipitate a vigorous confrontation. One thinks immediately of the disastrous confrontation 150 years later between Jeremiah and Hananiah, both ostensibly prophets of Yahweh but with diametrically opposite messages for king and people (cf. Jeremiah 28). In this case, there is no story; the reference in Hosea is meager and the blow glancing, but the juxtaposition of Jonah ben-Amittai as he appears in II Kings 14:25–26, and Hosea ben-Beeri as he appears in the Book of Hosea is intriguing. If "The Prophet" in Hosea 4 is not Jonah, he must have been someone much like him. And the same may be said of "The Priest" in Hosea 4; if he is not Amaziah of Bethel, he must have been a counterpart, perhaps in Samaria, perhaps at another cult center.

With respect to the other correlations cited, we may be more brief. If, as we suppose, Hosea 7:3–7 is a sketchy version of a palace intrigue resulting in the murder of a king, there are several possibilities, beginning with Zechariah and continuing with Shallum, but not excluding Pekahiah and Pekah, though the latter two are less likely in our judgment. While the account of Zechariah's death in Kings (II Kings 15:10) implies military action, the language is laconic, and all that is required to meet the terms used is the blow of a dagger or sword. Our preferred candidate would be Zechariah as the only legitimate king of the lot — and this fits with the "year of the four kings" which is central in our thinking.

Hosea 8:4–10 presents the revolving door. For people accustomed to one king securely in power for a long time (Jeroboam reigned more than forty years), the bewildering succession of assassinations and the crowning of assassins must have had an extraordinary shock effect. Surely this year of the four kings is reflected by Hosea in c 8; later there would be something similar with the sequence: Menahem, Pekahiah, Pekah, and Hoshea — but not quite as sudden or dramatic.

The oracle in Hosea 13:10–11 reflects divine disgust and outrage at the desecration of the institution of the anointed king in Israel. While the statement is indefinite, it is a parody of the traditional mode of divine selection, reflected for example in the case of Saul (and his successor David), who was chosen to be king of Israel and then rejected as unfit. Here the choice is an act of divine anger, and the removal is in the same category. While normally we would expect the object, *melek,* "king," of the verbs to be the same, especially as it is not expressed after the second verb, two kings may be involved here, and both actions express divine outrage. In each case what is done is contrary to the usual expectation that God acts for his people, and not against them, as here. Giving a king in anger means that he is a bad choice; this could apply to any of the kings after Zechariah; Shallum is the most obvious candidate. Removing him or any of the others would hardly be regarded as an act of wrath, so here the second verb ought to refer to Zechariah. The sequence seems to be inverted, but in fact it is the giving of the new king that involves the removal of the incumbent. So the two verbs together may describe the violent displacement of Zechariah by Shallum. There are other, equally bloody possibilities, but for the reasons adduced above this seems the most likely.

Hosea the Prophet

The Eighth-Century Prophets

Prophecy as an institution and prophets in groups or as individuals had long been a familiar element in the drama of Israel's ongoing experience as the people of God, when the eighth century B.C.E. brought new challenges and crises, new threats and even new hopes to the beleaguered inhabitants of the small nations of Israel and Judah. For centuries prophets had played a major role in the life of the nation, in fact were key figures in the formation of the monarchy, the division of the kingdoms, and in socioeconomic and political decisions. As critics and censors of the spiritual well-being of the worshiping community, they kept a close watch over the ecclesiastical and royal representatives, initiating and effecting reforms, and continuously deploring the inevitable failure on all sides to meet their exacting standards, and warning about the consequences of intermittent, to say nothing of persistent, backsliding.

We can trace the prophetic movement in Israel to its historic origin in the time of Samuel (eleventh century) and recognize in his personality and activity those factors which characterize the later history of prophecy: the charismatic leader, called by God, and bearer of the authoritative self-effecting message; and the community of followers and disciples, from whose ranks successors would come, as dramatically instanced in the case of Elisha, the faithful follower and successor of Elijah (Albright 1961). As we know from the stories and incidental references in Kings and Chronicles, prophets, in schools and as individuals, figure prominently in pivotal and decisive events from Samuel on, advising and admonishing kings and priests, military and civilian leaders. They are king-makers and king-breakers; they molded a nation, and fractured it. Without a formal power base, they served the most powerful master of all as messengers and spokesmen for God himself. Their word was his word, stronger than all human words and works, but dependent upon human structures and frail members of the species to carry out the pronouncements.

The message of the prophets was an original mixture of the ancient tradition of the One of Sinai who had revealed himself to Moses, and through him to Israel, coupled with a commandment or prescription for the nation and its population in the day of the prophet, a new meaning, or change of purpose and direction, a challenge to the established order of things or way of doing politics and business. The prophet was the messenger of the most high God to his people with a word, whether of admonition or comfort, of threat or reassurance, for this crisis or that opportunity. By the rules of the covenanted community, all, from the greatest to the least, from king to commoner or slave, from the powerful to the penniless, were bound to listen, and if the message was true — if the source was the heavenly palace and the messenger was faithful to his charge — then the whole nation was obliged to take the commanded action and fulfill the divine demands at the risk of irredeemable losses: status, possessions, life.

As the stories also make clear, the prophets, while exercising a unique office, nevertheless did not operate in a vacuum. Powerful figures in palace and temple exerted influence on the prophets in addition to being influenced by them. Political and ecclesiastical power had their effect; prophets, being human, could be bribed and bought, or threatened and manipulated, and often were. The familiar story of Micaiah and the four hundred prophets of Ahab (I Kings 22) is an object lesson in the corrupting effects of the monarchy on prophecy and the contrasting consequences of being honest and faithful to one's calling. There were prices to be paid, as well as rewards to be won in the delivery of messages, which could be or were changed to suit the circumstances.

By the eighth century, prophecy and prophets had run a gamut of experiences, and both those who brought the divine message and those to whom it came were worldly-wise and well-seasoned in the practice of giving and receiving, in measuring out and counting in. Nevertheless, more than ever there was a word to be spoken, and to be heard. In the mounting crises of that century, traditional wisdom and the appeal to precedent could hardly suffice, and the ingenious makeshifts of generals and kings, even of priests and wise men, would not save the kingdoms. Only the word of God, drastic and devastating as it might be, could avail against the forces both internal and external which threatened the life of the nations and their inhabitants severally.

It was in such a critical situation that the voices of the eighth-century prophets were raised: Amos, Hosea, Isaiah, and Micah. They were presumably a few among many; they stand out because their words — or the words of God which they proclaimed — were not only heard but remembered and ultimately transcribed and preserved for later generations and all posterity.

They were the first of the so-called literary or writing prophets. The term is probably a misnomer, since it is not likely that these four prophets were markedly different from either their non-writing predecessors of previous centuries, or their contemporaries. As with the others, named and unnamed, these four doubtless were called to their mission in some unusual experience and received messages which they delivered in turn to a variety of audiences. What made their experiences and oracles distinctive and memorable were the circumstances and times in which they lived, and the meaning and bearing the messages had on those of a later time, and for whom it was necessary and important to preserve the message. The difference came later — although no one would want to deny the commanding presence and insistent importance of these particular men who doubtless stood out from their colleagues as strikingly as Elijah and Elisha and Samuel and Nathan did from theirs — when editors and scribes selected and organized, put together and pulled apart the messages of a previous age so that a later generation could learn wisdom from the past, find truth and consolation in unrepeatable and vital experiences of an earlier time. The final loss of statehood and the end of national existence required drastic measures if the community was to survive as the people of God. To replace land and government, temple and palace, the cities and villages and farms which made up Israel and Judah, there had to be a Bible: a book which would embody all those things, relate history and justify the ways of God to people. Necessary to this last task was the message of the prophets who had given due warning and hence were vindicated as representatives of the true God in spite of the tragedy which overcame his people. Without this faithful witness duly recorded and glossed, there could have been no survival, no identity, no return, no restoration. This is what made the prophets of the eighth century "writing" prophets: the imminence of the crisis and its aftermath.

We leave to one side entirely the question of actual writing in the eighth century. That the people of Israel and Judah could write and did write is beside the point. Whether or not these prophets wrote or used scribes to record imperishable thoughts, as Jeremiah was to do a hundred years later, cannot be answered specifically, even if all the necessary tools were at hand. It hardly matters, since prophetic oracles were made to be delivered orally, and so doubtless they were. Given their basically prosodic form, they could easily be remembered, both by the speaker and the hearers. It is altogether likely that the prophets gave essentially the same speech many times over, and anyone who heard it two or three times was not likely to forget it. When the time came to record the utterances permanently, relevant materials, both oral and written, would have been available. As for the prophets themselves, they were speakers of the word — whether they made notes before or after delivery is an interesting question which cannot now be answered.

Just these factors show that the eighth-century prophets, their message and the setting in which it was given, were different. The nature and magnitude of the crisis confronting Israel and Judah set this age apart from what had gone before, and the mood and message of the prophets were adapted accordingly. The essentials remained the same from the time of Moses or of Samuel: the covenant relationship between God and Israel, the demands of the former and the obligations of the latter, the conditional character of national existence, and the dependence of Israel upon the mercy and justice of God. But whereas in times past, there was a basic confidence in national survival, and a certain leeway for repentance and reform to allow the situation to be rectified without permanent and ultimate damage, now the stakes were escalated, and it was literally life or death for the nation. For the first time the threat of national destruction was serious and real, and captivity loomed for the survivors of the impending disaster. Loss of the land and the end of the state were not remote and theoretical possibilities but present and impending realities. The fundamental assumptions of Israelite faith and practice were in question. Whereas it had always been taken for granted that God's commitment was not only the foundation of national life, but also a continuing guarantee of the nation's permanent existence, the prophets maintained that was no longer the case. The God who had created the people and the state could dissolve them and would, if conditions and practices persisted. The great states hovering on the borders of both nations could and would destroy them, not in defiance of God, but as instruments and agents of his will and judgment.

A much more complex and problematic view of the future of the two nations was held by these prophets than had obtained in the past. The divine promise to the fathers was no blank check for the present or future. Israel's responsibilities in fulfilling the demands of the covenant, as a people, a community of faith and works, as individual worshipers and sinners, formed a counterpoise to the divine commitment in grace and love. God could not abandon the people whom he had led out of slavery in Egypt and whom he had settled in a land flowing with milk and honey, but he could and would punish them for their rebellion against him and his will, their apostasy and idolatry, their mistreatment of their fellow human beings, especially the poor, the stranger, the widow, and the orphan. Persistent violation would bring drastic consequences; natural calamity would signal political and military catastrophe. In a variety of ways and with differing emphases the prophets of the eighth century brought home a message to the people of their own day which has proved to have permanent value for all days and all people, but especially for the nucleus of Israel which ultimately survived; it had to learn again and again the bitter lesson of divine election, love, and justice, to know forever what it meant to be the people of God, and what was required for survival, not to speak of return and restoration.

It is safe to say that these prophets and their successors were the difference for an Israel and Judah that otherwise would have been swept away in the tides from east and west which rolled over all the nations of greater Syria-Palestine. Against the political and military leaders of their day, and the ecclesiastical authorities, they correctly warned of the coming collapse, and accurately predicted what did in fact happen. Theirs was an

insight into political realities engendered not by special training in the eso-
teric fields of diplomacy and military strategy, but by an intimate acquaintance with the God who is the breaker of battles and the decider of
human affairs. Theirs, moreover, was not exclusively a word of doom,
since it would be an exercise in futility or irrelevance merely to keep the
record straight on the roles of God and his people in the debacle which
was inevitable and resulted in the destruction of both nations. In spite of
their certainty about what would happen — given the covenant structure
and the behavior patterns of the principals both divine and human — the
proclamation of divine judgment could not be separated from a call to repentance. However futile that expectation might be, the message was nevertheless intended to produce effects, or at least offer the hearers a choice
or a chance to change their ways. Even if punishment were their lot, if
ruin and exile were their future, still there was a future, there would be
survivors; they would have a role in exemplifying divine justice and mercy,
and they would have a responsibility to transmit and interpret to their
posterity the meaning of all that had transpired, and of what they had experienced. In spite of the terrible message of doom, there was a structure of
ongoing reality of which it was only a part and a phase. Beyond doom and
death were resurrection and life. For those who could endure the destruction of the state, survival would also mean restoration and renewal; for
those who would be taken into captivity, there was promise of a return to
the land, and of the land to them.

Hosea

Hosea was one of these prophets, and his mission and message are an integral part of the eighth-century B.C.E. prophetic corpus. As with each of
the others, there are distinctive elements and emphases in his prophetic
ministry, and as he comes near the beginning of the sequence, some of the
components are less well defined.

Whatever his background, training, and circumstances, of his family
and lineage, of his residence and locality we know next to nothing — only
his patronymic: Hosea ben-Beeri. What sets him apart is his calling as a
prophet: it places him in that select company of men and women who
held this office, who were messengers of God to his people. Typical of
prophets was an initial call and commission, often of a dramatic nature.
A typical account of a prophetic call is Micaiah's vision in I Kings 22;
the setting, dramatis personae, and procedures used there are probably
standard. The prophet describes his vision of the divine council: Yahweh
surrounded by the heavenly beings who serve him. The prophet is present
to witness the proceedings and report, even to participate by intercession.
The prophetic summons to service, commonly accompanied by an inaugu-

ral vision, which sets it off dramatically, is illustrated by the vivid and colorful accounts from the prophets Isaiah, Jeremiah, Ezekiel, Amos, and
Zechariah. Sometimes it is difficult to be sure that the great vision narrated
was in fact the first. In any case, the later experiences were probably not
much different from the inaugural one, and did not need to be redescribed
each time. It was enough to say, "The word of Yahweh came to me," or
the like.

This phrase occurs only at the opening of Hosea. There is reference to a
dramatic call to prophetic service but no inaugural vision is recorded. Actually, no visions as such are described in the Book of Hosea, unlike the
reports in the books of the prophets just mentioned. The omission of such
reports in the case of other minor prophets (and others in the historical
books) can be explained on the basis of the brevity of the material
preserved. But Hosea is one of the longer books, and a good deal is
revealed there about his personal and family history.

Whereas in other cases of omission it is not clear whether there were
such stories and they have been lost, or there simply was none to begin
with, for Hosea none is recorded, and perhaps the conclusion is that none
occurred. It is also possible that some initial vision would be taken for
granted by the book's audience. There is evidence in the text that Hosea,
like Micaiah and other prophets, did gain the word of Yahweh through visionary experience.

The Book of Hosea does not present us with finished oracular utterances, ready for public delivery; rather it offers material from an earlier
stage in the process, from the actual deliberations of Yahweh in the divine
council. In fact, since Yahweh does not consult the council, these talks
seem to be his preliminary reflections or soliloquies. This hypothesis accounts for many puzzling literary features of the oracles, and goes a long
way toward liberating readers from the impasse and frustration of inconclusive form-critical studies. In particular, it explains the turbulent vacillation of many of the reflections, and the abrupt shifts from direct address to
the people (rare in any case) to third-person description. Such soliloquies
have not reached the stage of composition at which form-critical analysis
would be profitable.

It may be that visions are also indirectly substantiated or alluded to in
the rich metaphoric imagery of the oracles. Behind the similes and metaphors there may be not merely literary conventions but visions of the
prophet. There are similarities between visions of prophets such as Amos
and Jeremiah and the language of identification and comparison used by
Hosea. Whatever correlation there may be between visionary experience
and linguistic imagery, we should look more closely at the central image
of Hosea's ministry, the substance of his call, and the symbolism of his
family. These come out of the whole experience of his personal life: his

marriage and family are the vehicle of his message and the two are so closely intertwined that the meaning of the one is the focus of the other. We must conceive of his personal life, especially in terms of his wife and children, as an ongoing process of revelation, and find in this experience a partial equivalent of the visions of the other prophets.

The dramatic call to marry a promiscuous woman is unmatched in Scripture; it provides a sharp characterization of his message, as subsequent words of comparison with Israel as the unfaithful marriage partner of God show. In our view (explained in detail in the commentary) the significance of the words and in fact the particular formulation could only have gained their real force in retrospect, when much later in life the prophet could gauge the meaning of his own experience with wife and children in relation to that of Yahweh and Israel. For Hosea therefore, the meaning of his message, and to some degree its form, was in part revealed and shaped by his life, and the history of his marriage and children became a continuing source of insight into and understanding of the story of God and his people. Subsequently other prophets, especially Jeremiah and Ezekiel, would use the same basic marriage figure for the relationship between God and his people, but for them it was simply one of many different metaphors available to convey an aspect of a hidden truth. There is no correlation with the personal life of these prophets, whereas in the case of Hosea it seems clear that the theological imagery arises out of his personal tribulation. The nature and extent of the analogy, the points of contact, and the sequence in which the various components fit together are discussed at length in the commentary. Here it will suffice to say that the lifetime experience of the prophet served as source and model for his message, and specifically that his marriage and family were an analogy to the relationship between God and Israel, although the reverse is also true. By combining description and analysis and seeing the latter in the light of the former, the prophet articulated a message of dire threat and warning. If the relationship between God and Israel was to be compared to that between Hosea and his faithless wife, then the consequences were clear, and the message could not be in doubt. Israel would reap the same reward for its conduct that a straying wife deserved. At the same time a relationship as profound and deeply rooted in mutual commitment and radiant experience of the past could not easily be dissolved, and might one day be restored; at least that would be true of God and Israel, even if the case of Hosea and Gomer was more doubtful. Nevertheless, the children whose names signify the progressive deterioration of the marriage, and the dissolution of the bond between God and his people, will also symbolize the renewal and restoration of that relationship in the end time when their names are reinterpreted or changed. So intricately combined and blended are the two stories — of God and Israel, and Hosea and Gomer — that it is impossible to tell always where one stops and the other picks up. Without being able to say just what the outcome was for Hosea and Gomer, it seems fair to postulate that the parallelism was intended to be wide-ranging, and that the entire scope of experience — from the wife's defection and abandonment of her husband to her reclamation and ultimate restoration and rehabilitation — was as true of the prophet as of God.

Aside from this elaborate construction incorporating the marital experience of the prophet into his message, we know little of the prophet's life. Occasional references to the difficulties of the prophetic calling and duty suggest a link to the prophet himself, but these seem rather stereotyped, and reveal little in detail. We turn then to his message.

As already indicated, Hosea belongs to the group of eighth-century prophets including Amos, Micah, and Isaiah of Jerusalem, and shares with those prophets the main themes of the divine proclamation for that time. Firmly rooted in the tradition of divine grace and guidance, Hosea, like the others, emphasizes the unobligated action of God in the creation of his people and their settlement in the promised land. The twin themes of the promise to the patriarchs and the deliverance from Egyptian bondage form the basis both for the uniqueness of Israel's existence and its responsibility for its behavior to God. In spite of constant care and repeated warnings, Israel failed to keep its part of the commitment, failed to maintain unquestioning obedience to the Lord of the covenant, and to fulfill the demands of the righteousness essential to being the people of God. Repeated and persistent violation of the requirements of that status have brought Israel into crisis, brought it literally under the judgment of God himself. The chosen people is threatened with divine repudiation. That rejection will take the form of defeat in battle and conquest by aliens. The nation will be overrun and its population dispersed to the four winds. Nor are these theoretical considerations. Egypt and even more powerful Assyria are being prepared to swallow up the small nation states between them, a threat which only the foolhardy or naive could ignore. While the possibility of either repentance and rescue of the people or the survival of a remnant could not be dismissed entirely, in practical terms no real hope of serious or permanent reformation was held and ultimate destruction loomed over the nations. Along with the central theme of judgment, to be signaled by natural catastrophes and executed by foreign armies, were accompanying theses of survival and restoration, captivity and return.

For Hosea the primary image, as conveyed in cc 1–3, is that of marriage, the marriage of God and his people, its consummation in the idyllic period in the Exodus and wilderness wandering, and then its corruption in the settlement of the land and the abandonment of her husband by the nation-wife in favor of other gods (her lovers). Promiscuity and idolatry are interchangeable terms, as the focus shifts back and forth between the contamination of domestic family life and the same failure in the public sphere of worship and diplomacy. For the eighth century this imagery is unique to Hosea, but it exerted a powerful influence in subsequent thought and speech on the subject, and we find the theme of Israel as the faithless partner of Yahweh central in the proclamations of Jeremiah and Ezekiel. For Hosea, his own marital experience apparently provided both the symbolism and the analysis necessary to an understanding of the present predicament of Israel. His private tragedy is a paradigm for that of Israel, and the comparable stages of corruption and degradation are traced in both areas. At the same time hope of renewal and recapitulation, of a reconciliation and revival of the marriage pact in both spheres, is announced, not to console or comfort those facing the just punishment for their sins but to affirm the prevenient and countervailing grace of God, whose purpose for his people could not and would not finally be thwarted. This theme — that beyond the menacing judgment of the present age, there would be a new age of beginnings to catch up the old beginnings of peoplehood and nation state — while challenged by many scholars, and awkward on the face of it, is so persistent in the surviving texts of the prophetic books that we must attribute it either to the prophets themselves, including Hosea, or to some master editors who were determined to reverse the message of the prophets whom they held in awe and turn them one and all into mediators of a doctrine of overarching divine grace. Since we find this paradox of irreversible judgment and irresistible redemption in the undoubted teaching of Ezekiel, who could hardly be accused of modifying his message to mollify his audience, and something approaching the same view in Jeremiah, it seems the better part of valor as well as common sense to acknowledge this peculiarity in other prophets as well, including Hosea.

Part II of Hosea, cc 4–14, also has distinctive features which set Hosea apart from his fellow prophets even while establishing his kinship with them. In this part of the book, which on the face of it is a heterogeneous collection of oracles without clear continuity or obvious linkage, there are nevertheless dominant elements, which are repeated in a variety of images and figures. The major aberrations are cultic, in the most basic sense of the term, and political. False worship of the true God or true worship of false gods — one leads to the other — has its counterpart in false politics, to seek power rather than justice in internal affairs, and externally to seek security in armed might, whether one's own or another's, in preference to the service of God and his purposes.

In the sphere of religion, Hosea levels the heavy charge of idolatry at the people of Israel, and more crucially at their leaders. Whatever may have been the original intent or meaning behind the golden calves installed at Dan and Bethel, the worship at those sanctuaries is flatly called idolatrous. And whatever the people and their priests understood about such worship, it is as much the worship of Baal as of Yahweh. It is not always clear whether Hosea is condemning a false (idolatrous) worship of Yahweh, or an apostate worship of Baal, or even whether the two are identified in the official cult, with Baal used as a title of Yahweh. In any case, apostasy and idolatry are parts of the same defection from and rebellion against the true God.

The cultus described in Hosea has sometimes loosely been referred to as distinctively Mesopotamian. Our examination of the text leads us to agree with the conclusion of a recent study of relevant cuneiform material: "There is no evidence of Assyrian interference in the Israelite cult prior to the 720 B.C.E. annexation of Samaria. . . . [Even] as an independent vassal state [after Hosea prophesied], Israel was free of any cultic obligations" (Cogan 1974:103–104). Our ignorance of Iron Age religion has recently been pointed up by the as-yet unpublished finds at Kuntillat 'Ajrud, which show that toward the end of the ninth century there was a flourishing cultus of Yahweh, with Baal as either an alternative name or a co-god; and a consort called *šrth*, "his Asherah." The site is an isolated shrine at the intersection of wilderness tracks in the easternmost part of the Sinai; for a preliminary description, see Meshel and Meyers (1976). At present, it is crucial that we yield to the text's lead and recognize that the religion of Moses in Hosea's time had been diversified, distorted, and dragged into direct support of the state apparatus to a dangerous degree.

Idolatrous and apostate worship has two outstanding features, on both of which the prophet pours out his vehemence. Sexual promiscuity in the fertility cult undermines the moral structure of the covenant, and is a gross violation of the basic requirements of community life under God. Furthermore it leads in some circuitous way to the culminating sin against God and people, that is, the shedding of innocent blood. This is not ordinary murder, itself an ultimate crime, but officially sanctioned human sacrifice. The language of the prophet is obscure, perhaps deliberately so, but the hints and clues point to a conclusion which Ezekiel later makes quite explicit. It is hard to escape this horrifying inference about the central pattern of official worship in eighth-century Israel, and it helps to explain the adamantine harshness with which Hosea condemns his fellow Israelites, especially those in major ecclesiastical posts.

The false politics of Israel are also analyzed and condemned in distinctive terms. Hosea speaks repeatedly of defections in two areas: internal and external, also linked by a fundamental apostasy from the true faith. The latter is defined most completely by Hosea's contemporary, Isaiah of Jerusalem, but the theme is present in Hosea's work too: to have faith in God, not in armaments, to be bound to the one true God, the redeemer, and not to other nations in entangling alliances. There are two great political crimes. The first is the desecration of the holy office of king. In Hosea's day kings came and went, usually by assassination. Contrary to traditional wisdom, crime paid and the payoff was immediate. Repeatedly, the assassin of the incumbent king himself became the king. But a kind of crude justice prevailed, and the usurper was himself murdered by his successor. We can count four Israelite assassinations within the space of twenty years, and in each instance the assassin himself usurped the throne. Twice the assassin-become-king was himself assassinated, and only once in this bloody period did a son succeed his father (and then only for a brief time before he was assassinated). Such callous disregard of the office, and the unbridled ambition of mere men in anointing themselves with the blood of their predecessor could only ensure the swift demise of the nation. The breakdown of the monarchy and the ensuing anarchy led directly to Assyrian domination and later conquest — and the permanent destruction of the northern kingdom.

Along with this internal collapse went an equally suicidal foreign policy. Hosea frequently describes and roundly condemns the incessant quest for security in political and military alliances. Ephraim is a silly dove who flutters between Northeast and Southwest — Assyria and Egypt — suing for peace and support from one or the other or both. In the face of threats on all sides, it is hard to see a practical political alternative to seeking out a patron and protector such as the great powers which dominated the small nations in Syria-Palestine. But the prophets were not political commentators as such — they were messengers of God with a word for their people and its leaders. It was not merely political folly to invite the dominance of powers like Assyria and Egypt; it was also apostasy from God, the only true sovereign of Israel. If we cannot translate such counsel immediately into a practical course of action, that failure only accentuates the dilemma of those unfortunate enough to exercise the limited authority left to Ephraim and Judah. But that faith in God and reliance upon him was meant as national policy by a prophet like Hosea is confirmed by the advice given by Isaiah to Ahaz of Judah, advice promptly rejected by the king in favor of a treaty of surrender to the Assyrian emperor (Isaiah 7).

With faithlessness and falsity so deeply embedded in Israel at every level and in every sphere of action, thoughts of the end of existing social structures and of immediate disaster could not be avoided. Perhaps such a conclusion could have been foreseen by any competent observer of the scene. After all, the same fate befell most, if not all, of the small nations between the two great powers, and this happened without benefit of the Israelite prophets, even though those peoples had their own theology, and the Israelite prophets had a profound interest in the fate of the neighboring peoples and the great powers. All came within the jurisdiction of the almighty suzerain to whom all owed allegiance.

For the prophets history was not an autonomous process, but the working out of the divine purpose and will. Hence it was necessary to explain the premises and reasons for the judgment which had been pronounced and would shortly be executed. The roots of that decision lay in the distant past when the intricate relationship between God and his people had been formed and its moral character defined. In the confusion of alliances and battles, and the ambiguities of public action, there was a constant truth, a continuity to which the denouement belonged as the consequence of a long history of behavior and attitude. The present outcome was the necessary result of previous decisions and actions. From the same source, and from the same history, the outlines of the more distant future also emerged. The interaction of the same persons and operative factors which produced or would effect the imminent judgment on the nation, would with other active components produce a dramatically different resolution.

The proclamations of judgment are not the impartial, impersonal verdicts of a God of justice; the expressions of wrath do not come from an implacable avenger. God is the outraged partner to a violated agreement created by his own generosity. He is grieved by the ingratitude of his people. The passion of God revealed in these speeches is often that of a heartbroken husband and father. These roles are more prominent than those of ruler and judge, and they give to the prophetic messages a poignancy matched by Hosea's corresponding distress over his own family.

It has sometimes been said that Hosea's unquenchable love for his wife gave him the fundamental insight into the love of God that never gives up. It is just as likely that the prophet's belief that heroic measures might still restore his broken marriage arises, at least in part, from faith that God's will to love can overcome all barriers. He is commanded to love the woman "just as Yahweh loves the Israelites" (3:1), i.e. in spite of everything.

This seemingly impossible task confronts God and his prophet. Some of the speeches have the tone of soliloquies. God searches in his own mind for what to do, revealing a conflict of emotions as every course of action proves unacceptable. God cannot bring himself to carry out the punishment demanded by every consideration of justice, yet he cannot condone the treachery and depravity of his people.

One door of hope remains open. If the wife (or Israel) would change her mind and come back, the relationship might yet be repaired. Hence the call to repentance is sounded along with the threats, right up to the end.

God's will to punish and his will to pardon do not neutralize each other. Rather they are expressed together in the strongest terms, savage and tender. This gives the speeches a turbulence, a seeming incoherence, in which we reach the limits of language for talking about the goodness and severity of God.

In the case of Israel and perhaps in the case of Gomer also, there was no significant repentance. Hosea stands at a crisis point in history where the destruction of the nation is increasingly inescapable. Repentance is so unlikely that other, more drastic remedies must be found. Even when death comes as the end, national or personal, the living and creating God has not finished his work. By fresh acts of redemption he will rescue them from death itself (6:1–3; 13:14). In the end those who had been alienated will be reconciled, and the new age will begin as did the old, with a great universal chorus of praise and joy and peace (2:20–25).

HOSEA AS LITERATURE

Literary History

Considered as a literary work, the Book of Hosea is best described as an anthology, consisting of both narrative (mainly in cc 1–3) and oracular material (cc 2 and 4–14). In this respect it is much like the books associated with contemporary prophets, Amos and Isaiah of Jerusalem; Micah also belongs to this group of prophets but there is no discernible narrative in his book. While later prophets, in addition to providing the contents of their books, may have had a hand in compiling them as well, that is unlikely in any of these cases. The probability is that some disciple or group of followers was responsible for collecting, preserving, organizing, and editing the surviving materials. When this may first have occurred is difficult to determine, but the preservation of many oracles in their original form argues for an early date, while the heterogeneous nature of the material, and some signs of editing, argue for a later date.

It should be possible to identify different periods of literary and editorial activity. As noted below, the rubrics or headings of these four prophetic works reflect a discriminating concern for dynastic chronology in the eighth century and point to a compiler of the works (whether separately or together) during the first half of the seventh century, the period immediately following the era of the four prophets. Oracles of each prophet were combined with limited narrative material to form the nucleus or perhaps even bulk of the books as we know them.

The reason for and operating principle behind these collections doubtless were the importance of the message for those who lived at a later time, and its applicability to their day. These prophets, against the prevailing mood of their time, and in defiance of civil and ecclesiastical leadership, had shrewdly challenged conventional wisdom, had foreseen the catastrophe which threatened the existence of the state, and had warned the people, from king to commoner, of their peril. When the threats materialized, and events came to pass as predicted, the standing of the prophets was enhanced accordingly. Not only had the course of history ratified the insights and claims of the prophets as messengers of almighty God, but their words set in a later context gained new and ominous force. For the reduced southern kingdom which had precariously survived the Assyrian onslaught of the eighth century, and for which the future was bleak, the words of the prophets of that period had special importance and impact. Survival itself, after the dismantling of the northern kingdom, was a sign of hope, but the rise of the Assyrian empire, more powerful and dangerous than ever in the final century of its hegemony, boded poorly for all of western Asia; the success of the empire threatened small states with complete dissolution and amalgamation into the imperium, while the structural weaknesses and ultimate collapse of the great political edifice would bring chaos and upheaval throughout its territories with consequences too terrible and uncertain to contemplate with equanimity.

The warnings of the prophets to an earlier age, when flirtation with the great powers and dabbling in pagan worship seemed appropriate responses to a complex and difficult religio-political crisis, in retrospect were seen to be not only a pillar of fiery truth for the unheeding generation which perished in the destruction which overtook them, but also a message for waverers and those who were smug about the political and religious accommodation made with the ruling authority.

If, as we believe, the initial compilation of oracles and narrative was made by faithful conservators of the tradition of inspired messengers of the eighth century in the first half of the seventh century, when the infamous Manasseh controlled the destiny of Judah and bought peace with the Assyrians, at a price these faithful and others considered much too high, then the literary work which resulted served as a rallying point for them and other adherents of the reform party. This party had been in the ascendancy during the reign of Hezekiah, Manasseh's father and predecessor. Then, as a result of the disasters which attended his reign, especially the loss of territory and treasure, not to speak of status and independence, which followed the thoroughly devastating invasion by Sennacherib in 701 B.C.E., it fell out of power.

Manasseh, who reigned independently from 687 to 642, brought peace and stability and a measure of prosperity through a treaty of submission to Assyria. This procedure involved submission also to the gods of Assyria and the subordination and contamination of the worship of Yahweh in the Temple at Jerusalem. According to the Deuteronomic historian, Manasseh was never forgiven for this and other heinous defections from the religious and cultic standards of the reformers. (Contrast II Chron 33:12–19; the

Chronicler's more sequential view of divine judgment suggested that since Judah did not suffer under Manasseh's reign, he must have repented and been forgiven.) The charter of the reformers, held firmly if secretly during the long years of Manasseh's reign, was the code of Deuteronomy (or something similar to it, which must have served as the marching plan for Hezekiah's great reform, as it also did for that of his great-grandson, Josiah) and the words of the eight-century prophets, preserved and ordered for this purpose. Here was a prescription for the present intolerable but also unchangeable conditions: to hold fast to the tradition of Moses and the prophets, and prepare for a day of reckoning and reform. If the prophetic denunciation of the kings and priests of the eighth century had been vindicated by the destruction of Israel, and the devastation of Judah, how much more did they apply to the arch-apostate and idolater, Manasseh! The message which had failed to save Israel might yet bring Judah to repentance, and a timely change of kings might bring to the throne someone who was, like Hezekiah, a faithful reformer. Along with threats there were promises. Those other words of the prophets, tied to the changing fortunes of the House of David but aimed at a renewal of the reign of David and a revival of the kingdom of Solomon, might yet prevail.

All the warnings and hopes, perseverance and promises, found fulfillment in Josiah and the reform associated with the eighteenth year of his reign (ca. 622/21). The centralization of worship in Jerusalem, and the corresponding destruction of the high places and their pagan cultic practices (spelled out in the charges against Manasseh) purified religion in Judah at a stroke. The program of the Deuteronomists and the classical prophets was carried out on a national scale, by a king as dedicated to the service of Yahweh and the Mosaic revelation (at least as presented in the farewell sermons of Moses recorded in Deuteronomy) as his grandfather Manasseh had been to the gods of Assyria and Canaan, and the abominable practices associated with their worship. The new order in Judah was a success, as the enthusiastic reports of the historian of the Books of Kings attest. Domestic renewal and reform were accompanied by national liberation and foreign conquest — or the recapture of territories which in former times belonged either to Israel or to Judah, essentially the united kingdom of the halcyon days of David and Solomon. Although short-lived, this sensational restoration confirmed the reformers and the followers of the prophets in all their zeal and urgency. The new age was now, and the era of the future was already present. But it did not last. Already new prophets had appeared to announce the failure of reform and the last days of Judah. The first in importance of these spokesmen was Jeremiah, followed closely by the even more insistent and obdurate Ezekiel. More penetrating and not less passionate students of the older prophets could read their message as spelling out the same doom upon the surviving kingdom.

Once again the words of the Deuteronomic historians and the prophets converged to explain and to justify the latest tragedy in the story of God's people. Josiah was slain in battle with the Egyptians and his successors were either picked off or carried captive to Egypt and Babylon respectively. In the end Judah fell as Israel had before it, and the nation states established centuries before ceased to exist.

In the context of the Babylonian captivity there was an even greater urgency for an adequate interpretation of the present situation in which the remnant of survivors of the catastrophe found themselves. They were almost literally back where their patriarchal ancestors had begun the great adventure of faith. It could be and was argued that the story had indeed come to an end; it was all over. The God who had summoned the forefathers and created from their progeny the new nation, Israel, had now in these last days destroyed his own people. The more stress that was placed on the reasons for this disastrous action, and the justification of God's wrath at the rebellion and misbehavior of his people, the more desperate the resultant mood. On the one hand it was necessary to establish that the history of Israel was not pointless, that Israel had not merely been the victim of more powerful forces (or gods), that its destiny was morally conditioned, and that it merited its reward, good or bad. On the other hand, since the outcome was an unrelieved tragedy, the further consequence could well have been the demise of the community altogether. And this would have been an even greater tragedy. If judgment and defeat, loss of freedom, loss of nationhood, were no accident, neither was the survival of the community nor its banishment to Babylonia.

They were chosen to survive, and to return and rebuild the community which had been shattered. The written record, the message of the prophets and historians preserved for study and reflection was to perform a unique function. The story of Israel from its origins until its end in defeat and captivity was to serve as a permanent and definitive lesson in theology, emphasizing the role of God as creator and redeemer, and as commander and judge. People could read the record and discover how and why Israel had come to be and also to be no more. They would learn that the relationship between God and his people was grounded in divine love and election but that its ongoing character was moral, requiring responsible behavior on the part of Israel, commensurate with the grace and revelation which it had received. Justice and mercy dominate the interaction between God and people, and in the end the people receive what they deserve. The story in all its variety and complexity is the frame of reference, the essential pattern on the basis of which and within which the message of the prophets, with its own particularity and time-bound quality, is to be fitted and understood. This message affirms the basic points about the nature of God, his will and his action; about the people, their behavior, and the consequences of their behavior. But there was an addendum, barely touched on though present in the Primary History (the Pentateuch and Former Prophets). Moses in his lengthy prophetic sermons in Deuteronomy had asserted that after the judgment there would be mercy and grace, pardon and renewal. The prophets who denounced a self-righteous arrogance, and a calculated repentance designed to trigger forgiveness, rather than genuine sorrow and regret, also tried to prevent a mood of despair and resignation. That was equally bad or worse. Just as surely as their grim warnings had proved utterly realistic as predictions became facts, so now they must also be believed when they promised return to the land, and its restoration to the people of God.

During the Exile a substantial part of the prophetic corpus was assembled and edited to provide a complementary work to the Primary History. Just as the latter explained, for those who seemed to be beyond that history in their captivity, the meaning of the long experience between God and his people, so the prophetic corpus could and would provide a message for this latter day. These prophets and their message had been vindicated by events; now there was another message to give them courage and hope for a better day. This, too, required a commitment in faith if it was to come to pass. In this way the older corpus of eighth-century prophecies was blended with the utterances of later prophets, and interwoven with them to produce a message for the Exiles, primarily. In this manner we can explain the intrusion of sixth-century matters into prophetic books of the eighth century (notably in Micah 4–7 and Isaiah 13–14), and the commingling of themes and events of both periods. The parallel between the fall of Israel in the latter part of the eighth century, and the fall of Judah in the early part of the sixth century was drawn so often and so explicitly by the later prophets such as Jeremiah and Ezekiel that it became a commonplace of biblical and prophetic speech. Thus the denunciations of Israel by the eighth-century prophets became paradigms of Judah's predicament more than a century later. The great prophets of the eighth century were co-opted by their successors, and also by the editors of their books for service in a larger cause involving the fate of Judah and not only Israel.

We conclude from this that it was during the Babylonian Exile that the final shape of the Book of Hosea was worked out. While the orientation is similar to that of other prophetic books, with repeated emphasis on judgment and survival, repentance and renewal, it is difficult to say how much is owed to the sixth-century reenactment of defeat and captivity, and how much belongs to the original eighth-century composition. The analogies are both obvious and powerful; in fact, the eighth-century assertions, positive and negative, so closely fit the sixth-century situation, except in details, such as names and dates, and the specifics of personalities and events, that little deliberate change need have occurred.

As part of a prophetic manual on the causes of the recent series of disasters and on the possibilities of restoration in the future, the Book of Hosea, in our opinion, was put in final form during the Babylonian captivity. Beyond that point, Hosea and its companion volumes seem to have remained intact. There is no reason to imagine that there were either major or wholesale changes in any subsequent period, although we must always allow for marginal alterations as the result of copyists' errors, or the hypercorrections of fussy editors.

The corpus of minor prophets consists of the oracles of the three minor eighth-century prophets and the oracles of later prophets as well, clearly compiled and presented during the Exile. There is a sixth-century cast to the Book of the Twelve, and its function and objective are to be sought in a study of the needs and desires of the audience of that period and of the interests of those who were responsible to and for them. One more major revision or reorganization of the prophetic material should be mentioned. After the return, which cannot be disentangled from the oracles of so-called Second or Babylonian Isaiah, there was added a group of prophets including, in addition to that unknown prophet of the Exile, Zechariah, Haggai, and perhaps Malachi. These materials reflect the renewed occupation of the land and set the stage for the next step. Just as the fall of Judah confirmed the second phase of prophecy, which predicted just such an end of the nation, so these new oracles confirm the predictions of the return and restoration of the community, and prepare the way not only for the actuality of the return, but the next stage of prophecy, the establishment of the new order and the confirmation of God's reliability and overarching mercy. With the addition of Second Isaiah and the prophecies of Zechariah, Haggai, and Malachi, the corpus was complete.

It is not clear to us how much the two major expansions and editions affected the content or structure of the earlier books such as Hosea. For the moment we can speak only of possibilities, since the reality of such adaptation of the text to ever changing new conditions is difficult to determine. Suffice it to say that while a sixth-century setting is not unlikely for the final editing and publication of Hosea as part of a larger corpus, there is little evidence of any tampering with the text in the interest of updating its material. For the most part it remains archaic, fitting better into an eighth-century setting than anywhere else, and more acceptably than some of the other literature traditionally associated with this period.

The Texture of Hosea

The Book of Hosea can be divided into two unequal parts: I, cc 1–3, and II, cc 4–14. They are quite distinct, though not so different as to constitute separate works of two prophets living decades or even a century apart. We believe there is only one prophet and that the first part of the book is biographical (cc 1–2) with an autobiographical appendix (c 3), while the second has few personal references and consists mainly of a collection of prophetic utterances, autonomous but related by subject matter, setting, style and vocabulary.

Part I was composed by someone who was close to the prophet or had access to his family history. It was known that his marriage and children, and his family life, were closely bound up with his calling to be a prophet and his ministry as a messenger of God. Not only was this the point of departure for his mission and message, but it was a model and metaphor for Yahweh's marriage to his bride Israel and the history of their relationship. Chapters 1 and 2 form a continuous whole built around the prophet's family, the story of which is projected onto the story of Israel as the errant wife of Yahweh. Marriage, conflict, separation, disgrace and degradation, followed by the crisis of forgiveness conjoined with repentance and resolution, reconciliation and renewal — this is the pattern for the prophet and his wife and children, and for Yahweh and his people. The stories are so intertwined and involved that separation is not always easy or even possible, and the language belonging to one set of characters and experiences is regularly adapted to the others. Reality and symbolism merge and divide, leaving an impressionistic design in which past, present, and future flow into one another, without clear demarcations. While different strands of thought can be traced, and different images can be isolated and identified, it would be difficult if not impossible to rearrange or reorganize the material in more rational patterns without changing its fundamental character or altering its essential texture.

Without denying the possibility of editorial changes and additions, we contend that Part I as we have it is the original composition of a disciple or follower, whose primary purpose was to portray the mission of the prophet as an expression of his personal experience, especially in terms of his marriage and his children. These events furnish the decisive moments in an account of Yahweh's experience with his people, also described as the relationship of husband and wife. The first two chapters form a unit founded and bonded by the names of the children, which change in form and meaning as the story unfolds, and as the message changes from threat and judgment to promise and redemption. The third chapter, in the first person, is not a doublet but an epilogue to the longer presentation, reflecting a later stage in the experience of the prophet, which presupposes the earlier account. While c 3 is too short to reveal fully its literary affinities, it seems to derive from the prophet himself. It was attached to the longer introductory account by the composer of that account, or some editor down the line.

Part II shows little superficial evidence of careful composition or organization. The individual oracles — it is not always easy to separate them, since openings and closings, with few exceptions, are not clearly marked — are sophisticated compositions employing a variety of literary devices, and reflecting the creative genius of the prophet himself. Presumably another hand has been at work in this material as well, but identifying particular verses as editorial comments is difficult; proposals are largely speculative.

It is possible that the two sections circulated independently for a while before they were joined. There are many thematic links between the parts, and some editorial supervision of the whole can be postulated. This basic work, containing the substance of the present Book of Hosea, was compiled within a generation or two of the time of the prophet. At the same time it may have been combined with other eighth-century prophecies to form a small corpus, the nucleus of the Minor Prophets, itself a product of the Exilic period. The use of the eighth-century prophecies in that later period resulted in some editorial reworking or commentary tying the oracles of one century to the circumstances of another. Through all these developments Hosea remained essentially untouched. Here and there we may find allusions to or echoes of another age, or reflections of dramatically changed conditions; references to Davidic restoration and return from exile are the most obvious. For the most part, however, the setting is that of the eighth century, and the pronouncements fit the situation as we know it from other sources. The obscurities, which are many, do not point us away from that era or in any direction in particular; they only expose our ignorance of the circumstances generally, and emphasize repeatedly that the Book of Hosea is maddeningly difficult to grasp, no matter how we approach it.

As we turn to the question of the literary character of the work, we must consider two anterior issues: the unity of the work, and the integrity of the text. In both cases, our premise and point of departure are conservative, that the book is essentially the work of a single person, and that the text is basically sound. These are hardly ringing affirmations; they are more like defensive desperation. If the opposite were true, if many hands and voices could be found in the book, then we would have the thankless and ultimately fruitless task of apportioning the work among a variety of people whose existence is hypothetical, and whose only distinguishing mark is some obscurity or inconsistency in the text. That the text in the Hebrew Bible is difficult is widely agreed; that it is also corrupt is maintained by many scholars, but this is less certain. It is true that to make Hosea read like typical classical Hebrew prose or poetry would require extensive emendation, which is the common procedure. But is it justifiable? There may be errors in the text, and if possible these should be corrected. There are peculiarities as well, and these should be respected. How to distinguish the two groups of phenomena and deal with them appropriately is the major task of the exegete or interpreter. The initial presumption must be in favor of peculiarities, since we know that the book is the work of serious people who endeavored to reproduce faithfully the utterances of the prophet, while weaving oracles and narrative into a totality for the edification of hearers and readers. Did they succeed or are we faced with wholesale corruption in the transmission of the text?

There are more than enough oddities and peculiarities which can be defended, interpreted, and explained to undermine the hypothesis of extensive corruption. While the versions often differ from the MT, it is doubtful that they reflect superior readings, since they do not make much sense or command automatic assent either. While it would not advance the cause of scholarship to hold a difficult text sacrosanct, or contrariwise to emend away the prophet's deliberate deviation from normality and conventionality whether in the order and arrangement of words, or the selection of strange terms in preference to common ones, it is perhaps better to stay with the text in cases of doubt than to increase the doubt by resorting to emendation.

What is preserved is odd enough. It seems to have features both of prose and poetry in varying degrees, but the boundaries are not clearly marked, and it is not feasible or desirable to attempt the separation on the grounds that the prose is secondary and editorial and, once stripped away, will leave the pristine and uncontaminated verse of the author, poet and prophet. While there are some prosaic elements, especially in the early chapters, which serve as introduction, bridges, or asides, the practice is not widespread and more often prose and poetry are intertwined. The effects, which to some degree are measurable, can be compared with similar usage in other prophets, especially Amos and Micah, but not excluding Isaiah. What seems to emerge from some statistical studies is a prophetic literary pattern, characteristic at least of the eighth-century prophets. This style or quality of literature does not fall obviously into either of the classical categories of prose or poetry, but seems to be a mixture, in which the parts are blended rather than being separated either by form or content.

This blend can be illustrated through the results of a statistical study of the use of certain "prose particles" in the books of the Bible. It has long been believed that the particles 'ēt, 'ăšer, and the definite article are typical of Hebrew prose and atypical in Hebrew poetry. This basic position can now be confirmed statistically on a broad scale. A simple count of these particles in the Masoretic Text shows a striking divergence between prose and poetry in the frequency with which these particles occur. (For our purposes, we count only the article written with h; see further on this point Freedman 1977:8 n 9.) In standard prose, the frequency is high (on a percentage basis, 15% or more of all words), while in poetry, as the category is recognized by most scholars, it is much lower (5% or less). The gap is a fairly wide one and while some pieces fall between the two categories, most cluster at the high and low ends of the scale. The prophetic literature, especially of the eighth century, is exceptional in that much of the material comes in the middle, between prose and poetry. It is not a matter of an obvious mixture of prose sentences and poetic verses, but rather a distinctive oratorical style which blends features of both. That characteristic is clearly reflected in the frequency patterns of these particles. With respect to Hosea there is a marked difference between cc 1–3 and 4–14. The former is much closer to the prose end of the scale with an 11 per cent frequency. Chapters 4–14, on the other hand, are closer to the poetry end of the scale: about 3 per cent. The average for Hosea as a whole would be about 5 per cent, which would put it toward the upper limit for poetry. Individual chapters vary considerably so that according to this criterion the literary character of the material varies from pure poetry (cc 8, 11, 13, 14 = 1% or less) to something more like prose poetry or free verse (cc 4–5, 12, between 5% and 7%) while several chapters fall in between, around the average for the unit as a whole (cc 6–7, 9–10). In the first part, c 3 has a ratio of 5 per cent, but it is too short to be an adequate sample; it seems to contain both prose and poetry. Hosea 1:2 – 2:3 has a frequency of 7.4 per cent, which suits the narrative-dialogue style of the material, whereas in 2:4–25, which is a major unified oracle, the frequency climbs to 15.1 per cent, which is much too high for poetry, and well within the range for standard prose. (For the purposes of this brief sketch we can ignore the age of the material involved. Forthcoming results of the work of Andersen and Forbes show that later poetry uses more particles than early poetry, and early prose is more sparing in their use than later prose; the slight differences do not materially affect our argument here.)

In Part I (Hosea 1–3) we can distinguish two kinds of literary construction. Chapters 1:2 – 2:3 and 3:1–5 are essentially narratives concerning the prophet and his family. The framework is prose, while the content is in the form of speeches. The utterances tend to be poetic in structure, with a certain rhythm or meter, though not repeated or regular. This phenomenon is fairly common in biblical rhetoric and writing; it has been noticed that speeches tend to be more poetic or elevated in style than ordinary narrative. The distribution pattern for prose particles (h, $'t$, $'šr$) shows a frequency of 7.4 per cent for the first unit and 4.9 per cent for the second, for a weighted average of 6.6 per cent. The inclusion of 1:1 (4.8%) does not materially affect the results. The data are summarized in the following table:

Hosea	Words	$'šr$	$'t$	h	Totals	Percent
1:1	21	1	0	0	1	4.8%
1:2 – 2:3	162	2	6	4	12	7.4%
3:1–5	81	0	3	1	4	4.9%
	264	3	9	5	17	6.4%

The final average is near the upper limit for poetry, and well below the average for prose, essentially what we would expect of a mixture of narrative and dialogue.

The long central section (2:4–25) of this part exhibits a strikingly different pattern. It consists of a sustained description of marital breakdown reflecting both the experience of the prophet and his wife and that of Yahweh and his people. It moves through different time phases from present to past to future and traces the progress of thought from fact to threat or hope. The style is uniform but the character of the material is not easy to describe. Since it is mostly speech, whether articulated or not, dialogue or monologue, there is a certain rhythm; rhetorical devices are numerous and stylistic features are elaborate and intricate. The extensive use of inclusion, echo, catchwords, and chiasm, shows that the composition is a carefully crafted whole. But is it prose or poetry? Perhaps the most convenient evasion of this thorny dilemma is to designate it prophetic speech of the eighth century, orotund, ornate, hardly conventional narrative or exposition, but not lyric poetry either. The data for the frequency of prose particles show that this material is out of the poetry sector entirely and belongs solidly with standard prose. The information may be summarized as follows:

Hosea	Words	'šr	't	h	Total	Percent
2:4–15	168	3	9	6	18	10.7%
2:16–25	124	0	11	15	26	21.0%
	292	3	20	21	44	15.1%

The piece can be divided at the end of v 15, and there is a marked difference in the frequency of prose particles between the two units (proportionately there are twice as many in the second part on restoration as in the first part on condemnation). The latter unit, vv 16–25, has many affinities with the priestly style in the Pentateuch, especially Genesis, but there are striking differences both in imagery and rhetorical flourishes. The first part is less prosaic, and here and there we find typical poetic parallelism and traditional pairs which are characteristic of classical Hebrew poetry. There is no reason, however, to chop up the unit in terms of literary style, since whatever the internal variations the piece as a whole has a distinctive character and is unified in concept and content. Perhaps the designation prose poetry, or prophetic discourse (or more properly soliloquy, since the prophet — or God — only imagines the dialogue) would be equally appropriate.

The statistics for Part II of Hosea may be tabulated as follows:

Hosea	Words	'šr	't	h	Total	Percent
4:1–3	45	0	0	5	5	11.1%
4:4–19	178	0	2	8	10	5.6%
	223	0	2	13	15	6.7%
5:1–7	86	0	3	3	6	7.0%
5:8–11	37	0	0	0	0	0.0%
5:12–15	56	1	2	0	3	5.4%
	179	1	5	3	9	5.0%
6:1–3	31	0	1	1	2	6.5%
6:4–6	32	0	0	0	0	0.0%
6:7 – 7:2	68	0	0	0	0	0.0%
	131	0	1	1	2	1.5%
7:3–7	54	0	1	1	2	3.7%
7:8–16	108	1	0	1	2	1.9%
	162	1	1	2	4	2.5%
cc 4–7	695	2	9	19	30	4.3%
8:1–8	86	0	0	0	0	0.0%
8:9–14	68	0	1	0	1	1.5%
	154	0	1	0	1	0.6%
9:1–9	114	0	0	5	5	4.4%
9:10–17	99	1	1	0	2	2.0%
	213	1	1	5	7	3.3%
10:1–8	104	0	2	1	3	2.9%
10:9–15	97	0	1	1	2	2.1%
	201	0	3	2	5	2.5%
11:1–11	122	0	0	0	0	0.0%
cc 8–11	690	1	5	7	13	1.9%
12:1–15	160	1	3	4	8	5.0%
13:1 – 14:1	174	1	0	1	2	1.1%
14:2–10	105	1	0	0	1	1.0%
cc 12–14	439	3	3	5	11	2.5%

Summary:

Part I	Hosea 1–3	Words	Particles	Percentage
	1:1 – 2:3	183	13	7.1%
	2:4–25	292	44	15.1%
	3:1–5	81	4	4.9%
	cc 1–3	556	61	11.0%

Part II Hosea 4–14	Words	Particles	Percentage
4	223	15	6.7%
5	179	9	5.0%
6:1 – 7:2	131	2	1.5%
7:3–16	162	4	2.5%
cc 4–7	695	30	4.3%
8	154	1	0.6%
9	213	7	3.3%
10	201	5	2.5%
11	122	0	0.0%
cc 8–11	690	13	1.9%
12	160	8	5.0%
13:1 – 14:1	174	2	1.1%
14:2–10	105	1	1.0%
cc 12–14	439	11	2.5%
cc 4–14	1,824	54	3.0%
Hosea 1–14	2,380	115	4.8%

It will be seen at once that there is a marked difference in the occurrence of prose particles between Parts I and II of Hosea. While cc 1–3 have 556 words, less than one-third of the 1,824 words in cc 4–14, there are actually more prose particles in the former (61) than in the latter (54). Proportionately the contrast is so great (11% for 1–3 versus 3% for 4–14) that some explanation is called for. On the scale we have used to distinguish prose from poetry, the frequency in cc 1–3 (11%) is well above the category of poetry but substantially below the standard range for prose; the frequency in cc 4–14 (3%) is well within the range for poetry. It would appear that not only are the literary forms of the two parts markedly different, but that they have different literary histories. It would be reasonable to conclude that cc 4–14 stem directly from the utterances of the prophet and have retained their original poetic character. Chapters 1–3, on the other hand, derive from the experience and teaching of the prophet, but have been put together by someone else, especially the large central section (2:4–25), which stands apart from the rest of the book not only in its literary style and intricate construction, but also with respect to the frequency of the prose particles (15% or five times the frequency of cc 4–14 and almost 2.5 times the frequency of cc 1 and 3). At the same time the strong thematic and verbal associations between c 2 and the latter part of the book, especially cc 4–5, militate against the views that the parts of the book belong to different centuries or refer to different prophets.

With respect to cc 4–14, most are well below the 3 per cent average of the whole: cc 6, 7, 8, 11, 13, 14; two others are close to the average: 9 and 10; while three are substantially above it: 4, 5, 12. The latter two are at 5 per cent, which is barely on the side of poetry.

As it stands, c 4 is apparently intermediate. The problem lies in the first unit, vv 1–3, which has a frequency of 11.1 per cent, compared with the rest of the chapter at half of that figure or 5.6 per cent, on the high side for poetry but comparable to cc 5 and 12 (the latter has more than its share of narrative prose) at 5 per cent each. The opening verses of c 4 constitute the introductory oracle of this part of the book. The vocabulary is related to the Decalogue and priestly or deuteronomic prose of the Pentateuch; it also has close ties with material in c 2 of Hosea (especially vv 20ff). The frequency in 4:1–3 is 11.1 per cent, which corresponds almost exactly with that of cc 1–3 as a whole, and might point to a common authorship, or the same editor.

In Part II, there is less prose generally according to the evidence presented by our indicators, and more homogeneity of style, although there is considerable variation from section to section. Once again we ar-, rive at the provisional judgment that the material is not classical poetry in the sense in which we apply the designation to the early poems of the Pentateuch and Former Prophets or the lyrics of the Psalter; certainly it is not like the standard couplets of the Wisdom books. While occasional passages have good parallelism and a strong rhythm (which can be quantified in terms of stresses or syllables or words), for the most part Hosea goes off on its own bent, a kind of free verse, or unregulated rhythmic pattern. It would be impossible to achieve any sort of regularity in rhythm or consistency in stanza construction without wholesale emendation of the text. At the same time, we are not dealing with ordinary prose, or even elevated, sonorous prose as in the sermons of Deuteronomy.

The combination of poetic and prosaic elements is distinctive and deserves recognition. There are affinities among the prophets of the eighth century, but there is wide variation as well: Amos and Isaiah make extensive use of refrains in marking off strophic divisions and generally their oracles are more clearly poetic in the classical sense; Micah is closer to Hosea, although differences in structure and style are to be noted as well. It is important to study the features of this style and the actual way in which the material is presented so that a variety of errors in treating and interpreting the material may be avoided. Chief among these is the notion that the prophet himself spoke in a lyric poetic style and therefore we must attempt to disentangle the pristine material from the accretions which have crept in, or the paraphrases provided by editors and commentators. Efforts have been made along these lines, but in the case of Hosea they have been singularly unsuccessful. In order to achieve symmetry and uniformity, excessive tampering is required; confidence in the results is undermined by the absence of evidence. Less drastic treatment is more cosmetic in character and a matter of scholarly predilection or taste and does not affect the basic character of the material.

At the heart of the problem is the difficulty in understanding the text at all. Because of the many subtleties and intricacies in the text which are noted below, and which make it clear that the Book of Hosea is not a mere hodgepodge, extreme caution is advisable in dealing with materials where patterns are not discernible. For the present it seems best to describe the phenomena, examine them, draw what inferences seem appropriate, identify rhetorical devices and literary features as clues to the purpose of the prophet (and his editor), and the manner or style of presentation. Eighth-century prophecy, and the Book of Hosea in particular, is a manifestation of the classic prophetic experience, formulated in a literary style which is a creative adaptation of earlier oracular poetry on the one hand (reflected in pieces like the Oracles of Balaam and the Song of Hannah) and the great prose narrative tradition of Israel (reflected in the work of J and E, and the so-called court history of the reign of David).

The Text of Hosea

The text of Hosea competes with Job for the distinction of containing more unintelligible passages than any other book of the Hebrew Bible. Concerning this text, there is not very much that can be said, at least of a constructive nature, beyond our earlier remarks. For the Hebrew original we have the Masoretic Text, and not much else. Bits and pieces of the Minor Prophets have turned up at Qumran (Testuz 1955), but the total is not impressive, and the text does not differ in any significant way from the MT. An occasional reading may be of interest, but none helps to resolve basic or serious problems. There are many of the latter, and it is difficult to avoid the conclusion that the surviving Hebrew is corrupt and defective. That at least has been the opinion of most critical scholars, and our commentary confirms the fact that the text bristles with difficulties. What to do about the situation is another question altogether, because whatever the deficiencies of the Hebrew text, the versions are no better, and in general are not so good. The only one that is worth serious thought is the Greek, but the LXX can hardly be construed as a witness to a different Hebrew Vorlage. For the most part, the Greek translator seems to have faced the same problems in the Hebrew text before him, and did no better than most scholars in trying to solve its many riddles. No doubt there are places where he had a Hebrew text different from the MT (where it is not the result of a common scribal error) and rendered accordingly. As to whether particular readings presupposed by the Greek translation are better than those preserved in the MT, or the other way around, such matters can only be decided on their merits in individual cases. By and large, the MT is superior to all the versions.

We have proceeded on that basis and have tried to work out translation and comments on the basis of the received Hebrew text. We wish there were a broader base for determining the Hebrew original such as is available in treating the Pentateuch and Former Prophets. But we have felt that it was more consistent with good scholarship to deal as faithfully as possible with a text that exists, than to create one which might serve our purposes better, but the interests of serious scholarship and study of this book less well. In the end, however, it must be confessed that many problems remain unsolved, and that a good deal of the content of Hosea and its real meaning remain beyond reach.

The difficulties of the text of Hosea were universally recognized by older scholars. This state of affairs they blamed on extensive corruption owing to a long history of transmission. It was the accepted task of scholarship in previous generations to solve as many of these problems as possible by repairing the damaged texts. This activity was particularly prominent in the great German commentaries of the last century. Wellhausen's notes on the Minor Prophets (1893) are still a rich mine for such ideas and the tradition persists. Even if many of these proposed emendations are too conjectural to carry conviction, enough of them have won their way into general acceptance to justify the enterprise and to excuse its excesses. If we have been restrained in our own resort to such means to solve problems, it is not out of blind veneration for the Masoretic Text. The knowledge of ancient Hebrew gained through epigraphic studies and related disciplines has provided new ways of explaining the text without changing it. Willingness to recognize such grammatical phenomena as the broken construct chain, double-duty prepositions, suffixes, and conjunctions, poetic sequences of the verb-tense forms, archaic spellings, as well as particles such as asseverative *l'*, asseverative *k*, and enclitic *m*, supplies the investigator with a wider range of options. As a result, there is less need to alter the text to remove a supposed difficulty.

Another explanation of the linguistic peculiarities of Hosea has often been broached. It has been supposed that, as the only prophet native to the northern kingdom, Hosea's language is regional, with peculiarities of the dialect of Samaria (or Ephraim). While our knowledge of the dialects of Hebrew spoken in Israel during the monarchical period is still meager, epigraphic materials such as the Samaria Ostraca give some controls; knowledge of ancient neighboring cognate languages, notably Phoenician and Ugaritic, adds a further perspective. The supposition that Hosea is written in a distinctive dialect of Hebrew has not been confirmed, and the hope that light from Ugaritic would illuminate dark places in the text has been fulfilled only to a limited degree. The study of Kuhnigk (1974) has shown the usefulness of such research, but the yield in the case of Hosea has not been significantly greater than from other poetic books of the Bible.

THE STUDY OF HOSEA

The position of this book among the "writing" prophets, the power of its "message," and the fascination of the prophet himself have attracted the attention of many students of the Hebrew Bible, so that nearly every notable name has appeared in the literature. Previous study is too extensive for a complete inventory here, and a detailed history of Hosea studies has yet to be written. We will review major trends, mentioning only the more significant contributions. Craghan (1971) supplies a useful supplement to what is here and to our Bibliography.

The differences between Parts I and II, cc 1–3 and cc 4–14, are so marked that each part may be discussed on its own terms. The great contrast between the parts has even suggested that two distinct works of widely separated date are involved (Kaufmann 1960:309; Ginsberg 1971). Deutero-Hosea has not, however, attracted the kind of credence enjoyed by Deutero-Isaiah and Deutero-Zechariah, and most scholars acknowledge the general unity of the book. Even when a considerable amount of the text is treated as the work of later editors, it is still recognized that the core of both parts goes back to Hosea himself.

Hosea's family tragedy, which provides the setting for cc 1–3, is a perpetual challenge to interpreters, and the publications on the subject show no signs of abating. The problems are numerous and urgent, for the interpretation of the whole book is influenced by the way they are resolved. The major questions are: Were the events real, or is the story a vision or an allegory? Was only one woman involved, or two? Much is at stake here, and scholars have been emphatic in declaring for the alternate positions. Although we are convinced that Gomer is the only woman involved, the problems of putting cc 1, 2, and 3 together into one coherent narrative are great. The two-woman theory is still affirmed, for example, by Fohrer (1968b:421), following a number of previous scholars. Was Hosea's wife promiscuous from the first, and did he know it? Or did she only become promiscuous later on (and, if so, how many of the children were not his)? What is the explanation for the different mode of narration in c 3 (first person) and c 1 (third person), especially since c 3 says nothing about the children? How does c 2 fit in? To what extent does theological motivation steer the narration in the direction of fantasy, complicated by an overlay of later additions?

There is plenty of room for speculation, and almost every imaginable solution seems to have been tried. Since Hosea 1–3 constitutes a famous problem, there is no need to go over the well-trodden ground here; our notes on the text are extensive. The whole subject was reviewed comprehensively by Rowley (1956), with rich documentation. Additional contributions are by Eybers (1964–65), Ginsberg (1960), Gordis (1954), Hendriks (n.d.), McDonald (1964), Rudolph (1963), and van Selms (1964–65). In addition to these specialized studies, extended discussions of the question of Hosea's marriage are to be found in standard Introductions to the Old Testament. Eissfeldt (1965:387–390) and Harrison (1969:861–868) have detailed summaries along with long lists of scholars who hold the seemingly innumerable theories.

The main conclusions reached in our notes are that the events of cc 1 and 3 did take place and that these chapters contain parts of a single, although complex, story, from which grows the fantasy of c 2. Our belief that Gomer was guilty of adultery through involvement in the Baal cult after a good start in marriage is not new. It was Wellhausen's position (1893), for instance. But, in addition to the general arguments that have been heard before, we have examined more thoroughly the precise meaning of the language used by Hosea to support our case.

The major literary problem encountered in cc 4–14 is its apparent incoherence. It is amorphous, on first sight. This has long been observed, and the opinion of Jerome is often quoted: *Osee commaticus est, et quasi per. sententias loquens* (Jerome 1845:1015). A similar impression was recorded by the popular English devotional commentator, Matthew Henry: "The style is very concise and sententious, above any of the prophets; and in some places it seems to be like the book of Proverbs, without connexion, and rather to be called Hosea's *sayings* than Hosea's *sermons*. And a weighty adage may sometimes do more service than a laboured discourse" (1827:739).

Modern study, in the main, has confirmed these impressions, and has supplied a theoretical explanation of the phenomena, largely through form criticism and the history of prophetic speech. The course of twentieth-century research into this matter has been charted by Westermann (1967) and Hayes (1974:157–175). Beginning early in this century, the prevailing opinion, in spite of numerous minor variations, has been that prophetic speeches, in the early stages of Israelite prophecy at least, and certainly still in the time of Hosea, consisted of short complete utterances, each quite independent. Hosea's has been taken as an extreme case, since his collected sayings, lacking the protection supplied to sustained discourse by contextual controls, were especially vulnerable to injury in transmission. T. H. Robinson said (1954:1): "In no other prophetic book are there so many mangled pieces as in Hosea. . . . Sometimes the damage is so great that we have only little bits, *of one or two lines*" (italics added). Even when these little sayings were gathered together, they remained a loose agglomeration, united only accidentally insofar as the speaker returned to the same themes at different times, or an editor assembled similar pieces with the aid of catchwords.

A different opinion has often been expressed, a suspicion that there is considerable coherence in the collections of sayings, even though the principle of organization is hard to detect, and it is impossible to tell who is responsible, the prophet himself, or some disciple. Eissfeldt (1965:385–387), for instance, finds a difference between 4:1–9:9 and 9:10–14:10. The former contains nine speeches of considerable scope, most of which can be characterized as diatribe and threat; the latter has about ten speeches of varying length, in which Israel's sinfulness is viewed in historical retrospect.

We have found it convenient to work with units of substantial size, recognizing a degree of cohesion within each unit on the basis of its internal literary (rhetorical) organization, and at the same time not marking the boundaries with great confidence, since the reappearance of the same theme, often with further elaboration, suggests continuity. In fact, we have often wondered if the whole of cc 4–14 is really a single sustained prophetic discourse. In any case, our continual discovery of more and more structural devices of many different kinds — linguistic, thematic, and poetic — some of which operate over a long range (such as inclusion and elaborate introversions), increasingly convinced us, not only that there was a high level of coherence in the composition, but that it is the deliberate result of an artistry far more sophisticated than anything previously suspected.

This brings us back to Hosea's own genius as an author. In spite of dismay over the numerous problems of the text, its literary excellence is frequently praised. Noting "the way wisdom has influenced his language," Fohrer (1968b:419) suggests "that he was educated in a wisdom school, which served primarily for the training of royal officials." Such an inference is not so precarious as Knight's argument (p. 13) that Hosea's knowledge of baking, shown in 7:4–7, proves that he was trained in that trade, but it can no more be proved than earlier proposals that Hosea was a priest (Duhm 1911).

Attempts to account for Hosea's literary ability by education are not much better than the theories which explain his prophetic insight by psychology (Allwohn 1926). In particular, many writers, especially preachers, have expanded his meager biography along sentimental lines, making it into a great romance in which Hosea's indestructible love for Gomer gives him the clue to God's love for his people. Our study of c 2 shows how intimately these two things were fused in his thought; 3:1 seems to turn the process around the other way, as if Hosea drew the inspiration for his personal struggle from his belief in the love of God. In any case, recognition of love as an elemental motivation in the prophet and in his God makes the emotional complexity of the book more credible, a point well made by Mauchline (p. 563). Brown (pp. xxix–xxx, 25–27) uses this feature to argue for the authenticity of the "hopeful" passages.

There is certainly a turbulence in Hosea's thought that would seem to interfere with the composure of mind needed for composition in classical forms; this circumstance could, however, make for a flow of lyrical expression as sublime as more formal work. Without claiming too much for the perfection of his art, we feel at least that Hosea's abilities should not be restricted in advance of studying his work, whether by the constraints of such conventional forms as genre, or by the supposed primitive stage of prophetic discourse in his times.

The problem of the literary character of the discourse in Hosea involves consideration of whether it is poetry or prose, discussed above; as well as consideration of the formality of the genres of prophetic speech and their rules of (poetic) composition; and the injury to these forms by editorial changes or scribal errors. The dangers introduced by a priori judgments are grave; for, if one supposes a high degree of poetic regularity in genuine prophetic composition (a widespread belief, almost an axiom in present-day scholarship), then all prose-like material will have to be deleted as spurious. This is commonly done.

There is a paradox here; the supposed processes of literary development of primitive oral traditions work in contrary ways. On the one hand, editors are credited with bringing originally miscellaneous materials into some kind of system, however contrived and however detrimental to the true formal character of the ingredients. On the other hand, scribes are suspected of upsetting this order by adding incongruous comments of their own, as they copied the text. In this way, both order and disorder are attributed to secondary hands.

We have found it impossible to draw a line between poetry and prose in Hosea. The text is not simply a mingling of both, too intricate to be separated out. Rather we have an intermediate mode for which a special name is needed. While most of the discourse is poetic in many and various ways, the prosody is diverse, and regular patterns are rarely sustained for long. The poetic and prosaic lines are usually woven together by means of numerous and intricate verbal patterns which make it impossible to separate one from the other without dismantling the whole structure.

The observations we have made so far will help to explain why the major thrust of critical investigation of Hosea during this century — form criticism — has proved disappointing, or at least has not yet yielded agreed results, as a comparison of current proposals soon shows. This is said, not to decry the method, but to caution against overassurance in its use.

The form critic asks first of all, "What is the form (*Gattung*)?" of any given piece, assuming that an item embodying a form can be isolated. The investigator is looking for a conventional form whose appropriate use in some institutional setting, on some community occasion, explains its communication function. If the concrete historical occasion for which the speech was made and in which, presumably, it was actually used, can be identified as well, so much the better. Such a goal has always been the hope of literary-historical interpretation, and it remains the only sound basis for biblical studies. But these prerequisites, insisted on too stringently, have proved stultifying in practice, if only because the knowledge required is unattainable by means available at present. Until form and date are settled, nothing further can be done. All too often, in order to go on, we have to guess.

In Hosea studies, it must be confessed, we still lack both the historical controls and the definitions of forms that alone would lead to conclusions commanding wide acceptance. Good's brilliant but unsuccessful attempt (1966b) to explain material in cc 5 and 6 in terms of a seasonal fertility ceremony, in contrast to Alt's reading of the passage (1919) as a narrative of the Syro-Ephraimitic War, shows how wide the disagreements can be.

Wolff's commentary (1974) is conspicuous for the determination with which he tackles the twin preliminary tasks of form and date, which must be settled before he proceeds to interpret any piece in terms of its function in the community. Unfortunately, the boundaries of the individual units he separates are not clearly marked in many cases; the forms they exhibit are rarely in agreement with theoretical norms. There is a limit to the degree that definitions of forms can be stretched to cater to the variety that is met, for they soon lose the distinctiveness essential to their use. The recognition of mixed forms grants more scope to the individual creativity of the speaker on each occasion; but the more one moves in that direction, the less chance he has of being certain about the life-setting of the form. If the originality of the author means a weakening of the constraints of custom, then the way is open to think of more literary uses of the material, liberated from institutionalized patterns (such as lawsuits); and an expectation of continued, rather than once-for-all, use. Indeed, one must ask if the preservation of the prophetic speeches was fostered by such a movement toward literature for repeated use, for more than the memory of a past moment. To the extent that this might be so, the obligation to account for all the references in a passage in terms of a given historical moment is correspondingly reduced.

In the case of Hosea, we know so little of the historical framework that we can rarely identify people and events with any confidence. In spite of the stout attempts of scholars, it is practically impossible to date or place any of Hosea's oracles with certainty; and, rather than guess, or, worse, force the passage into some selected historical occasion that we happen to know a little about, we have tried to manage without this aid, even though most of the time we are left groping. We have only to mention the remarkable fact that cc 4–14 do not contain the name of a single historical personage in Israel to underscore the scholars' predicament. Hence we have had to be content with a more modest task, simply describing the literary characteristics of each section, making only cautious guesses about what the historical circumstances might be.

Some other attitudes which pervade modern Hosea studies arise from preconceptions about the nature of the prophetic ministry, at least in the eighth century B.C.E. It is often supposed that the prophet brings a message for the moment, primarily if not exclusively for his immediate audience. His focus is narrow in both space and time. Hosea, as a prophet of the north, addressed Israel; therefore it is assumed he had nothing to say about Judah. He announced imminent and inevitable disaster as judgment; he had no message of hope, whether of averting the calamity or of restoration after it. (For the latest review of this feature in general terms, see Warmuth 1976.) Except for the threat of immediate destruction, the element of prophecy as foretelling coming events is not present; the prophet's vision does not extend far into the future, so that anything that sounds eschatological cannot be his word.

This view of the limited scope of the prophetic "message" has often led to the removal of a number of verses as not belonging to Hosea. It has been common practice for a long time to remove all, or nearly all, references to Judah as spurious. They are either deleted or changed to "Israel," Hosea's sole interest. Some of the explanations of the alteration to "Judah," such as that of Ginsberg, based on a theory of scribal abbreviations (1971), are too ingenious to be convincing, especially since there is no supportive textual evidence. Many scholars, hesitating to go to this extreme and following Alt (1919), retain at least the references to Judah in 5:10 – 6:4. We find no compelling reason for abandoning any of the references to Judah, though each case must be judged on its merits, and certainty should not be claimed by anyone.

Harper (pp. clviii–clxii) provides a list of what he regards as the more important "secondary" additions. He is cautious; even so, over fifty verses or parts of verses (out of 197 verses) are deemed not original. In addition to the references to Judah (whether the word itself, or the whole sentence in which it is found), most of the suspect passages are hopeful references to the future, which "are entirely inconsistent with Hosea's point of view, and directly contradict the representations that are fundamental to his preaching" (pp. clix, clxi). In addition, Harper has a group of "expansions and explanations" and another collection of unexplained glosses.

The eschatological, or, to put it more moderately, "hopeful" passages are the most substantial of the suspected interpolations, and their removal or retention makes a major difference in our understanding of Hosea as a whole. Since their wholesale rejection by Marti (1904), there has been a steady retreat from that extreme position, so that now Fohrer (1968b:422) is able to maintain that "most of these oracles are shown by their style and content to be Hoseanic." We, too, are inclined to retain them on largely formal literary grounds. Form critics have been inclined to doubt that the early prophets had "salvation" oracles in their repertoire, but entrenched doubt about the antiquity of eschatological passages (using the term in the broadest possible sense) goes back to a belief that such ideas were absent in pre-exilic Israel. Their ascription to a later age was partly based on a correct perception that apocalyptic terminology is a late development; and also on the questionable assumption that Israel's religion evolved in strictly unilinear fashion.

Mowinckel (1956:126) has a chapter heading "No Pre-prophetic or Prophetic Eschatology." His subsequent discussion moderates somewhat the bluntness of this assertion; for, while he says "the prophet of doom had no eschatological message" (p. 134), he recognizes that there was an ancient "hope for the future" in the covenant itself. Definition of "eschatology" has a lot to do with this problem. Hosea's so-called eschatological passages do not refer to the end of the world. Taken at face value, the promises of restoration are not a program merely to reconstitute a lost past; they seem to strain beyond the possibilities of the historical, and they sound a note of finality. Particularly prominent in Hosea are promises of deliverance from death in which the motifs of later apocalypses can already be discerned. Arguing in a manner different from ours, Hecht (1971) has found an eschatological component in the cultic expression of the covenant, and offers this as background for the future expectations of the reforming prophets.

Hosea's key position at the beginning of "written" prophecy, and the richness of his stimulating ideas left their mark on prophets of a later age. Willi-Plein (1971) has examined this general question. In the case of Jeremiah and Ezekiel, the direct influence is palpable (Hendriks n.d. has the latest extended treatment), although not as sustained as that of Isaiah on "Deutero-Isaiah." We are grateful for such evidence where it sheds light on a difficulty in Hosea; and it makes us aware that within little more than a century, Hosea's work was the subject of interpretation and application.

Of equal interest is Hosea's own dependence on more ancient traditions. Hosea seems to know a lot about Israel's ancient history, and to assume that his hearers will know what he is talking about without much explanation. His many allusions are all fragmentary, and the point being made often eludes us. It is also possible that in some of the obscure passages he is drawing on traditions now lost to us; available contemporary references may not always offer the proper explanation. The traditions we can recognize are drawn from three formative ages and concern the patriarchs (or Jacob at least), the Exodus (at least the wilderness), and the Judges. The use of historical retrospect by the pre-exilic prophets has been studied by Vollmer (1971), who devotes a quarter of his book to Hosea, and an ample section to the Jacob traditions in Hosea 12. See also Ackroyd (1963), Coote (1971), Gertner (1960), Ginsberg (1961), and the earlier studies of Vriezen (1941, 1942).

Hosea does not use the Sinai tradition, although he knows about Moses and the Decalogue. The relationship of Hosea to the deuteronomic tradition is more problematical, since it is generally supposed that the latter did not receive its definitive literary expression until the seventh century, and that influences from the eighth-century prophets, including Hosea, can be discerned (Weinfeld 1972). Hosea's discourses, however, are threaded with Deuteronomic ideas in a way that shows they already were authoritative in Israel. Whether already written in an early form, or still largely oral, Deuteronomic material served as background for much of Hosea's thought (Brueggemann 1968).

In nineteenth-century scholarship, the prophets were hailed as the creators of ethical monotheism, and the time of Hosea was regarded as the first major breakthrough in humanity's spiritual advance in that direction. This estimate cast the prophets in rather too narrow a role as doctrinal theologians and moral reformers. In particular, as critics of formal religion, their negative comments on its institutions — priest, temple, sacrifice, and other ceremonies — were regarded as a rejection of cultus in favor of a spiritual and ethical religion of almost pietistic inwardness.

Subsequent research showed that this picture was too simple. Israel did not move forward stage by stage. Monotheism and morality were a joint heritage from an earlier age, and were in fact the foundations of Israel's historic faith from the time of Moses onward. The historical problem of distinguishing the potential from its actual expression is a complicated one, not to be settled by asking what kind of "monotheist" Moses or David was; these details do not affect the essential point being made. What matters is that cultus was also integral to Israel's identity as the people of God, since the religious and political dimensions of life were not distinguished. In reaction to the polarized picture of the prophets in continuous confrontation with priests, with every possible contrast pushed to the limit, some scholars regarded the prophets as part of the establishment, officers of shrines whose messages were delivered in formal ceremonies as part of their public duties. Duhm (1911) suggested that Hosea himself was a priest; but because of his attacks on the priests of his own day, and on one of them in particular, this seems unlikely. The religious background of Hosea is unclear. In fact, it has not even been possible to work out exactly what kind of religion Hosea condemned.

Hosea's attitude toward the monarchy is equally unclear, and has been interpreted in various ways. At one extreme, his hard words against kings are seen as a rejection of monarchy as such, for all Israel at all times. Less extreme is the view that he only condemned the wicked kings of Israel in his own day. Since he names only the house of Jehu, and speaks positively of David in association with Yahweh (3:5 — commonly removed as a gloss), the evidence is mixed. For recent discussion of the issue in its historical context, see Gelston (1974) and Crüsemann (1978).

The late nineteenth century was a time of intensive interest in Hosea, and many text-critical commentaries were produced, notably by German scholars; Harper (1905) has a full list. While this tradition continued into the twentieth century, as in the commentaries of Nowack (1922) and Sellin (1930), the interest of research was directed more to form-critical investigations and Hosea was investigated along these lines together with the other prophets.

The scholastic tradition found its final expression in E. B. Pusey's great commentary (1885), although this spirit is still present in much conservative devotional writing, and also, on a less impressive scale, in Laetsch (1956). G. A. Smith's exposition (1899) represents a high point in the homiletical tradition.

W. R. Harper's contribution to the International Critical Commentary (1905) still holds its own, since it is full of detail and gathers together an enormous amount from earlier critical work. Brown (1932) assembled the accepted results of the criticism of his time on a smaller scale, and in a moderate tone; the impact of form criticism is not strongly felt. Mays (1969) pays more attention to form criticism, and has brought critical discussion up to date. Pride of place among commentaries goes to Wolff's contribution to the Biblischer Kommentar Altes Testament (1965), conveniently available in English in the Hermeneia series (1974). Its documentation is thorough. We have already remarked on the limitations resulting from Wolff's commitment to a strict literary-historical approach; but these are balanced by the positive and appreciative tone of his theological exposition.

A Note on Syllable Counting

In a series of papers on the poetry of the Torah, the Former Prophets, and the Psalter, Freedman has demonstrated the usefulness of syllable counting in the study of Hebrew poetry (Freedman 1960, 1968, 1971, 1972a, 1972b, 1972d, 1974, 1976, 1977; Freedman and Franke-Hyland 1973). Syllable counting does not apparently describe the meter of Hebrew poetry but provides a guide to its structure (cf. O'Connor 1980).

The method of syllable counting used here is discussed at length in the papers cited. In brief, the counts are minimal, systematically making allowance for certain features of Masoretic vocalization which would increase the number of syllables involved. Thus segolate formations are treated as monosyllables; auxiliary vowels associated with laryngeals, and furtive *patah* are ignored as secondary developments. Where a more ancient pronunciation is attested (as in the case of resolved diphthongs), it is adopted in preference to MT. Occasionally, our counts are higher than those of the MT, since we do not resolve combinations such as *wĕyĕ-* in *wyhwdh,* as MT does; thus we count four syllables here rather than three; and we do not allow for the complete reduction of an original stem thematic vowel. On the whole, the differences between our counts and those that would result from MT are small; whatever system is used, the underlying patterns of distribution emerge. In the commentary, we generally present the Masoretic Text along with our counts, rather than the forms on which they are based. The reader should be able to trace the sources of the differences easily, since they involve only the phonological processes noted here. No systematic emendation of the text is required.

We have used syllable counting here cautiously. The poetic character of Hosea is, as we have shown, a problematic matter. Useful as counting is, the results afford only occasional insights in the study of this difficult text.

BIBLIOGRAPHY

ABBREVIATIONS

Periodicals

AJSL	*American Journal of Semitic Languages and Literatures*
BASOR	*Bulletin of the American Schools of Oriental Research*
BZ	*Biblische Zeitschrift*
CBQ	*Catholic Biblical Quarterly*
EvT	*Evangelische Theologie*
HUCA	*Hebrew Union College Annual*
IEJ	*Israel Exploration Journal*
JAOS	*Journal of the American Oriental Society*
JBL	*Journal of Biblical Literature*
JNES	*Journal of Near Eastern Studies*
JTS	*Journal of Theological Studies*
OTS	*Oudtestamentische Studien*
OTWSA	*Die Ou Testamentiese Werkgemeenskap in Suid-Afrika*
RHPR	*Revue d'histoire et de philosophie religieuses*
RevQ	*Revue de Qumrân*
TSK	*Theologische Studien und Kritiken*
VT	*Vetus Testamentum*
VTS	Vetus Testamentum Supplements
ZAW	*Zeitschrift für die Alttestamentliche Wissenschaft*

Books and Series

ANET	*Ancient Near Eastern Texts*, ed. J. B. Pritchard 1969
BWANT	Beiträge zur Wissenschaft vom Alten und Neuen Testament. Stuttgart: Kohlhammer
BZAW	Beihefte zur Zeitschrift für die Alttestamentliche Wissenschaft. Giessen/Berlin: Töpelmann
CAD	*The Assyrian Dictionary of the Oriental Institute of the University of Chicago*, eds. I. J. Gelb et al. 1956–
EA	*Die El-Amarna-Tafeln*, J. A. Knudtzon 1915
GKC	*Gesenius' Hebrew Grammar*, ed. E. Kautzsch, tr. A. E. Cowley 1910
KAI	*Kanaanäische und aramäische Inschriften*, eds. H. Donner and W. Röllig 1971
UT	*Ugaritic Textbook*, C. H. Gordon 1965
VTS	Vetus Testamentum Supplements

COMMENTARIES

Commentaries are cited in text by author's name only, without date, except those with dates marked by an asterisk, below. The main commentaries of the nineteenth century are listed in Harper (1905: clxxviii–clxxxi).

Bewer, J. A.
    1949   *The Book of the Twelve Prophets in the Authorized Version.* Harper's Annotated Bible Series 1–2. New York: Harper's.
Brown, S. L.
    1932   *The Book of Hosea.* Westminster Commentaries. London: Methuen.
Cohen, A.
    1948   *The Twelve Prophets.* London: Soncino.
Harper, W. R.
    1905   *A Critical and Exegetical Commentary on Amos and Hosea.* International Critical Commentary. New York: Scribner's.
van Hoonacker, A.
    1908   *Les douze petits prophètes.* Etudes bibliques. Paris: Gabalda.
Jacob, E.
    1965*   "Osée." Pages 7–98 in E. Jacob, C.–A. Keller, and S. Amsler. *Osée, Joël, Abdias, Jonas, Amos.* Commentaire de l'Ancien Testament 11a. Neuchatel: Delachaux et Niestlé.
Knight, G. A. F.
    1960   *Hosea.* Torch Commentaries. London: SCM.
Laetsch, T.
    1956   *Bible Commentary: The Minor Prophets.* St. Louis, Mo.: Concordia.
Lindblom, J.
    1927*   *Hosea, literarisch untersucht.* Acta Academiae Aboensis. Humaniora 5. Åbo: Åbo Akademie.
McKeating, H.
    1971   *The Books of Amos, Hosea and Micah.* The Cambridge Bible Commentary: New English Bible. Cambridge: Cambridge University Press.
Marti, K.
    1904   *Das Dodekapropheton.* Kurzer Hand-Commentar zum Alten Testament 13. Tübingen: Mohr.
Mauchline, J.
    1956   "Hosea." Pages 553–725 in *The Interpreter's Bible.* Vol. 6. Eds. G. A. Buttrick et al. Nashville: Abingdon.
Mays, J. L.
    1969   *Hosea.* Old Testament Library. Philadelphia: Westminster.

Nowack, W.
1922   *Die kleinen Propheten.* Göttinger Handkommentar zum Alten Testament 3.4. Göttingen: Vandenhoeck und Ruprecht.

Nyberg, H. S.
1935   *Studien zum Hoseabuche. Zugleich ein Beitrag zur Klärung des Problems der alttestamentlichen Textkritik.* Uppsala Universitets Årsskrift 1935:6. Uppsala: Almqvist und Wiksells.

Robinson, Th. H.
1954*   "Hosea." Pages 1–54 in Th. H. Robinson and F. Horst. *Die Zwölf kleinen Propheten: Hosea bis Micha.* Handbuch zum Alten Testament 1.14. Tübingen: Mohr.

Rudolph, W.
1966*   *Hosea.* Kommentar zum Alten Testament 13.1. Gütersloh: Gerd Mohn.

Sellin, E.
1930   *Das Zwölfprophetenbuch.* Kommentar zum Alten Testament 12.1. Leipzig: Deichert.

Smith, G.A.
1899   *The Book of the Twelve Prophets Commonly Called the Minor. I. Amos, Hosea and Micah.* The Expositor's Bible. New York: A. C. Armstrong.

Snaith, N.
1953   *Mercy and Sacrifice. A Study of the Book of Hosea.* London: SCM.

Ward, J. M.
1966*   *Hosea. A Theological Commentary.* New York: Harper & Row.

Weiser, A.
1964   *Das Buch der zwölf kleinen Propheten I.* Alte Testament Deutsch 24. Göttingen: Vandenhoeck und Ruprecht.

Wellhausen, J.
1893   *Die kleinen Propheten übersetzen, mit Notizen.* Skizzen und Vorarbeiten 5. Berlin: Töpelmann.

Wolff, H. W.
1965*   *Dodekapropheton 1. Hosea.* Biblischer Kommentar Altes Testament 14/1. Neukirchen-Vluyn: Neukirchener Verlag = Wolff 1974.

1974*   *Hosea,* tr. G. Stansell. Hermeneia. Philadelphia: Fortress Press = Wolff 1965.

BOOKS, MONOGRAPHS, AND ARTICLES

Aberbach, M., and L. Smolar
1967   "Aaron, Jeroboam and the Golden Calves," *JBL* 86:129–140.
Ackroyd, P. R.
1963   "Hosea and Jacob." *VT* 13:245–259.

Aharoni, Y.
1965   *The Land of the Bible: A Historical Geography.* Tr. Anson
            Rainey. Philadelphia: Westminster.
Albright, W. F.
1950/51   "A Catalogue of Early Hebrew Lyric Poems (Psalm
            LXVIII)." *HUCA* 23 Part I: 1–39.
1955   "The Son of Tabeel (Isaiah 7:6)." *BASOR* 140: 34–35.
1957   "The High Places in Ancient Palestine." VTS 4: 242–258.
1961   *Samuel and the Beginnings of the Prophetic Movement.* Cin-
            cinnati: Hebrew Union College Press.
1965   "The Role of the Canaanites in the History of Civilization."
            Pages 438–487 in Wright 1965.
1969   *Archaeology and the Religion of Israel.* Garden City, N.Y.:
            Doubleday Anchor.
———— and C. S. Mann
1971   *Matthew.* Anchor Bible 26. Garden City, N.Y.: Doubleday.
Allwohn, A.
1926   "Die Ehe des Propheten Hosea in psychoanalytischer
            Beleuchtung." BZAW 44.
Alt, A.
1919   "Hosea 5,8 – 6,6. Ein Krieg und seine Folgen in prophetischer
            Beleuchtung." *Neue kirchliche Zeitschrift* 30: 537–568 = Alt
            1953 II: 163–187.
1929   "Der Gott der Väter." BWANT III, 12 = Alt 1953 I:
            1–78 = Alt 1968: 3–100.
1945   "Gedanken über das Königtum Jahwes" = Alt 1953 I:
            345–357.
1951   "Das Königtum in den Reichen Israel und Juda." *VT* 1:
            2–22 = Alt 1953 I: 116–134 = Alt 1968: 311–335.
1953   *Kleine Schriften zur Geschichte des Volkes Israel.* I, II.
            München: Beck.
1954   *Der Stadtstatt Samaria.* Berichte über die Verhandlungen der
            Sachsischen Akademie der Wissenschaften zu Leipzig. Philo-
            logisch-historische Klasse. 101.5. Berlin: Akademie Ver-
            lag = Alt 1959: 258–302.
1959   *Kleine Schriften zur Geschichte des Volkes Israel* III. Ed. M.
            Noth. München: Beck.
1968   *Essays on Old Testament History and Religion.* Tr. R. A. Wil-
            son. Garden City, N.Y.: Doubleday.
Ambanelli, I.
1973   "Il significato dell espressione *da'at 'ĕlōhîm* nel profeta Osea."
            Rivista Biblica Italiana 21: 119–145.
Andersen, F. I.
1966a   "Moabite Syntax." *Orientalia* 35: 81–120.
1966b   "The Socio-Juridical Background of the Naboth Incident." *JBL*
            85: 46–57.

1966c   "A Lexicographical Note on Exodus XXXII:18." *VT* 16: 108–112.

1969a   "A Note on Genesis 30:8." *JBL* 88: 200.

1969b   "A Short Note on Construct *k* in Hebrew." *Biblica* 50: 68–69.

1970a   *The Verbless Clause in the Hebrew Pentateuch.* JBL Monograph Series 14. Nashville: Abingdon.

1970b   "Biconsonantal Byforms in Biblical Hebrew." *ZAW* 82: 270–274.

1971   "Passive and Ergative in Hebrew." Pages 1–15 in Goedicke 1971.

1974   *The Sentence in Biblical Hebrew.* Janua Linguarum, Series Practica No. 231. The Hague: Mouton.

1976a   *Job.* Tyndale Old Testament Commentaries. Downers Grove, Ill.: Inter-Varsity Press.

1976b   Rev. Kuhnigk 1974. *Biblica* 57: 573–575.

Ap-Thomas, D. R.
1970   "All the King's Horses?" Pages 135–151 in *Proclamation and Presence: Old Testament Essays in Honour of Gwynne Henton Davies.* Eds. J. I. Durham and J. R. Porter. Richmond, Va.: John Knox.

Astour, M. C.
1971   "841 B.C.: The First Assyrian Invasion of Israel." *JAOS* 91: 383–389.

1976   "Shalman." Page 821 in Crim et al. 1976.

Auerbach. E.
1953   "Die grosse Überarbeitung der biblischen Bücher." VTS 1: 1–10.

Bailey, L. R.
1971   "The Golden Calf." *HUCA* 42: 97–115.

Baltzer, K.
1971   *The Covenant Formulary in the Old Testament, Jewish and Early Christian Writings.* Tr. D. E. Green. Philadelphia: Fortress.

Barth, C.
1966   "Zur Bedeutung der Wustentradition." VTS 15: 14–23.

Barré, M. L.
1978   "New Light on the Interpretation of Hosea vi 2." *VT* 28: 129–141.

Barthélemy, D.
1963   *Les Devanciers d'Aquila. Première publication intégrale du texte des fragments du Dodécaprophéton trouvés dans le désert de Juda. Précédée d'une étude sur les traductions et récensions grecques de la Bible réalisées au premier siècle de notre ère sous l'influence du rabbinat palestinien.* VTS 10.

Batten, L. W.
1929   "Hosea's Message and Marriage." *JBL* 48: 257–273.

Baumann, E.
1956 "Das Lied Mose's (Dt. XXXII 1–43) auf seine gedankliche Geschlossenheit untersucht." *VT* 6: 414–424.

Baumgärtel, F.
1961 "Die Formel *nĕ'um-jahwe.*" *ZAW* 73: 277–290.

Baumgartner, W.
1913 "Kennen Amos und Hosea eine Heilseschatologie?" *Schweizerische theologische Zeitschrift* 30, Heft 1–4: 13–42; 95–124.
1940–41 "Was wir heute von der hebräischen Sprache und ihrer Geschichte wissen." *Anthropos* 35/36 (1940/41): 593–616 = Baumgartner 1959: 208–239.
1959 *Zum Alten Testament und seiner Umwelt.* Leiden: Brill.

Begrich, J.
1929 "Der Syrisch-Ephraimitische Krieg und seine weltpolitischen Zusammenhange." *Zeitschrift der Deutschen Morgenländische Gesellschaft* 83: 213–237.
1934 "Das priestliche Heilsorakel." *ZAW* 52: 81–92 = Begrich 1964: 217–231.
1944 "Berit. Ein Beitrag zur Erfassung einer alttestamentlicher Denkform." *ZAW* 60: 1–11 = Begrich 1964: 55–66.
1964 *Gesammelte Studien zum Alten Testament.* Ed. Walther Zimmerli. Theologische Bücherei 21. München: Chr. Kaiser Verlag.

Behrens, E. K.
1971 ". . . like those who remove the landmark (Hosea 5:10a)." *Studia Biblica et Theologica* (Pasadena) 1:1–5.

Beltz, W.
1974 *Die Kaleb-Traditionen im Alten Testament.* BWANT 98.

Bentzen, A.
1948–49 *Introduction to the Old Testament.* 2 vols. Copenhagen: Gad.

Bergren, R. V.
1974 *The Prophets and the Law.* Monographs of the Hebrew Union College, No. 4. Cincinnati, New York, Los Angeles, Jerusalem: Hebrew Union College — Jewish Institute of Religion.

Berman, H.
1972 "A Hittite Ritual for the Newborn." *JAOS* 92: 466–468.

Beuken, W. A. M.
1974 "Isaiah LIV: The Multiple Identity of the Person Addressed." *OTS* 19: 29–70.

Bewer, J. A.
1905–6 "The Story of Hosea's Marriage." *AJSL* 22: 120–130.

Beyer, K.
1969 *Althebräische Grammatik. Laut- und Formenlehre.* Göttingen: Vandenhoeck und Ruprecht.

Biggs, R. D.
1967 *šà.zi.ga, Ancient Mesopotamian Potency Incantations.* Texts

from Cuneiform Sources 2. Locust Valley, N.Y.: J. J. Augustin.

Bitter, S.
1975   *Die Ehe des Propheten Hosea: ein auslegungsgeschichtliche Untersuchungen.* Göttinger Theologische Arbeiten 3. Göttingen: Vandenhoeck und Ruprecht.

Blau, J.
1955   "Etymologische Untersuchungen auf Grund der palaestinischen Arabisch." *VT* 5: 337–344.
1957   "Über homonyme und angeblich homonyme Wurzeln II." *VT* 7: 98–102.

Blommerde, A. C. M.
1969   *Northwest Semitic Grammar and Job.* Biblica et Orientalia No. 22. Rome: Pontifical Biblical Institute.

Boecker, H. J.
1964   *Redeformen des Rechtsleben im Alten Testament.* Wissenschaftliche Monographien zum Alten und Neuen Testament 14. Neukirchen-Vluyn: Neukirchener Verlag.

de Boer, P. A. H.
1946–47 "Genesis XXXII 23–33. Some Remarks on the Composition and Character of the Story." *Nederlandsch Theologisch Tijdschrift* 1: 149–163.

Boling, R. G.
1965   "Prodigal Sons on Trial: A study in the prophecy of Hosea." *McCormick Quarterly* 19: 13–27.
1975   *The Book of Judges.* Anchor Bible 6A. Garden City, N.Y.: Doubleday.

Bottéro, J.
1957   *Archives Royales de Mari VII. Textes économiques et administratifs.* Paris: Imprimerie Nationale.

Bright, J.
1965   *Jeremiah.* Anchor Bible 21. Garden City, N.Y.: Doubleday.

Brockelmann, C.
1956   *Hebräische Syntax.* Neukirchen: Kreis Moers, Verlag der Buchhandlung des Erziehungsvereins.

Brongers, H. A.
1965   "Bemerkungen zum Gebrauch der adverbialen *wĕ'attāh* im Alten Testament (Ein lexikologischer Beitrag)." *VT* 15: 289–299.

Bronner, L.
1968   *The Stories of Elijah and Elisha as Polemics against Baal Worship.* Pretoria Oriental Series 6. Leiden: Brill.

Brown, R. E.
1966   *The Gospel According to John (i–xii).* Anchor Bible 29. Garden City, N.Y.: Doubleday.
1977   *The Birth of the Messiah.* Garden City, N.Y.: Doubleday.

Brueggemann, W.
1968   *Tradition for Crisis: A Study in Hosea.* Richmond: John Knox.

Buber, M.
1960   *The Prophetic Faith.* Tr. C. Witton-Davies. New York: Harper.
——— and F. Rosenzweig
1934   *Die Schrift XIII. Das Buch der Zwölf.* Berlin: Lambert Schneider.

Buccellati, G.
1966   *The Amorites of the Ur III Period.* Seminario di Semitistica Pubblicazioni Richerche I. Naples: Instituto Orientale di Napoli.

Buchanan, G. W.
1972   *To the Hebrews.* Anchor Bible 36. Garden City, N.Y.: Doubleday.

Budde, K.
1925   "Der Abschnitt Hos 1–3 und seine grundlegende religionsgeschichtliche Bedeutung." *TSK* 96/97: 1–89.
1926   "Zu Text und Auslegung des Buches Hosea (4:1–19)." *JBL* 45: 280–297.
1934   "Hosea 1 und 3." *Theologische Blätter* 13: 337–342.

Burrows, M.
1938   *The Basis of Israelite Marriage.* American Oriental Series 15. New Haven: American Oriental Society.

Buss, M. J.
1969   *The Prophetic Word of Hosea, a Morphological Study.* BZAW 111.

Buttrick, G. A. et al.
1962   *The Interpreter's Dictionary of the Bible.* Nashville: Abingdon.

Campbell, E. F.
1976   *The Book of Ruth.* Anchor Bible 7. Garden City, N.Y.: Doubleday.
——— and D. N. Freedman, eds.
1964   *The Biblical Archaeologist Reader II.* Garden City, N.Y.: Doubleday Anchor. Rpt. 1978. Ann Arbor: American Schools of Oriental Research.

Caquot, A.
1961   "Osée et la Royauté." *RHPR* 41: 123–146.

Carmignac, J.
1969   "La notion d'eschatologie dans la Bible et à Qumrân." *RevQ* 7: 17–31.

Cassuto, U.
1927   "The Second Chapter of the Book of Hosea." Pages 101–140 in Cassuto 1973.

1970   *The Goddess Anath. Canaanite Epics of the Patriarchal Age.* Tr. I. Abrahams. Jerusalem: Magnes.

1973   *Biblical and Oriental Studies.* Volume I. Bible. Tr. I. Abrahams. Jerusalem: Magnes.

Cazelles, H.

1949   "The Problem of the Kings in Osee 8:4." *CBQ* 11: 14–25.

1969   "Les origines du décalogue." *Eretz-Israel* 9: 14–19.

Ceresko, A. R.

1978   "The Function of Chiasmus in Hebrew Poetry." *CBQ* 40: 1–10.

Černy, L. J. Krušina

1948   *The Day of Yahweh and Some Relevant Problems.* Práce z Vĕdeckých Ústavů 53. Prague: Nakladem Filosofické Fakulty University Karlovy.

Charles, R. H.

1913   *The Apocrypha and Pseudepigrapha of the Old Testament. II. Pseudepigrapha.* Oxford: Clarendon.

Childs, B. S.

1962   *Memory and Tradition in Israel.* Studies in Biblical Theology 37. Naperville, Ill.: Allenson.

Chmiel, J.

1971   "Problemy struktury literackiej Ozeasza 6, 1–6." *Analecta Cracoviana* 3: 183–199.

Coats, G. W.

1968   *Rebellion in the Wilderness.* Nashville: Abingdon.

1972   "An Exposition for the Wilderness Traditions." *VT* 22: 288–295.

Cogan, M.

1974   *Imperialism and Religion: Assyria, Judah and Israel in the Eighth and Seventh Centuries B.C.E.* Society of Biblical Literature Monograph 19. Missoula, Mont.: Scholars Press.

Coote, R. B.

1971   "Hosea XII." *VT* 21: 389–402.

1974   "Hos 14:8: 'They who are filled with grain shall live.'" *JBL* 93: 161–173.

Cornill, D.

1887   "Hosea 12:1." *ZAW* 7: 285–289.

Cowley, A. E.

1923   *Aramaic Papyri of the Fifth Century B.C.* Oxford: Clarendon.

Craghan, J. F.

1971   "The Book of Hosea, a Survey of Recent Literature on the First of the Minor Prophets." *Biblical Theology Bulletin* 1: 81–100, 145–170.

Crim, K. et al., eds.

1976   *The Interpreter's Dictionary of the Bible: Supplementary Volume.* Nashville: Abingdon.

Cross, F. M.

1947 "The Tabernacle: A Study from an Archaeological and Historical Approach." *Biblical Archaeologist* 10:45–68 = Pages 201–228 in Wright and Freedman 1961.

—— and D. N. Freedman

1947 "A Note on Deuteronomy 33:26." *BASOR* 108: 6–7.

1948 "The Blessing of Moses." *JBL* 67: 191–210 = Cross and Freedman 1975: 97–122.

1953 "A Royal Song of Thanksgiving: II Samuel 22–Psalm 18." *JBL* 72: 15–34 = Cross and Freedman 1975: 125–158.

1955 "The Song of Miriam." *JNES* 14: 237–250 = Cross and Freedman 1975: 45–65.

1975 *Studies in Ancient Yahwistic Poetry.* Society of Biblical Literature Dissertation Series 21. Missoula, Mont.: Scholars Press.

Crüsemann, F.

1978 *Der Widerstand gegen das Königtum.* Wissenschaftliche Monographien zum Alten und Neuen Testament 49. Neukirchen-Vluyn: Neukirchener Verlag.

Dahl, M. E.

1962 *The Resurrection of the Body.* Studies in Biblical Theology 36. Naperville, Ill.: Allenson.

Dahood, M.

1953 "The Root GMR in the Psalms." *Theological Studies* 14: 595–597.

1964 Hebrew-Ugaritic Lexicography II. *Biblica* 45: 393–412.

1966 *Psalms I: 1–50.* Anchor Bible 16. Garden City, N.Y.: Doubleday.

1968 *Psalms II: 51–100.* Anchor Bible 17. Garden City, N.Y.: Doubleday.

1969 "Ugaritic-Hebrew Syntax and Style." *Ugarit-Forschungen* 1: 15–36.

1970 *Psalms III: 101–150.* Anchor Bible 17A. Garden City, N.Y.: Doubleday.

1971 "Causal Beth and the Root NKR in Nahum 3, 4." *Biblica* 52: 395–396.

1972 "Hebrew-Ugaritic Lexicography X." *Biblica* 53: 386–403.

1976 "The Conjunction *pa* in Hosea 7, 1." *Biblica* 57: 247–248.

1978 "New Readings in Lamentations." *Biblica* 59: 174–197.

—— and T. Penar

1970 "The Grammar of the Psalter." Pages 361–456 in Dahood 1970.

1972 "Ugaritic-Hebrew Parallel Pairs." Pages 71–382 in *Ras Shamra Parallels I.* Ed. L. R. Fisher. Analecta Orientalia 49. Rome: Pontifical Biblical Institute.

Dales, G. F.

1963 "Necklaces, Bands and Belts on Mesopotamian Figurines." *Revue d'Assyriologie* 57: 21–40.

Dalman, G.
1928–42   *Arbeit und Sitte in Palästina.* 7 vols. Gütersloh: Bertelsmann.
           Rpt. 1964. Hildesheim: Georg Olms.
David, M.
1955   "Adoptie in het Oude Israël." *Mededelingen der Koninklijke
           Nederlandse Akademie van Wetenschappen Afd. Letterkunde*
           NR 18: 85–103 (= NR 18 ⚡4).
Davidson, A. B.
1894   *Hebrew Syntax.* Edinburgh: T. and T. Clark.
van Dijk, H. J.
1968   *Ezekiel's Prophecy on Tyre* (Ez. *26, 1–28, 19*): *A New Ap-
           proach.* Biblica et Orientalia No. 20. Rome: Pontifical Biblical
           Institute.
Dion, H. M.
1967   "The Patriarchal Traditions and the Literary Forms of the Or-
           acle of Salvation." *CBQ* 29: 198–206.
Donner, H.
1964   *Israel unter den Völkern. Die Stellung der klassischen Prophe-
           ten des 8. Jahrhunderts v. Chr. zur Aussenpolitik der Könige
           von Israel und Juda.* VTS 11.
Donner, H., and W. Röllig
1971   *Kanaanäische und aramäische Inschriften.* Wiesbaden:
           Harrassowitz.
Driver, G. R.
1936   "Confused Hebrew Roots." Pages 73–83 in *Occident and
           Orient. . . . Gaster Anniversary Volume.* Eds. B. Schindler
           and A. Marmorstein. London: Taylor's Foreign Press.
1953   "Hebrew Poetic Diction." VTS 1: 26–39.
1954a   *Semitic Writing: From Pictograph to Alphabet.* Rev. ed. Lon-
           don: The British Academy.
1954b   "Reflections on Recent Articles." *JBL* 73: 125–136.
1958   "Notes on Isaiah." Pages 42–48 in Hempel and Rost 1958.
Driver, S. R.
1885–86   "Grammatical Notes." *Hebraica 2:* 33–38.
1896   *Deuteronomy.* International Critical Commentary. Edinburgh:
           T. and T. Clark.
Duhm, B.
1911   "Anmerkungen zu den zwölf Propheten II. Buch Hosea."
           ZAW 31: 18–43.
Du Mesnil du Buisson, R. le Compte
1947   *Le Sautoir d'Atargatis et la chaine d'Amulettes.* Documenta et
           Monumenta Orientis Antiqui. Études d'iconographie orientale
           1. Leiden: Brill.
Dumbrell, W. J.
1974–75   "The Role of Bethel in the Biblical Narratives from Jacob to
           Jeroboam I." *The Australian Journal of Biblical Archaeology* 2
           No. 3: 65–76.

Durr, L.
1935 "Altorientalisches Recht bei den Propheten Amos und Hosea."
BZ 23: 150–157.

Dussaud, R.
1920 "Jupiter Heliopolitain." *Syria* 1: 3–15.
1927 "Nouveaux renseignements sur la Palestine et la Syrie vers
2000 avant notre ère." *Syria* 8: 216–233.

Edwards, I. E. S.
1955 "A Relief of Qudshu-Astarte-Anath in the Winchester College
Collection." *JNES* 14: 49–51.

Ehrlich, A. B.
1912 *Randglossen zur hebräischen Bibel V.* Leipzig: J. C. Hinrichs.
Rpt. 1968. Hildesheim: Ohms.

Eichrodt, W.
1961 "The Holy One in Your Midst, the Theology of Hosea." *Interpretation* 15: 259–273.

Eissfeldt, O.
1928 "Yahwe als König." *ZAW* 46: 81–105 = Eissfeldt 1962:
172–93 = Eissfeldt 1969: 353–374.

1935 *Molk als Opferbegriff im Punischen und Hebräischen und das
Ende des Gottes Molk.* Beiträge zur Religiongeschichte des Al-
tertums 3. Halle: Max Niemeyer.

1945–48 "'Mein Gott' im Alten Testament." *ZAW* 61: 3–16 = Eissfeldt 1966: 35–47 = Eissfeldt 1969: 396–408.

1957 "Non dimittam te, nisi benedixeris mihi." Pages 77–81 in
Mélanges Bibliques . . . A. Robert. Ed. J. Trinquet. Travaux
de l'Institut Catholique de Paris. Paris: Blond et Gay = Eissfeldt 1966: 412–416.

1962 *Kleine Schriften I.* Eds. R. Sellheim and F. Maass. Tübingen:
Mohr.

1965 *The Old Testament: An Introduction.* Tr. P. R. Ackroyd. New
York: Harper & Row.

1966 *Kleine Schriften III.* Eds. R. Sellheim and F. Maass. Tübingen: Mohr.

1969 *Kleine Schriften zum Alten Testament.* Eds. K.-M. Beyse and
H. J. Zobel. Berlin: Evangelische Verlagsanstalt.

Elliger, K.
1951 "Der Jacobskampf am Jabbok. Gen. 32, 23ff. als her-
meneutisches Problem." *Zeitschrift für Theologie und Kirche*
48: 1–31.

1957 "Eine verkannte Kunstform bei Hosea (Zur Einheit von Hos
5, 1f.)." *ZAW* 69: 151–160.

Engnell, I.
1970 *Critical Essays on the Old Testament.* London: SPCK.

Eybers, I. H.
1964–65 "The Matrimonial Life of Hosea." *OTWSA* 7/8: 11–34.

Farrar, F. W.
1890   *The Minor Prophets, their Lives and Times.* Men of the Bible 14. New York: A. D. F. Randolph.

Fensham, F. C.
1962   "Malediction and Benediction in Ancient Near Eastern Vassal Treaties and the Old Testament." *ZAW* 74: 1–9.

1963   "Common Trends in Curses of the Near-Eastern Treaties and *kudurru*-Inscriptions compared with Maledictions of Amos and Isaiah." *ZAW* 75: 155–175.

1964–65   "The Covenant-Idea in the Book of Hosea." *OTWSA* 7/8: 35–49.

1966a   "The Burning of the Golden Calf and Ugarit." *IEJ* 16: 191–193.

1966b   "A Possible Origin of the Concept of the Day of the Lord." *OTWSA* 9: 90–97.

1967   "Legal Aspects of the Dream of Solomon." Pages 67–70 in *Fourth World Congress of Jewish Studies: Papers I.* Jerusalem: World Union of Jewish Studies/The Hebrew University.

1969   "The Son of a Handmaid in Northwest Semitic." *VT* 19: 31–32.

1971   "Father and Son as Terminology for Treaty and Covenant." Pages 121–135 in Goedicke 1971.

Finesinger, S. B.
1926   "Musical Instruments in the Old Testament." *HUCA* 3: 21–76.

Finkelstein, J. J.
1956   "Hebrew ḥbr and Semitic *ḫbr." *JBL* 75: 328–332.

1966   "Sex Offences in Sumerian Laws." *JAOS* 86: 355–372.

Fishbane, M.
1971   "Studies in Biblical Magic. Origins, Uses and Transformations of Terminology and Literary Form." Brandeis University Dissertation.

Fisher, L. R., ed.
1972   *Ras Shamra Parallels I.* Analecta Orientalia 49. Rome: Pontifical Biblical Institute.

1976   *Ras Shamra Parallels II.* Analecta Orientalia 50. Rome: Pontifical Biblical Institute.

Fitzmyer, J. A.
1967   *The Aramaic Inscriptions of Sefîre.* Biblica et Orientalia 19. Rome: Pontifical Biblical Institute.

1971   *The Genesis Apocryphon of Qumran Cave I.* Biblica et Orientalia 18A. Rome: Pontifical Biblical Institute.

Fohrer, G.
1955   "Umkehr und Erlösung beim Propheten Hosea." *Theologische Zeitschrift* 11: 161–185 = Fohrer 1967: 222–241.

1967   *Studien zur Alttestamentlichen Prophetie (1949–1965).* BZAW 99.

1968a   *Geschichte der Israelitischen Religion.* Berlin: Walter de Gruyter = Fohrer 1972.

1968b   *Introduction to the Old Testament.* Tr. D. E. Green. Nashville: Abingdon.

1972   *History of Israelite Religion.* Tr. D. E. Green. Nashville: Abingdon.

Forbes, R. J.

1956   *Studies in Ancient Technology.* IV. Leiden: Brill.

Fox, M.

1973   "*Ṭôb* as Covenant Terminology." *BASOR* 209: 41–42.

Freedman, D. N.

1955a   "God Compassionate and Gracious." *Western Watch* 6: 7–24.

1955b   "*Pšty* in Hos 2:7." *JBL* 74: 275.

1960   "Archaic Forms in Early Hebrew Poetry." *ZAW* 72: 101–107.

1964   "Divine Commitment and Human Obligation." *Interpretation* 18: 419–431.

1965a   "The Biblical Idea of History." Pages 11–16 in *The Shape of the Church and the Future.* Gross Pointe Farms, Mich.: United Presbyterian Church in the U.S.A.

1965b   "The Chronology of Israel and the Ancient Near East: Old Testament Chronology." Pages 265–281 in Wright 1965.

1968   "The Structure of Job 3." *Biblica* 49: 503–508.

1971   "The Structure of Psalm 137." Pages 187–205 in Goedicke 1971.

1972a   "The Refrain in David's Lament over Saul and Jonathan." Pages 115–126 in *Ex Orbe Religionum: Studia Geo Widengren.* Eds. C. J. Bleeker et al. Studies in the History of Religions/Supplements to Numen 21. Leiden: Brill.

1972b   "Prolegomenon" (pp. vii–lvi), in *The Forms of Hebrew Poetry* by George Buchanan Gray. Library of Biblical Studies. New York: KTAV.

1972c   "The Broken Construct Chain." *Biblica* 53: 534–536.

1972d   "Acrostics and Metrics in Hebrew Poetry." *Harvard Theological Review* 65: 367–392.

1974   "Strophe and Meter in Exodus 15." Pages 163–202 in *A Light unto my Path: Old Testament Studies in Honor of Jacob M. Myers.* Eds. H. N. Bream, R. D. Heim, and C. A. Moore. Philadelphia: Temple University Press.

1975   "Early Israelite History in the Light of Early Israelite Poetry." Pages 3–35 in *Unity and Diversity (Essays in the History, Literature, and Religion of the Ancient Near East).* Eds. H. Goedicke and J. J. M. Roberts. Baltimore: The Johns Hopkins University Press.

1976   "The Twenty-third Psalm." Pages 139–166 in *Michigan Oriental Studies in Honor of George G. Cameron.* Eds. L. L. Orlin et al., Winona Lake, Ind.: Eisenbrauns.

1977   "Pottery, Poetry, and Prophecy." *JBL* 96: 5–26.
———— and C. Franke-Hyland
1973   "Psalm 29: A Structural Analysis." *Harvard Theological Review* 66: 237–256.
———— and M. O'Connor
forthcoming   "Yahweh." In *Theologisches Wörterbuch des Alten Testaments*. Eds. G. J. Botterweck and H. Ringgren. Stuttgart: Kohlhammer.
———— and A. Ritterspach
1967   "The Use of *Aleph* as a Vowel Letter in the Genesis Apocryphon." *RevQ* 6: 293–300.
Frey, H.
1957   "Der Aufbau der Gedichte Hoseas." *Wort und Dienst* (NF) 5: 9–103.
Fritz, V.
1970   *Israel in der Wüste. Traditionsgeschichtliche Untersuchung der Wüstenüberlieferung des Jahwisten.* Marburger Theologische Studien 7. Marburg: N. G. Elwert Verlag.
Fück, J.
1921   "Hosea Kapital 3." *ZAW* 39: 283–290.
Funk, R. W.
1959   "The Wilderness." *JBL* 78: 205–214.
Galbiati, E.
1967   "La struttura sintetica di Osea 2." Pages 317–328 in *Studi sull'Oriente e la Bibbia offerti a Giovanni Rinaldi.* Eds. G. Buccellati et al. Genova: Editrice Studio e Vita.
Gaster, T.
1954   "Old Testament Notes." *VT* 4: 73–79.
1964   *The Dead Sea Scriptures.* Garden City, N.Y.: Doubleday.
Gelb, I. J.
1942   "A Tablet of Unusual Type from Tell-Asmar." *JNES* 1: 219–226.
———— et al.
1956   *The Assyrian Dictionary of the Oriental Institute of the University of Chicago.* Chicago/Glückstadt: Oriental Institute/ J. J. Augustin Verlagsbuchhandlung. Cited as *CAD.*
Gelston, A.
1974   "Kingship in the Book of Hosea." *OTS* 19: 71–85.
Gemser, B.
1955   "The *Rîb* or Controversy Pattern in Hebrew Mentality." VTS 3: 124–137.
Gerleman, G.
1974   "Der Nicht-Mensch. Erwagungen zur hebräischen Wurzel *NBL.*" *VT* 24: 147–158.
Gerstenberger, E.
1962   "The Woe Oracle of the Prophets." *JBL* 81: 249–263.

Gertner, M.
1960   "An Attempt at an Interpretation of Hosea XII." *VT* 10:
            272–284.
Gilula, M.
1974   "An Offering of 'First Fruits' in Ancient Egypt." *Tel Aviv*
            I/1: 43–44.
Ginsberg, H. L.
1960   "Studies in Hosea 1–3." Pages (50)–(69) in Haran 1960.
1961   "Hosea's Ephraim, more Fool than Knave. A New Inter-
            pretation of Hosea 12:1–14." *JBL* 80: 339–347.
1967   "Lexicographical Notes." VTS 16: 71–82.
1971   "Hosea." Columns 1010–1024 in *Encyclopedia Judaica* 8.
            Jerusalem: Encyclopedia Judaica/Macmillan.
Glueck, N.
1927   *Das Wort ḥesed im alttestamentlichen Sprachgebrauche als
            menschliche und gottliche gemeinschaftsgemässe Verhältungs-
            weise.* Giessen: Töpelmann = Glueck 1967.
1967   *Hesed in the Bible.* Tr. A. Gottshalk. Cincinnati: Hebrew
            Union College Press.
Goedicke, H., ed.
1971   *Near Eastern Studies in Honor of W. F. Albright.* Baltimore:
            The Johns Hopkins University Press.
Goetze, A.
1944   "Diverse Names in an Old Babylonian Pay-List." *BASOR* 95:
            18–24.
1949   "Mesopotamian Laws and the Historian." *JAOS* 69: 115–120.
1957   *Kulturgeschichte des vorgriechishen Kleinasien.* Handbuch der
            Altertumswissenschaft. Kulturgeschichte des Alten Orients 3.1.
            München: Beck.
Good, E. M.
1966a   "The Composition of Hosea." *Svensk Exegetisk Årsbok* 31:
            21–63.
1966b   "Hosea 5.8–6.6: An Alternative to Alt." *JBL* 85: 273–286.
1966c   "Hosea and the Jacob Tradition." *VT* 16: 137–151.
Gordis, R.
1933a   "A Rhetorical Use of Interrogative Sentences in Biblical He-
            brew." *AJSL* 49: 212–217 = Gordis 1976: 152–157.
1933b   "Some Hitherto Unrecognized Meanings of the Verb *shub*."
            JBL 52: 153–162 = Gordis 1976: 218–227.
1934   "A Note on *ṭwb*." *JTS* 35: 186–188 = Gordis 1976: 313–314.
1943   "The Asseverative *Kaph* in Ugaritic and Hebrew." *JAOS* 63:
            176–178 = Gordis 1976: 211–213.
1954   "Hosea's Marriage and Message. A New Approach." *HUCA*
            27: 9–35 = Gordis 1971: 230–254.
1955   "The Text and Meaning of Hosea 14:3." *VT* 5:
            88–90 = Gordis 1976: 347–349.

1970   "On Methodology in Biblical Exegesis." *Jewish Quarterly Review* 61: 93–118 = Gordis 1976: 1–26.

1971   *Poets, Prophets, and Sages.* Bloomington: Indiana University Press.

1976   *The Word and the Book: Studies in Biblical Language and Literature.* New York: KTAV.

Gordon, C. H.

1936   "Hosea 2:4–5 in the Light of New Semitic Inscriptions." *ZAW* 54: 277–280.

1937   "Zu *ZAW* 1936. 277*ff*." *ZAW* 55: 176.

1949   *Ugaritic Literature. A Comprehensive Translation of the Poetic and Prose Texts.* Rome: Pontifical Biblical Institute.

1965   *Ugaritic Textbook.* Analecta Orientalia 38. Rome: Pontifical Biblical Institute. Cited as *UT*.

1966   *Ugarit and Minoan Crete. The Bearing of Their Texts on the Origins of Western Culture.* New York: Norton.

1967   *Homer and the Bible.* Ventnor, N.J.: Ventnor Publishers.

Gray, J.

1961   "The Kingship of God in the Prophets and Psalms." *VT* 11: 1–29.

Green, A.

1975   *The Role of Human Sacrifice in the Ancient Near East.* American Schools of Oriental Research Dissertation Series 1. Missoula, Mont.: Scholars Press.

Greenberg, M.

1960   "Some Postulates of Biblical Criminal Law." Pages 5–28 in Haran 1960.

Greenfield, J. C.

1959   "Lexicographical Notes II." *HUCA* 30: 144–150.

1965   "Studies in West Semitic Inscriptions I. Stylistic Aspects of the Sefire Treaty Inscriptions." *Acta Orientalia* 29: 1–18.

Greengus, S.

1969   "A Textbook Case of Adultery in Ancient Mesopotamia." *HUCA* 40: 33–44.

Grether, O.

1934   *Name und Wort Gottes im Alten Testament.* BZAW 64.

Grimm, D.

1973   "Erwagungen zu Hosea 12.12 'in Gilgal opfern sie Stiere.'" *ZAW* 85: 339–347.

Guillaume, A.

1964   "A Note on Hosea 2:23,24(21,22)." *JTS* 15: 57–58.

Gunkel, H.

1895   *Schöpfung und Chaos in Urzeit und Endzeit. Eine religionsgeschichtliche Untersuchung über Gen und Ap Joh 12.* Göttingen: Vandenhoeck und Ruprecht.

Guttmann, M.

1926   "The Term 'Foreigner' (*nkry*) Historically Considered." *HUCA* 3: 1–20.

Habel, N. C.
1964   *Yahweh versus Baal: A Conflict of Religious Cultures.* Concordia Theological Seminary Graduate Study 6. New York: Bookman Associates.

Halévy, J.
1902   "Le Livre d'Osée." *Revue Semitique* 10: 1–12; 97–133; 193–212; 289–304.

Hallo, W. W.
1960   "From Qarqar to Carchemish." *Biblical Archaeologist* 23 ⚹2: 33–61 = Campbell and Freedman 1964: 152–188.

Haran, M.
1967   "The Rise and Decline of the Empire of Jeroboam ben Joash." *VT* 17: 266–297.

——— ed.
1960   *Yehezkel Kaufmann Jubilee Volume.* Jerusalem: Magnes.

Harrelson, W.
1970   "About to be Born." *Andover Newton Quarterly.* 11/2: 56–61.

Harrison, R. K.
1969   *Introduction to the Old Testament.* Grand Rapids: Eerdmans.

Hartman, L. F., and A. A. Di Lella
1978   *The Book of Daniel.* Anchor Bible 23. Garden City, N.Y.: Doubleday.

——— and A. L. Oppenheim
1950   *On Beer and Brewing Techniques in Ancient Mesopotamia.* Supplement to the Journal of the American Oriental Society 10. Baltimore: American Oriental Society.

Harvey, J.
1962   "Le *Rîb*-Pattern. Requisitoire prophetique sur la rupture de l'alliance." *Biblica* 43: 172–196.

Haupt, P.
1915   "Hosea's Erring Spouse." *JBL* 34: 41–53.

Hayes, J. H., ed.
1974   *Old Testament Form Criticism.* Trinity University Monograph Series in Religion, Vol. 2. San Antonio: Trinity University Press.

Hecht, F.
1971   *Eschatologie und Ritus bei den "Reformpropheten." Ein Beitrag zur Theologie des Altes Testament.* Pretoria Theological Studies 1. Leiden: Brill.

Heermann, A.
1922   "Ehe und Kinder des Propheten Hosea; eine exegetische Studie zu Hosea 1, 2–9." *ZAW* 40: 287–312.

Hempel, J.
1926   *Gott and Mensch im Alten Testament: Studie zum Geschichte der Frömmigkeit.* BWANT 38.

———— and L. Rost., eds.

1958   *Von Ugarit nach Qumran: Beiträge . . . Otto Eissfeldt . . . dargebracht*. BZAW 77.

Hendriks, H. J.

n.d.   "Juridical Aspects of the Marriage Metaphor in Hosea and Jeremiah." Doctoral Dissertation. University of Stellenbosch, South Africa.

Henry, M.

1827   *An Exposition of the Old and New Testament. III. The Prophetical Books*. New York: Robert Carver.

Hillers, D.

1964a   *Treaty-Curses and the Old Testament Prophets*. Biblica et Orientalia 16. Rome: Pontifical Biblical Institute.

1964b   "A Note on Some Treaty Terminology in the Old Testament." *BASOR* 176: 46–47.

1969   *Covenant: The History of a Biblical Idea*. Baltimore: Johns Hopkins University Press.

Hoffner, H. A.

1966   "Symbols for Masculinity and Femininity: Their Use in Ancient Near Eastern Sympathetic Magic Rituals." *JBL* 85: 326–334.

Holladay, W. L.

1958   *The Root Šubh in the Old Testament*. Leiden: Brill.

1961   "On Every High Hill and under Every Green Tree." *VT* 11: 170–176.

1962   "Style, Irony, and Authenticity in Jeremiah." *JBL* 81: 44–54.

1969   " 'EREṢ — Underworld: Two More Suggestions." *VT* 19: 123–124.

Huesman, J.

1956a   "Finite Uses of the Infinitive Absolute." *Biblica* 37: 271–295.

1956b   "The Infinitive Absolute and the Waw + Perfect Problem." *Biblica* 37: 410–434.

Huffmon, H. B.

1959   "The Covenant Lawsuit in the Prophets." *JBL* 78: 285–295.

1965   *Amorite Personal Names in the Mari Texts*. Baltimore: The Johns Hopkins Press.

Humbert, P.

1921   "Osée, le prophète bedouin." *RHPR* 1: 97–118.

1934   "La formule hebraïque en *hineni* suivi d'un participe." *Revue des Études Juives* 97: 58–64 = Humbert 1958: 54–59.

1958   *Opuscules d'un Hebraïsant*. Memoires de l'Université de Neuchatel 26. Neuchatel: Secrétariat de l'Université.

Hummel, H. D.

1957   "Enclitic *Mem* in Early Northwest Semitic, especially Hebrew." *JBL* 76: 85–107.

Hvidberg, F. F.
1962   *Weeping and Laughter in the Old Testament. A Study of Canaanite-Israelite Religion.* Leiden: Brill.
Jacob, E.
1963   "L'héritage cananéen dans le livre du prophète Osée." *RHPR* 43: 250–259.
1964   "Der Prophet Hosea und die Geschichte." *EvT* 24: 281–290.
James, F.
1947   *Personalities of the Old Testament.* New York: Scribner's.
Jenni, E.
1952–53   "Das Wort '*ôlām* im Alten Testament." *ZAW* 64: 197–248; 65: 1–34.
1956   *Die politischen Voraussagen der Propheten.* Abhandlungen zur Theologie des Alten und Neuen Testaments 29. Zürich: Theologischen Verlag.
Jerome
1845   "Praefatio S. Hieronymi in Duodecim Prophetas." Cols. 1013–1016 in *Divinae Bibliotheca Pars Prima. Hieronymi Opera 9.* Patrologiae (Latinae) Cursus Completus 28. Ed. J. P. Migne. Paris: Vrayet de Surcy.
Johnson, A. R.
1949   *The Vitality of the Individual in the Thought of Ancient Israel.* Cardiff: University of Wales Press.
Joüon, P.
1933   "Divers emplois métaphoriques du mot *yad* en Hébreu." *Biblica* 14: 452–459.
1947   *Grammaire de l'Hébreu Biblique.* Rome: Pontifical Biblical Institute.
Junker, H.
1906   "Textkritische, formkritische und traditiongeschichtliche Untersuchung zu Os 4, 1–10." *BZ* 4: 165–173.
Kapelrud, A. S.
1955   *Baal in the Ras Shamra Texts.* Copenhagen: Gad.
1978   "The Spirit and the Word in the Prophets." *Annual of the Swedish Theological Institute* 11: 40–47.
Kaufmann, Y.
1960   *The Religion of Israel.* Tr. M. Greenberg. University of Chicago Press.
Kautzsch, E., ed.
1910   *Gesenius' Hebrew Grammar.* Tr. A. E. Cowley. Oxford: Clarendon. Cited as *GKC.*
Kimron, E.
1974–75   "Medial 'Alef as Matres Lectionis in Hebrew and Aramaic Documents from Qumran Compared with Other Hebrew and Aramaic Sources." *Leshōnēnû* 39: 133–146.
Klopfenstein, M. A.
1972   *Scham und Schande nach dem Alten Testament. Eine be-*

griffsgeschichtliche Untersuchung zu den hebraischen Wurzeln boš, klm und bḥr. Abhandlungen zur Theologie des Alten und Neuen Testaments 62. Zürich: Theologischer Verlag.

Knudtzon, J. A.
1915   *Die El-Amarna Tafeln.* Leipzig: Hinrichs.

Koch, K.
1967   *Was ist Formgeschichte?: Neue Wege der Bibel-exegese.* Neu-kirchen-Vluyn: Neukirchener Verlag = Koch 1969.

1969   *The Growth of the Biblical Tradition: The Form-Critical Method.* Tr. S. M. Cupitt. New York: Scribner's = Koch 1967.

Koehler, L., and W. Baumgartner
1958   *Lexicon in Veteris Testamenti Libros.* Leiden: Brill.

Kotting, B.
1964   "Tier und Heiligtum." Pages 209–214 in *Mullus: Festschrift Theodor Klauser.* Eds. A. Stiber and A. Hermann. Jahrbuch für Antike und Christentum Ergänzungsband 1. Münster Westfalen: Aschendorff.

König, E.
1900   *Stilistik, Rhetorik, Poetik.* Leipzig: Hinrichs.

Kramer, S. N.
1943   "Man's Golden Age: A Sumerian Parallel to Genesis XI 1." *JAOS* 63: 191–194.

Krszyna, H.
1969   "Literarische Struktur von Os 2, 4–17." *BZ* 13: 41–59.

Kuhl, C.
1934   "Neue Dokumente zum Verständnis von Hos. 2:4–15." *ZAW* 52: 102–109.

Kuhnigk, W.
1974   *Nordwestsemitische Studien zum Hoseabuch.* Biblica et Orientalia No. 27. Rome: Pontifical Biblical Institute.

Labuschagne, C. J.
1964–65   "The Similes in the Book of Hosea." *OTWSA* 7/8: 64–76.

Lagrange, A.
1892   "La nouvelle histoire d'Israel et le prophète Osée." *Revue biblique* 1: 203–238.

Lambert, W. G.
1960   *Babylonian Wisdom Literature.* Oxford: Clarendon.

Lescow, T.
1973   "Jesajas Denkschrift aus der Zeit des syrisch-ephraimitischen Krieges." *ZAW* 85: 315–331.

Levi della Vida, G.
1942   "The Phoenician God Satrapes." *BASOR* 87: 29–32.

Lindblom, J.
1953   "The Political Background of the Shiloh Oracle." *VTS* 1:78–87.

1963   *Prophecy in Ancient Israel.* Oxford: Blackwell.

Lohfink, N.
1961   "Zu Text und Form von Os 4:4–6." *Biblica* 42:303–332.
1963   "Hate and Love in Osee 9:15." *CBQ* 25:417.
Lundbom, J.
1979   "Poetic Structure and Prophetic Rhetoric in Hosea." *VT* 29: 300–308.
McCarter, P. K.
1980   *I Samuel.* Anchor Bible 8. Garden City, N.Y.: Doubleday.
McCarthy, D. J.
1964   "Hosea XII 2: Covenant by Oil." *VT* 14: 215–221.
1972a   *Old Testament Covenant; A Survey of Current Opinions.* Oxford: Blackwell.
1972b   "Běrît in Old Testament History and Theology." *Biblica* 53: 110–121.
McDonald, J. R. B.
1964   "The Marriage of Hosea." *Theology* 67: 149–156.
McKenzie, J. L.
1955a   "Divine Passion in Osee." *CBQ* 17: 287–299.
1955b   "Knowledge of God in Hosea." *JBL* 74: 22–27.
1968   *Second Isaiah.* Anchor Bible 20. Garden City, N.Y.: Doubleday.
McLean, H. B.
1962   "Pekah." Volume 3, p. 708, in Buttrick et al. 1962.
Malamat, A.
1955   "Doctrines of Causality in Hittite and Biblical Historiography. A Parallel." *VT* 5: 1–12.
1962   "Mari and the Bible: Some Patterns of Tribal Organization and Institutions." *JAOS* 82: 143–150.
Mansoor, M.
1961   *The Thanksgiving Hymns.* Studies on the Texts of the Desert of Judah 3. Leiden: Brill.
Martin, J. D.
1969   "The Forensic Background to Jeremiah 3:1." *VT* 19: 82–92.
May, H. G.
1931–32 "The Fertility Cult in Hosea." *AJSL* 48: 73–98.
1936   "An Interpretation of the Names of Hosea's Children." *JBL* 55: 285–291.
Mendenhall, G. E.
1973   *The Tenth Generation.* Baltimore: Johns Hopkins University Press.
Mercer, S. A. B.
1939   *The Tell el-Amarna Tablets.* 2 vols. Toronto: Macmillan.
Meshel, Z., and C. Meyers
1976   "The Name of God in the Wilderness of Zin." *Biblical Archeologist* 39: 6–10.
Mezger, F.
1948   "The Origin of a Specific Rule on Adultery in the Germanic Laws." *JAOS* 68: 145–148.

de Moor, J. C.
  1969   "Ugaritic   *hm* — Never 'Behold.'"   *Ugarit-Forschung* 1:
              201–202.
Moran, W. L.
  1963   "A Note on the Treaty Terminology of the Sefire Stelas."
              JNES 22: 173–176.
Morgenstern, J.
  1929   *"Beena* Marriage (Matriarchat) in Ancient Israel and its His-
              torical Implications." *ZAW* 47: 91–110.
  1931   "Additional Notes on *Beena* Marriage (Matriarchat) in An-
              cient Israel." *ZAW* 49: 46–58.
Motzki, H.
  1975   "Ein Beitrag zum Problem des Stierkultes in der Religionsge-
              schichte Israels." *VT* 25: 470–485.
Mowinckel, S.
  1956   *He That Cometh*. Tr. G. W. Anderson. Oxford: Blackwell.
  1959   "General Oriental and Specific Israelite Elements in the Isra-
              elite Conception of the Sacral Kingdom." Pages 283–293 in
              The Sacral Kingship/La Regalità Sacra. Studies in the History
              of Religions. Supplements to Numen IV. Leiden: Brill.
  1962   *The Psalms in Israel's Worship*. Tr. D. R. Ap-Thomas. Nash-
              ville: Abingdon.
Muilenburg, J.
  1953   "A Study in Hebrew Rhetoric: Repetition and Style." VTS 1:
              97–111.
  1961   "The Linguistic and Rhetorical Usages of the Particle *kî* in the
              Old Testament." *HUCA* 32: 135–160.
Muntingh, L. M.
  1964–65   "Married Life in Israel according to the Book of Hosea."
              OTWSA 7/8: 77–84.
North, F. S.
  1957   "A Solution of Hosea's Marital Problems by Critical Analysis."
              JNES 16: 128–130.
Noth, M.
  1928   *Die israelitischen Personennamen im Rahmen der gemein-
              semitischen Namengebung*. BWANT 46.
  1960   *The History of Israel*. Tr. P. R. Ackroyd. New York: Harper
              & Row.
  1971   *Aufsätze zur biblischen Landes- und Altertumskunde*. Ed.
              H. W. Wolff. I, II. Neukirchen-Vluyn: Neukirchener Verlag.
O'Connor, M.
  1977   "The Rhetoric of the Kilamuwa Inscription." *BASOR* 226:
              15–29.
  1980   *Hebrew Verse Structure*. Winona Lake, Ind.: Eisenbrauns.
Oded, B.
  1970   "Observations on Methods of Assyrian Rule in Transjordania

after the Palestinian Campaign of Tiglath-Pileser III." *JNES* 27: 177–186.

1972   "The Historical Background of the Syro-Ephraimite War Reconsidered." *CBQ* 34: 153–165.

Oldenburg, U.

1969   *The Conflict between El and Baal in Canaanite Religion.* Leiden: Brill.

Ostborn, G.

1956   *Yahweh and Baal. Studies in the Book of Hosea and Related Documents.* Lunds Universitets Årsskrift, N. F. Avd. 1. Bd. 51. No. 6. Lund: Gleerup.

Paton, L. B.

1896   "Notes on Hosea's Marriage." *JBL* 15: 9–17.

Paul, S. M.

1968   "The Image of the Oven and the Cake in Hosea VII 4–10." *VT* 18: 114–120.

1970   *Studies in the Book of the Covenant in the Light of Cuneiform and Biblical Law.* VTS 18.

Pettinato, G.

1976   "The Royal Archives of Tell Mardikh-Ebla." *Biblical Archeologist* 39: 44–52.

Phillips, A.

1970   *Ancient Israel's Criminal Law.* Oxford: Clarendon.

Plautz, W.

1964   "Die Form der Eheschliessung im Alten Testament." *ZAW* 76: 289–318.

Plöger, O.

1959   *Theokratie und Eschatologie.* Wissenschaftliche Monographien zum Alten und Neuen Testament 2. Neukirchen-Vluyn: Neukirchener Verlag.

Pope, M. H.

1953   " 'Pleonastic' *wāw* before Nouns in Ugaritic and Hebrew." *JAOS* 73: 95–98.

1970   "The Saltier of Atargatis Reconsidered." Pages 178–196 in *Near Eastern Archaeology in the Twentieth Century: Essays in Honor of Nelson Glueck.* Ed. J. A. Sanders. Garden City, N.Y.: Doubleday.

1973   *Job.* 3d ed. Anchor Bible 15. Garden City, N.Y.: Doubleday.

1977   *Song of Songs.* Anchor Bible 7C. Garden City, N.Y.: Doubleday.

Preuss, H. D.

1971   *Verspottung fremder Religionen im Alten Testament.* BWANT 92.

Pritchard, J. B.

1969a   *Ancient Near Eastern Texts Relating to the Old Testament.* Princeton: Princeton University Press. Cited as *ANET.*

Rabin, Ch.
1973   "Hebrew *baddîm*, 'power.'" *Journal of Semitic Studies* 18: 57–58.

Rabinowitz, J. J.
1959   "The 'Great Sin' in Ancient Egyptian Marriage Contracts." *JNES* 18: 73.

Reines, Ch. W.
1950   "Hosea XII, 1." *Journal of Jewish Studies* 2: 156–157.

Ribar, J. W.
1973   "Death Cult Practices in Ancient Palestine." University of Michigan Dissertation.

Rice, J. A.
1921   *The Old Testament in the Life of Today*. New York: Macmillan.

Richter, W.
1964   *Bearbeitungen des "Retterbuches" in der deuteronomischen Epoche*. Bonner Biblische Beiträge 21. Bonn: Peter Hanstein.

1966   *Traditionsgeschichtliche Untersuchungen zum Richterbuch*. Bonner Biblische Beiträge 18. Bonn: Peter Hanstein.

1970   *Die sogenannten vorprophetischen Berufsberichte. Eine literaturwissenschaftliche Studie zu 1 Sam 9, 1–10, 16, Ex 3f. und Ri 6, 11b–17*. Forschungen zur Religion und Literatur des Alten und Neuen Testaments 101. Göttingen: Vandenhoeck und Ruprecht.

Robinson, H. W.
1949   *The Cross of Hosea*. Philadelphia: Westminster.

Robinson, Th. H.
1935   "Die Ehe des Hosea." *TSK* 106: 301–313.

Roth, W. M. W.
1962   "The Numerical Sequence x/x + 1 in the Old Testament." *VT* 12: 300–311.

1965   *Numerical sayings in the Old Testament. A form-critical study*. VTS 13.

Rowley, H. H.
1956   "The Marriage of Hosea." *Bulletin of the John Rylands Library* 39: 200–233 = Rowley 1963: 66–97.

1963   *Men of God*. London: Nelson.

Rudolph, W.
1963   "Präpariete Jungfrauen?" *ZAW* 75: 65–73.

Rupprecht, K.
1970   "*'lh mn h'rṣ* (Ex 1,10, Hos 2,2): 'sich des Landes bemachtigen?'" *ZAW* 82: 442–447.

Sanders, J. A.
1975   "Palestinian Manuscripts, 1947–1972." Pages 401–413 in *Qumran and the History of the Biblical Text*. Eds. F. M. Cross and Shemaryahu Talmon. Harvard University Press.

Schildenberger, J.
1953   "Jakobs nächtlicher Kampf mit dem Elohim am Jabbok (Gn
        32, 23–33)." Pages 69–96 in *Miscellanea Biblica B. Ubach.*
        Scripta et Documenta 1. Ed. R. M. Díaz Carbonell. Montisser-
        rati/Barcelona: Casa Provincial de Caridad.
Schmidt, H.
1924   "Die Ehe des Hosea." *ZAW* 42: 245–272.
Schottroff, W.
1964   *'Gedenken' im Alten Orient und im Alten Testament; die Wur-
        zel zākar im semitische Sprachkreis.* Wissenschaftliche Mono-
        graphien zum Alten und Neuen Testament 15. Neukirchen-
        Vluyn: Neukirchener Verlag.
Schreiner, J.
1977   "Hoseas Ehe, ein Zeichen des Gerichts." *BZ* 21: 163–183.
Schunchk, K.-D.
1963   *Benjamin. Untersuchungen zur Entstehung und Geschichte
        eines israelitischen Stammes.* BZAW 86.
Scott, R. B. Y.
1965   *Proverbs • Ecclesiastes.* Anchor Bible 18. Garden City, N.Y.:
        Doubleday.
Sellers, O.
1924–25 "Hosea's Motives." *AJSL* 41: 243–247.
1941   "Musical Instruments of Israel." *Biblical Archaeologist* 4 ※3:
        33–47 = Wright and Freedman 1961: 81–94.
van Selms, A.
1950   "The Best Man and Bride — From Sumer to St. John with a
        new Interpretation of Judges, Chapters 14–15." *JNES* 9:
        65–75.
1964–65 "Hosea and Canticles." *OTWSA* 7/8: 85–89.
Shea, W. H.
1977   "The Date and Significance of the Samaria Ostraca." *IEJ* 27:
        16–27.
1978   "Menahem and Tiglathpileser III." *JNES* 37: 43–49.
Skipwith, G. H.
1894–95 "Note on the Order of the Text in Hosea i–iii." *Jewish Quar-
        terly Review* 7: 480.
Smith, J. M. Powis
1925   *The Prophets and Their Times.* University of Chicago Press.
Speiser, E. A.
1964   *Genesis.* Anchor Bible 1. Garden City, N.Y.: Doubleday.
1967   *Oriental and Biblical Studies: Collected Writings.* Eds. J. J.
        Finkelstein and M. Greenberg. Philadelphia: University of
        Pennsylvania.
Sperber, A.
1966   *A Historical Grammar of Biblical Hebrew.* Leiden: Brill.
Sperber, J.
1918   "Der Personenwechsel in der Bibel." *Zeitschrift für As-
        syriologie* 32: 23–33.

Tadmor, H.
1961 "Azriyau of Yaudi." *Scripta Hierosolymitana* 8: 232–271.

Talmon, S.
1963 "The Gezer Calendar and the Seasonal Cycle of Ancient Canaan." *JAOS* 83: 177–187.

Testuz, M.
1955 "Deux fragments inédits des manuscrits de la Mer Morte." *Semitica* 5: 37–38. Testuz ⅟1 = Hos 13:15 – 14:6, now siglaed 4QXIIᶜ, according to Sanders (1975:406), who miscites the *editio princeps*.

Thiele, E. R.
1965 *The Mysterious Numbers of the Hebrew Kings.* Grand Rapids: Eerdmans.

Thompson, H. O.
1970 *Mekal, the God of Beth-Shan.* Leiden: Brill.

Thompson, J. A.
1965 "Expansions of the 'd Root." *Journal of Semitic Studies* 10: 222–240.

Thureau-Dangin, F.
1910 *Lettres et contrats de l'époque de la première dynastie Babylonienne.* Textes cuneiformes 1. Paris: Geuthner.

Torczyner, H.
1938 *Lachish I: The Lachish Letters.* London: Oxford. *See also* David Diringer. 1953. Early Hebrew Inscriptions. Pages 331–339 in Olga Tufnell. *Lachish III.* London: Oxford.

Toy, C. H.
1913 "Note on Hosea 1–3." *JBL* 32: 75–79.

van Tright, F.
1958 "La signification de la lutte de Jacob près du Yabboq. Gen. xxxii 23–33." *OTS* 12: 280–309.

Tromp, N. J.
1969 *Primitive Conceptions of Death and the Nether World in the Old Testament.* Biblica et Orientalia No. 21. Rome: Pontifical Biblical Institute.

Tushingham, A. D.
1953 "A Reconsideration of Hosea, Chapters 1–3." *JNES* 12: 150–159.

Tuttle, G. A.
1973 "Wisdom and Habakkuk." *Studia Biblica et Theologica* (Pasadena) 3:3–14.

de Vaux, R.
1961a *Les Institutions de l'Ancien Testament* I. Paris: du Cerf = de Vaux 1961b.

1961b *Ancient Israel: Its Life and Institutions.* Tr. J. McHugh. New York: McGraw-Hill = de Vaux 1961a, 1967.

1967 *Les Institutions de l'Ancien Testament* II. Paris: du Cerf = de Vaux 1961b.

Vincent, A.
1937   *La Religion des Judeo-Araméens d'Elephantine.* Paris:
        Geuthner.

Virolleaud, C.
1968   "Les nouveaux textes mythologiques et liturgiques de Ras
        Shamra." Pages 545–606 in J. Nougayrol et al. *Ugaritica V.*
        Mission de Ras Shamra 16. Institut Français d'Archéologie de
        Beyrouth, Bibliothèque Archéologique et Historique 80. Paris:
        Geuthner.

Vollmer, J.
1971   *Geschichtliche Ruckblicke und Motive in der Prophetie des
        Amos, Hosea und Jesaia.* BZAW 119.

de Vries, S. J.
1962   "Chronology of the Old Testament." Volume I, pp. 580–599,
        in Buttrick et al. 1962.

Vriezen, T. C.
1941   "Hosea 12." *Nieuwe Theologische Studien* 24: 144–149.
1942   "La tradition de Jacob dans Osée 12." *OTS* 1: 64–78.
1953   "Prophecy and Eschatology." *VTS* 1: 199–229.
1958   "Einige Notizen zur Übersetzung des Bindeswortes *ki.*" Pages
        266–273 in Hempel and Rost 1958.

Vuillenmier-Bessard, R.
1958   "Osée 13:12 et les manuscrits." *RevQ* 1: 281–282.

Ward, J. M.
1969   "The Message of the Prophet Hosea." *Interpretation* 23:
        387–407.

Warmuth, G.
1976   *Das Mahnwort. Seine Bedeutung für die Verkündigung der
        vorexilischen Propheten Amos, Hosea, Micha, Jesaja und
        Jeremia.* Beiträge zur biblischen Exegese und Theologie 1.
        Frankfurt am Main: Peter Lang.

Waterman, L.
1918   "The Marriage of Hosea." *JBL* 37: 193–208.
1955   "Hosea, Chapters 1–3, in Retrospect and Prospect." *JNES* 14:
        100–109.

Wehr, H.
1953   *Der arabische Elativ.* Akademie der Wissenschaften und der
        Literatur in Mainz. Abhandlungen der geistes- und sozialwis-
        senschaftlichen Klasse 1952: 567–621 (= ✳7). Wiesbaden:
        Franz Steiner.

van der Weiden, W. A.
1966   "Radix hebraica '*rb.*" *Verbum Domini* 44: 97–104.

Weider, A. A.
1965   "Ugaritic-Hebrew Lexicographical Notes." *JBL* 84: 160–164.

Weinfeld, M.
1972   *Deuteronomy and the Deuteronomic School.* Oxford: Claren-
        don.

Weingreen, J.
1961   "The Title *Môrēh Ṣedeḳ*." *Journal of Semitic Studies* 6: 162–174 = Weingreen 1976: 100–114.
1976   *From Bible to Mishna*. Manchester University Press.

Weippert, M.
1961   "Gott und Stier: Bemerkungen zu einer Terrakotte aus Jāfa." *Zeitschrift des Deutschen Pälastina-Vereins* 77: 93–117.

Weiss, D. H.
1962   "A Note on *'šr l' 'ršh*." *JBL* 81: 67–69.

Westermann, C.
1967   *Basic Forms of Prophetic Speech*. Tr. H. C. White. Philadelphia: Westminster.

Wijngaards, J.
1967   "Death and Resurrection in Covenant Context (Hos 6:2)." *VT* 17: 226–239.

Wildberger, H.
1960   "Die Thronnamen des Messias, Is 9, 5b." *Theologische Zeitschrift* 16: 314–332.

Willi-Plein, I.
1971   *Vorformen der Schriftexegese innerhalb des Alten Testaments. Untersuchungen zum literarischen Werden der auf Amos, Hosea und Micha züruckgehenden Bücher im hebräischen Zwölfprophetenbuch*. BZAW 123.

Wolff, H. W.
1952-53a   "Der grosse Jesreeltag (Hosea 2, 1–3)." *EvT* 12: 78–104 = Wolff 1964: 151–181.
1952–53b   "Wissen um Gott: bei Hosea als Urform von Theologie." *EvT* 12: 533–554 = Wolff 1964: 182–205.
1956   "Hoseas geistige Heimat." *Theologische Literaturzeitung* 81: 83–94 = Wolff 1964: 232–250.
1961   "Guilt and Salvation. A Study of the Prophecy of Hosea." *Interpretation* 15: 274–285.
1964   *Gesammelte Studien zum Alten Testament*. Theologische Bücherei 22. München: Kaiser Verlag.
1970   "Das Ende des Heiligtums in Bethel." Pages 287–298 in *Archäologie und Altes Testament: Festschrift für Kurt Galling*. Eds. A. Kuschke and E. Kutsch. Tübingen: Mohr.

Worden, T.
1953   "The Literary Influence of the Ugaritic Fertility Myth on the Old Testament." *VT* 3: 273–297.

Wright, G. E.
1969   *The Old Testament and Theology*. New York: Harper & Row.
1971   "The Divine Name and the Divine Nature." *Perspective 12*: 177–185.
———— ed.
1965   *The Bible and the Ancient Near East*. Garden City, N.Y.: Doubleday Anchor.

110 HOSEA

────── and D. N. Freedman, eds.
1961   *The Biblical Archaeologist Reader I.* Garden City, N.Y.:
        Doubleday Anchor. Rpt. 1978. Ann Arbor: American Schools
        of Oriental Research.
Yaron, R.
1957   "On Divorce in Old Testament Times." *Revue International
        des Droits d'Antiquité* 4: 117–128.
1963   "A Royal Divorce at Ugarit." *Orientalia* 32: 21–31.
Young, D. W.
1960   "Notes on the Root *ntn* in Biblical Hebrew." *VT* 10: 457–459.
Zayadine, F., and H. D. Thompson
1973   "The Ammonite Inscription from Tell Siran." *Berytus* 22:
        115–140.
Ziegler, J.
1943   *Duodecim Prophetae.* Septuaginta Vetus Testamentum Grae-
        cum 13. Göttingen: Vandenhoeck und Ruprecht.
van Zijl, P. J.
1972   *Baal: A Study of Texts in Connection with Baal in the Ugaritic
        Epics.* Alter Orient und Altes Testament 10. Kevelaer —
        Neukirchen-Vluyn: Verlag Butzon und Berker and Neukir-
        chener Verlag.

PLATES

P. Albenda. 1974. "Grapevines in Ashurbanipal's Garden." *BASOR* 215:5–17.
────── 1977. "Landscape Bas-Reliefs in the *Bīt Ḥilāni* of Ashurbanipal."
BASOR 225:29–48.
R. D. Barnett. 1970. *Assyrian Palace Reliefs in the British Museum.* London:
BM.
────── 1976. *Sculptures from the North Palace of Ashurbanipal at Nineveh
(668–627 B.C.).* London: BM.
────── and M. Falkner. 1962. *The Sculptures of Aššur-naṣir-apli II (883–859
B.C.), Tiglath-Pileser III (745–727 B.C.), Esarhaddon (681–669 B.C.)
. . . at Nimrud.* London: BM.
E. A. Wallis Budge. 1914. *Assyrian Sculptures in the British Museum . . .
Ashur-nasir-pal.* London: BM.
M. Dothan. 1956. "The Excavations at Nahariyah." *IEJ* 6:14–25.
C. Meyers. 1978. "The Roots of Restriction: Women in Early Israel." *Biblical
Archeologist* 41:91–103.
J. B. Pritchard. 1969b. *The Ancient Near East in Pictures.* Princeton Univer-
sity Press.
C. F. A. Schaeffer. 1933. "Les Fouilles de Minet-el-Beida et de Ras-Shamra,
Quatrième Campagne (Printemps 1932)." *Syria* 14:93–127.
────── 1949. *Ugaritica II.* Mission de Ras Shamra 5. Institut Français

d'Archéologie de Beyrouth Biliothèque Archéologique et Historique 47. Paris: Geuthner.

H. Shanks. 1977. "A Jerusalem Celebration—of Temples and Bamot." *The Biblical Archaeology Review* 3 ⚒3:22–24.

F. Thureau-Dangin et al. 1931. *Arslan-Tash. Atlas.* Haut-Commissariat . . . Française en Syria et au Liban . . . Bibliothèque Archéologique et Historique 16. Paris: Geuthner.

PART I

Hosea's Marriage

(Chapters 1–3)

INTRODUCTION

The Story of Hosea's Marriage

The first part of the Book of Hosea encompasses cc 1–3.* The division between this part and the remainder of the work is so marked that some scholars, e.g. Kaufmann (1960:368–371) and Ginsberg (1971), have concluded that two different prophets of two different periods are involved. So drastic an analysis of the text is not required by the evidence, and we prefer the traditional view that the book as a whole stems from one era, the eighth century, and contains substantially the work of one prophet, Hosea ben-Beeri. The proposal at least points up the radical disjuncture between cc 3 and 4. It is only in the earlier part that the prophet himelf appears, along with other members of his family: his wife Gomer bat-Diblaim and their children. The style is distinctive as well; the prosaic quality of cc 1–3 contrasts with the poetic character of the remainder. Further, the extended analogy between the life of Hosea and his family on the one hand and the historical relationship of Yahweh to his people on the other in the earlier part finds no consistent counterpart in the latter part of the book.

The first part can be divided into two unequal portions, each introduced by the words, *wy'mr yhwh 'l*, "Then Yahweh said to," at 1:2b and 3:1a. The title (1:1) is followed by the enigmatic preface (1:2a), which may stand as a prologue to the entire book, to the first part (cc 1–3), or, perhaps more pointedly, as the introduction to the second part of the book, which begins at 4:1 with the proclamation: "Hear the word of Yahweh, Israelites . . ." (cf. 5:1, and especially Amos 3:1; 4:1; 5:1), on which see the NOTES ad loc. The narrative proper begins with a divine instruction to the prophet (1:2b). The godly imperative is both so startling and commonplace as to require two chapters of the book to elucidate. The first part of it is commonplace: "Go, take . . . a . . . wife . . . ," so much so

* The Hebrew numeration (used by the LXX, and some modern versions, e.g. *NAB* and *JB*) differs from the English numeration (derived from the Vulgate and followed by, e.g. *RSV* and *NEB*). In the Hebrew system, c 1 has nine verses; in the English, the first two verses of the Hebrew's second chapter are included in the first. So, Heb 2:1 = Eng 1:10, Heb 2:2 = Eng 1:11, and Heb 2:3 = Eng 2:1, etc. The Hebrew numeration is used here. (There is a third major numeration tradition which is not reflected in any current English version; the Bomberg Rabbinic Bible includes the first three verses of the Hebrew numeration's second chapter in the first.)

as to be unnecessary in a society in which marriage and family were regarded as among the highest goods and as essential elements of social life. By contrast, a special word was addressed by God to the prophet Jeremiah forbidding him to marry, as a symbol of the parlous state of affairs in his days and of the imminent threat to all social structures and the ongoing life of the nation (Jeremiah 16).

The first chapter of Hosea elaborates the initial instruction and details the marriage and the arrival of children. All of this follows a predictable pattern and is paralleled in the experience of a roughly contemporary prophet, Isaiah ben-Amoz of Jerusalem (Isa 8:1–4). In both cases, the children bear symbolic names which, as the comments make clear, are minatory in character. A calculated ambivalence is built into the names and the accompanying interpretations in Hosea, so that at the end of c 2 there is a complete reversal of meanings: out of the disaster which will overwhelm the country there will come a renewal of life and restoration of good things to fulfill the original intention and basic desires of the deity. With the conclusion of the account of the prophet's three children the central message of the book has been delivered, and a sketch of the entire literary enterprise presented. But much explaining remains to be done.

The balance of the call or charge to the prophet is to marry a promiscuous woman, certainly one of the more startling divine allocutions recorded in the Bible. The precise expression (*'št znwnym*) is unique to Hosea, and opinions differ as to its exact meaning; but other uses of the key term refer to the behavior of married women, thus reflecting a compound involvement in both promiscuity and adultery, an interpretation also validated by specific terms in cc 2 (v 7) and 3 (v 1). The implication is that the illicit activity of the woman chosen by the prophet only commenced after the marriage was consummated; the injunction was proleptic in nature, its full content not realized until years later with the deterioration and effectual collapse of the marriage relationship. That the development was gradual is shown by the account in c 1 in which the story of Hosea's children is told without reference to the initial characterization of both wife and children, and is simply the record of names and their symbolic meanings. Only in the course of c 2 (confirmed by the summary statements in c 3) do we learn about the unseemly side of the family's life, the disastrous effects of the behavior of the wayward wife, and the disruption of the covenanted relationship to her husband, ending in desertion of his bed and board as she, decked out in all her finery, heads off in pursuit of her lovers.

The section 2:4–25 itself divides conveniently into two subsections, the first (vv 4–15) dealing with the status of the marriage, the willful activity of the wife-mother who compounds adultery with promiscuity, apparently in the context of officially approved Baal worship. We need not doubt the accuracy or reality of the description of her behavior: in a remark about the precarious status of the children, the prophet asserts that their mother has been promiscuous; corresponding to this is the equally explicit statement that she has deserted them and left their home.

This is the occasion for a long address by the prophet: 2:4–25 is essentially a monologue in which the prophet speaks to the children first and later to their mother as he reflects on the situation and ponders what he should do about it. Throughout he speaks in the name of God, and often, in the first person, for God himself in his relationship with his people Israel, which is an analogue to that between Hosea and his wife. The prophet considers the countermeasures he must take, mainly of a punitive and retributive nature, in the form of threats should she fail to repent and, suitably chastened, return. The hope is expressed that punishment, or the threat of it, will lead her to repentance, and that the deserter will come to her senses, be stricken in her conscience, and return with contrition to her original husband (v 9). This move will provide both occasion and opportunity for the restoration of the fallen woman, the renewal of marriage ties and the restoration of the family to its pristine splendor. The second subsection (vv 16–25) describes the consequences of repentance and renewal and reaches a climax with the inauguration of the eschatological age of fulfillment. A grand chorus, consisting of heaven and earth and all of their inhabitants, celebrates the new order.

In brief, 2:4–25 portrays the actual situation of the prophet and his family already foreshadowed and assumed by the opening command to the prophet: "Take for yourself a promiscuous wife and children of promiscuity." The history and meaning of this extraordinary pronouncement are explored and analyzed. In the chapter, the scene is set dramatically at the low point in the relationship between an unfaithful wife who has deserted her husband, and an angry but heartbroken husband, who is determined by all means to hang on to the one who has abandoned him. He recounts what has led to the present state of affairs, but centers his thought mainly on what may yet transpire, and how through a program of retribution leading to repentance the guilty one may yet be saved and the marriage restored. Repentance and return will lead to renewal and restoration. The names of the children, which symbolized the destruction of the relationship between God and his people, will be reversed so that at the end of days they will symbolize the reparation of the relationship, and the realization of an Edenic existence on earth. With this climactic reversal of fortune and names, the unit of the first two chapters closes. The children and their symbolic names constitute the link among the parts of the unit, and in particular bind the last verse of c 2 with the opening verses of c 1.

Chapter 3 serves as a historical footnote or postscript to the extraordinary monologue in c 2. It is introduced as a later summons or charge of

Yahweh to the prophet and describes what actually happened after the scene in c 2. In place of the theological speculation and prophetic recitation about the future which culminated in the cosmic chorus welcoming the new age, we have the prosaic aftermath of this spiritual and emotional event. Instead of the richly decorated scene of punishment, repentance, and restoration which we found in c 2, there is a brief statement about what really happened, as well as some hope and expectation about the future. The prophet retrieved his lost wife for a payment partly in cash, partly in kind. They are once again together but the period of rehabilitation has only begun. There is hope for the future, but the goal is a long way off. The present reality reflects progress but the fulfillment of hopes and dreams is still to be achieved, both for the prophet and his wife and for their analogues, God and his people Israel.

The Character of the Narrative

In each succeeding section of Part I the narrative proceeds to a point in time later than the preceding one, while the ultimate goal, still indefinitely in the future, remains essentially the same: reconciliation, restoration, fulfillment. Thus the first section describes first (1:2–9) the initial phases of married life and the birth of the children with their ominous names. In the future (2:1–3) the circumstances will be altered, and the names reversed to fit the new, restored relationships between Yahweh and his people. The second section (2:4–25) carries the story further, in a description of the depravity and dissolute behavior of the mother and her desertion of her husband as she chases after her lovers. The abused husband contemplates various forms of discipline and punishment designed to bring back the errant wife and lead her to repentance — the necessary prerequisite to the restoration of harmonious relations. Given that vital ingredient, the world's new age will dawn, along with the renewal of the marriage and the realization of a covenant of peace and well-being among all the inhabitants of the created universe. Again the names of the children are reversed to reflect the reversal of fortunes and the fulfillment of divine intention and promise.

The final section, c 3, is autobiographical — perhaps the most original and authentic part of the preserved material — and picks up the story where it was left in the preceding section. It describes not the hoped-for repentance and return of the wife, but more matter-of-factly the recovery of his wife by the prophet in some obscure commercial transaction. The immediate prospects seem grim: solitary confinement for a long but indeterminate period. Faith and hope, however, remain indomitable, and ultimate reconciliation and restoration are confidently affirmed, at least for Israel and Yahweh, if not explicitly for Hosea and his wife.

In barest outline, the story describes the marriage of Hosea, and the children of that union; the subsequent desertion by the wife, and her reclamation by the husband. This commonplace sequence of events is interpreted as symbolic of Yahweh's experience with his people Israel, and preparatory for the ultimate resolution of tension and conflict in the eschatological fulfillment of hope and promise. The material may be outlined as follows:

1:1 *Title*
1:2 – 2:25 *Hosea and his Family*
   1. 1:2 – 2:3 Hosea's Wife and the Naming and Renaming of the Children
      a. 1:2 The Divine Imperative
      b. 1:3–5 Jezreel
      c. 1:6–7 Lo-Ruhama
      d. 1:8–9 Lo-Ammi
      e. 2:1–3 The Great Day of Jezreel: the Restoration of Israel and the Reversal of Names
   2. 2:4–25 Defection and Retribution; Reconciliation and Renewal
      a. 2:4–15 Desertion and Discipline
         1) 4–7 The dissolute behavior of wife
         2) 8–9 The hoped-for repentance
         3) 10–15 The punishment and consequences
      b. 2:16–25 Renewal and Restoration
         1) 16–17 The new exodus
         2) 18–19 The end of Baal worship
         3) 20–22 Covenant and betrothal
         4) 23–25 Consummation: the great chorus
3:1–5 *Hosea and the Woman*
   1. 3:1–3 The Recovery of Hosea's Wife
   2. 3:4–5 Israel: Repentance and Restoration

In dealing with cc 1–3 in their present form we proceed on the assumption that it has been arranged deliberately and should make sense when rendered and treated in consecutive fashion. In the translation and NOTES primary consideration is given to this circumstance. At the same time the structure of the sections shows that beneath the surface other arrangements and connections have also been contrived. In each section there is a movement from present or past reality to an unrealized future, and each narrative echoes or evokes the others. In each section there is a pattern of inclusion whereby the closing remarks are linked by vocabulary and morphology with the opening. Many similar devices are used to set off smaller units and to link passages in different sections. While one speaks hesitantly of code language and ciphers, nevertheless it must be suggested that there is more here than meets the eye — whether these complexities and insin-uations derive from the prophet or have been built into the final literary form of the work by the author-editor-compiler can hardly be decided. For our purposes the important thing is to identify the phenomena and in-dicate their significance in interpreting and evaluating the whole.

While the basic narrative is straightforward and superficial, the underly-ing, or second, level is fragmentary and discontinuous, visible here and there where a literary device of one kind or other is more in evidence, or where the connections are more obvious. The reader will have to judge the validity and importance of such contentions and speculations, though in certain instances the collocation of significant items is too detailed and ex-tensive to be a matter of happenstance. A few examples must suffice here; all cases of remote or hidden linkage so far found are discussed below and in the NOTES.

The distribution of the 3 m pl pronoun in c 2 is revealing. In 2:24b we read: "And they themselves will respond to Jezreel." Since the inde-pendent pronoun *hēm* is used in addition to the verb *y'nw* it is clear that "they" is a matter of special interest. In order to identify the antecedent to which the pronoun refers, one would normally look to the nearest qualified nouns, in this case, "the grain and must and oil," and interpret the phrase as the concluding link in the chain of responses which begins with Yahweh and includes the heavens and the earth and these products of the soil. So far, so good. One would not doubt the correctness of this superficial arrangement, except that the list, which begins appropriately with God and then extends to the major components of creation, grows less obviously intelligible as it proceeds and finally comes to Jezreel, the oldest son.

While pondering this matter we are reminded that at the end of the pre-vious section (it may be that 2:3, which serves to end the section begin-ning with 1:2, also introduces the second section, 2:4–25), the same Jezreel is apparently instructed to speak to his siblings and revise their names positively to Ammi and Ruhama. The same theme is articulated in the last verse of the chapter (2:25), i.e. the change of the names of the younger siblings, and this follows immediately upon the expression at the end of v 24. Considered by itself, 2:24b could be regarded as a link to v 25 as well as with the earlier sentence in v 3. The pronoun *hm* might refer to the other children, who were named in 2:3 and will figure also in v 25. In response to their brother's statement (v 3) they will make a suitable answer.

Pursuing a more complex set of data concerning the children and the 3 m pl pronoun, we observe that the mother speaks in 2:14a: "They are my wages, which/whom my lovers paid me." We look for the antecedent to the pronoun (*hēmmâ*) in the preceding clause and find the words, "her vines and her fig trees." Such an association is entirely appropriate because the woman previously identified her lovers as those who provide her with food and water, wool and flax, oil and drink (v 7). The continuation in v 14 is likewise superficially consistent: "I shall consign them to the jungle, and wild animals of the countryside will devour them." There can be no quarrel with the analysis and interpretation thus far, though a second line of investigation may be pursued. The expression *ḥyt ḥśdh* commonly refers to "wild animals," characteristically carnivores, and it may be wondered whether devouring figs and grapes adequately describes their activities. The question is whether a more remote antecedent of the pronoun *hmh* is not indicated. It may be noted that the pronoun *hmh* is used in v 6 to refer to the children: "To her children I shall not show pity because they are children of promiscuity." What will happen to them is not further specified, unless their destiny is concealed in v 14. In our opinion, v 14 may explicate the meaning of the peculiar expression *bny znwnym* as well as define the force of the implied threat in v 6: the children inevitably share the contamination of the mother, and hence also share in the consequences of her sin. If we understand *hmh* in v 14 as resuming the *hmh* in v 6, then a second level of meaning and significance for the passage is opened up: referring now to the children, the wife says, "They are my wages, which my lovers paid me" (v 14). The notion that children are a reward from God for faithful worship and service is not alien to the Bible; the apostate wife would attribute her fertility to the benign intervention of the appropriate gods (especially Baal). There is no need to suppose that this implies that the later children were illegitimate, though the question remains open. The following words then express a judgment against the children: "I shall consign them to the jungle and wild animals of the countryside will devour them." This picture of violent destruction is in keeping with what is said throughout about the fate of Israel and Judah, with whom the children (and the mother) are identified. In support of this analysis establishing links between v 14 and v 6, we note that *wśmtym* picks up *wśmtyh* in v 5 (which describes the threatened punishment of the mother) and that in v 15a, the clause "and she went after her lovers" completes the preliminary statement in v 7, "for she said, 'Let me go after my lovers.'" The envelope construction, in which terms and themes introduced in the opening lines of the unit (vv 4–7) are then resumed or completed in the closing lines (vv 14–15), is characteristic of literary style in the Bible, and is especially noteworthy in the Book of Hosea.

We can carry the present discussion one step further. In 2:20 Yahweh says, "I shall make for them a covenant"; and at the end of the verse, "I shall make them lie down in safety." Once again the question of antecedents must be considered. For the pronominal suffix "them" (*lhm*) in v 20a the apparent antecedent is *hb'lym* "the Baalim" in v 19a, but this clearly cannot be correct; nor is it easy to find a suitable noun in the vicinity with which to connect this pronoun. The word "her vineyards" (v 17) is the next nearest m pl noun but this is hardly an improvement. Generally scholars have interpreted the expression generically, as referring to the Israelites or mankind. We suggest, however, that the pronoun here also refers to the children of the story (who stand for the Israelites, it is true). It is noteworthy that the covenant will be made by Yahweh with the beasts of the field (among others) to ensure domestic tranquillity, and it is fitting to suppose that traditional enemies will be at peace with each other. If the pronoun hmh in v 14 refers to the children, then the corresponding pronominal element may have the same force in v 20. Similarly the suffix on the verb "I shall make them lie down" has no obvious antecedent to fall back on — the nearest nouns would be the beasts of the field, the birds of the sky, and the reptiles of the ground. None of them is a very suitable candidate: ḥyt hśdh, because it is f s and the pronoun is m pl; and neither birds nor reptiles are usually described as lying down. In fact, the verb is almost always used with human beings and it seems logical to identify the pronominal element here with the same 3 m pl element at the beginning of the verse. Once again we can argue that the most likely association is with the children; they are mentioned explicitly only in v 6 but are present both at the beginning (v 4) and the end (v 25) — and as we have suggested, they appear subliminally in several other places. It may finally be asked whether the 3 m pl pronoun, independent or suffixal, is not a code word for the children as well as fitting in its ordinary context throughout the chapter.

Another example of second-level usage, in this case dispersion or scattering, may be seen in a comparison of a straightforward affirmation in v 10a of the first subsection of c 2 and the dispersion of the component parts in the second part. In v 10a Yahweh says, "She didn't know that it was I who provided her with grain and must and oil." We note again the occurrence of grain and must and oil in v 24, the same words in the same order as in v 10, though here each has the sign of the direct object, missing in v 10. In v 17a we have the phrase "I will assign to her" and in v 16a the independent 1 c s pronoun. On the surface each element serves satisfactorily where it is, but one wonders whether the author had a secondary objective in mind, hinting that these scattered elements should be brought together by the reader as another sign or mark of the new age of redemption. An attentive reader would note these and similar secondary phenomena.

The Texture of the Narrative

Before considering the integrity of the first three chapters of Hosea in detail, we should discuss briefly the opening of the book and the role of the entire section in the book. Hosea 1:2a is in one sense a title for the prophecy proper, the public proclamation, which does not begin until the first formal oracle of 4:1. The intervening biographical and autobiographical material is not, however, irrelevant to the prophecy: the names of Hosea's children are messages, albeit enigmatic ones, explained only after they are introduced.

The rest of c 1 (vv 2b–9), and cc 2 and 3 supply the background and circumstances of the prophet's proclamation. The narrative is a literary, not an oral, composition. The introductory personal material helps to make the significance of the discourse in Hosea 4–14 more meaningful. A distinction can be made between the biographical passage in c 1, the autobiographical verses in c 3, and the discourse of c 2. The material does not amount to a coherent life of Hosea, but it is not so subservient to the "message" (Hendricks n.d.:98; Waterman 1955:102) as to be useless for historical purposes. The formal diversity of the three chapters could be the result of varying sources, some closer to the prophet than others. Thus c 3 could be genuine autobiography; c 1, the work of an intimate friend; and c 2, the labor of the compiler of the whole book, himself still close to the situation. Such a description does not "explain" the material itself in detail. Nonetheless, the diversity in motifs and literary form does not eliminate the thematic unity within the entire section and its verbal links with the rest of the book.

In approaching the first three chapters, two extreme positions must be avoided. The first is Toy's: "The section chaps. 1–3 is a mass of separate prophetic productions, originating in different periods, and put together, as was the manner of scribes, by a late editor who made no rigorous attempt at coherency" (1913:77). There is abundant evidence of coherence throughout the passage, as will be shown below. The other extreme is represented by Allwohn (1926:4), who thinks that Hosea 1–3 falls entirely within the reign of Jeroboam II. Related to Toy's approaches are the labors of recent translators and commentators who shunt materials around within the three chapters in an effort to find more logical connections. Thus the first three verses of the second chapter are often shifted to the end of the third chapter, as in the *NAB,* or to the end of the second chapter; Wolff places Hos 2:1–3, 23–25 during the reign of Hoshea, the last king of Israel (1974:4). These commonly accepted conclusions are the result of hasty judgment too much preoccupied with superficial formal harmony as a sign of unity, coupled with serious underestimation of the author's capacity for sustained artistic composition. Let us review in some detail a variety of arguments for taking the received text in substantially its present form as the base for further study.

In keeping with the rest of the prophecy, cc 1–3 have the general theme of redemption by rejection and rehabilitation. Hosea's statements on both

sides are extreme. Rejection is total; renewal requires the miracle of resurrection. The paradoxical basis for this is the fact that an indissoluble marriage has dissolved, an inviolable covenant has been violated. The matter
lies beyond law and logic; the question whether Hosea divorced Gomer
(Yahweh renounced his covenant with Israel) does not have an either/or
answer. Modern ideas of "divorce" are not adequate to describe such a
breakdown in relationships. The impasse in the present case consists of
two simultaneous realities — the wife has decisively left her husband; the
husband absolutely refuses to relinquish her.

The story of Hosea and his family is not told in a straightforward —
certainly not in a chronological — way; neither is the theological history
that becomes incarnate in Hosea's life set out systematically. The ingredients are not arranged in a line of consecutive events but are scattered
through the composition to set the contrasts side by side in a way that
finally achieves balance and harmony.

Practically everything that is said in these chapters makes sense as applied to Hosea's family life. The facts are clearest in 1:2–9 and 3:1–3; it
is less clear how much in 2:4–25 reflects real events. Everything seems to
be a metaphor of Yahweh and Israel. The comparison is openly made
from the beginning, since the names of the children say things about Israel, and the wife is compared with the nation at the outset (1:2) as well
as at the end (3:1).

The story is not allegory in the strict sense. It is prophecy. It does not
contain a well-wrought narrative which can be read on two levels. There
are not two stories running parallel. Hosea's love for his wife is "like"
Yahweh's love for his people. The similitude is vast, and equations are not
to be sought in minute details. We have only to mention the fact that either the wife or the children can represent Israel in order to indicate that a
neat scheme is not possible. At the same time some distinctions are made.
The mother represents Israel in general, but is sometimes compared with
the land (1:2, and also, most likely, in 2:24). (In 2:2 and 2:23, hā'āreṣ
may be the Underworld.) In 2:25a she represents Israel in the land. All
the children together (2:6) also represent Israel in general. But when the
three children are distinguished, they severally represent Israel under three
aspects. Jezreel stands over against the other two as united Israel of the
first monarchy and of the end time (2:2). In 1:4, however, which is in a
sense definitive, Jezreel is identified more narrowly with the house of Jehu,
the ruling dynasty of the northern kingdom. Lo-Ruhama, the daughter, is
equated with Jezreel's sisters in 2:3, while Lo-Ammi, the younger son, is
Jezreel's brothers, standing respectively for the northern and southern
halves of Israel (2:2). Together they greet their older brother in 2:24b.
The three children, then, enable Hosea to talk about the nation as a whole
(Jezreel) or divided (Lo-Ruhama and Lo-Ammi).

Most of the material is oracular, except where statements are made about the wife's conduct. The oracular names of the children (1:2–9) and the symbolic redemption of the wife (3:1–3) stand side by side with prophetic utterances about the nation, often introduced by *kî*. These pass into eschatological passages, introduced by *wĕhāyâ* (*bayyôm hahû'*), e.g. 2:1–3, in which application to Israel is paramount.

In the central section (2:4–25), on the other hand, where everything is treated in detail, an analysis of Israel's covenant history is glimpsed through the story of Hosea's family. Yet that story is not told in a self-contained way. It does not have the kind of realism that permits it to be used as a document of Israel's marriage laws and family customs; we could not, for instance, infer from the available data just what the status of children in a broken marriage was. At points like this the balance shifts almost imperceptibly so that it is Yahweh rather than Hosea who is to the fore.

In a proper allegory there are no necessary connections between the two stories that run side by side. In Hosea's parable, on the contrary, there is in effect but one story. The fact that the wife and children *are* Israelites unifies the two aspects. Gomer's misconduct is not just *like* the sin of Israel that infuriates God and breaks his heart; it *is* that sin. Her infidelity was not simply adultery committed against Hosea, and so an allegory of Israel's spiritual adultery against Yahweh. Her prostitution in the Baal cult was the very epitome of Israel's apostasy. Yahweh's judgment of her as a sinner is indistinguishable from his condemnation of the whole nation's societal sin. Hence it is impossible to disentangle the double thread that runs through these three chapters. They are, in fact, a highly sophisticated composition, and the subtle effects are lost in simplistic solutions. The technique is not found in Hosea alone. In Isaiah 54, Zion is discussed with reminiscences of Israel's progenitresses, notably Sarah. The layers of meaning are evident in *riḥamtîk* (Isa 54:8) (Beuken 1974), a word that suggests that the lesson was learned from Hosea. The artistry of Second Isaiah resembles Hosea's in two ways not noted by Beuken. First, the focus in both changes imperceptibly from the individual woman to the city, whose reconstruction climaxes the poems. Secondly, the promise of children places a limitation on the symbol of the wife/mother as comprising all Israel. Historical reality cuts across the metaphor. Thus "I deserted you (singular)" (Isa 54:7) is not followed by the expected or logical "I will return to you," but by "I will reassemble you," the gathering of a scattered people.

Besides the shifting of the focus back and forth from Hosea to God and from family to nation, the presentation is variegated even further, but also unified, by the fact that the children alone or the mother alone, and not just the family as a whole, also represent Israel.

The whole matter is rehearsed completely three times. In 1:2–2:3 there are three oracles about the children, and in each of them there is something about Israel, so each child alone can signify Israel. In 3:1–5 there is one oracle about the wife, who is compared to Israel. The effort to explain these two sections as doublets founders on the substantial differences between them. It also misses their structural relationship to each other and to the central section (2:4–25) which they encompass. There is also a temporal shift, since c 3 reflects a later moment in the life of the family, a gap apparently bridged by c 2.

In all four oracles about the four members of Hosea's family (1:2–2:3), the discourse moves from the individual to the nation. In the central section the effect is more kaleidoscopic; but there is a gradual shift of focus from Hosea and his family (2:4–15) to Yahweh and his people (2:16–25), even though the entire text is about both throughout. And whereas 1:2–2:3 is mainly about the children and 3:1–5 is about the mother, in 2:4–25 the writer's attention switches back and forth from "them" to "her" so that another double thread runs through it all. The highlighting of the pronouns, discussed earlier, is a vital key to this alternation. The process of winning back the wife and (so) reinstating the children is traced in some detail in 2:4–25. But the action does not advance in a straight line: the events are not in chronological order; the development is not logical. The material is broken up and intermingled, so that a clause about the children (such as 2:6) is embedded in a passage dealing with the wife, and a clause about the wife (such as 2:25aA) is embedded in a passage dealing with the children.

Because of the architectonic use of balancing structures and the intricate use of inclusion, material which goes together logically or chronologically is often discontinuous. Many commentators have observed this and have tried to reassemble the scattered pieces. We believe this procedure to be mistaken. It achieves a kind of clarity; but it destroys the artistry which we believe to be original and intentional, already noticed by Cassuto (1927). If the text is left as it is, there are several climactic moments, and the outcome is often stated before the events which precede it, so that sometimes the narrative seems to unfold backward. Not that the history is recounted in reverse order; it is more complicated than that. Because of the separation of clauses that belong together, the same point in the story is sometimes reached more than once.

The composition gives a superficial impression of grammatical incoherence: 1:2–2:3 is an objective biographical narrative (i.e., third person), whereas the balancing 3:1–5 is autobiographical (i.e. first person). The central section is mostly in the first person; it consists of a monologue initially addressed to the children about their mother, which continues as a series of reflections about the future, and the possibilities of punishment, repentance, and reconciliation culminating in an awesome picture of the new age of redemption and renewal. The "I" is the speaker throughout but without clear signals; it must be the prophet at times and at other times the God of the prophet. In spite of the fact that this speech (2:4–25) begins by addressing the children in the second person (v 4a), it later talks about them in the third person (v 6, etc.). While the speech describes the mother's doings in the third person, she is occasionally addressed directly (vv 8, 18, and 21–22) in the second person.

It is easy to regard such inconcinnities as blemishes and to make the text homogeneous by excising them. But, as we have already indicated and shall point out in more detail below, the removal of such heterogeneous passages as the second-person vv 8, 18, 21–22 rends the fabric, because these very passages are necessary for connections and continuities of other kinds.

Form criticism does not offer much help for the control of this discourse. The oracular character of 1:2 – 2:3 and of 3:1–5 is clear enough; but 2:4–25 cannot be forced into any stereotype. It begins with a command to the children to contend against or plead with (*ryb b*) their mother. But the *rîb* pattern is not developed along recognizable juridical lines. The usual dramatic features of the court setting are absent (unless we are to discover in the heavens and the earth in v 23 the traditional adjudicators in a covenant dispute). There is no doubt about the woman's guilt. No provision is made for defense. There is no clear statement about divorce in spite of the formula often supposed to exist in v 4; the death penalty for adultery is mentioned in v 5, but the usual mode, stoning, is not. The reason for killing the woman with thirst is historical, not juridical.

The search for a *Sitz-im-Leben* is even more baffling when we try to understand why the children, not the husband, take the initiative in the indictment, or in pleading with their mother for a change of heart. Where in the ancient Near East can a parallel be found for such a proceeding? The evidence brought by Kuhl (1934) and Gordon (1936, 1937) is tangential. The situation is obscured further by the fact that later (2:21) the husband does address his wife directly. Indeed, after 2:4a, which is purely introductory and has no counterpart in what follows, the children play little active part at all, until the end of the chapter.

The recognition that 2:8 and 2:11–15 have features of the "sentence" in a "speech of judgment," and that 2:16–25 is like a message of promise in an "oracle of salvation" (Brueggemann 1968:55–90) does not get us far. These designations are too vague to do justice to the intricacy and the uniqueness of Hosea's writing.

In spite of these difficulties, the general movement in 2:4–25 can be traced. The husband will take steps of increasing severity to bring his errant wife to a better mind (2:4–15); then there will be a new courtship, engagement, and marriage (2:16–25). The children will be reinstated along with their mother. The several themes which are scattered and interwoven may be consolidated.

A. Hosea insists that the marriage is no longer functional, though there is no evidence of a formal divorce. After repeated violations of the prescribed code, she has gone off entirely (vv 4a, 7b, 10, 15b). Other statements about the woman's activities occur in vv 7a and 15a, but these are included in clauses dealing with different matters.

The purpose of this narration is not clear. Is it to express the husband's outrage or heartbreak? Is it an indictment to condemn her? Is it a reproach, to move her to shame and repentance? Perhaps it is all of these, and it is artificial to try to decide between one or another. The passage expresses both an ardent will to reconciliation and an indignant determination to use coercive or punitive measures to correct or even to destroy her. Such a combination of contrary moods and motives is psychologically convincing. Catastrophic deprivation produces mingled rage and grief.

B. There is a statement of what Hosea's wife should do to retrieve the situation and so avoid more drastic discipline (2:4b). This clause could stand alone; it is possible, but not likely, that it is continued in v 9b. The latter, however, stands in an important structural relationship to v 4b. It represents the final outcome of the process whose point of departure is v 4b, and forms a structural inclusion.

C. There are threats of what her husband will do to her if she does not mend her ways (2:5). It is not clear whether this theme is continued in any later passages. In v 5 the opening imperfect is followed immediately by a series of four consecutive future verbs. Later on there are more such verbs, notably in v 8 and throughout vv 11–15, all saying what the husband will do. The question is whether any of them picks up the theme that begins in v 5. In a sense they do, for they are all threats. However, the introductory conjunctions for some of these verbs — *lākēn hinnēh* (v 8; cf. v 16); *lākēn* (v 11); *wĕʿattâ* (v 12) — indicate that new paragraphs begin at these points. It is likely that v 15a, which lacks such a conjunction, does pick up v 5. This connection will be supported further below by arguments from general structure.

D. Side by side with the threat against the wife, the husband says what he will do to the children if she does not mend her ways. Although the children are given a label similar to their mother's ("children of promiscuity"), the fault is entirely hers, and it is she, not they, who must repent. The children themselves are not asked to fulfill any conditions for reinstatement. There is nothing for them corresponding to B above; D is linked directly to C. The treatment of the children is not an independent train of thought; they are dependent upon their mother. Because she said that they were wages paid to her by Baal for her harlot services, they are "children of promiscuity" (v 6). This is a theological rather than a moral or biological designation. This is why there is further material about the mother in the passages which deal more specifically with the children (vv 7a, 14aB, 25aA).

E. According to the discussion under C above, the implementation of the threats passes through more than one phase. The threat first announced is, in fact, the most harsh, namely, to kill her with thirst. It is equaled in severity by the parallel threat to abandon the children for the wild animals to eat. That is final. Before it comes to this, the husband will try other means. There are three stages, forming a figure we may call a pseudo-sorites. (1) I will hamper her movements (v 8), so that she won't find her paramours (v 9a); (2) but if she does find them I will take away her food and clothing (vv 11, 13, 14), and then she will understand that it is I, not Baal, who gives such things (v 9b); (3) but if she doesn't understand (v 12a), I'll expose her in front of her lovers and prove their worthlessness and helplessness (v 12b). Then she will return to me — the desired outcome of all this. A fourth possible stage, death, threatened in v 5, is apparently never reached (but see 6:5).

Admittedly this analysis of the threats is speculative. The speech is emotional and fantastical; its imagery is evocative, not analytical. It is not certain that these stages in the correction of the woman should be distinguished. It is probably introducing too much order into the themes in their logical development to link v 11 with vv 13 and 14aA (Stage 2), just because the subject matter is similar. Nor does it follow that v 9b should be seen as the result of Stage 2, although it fits logically, completing a line of thought that runs from v 10 through v 17. She did not know that Yahweh was the real giver (v 10); she said that Baal was the giver (v 7); so Yahweh takes his gifts back (vv 11, 13, 14aA). Verse 9b does not explicitly complete this educative discipline, because she does not exactly say, "Now I know that Yahweh is the giver."

F. If there is an eventual change of heart, the only expression of it is found in v 9b, and even this is not very impressive as a recovery of the richness and confidence of a good marriage. This is the positive outcome of the procedures outlined in 2:4–15, whether it corresponds to anything real in the life of Hosea or not. The steps taken in 3:2 suggest that in the end reconciliation was the result of direct personal initiative, corresponding to the activity of Yahweh in 2:16. In any case the whole of 2:4–25 is predictive and phantasmic, not descriptive and historical.

Verse 9b occupies a central position in the balanced structure of 2:4–15, and so represents the point of departure, in thought if not in fact, for the constructive phase that follows in 2:16–25. The tapestry effect we observed in 2:4–15 (A–F above) is found also in 2:16–25. It is all consistently disjointed in a way that suggests deliberate artistry and so points to the unity of the whole.

As in 2:4–15, the mother and the children are dealt with alternately, but not systematically. There is an incongruity also in the new arrangements. For the woman, there is to be a new courtship and marriage; for the children, a new covenant and new names. Both are symbolic figures of Israel. In fact, at many points the subjects are more patently Yahweh and Israel than Hosea and his family. The themes in this section are these:

Wooing, betrothal and endowment (vv 16, 21, 17a).
The marriage (vv 19, 17b, 18, 25aA).
A new covenant for the united children (vv 20, 23, 24a).
New names for the children (v 25b).

There is much in this analysis that is uncertain. The use of the verb ʿānâ in v 17b and in vv 23–24 suggests that the woman also joins in the covenant-making ceremony, if that is what is happening in vv 23–24. It is not clear whether this ceremony includes the grain, must and oil, and Jezreel. We have linked the last response to Jezreel, with the following names of the other children. It could face both ways, as could the occurrence of ʿny in v 17, which may refer both to the woman's response to her lover's words in v 16 and to her marriage declaration in v 18. We then obtain the following scheme:

v 17 The mother answers Yahweh.
v 23 Yahweh answers (the mother?).
     Yahweh answers the skies.
     The skies answer the earth.
v 24 The earth answers (Yahweh?).
     They (the other children) answer Jezreel.

We are not at all suggesting that these thematic materials should be separated out and arranged in this way. We have compared the action of restoring the vineyards (to which we have joined the grain, the must and the oil of v 24) to endowment. Perhaps it should come after the marriage, to correspond to the original history of the Exodus, in which the wilderness period was the honeymoon and the Conquest, the groom taking the bride into his home. Verse 25aA would then follow v 17a in a sense.

We have presented this analysis simply to show the themes of 2:4–25. To isolate these constituents we have sometimes cut across the grammatical structure of a clause which combines different themes in order to bring together material that deals with the same topic. This should not be mistaken for documentary analysis. On the contrary, we recognize that there are different levels of narration in the text, that there is a basic reading to be conserved as well as an associative reading that reflects another aspect of the prophet's thought. Its unevenness is not to be smoothed out by gathering together all the passages of one sort (for example, the eschatological ones), and assigning them to a distinct source. Harper (1905:206), for instance, segregates 2:8–9, 16–18, 20–25, and 3:1–3 as "later voices describing Israel's return to Yahweh and his acceptance of her." The abrupt changes do not have to be thus explained as the seams of editorial additions. Adopting this stance does not mean that we suppose that the text has been preserved from error or alteration. Residual difficulties in any scheme of interpretation confirm the fallibility of compilers and scribes. But wholesale emendations, restorations, or rearrangements subvert the scholarly process, and in challenging the integrity of the transmitted text undermine the credibility of any reconstruction, i.e. if the text has become so corrupt, then there is no chance of recovering the original. In the long run it is better to work with the text than against it; better to understand and cope with what is there, than to create something more congenial to the critics.

All of cc 1–3 is pervaded by memories of Israel's past which give the text another kind of unity. These memories are evoked by the skillful use of heavily freighted words found in the traditions. The language is rich with connotations of the covenant; the whole scheme is an elaborate *recapitulatio* of the Exodus.

The threat that God will visit something on someone (*pqd . . . 'l . . .*) comes from the Decalogue (Exod 20:5; Deut 5:9). The affinities of Hosea with Deuteronomy are well-known. They extend to verbal equations. Questions of literary dependence are vexing and perhaps beyond solution, and it is safer to speak of a common tradition from which both draw. Whatever the solution adopted, it is a striking fact that parts of Hos 2:4–25 read like a pastiche of deuteronomic phrases. These are more prominent here than anywhere else in Hosea, in a merger of the tradition of hortatory prose with Hosea's prophecy. Not only such phrases as "other gods," "grain and must and oil," "vine and fig," but peculiar expressions such as "in its time" (found only in Deuteronomy in the Pentateuch) and "in its season" betray Hosea's favorite sources. The idiom "multiply silver and gold" occurs only in Hosea and Deuteronomy. This is an interesting link, because the (silver and) gold that was used to make the bull image in the desert was the spoil that Yahweh had given the people when they escaped from Egypt. Deuteronomy 8 contains a number of phrases found also in Hosea 2, suggesting that Hosea interprets Israel's present condition in the light of this tradition. The reiterated warning in Deuteronomy 8 against forgetting (*škḥ*) Yahweh finds its echo in the crucial use of the same word in Hos 2:15. The use of *raḥămîm* in 2:21 fulfills the promise of Deut 13:18. The boast of Deut 32:39 is echoed in Hos 2:12.

The list could be extended. The only inference that we make for the present is that this way of using the tradition is integral to the compiler's method and unified his work.

Hos 1:2–3:5 does not have poetic form in the usual Hebrew sense. It is not written in pairs of parallel lines which are easily scanned and which can be arranged in strophes. But if it is not poetry, it is not necessarily prose. It ranges from well-formed bicola which realize the classical norms of parallelism to lines which cannot be taken as anything but prose. Such writing cannot be described as a mixture of poetry and prose. We certainly cannot separate the two as if the verse were original and the prose scribal. There is unbroken continuity between one kind and the other. Even the lines which seem to be prose often include quasi-poetic patterns. The result is a special literary style, characteristic of the prophets.

There is a distinction between Hos 1:2–3:5 and Hosea 4–14 in this matter. Using the incidence of the particles *h*, *'et* and *'ăšer* as an index of prose, Hosea 4–14 is the most "poetic" of all prophetic writings. By the same measure Hosea 2 is "prose." Using the incidence of parallelism as an index of poetry gives a similar distribution. But neither index is precise enough, for "prose," according to the particles, may achieve poetic cadences, and the particles might be used sparsely in spoken, as distinct from written, prose. What we have here is what Farrar (1890) called the "intermediate style," partaking of both prose and verse, which has its roots in oratory. It also has affinities with spoken dialogue in epic narrative. This has already been discerned in part by Gordis (1971:76) who said, "There is no iron curtain between prose and poetry in the ancient world." What is needed is the recognition of a distinct third category—rhetorical oratory.

Hos 1:2–3:5 owes much of its poetic quality to the use of traditional verse forms. The bicola usually describe actions which are simultaneous, similar, or closely related (cf. those in 2:2,8,10,12,15,20,23–24,25; 3:1,3,5).

Among the bicola dispersed throughout Hos 1:2–3:5 are found many distinct poetic patterns. There is synonymous parallelism in 2:5b and 2:7a (the latter example rhymes), and antithetical parallelism in 2:4aB. There is incomplete parallelism in 2:4b and 2:11a, in both cases with rhyme. In 2:21–22 and in 2:23–24 there is effective use of repetition in parallelism.

Another thing that is often done in this kind of rhetoric is the coordination of nouns in patterns. There are sets of three: *bow, sword, and weapons of war* (2:20; cf. 1:7); *wild animals, birds, and reptiles* (2:20); *grain, must, and oil* (2:24; cf. 2:10). There is a set of four, arranged as two pairs: *grain and must, wool and flax* (2:11). Sets of five are set out symmetrically: one-three-one (2:13) or three-two (1:7; LXX reads here a three-three; and 2:10). A set of six may be arranged in three pairs (2:7; 3:4; cf. LXX of 1:7), or as one-two-two-one (2:21). Other, more intricate patterns are discussed in the NOTES.

One of the devices most frequently used in the narrative is the repetition of key words or ideas. They also serve to unify the whole and they enable the same theme to be enumerated more than once. These patterns do not necessarily correspond to poetic parallelism, nor do they always follow the thematic motifs, although they often link together passages with the same theme. The same idea sometimes recurs in the same words; for example, the occurrences of the word *m'hbym,* "lovers." Sometimes different words are used; for example, the idea of shameful nakedness is expressed by means of *'ǎrummâ* (2:5), *'erwātâ* (2:11), and *nablutâ* (2:12). Such variation is part of the art of repetition. In transmission such variants tend to converge, not diverge, so the text should not be normalized to a uniform vocabulary. There is a skillful play on the meaning of the word *hiṣṣîl* in its two occurrences in 2:11,12. Yahweh is able to "rescue," i.e. "retrieve," his wool and flax, but no one is able to "rescue," i.e., "save," a victim from his power.

Such matching ideas and repeated words do not necessarily occur at symmetrical points in the total structure. The system is not geometrical. Sometimes the same clause has several links, some near, some far. The final effect is an intricate extended network of correspondences.

The following are some of the major repetitions and correspondences.

A. *Repetition of the same word or root with the same meaning* (※※1–52). In most instances the word is important, and occurs just twice. In this list we do not include the numerous examples in which the same word occurs twice in immediate poetic parallelism, as with *bêt* and *yizrě'e'l* in 1:4b–5; *'ăraḥēm* in 1:6–7; the threefold *wě'ēraśtîk* of 2:21–22.

※1. The command *lēk qaḥ* (1:2) is followed by a description of obedience in the same words *wayyēlek wayyiqqaḥ* (1:3). Cf. ※29. A similar command *lēk 'ěhab* in 3:1 is not followed by an account of its performance using the same words; the play on the root *'hb* is developed differently. And *lēk* in 1:2 is linked with *lēk* in 3:1 to bring the opening and closing sections of Part I into balance.

※2. "To be promiscuous away from Yahweh" (1:2) contrasts with "going after lovers" (2:7,15).

※3. The word *'šh* "woman, wife" runs like a thread from 1:2 through 2:4 to 3:1, occurring each time in the first clause of the three main sections (1:2 – 2:3; 2:4–25; 3:1–5).

※4. *Yaldê zěnûnîm* (1:2); *běnê zěnûnîm* (2:6).

❋5. *Zānōh tizneh* (1:2); *zānĕtâ* (2:7).

❋6. "The land" occurs in 1:2 and 2:25, referring to Palestine.

❋7. Apart from its use in narrative (1:1,2 bis,4; 3:1) and in the formula *nĕ'ūm yhwh* (2:15,18,23), the sacred name occurs in 1:2, where it is disowned by Israel, and in 2:22, where it is acknowledged climactically; it also occurs in 3:5 at the end, where turning back to Yahweh matches the turning away in 1:2.

❋8. The longer (and deuteronomistic) phrase "Yahweh their God" occurs twice: negatively in 1:7, positively in 3:5 (Driver 1896: lxxix–lxxx).

❋9. The key name Jezreel occurs twice in the oracle in 1:4–5, where it serves as an inclusion. Its opening occurrence in 1:4a is balanced by terminal mention in 2:24. It also occurs in 2:2 along with the names of the other two children (transparently present in v 3).

❋10. *Ûpāqadtî 'et-dĕmê yizrĕ'e'l* (1:4) is balanced by *ûpāqadtî . . . 'et-yĕmê habbĕ'ālîm* (2:15).

❋11. *Wĕhišbattî* (1:4; 2:13).

❋12. The threat to break (*šbr*) Israel's bow, leaving her defenseless (1:5), is offset by the promise to break (*šbr*) the bow and other weapons of enemies, making Israel secure (2:20).

❋13. *'Ēmeq yizrĕ'e'l* (1:5); *'ēmeq 'ākôr* (2:17).

❋14. *Lō' ruḥāmâ* (1:6; 2:25); *raḥămîm* (2:21). The verb is used with the name in 1:6,7 and 2:25.

❋15. "Bow, sword, and weapons of war" (1:7; 2:20).

❋16. *Lō' 'ammî,* as the last and most horrible of the names, comes in for the most attention (1:9 bis; 2:1,25). It carries a heavy load of covenant connotations.

❋17. "You" (emphatic) — *'attem* (1:9); *'attâ* (2:25), both referring to *lō' 'ammî,* the only occurrences of these pronouns. See ❋20 below.

❋18. To come up from the land of Egypt (2:17) is the historical Exodus. To come up from the land (2:2) is some sort of second exodus; ascent may be eschatologized to refer to the raising of the dead from Sheol.

❋19. "Your mother" (2:4); "their mother" (2:7).

❋20. The independent personal pronouns often come in pairs. "She" and "I" in 2:4 are resumed by "she" and "I" in 2:10. *Hēmmâ* in 2:6 is resumed by *hēmmâ* in 2:14, the former referring to the children, the latter superficially to the vine and the fig tree, but as we have suggested, at another level to the children. The two occurrences of *hēm* (note the variant form) in 2:23 and 2:24 also go together, and may represent the children in another context.

❋21. *'Îšāh* (2:4); *'îšî* (2:9b,18).

❋22. In 2:4 the wife is to cleanse herself by removing (*swr*) her promiscuity; in 2:19 Yahweh purifies Israel by removing (*swr*) the names of the Baals from her mouth.

✳23. The hapax legomenon *na'ăpûpîm* (2:4) matches the related *mĕnā'epet* in 3:1.

✳24. The mother's *zĕnûnîm* (2:4) are the reason why the children are children of *zĕnûnîm* (2:6) — a pairing like that in 1:2.

✳25. *Wĕśamtîhā* (2:5); *wĕśamtîm* (2:14) — the first refers to the mother, while the second has as its apparent antecedent the vine and the fig tree and, as ultimate point of reference, the children.

✳26. *Midbār* (2:5,16).

✳27. "Like the day of her birth" (2:5) is echoed by "like the day she came up from the land of Egypt" (2:17), the birth of the nation. The connection is important thematically.

✳28. The first clause of 2:6 resembles the first clause of 1:7, especially if the latter is elliptically negated, as we argue.

✳29. "I will go after my lovers" (2:7) is completed by "and she went after her lovers" (2:15). Cf. ✳1. In another direction this resolve to depart (*'ēlĕkâ*) stands in contrast with the resolve to return (*'ēlĕkâ*) in 2:9b. The latter clause, unique in the structure of 2:4–15, is linked with 2:16 (*hlktyh*), since it was in the desert that Israel "went after Yahweh." Thus, 2:9b is the midpoint of 2:4–15 and the starting point for the fresh development in 2:16–25.

✳30. The use of *'āmĕrâ*, "she said," twice (2:7,14) signals the close connection of two widely separated passages. They list the two prime charges against the woman: (1) the moral fault of adultery; (2) the theological error of supposing that Baal gave her her children. *'Āmĕrâ* occurs again in 2:9b; but here the time reference is different, and the meaning is opposite. As the correction of these two faults, 2:9b is thematically unique, just as it is structurally central in 2:4–15. In fact, the whole of 2:4–15 focuses on this line, and 2:16–25 emerges from it.

✳31. The key word "lovers" occurs six times (*m'hbym* in 2:7,9,12,14,15; *'hbym* in 3:1). Cf. ✳29. The occurrences in 2:9 and 2:12 belong together. They describe two stages in discrediting the lovers. The fourth occurrence (2:14) seems to match the equation of "lovers" and "givers" in 2:7; "givers" is otherwise unpaired. In 3:1–5, *rēa'*, "friend, someone else, neighbor," is used for the paramour. The root *'hb* is still prominent in 3:1, where it occurs four times. While not strictly synonymous with *m'hbym*, the *Qal* participle used there has the same referent, clearly identified as "other gods" (3:1). Hence in c 2, the plural "lovers" matches the plural "Baals" (2:15,19).

✳32. There is important play on the root *ntn*, with its two meanings "give/pay." The lovers "pay" the prostitute (2:7,14); Yahweh "gives" (2:10,17). The doctrine that Yahweh is the sole source of all gifts dominates Deuteronomy; statements that "Yahweh your God gave/gives, etc." occur more than one hundred times. So the twofold statement that the lovers did the like (2:7,14) casts Baal in the role of Anti-Yahweh, and requires the reaffirmation of the deuteronomic truths (2:10,17).

※33. *Şmry wpšty* (2:7,11).

※34. The construction *lākēn hinnēh* + pronoun + participle occurs in 2:8 and 2:16.

※35. *Lō' timṣā'* (2:8,9), both with the same implied object, that is, "her lovers."

※36. Seeking (*bqš*) the lovers (2:9) contrasts with seeking (*bqš*) Yahweh (3:5).

※37. The husband says *'āšûb* (2:11); the wife says *'āšûbâ* (2:9b) — this is the logical order — even though the referents are not the same.

※38. *'Îšî* (2:9b,18). Cf. ※21.

※39. *Ţôb* (2:9); *ţûbô* (3:5).

※40. What she didn't know (*yd'*) (2:10) is counterpoised by whom she will know (*yd'*) (2:22); by knowing Yahweh she will know everything needful; but cf. Speiser (1964:132–133).

※41. "The grain and must and oil" (2:10,24); "grain . . . and must" (2:11).

※42. The name Baal and its plural occur twice each, first in devotion (2:10,15), then in renunciation (2:18,19); singular and plural alternate.

※43. Yahweh's ability to retrieve his property (2:11) contrasts with Baal's inability to retrieve his (2:12).

※44. The various predatory animals in 2:14 are restrained by treaty in 2:20.

※45. The days of the Baals (2:15) are offset by the days of her youth (2:17).

※46. There is play on *'ny,* "to respond," which comes once in 2:17, and five times in 2:23–24.

※47. *Miššām* and *šāmmâ* in 2:17 seem to go together, although their referents are not clear.

※48. "The skies" in 2:23 may match "the birds of the skies" in 2:20.

※49. The threefold use of *lî,* "for myself," in 2:21–22 continues as a theme through 2:25; 3:2; and 3:3.

※50. *Yāmîm rabbîm* (3:3,4).

※51. *Yšb* (3:3,4).

※52. King (3:4,5).

B. *Closely related ideas expressed in different words and other linkages of vocabulary* (※※53–73).

※53. "To be promiscuous away from Yahweh" (1:2) matches "to turn away (*pny*) to other gods" (3:1).

⚹54. The threat never to forgive (1:6) is cancelled by the assurances of 2:16–17, but the language is quite different.

⚹55. "I am not Ehyeh" (1:9) matches "my god" (2:25), which in turn balances "the living God" (2:1).

⚹56. The "place" where everything is reversed (2:1b) might be the mysterious "there" of 2:17.

⚹57. The use of both qr', "to call," (1:4,6,9; 2:18) and 'mr, "to say," (2:1,25) with evidently the same meaning "to name" constitutes an interesting isogloss.

⚹58. "One head" (2:2) matches "David their king" (3:5).

⚹59. Israel and Judah can be referred to as "house/state of" (1:4,6,7) or "children of" (2:2; 3:1,5).

⚹60. The day when they come up from the land (2:2) is like "the day" when Israel came up from Egypt (2:17).

⚹61. Note the balance of "brothers" and "sisters" in 2:3. The sequence is chiastic with the birth order in c 1.

⚹62. Different words are used for nakedness in 2:5 and 2:11.

⚹63. Shame (2:7) parallels lewdness (2:12).

⚹64. To make her a public spectacle (2:5) is like uncovering her in the sight of her lovers (2:12), although the vocabulary is different.

⚹65. Killing her (the mother) with thirst (2:5) may parallel having the wild animals eat the children (2:14).

⚹66. The various negatives are used in parallelism many times, and occur over twenty times in all.

⚹67. The word "the first" (2:9b) does not occur elsewhere; it matches "the days of her youth" in 2:17.

⚹68. The references to the way, the thornbushes, the wall, and the pathways (2:8) are obscure and have no apparent counterparts elsewhere. Since her movements are impeded, perhaps the opposite is found in 2:16, where she is now escorted by her reconciled husband.

⚹69. The word mô'ēd has different connotations in 2:11 and 2:13.

⚹70. The deprivation of the woman of her festivals (2:13) is matched by the suspension of the cult in Israel (3:4).

⚹71. The vine and fig tree (2:14) do not recur; but their destruction is offset by the provision of vineyards in 2:17.

⚹72. If the zĕnûnîm on the face and the na'ăpûpîm between the breasts (2:4) are ornaments, they are equivalent to the jewelry of 2:15.

⚹73. If the cult suspended in 3:4 is not the worship of Yahweh but the religion of Baal, this implements the threat to eliminate the names of the Baals (2:19).

C. *There is very little in these chapters that stands by itself and has no counterpart (⚹⚹74–76).*

⋕74. Some unique phrases occur as poetic parallels. "Lest I deal with her as in the arid land" occurs only in 2:5. But its parallel does occur elsewhere, "wilderness" in 2:16. "Pursue" and "overtake" occur only in 2:9a. But their parallels occur elsewhere, "seek" in 3:5 and "find" in 2:8.

⋕75. When a list is repeated, it tends to be shorter. The list of five items in 1:7 reappears as three in 2:20, so that "horses and horsemen" are mentioned only once. The list of five items in 2:10 reappears as three in 2:24, so that "silver and gold" are mentioned only once. (The silver in 3:2 is not material but money.) In 2:11 there is a list of four items in two pairs: one pair from a list of six in 2:7 and one pair from a list of five in 2:10; thus some items in the longer lists occur only once.

⋕76. Certain key expressions occur only once, perhaps to point up their importance in the narrative: *'etnâ,* "pay," in 2:14 links the themes of apostasy and promiscuity but occurs only once, as does *taqṭîr,* "she burned incense," in 2:15, a feature of Baal worship. The curious but significant expression *petaḥ tiqwâ,* "a doorway of hope," occurs in 2:17 (and not elsewhere in the Hebrew Bible). In 2:20 there is the well-known expression *krt bryt,* "to cut a covenant," basic to the biblical narrative but rare in the prophetic writings (Hosea is the striking exception in the eighth century), while in 3:2 we have the problematic *w'krh,* which is variously interpreted but does not occur again in Hosea. Much of the material in 2:1 is isolated. The expression *běnê 'ēl-ḥāy,* "children of the living God," is unique but seems to be a play on the common term *běnê yiśrā'ēl,* which occurs earlier in the verse. At the same time there is a link with *lō' 'ammî,* "Not my people," the third child, though the expected name *'ammî,* "my people," does not appear until v 3. The expression *'ēl-ḥāy* is to be compared with the closing word of c 2, *'ĕlōhāy,* "my God," with which it alliterates and rhymes. Finally in 1:8 we have the verb *wtgml,* "and she weaned," an incidental touch without special importance; it may reflect the popular view that nursing an infant tends to inhibit pregnancy.

To sum up. Out of a repertoire of approximately one hundred words and ideas, there are only a handful which do not occur at least twice. The upshot of this manifold use of repetition is that there is no verse, and hardly a clause or a phrase, that does not have verbal links with the surrounding material.

These repetitions serve various rhetorical and structural purposes. Some of them occur *within* one or another of the three main sections (1:2–2:3; 2:4–25; 3:1–5). When this happens, there may be one reference to Hosea and his family and a parallel allusion to Yahweh and Israel. The matching items may refer to the parallel treatment of the mother and her children, a feature well developed in 2:4–15. Again, a pair of similar words may be used first as a threat, then as a promise which inverts the threat. This is seen in the use of opposite names for changed status in 1:2–2:3, and again in the sustained juxtaposition of contrasting statements in 2:4–15 and 2:16–25.

In most of the instances of repetition discussed above, a word or an idea was stated in one place, and an equivalent or opposite expression was used in another place outside the range of the usual poetic parallelism. There is another way in which related materials are set in juxtaposition: a piece of discourse normally continuous is broken in the middle; the first part is held in suspense, and the sequel needed to complete it is delayed until after another passage. The effect of this is to make a sandwich.

A. "Lest I strip her naked
  and set her out
   as on the day of her birth" (2:5).
It is being naked, not being born, that makes one a spectacle; the reference to the day of birth qualifies nakedness discontinuously.

B. The comparison in 3:1 is similarly detached and delayed. Yahweh's love for Israel shows how Hosea is to love his wife, not how she is loved by her "friend."

C. In 2:16 a tricolon is arranged so that the first and third lines correspond, and the second one is intrusive.

D. In 2:8 the parallel references to "way" and "path" are separated by a statement about a wall.

E. In 2:3 the nation, in the character of Jezreel, gives new names to the brothers and sisters. It is not until 2:24 that they answer Jezreel, giving his unchanged name its new meaning, "God sows."

F. The whole of the unit 2:4–15 is embraced by an extended inclusion.

    2:4 "she is not my wife . . ."
    2:15 "and she forgot me."

G. We suggest that the more remote antecedents of *'amĕrâ* in 2:14 are *'immām* and *hôrātām* in 2:7.

   2:6 "Because children of promiscuity are they."
   2:7 "Indeed their mother was promiscuous,
     she who conceived them behaved shamefully, . . ."
   2:14 "She who said, 'They are my wages . . .'"

H. The sequel to 2:7 is found in 2:15.

I. The marriage scenes in the early part of 2:16–25 are not consummated until we reach "I will inseminate her for myself . . ." (2:25a), which is otherwise isolated within material dealing with the children.

J. It is possible that the products in 2:24a are not only the objects of the verb "to respond" that immediately precedes, but also delayed objects for "and I shall give her" in 2:17a. Strained as this may seem, it can be supported by several arguments. Linking the objects with the verb in v 17 retrieves a clause identical with that in v 10. The detachment of an object from its verb is no more anomalous than the disarticulation of a prepositional phrase from what it modifies or of a relative clause from its antecedent, phenomena that also occur here. The detailed analysis of 2:4–25 above shows that thematically related materials are dismembered and scattered over the whole passage.

K. Recognition of a similar envelope construction in v 20 helps to explain some of its features. An inclusion is made by dividing a bicolon made up of the first and last clauses of the verse. That is, "I shall make for them a covenant," and "I shall make them lie down in safety" are the closest parallels, and the pronouns are the same, referring to the children, not the animals. Because the intrusive material breaks this continuity, the imperfect verb 'ešbōr is used rather than the expected *wěšābartî.

One result of this elaborate use of repetitions and inclusions is the creation of a vast introverted structure. This is seen most clearly in 2:4–15.

v 4a	she is not my wife	me she forgot	v 15b
	I am not her husband	she went after lovers	v 15a
v 4b	so that she remove her promiscuity from her face and her adultery from between her breasts	she decked herself with nose-ring and necklace	v 15a
v 5a	lest I strip her . . .	I shall punish her	v 15a
v 5b	and treat her as in the wilderness	and consign them to jungle	v 14b
v 6	to her children I shall not show pity	"they are my wages"	v 14a
v 7	"my lovers . . . provide me" wool and flax	I shall expose her lewdness	v 12
vv 8–9a	therefore . . .	therefore . . .	v 11
v 9b	it was better for me then	I . . . provided her	v 10

Some of the connections are clearer than others. The layers of inclusions in vv 14–15 correspond remarkably in reverse to the opening development of the topics in vv 4–6. The relationships between the materials in the middle (vv 7–13) are more confused, except for the clear break between v 9 and v 10.

There are other linkages which cut across the introverted structure shown above. The theme of exposure in v 5a is picked up in v 12. The theme of providing in v 7 comes again in v 10. Verse 11 has verbal links with vv 5,7,8,9,10,12, and 13. Verses 6a,7a,9b, and in part 15a have major links outside this section. Verse 10 is also clearly marked as the beginning of a new section by the use of personal pronouns to match those in v 4.

Cassuto (1927) drew attention to some of these features fifty years ago. Two recent studies of the structure of Hosea 2 have noticed some of these introversion patterns. Galbiati (1967) observes the structure of Hos 2:4–12. Krszyna (1969) searches out the patterns of Hos 2:7–15. We have recognized these and more, and traced their connections more widely throughout cc 1–3. This simultaneous use of overlapping introversions means that the whole does not end up with simple geometrical symmetry. In Hosea 1–3, and again in Hosea 4–7, interlocking patterns of introversion unify extended stretches of text. There is a kind of organic growth. As each theme is worked out, new themes develop from it; there are no abrupt transitions to new material, with no further mention of matters already discussed. Hence it is impossible to analyze the text into completely distinct parts.

Alongside this intricate network of interwoven themes and verbal signals, the composition is unified by an architectonic arrangement of great blocks of material which balance one another quantitatively. For example, the section 2:4–9 has 221 syllables, and the matching 2:10–15 has 222 syllables.

The several kinds of structuring we have observed do not coincide. There are parallels, repetitions, chiasms, introversions, inclusions; but they do not add up to a neat geometrical scheme. The resulting structures are not congruent with thematic development, which sometimes cuts across grammatical, poetic, and strophic structure.

We conclude from these observations that Hos 1:2–2:25 is a literary whole, with an appendix or postscript (3:1–5). On careful examination the apparent confusions and inconcinnities fall into place as parts of a highly artistic arrangement. Solving supposed problems by sorting out similar material and rearranging it in logical sequences misses the point and destroys the art. The power of the writing lies in the energy with which its several themes are all kept going at once, in the juxtaposition of contrary modes, in breaking away from a point that is hardly made and leaving it in suspense. There effects are lost if the fractures are mended. The lack of order, the sudden changes of focus, the alternation of rage and compassion, the use of words heavily loaded with the most sacred memories — all this builds up emotionally to some terrific climaxes. Because the eschatological material is interspersed with the rest, the final outcome can be stated more than once: "Children of Living El!", "My God!"

I. TITLE AND HOSEA'S WIFE AND THE NAMING AND RENAMING OF THE CHILDREN
(1:1–2:3)

1:1 Title

1 ¹The word of Yahweh which came to Hosea ben-Beeri in the era of Uzziah, Jotham, Ahaz, Hezekiah, the kings of Judah, and in the era of Jeroboam ben-Joash, the king of Israel.ᵃ

1:2–2:3 Hosea's wife and the naming and renaming of the children

1:2 The divine imperative

²At the beginning, when Yahweh spoke with Hosea, then Yahweh said to Hosea: "Go, take for yourself a promiscuous wife and children of promiscuity, for the land has been promiscuous away from Yahweh."

3–5 Jezreel

³So he went and took as his wife Gomer bat-Diblaim; then she conceived and bore him a son. ⁴Yahweh said to him, "Call his name Jezreelᵇ: for in a little while I shall surely punish the dynasty of Jehu for the blood shed at Jezreel, and I shall put an end to its rule over the state of Israel. ⁵It will happen on that day that I will break Israel's bow in the Jezreel Valley."

6–7 Lo-Ruhama

⁶Then she conceived again and bore a daughter. He said to him, "Call her name Lo-Ruhama,ᶜ because I — as Yahweh their God —

ᵃ The Hebrew numeration (used by the LXX, and some modern versions, e.g. *NAB* and *JB*) differs from the English numeration (derived from the Vulgate and followed by, e.g. *RSV* and *NEB*). In the Hebrew system, c 1 has nine verses; in the English, the first two verses of the Hebrew's second chapter are included in the first. So, Heb 2:1 = Eng 1:10, Heb 2:2 = Eng 1:11, and Heb 2:3 = Eng 2:1, etc. The Hebrew numeration is used here.
ᵇ Jezreel means "God sows/seeds." Cf. 2:25.
ᶜ Lo-Ruhama means "(She is) not pitied." Cf. 2:3.

never again shall I show pity for the state of Israel, or forgive them at all; [7]nor for the state of Judah will I show pity, or save them. I will not save them from bow and sword and weapons of war, from horses and horsemen."

8–9 Lo-Ammi

[8]When she had weaned Lo-Ruhama, she conceived and bore a son. [9]He said, "Call his name Lo-Ammi,[d] for you are not my people, and I am not Ehyeh[e] to you."

2:1–3 The great day of Jezreel: the restoration of Israel and the reversal of names

2 [1]Then it will happen that the number of the Israelites will be like the sands of the sea, which cannot be measured and cannot be counted. And it will happen in the place where it was said to them, "You are not my people," it will be said to them, "(You are) children of the Living God." [2]The Judahites and the Israelites will gather themselves together, and they will appoint for themselves one head, and they will come up from the land. How great is the day, O Jezreel— [3]you will say to your brothers, Ammi, and to your sisters, Ruhama.

NOTES

1:1. *The word of Yahweh.* There is a surprising diversity among the opening words of the prophetic books. We may leave aside the works which have no formal title but begin abruptly in narrative mode — Haggai and Zechariah; Daniel and Ezra-Nehemiah are in the same tradition. Jonah is different again, resembling in its opening words the stories about prophets embedded in the Books of Kings.

Although no one book has all of them, as many as eight distinct features may be included in the prefatory remarks.

[d] Lo-Ammi means "Not my people." Cf. 2:3.
[e] Ehyeh is a divine appellation which appears in Exod 3:14; it is related to the proper name of the God of Moses, Yahweh, and has the same form as a first-person form of the verb *hāyâ*, "to be, become."

1) A name for the work
2) The prophet's name
3) The prophet's patronymic
4) His hometown
5) A reference to his call, however vague
6) The time of his activity
7) A precise date (of his call or first oracle)
8) The subject matter of his prophecy

The titles vary in the number of these items that are included, in their sequence and in vocabulary. Considering the variety that this makes possible, the titles of the books of the four eighth-century prophets — Amos, Hosea, Isaiah, and Micah — display enough similarity to suggest that they were shaped by a common editorial tradition. Yet each shows its own peculiarities, suggesting that the editor(s) devised and applied the front matter for each book with care and deliberation. The differences doubtless reflect certain knowledge or recollections about the life and career of each prophet, and in all likelihood, conserve reliable traditions of their activities. The titles of Zephaniah, Jeremiah, and in part, Ezekiel (about a century later) have features similar to the four eighth-century prophets, but they are markedly different in other respects. The remainder — Obadiah, Nahum, Habakkuk, and Joel — are different again, both in having meager titles in contrast to the ample information in the first seven mentioned, and also in the greater diversity they display among themselves. Malachi is different from them all; in fact, its title is not the same as that of any other prophetic book in the canon.

1) The preferred title is *the word of Yahweh* (Hosea, Micah, Zephaniah, Joel, Malachi). No book is called the word of the prophet himself. A title such as "the words of Amos" reminds us of the histories cited in such books as Kings and Chronicles, where something like "matters" or "affairs" is intended, as the title of Nehemiah shows.

The prime title of Isaiah is "The vision of Isaiah . . . ," and the verb *ḥāzâ,* "he had a vision," is used there. Both Obadiah and Nahum use the expression "the vision of" the prophet; the verb is also used to describe the prophetic call of Amos, Micah, and Habakkuk. The idea of "vision" is thus associated with six prophets, three of them in the eighth century.

2) If the prophet's name is not given in the opening phrase, he is named as the recipient of the word in a title such as "the word of Yahweh which came to/was unto Hosea" (also Joel, Micah, Zephaniah). Only Malachi identifies the prophet as agent, using *běyad,* "by the hand of," and this is also the only instance in which the name itself is suspect (the word *mal'ākî* means "my messenger," a suitable description of any prophet — it does not occur anywhere else as a name).

3) A patronymic is often added to the name—Hosea, Isaiah, Jeremiah, Joel. Zephaniah is unique in having a genealogy for four generations.

4) The eighth-century prophets who are not given patronymics (Amos and Micah) are identified by information about their hometown —Amos from Tekoa, Micah from Moresheth. Since Jeremiah is identified by both patronymic and home address (Anathoth), it is not likely that the one is supplied only to compensate for ignorance of the other. The patronymic or hometown is simply part of a person's identification and is in no sense intended as a credential.

Only Habakkuk is called "the prophet" in the book title; others, especially Jeremiah, are frequently styled thus in the narrative.

5) The titles of all eighth-century prophetic works, as well as those of Zephaniah and Jeremiah, include a statement about the call of the prophet to his mission. There are three ways of doing this: (1) after the title "The word of Yahweh . . ." there is a relative clause ". . . which came to/was unto Hosea . . ." (Joel, Micah, Zephaniah); (2) after the prophet's name there is a relative clause ". . . who had a vision . . ." (Amos, Isaiah, Micah); in Jeremiah, the clause "to whom was the word of Yahweh . . ." is added after his name. Because relative clauses have an unobtrusive role, the prophetic call is not highlighted by these statements. They serve rather to carry information about the period of prophetic activity or about the subject matter, or both. Only in Micah do both statements appear: "the word of Yahweh was unto him," and "he had a vision." Since the information about the period of activity or the subject matter could apply to the prophet's entire career, it weakens the perfective, punctiliar, aspect of the verbs (*hāyâ, hāzâ*), which might otherwise pinpoint a decisive moment of prophetic receptivity. But this does not settle any questions about the patterns of prophetic life. Though distinctive, experiences such as those reported in Amos 7:14; Hos 1:2; Isaiah 6; Jeremiah 1; Ezekiel 1–2 do not automatically confer permanent prophetic status or constant access to the mind and word of God. The frequency with which the formula "the word of Yahweh came to/was unto X" occurs in relation to particular oracles in the prophetic literature shows that communication from the deity was occasional rather than continual, and regardless of the prophet's desire or intentions came at the initiative of God, in conformity with the original call and commission. The perfective verbs then describe the totality of the experience.

6–7) The time of the prophet's activity is specified for the eighth-century prophets, as for Zephaniah and Jeremiah. Names of kings are mentioned, permitting the prophets to be dated according to the information provided by the compiler. Books which lack such notices have to be dated by internal evidence, which is seldom sufficient to be decisive.

Prophets are linked either with kings of both Judah and Israel (Amos, Hosea) or to kings of Judah only (Isaiah, Micah, Zephaniah, Jeremiah). The king style for the seventh-century prophets is different from that used in the eighth century. Zephaniah is located "in the reign of Josiah ben-Amon, king of Judah." The various titles of Jeremiah show exactly the same pattern: the monarch is given his full style — name, patronymic, royal title.

In descriptions of the eighth-century kings of Judah, the names are always given in a list, *without conjunctions* — by no means a trivial detail, but an important sign of affinity among them. It could be argued that the later names in these lists were supplied subsequently and were not original. It is not common in Hebrew to have a noun (viz. *yĕmê*) in construct relationship with a list of coordinated nouns, and it is rare to have such coordination without the use of the conjunction "and" before each noun. The repetition of the pattern in the cases of Hosea, Isaiah, and Micah establishes its validity, but also points to a common source of the oddity, namely the editor or compiler of these particular works. Furthermore, in Hosea there is another example of such a construction in 2:7, where six nouns in the *nomen rectum* of a construct chain are coordinated in three pairs. LXX has "and" throughout; since the absence of the conjunction is less harsh in Greek than in Hebrew, LXX probably translated literally from a Hebrew recension with the "and's"; MT is to be retained as the more difficult and hence more original reading. In Jeremiah, on the other hand, the construct form *yĕmê* is repeated for each king. Its use only once in Hosea, Isaiah, and Micah may imply that the successive reigns were considered by the editor to constitute one era. Secondly, no patronymics are supplied for the eighth-century Judean kings. Thirdly, the group as a whole is designated *kings of Judah,* strengthening our impression that a single age is in mind. This does not apply to Amos, where only "Uzziah, king of Judah" is mentioned. When Jeroboam (II), king of Israel, is mentioned in both Amos and Hosea, his patronymic (*ben-Joash*) is given as well as his royal title, to distinguish him from the other Jeroboam. Dating by Judean kings is the only reference point for Micah and Isaiah, even though there were still kings of Israel in their days, and both Micah and Isaiah paid considerable attention to the northern kingdom in their prophecies, a fact made explicit in the title of Micah. It is therefore remarkable that the contemporary Israelite kings are not listed. Even more remarkable is the case of Amos and Hosea, whose activity was primarily, if not entirely, in the north. Although Jeroboam is mentioned, his name comes after the Judean king(s) in each instance.

In several respects, therefore, these four books show signs of common editing. The main point of reference is Judah, suggesting that the works of Amos and Hosea, as well as those of the Judahite prophets, Isaiah and

Micah, were preserved in the south after Israel had disappeared from history, *and that all four were considered parts of the same corpus.*

The numerous similarities among the titles of Amos, Hosea, Isaiah, and Micah, as we have displayed them, and the lack of most of these features in the titles to Zephaniah and Jeremiah (to say nothing of their total absence from the titles of the remaining prophetic books) makes it unlikely that this editorial work was carried out late in the seventh century or early in the sixth century, and still less likely that it is the work of editors during or after the Babylonian Exile. Such activity should rather be assigned to the period defined by the data in the titles within living memory of the men concerned. Wolff (1974:4) does not recognize the substantial differences between the titles of eighth- and seventh-century prophets. He suggests that they were all edited in the same Deuteronomic circles early in the Babylonian Exile.

The similarities of the titles of Amos, Hosea, Isaiah, and Micah should not obscure the fact that no two of them are identical. Isaiah's activity extended from Uzziah to Hezekiah, a claim confirmed by the contents of the book. He was called "in the year that king Uzziah died," evidently before his death. Isaiah 6 may well be the first event in the book. In any case, the collocation of the heading and the account in Isaiah 6 shows that Uzziah was recognized as king until his death, even though his son Jotham served as co-regent and governed the country during Uzziah's illness.

There is a slight difference in the king list in the Book of Micah. Uzziah's name is omitted, showing that the list was not merely copied from book to book, and also that information was available to fix the commencement of Micah's ministry in the reign of Jotham after the death of Uzziah.

In Hosea, the list of Judean kings is the same as that in Isaiah. Amos, in spite of its similarity to the others in most respects, lists only Uzziah. This would seem to indicate, at least in the belief of the editor(s), that Amos's ministry did not continue so long as Hosea's, and that it may have ended before Jeroboam's death (Uzziah outlived Jeroboam), and thus even before Hosea's began. While Hosea and Amos might have been active at the same time (neither mentions the other), what little success we have in reconstructing the background of their messages tends to suggest Amos's priority. In general Hosea's Israel seems to be further along the path to disaster than the nation described by Amos.

The impression left by the titling scheme is an awareness on the part of the editor(s) that the prophets appeared in the order Amos, Hosea, Isaiah, Micah. Jeroboam was still alive when Amos and Hosea prophesied but had died by the time Isaiah began his ministry. Without more precise year dates, we cannot say how much overlap there might have been.

The main problem is the Israelite kings in Hosea. Why is there no mention of the many kings of Israel who reigned during the more than twenty years between the death of Jeroboam and the fall of Samaria? The span of time represented by the four Judean reigns could be as little as twenty-seven years (from the end of Uzziah in 742 to the beginning of Hezekiah in 715) or as much as nearly a century (from the beginning of Uzziah, 783, to the death of Hezekiah in 687). We cannot believe that the discrepancy is due to the carelessness of an editor, or to the one-sidedness of a Judean patriot. It is not simply that the editor(s) did not recognize the upstart dynasties involved in the decline and fall of Israel; Jeroboam's own son Zechariah, who had as strong a claim as his father to the throne of Israel, is not listed.

From a purely practical point of view, however, Zechariah's reign was so short — only six months — that it may be that no prophecies occurred during it. More likely, the editor, like Amos and Hosea, may have believed that, with Jeroboam and his utter failure to meet the divine standard, the monarchy effectively ended in Israel, a contention which could only be strengthened by the sudden demise of Zechariah, to say nothing of the even more rapid exit of his displacer Shallum who lasted only one month before being assassinated in turn. The death of Zechariah, incidentally, confirms the prophecy to Jehu (II Kings 10:30; 15:12) that his descendants to the fourth generation would sit on the throne, which seems to have been more of a threat than a promise.

The time-span marked out by the Judean kings seems too long to match the contents of the Book of Hosea. Laetsch (p. 9) gives Hosea fifty years of activity. The minimal span would be about thirty years; allowing a few years at the beginning to include Jeroboam, who may have died in 746, and a year or two into the reign of Hezekiah, one could project a career for Hosea of about thirty to thirty-five years, which in itself would not be remarkable in comparison with Isaiah, Jeremiah, or Ezekiel. While some passages might reflect the political anarchy that set in after the death of Jeroboam, there are none that can be assigned with plausibility to the period after the fall of Samaria.

Since Hosea was not married when he was called, his prophetic career started when he was young (cf. Jer 1:7). Hos 1:4 only makes sense if the first child was born during the reign of Jeroboam II. A few more years must be allowed for all the events recorded in cc 1–3. If these provided the stimulus and insights for the public ministry that found expression in the oracles of cc 4–14, we do not need to come down far into Menahem's reign to find their background. In fact, the year of the four kings (746) provides a suitable date for many of the scenes. Given that there is little basis for the association of Hosea 5 with the Syro-Ephraimite War, as we hope to show, there is reason to date most of Hosea's activities in the decade 750–740.

It is also possible that the editor inadvertently used the same list of Judean kings as for Isaiah, and thus confounded the chronology; or if the inclusion was deliberate, then he may have been working with a tradition that brought Hosea, like Amos before him, to Judah at the conclusion of his work in the northern kingdom. The reference to Hezekiah in particular may have reflected a contemporary interpretation of the passages relating to the "one head" and "David their king" just as the well-known "messianic" passages in Isaiah probably articulated high hopes concerning Hezekiah's rule in Judah and the possibility of salvaging at least part of the lost kingdom in the north.

The upshot of all this is that the heading of the Book of Hosea offers apparently conflicting data on the true span of the prophet's ministry; we can only speculate about the source of the discrepancy. It is interesting, nonetheless, to note that according to the king lists, Hosea, Isaiah, and Micah ended their active ministries in the reign of Hezekiah. Prophetic activity ceased in the reign of Manasseh (687–642).

8) Some of the titles also give a general idea of the prophet's subject matter. Amos "had a vision concerning Israel" (Amos 1:1). The reference is presumably to Israel in the broadest sense, including both kingdoms, since the south is mentioned more than once, and is included in the prophetic denunciation. Micah "had a vision concerning Samaria and Jerusalem" (Mic 1:1). Here, in contrast to the sequence of kings in the titles to Amos and Hosea, the north comes first. The single use of the preposition binds the two nouns together as if there were but one tale of two cities. Isaiah "had a vision concerning Judah and Jerusalem" (Isa 1:1) — again one preposition and two nouns. In this respect again the titles of three of the four eighth-century prophets are much alike. In Hosea, no such notice appears.

1:1. *The word of Yahweh which came to.* In spite of its similarity to the common idiom *dbr 'el,* "to speak to," the idiom *dbr-yhwh hāyâ 'el* seems to be used to speak about the word of Yahweh in a way not used when other persons speak. It represents a slight retreat from the anthropomorphism involved in "Yahweh spoke," although such language remained in vogue. By saying "the word of Yahweh was unto X," the word becomes detached from the speaker, a quasi-independent entity befitting its divine status. (For the logical development of the thought, cf. Isa 55:11; the culmination is to be found in the famous *logos* passage in the Gospel of John, 1:1–18.)

Too much should not be made of the singular "word" which titles a whole book rather than a single oracle, as if it "signifies that with the variety of forms assumed by Yahweh's address there is a manifest uniformity of his will" (Wolff, p. 4). The Hebrew Bible knows nothing of the uniformity of Yahweh's will. More simply, a book of oracles can be called "the word of Yahweh" by using the title collectively. The plural "words of Yahweh," as a title for a book, would have the inappropriate connotation of "matters of . . ." as in the annals; compare Amos 1:1; Jer 1:1. When the phrase "words of Yahweh" is used (Exod 4:28; 24:3,4; Num 11:24; Josh 3:9; I Sam 8:10; 15:1; Amos 8:11; and several times in Jeremiah), it identifies a single oracle, and does not seem to be different from *děbar-yhwh*. In fact, the expression *dbry-yhwh* may be limited to Num 11:24 and Jeremiah, since (a) the versions read *dbr* in Josh 3:19 and Amos 8:11; (b) Exod 4:28; 24:3,4; I Sam 8:10 prefix *kl;* and (c) the phrase in I Sam 15:1, *qwl dbry* (omitted in LXX[B]) *yhwh,* should probably be emended to agree with the (b) cases.

The prophet is entrusted with the word, which he must then deliver verbatim (Num 22:20, cf. 38; 23:12,26; 24:13); this makes the person of the prophet unimportant. He is completely subservient to the word. In another sense, he acquires an exalted stature, since only in his mouth (Jer 1:9; Num 23:5,16) can the word of Yahweh be found (I Kings 17:24; 18:36).

That the word of Yahweh has a different quality from the speech of other persons is seen in another aspect of this usage. In contrast with the teeming examples of "the word of Yahweh," *děbar* comes before other persons' names only with the meaning of "matter, affair," as in I Kings 15:5 — "the business of Uriah the Hittite." Otherwise it means utterance of a human speaker only in I Sam 4:1; I Kings 17:1; in II Sam 14:17 this terminology is court flattery. In II Kings 18:28–29 we have a rare instance in the Hebrew Bible of someone imitating Yahweh. Here, Rabshakeh, the messenger of the king of Assyria, opens his speech with the command, "Hear the word of the Great King, the King of Assyria," similar to Hos 4:1; Amos 3:1; 5:1 and numerous other oracles. Rabshakeh's patently blasphemous utterance reflects royal style; Israelite prophets are like him in being messengers of a monarch and heralds of court decrees. The term *ně'um* is similarly restricted in distribution (cf. Ps 36:2, Dahood 1966:218). It is almost always used of Yahweh; when used of Balaam (Num 24:3,4,15,16), David (II Sam 23:1), and a proverb maker (Prov 30:1), divine inspiration is implied.

came to. Literally "was/became unto." The idiom may be used technically to describe some decisive moment in prophetic communication, or in a more general way (Grether 1934). We have already noted its occurrence in the titles to Hosea, Micah, and Joel. Stories about prophets often begin "And the word of Yahweh came to" the prophet, whether the word comes as a personal message or is intended for someone else, as is more often the case: I Sam 15:10 (Samuel, a decree deposing Saul); II Sam 7:4 (Nathan, a message to David); I Kings 12:22 (to Shemaiah, a message for Rehoboam); 13:20 (an anonymous prophet, a message for his guest, who although a prophet himself, does not receive the word directly); 16:1 (Jehu the prophet, a message addressed directly to Ba'sha'; note that in v 7 'el- designates the eventual recipient běyad through the agency of the prophet; compare the title to Malachi and Judg 3:19); I Kings 21:17,28 (Elijah, a message for Ahab); etc.

In some occurrences of the idiom, the message is for the prophet himself: I Kings 17:2,8; 19:9 (Elijah). In this sense, the word is said to have "come" to three persons who were not technically prophets — Abram (Gen 15:1, although he is called a prophet in Gen 20:7); Jacob, telling him his name would be Israel (Gen 32:28); and Solomon (I Kings 6:11–13).

The idiom is used profusely in Jeremiah and Ezekiel, covering both messages to be delivered to someone else and instructions for the prophet himself to obey. It is accordingly impossible to tell whether Hos 1:1 refers to a specific word for Hosea or is used more generally of his entire ministry. In most occurrences the idiom describes a specific event. So, in Hos 1:2 the speech with the command to marry seems to be identified with the call to prophesy, whereas in the editorial title the word seems to have a more general meaning. Hos 1:2b – 2:25, and perhaps 3:1–5, supply the background and experience out of which the word came to Israel through Hosea. These chapters are retrospective and explanatory; but they do not contain the immediate oracles. Unlike Jeremiah, Ezekiel, and Zechariah, individual oracles in Hosea are not introduced by this formula, and this is one of the reasons why it is difficult to define their boundaries.

In the Hebrew Bible only prophets or other inspired people received the word in this way; others received it from the one inspired. The translation *came to* is inadequate if it gives the impression of the transmission of the word from God to the prophet. There is no gap to be bridged, because through his call, the prophet finds himself immediately in the divine presence. The prophet never acquires the word; he merely reports what Yahweh has said in his hearing. What Yahweh says does not lose its distinctiveness when it is repeated by human lips. "The word of Yahweh" is a parallel of *tōrâ*, "instruction," in Mic 4:2, and is paralleled by *miṣwâ*, "commandment," in Num 15:31. The word is often a command, as in v 2, and not just information, as is shown by the expected response of obedience in addition to understanding and acceptance. Since Hosea mentions "the knowledge of Yahweh (or God)" (4:1,6; 6:3,6), it is worth noting that Samuel did not "know Yahweh" before "the word of Yahweh was revealed to him" (I Sam 3:7).

Hosea. Five persons have this name in the Hebrew Bible. According to Num 13:8, this was Joshua's original name, changed to *Yĕhōšūa'* by Moses (Num 13:16). Besides the prophet, *Hōšēa'* is the name of an officer of David (I Chron 27:20), the last king of Israel (II Kings 17:1), and a post-exilic covenanter (Neh 10:24). Most of these were Ephraimites, but there is no proof that Hosea himself was (Laetsch, p. 9), although this is quite likely; the name Ephraim occurs more often in Hosea than in any other prophet. The name Hosea was common in the Jewish community at Elephantine. In the papyri it is spelled either *hwš‘* or *hwš‘yh,* the first vowel always plene; the name of the same individual can be spelled both ways (Cowley 1923:283).

The history and meaning of the name are far from clear. It has the form of a *Hip‘il* infinitive of *yš‘,* "to save" (Jer 11:12; I Sam 25:26,33). Noth (1928:175ff) identifies it as a perfect form. On this basis Wolff calls it "a name of thanksgiving" meaning "He has helped," a witness to divine help given at Hosea's birth (p. 4). Rather than an infinitive form, the name may be derived from **yahawši‘,* "Let him save!" A likely original is **yahawši‘-’ēl,* "May El rescue!" Koehler's derivation (Koehler and Baumgartner 1958:228) from *yĕhō-* plus *yōšī‘* is open to several objections. The usual development would be **yĕhōyōšī‘* > *yōyōšī‘,* and one might suppose that the first syllables would be simplified by haplology; a change from *yōšī‘* > *hōšē‘* is harder to accept. The theory supposes that the name is a late Yahwistic coinage, but as we shall see, the name never had a Yahwistic element. Normal phonetic development of **yahawši‘* would contract the diphthong, and elide the intervocalic *-h-* giving indicative *yōšī‘* or jussive *yōša‘* (Prov 20:22), the *-a-* in the latter due to secondary influence of the laryngeal. In its evolution the name did not follow the same path as the verb, but diverged in three different directions. Remarkable is the supposed loss of initial *yĕ-* to yield *Hōšēa‘,* although the variation in the forms of Hezekiah's name, *yĕḥizqîyāhû* and *ḥizqîyāhû,* is similar, and Num 13:16 suggests the reverse, i.e. *hôšēa‘* > *yĕhôšūa‘.* The *-ē-* is a tone-lengthened *-i-,* so this feature is primitive; the length is confirmed by contemporary Assyrian transcriptions — *a-ú-si-i’.*

A related Yahwistic name is attested: *hōša‘yāh* (Jer 42:1; Neh 12:32), attested in the longer form **hôša‘yāhû* (*hwš‘yhw*) in the Lachish Letters (Letter 3, Torczyner 1938 = *KAI* 193) and in the Meṣad Ḥašabyahu (or Yavneh Yam) text (*KAI* 200). Here the original *-i-* has not been so tenacious. It is not likely, in view of its retention of the archaic *-h-* and its attestation in the Mosaic age, that Hosea is a hypocoristicon of the Yahwistic name, although it was doubtless interpreted as such. (Apropos of the Mosaic age, recall that none of the names in Numbers 1 is Yahwistic.) In spite of the contrast in the stem vowel, *Hōšēa‘* could later have been taken as imperative. Cf. Ps 118:25; *Šūb-nā’* (English Shebnah) is an analogous imperative construction used as a personal name. Thus apart from the change of person, the meaning would not be far from the original jussive.

The prophet Hosea is not mentioned anywhere else in the Bible. All we know about him is derived from this book. Although Hosea's children were given strange names, there is no indication that his own name was intended to be symbolic, although it is a good name for a person with a message of liberation, and Jesus shares it (Matt 1:21).

It is ironic that the last king of Israel had the same name. As an omen of salvation it did him no good. After becoming a vassal of Shalmaneser V, he rebelled and was eventually dethroned (II Kings 17:1–4).

Beeri. Nothing is known of Hosea's father. Esau's father-in-law, a Hittite, had the same name (Gen 26:34). There are many names in the Hebrew Bible ending with -*ī*, and many are the names of Levites or northerners. The name *Bi-e-ri,* "the man of Ḥašabu," which occurs once in the El Amarna Letters (*EA* 174:3), is not demonstrably Semitic; the ending is as in Hebrew. A gentilic or vocative (Noth 1928:224) meaning for the suffix is not indicated, so nothing is gained by speculating that his father was from a town called "Spring" (compare Be'erot, Josh 18:25; II Sam 4:2). I Chron 5:6 notes that a Reubenite called Beerah was taken into exile by Tiglath Pileser, and the rabbis suggested that this was Hosea's father. An Aramaized spelling of this name occurs in I Chron 7:37. Early Christian scholars had traditions that Hosea belonged to the tribe of Issachar, with several suggestions about his hometown. These have no historical value, and cast no light on the Book of Hosea itself.

the era. Literally "the days of." *Yāmîm,* "days," refers to a definite span of time, such as a year or a lifetime. Applied to one king, it means his reign. Since the four Judean kings are linked closely together here, they are regarded as belonging to a single era, the time setting of Hosea's work.

2. *At the beginning, when Yahweh spoke with Hosea.* Literally "the-beginning-of [construct] spoke Yahweh," the *nomen rectum* being a verbal clause. This is an acceptable construction, and there is no reason for preferring the versions, which render *dbr* as a noun. Davidson (1894:§25) lists thirty-five examples, a conservative count; cf. *GKC* §130d. The most famous instance, Gen 1:1, illustrates the epic use of this construction to mark a major onset in narrative. This construction probably marks the original beginning of the prophecy; i.e. the editorial title of the whole work is 1:1 and 1:2a is the beginning of the narrative proper. It is a distinctively literary, rather than an oral, device. The absence of a preposition with such a paragraph-initial time reference is striking; contrast *b* in Gen 1:1; 2:4b; etc. It is another archaic, quasi-poetic touch, matched only by II Sam 21:9; this good example is enough to protect Hos 1:2a from gratuitous emendation. It is conceivable that the opening phrase should not be run on with the next clause, which can stand by itself and is paralleled by 3:1; and that this phrase leads into c 4 (cf. Amos 3:1; 4:1; 5:1).

At the beginning. *Tĕḥillat,* "initiation," indicates that what follows took place at the inauguration of Hosea's prophetic career, and amounts to his call to prophetic office. The word does not occur again in Hosea. No circumstances or date are given, as they are in other stories of prophetic ordination. Nor does Hosea respond, as other prophets do, with objections or attempts to dissuade God. The dramatic callings of Isaiah, Jeremiah, and Ezekiel are related autobiographically, and Amos's testimony (Amos 7:14–17) is in the same vein; cf. I Kings 22; Hab 2:1–2. The first person is used to describe Hosea's experiences only in c 3.

Some scholars (e.g. Allwohn 1926:5) find a connection between *tehillat* and *'ôd* in 3:1, connecting a "first" with a second stage of the story. This may be the case, but it is also to be noted that there is a break between 1:2a and 1:2b, already reflected in the Masoretic punctuation with *pisqā'* (a major pause). The idiom *dibber bĕ* is in itself ambiguous and may designate speaking *with, to,* or *by* another person. If it means "Yahweh spoke *by* (the agency of)" in public proclamation, then we would look to Hos 4:1 and the beginning of formal prophecy as the continuation of this statement. Otherwise Yahweh is speaking *to* Hosea and 1:2b follows. In the first case, 1:2b – 3:5 would be a vast but pertinent parenthesis. It does not follow, in the second case, that c 3 documents a "second" episode. Quite apart from the change to first person, the connections of *'ôd* are not certain.

with Hosea. The preposition *b* means usually "in"; it can also indicate an instrument — "by (means of)," or "through (the agency of)." Its use here contrasts with the idiom *dbr 'el,* "to speak *to.*" Neither oracle nor command to deliver an oracle follows, only instructions concerning Hosea's personal life. The messages come later, indirectly in the names of his children, each of which requires its own interpretation.

A spatial meaning for *b,* "in," can be ruled out; the Israelites never thought of the prophet as the speaking instrument of a deity; rather he is one who hears the word of Yahweh by various means, and repeats it. Nor could "in" refer to the inner voice of a person's own thoughts or conscience, equated with the voice of God. According to Jeremiah, prophets who rely on their own thoughts are false prophets. The true prophet is aware of God as an Other.

A distinction needs to be made between the instrumental and agential uses of *b.* The former use, with inanimate instruments (sometimes animals) is well established. The latter, applicable to persons, is dubious, or at least marginal to Hebrew usage (Andersen 1966a:108; 1971:13). Because of its rarity, each case requires individual demonstration. *NEB* has now disposed of the parade example in Gen 9:6 by translating a *b* of price, not agency, "for that man his blood shall be shed." Instances with a passive participle such as *nôśa' byhwh,* "rescued by Yahweh," do not establish a universal rule. In the idiom *dbr b* the verb is active, and in all known occurrences there is no other object. The idiom is a technical expression for the peculiar function of the prophet as agent of God; see Budde (1925:8).

The idiom *dbr b* occurs also in Num 12:2,6,8; II Sam 23:2; I Kings 22:28; Hab 2:1. All these examples involve emphatic or unusual assertions of prophetic status. In some, Yahweh speaks by, and in others with, the prophet. Compare Zech 1:9,13,14; 2:2,7; 4:1 in which the angel is not speaking "through" the prophet. The Habakkuk case offers a close parallel to the present passage, for the context there makes it clear that Habakkuk is waiting for God's reply to him, not for some message through him. All these passages suggest intimate conversation between God and the prophet in the divine council, to which he has been admitted by his call and to which he is summoned again from time to time as his work requires (cf. Num 12:8). Amos 7:2 shows that the prophet participated in the discussion in the heavenly assembly and was not merely permitted to overhear it (cf. Amos 3:7–8). On the other hand, the interpretation of the preposition *b* as instrumental has been supported by comparison with *bĕyad,* "by the hand of" (Joüon 1933); cf. Mal 1:1. The expressions are, however, distinct, nor is *b* here a dialectal variant of the common *'el,* "unto," which is used in the clauses which precede and follow, for example. Some LXX manuscripts read *pros Osēe* in both places; this is evidently a normalization of the more difficult reading. These Greek renditions could indicate a Hebrew Vorlage already normalized; but LXX[B] reads *en,* supporting MT.

Only in II Sam 23:2 ("The Spirit of Yahweh spoke by [*b*] me" or "By his Spirit, Yahweh spoke by me") does the context suggest entrustment with a message: "and his word was upon my tongue." In the next verse we read *lî dbr,* "to me he spoke," which can only mean that David was a transmitter of the divine word. The New Testament tradition that he was a poet-prophet is thus accurate. The language of divine inspiration is applicable to poet and prophet alike.

Hos 1:2a marks first, the beginning of the ministry as proclamation and second, the beginning of the story as experience. Hos 1:2b–9 describes the spiritual formation of a prophet. His biographer is not the realist that Baruch was; we know nothing of Hosea's public life. But what we lack in external fact is made up for by the glimpses given here of Hosea's family life and the anguish of his mind.

then Yahweh said to Hosea. A series of four commands, each separately communicated to Hosea, follows. Verse 2a provides a time reference, hence our use of "then," which corresponds to no word in the Hebrew. The saying is grammatically dependent on the speaking, but it is thematically distinct. *Yahweh said to Hosea* is not repetitious; it is necessary to use *'mr* to quote the speech; the formula "spoke and said" is quite common in Hebrew. It has been argued that the occurrence of both names (Yahweh and Hosea) twice shows that the first clause is a clumsy later addition. We have already noted the grammatical peculiarities of v 2a and found in them an epic formula; the repetition of names in v 2b is similarly epic. Compare the use of the names Yahweh and Sarah in Gen 21:1. Furthermore, v 2b has an important place in the total narrative structure that follows. It introduces the first of four speeches, and the introductory formula is successively shortened with each.

> 1:2 Yahweh said to Hosea
> 1:4 Yahweh said to him (*'ēlāyw*)
> 1:6 He said to him (*lô*)
> 1:9 He said

The repetition of Yahweh in v 2 is no more remarkable than its repetition in v 4.

Go, take for yourself. *Lēk* intensifies the command; it does not imply a journey. Nathan says to Bath-Sheba, "Go (*lĕkî*) and come (*bō'î*)" (I Kings 1:13), having already said *lĕkî* in v 12, when he clearly wishes her to stay and listen to his scheme. Compare *lēk bō'* in II Kings 5:5, and the discussion in Andersen (1974:56–57).

While *lqḥ* often means more precisely "buy," it is also used simply for the acquisition of a wife. In Gen 24:67 it seems to describe first intercourse. In other places, however, it is quite general (Gen 4:19; I Sam 25:40–43). In Jer 29:6 the same verb describes both the act of a bridegroom and the act of the bridegroom's father; similarly, Hagar "gets" a wife for Ishmael (Gen 21:21) and Abraham's slave "gets" a wife for Isaac (Gen 24:4). Among Bedouin, the payment of the *mahr* finalizes the marriage, and Akkadian documents call the bride "wife" as soon as the *terḫatu* is paid. *Lqḥ* sometimes refers to the action whereby the woman becomes a wife rather than the settling of a contract. Ezekiel 16 does not include any negotiations between parents or by any go-between. Verse 8 describes several acts of the bridegroom:

> A. I spread my "skirt" over you;
> B. I covered your nakedness (cf. Hos 2:11b);
> C. I swore to you;
> D. I entered a covenant with you;
> E. And you became mine.

In Deut 20:7, to take (*lqḥ*) a wife means to consummate the marriage after betrothal (*'rś;* cf. Hos 2:21–22) is arranged. Thus, if the marriage process is divided into parts, *lqḥ* can describe the formal settlement (often the act of a third party) or the consummation; when used alone, it can describe the whole process. If *lqḥ* has a technical meaning here, it would most likely be "to get married" rather than "to arrange a marriage," or "to buy a wife." The distinction would not be relevant were it not important to decide whether the implied payment was the original bride-price or the ransom purchase of Gomer from the slave market, mentioned in 3:2. If there was only one payment, then the two passages are a doublet; but the rest of c 1 indicates that Hosea fathered the children one after the other, and did not buy them with their mother. In 3:1, Hosea is told to go and *love* (not *take*) a woman, and a special verb is used for the slave purchase in Hos 3:2. As we shall suggest further in the following note, the language of v 2b is anticipatory and *take* is quite general — "acquire a family (wife and children)." The children are mentioned along with the bride, not because she already had them, but because it was Yahweh's purpose for Hosea's marriage that he should raise a family, and more particularly so in the context of a call to prophesy, for these children were intended by Yahweh to be oracles.

a promiscuous wife and children of promiscuity. Both phrases are unique, occurring only here in Hosea. The key term, *znwnym,* occurs several more times, only in the plural; it may be regarded as an abstract formation, like *raḥămîm,* "pity," *ḥayyîm,* "life," etc. Its essential meaning centers in sexual misbehavior, and as the verbal root *zny* and related nouns show (see below), it refers to sexual activity outside the bounds of marriage. It would be a mistake in analyzing the word *znwnym* to separate the idea from the action, since these are organically related in biblical thought. Anyone described as "a promiscuous wife" is engaged in activity consistent with her character, which is expressed by the word *znwnym.* The precise nature of the misbehavior described by *znwnym* must be determined from context, the use of synonymous expressions, and other clues.

While *zĕnûnîm* is characteristic of Hosea, this is not the only book in which the word is used. Its occurrence in Ezek 23:11,29 (otherwise *taznût,* a synonym, is used abundantly in Ezekiel 16 and 23), could be derived from Hosea. It occurs in Gen 38:24 (Tamar), II Kings 9:22 (Jezebel), and Nah 3:4 (Nineveh); the last two passages are powerfully abusive. Its ascription to Jezebel is particularly germane, infamous devotee of Baal that she was. Jehu told Joram that there was no prospect for peace, because of his mother's "numerous *zĕnûnîm* and *kĕšāpîm,*" tying together promiscuity and sorcery. The same tie is found in Nah 3:4, where Nineveh is called a *zônâ,* and a "mistress of spells" (*zĕnûnîm* and *kĕšāpîm* occur twice in parallel in this verse). While both practices are reprobated, and each deserves death, their linkage points to a complex of interrelated activities. Exod 22:17 affirms that witchcraft, like adultery, was a capital crime in Israel. It is associated with bestiality and idolatry in a group of anti-Canaanite measures. The perversion of sex, and an excessive preoccupation with it, are common factors in Canaanite religion and much ancient magic. Mal 3:5 similarly lists magicians and adulterers with those who swear by "the lie," that is, the false god. Idolatry, sexual license, and the black arts are three overlapping spheres; Mic 5:11–13 has the same combination. That sorcery was sometimes ancillary to sex among non-Yahwists is indicated by Isa 47:9. In spite of Babylon's numerous spells and powerful enchantments, she will suffer both childlessness and widowhood; the implication is that the unavailing magic was intended to secure a healthy husband and abundant offspring. Protreptic fertility rites have a large ingredient of sympathetic magic; something more sinister than fooling around with love potions is involved. Hos 4:12 is another pointer to the combination of magic, sex, and idol worship. Whoring away from their god is the work of the spirit of zĕnûnîm, as is resorting to a wooden pole for divination. This "wood," an image of Asherah, a symbol of fertility, a tree of vitality (perhaps a phallic sign), could be a complex of ideas; more than one kind of divination may be involved.

The most comprehensive information about such proceedings is supplied by Deut 18:10. II Chron 33:6 has six of the same items in the same sequence. The five functionaries in Jer 27:9 include three found in Deut 18:10–11 in the same sequence; some magicians appear in all three lists.

	Deut 18:10–11	II Chron 33:6	Jer 27:9
1)	Passing children through fire	same	(prophets)
2)	Fortune telling	---	same
			(dreams [?])
3)	Soothsayer	same	same
4)	(Snake?-) augury	same	---
5)	Sorcerer (mĕkaššēp)	same	kaššāpîm
6)	Tier of magic knots (?)	---	---
7)	Consulter of spirits	same	---
8)	Wizard	same	---
9)	Necromancer	---	---

The root kšp is prominent, occurring in all these lists; the cognate Akkadian root refers to the casting of spells (kišpū). An instance in which a man is rendered sexually impotent by magic is particularly instructive: "A man is bewitched (kāšip) so that his flesh is flaccid, his semen flows when he walks, stands, lies, or when he urinates" (CAD K:284). On ancient Mesopotamian attitudes toward sexual performance and remedies for failings, see Biggs (1967).

In every case of znwnym the women involved had engaged in illicit sexual activity or were suspected of doing so. The women were married or betrothed, so that the sexual activity involved adultery; none was a typical prostitute. Strictly speaking, Tamar masqueraded as one, but the term znwnym occurs in a context which does not refer to her prostitution, and is rather a general term for her behavior in becoming pregnant by an unknown man, rather than her betrothed husband.

In considering the structure of the phrase *'št znwnym,* we note others of the same type: (1) *'ēšet bĕrît,* "covenant wife" (Mal 2:14) is the betrothed; (2) *'ēšet nĕ'ûrîm,* "wife of youth" (Prov 5:18; Isa 54:6; Mal 2:14,15), the wife of early marriage or first love; thus Beuken (1974:37) cautiously proposes to translate Isa 54:6, "She was the first choice of God, she was the wife of his youth"; this connotation enriches the use of *nĕ'ûrîm* in Hos 2:17 and Jer 2:2; (3) *'ēšet ḥēq,* "bosom wife," is the beloved one of mature trustful marriage (Deut 13:7; 28:54; cf. II Sam 12:8 for its sexual connotations); (4) *'ēšet midwānîm* (or *midyānîm* or *midwōnîm*), "wife of contentions" (Prov 21:9; 25:24; 27:15), is the shrew of a soured marriage. These epithets describe the woman's relationship to her husband. Hence *'ēšet zĕnûnîm* describes a wife who becomes promiscuous, not a prostitute or promiscuous woman who becomes a wife, in a parody perhaps of the phrase *'ēšet nĕ'ûrîm.*

The terms emphasize the woman's character rather than her activity, but it would be a mistake to separate the two. Of the terms, the one most like *'št znwnym* is *'št mdwnym;* both expressions presuppose a series of actions consistent with the idea inherent in the term — a contentious woman is one who has demonstrated this quality or characteristic over the years. Likewise a promiscuous woman is one who has misbehaved frequently and in the same fashion for a considerable length of time.

Both terms, *'št* and *znwnym,* are used of married women; in Hosea, *znwnym* appears in parallel with *na'ăpûpîm,* "adultery." The terms are related rather than synonymous; the second (*n'pwpym*) defines the former: it particularizes the misconduct charged in the more general expression. Adultery, in the Bible at least, requires that the woman involved be married. The prime emphasis in the story of the woman in Hosea is that she has violated her marriage vows and in the pursuit of her lovers she has committed adultery. Along with this, certain other activities are alluded to or hinted at: the use of the word *'tnh* in 2:14 suggests pay or reward for services, and the identification of the "lovers" with Baal or Baalim suggests involvement with or participation in the fertility cult. We may speak provisionally and tentatively of cultic sexual activity as the specific form of her adultery.

The standard term for prostitute, *'iššâ zônâ* or just *zônâ,* does not occur in Hosea, though there would have been ample opportunity to use it in connection with the woman's activities. It may be concluded therefore that she was never a common streetwalker or professional prostitute. The passages relating to Tamar in Genesis 38 are instructive at this point: during her masquerade as a prostitute she is called *zônâ* and *qĕdēšâ,* an equivalent term. But when she is under suspicion of misbehavior after her pregnancy is discovered, the term *znwnym* is used. Similarly in Ezekiel 16, the prophet goes into great detail in describing the sexual misbehavior of Jerusalem represented as a dissolute wife — the point he makes is that she was guilty of adulterous misbehavior with her lovers but that, unlike ordinary prostitutes, she accepted no pay or favors from her lovers. On the contrary, she bestowed gifts upon them. Ezekiel's story represents a more advanced stage of depravity than the one described in Hosea, though the pictures and vocabulary are much the same.

The root *zny* is the most general term in Hebrew to describe sexual misconduct, especially on the part of women. It describes prostitution as a remunerative profession only in a small fraction of its occurrences. The practice of English translations in always rendering it by the derivatives of the words whore, harlot, etc., fails to cover the range of its denotations, and gives a misleading connotation in many passages. In its coverage of all kinds of minor crimes, it resembles Greek *pornē*. Because the feminine participle, *zônâ*, is so general, other terms with more precise meanings are often used in conjunction with it. They include *'iššâ 'aḥeret*, "another woman" (Judg 11:1–2); (*'iššâ*) *zārâ*, "foreign (woman)," *nokriyyâ*, "foreigner," (*'iššâ*) *měnā'epet*, "adulterous (woman)" (Prov 30:20); *nô'epet*, "adulteress," *qědēsâ*, "holy woman," and *'ôněnâ*, "sorceress" (Isa 57:3). Certainly the verb *zānâ* describes every aspect of sexual misconduct. As an activity of females primarily, the verb is rarely used in masculine forms, and then figuratively to describe Israel's infidelity (Num 25:1; Deut 31:16; Judg 2:17; Hos 9:1). In allegories, Israel is feminine. For masculine subjects the *Hip'il* is preferred, implying that men cause women to be promiscuous.

The other side of this coin is the general use of *n'p* to describe the adulterous act of a man with a married woman, while its occurrence in feminine forms is rare. In Jer 5:7 a *bêt zônâ* is where men *n'p*. This is not a brothel, but the home of a married woman.

More distinctions are made regarding the sexual misconduct of women than of men. A girl who loses her virginity before marriage (Lev 21:9; Deut 22:21), even by rape when honorable marriage is intended (Gen 34:31), is a *zônâ*. The same verb describes the premarital intercourse of a single woman (Ezek 23:3) and the adultery of a married woman (Gen 38:24; Jer 3:1). A curious use is met in Judg 19:2, where it describes the return of a woman (a concubine) to her home, with no hint of adultery and no breach of marriage. The verb *zānâ* is the only one used to describe professional prostitution.

In a figurative sense *zānâ* is commonly used to describe turning away (*pānâ* in Hos 3:1, *swr* in Ezek 6:9) from Yahweh to engage in illicit devotion to rival gods (Exod 34:15,16; Lev 17:7; 20:5; Num 15:39; Deut 31:16; Judg 2:17; Ezek 6:9; 20:30; Ps 73:27). Since, in Canaanite religion, worship may have involved sexual unions, the verb is not entirely figurative in that context, but it does not imply prostitution as distinct from adultery.

A *qĕdēšâ* (Gen 38:21–22; Deut 23:18; Hos 4:14) is specifically a cult person; and Deut 23:19; Gen 38:15; and Hos 4:14 show that such a person could also be called a *zônâ*. Inasmuch as this was her profession or means of livelihood, she was a "prostitute," but the institutional setting makes the term rather inappropriate. One of our main difficulties in interpreting many details in the Book of Hosea is our ignorance of Gomer's status in this regard — whether she was attached to the Baal cult as a worshiper, like any other laywoman who attended the shrines, or whether she was appointed to perform sacred functions in the temples. In the former case her "lovers" would be the priests; in the latter they would be lay worshipers. But we do not even know whether ritual sex was performed by male and female clergy on behalf of the people, or with the people, or whether lay men and women attended the shrines in order to copulate there outside their own marriages.

The words used to refer most plainly to an ordinary prostitute are (*'iššâ*) *zārâ* and *nokriyyâ*. Both mean "foreigner" as if it were taken for granted that no Israelite woman would be a prostitute; here we might have no more than the all too familiar economic consequences of the social disadvantages of being an alien, to say nothing of ethnic prejudice. Both terms occur in parallel in Prov 2:16; 5:20; 7:5. Warnings against "the strange woman" are given to men in Proverbs 5–7. Prov 7:19 makes it clear that this seducer is a married woman committing adultery in her own home. (This involves an important legal distinction in the Middle Assyrian Laws; see *ANET* 181 at A13–14; the guilt of a woman who commits adultery in another man's house is beyond dispute.) There is no talk of payment; she seems to be the wife of a wealthy merchant, perhaps a resident alien. The word *nokriyyâ* itself can be used without unsavory associations (Ruth 2:10). The disapproval of marriages with "foreign women" voiced throughout Ezra and Nehemiah is based on ethnoreligious rather than moral grounds. No hint is given that prostitution was a danger. In Gen 31:15 the plural probably means "prostitutes," for Laban is accused of selling his daughters and living on the proceeds. Nevertheless, the language is still figurative, for the charge was not strictly true, as they had been sold to Jacob as wives.

In all its occurrences, the phrase *'iššâ zônâ* means "prostitute" in the strict sense. If she is also married, she is an adulteress as well; the focus is on greed rather than venery as the driving force. While *zônâ* alone, as we have shown, refers to any woman guilty of sexual misconduct of any kind, there are many occurrences of *zônâ* where associated evidence shows that it is short for the more technical *'iššâ zônâ,* and equally means "prostitute." The complete phrase *'iššâ* . . . *zônâ* can be recognized in the bicolon of Prov 7:10, broken up and distributed over the two lines. Prov 6:26 provides evidence in the statement that an *'iššâ zônâ* may be hired for a loaf of bread, although the text is unclear; compare the fee of "a kid from the flock" (Gen 38:17; Judg 15:1). Otherwise the harlot's fee is called *'etnan zônâ* (Deut 23:19; Mic 1:7), a rejected source of temple revenues. Hos 2:14, using a slightly different but related noun, suggests that this element may have been present in Gomer's case.

Many known prostitutes, or cities described as prostitutes, are called *'iššâ zônâ* in the Old Testament. They include Rahab (Josh 2:1; 6:17,22), Jephthah's mother (also called *'iššâ 'aḥeret*) (Judg 11:1–2), Samson's contact in Gaza (Judg 16:1), the women who came to Solomon (I Kings 3:16), Israel (Jer 3:3; cf. 2:20), Jerusalem (Ezek 16:30; cf. v 35), Jerusalem and Samaria (Ezek 23:44). Tyre (Isa 23:15–17) and Nineveh (Nah 3:4) are called simply *zônâ;* compare Isa 1:21. (A priest was not permitted to marry an *'iššâ zônâ,* Lev 21:7).

In the light of this consistent usage we can see why Hosea uses the verb *zānâ* to describe Gomer's activity, but not (*'iššâ*) *zônâ* to describe her; *'ēšet zĕnûnîm,* which is found only in Hos 1:2, means something else, a married woman who is promiscuous.

There is no basis in the meaning and usage of the expressions to mitigate the force of the terms: *'št znwnym* cannot mean a woman with tendencies toward promiscuity, or a potential adulteress or prostitute. This would have to be the case if the words are to be applied to Gomer bat-Diblaim, who had neither husband nor children before Hosea married her. A literal reading of the passage *'št znwnym wyldy znwnym* would require her to be an adulteress with several children before even meeting Hosea, a highly unlikely proposition especially in view of 1:3–9, which describes the birth of her children after marriage to Hosea. Common sense, if not more complex laws of evidence and probability, dictates that we keep the number of wives and children to a minimum. The story of the children makes it clear that 1:2 must be understood proleptically — Hosea did not acquire them all at once but only after several years. Similarly his wife only became an adulteress after marriage and, if we can take 2:7 as a description of domestic reality, only after the children were born. If we are right in insisting, in connection with *'št znwnym wyldy znwnym,* that *znwnym* involves actual, repeated, and persistent sexual activity — in this case adulterous ritual or cultic behavior — then the initial statement, 1:2, can only describe a reinterpretation of the first command after the marriage and family of Hosea were constituted. The original call must have been simply: "Go take for yourself a wife and build a family with her."

Later it became apparent that this wife was guilty of sexual misconduct — which immediately put her in the capital class of adulterers. This seems the best way out of the maze of conflicting data about the relationship of cc 1 and 2 to c 3.

The most important alternative explanation is that of Wolff, who contends that *'ēšet zĕnûnîm* "refers to any young woman ready for marriage who had submitted to the bridal rites of initiation then current in Israel" (1974:15). This act, "occurring only once in a person's lifetime" (p. 14), represents the degree to which the *hieros gamos* had been democratized, according to Wolff. The comparative evidence he adduces from classical Greek and Roman authors (there are no biblical allusions) gives the impression that this custom, where practiced, involved a father's dedicating his daughter to the god to make her fit for marriage, a practice which has no counterpart in Hosea. The act envisioned by Wolff was part of puberty rites, and hardly a matter for which the girl herself bears the main responsibility; this seems to have no bearing on the situation in Hosea (Rudolph 1963). It is the woman who takes the initiative and goes off after lovers (Hos 2:7,15). Her behavior was not restricted to the marriage ceremony; there is no indication that Hosea himself took any part in the Baal cult, receiving his bride from the arms of the god. The total impression of cc 1–3 is of repeated and flagrant acts, deliberately performed by a married woman, acts therefore at once of adultery and of prostitution. This is seen from Hos 2:4, where "adulteries" is in parallel with *zĕnûnîm* (as complementary rather than synonymous terms), and from 4:13*f*, where the same roots occur twice in parallel construction, and where it is precisely "daughters and daughters-in-law," that is, married women, who are guilty of adulterous promiscuity.

Go, take for yourself a promiscuous wife. In ancient Israel it was usual for a man to be married. It required special instructions to Jeremiah to restrain him from taking a wife (Jer 16:1–4). Hosea's case was the opposite. He had to be told to get married, as if he were not disposed to do so, or had even made up his mind to remain single. Such an aversion could have been due to his loyalty to Yahweh; if the whole land had abandoned Yahweh, no pure woman could be found in the country and any marriage would involve him with a Baal worshiper. His wife would turn out to be "a promiscuous wife" from the outset.

Some commentators have found it impossible to believe that Yahweh would ever command one of his prophets to do such a thing in actuality.

> These words [the command in 1:2 and 3:1] cannot represent Hosea's direct perception of an ethical God's commands to him to commit moral pollution whether for the purpose of teaching the people of his day, who were guilty of that very thing, or for any other reason whatever. Such a direct command and compliance therewith cannot be conceived to originate with the writer of Hos 6:6 (Waterman 1955:100–101).

Such squeamishness is not justified. Yahweh was not above asking his servants to do things generally regarded as morally abhorrent. Thus Isaiah paraded in public completely naked (Isaiah 20); Ezekiel was told to prepare food by disgusting methods (Ezek 4:12).

The problem cannot be sidestepped by theories that it all happened only in a vision or that the prophet made up the story as an instructive parable. The vision theory starts with Origen; Jerome preferred allegory. The theory of prophetic visions appealed to medieval Jewish scholars (Ginsberg 1971:1012). (Among the Fathers, Irenaeus took the text as history.) It is doubtful if Israelites would have thought immorality more palatable in fiction. In the real life of a man and a woman and their children, the word of Yahweh became human and historical. It was never abstract, an idea without flesh.

The attractiveness of a vision solution is a testimony to the realism of the story. It is only by removing derogatory comments as glosses that Batten (1929:266) was able to conclude that "study as minutely as we will, we can in the text itself find no hint of anything abnormal in the family life of the prophet. . . . There is not the slightest suggestion that Gomer ever had been or ever would be any other than a virtuous woman."

We must admit that it is impossible to reconstruct any kind of biography from Hosea 1–3. There are several reasons for this. First, the details given are too meager. Secondly, the account we now have lacks coherence and continuity, so no clear sequence of events can be recovered. Thirdly, the background in Israelite custom and law, which would have made the circumstances clear to people of that culture, is now lost to us; we can only guess. Finally, the intertwining of the allegorical parallels of Yahweh's "marriage" with Israel continually deflects the focus from the individual and his family to the nation and its Lord. There were some features of the covenant history with no human counterpart, and some aspects of human marriage not applicable to Yahweh and his people.

Chapter 3 is so different from c 1 that they cannot be two accounts of the same sequence of events. At the same time, if they are part of the same story, they are hard to integrate. The word "again" in Hos 3:1 suggests that this narrates a distinct stage in Hosea's life. For various reasons some scholars have suggested that a different woman was involved this second time (e.g. Kaufmann 1960; Ginsberg 1971; Rudolph; Hendricks n.d.). Gordon (1966:21) has even argued from Ugaritic evidence that two wives are required in such a story. It is true that Ezekiel describes a bigamous marriage between Yahweh and the two kingdoms of Israel (Ezekiel 23), but that detail is dictated by the historical facts, which provide no explanation relevant to Hosea. The first claim in Hosea studies belongs to an interpretation involving only one woman. The presence of two women complicates matters without clarifying or resolving difficulties.

While much remains obscure, most of c 3 can be accounted for as an attempt to remedy the tragedy described in cc 1–2. The argument that the story begins in c 3 and thus that there can be no doubt that Hosea married a known prostitute is unwarranted.

Yahweh's identification of Hosea's intended wife as "a promiscuous wife" is by way of anticipation. The compelling thought for Hosea was that Yahweh had commanded him to get married. If it turned out later that the woman he chose was or became promiscuous, then it was the will of God that he take "a promiscuous wife."

It is possible to become sentimental about an act at first sight shocking to the puritanical mind. Romantic love is ascribed to Hosea, making him blind to all faults, or hopeful of reforming them. Scholars who think that Hosea was fully aware that Gomer was already a prostitute when he married her include J. M. P. Smith (1925:59). By contrast, Toy (1913:76) points out "the calm tone" of 1:2–9, and also the fact that here "the names convey in themselves no slur on wife or children." Theological arguments can be brought in support of Hosea's romantic love. First, there is Yahweh's sovereign freedom, noted earlier; he is likely to do anything, unpredictably and unaccountably. We remember Job's agonized doubts about God's morality. Since it suited his purpose, Yahweh involved Samson with a pagan woman — a forbidden thing. "She was from Yahweh," the historian comments (Judg 14:4), because Yahweh was looking for a pretext to make war against the Philistines. In Hosea Yahweh is looking for a pretext to make a case against the Israelites. A further theological argument is found in the plan to have Hosea recapitulate the covenant history of the people of God by means of a marriage to an undeserving and incorrigible woman. According to a tradition found most clearly in Ezekiel 16 and 23, Israel was defiled even before Yahweh took her. The wilderness was the courtship period or honeymoon, the crossing of the Sea of Reeds was the cleansing bath before marriage. The covenant was an undeserved gift of Yahweh from the outset, its aim the purification of the sullied bride by love in marriage. So Hosea is said to be an image of the Redeemer, uniting to himself what was unholy, in order to make it holy. If Gomer were already involved in Baal ceremonies before her marriage, her condition would resemble that of Israel's remotest ancestors, who served idols on the other side of the River (Josh 24:14), before the call of Abram; or it would match the tradition that Israel was already defiled with idols in Egypt before Yahweh called her.

A second line of interpretation, which we prefer, is that Gomer was not promiscuous when Hosea married her. We do not say this because we believe, a priori, marrying a promiscuous woman is precluded as morally unthinkable. As we have seen, there are theological ways of getting over that objection. But what she was when he married her is not the main point of interest. The prophecy grows from the marriage. It is what she became in marriage that makes the oracles. Her behavior recapitulates Israel's conduct with Yahweh in the covenant, not the origins of the covenant. The focus is on the contemporary situation. The statement that "their mother was promiscuous" (Hos 2:7) suggests that the immorality started some time after the marriage. The fact that it is also called "adultery" shows that it is the act of a married woman. The repeated acts were not the helpless submission of a young girl to social custom (so Wolff), not the lapse of a weak woman who for once could not resist temptation and then repented, restrained forever now by the horror of her memory. Gomer/ Israel committed adultery, a primary violation of the covenant, and a capital offense. For the hierarchy of values, reflected in 2:9, compare Ezek 16:30–43, especially vv 32 and 38; cf. Prov 7:10–23, especially vv 18–20.

The misconduct was in one and the same act both infidelity and apostasy. Since everything points to her promiscuity as participation in the ritual sex acts of the Baal cult, it was doubly wicked, against both Hosea and Yahweh. Such a combination had already occurred in the Baal-Peor incident (Numbers 25). In historical perspective that crisis looms large in Hosea's mind. It was a major defection, soon after the covenant had been made. It was a portent and paradigm of Israel's later history. The parallels with the religious crisis of Hosea's day are close. Hosea's heartbreak was then like Yahweh's disappointment. The relationship that began well parallels Jeremiah's account (different in this respect from Ezekiel's) of the Wilderness period as the time of joyful bridal love (Jer 2:2), which Hosea also speaks about in glowing words. That Yahweh can also speak of Israel as his dear child at that stage shows how inseparable family relationships are in the thought of Hosea and Jeremiah. Nonetheless, Vollmer's assertion that it is Hosea's interpretation of the traditions that sets up the contrast between a "positive judgment on the Wilderness period" and a "critical judgment of Israel's conduct in civilized territory" (1971:126) is overdone. He supposes that Hosea treated the traditions with considerable liberty for theological purposes; and he fails to do justice to Hos 9:10. Baal Peor does not belong to the Wilderness period, but marks the beginning of Israel's decline through contact with Canaanite cultures.

We conclude that the marriage was real, and so were the children, in spite of their unusual names. The marriage was also a symbolic action under the express direction of Yahweh from the outset, and new oracles were given at each decisive stage. Part of Hosea's prophetic activity was his marriage and family life. Since Hosea 1–3, or more particularly Hos 2:4–25, was written from the perspective of a developed ministry, the integral connection between his marriage and his message makes it appropriate that his career as a prophet be traced to his wedding. There is no need to deny to Hosea a consciousness of divine guidance, for the call to office is matched by a personal commitment to Yahweh which is deep and intense. This awareness of his "call," sealed in him when Yahweh first spoke with him, was as binding as the irrefragable covenant of Yahweh. It enabled him later to see his wife as possessing her true character from the first, or to tell the story from this perspective; for whatever emerges as a result of the word of Yahweh in history is perceived by biblical faith as intended all along in the counsel of God. The epithet "promiscuous wife" is proleptic; the inclusion of the children in the marriage command, and their equation with "the land," anticipates the analogy of Israel as Yahweh's family. Verse 2 does not preserve the actual words of the original call; it records Hosea's mature understanding (or the understanding of a disciple, for the narrative is in the third person) in retrospect. This is what Yahweh's call to take a wife would later lead to.

The words of Hos 1:2 are an answer to a question the prophet could only ask after his marriage was ruined: "Why did Yahweh tell me to get married, if it was all to end up like this?" Such reflection would bring the horrified insight "What has happened to me with Gomer is what is happening to Yahweh with Israel, has been happening for centuries. The whole land has abandoned Yahweh." Yahweh had deliberately led Hosea into a marriage like his own. And the moral justification of that astounding guidance is found in the fact that he is not asking Hosea to endure anything that Yahweh himself has not endured. Furthermore, if Yahweh is still making an effort to save his marriage, Hosea might well be inspired to attempt to retrieve his own.

Since the last clause of 1:2b gives the reason for calling the wife and children *zĕnûnîm,* it depends on the previous clause; if the latter was not actually spoken at the original call, neither was the former. These words represent an expansion and interpretation of the original simple command in the light of later developments. In point of time this perception could not come before the end of c 1. Hos 1:2 is then the latest message; it sums up the meaning of the whole experience. From the point of view of literary composition it rightly comes where it is now, for it announces the major theme of cc 1–3 as a whole.

children of promiscuity. By supplying another verb — "have children of harlotry" — *RSV* suggests two distinct acts and divides the family. By saying "take a wife and children" Yahweh looks on the family as one, and especially as one with the mother. The phrase does not mean that the bride already had (illegitimate) children, nor that the children, like their mother, were later promiscuous. No such reproach is brought against them elsewhere.

Nor does this term necessarily mean that the children were besmirched with their mother's promiscuity in the crude sense of being conceived in her illicit liaisons (*pace,* e.g. Harper 1905:207). The story, it is true, lacks the conventional formula, "And he went in to her, and she conceived, and. . . ." Just because there is no explicit statement that Hosea had intercourse with her, it cannot be inferred that the parentage of the children was in doubt. In Genesis 29–30 the formula is not repeated with each successive pregnancy of the same wife; but when there is a new beginning, or a new wife, the commencement of sexual relations will be described in those terms. Verse 3 says, "She bore him a son," the usual indication of the father. Furthermore, Hosea names them all, as any father might do, expressing no doubts as to their legitimacy in the legal sense. But, although these formalities were maintained, some scholars have seen in the menacing names of at least the second and third children evidence that Hosea had by now discovered that the children were not his, or not certainly his. The names express his outrage, even though he keeps his family intact (Rice 1921:42). It is more likely that the names, being artificial and intentionally oracular, tell us nothing about Hosea's private life or the characters of his children. Even supposing that his wife was already wayward, and even if Hosea knew it, he does not deny that she is his wife and he accepts her children as his. This has a bearing on the question of whether there was ever a formal divorce.

The title "children of promiscuity" and their symbolic names link mother and children together as representing the nation, having the same character. The description of Hosea's fulfillment of the command, which follows immediately in v·3, does not say that he acquired a wife and children, but simply that he married Gomer. The children follow later: *yaldê zĕnûnîm* means "children of (a wife of) promiscuity," in recognition of this family solidarity. In the same way *bĕnê hannĕ'ûrîm* (Ps 127:4) does not mean "young children" (Prayer Book), "children of the youth" (*KJV*), "the sons of one's youth" (*RSV*), or "the sons you father when young" (*JB*), but rather the children of a wife married in youth ('*ēšet nĕ'ûrîm*). Compare *ben-zĕqûnîm* (Gen 37:3; 44:20; cf. Gen 21:2,7), which describes the character of the father.

Hosea's children were also children of promiscuity in another sense if, as we shall point out in the NOTE on '*etnâ* in Hos 2:14, they were regarded by their mother as her reward from the Baals for her services to them in the cult, whoever their real father was. In this they contrast with the children in Psalm 127 who are Yahweh's *śākār,* the wages of honest work. Ahab's children, without having doubt thrown on their legitimacy in the legal sense, forfeit their right to the throne because of the excessive "promiscuity and sorceries" of their mother (II Kings 9:22).

In keeping with his main line of interpretation, Wolff explains the term "children of whoredom" as the result of the bridal initiation by the sacral marriage: "The mother had acquired her ability to bear children in marriage by her participation in a pagan rite" (1974:15). Such an act, once performed, could never be undone. Both these points are contradicted by Hosea 2. First, the way is open to reconciliation if the wife will desist from her adulteries; secondly, the remedial measures taken by the husband only drive her to be more blatant and defiant. Hence her promiscuity is not simply in the past.

the land. See Lev 19:29. This comprehensive word, with sacred associations, covers everybody — kings, priests, people. Also, *pace* Harper (1905:210), Judah as well as Israel (Ephraim) is included in the term. The noun "land" happens to be feminine, but we ought not to mythologize the word into identity with the Earth Mother or "Mother Israel" (Waterman 1955:102, 104). The female fertility deities of the Canaanite pantheon were not earth goddesses. Asherah was "Lady Athirat of the Sea." In other places in Hosea, "the land" is paralleled by "all its inhabitants," pointing to the people. The cult has not only been democratized, it has been politicized. "The land" has been promiscuous away from Yahweh because the state, led by the king, has made some form of Canaanite religion official instead of Yahwism. At least that is how it was in the days of Ahab and Jezebel. Hosea contains no statement of the persecution of Yahweh's prophets, but compare Hos 4:1 and Amos 7. It is more likely that there had developed a syncretism which enabled the pretense of Yahwism to be officially maintained; in Hosea's eyes this was plain Baalism. In effect, Jeroboam was following Ahab's lead, and deserved the same fate.

has been promiscuous. A verb is used with its intensifying cognate infinite absolute. The effect of this repetition is that the root *zny* occurs four times in a single verse; cf. the four occurrences of *'hb* in Hos 3:1. We have chosen a past tense for the imperfect verb, which is often future (Ginsberg 1971:1010). This is not prophecy, but narrative. A present, iterative tense would have served equally well, suggesting repeated and ongoing acts of unfaithfulness (the imperfect is occasionally used in this sense). Each of the four prophetic acts — taking a wife and naming three children — is accompanied by an explanatory clause, beginning with *kî,* "for," in which Yahweh gives the reason for his instructions.

away from Yahweh. In the Bible, loyalty is often described as "following Yahweh," or "walking in his ways," and religious defection is "turning aside." Cf. Hos 3:1. This language is prominent in the Deuteronomic writings, a tradition that Hosea knows well, cf. Deut 31:16 and Hos 9:1 (Weinfeld 1972:320–324, 367–370). In Judg 2:17 resorting to a Canaanite shrine is described as being promiscuous (*zānû*), "after other gods." While our text falls short of saying that they commit adultery against Yahweh, the image is daring enough, for Yahwism generally avoided all language that suggested sexual activity in connection with

Yahweh. Political vocabulary is preferred in describing Yahweh's relationship to his people (Wright 1969). Hosea finds the legal and constitutional terms of the covenant inadequate for describing Yahweh's tenacious love (both tender and violent), and, more than any other biblical writer, he exploits the most intimate of human relationships to present the personalism of Yahweh. The language of Lev 20:2–6 is relevant. There it is not the sexual side of a pagan cult that is called whoring after; it is child sacrifice and wizardry. As we shall see, the three go together.

The Deuteronomistic background of Hosea's language takes the expression "to walk behind Yahweh" back to holy war theology, where it meant to follow Yahweh into battle as the one "who goes before you" (Deut 1:30,33; etc.). To "turn aside" is to prove disloyal in the time of testing, such as deserting on the eve of battle (Ps 78:9–11). In the Psalm, as in Hos 2:15, the accusation that "they forgot" implies more than a lapse of memory. To follow another god means to turn traitor, to fight against God. Israel has not only deserted her covenant partner; she has gone over to his chief rival, the anti-Yahweh, Baal. This describes total defection, not just walking behind the statue of the god in ceremonial processions, or going on pilgrimage to the shrines.

The fact that the message says "away from Yahweh" rather than "away from me" is not evidence that this part of the verse is a remark of the compiler, and not part of Yahweh's speech. It is not uncommon in exalted address to speak about oneself in the third person. Note the phenomenon in Yahweh's speech in Num 32:11–12:

$$kî\ lō'\text{-}mil'\hat{u}\ 'ah\breve{a}r\bar{a}y$$
$$kî\ \ \ \ mil'\hat{u}\ 'ah\breve{a}r\hat{e}\ yhwh$$

3. *he went and took.* It is characteristic of Hebrew narrative style to have a command followed by its fulfillment described in the same words. Cf. 2:7 and 2:15. We have used this to argue that not all of the words now in v 2 were part of the original "call." The pattern is not invariable; for instance, in Hos 3:1*f*, otherwise similar to the present passage, the repetition does not occur.

Since the verb "he took" is followed immediately by the statement "then she conceived," it is more likely that it means "he got married" rather than "he got engaged" (Gen 25:20; Deut 20:7; Ruth 4:13; etc.). The full expression, *lqh 'ōtāh lô lĕ'iššâ,* "to take her for himself as (his) wife" (Deut 21:11; 25:5), is shortened here, as is the full sequence of events from engagement to first birth, which includes:

He took her
She became his wife
He went in to her

She became pregnant
She gave birth to a child

Often one or more of these details are missing, though Ruth 4:13 has all
five. Gen 25:1–2, for example, has only the first and last; our text has the
first and the last two. The nuances of *lqḥ* in command and fulfillment portions of the narrative are slightly different.

Gomer. Yahweh had not designated the intended bride; presumably the
choice was Hosea's. This is the only place where the name is mentioned;
apparently no significance is attached to its meaning. The root means "ac-
complish, complete" (cf. Dahood 1953). Koehler and Baumgartner
(1958:189) list either "Perfection" or "Burning coal." *CAD* (G:133)
doubts if the latter has any connection with the Semitic root *gmr*. Wolff
(1974:16–17) compares *gĕmaryāhû*, meaning "Yahweh has accomplished it [i.e. the child's birth]." The segolate form of Gomer points to a
different stem; and this question should not be begged by explaining the
vocalization as scribal assimilation to the ethnic Gomer (Gen 10:2, so
Noth 1928:175, 195). LXX confirms MT in this regard. The name does
not seem to be symbolic; there is no wordplay on it as there is on the
names of the children.

bat-Diblaim. Gomer's patronymic is no more than a concrete historical
fact; there is no need to suppose that it is fanciful or intended to be
allegorical. Attempts to find its significance in the word *dĕbēlâ,* "a compressed cake of figs," are desperate. Comparison with the raisin cakes used
in the Baal cult (Hos 3:1) has suggested that the apparent patronymic is
the appellative of a cult prostitute, but there is no confirming evidence.
Furthermore, the dual of the word for cake would be **diblatayim;* and
why two? Nor is the proposal that "daughter of two fig cakes" means a
prostitute who can be bought for this price any more probable (cf. Wolff
1974:17). There is no need to resort to this meaning for *bat* unless a patronymic is proved impossible; and we have already concluded that
Gomer was not a prostitute in this commercial sense. The obvious explanation is that Diblayim was her father's name. Although otherwise unknown, and of a strange form (the apparent dual may point to a word
originally not Hebrew), it is not unparalleled (compare *'Eprayim*).

If Diblayim is not the name of Gomer's father, it would have to be the
name of her hometown. The use of such a designation instead of the normal patronymic suggests a person without family, or whose status is not
secured by family membership, identified as a nobody, a foreigner.
(Albright 1955). There is no hint of this in Hosea. And would not the
point of the marriage for prophecy be spoiled by marrying a foreigner instead of an Israelite? Further, no such place is known. The name suggests
the Moabite town of Diblatayim, an Israelite staging place in the desert

journey (Num 33:46,47), cursed by Jeremiah (48:22). This could be significant, since the site was near the location of the fatal Peor incident which looms large in Hosea's mind. Yet the equation is tenuous, and Hosea does not make the connection. It is simpler to conclude that the names were real. The only portentous names are those of the children, divinely given to yield prophetic messages.

she conceived. The account is terse; it does not include the usual "and he went in to her" and "he knew her." We should not infer from this brevity that there was any doubt that Hosea was the real father of the child. The use of *lô,* "for him," in what follows, suggests the reverse (Andersen 1971). Some commentators, however, consider that Jezreel was a bastard, arguing from the phrase "children of promiscuity" in v 2, and pointing to the omission of *lô* from some MSS of both MT and LXX (Harper 1905:211); this evidence is better accounted for as a normalization of v 3 to the shorter repetitions in vv 6 and 8. And, since *lô* is authentic in v 3, it must also be understood in vv 6 and 8, by the principle of successive abbreviation noted above at 1:2. The second and third children have negative names; there may have been some doubt about their paternity, but the evidence of the names is insufficient to prove that only the first child was Hosea's in fact.

4. *Yahweh said to him.* The selection of a name for a child was the prerogative of the parents, either the mother (Gen 4:1; Judg 13:24; I Sam 1:20; Isa 7:14; etc.) or the father (Gen 16:15; 17:19; 21:3; Exod 2:22; II Sam 12:24; Isa 8:3). Most of these examples are exceptional in some way; in several instances the woman had been barren and commemorated the answer to prayer in the child's name. The name can be prescribed by God to the father before birth. In Genesis 16, Hagar is granted an oracle on the destiny of her unborn child, and supplied with his name (v 11); in the event the name is actually conferred by Abram (v 15). The placing of the child on the father's knees is part of the ritual for naming the newborn in a Hittite text (Berman 1972); cf. Gen 50:23; Job 3:12. If the recording of such details points to exceptional circumstances, they are not a safe guide to common custom. Gen 35:18 suggests that the father could override the mother's choice; compare Luke 1:59–63. Hosea and Isaiah were told by Yahweh what to call their children, apparently after the births. The bizarre names served as messages from God to be elaborated and explained by the prophet.

Jezreel. Literally "May God sow!" Although best known as a place name, the form is not strange for a person. An analogous form is attested from Tirqa: *Iz-ra-aḫ* ᴰᴵᴺᴳᴵᴿ*DAGAN* (Thureau-Dangin 1910: No. 238:33). A West Canaanite variant **yizra'-'ēl,* "May El sow!" would represent an early stage of West Semitic religion when El was still preeminent as the fertility god (Oldenburg 1969); although the *'ēl* could be generic, viz. "the god," this seems unlikely. No similar name is known from Ugarit. Apart from Hosea's son, the only person with this name is a Judahite mentioned in I Chron 4:3; this could be no more than an eponym for the town of Jezreel in Judah (Josh 15:56), the home of David's wife Ahinoam (1 Sam 25:43; 27:3; 30:5).

The reference to "the blood shed at Jezreel" makes it certain that Hosea's son was named for the town of Jezreel in the valley of the same name. The occurrence of the Valley of Jezreel in v 5 (which is not secondary; cf. Wolff 1974:12, 19) shows that this region is meant; this does not exclude the possibility that the name was also intended to have other associations. Jezreel was the scene of many memorable events in Israel's past. It became a second capital of the Omride dynasty, although Samaria continued to be the main center; for the political history see Alt (1954). Ahab seems to have transferred his administration there, and developed his estate by murdering Naboth (I Kings 21) (Andersen 1966b). It was at Jezreel that Jezebel, Joram, and Ahab's bureaucrats were murdered by Jehu. The heads of Ahab's seventy sons were sent there from Samaria (II Kings 9–10).

The name Jezreel thus conjures up two opposite ideas — the beneficence of God in fruitfulness of plants, animals, and people, and the crimes and atrocities of the Israelite kings (Gelston 1974). In both respects the name is suggestive. In its positive aspect it hints that Yahweh (= El), not Baal, is the one who gives seed for people, animals, and plants. In what concerned Israel most, Yahweh was so different from Baal that he was in no sense a competitor; it was not in the fertility of nature, but in his mighty acts in history, that Yahweh revealed himself, fulfilling his covenant promises which stemmed from the plan to make "the seed of Abraham" innumerable; cf. Hos 2:1. Jezreel was also a scene of dreadful destruction. The mystery of the child's name lay in its ambivalence: it refers to both hope and terror. Hosea will exploit the double meaning to bring out both the threat and the promise of God.

in a little while. The reason for the name is introduced by the conjunction *kî.* The name is taken as a threat of punishment. It was not necessary for a child to have the name Jezreel in order for the prophet to make a statement like 1:4b. The technique would be more effective if the name were announced first, and its meaning given later, after people had had time to puzzle over the name. The name was a riddle; and like many riddles in ancient Wisdom talk, capable of more than one meaning. While we think that the child's name eventually yielded a public oracle, it is likely that the revelation of its meaning was intended only for Hosea in the first place.

The phrase "in a little while" is a time modifier of the entire following paragraph, which extends to the end of v 5. The punctuation in translations like the *RSV* spoils the effect of the speech as a closely woven rhetorical unit.

		Syllable Count	
A	*kî-'ôd mě'aṭ*	4	
B	*ûpāqadtî 'et-děmê yizrě'e'l*	10	
C	*'al-bêt yēhû'*	4	18
B'	*wěhišbattî mamlěkût*	7	
C'	*bêt yiśrā'ēl*	4	
A'	*wěhāyâ bayyôm hahû'*	7	18
B"	*wěśābartî 'et-qešet yiśrā'ēl*	9	
C"	*bě'ēmeq yizrě'e'l*	5	14

Speech in the Bible is often poetic in quality, if not in prosodic structure, and shares the literary and rhetorical features of verse. The present statement belongs to that category; it should be classified as prose, both with respect to sentence structure and word order, as well as the use of *'et* and *h* (the definite article), which are diagnostic. At the same time, rhetorical devices such as parallelism, chiasm, and inclusion or echo patterns are prominent. The introductory time statement (A) is matched by the eschatological formula (A'). Note how *wěhāyâ* is used twice in Hos 2:1 to achieve the same effect. The first time reference here (A) introduces two threats, the second (A') one. All the subsequent clauses begin with consecutive future (perfect) verbs — B (*ûpāqadtî* . . .), B' (*wěhišbattî* . . .), B" (*wěśābartî* . . .). The speaker is Yahweh, announcing his intention. There is no indication of the audience addressed, although the message is aimed at Israel. The phrase "in a little while" indicates how short the interval will be between the moment of speech and the fulfillment of the threat. This is the case in its other occurrences — Exod 17:4; Isa 10:25; 29:17; Jer 51:33; (cf. *m'ṭ* in Ps 37:16 and *'wd 'ḥt m'ṭ* in Hag 2:6). In these cases the phrase is followed, as in Hos 1:4, by the consecutive future (perfect) verb. The meaning "any moment now" points to the authenticity of the oracle since in point of fact, this threat was not carried out immediately. The threat of "Jezreel" seems to have been held in suspense while the other children were born.

The three verbs constitute a climactic series of increasing severity. The first and second threats are linked by the word *bêt*, "house," viz. Jehu's dynasty and the state of Israel. The second and third have a measure of assonance in the verbs and have in common the word "Israel." Together they give a specific exposition of the form that the punishment announced in the first threat will take. The first and third have the word "Jezreel" in common; by beginning and ending the speech, it serves as an inclusion. The relationship between the names is more intricate, involving the chiasm Jezreel . . . Israel . . . Israel . . . Jezreel. Each of the three threats has verbal links with each of the others, integrated into a single word of judgment. No line is without some kind of rhetorical connection with the rest of the oracle. The closely woven texture of vv 4 and 5, together with the climactic position of the final "Jezreel," makes it impossible to discard v 5 as a later addition. Mays calls v 5 "a Hosea fragment introduced by a redactor into the narrative because of the common catch-word, Jezreel" (p. 28). But it is not just a question of one catch-word. One wonders how v 5 could possibly have survived in isolation as a meaningful fragment. It is even more difficult to comprehend how Wolff can speak of the "different structure and vocabulary" of this verse (1974:19).

Note that the structure of B – C and B″ – C″ is the same exactly — w + Qal perfect + 'et with the two-word construct chain followed by prepositional phrase; and each line has fourteen syllables.

The sequence of anticipated actions may be described as follows: In a little while, on a momentous day (i.e. Yahweh's day), Yahweh will punish the house of Jehu for blood shed at Jezreel, by defeating the army of Israel in the Valley of Jezreel; not only will the dynasty of Jehu come to an end, but kingship itself will end in Israel, i.e. the independent state will be destroyed.

I shall surely punish. The biblical cliché "visit sins upon" has been avoided; its vacuity misses the juridical connotations of the idiom. The verb *pqd* sometimes means "appoint"; a *pāqîd* is a military or civil official ("appointee"). More commonly it means "to investigate," as in the inspection of a military muster, or an audit of livestock (Job 5:24). If something is found to be wrong, the *pôqēd* could conduct an inquiry and set things to rights; his duties are like those of a magistrate; cf. LXX *ek-dikēsō.* Such a visitation could result in either the deliverance of the oppressed or the punishment of culprits, or both. "Visit blood upon" is an idiom found only in this verse. In other passages iniquity or sin of some kind is the object of the verb, visited "upon" the guilty; hence "blood" refers to some kind of crime. In other texts different verbs (*nqm, drš, bqš*) are used to describe punishment for blood crimes. Clearly *pqd dām 'al* means to punish the house of Jehu for murder. Note the Pentateuchal use of the idiom *pqd 'āwôn 'al:* Exod 20:5; 34:7; Num 14:18; Deut 5:9.

the dynasty of Jehu. The reigning king, Jeroboam II, Jehu's great-grandson, is not mentioned by name, but seems to be meant. David's successors could similarly be called "house of David" (Isa 7:13), or simply "David" (I Kings 12:16). In Jer 21:12, the king of Judah is addressed as "house of David." In Amos 7:9–11 "house of Jeroboam" and "Jeroboam" seem to be interchangeable, although there may be a shift in the prophetic judgment from the royal house to the person of the king.

The phrase "house of Jehu" could also mean Jehu's realm, that is, the country of Israel as a political entity: Israel is referred to in the Assyrian annals as *Bit Ḫumri*, "House of Omri" (*ANET* 284, 285), and similar examples are easy to find. The question is important here, because some translations of the last clause in v 4 ("and I will put an end to the kingdom of the house of Israel," *RSV*) suggest that it is the destruction of the whole country as such, and not merely of the monarchy, or more narrowly of the Jehu dynasty, that is being threatened. Poetic parallelism then suggests that "the house of Jehu" may also mean the nation. We do not think so, preferring to apply the poetic parallelism the other way, to the interpretation of *mamlākût* (kingship, not kingdom). The oracle is directed against Jehu's line; its rule must come to an end. The judgments associated with the three children are of increasing scope and severity: first the fall of the royal house, then the defeat of the nation, finally its total rejection.

the blood shed at Jezreel. Literally "bloods," in the sense of blood violently shed, that is, murder; this is the meaning of *dāmîm* in 4:2 as well. The insults "man of bloods" (= murderer) (II Sam 16:7,8; cf. Ps 59:3), "city of bloods" (Ezek 22:2; Nah 3:1), and "house of bloods" (= murderous family) (II Sam 21:1), are similar. Its occurrence in juridical or penitential writings (e.g. Ps 51:16) gives the term "bloods" the meaning of "guilt for murder." In the phrase *dĕmê*-X, X is often the name of the murdered person, so "Jezreel" suggests a person, not a place. If it were not that the phrase "Valley of Jezreel" (v 5) points to the latter, the context would suggest that the house of Jehu was to be held accountable for the murder of someone named Jezreel.

Much blood flowed in Jezreel. First there flowed the blood of Naboth and of his sons (II Kings 9:26; contrast I Kings 21:13); Naboth's lèse majesté involved blood taint, requiring extirpation of the family. Naboth's vineyard was then forfeit to the crown, not as penalty for blasphemy, but because there was no surviving heir (Andersen 1966b). Later Ahab's blood flowed there (I Kings 22:38); finally Jezebel's did (II Kings 9:33).

The name of the firstborn child serves as a reminder of the bloods of Jezreel. The message conveyed by the name is a typical oracle of divine judgment, or punishment threatened against the "House of Jehu," the ruling dynasty of Israel. The nature and extent of the judgment are indicated in the parallel clause: "and I shall put an end to its rule over the state of Israel." The punishment will be the violent termination of the royal house, a threat made even more explicitly by Amos in a contemporary utterance: Amos 7:9, "And I will attack the house of Jeroboam with the sword"; cf. 7:11 where the prophet is misrepresented as saying that the fatal consequences will befall Jeroboam himself.

We normally would look for a causal or occasional nexus between the sign and the event, i.e. between "the blood of Jezreel" (represented by the prophet's son) and the violent end of the house of Jehu. The latter actually occurred in the reign of Zechariah, son of Jeroboam, who after six months on the throne was summarily assassinated by his successor, Shallum. The account is brief but to the point: "Shallum the son of Jabesh conspired against him [Zechariah] and struck him down in Ibleam, and killed him; then he reigned in his stead" (II Kings 15:10). The reading "Ibleam" is derived from LXX[L]: MT has *qbl-'m* which is incomprehensible in this context; it is curious and perhaps significant that Ibleam is also mentioned in connection with the killing of Ahaziah of Judah by Jehu (II Kings 9:27). Both the content and style of this report evoke memories of the assumption of power by the founder of the dynasty just ended, Jehu, and the link is made more secure by the historian's citation of the divine promise to Jehu: "Your sons of the fourth generation will sit upon the throne of Israel" (II Kings 15:12, cf. II Kings 10:30 — the quotation in Hebrew is exact).

The superficial correlation between the end of the dynasty of Jehu and the end of the preceding one, that of Omri and Ahab, is evident. Each was ended by the assassination of the reigning king, with the perpetrator of the deed succeeding to the throne. In the case of the dynasty of Ahab, the successor was the commander of the armies, Jehu; we are not told much about Shallum, but it is likely that he, too, was a military leader.

Often in the biblical tradition, the nature and extent of the punishment is prefigured in the character and degree of the crime. Thus those who use the sword will find it used against them, those who live by it will also die by it. As Jehu came to power through murder, his dynasty will lose power through the same means. Such a correlation has dramatic impact as well, and the biblical authors were not slack at making the point: condign retribution and poetic justice form an irresistible pattern in biblical narration, and both actors and speakers were fully aware of the possibilities of this genre.

The initial oracle in Hosea, linked to the child with a symbolic name, and expressive of a historically conditioned doom, is in the classic mold. The royal house of Jehu will go out the way it came in, with blood. It began as the instrument of divine judgment, and will end as the object or target of the same kind of judgment. The resultant picture is neat, clean, and well-balanced, but something is lacking, or badly askew, since the implication of this line of reasoning is that the "blood of Jezreel" is not only descriptive of the coming fall of the house of Jehu (i.e. assassination and displacement), but that the blood is causative, that it is the reason for the condemnation of that dynasty.

To the question of why the house of Jehu will be terminated, the answer seems to be "the blood of Jezreel." This would be the obvious inference, and many scholars have so interpreted the matter, but we may be uneasy about the implications as well as the inferences to be drawn. A great deal of blood was shed at Jezreel, and much of it was spilled by Jehu or at his command. From a modern point of view, his zeal for his task seems excessive, and most of us would regard his behavior as outrageous, especially in the indiscriminate slaughter of the royal house of Ahab, and the almost incidental extermination of Ahaziah of Judah and many of his relatives. The biblical writers did not see things in this fashion at all. Jehu is praised enthusiastically for carrying out the will of Yahweh in this slaughter, as expressed by the redoubtable prophet Elisha. While the Deuteronomic historian is less enthusiastic about Jehu's other behavior (especially with regard to the golden calves at Bethel and Dan) he supports the standard view: "Yahweh said to Jehu, Because you have done well in carrying out what is right in my eyes, and have done to the house of Ahab according to all that was in my heart, your children of the fourth generation shall sit on the throne of Israel" (II Kings 10:30).

It is difficult, therefore, to square the statement in Hosea that the blood of Jezreel will be visited upon the house of Jehu with the strong theological support of that bloodbath given elsewhere in the Bible. It may be that only the superficial correlation pointed out above is intended, namely that the house of Jehu will suffer the same fate it inflicted on the house of Ahab, and that the crimes for which the dynasty of Jehu is to be punished are unrelated to that episode. That there are such crimes is made clear not only by the historian who repeats monotonously that Jehu and his descendants along with all the kings of the north perpetuated the original and unpardonable sin of Jeroboam I and hence are under divine judgment, but by the prophets Amos and Hosea who vehemently attack the current administration as a source of political and religious corruptions and find ample justification in its behavior for divine punishment.

All this may be true, but it still does not explain the statement in Hos 1:4 which clearly links the blood of Jezreel with the destruction of the royal house. How are we to explain this apparent discrepancy? Many scholars believe that this statement in Hosea represents a dramatic turnaround from the days of Elijah and Elisha, and reflects a more penetrating insight into the nature of God's dealings with people. Far from approving the bloodbath at Jezreel, Hosea establishes a higher and morally more sensitive standard of evaluation and judgment. Jehu was wrong in what he did, and now at last his dynasty is paying the price of his brutality. "A hundred years later Hosea was to look back on the 'blood of Jezreel' as a crime to be atoned for only by the fall of Jehu's house (Hos 1:4)" (James 1947:190). So also Wolff (1974:18), following the same line, though he suggests that Hosea was not acquainted with the Elijah traditions; it is scarcely conceivable that any knowledge of Jehu's accession would come down without including the key roles of Elijah and Elisha. There may be some truth in this general analysis, but it seems detached

from the realities of the ninth–eighth centuries B.C.E. in the Near East—
or of any other period in ancient (or more recent) history. An adequate
solution may be found in a more nuanced form of this interpretation.

There is no reason to suppose that Hosea's view of Israel's history in
relation to its God was significantly different from that of the biblical historians or the prophets who preceded or were contemporary with him. In
the rest of his book we find numerous points of contact and agreement, although emphases and tendencies vary from the norms. In this case as well,
we may suppose his full agreement with the thundering condemnation of
Ahab and his house, and the necessity for the violent overthrow of that infamous regime. While therefore he, along with the other prophets and historians, could approve Jehu's action in overthrowing the house of Ahab,
that in itself does not require automatic approval of Jehu and his dynasty
in other matters. Thus the historian condemns Jehu and his house in the
stereotyped fashion after granting the inexorable divine oracle and promise. The house of Jehu has turned out to be no different from the house of
Omri; it will come to the same bloody end for the same reasons. James
asks, "Would Hosea have hewed Agag in pieces before Yahweh?"
(1947:94); the answer is probably that he would have recommended it,
even if he did not do it himself. He would have approved in principle,
even if the technique of his day was to bring about the downfall of kings
by the word. The language of Hos 6:5 may refer to the execution of Agag;
cf. I Sam 15:33. Amos's thought was similarly in line with that of Samuel
and Elijah (Amos 7:11). Jeremiah's severity on such a matter was undiminished (Jer 22:18f). Micah continued to refer directly to Ahab's
deed and his end as a gauge for measuring later kings (Mic 6:16).

Hosea turns the promise to Jehu that his dynasty will continue through
four generations (the longest of any in the northern kingdom) into a
threat—that it will perish in the fourth generation. In the same way we
may suppose that along with approval there was criticism of the bloodbath
at Jezreel and surrounding areas itself. We need only call to mind the
Deuteronomist's view of the Israelite conquest of Canaan: it was commanded by God and justified on the basis of the wickedness of the present
inhabitants, and the promise of the land to the fathers whom God loved
and chose. At the same time Israel was warned not to misunderstand its
position in the matter: by misinterpreting its election, by supposing later
that the conquest was its own doing, or that its success gave it license to
behave as it pleased, or both, it could forfeit both election and promise,
and even in the act of gaining the land (or by its immediate subsequent
behavior) lose its right to it—and ultimately suffer the same fate as those
whom it had dispossessed.

In similar fashion, Assyria (and later Babylonia) was called to be the
instrument of God in chastising his own people, Israel and Judah. No

opprobrium could attach to the great power for carrying out the judgment of God against Israel and Judah. Nevertheless the Assyrians ran a risk in executing the divine judgment. By misunderstanding their role as instrument, they could imagine the conquest as their own doing, grow proud and defiant, and thus gloat over the defeated people of God, or mistreat them more than God intended. God could not hold them guiltless for this attitude and behavior but would judge and punish them too. So in the very act of carrying out the will of God, first Assyria and then Babylonia sinned against the Lord of heaven and earth, and thus merited the destruction which overtook them subsequently.

It may be therefore that a prophet like Hosea viewed the behavior of Jehu in a dual light: in the very act of carrying out the divine judgment against the house of Ahab, he overstepped the bounds of his mandate and showed that arrogance and self-righteousness which was the undoing of the preceding dynasty. Already the seeds of destruction were sown in the terrible slaughter initiated by Jehu. If we may try to be more specific in this case we note that Jehu, in the process of making a clean sweep, not only wiped out the whole dynasty of Ahab, but nearly did the same to the royal house of Judah. Just how Hosea felt about this is not clear, and certainly he had no special brief for Judah — but he may have detected here a sign that all was not well with Jehu, that he had already begun to bring judgment on his own house by these violent actions.

The connection between the blood of Jezreel and the fall of the dynasty of Jehu is a patterned one: doom and succession by assassination. The house of Jehu will be destroyed as it destroyed its predecessor. In all likelihood we should see more here than correlation, namely alternate causation. Something in the manner or attitude with which the feat was accomplished boded ill for the future of the dynasty. Paradoxically the act of carrying out the will of Yahweh also violated it.

We should not suppose that in the thought of the prophet(s) it was Jehu's sin which doomed his great-great-grandson. No one is condemned for the sins of others, especially his ancestors — there was ample evidence to document charges against the later kings of the dynasty, so it was contemporary behavior, namely that of Jeroboam, which brought matters to a head. Judgment came to those who richly merited it, but the beginning was back with the founder of the dynasty; it all started with "the blood of Jezreel."

The punishment of a later generation for the sins of its ancestors (Exod 20:5; Deut 5:9), which the Decalogue makes prominent precisely in the matter of idolatry, never involved the exculpation of the fathers and the transference of their guilt to their innocent children. As the case of Achan shows (Joshua 7), the rule was based on family solidarity. The extension of responsibility, or at least involvement, to the fourth generation (five generations in all, Exod 34:7; Weinfeld 1972:25) would include all the members of a family alive at one time (Job 42:16). The qualification "the children to the third and the fourth generation *of those who hate me*" (Exod 20:5) suggests children's knowing persistence in parents' misconduct. In Hos 4:4–6 the prophet includes both the preceding generation (the mother) and the following (the children) in the judgment of an apostate priest.

Accordingly we reject the modern interpretation of Hos 1:4 which maintains that the prophet here repudiates Jehu's extermination of Ahab's line and sees this as a crime for which his descendant must now pay. On the contrary, the main target of Hosea's criticism (in contrast to that of Amos) of the royal house of his day is precisely the sin of the Omrides; and there is no hint that he believed that an unpunished sin could be expiated by punishing a later generation. Rather Hosea is saying that what God did to Ahab and his brood by means of Jehu is exactly what he will now do to Jeroboam and his family, *and for similar reasons.* That Hosea thinks that Jeroboam is following in Ahab's footsteps is shown by his application to Jeroboam of language that Elijah used with Ahab (I Kings 18:18). Jeroboam is blamed, not for resembling Jehu, but in part for the opposite. He was a traitor to the good done by his great-grandfather; he did not maintain Jehu's "zeal for Yahweh," zeal shown in his merciless extermination of the Baal cult and all its devotees.

This problem has been solved in other ways. For example, Kaufmann (1960:368–371), assuming that the doctrine of Deut 24:16 and II Kings 14:6 must be applied, suggested that it is Jehu himself who is here threatened by a prophet of his own day, whom he calls "First Hosea." In other words, this is an oracle of doom from an otherwise unknown prophet (was he also called Hosea, hence the confusion?) of about 840 B.C.E. who was horrified at Jehu's violence and took a point of view the opposite to that in II Kings 9–10. This is a flimsy argument. The phrase "house of Jehu" is more appropriate to the dynasty than its head. There is no trace of any prophet in disagreement with Elisha, no trace of any sentiment disapproving of Jehu, although it is possible that there was some revulsion against the excessive use of violence. We must find in the reign of Jeroboam the real source of the trouble. Both Amos and Hosea hated the incumbent with a fine passion because of his support for rampant Baalism and lip-service Yahwism. Hosea and Amos between them refer to Bethel nine times; Amos refers to Dan once (8:14). Hosea's three references to Beth Awen, perhaps another term for Bethel, increase the number. Their opinion is not dissimilar from that of the historian. Hosea denounces "the calf of Samaria" (8:6) and the "heifers of Beth Awen" (10:5), a Baal and his female counterpart made of gold, it would seem (Hos 2:10).

All in all, there is no indication that Hosea disagreed substantially with Deuteronomistic theology. Jeroboam inherited the promise made to Jehu, but his son will be the last of the line unless that promise is renewed by deeds of zeal for Yahweh. The same crisis emerged in Judah a century later. The outstanding Josiah had no one after him who was like him (II Kings 23:25); if there had been, the house of David would have endured.

I shall put an end to. In nearly half of the occurrences of the *Hip'il* of *šbt* it is found in a clause of this kind, beginning, literally, "and I shall cause to cease . . . ," and the speaker is Yahweh. Although the basic meaning of the root *šbt* is rest, as in sabbath, the *Hip'il* has vigorous transitive force and means to abolish, not just render inactive; cf. Hos 2:13. The use of the verb *hišbît* conveys no idea of the means to be used to bring an end to the kingship. More precise or more colorful interpretations have been attempted. The validity of any proposal must be tested by the general usage of the idiom elsewhere and its congruency with the context here. A wide departure from a generally attested meaning can be taken seriously only when the usual meaning does not fit at all, and when a special meaning is demanded and defined by a context manifestly different from the context of other occurrences. The next line, if related, provides the only hint as to how the kingdom is to be terminated, by breaking the bow of Israel. *Ausrotten* (extirpate) (cf. Wolff 1974:8) resorts to an image, but does not say what political or military activity is described as "uprooting." *Verabschieden* (dismiss) or even *Zurruhesetzung* (pensioning off) (Buber and Rosenzweig 1934), which preserve an adroit etymological connection with *šbt,* are misleading if they suggest honorable discharge. There is something more seriously wrong with Jehu's house than outliving its usefulness.

Guided by parallelism, van Dijk (1968:34) has proposed the translation "I shall break the monarchy," on the basis of an appeal to biconsonantism; *šbb* "to splinter," *šbr* "to break," and *šbt* are all in the same word-field. (See also Kuhnigk 1974:2–3 and Andersen 1976b). This is unacceptable because of the following considerations: (1) It diverges too much from known meanings and clear idioms of *hišbît.* The *Hip'il* occurs forty times. Typical constructions are: A. to stop someone from doing something (Exod 5:5; Josh 22:25; Ezek 16:41; 34:10; Dan 9:27; Neh 4:5; II Chron 16:5; cf. Gen 2:2) — seven occurrences; B. to get rid of undesirable human beings or animals (means not specified) (Lev 26:6; II Kings 23:5,11; Jer 36:29; 48:35; Ezek 34:25; Amos 8:4; Pss 8:3; 119:119; Ruth 4:14); it is even used to describe banning God (Isa 30:11) — eleven occurrences; C. to bring about the cessation of a human activity — joy (Jer 7:34; 16:9; Hos 2:13); shouting (Isa 16:10; Jer 48:33); music (Ezek 26:13; 30:10); sighing (Isa 21:2); commemorating a name (Deut 32:26); quoting a proverb (Ezek 12:23) — ten occurrences; D. to eliminate a human attitude — pride (Isa 13:11; Ezek 7:24); insolence (Dan 11:18); lewdness (Ezek 23:27,48); dispute (Prov 18:18) — six occurrences. The verb "to break" is quite unsuitable with any of these as its grammatical object. Even when it describes the removal of material things — salt (Lev 2:13); leaven (Exod 12:15); wars (perhaps armies) (Ps 46:10); a scepter (Ps 89:45 — the text is difficult); or idols (Ezek 30:13) — (five occurrences) — the meaning "to break" is not applicable, while "to cause to cease" makes just as much sense as it does with all the others. There is no warrant for arguing that *hišbît* means "break" with an object like "idol" when it cannot mean that for all the other objects. This leaves Hos 1:4 as the only place where "kingship/ kingdom" is the object of the verb. The common meaning "to get rid of" makes sufficient sense. (2) The meaning of breaking the monarchy needs to be explained. Is it a figure of speech, implying some kind of simile, as in Ps 2:9? (3) It is adventurous to give a verb a special meaning when its only other occurrence in Hosea (2:13) is in line with standard usage. Furthermore, we have shown in the Introduction that much of the vocabulary in Hosea 1–3 occurs twice, with the same meaning each time.

its rule. That is, the rule of the house of Jehu over Israel. MT reads a construct phrase — "the kingdom of the house of Israel." If this is taken as appositive — "the kingdom which is the house of Israel" — the construction is awkward and redundant. Hebrew has several words for kingship/kingdom, both abstract and concrete: *mamlākâ, mĕlûkâ, malkût, mamlākût.* The last, used here, is the rarest. In Joshua 13 it is used concretely ("domain"); elsewhere its meaning is apparently abstract ("dominion"). In II Sam 16:3 it refers to royal rule as status and power; cf. Jer 26:1. In I Sam 15:28 the deposition of Saul is described as tearing away *mamlĕkût yiśrā'ēl* from him. The ripping of the rule "from upon" the king almost pictures stripping off the royal garments and insignia; but the imagery of I Kings 11:31 is ripping the kingship (*mamlākâ*) of the ten tribes "out of the hand of Solomon" (actually his son Rehoboam). In a similar manner, Hosea's prophecy was fulfilled in Jeroboam's son.

If, however, *mamlākût* is here concrete (the political state), then the clause could mean either that the kingdom of the house of Israel will cease to exist, or that the house of Jehu will be abolished "(from) the kingdom of the house of Israel," the preposition being understood and the object continuing from the preceding clause. Since the idiom for removal of either persons or things is *hišbît X min-Y,* such a construction can be discerned here only by supposing that it is highly condensed.

Another clue to the meaning is obtained from the fact that the object of the verb in other occurrences is either something evil (*zimmâ,* for instance), eliminated so as to purify, or something desirable (cf. Hos 2:13), whose removal serves to punish. The eradication of the house of Jehu from the kingdom of Israel would be an act of punishing the nation by depriving it of its ruling dynasty, a line of thought that does not fit the context well, for it is the monarchy, not the kingdom, that is the object of censure. It is likely that this clause follows the one before: the house of Jehu will be punished for the blood of Jezreel by abolishing its reign over the house of Israel. That is, *mamlākût* is the object of the verb, in spite of the lack of the *nota accusativi*, and it means "kingly rule." We have detached the final phrase, rendering it "(over) the state of Israel." A preposition is not needed; but its absence led the Masoretes to make a single construct phrase out of the three nouns.

A few more points can be made in support of this result. Hosea has a particular hostility to the monarchy, at least to the house of Jehu if not to the northern monarchy as such (7:3,7; 8:4; 10:3), and what is threatened here, namely the removal of the king, is referred to again in Hos 3:4. The nation will be spared, but it will be deprived of its king for a long time. (Dahood has suggested that *mamlākût* can mean king, 1968:151.)

Hosea's words, like those in Amos 7:9, are thus seditious. The purpose of Yahweh's judgment at this stage is to save the nation by destroying the evil kings. If the king does not achieve repentance by a change of heart, then the people must take the initiative (as Jehu did) and change the dynasty. We can understand why Amaziah was so alarmed at Amos's preaching (Amos 7:10–12), and why Hos 6:9 accuses the priests of complicity in current lawlessness. Older prophets had been known to take a hand in implementing their own predictions. A revolutionary such as Jehu was aided and abetted by Elisha (no friend of kings), a fact of history which Jeroboam could hardly have forgotten. The prophets dealt with particulars, not abstractions, with concrete historical realities and individuals, not with theoretical ideas. Hosea does not threaten the elimination of the monarchy as an institution, but the end of Jehu's dynasty. The mention of Jeroboam ben-Joash in Hos 1:1 makes it likely that Hosea's words are directed against him. His son Zechariah succeeded to the throne of Israel, but his death after reigning six months would seem to be a more impressive fulfillment of Hos 1:4 than his failure to succeed his father would have been. The ending of Jehu's dynasty does not mean the elimination of monarchy. It could mean no more than another revolution like Jehu's own insurrection. This is, in fact, how Jehu's line ended.

In predicting the downfall of Jehu's dynasty, it is not clear what Hosea had in view. Elisha had his agent anoint Jehu to replace Joram; there is no evidence that Hosea plotted in this way. Kaufmann (1960:263–264; 375–376) believed that Hosea did not reject the monarchical institution. He shrewdly remarks: "The current opinion that Hosea repudiates the monarchy in principle would be tenable had he advocated another political principle in its stead, as does Samuel. But Hosea does not call for a government of judges or prophets. His political idea can only have been a monarchy guided by the Word of God from the mouth of prophets" (p. 375). Wolff (1974:19) thinks that v 4 announces the end of the monarchy as such in Israel. He dismisses the six kings who came after Jeroboam II as being of no consequence. If, as we believe, Hosea 3 belongs with Hosea 1, the prophet anticipated a long period of catastrophic national deprivation, an interval "without a king" (3:4). But, after "many days" the reconstructed nation will be unified under "one head" (2:2), "David" (3:5). So if the monarchy is rejected, it will later be reinstated.

5. *It will happen on that day.* A familiar preface to an eschatological prediction. In connection with "a little while," an oracle so prefaced can be called eschatological only in the sense of "decisively final," not necessarily remotely future. In its full form the phrase is used three times in Hosea (here and in 2:18,23). The phrase "and it will happen" occurs twice in Hos 2:1, and since it is unmistakably eschatological in that context, it doubtless also contains the idea of "in that day." The pattern is consistent; the preface always comes twice — in the full form in 2:18,23, in the short form in 2:1, and in parallel with "in a little while" in 1:4,5. It is instructive that the expression "in that day" occurs in 2:20 with the same eschatological connotation. We may see in this phenomenon the breakup of a stereotyped phrase, designed to bind together separated parts in a unitary picture of the end time. These facts subvert the argument that the change to an eschatological style in v 5 sets it in contrast with v 4 and indicates that it is a later addition.

bow. Qešet is collective; cf. v 7, where it comes first in the catalogue of armaments. The bow was the weapon of princes (II Sam 1:22), perhaps of the royal bodyguard or palace troops. Hoffner (1966:329 n 12) suggests that the "bow" here is "a symbol of masculine physical powers and sexual potency." In Jer 49:35 "the bow of Elam" is in parallelism with "the head of their heroism," that is, their leading heroes or crack troops; cf. "the bow of warriors" (I Sam 2:4). The bow was prominent in the defeat of Babylon (Jer 51:56). The bow is also a poetic symbol of strength (Gen 49:24; Jer 49:35; Job 29:20). We hesitate to search for a historical event to supply the meaning of v 5. The threatened destruction of the army of Israel is associated with the fall of the house of Jehu in the same time frame: "In a little while" defines the imminence of the eschatological day of Yahweh (cf. Amos 5:18*ff*).

Whether military defeat will be the cause or effect of the sudden end of the line of Jehu is not clear. It is tempting to read the prophecy in the light of subsequent history. According to the record, Jeroboam did not die in battle; the dynasty ended with the assassination of Zechariah. After that there was a succession of palace revolutions and internal upheavals resulting in a bewildering rotation of kings and pretenders before the weakened nation collapsed completely under a series of Assyrian on-slaughts culminating in the capture of Samaria in 723/2. It may well be that Hosea presented a foreshortened version of the denouement with the end of the dynasty and the fall of the kingdom coming simultaneously or close together, and during the reign of the incumbent kings. It seems un-likely, however, that Hosea's vision extended that far. He probably thought the end was near, but did not bother to work out what would hap-pen next. Furthermore, cc 1–3 do not seem to contain reflections after the fall of Samaria. Amos seems to have had essentially the same picture in mind, for he is reported to have said that Jeroboam would die by the sword (7:11) — though 7:9 specifies the "house of Jeroboam," which is less precise — and that the nation would go into exile (7:11,17). The pre-dictions were not fulfilled in the case of Jeroboam II, or in any precise manner thereafter.

the Jezreel Valley. It is part of the tradition about "the blood of Jezreel" that Jezebel's blood was spattered there; where dogs had licked up Naboth's blood, they licked Ahab's blood and ate Jezebel (I Kings 21:19,24), even though I Kings 22:37 has the location in Samaria. The historian of Kings underscores the fact that the wounded Joram returned to Jezreel to recuperate (II Kings 9:15), but has him going out in his chariot so that Jehu can kill him "at the property of Naboth the Jezreelite" (v 21), apparently thought of as outside the town. In the case of Jezebel the fulfillment might have been more literal, since the vineyard was beside the palace (I Kings 21:1), and Jezebel was hurled from the window (II Kings 9:30–37). The word "Jezreel" occurs three times in this story. Yet there were limits to the liberties that the historian could take with his facts. Jehu killed Ahaziah, king of Judah, at the same time. But the narra-tor does not bring him to Jezreel to join the other victims; he was shot "at the ascent of Gur, which is by Ibleam" (II Kings 9:27); LXX reads *Ekblaam*. The coincidence is found in the circumstances of Zechariah's death. According to II Kings 15:8–12, Zechariah, fleeing from Shal-lum (?), was struck down in the same place. Though the word Ibleam in LXX of II Kings 15:10 (MT has Qabal-'am) may be a contrivance, the poetic justice is evident. Shallum was Hosea's Jehu, for Ibleam is very close to "the valley of Jezreel" (Hos 1:5) (Aharoni 1967:22). "The house of Jehu" ended where it began.

The sinister significance of Jezreel is now clearer. If the original "blood of Jezreel" included not only Naboth's but also Ahab's, then the text tells us not *why* Jehu's house was punished, but *how* it is to be punished. The pattern is not one of historical cause and effect, but a theological pattern in which the hidden hand of God is briefly glimpsed when something that once happened happens again in a similar way (cf. Gen 27:36 with 29:25

and 48:18; II Sam 12:11 with 16:22). Furthermore, these places, Jezreel and Ibleam, evoke associations with Mount Gilboa (I Sam 29:1), the scene of the disastrous defeat of Saul and Jonathan, and a song apparently called "The Bow" (II Sam 1:18) that was sung in lamentation for a dead king and prince and the end of a dynasty (Freedman 1972a). This memory, this dirge, and this place were a standing reminder that Yahweh had not spared Israel's first king when he became disobedient, and that his son Jonathan, even though he was a good man, perished with him. In view of what we have said above about sorcery, the reference to witchcraft in Samuel's denunciation of Saul (I Sam 15:23) is striking.

6. *Then she conceived again.* The absence of specific information about the father does not imply that the child was illegitimate, although that remains a possibility. It is more likely that such a point would be made by mentioning the abnormal, not by omitting the normal. While some scholars see the omission of "for him," which occurs in v 3, as a hint of doubtful parentage, the adverb *again* links the two pregnancies and suggests their similarity.

a daughter. No significance is attached to the sex of the second child.

He said. The identity of the speaker (Yahweh) is to be inferred from the preceding material.

to him. The idiom *'mr 'el,* "to speak to," is typical of Hosea (five times). In contrast *'mr l* means "to name" (2:1,3,25; 14:4); the action of naming Hosea otherwise expresses as *qr' šm,* "to call the name" (1:4,6,9). The unexpected *lw* here could be a precative particle before the imperative verb; the *l* in Hos 10:8 could be vocative; the idiom of 13:2 is not clear. This variation is probably not significant, however, as is confirmed by LXX, which consistently translates *'el* by *pros;* it reads *pros auton* in v 4, *autō* in v 6.

Lo-Ruhama. The understanding of this phrase cannot be separated from the most beautiful, and also the most elemental, of Yahweh's attributes (Freedman 1955a; Wright 1971). He is "a loving and generous god" (Exod 34:6; Deut 4:31; Joel 2:13; Jonah 4:2; Pss 86:15; 103:8; 111:4; 145:8; Neh 9:17,31; II Chron 30:9). As an expression of the most tender feelings of affection, it is one side of his character as "passionate" (*qannā'*). Yahweh is ardent in both love and justice. Thoughts of compassion or mercy are secondary, for these are evoked by a condition of misery, dejection, or contrition in their object; the *rhmym* of God is unconditional. To call the daughter "Not Pitied" suggests that pity is needed, but not forthcoming. Since Yahweh is always, in his deepest being, *rahûm,* the negation of his love cancels his most basic relationship with his people. The name is a verb in the perfect tense, with the negative. Since there is no *Qal* form, the verb is *Pu'al.* The marking of the stress on the second-last syllable makes it unlikely that the form is a participle; the word has a special pausal form. Since the form is not used anywhere else, it is possible that it was invented for this case; multiple inferences should not be drawn from grammar. If the form is what it seems, it implies a completed act of rejection (by Yahweh) with the focus on some past moment, rather than on the present state of affairs. She is not simply "unpitied"; a passive participle would express that better. Rather, she has been expelled from a relationship of love. There is an emptiness about this which would not be expressed had an antonym of *rḥm* been used. The term is also more concrete, suggesting an act of renunciation; note the following *lō' 'ôsîp 'ôd*. To suggest that the name is impersonal ("There is no mercy") (Wolff 1974:20) is insipid; the term could then be no more than a description of the state of society in the vein of Hos 4:2. But it is not an indictment; Yahweh is the hidden subject.

Since names can be ominous, it is possible that this one does not describe an accomplished fact, but announces a destiny — "Let her not be pitied." The use of a perfect verb as precative is known. We prefer to take the name to be a statement of the fact of a complete change in Yahweh's relationship with Israel. He has ceased to feel compassion toward them, and he will never love them again. The remainder of vv 6 and 7 expounds the meaning of the name; it does not give the reason for it.

never again. The entire explanation is a unity, and every clause in it is negated. We shall not enter directly into a debate with the widely held opinion that v 7 is favorable to Judah and (therefore) a later gloss (Harper 1905:205, 213). A demonstration of the rhetorical unity of the entire paragraph will be sufficient refutation.

Although the five constituent clauses are uneven in length, they are arranged in rhythmic patterns that achieve symmetry in the total construction.

6bA	*kî lō' 'ôsîp 'ôd*	5 syllables
	'ăraḥēm 'et-bêt yiśrā'ēl	8
6bB	*kî-nāśō' 'eśśā' lāhem*	7
7aA	*wĕ'et-bêt yĕhûdâ 'ăraḥēm*	9
7aB	*wĕhôša'tîm byhwh 'ĕlōhêhem*	11
7bA	*wĕlō' 'ôšî'ēm*	5
7bB	*bĕqašt ûbĕḥarb ûbĕmilḥāmâ*	10
	bĕsûsîm ûbĕpārāšîm	8

A common scholarly view of vv 6b–7 holds that it is composite and corrupt. The original message, an interpretation of the name of Hosea's second child, was a condemnation of "the house of Israel" playing on the verbal root *rḥm* and consisting of v 6b. The first two clauses combined a strong negative element (*l' 'wsyp 'wd*) with the verb *rḥm,* while the third clause was understood to reinforce the idea but required emendation since as it stands it affirms emphatically the certainty of forgiveness: "I will surely forgive them" — *ky nś' 'ś*. At the least a second negative must be added, or the verbs themselves must be altered. The whole of v 7 was then treated as a clumsy gloss added by a supposed "Judean" editor who insisted on gratuitously adding the assertion that "the house of Judah," unlike "the house of Israel," will be pitied and rescued. In our opinion none of these views is correct; they arise out of a failure to recognize the structure of the passage and its syntactic arrangements, as well as a misreading of its meaning and import. The text is neither composite nor corrupt, but, insofar as it is possible to judge these matters, has been preserved exactly as set down.

A cursory analysis of the passage shows that there are two major clauses, introduced by *ky l'* (6b) and *wl'* (7b); each is followed by the same form of a verb: *Hip'il* prefixing 1 c s. Syntactically the second of these poses no difficulties: after the verb there is a series of five prepositional phrases (divided into groups of three and two in the MT) which modify the verb. The first unit vv 6b–7a presents an anomaly; the auxiliary verb *ysp* "to add, do again" normally is followed by an infinitive form of the verb, whereas here it is followed by four finite forms, the first three being first-person prefixing forms and the fourth a perfect first-person form with the *waw*-consecutive. While unusual, the construction is not unacceptable, since there is some interchange between infinitive and finite forms of the verb, especially in poetry. Most if not all scholars agree both on the syntax and meaning of the first clause: "For I shall never again show pity for the state of Israel." If this is correct, as it must be, then it follows that the same syntactic pattern holds for the remaining three clauses of the unit and their verbs. In other words, the introductory clause (*l' 'wsyp 'wd*) controls all four following clauses and negates them individually and severally, e.g. never again will (1) I have pity on the house of Israel, (2) I make the slightest move to forgive them, (3) I have pity on the house of Judah, and (4) I, Yahweh their God, rescue them. Verse 7b picks up the verb in the fourth clause and elaborates on the theme of deliverance or victory in battle.

The application of the negative opening phrase *lō' 'ôsîp 'ôd* to every clause in vv 6–7 is validated by several arguments. First, the objection that such long-range flow of negation from one clause to the next without repeating *lō'* is not grammatical has no force. The construction has been recognized in other places where it has been found necessary to supply the double-duty negative in translation. An irresistible example is supplied by Jer 3:2.

> *'êpōh lō' šuggalt 'al-dĕrākîm*
> *yašabt lāhem . . .*
> *wattaḥănîpî 'ereṣ . . .*
> Where have you not been stretched out upon the roads?
> [Where have you not] sat for them . . . ?
> [Where have you not] defiled the land . . . ?

The opening words blanket all that follows, making each statement a question.

The syntax of Jer 22:10 is exactly the same as that of Hos 1:6.

> *kî lō' yāšûb 'ôd*
> *wĕrā'â 'et-'ereṣ môladtô*
> For never again shall he return
> and [never again] shall he see the land of his birth.

In Num 23:19a the opening *lō'* applies equally to the following clause.

> And El is not a human . . . . .
> and [he is not] a child of Adam . . . . . .

In a similar way the opening *'ên* in Mic 7:1b covers all that follows, not just the clause it is in. Isa 38:18 resembles Hos 1:6–7 in another structural feature. In a series of negative statements only the first and last have *lō'*. But all the translators recognize that the negative operates in the middle one as well; literal translation is impossible. There can accordingly be no objection to treating Hos 1:6–7 in the same way.

Secondly, the pressure to make v 6bB negative has been felt by some commentators, who wished to restore a missing *lō'*, "not," before *nāśō'* (Halévy 1902). There is no need for this, since the principle of double-duty operation of such particles is now well established (Dahood and Penar 1970:438).

Thirdly, the syntax of the entire unit shows that the construction is tightly knit; that is, "never again" does not have to be "understood" as present in each clause by ellipsis (although in English we have to supply it); it blankets all that follows as a single unit.

The anomalous or unusual sequence of auxiliary in the prefixing form followed by finite verbs may be explained by the fact that the negative first clause pervades the entire unit and negates each verb in sequence. An examination of the internal structure of vv 6b–7a shows that the four subordinate clauses divide into two pairs as they stand. Each pair is introduced by a clause with *'rḥm,* which in turn governs a direct object — state of Israel and state of Judah. These clauses are modified in turn by clauses with related themes (I will not forgive them; I will not rescue them). Closer examination reveals other interesting relationships: the *'rḥm* clauses are balanced in a perfect chiasm:

'rḥm 't-byt yśr'l

't-byt yhwdh 'rḥm.

Andersen (1974) has shown that chiasm is the most integrating form of coordination in Hebrew. Since 'eśśā' is embraced by the two occurrences of 'ăraḥēm, it is tied together with them in dependence on lō' 'ôsîp 'ôd.

The chiastic arrangement suggests an envelope construction for the interpretation of the name of the child: beginning with 'rḥm and ending with 'rḥm. The other clauses both end with the 3 m pl suffix -hem, producing a banal rhyme which nevertheless points to a deliberate linkage. The plural suffix in each case might refer to either the house of Israel or the house of Judah, or the two together. Since the author exercises special care in the agreement of pronouns and pronominal elements, we might have expected a singular pronominal suffix if the reference were simply to one house (whether of Israel or Judah); the use of the plural suggests that the connection is with both.

The sequence of introductory particles: ky, w, and w suggests a more subtle syntactic arrangement among the parts. It is clear that the second line of v 6bA is the opening clause in the series. It would be usual for the second balancing clause to begin with w and we may choose between vv 7aA and 7aB as the intended follow-up. The former would produce the tightly knit chiasm noted above, the latter an envelope pattern. In either case, the parallel unit would begin with v 6bB, balanced by the remaining w clause. The end results would be these:

A. 1) 'rḥm 't-byt yśr'l   6bA in part
      w't-byt yhwdh 'rḥm   7aA
   2) ky nś' 'ś' lhm   6bB
      whwś'tym byhwh 'lhyhm   7aB

B. 1) 'rḥm 't-byt yśr'l   6bA in part
      whwś'tym byhwh 'lhyhm   7aB
   2) ky nś' 'ś' lhm   6bB
      't-byt yhwdh 'rḥm   7aA

There is something to be said for both of these logical arrangements, as well as for the present rhetorical order. We do not suggest that any changes be made; this is the way the text has emerged from the hands of editors and scribes, if not the author himself; it is left to the perceptive reader to sort out the possibilities and see the variety of links and relations.

The idea that Hosea directed his fire exclusively at the northern kingdom and used only the term Israel and its equivalent Ephraim, while a Judean editor introduced the word Judah as a counterfoil to Israel, indicating that whereas the northern kingdom would surely fail, and fall, the southern one would survive and succeed, is questionable in both respects:

Judah is involved integrally in the prophecies of Hosea, and there is no essential difference in his attitude or predictions about the fate of either kingdom. The difference is that Israel and its condition are close at hand and of immediate concern to the prophet, whereas Judah is less immediately in the picture, and of less pressing concern. In the end the prophet does not neglect either. The same is true of Amos: to a somewhat greater extent the focus is on the north, but Judah is not neglected. The opposite is true of Isaiah and Micah, both of whom concentrate their attention on the southern kingdom but speak as well of the north, though with a different emphasis and interest. All this is quite understandable and reflects the physical circumstances of the prophets who lived in one or the other of the countries but were fully aware that both kingdoms were part of the people of God and had central roles in salvation history.

In every other place where Judah is mentioned in Hosea it is treated the same as Israel/Ephraim, sharing equally in culpability and awaiting the same judgment; there are the same possibilities for repentance and renewal, and ultimately the same hope for restitution and restoration. Regardless of whether these references are original or added by an editor, the status of Judah is essentially the same as that of Israel, so here we would be compelled to apply the negative prescription to the statement about Judah as much as to the statement about Israel. The identical sentences require the same interpretation; the perfect chiasm only emphasizes the coordination of the two clauses.

show pity. Both parts of the name *lō' ruḥāmâ* are used in the wordplay; note the recurrence of *lō' 'araḥēm* in 2:6. The Horeb incident (Exodus 33–34) provides a clue to Hosea's use of the root *rḥm*. Embedded in the mysterious theophany there is an equally mysterious "name"—

> And I will favor those I favor
> and I will pity those I pity (*'ăraḥēm*) (Exod 33:19).

Later on there is a grim warning about making a covenant with the inhabitants of the land, leading to intermarriage and the practice of Canaanite religion, which is called "being promiscuous after their gods" (Exod 34:15–16). The same words are used in Hos 1:2, language which hearers or readers would recognize as traditional.

the state of Israel. When this is linked to the similar remark about "the state of Judah" (literally "house" in each occurrence), it is clear that the second child, Lo-Ruhama, represents the whole nation, as the other children also may.

or forgive them at all. Assuming that the denial continues through v 6b, the *kî* must be resumptive or assertive. Wolff (1974:9) is emphatic that, after negation, *kî* must mean "on the contrary." It often but not always does; it can just as well be concessive (Vriezen 1958). On the range of possibilities that should always be considered when translating *kî,* see Muilenburg (1961). For a parade example of a construction in which *kî* continues the negation in the preceding clause, see the NOTE on Isa 43:22 in McKenzie (1968:58).

Although the words *nāśō' 'eśśā' lāhem* are common and mean roughly "lifting up, I will lift up to/for them," the sense of the construction is obscure. What is Yahweh not going to lift up? The verb *nś'* is used in many idioms, including some which mean "regard with favor," either by pardoning sin or by granting a petition. The Deuteronomic expression "to lift up faces" (Deut 10:17) describes the perversion of justice by favoritism ("respect of persons"). The same expression, ascribed to God, could here mean that hitherto he has treated Israel leniently, unjustly, because it is his favorite nation, but that the time for such partiality has now gone. This seems oversubtle. Society's respect for the prophet gave him power as an intercessor. This, and the idea of forgiveness, can be combined in a prayer, as in Hos 14:3. Moses' use of *nś'* in his prayer at Horeb (Exod 32:32) gives us the idiom God "carries away their sin." Comparison of Moses' usage with that of Hosea is invited because the sin is the same: worshiping the gold calf. Yahweh forgave Israel at Horeb, using *'ăraḥēm* to describe his compassion (Exod 33:19), though his acquiescence to Moses' daring and importunate plea seems reluctant, less than wholehearted. It is as if the punishment is not canceled, it is merely suspended, or even postponed, to be visited on them later (cf. Exod 32:34 and Hos 1:4). In other words, Moses persuaded Yahweh to forgive them that time, but next time will be different — "never again." Amos had a similar experience, and Yahweh said as much to him. Like Moses, he was successful once or twice in extending the deadline for punishment. But finally his prayers were silenced, and Yahweh said, "Never again" (*lō' 'ôsîp 'ôd* — Amos 7:8; 8:2). Time has run out; the historical wheel of repentance, forgiveness, and deliverance, followed by forgetfulness and fresh rebellion (the cycle of sin and redemption in Deuteronomistic history-theology) is about to stop. Before, when Yahweh was moved to compassion by his people's afflictions, he raised up a deliverer (*môšîa'* — Judg 3:9; the root of the latter is used in Hos 1:6–7). The phrase "never again" suggests that Hosea did not contemplate the replacement of Jeroboam's family by a new dynasty, a token of a fresh beginning. This background suggests that our text means "[Never again] will I lift up [their sin] for them." Isa 2:9 has the same idiom, also without the object. The inclusion of "never again," furthermore, is a final reminder of how many times previously Yahweh had had compassion on his undeserving and ungrateful people (Ps 78:38).

Many other attempts have been made to gloss this phrase, going back to LXX, which seems to be guessing: "But rather I shall opposing set myself against them," though this agrees with the drift of the passage. LXX seems to imply a *Nip'al* of *nś';* it does not support the conjectural use of *śn'*, "hate," in BH³, since LXX usually translates *śn'* by *misein.* Wolff (1974:8) retains a literal meaning "withdraw," but understands the object "my compassion." This is not so persuasive as "forgive," the interpretation which has appealed to most commentators. The difficulty Wolff complains of, the need for a modal translation, e.g. "that I should forgive them," certainly puts a strain on the conjunction, which, however, is removed when the clause is seen to be another negative statement. We think that "iniquity" is the most likely noun to be understood; Hosea elsewhere uses the full expression (Hos 14:3). In general, when a laconic expression is suspected, it is likely to be effective only when it abbreviates a cliché. Wolff's proposal is unlikely, since the idiom *nś' rḥmym* is nowhere attested. Unless *nś'* and MT can be shown to be impossible, there is no need to resort to another root (*nś/š'*) and an internal passive, as in "I will not be deceived by them" (Kuhnigk 1974:4).

7. *save them.* The clear statement "I won't save them" in v 7b, together with the generally negative thrust of the whole oracle, is the reason why we see v 7aB also as a negative statement, even though the negative particle is not explicit. The root of the verb *yš'*, "to save," is the same as that of the name Hosea, but there is no indication that a play on words is intended.

More apposite is the verb sequence *rḥm,* "pity" . . . *yš',* "save." In the historic tradition of Israel, compassion is the great motivation for Yahweh's most celebrated rescue acts. In its abundant use, *yĕšû'â,* "deliverance, salvation," is Yahweh's most typical achievement. Other gods do not have this ability (Jer 11:12). When there is neither compassion nor deliverance, the judgment of Yahweh does not take the form of an active destruction that he directly brings about. He deserts his people and they destroy themselves, or are destroyed by enemies. In this way they experience their weakness and helplessness without Yahweh, their Rescuer, the ultimate *môšîa'.* In many instances, as here, refusal to deliver is not the same as total rejection. It is intended to bring the people to their senses, to remind them that they are absolutely dependent on Yahweh, to bring them to contrition and new trust.

A Deuteronomic title, "Yahweh their God," appears in the original. The phrase, transposed to the start of the clause sequence from its end, could be rendered with the adjacent verb, "I will deliver them *by Yahweh their God,*" the preposition *b* indicating the agent; on agential *b,* see the NOTE on Hos 1:2. There are parallels to this usage, with the same verb, in Deut 33:29; Isa 45:17. Ps 33:16 stresses the futility of armaments for safety, since Yahweh alone has the power to rescue. This interpretation involves some strain, since the instrumental use (to rescue with weapons) is not the same as the agential (to rescue by Yahweh); but cf. Ps 44:4–8. We prefer to identify *b* as *beth essentiae,* used for apposition with the subject of the verb (GKC §119i). The alleged awkwardness (Harper 1905:213) in the switch from first to third person vanishes once it is realized that it is not uncommon, when Yahweh is using the formal *Hofstil* in an oracle, to refer to himself in the third person, and by the name Yahweh (cf. Hos 1:2 and Exod 6:3; Joüon 1947:404–405). The *beth essentiae* can indicate the capacity in which a person is acting. Yahweh will not rescue them *as* Yahweh their God, as they would have expected if he had continued to function as Yahweh their God. The statement then amounts to a renunciation of this relationship or at least a refusal to recognize its claims on him. This is very poignant, and prepares for the even more drastic severance of relationships to be declared in the name of the third child.

from bow and sword and weapons of war, from horses and horsemen. The use of *b* here poses the question: is the preposition used instrumentally, i.e. I will not save them *by* bow, etc. or protectively, i.e. *from* bow, etc.? The former, the standard interpretation, is tied to the previous clause, which has always been analyzed as a positive statement: "And I will save them by Yahweh their God—but I will not save them by bow or by sword," etc. The implication is that Yahweh will save them but not by military means. This accords with various passages in the Bible in which the contrast is made between reliance on conventional means of war and trust in God for survival and well-being.

On the surface at least, the juxtaposition of God, who can bring victory, with the weapons and matériel which do not, would seem to justify the traditional viewpoint. Closer scrutiny suggests that such considerations are hardly germane in this context. If the message is that Yahweh will no longer show pity to either of his peoples, Israel or Judah, and henceforth will not intervene to rescue or save them, then it would appear that the concern is not with means, that is, with the weapons with which he will not save them, but rather with circumstances, namely, when they are attacked. The weapons here are those of the enemy who will be permitted to overrun and destroy the kingdoms that had forfeited their claim to divine protection and intervention. This is close to the standard prophetic and Deuteronomic interpretation of history.

We follow Kuhnigk (1974:3) in rendering *mlḥmh* as a synecdoche, "(weapons of) war." The meaning "troops" is also possible (Gen 14:8; Exod 1:10; cf. Num 31:28; Judg 20:17). In the list of ordnance and military personnel in v 7b, the LXX adds a sixth to the five items in MT, *harmasin,* Heb *merkābâ,* "chariotry," after *milḥāmâ.* At first glance, the longer list is more appealing, as the omission of *mrkbh* can be explained as a result of haplography, or homoeoteleuton to be exact: the scribe's eye jumped from the final *he* of *milḥmh* to the final *he* of *mrkbh,* and *mrkbh* was omitted. It would be reasonable on the basis of LXX to group the items in pairs since they have elements in common both as to form and content: thus *qešet* and *ḥereb* are hand weapons and also segolate nouns; *milḥāmâ* and *merkābâ* are both three-syllable nouns ending in *-â* (here we might recognize a combination, chariots of war); and finally *sûsîm* and *pārāšîm* are both m pl nouns; and horses and horsemen together make up cavalry, one of the newer features of Iron Age warfare.

In spite of these data, there is evidence in favor of MT which must be considered. The reading in 2:20 of the first three items only (*wqšt wḥrb wmlḥmh*) supports MT against LXX, not because *mrkbh* is omitted but because the grouping of three cuts across the pairs we identified in LXX. Furthermore, MT has a break after *mlḥmh* since the next item, *bswsym,* is without the conjunction. The grouping of three things followed by a pair is thus confirmed. LXX, which has the conjunction with all of the items except the first, seems to be secondary whereas MT, without the conjunction at the beginning of the second group, seems to have the older and more difficult text.

The contempt expressed by Yahweh in this oracle for human armament as a safeguard for national security is probably intended as an answer to Israel's false confidence in recent military successes. Jeroboam had restored large parts of the old empire, almost rivaling David's achievement (II Kings 14:25). His conquests extended as far north as Hamat Rabbah (Amos 6:2). Damascus was for a time either a vassal or at least forced into a treaty economically favorable to Israel (II Kings 14:28). The scope of his conquests in southern Transjordan is not so clear. His main successes probably lay in the sphere of international trade, like Solomon's. Jeroboam's opulence, denounced more by Amos than Hosea, was offset by the appalling poverty caused among the common people by his successful commercial expansion. Here he is reminded that just as fertile soil gives no yield unless Yahweh decrees a good harvest, so the best equipped army is useless unless he gives victory. This gives us another reason for preserving the parallel references to Judah in v 7: they complete the larger picture, for Uzziah's contemporary military achievements matched those of Jeroboam II. Even if the account in II Chronicles 26 contains some exaggeration, there need be no doubt about its essential correctness. It notes the advances in military technology that aided Uzziah's conquests. He seems largely to have restored the southern part of David's original empire. If Jeroboam and Uzziah (like Ahab and Jehoshaphat before them) did not have a formal alliance, at least they must have had some kind of understanding concerning their respective spheres of influence. Their parallel successes and the forgetting of old quarrels must have fostered throughout both kingdoms the feeling that they were still one great nation, correctly referred to as "Israel (and Judah)." In a similar vein Hosea exactly parallels the impressive building projects of these two contemporary monarchs (Hos 8:14), and again comparison with Solomon is not far away.

As we have mentioned, in the old stories it was pity for his people's plight that moved Yahweh to indignation and mobilized his armies (Judg 10:16). When Israel is "not pitied," a more drastic method of saving the covenant relationship is required. The severity of this total rejection must be felt in order to understand Hosea's doctrine of salvation. Redemption is still possible, but not because Yahweh's drive to pardon overcomes his will to punish and not because he spares a faithful portion of his people, in this instance, Judah. Redemption does not begin until rejection is complete. The nation is created again after it is totally destroyed. Restoration comes by resurrection after dying; see Hos 2:1–3. The successive names of the three children show the mounting severity in Yahweh's attitude. "Jezreel" was a judgment within the covenant. When this is not heeded the nation is "not loved" and is left unaided. When this discipline is unavailing, Israel is pronounced "not my people," and the covenant is repealed.

horses. Joel 2:4 suggests that two kinds of horses might be involved in this phrase. The proposal that *pārāš* means "mare" has been discussed by ap-Thomas (1970).

8. *When she had weaned.* Such a detail was not mentioned in connection with Jezreel. A child could be suckled for two or three years; the time covered by the events recounted in Hosea 1 cannot be calculated, though five years would be minimal. Since the oracles are interrelated and the family is a unit, it is not likely that each child's name should be connected with specific contemporary events.

she conceived. LXX and Syriac read "again"; cf. v 6. The brief MT of 1:8 marks the end of the progressive shortening of the descriptions.

9. *Call his name Lo-Ammi.* The verb is singular, addressed to the father; the plural "you" is used in the comment on the name. This oracle is the shortest of the three namings. The parallel lines match grammatically, but they are unequal in length.

> *kî 'attem lō' 'ammî*   6 syllables
> *wĕ'ānōkî lō'-'ehyeh lākem*   9

"My people" was perhaps the most beloved title conferred on Israel by Yahweh, an intimate and honorable title; Yahweh was acclaimed with pride as "our God," "One Yahweh" (Deut 6:4). These titles had sacred associations; the entire story of the Exodus was built around them. The assertion "I am" (*'ehyeh*) is also highlighted there (Exod 3:12,14; 4:12,15; see below). The climax of covenant-making was a related promise.

wĕhayîtî lākem lē'lōhîm
wĕ'attem tihyû-lî lĕ'ām
And I will be for you as God,
and you will be for me as People (Lev 26:12).

The same language is used when the covenant is adapted to the monarchy.

'ănî 'ehyeh-lô lĕ'āb
wĕhû' yihyeh-lî lĕbēn
I will be for him as father,
and he will be for me as son (II Sam 7:14).

All this is now undone; a relationship hundreds of years old has been dissolved. This means the annihilation of Israel and the total disappearance of Yahweh from history. He had no other people. The shattering effect of this child's name is enhanced by addressing the people now for the first time directly: "You (are) *lō' 'ammî*." So far Hosea had spoken about Israel indirectly. Verse 9 apparently represents a public utterance. This "you" is resumed in the pronouns "your" in 2:3, an inclusion which joins all of 2:1–3 with 1:9. Whereas the comments on the names of the first two children are descriptive, this is oracular.

The title My People applies to Israel as a whole, the twelve tribes of the old confederacy and the united kingdom of the first three kings. The disruption after Solomon's death did not change that. Neither Samaria nor Jerusalem ever arrogated exclusively to itself this ancient title. Here the total nation, Israel and Judah, is renounced, just as in vv 6–7.

In Deut 32:21 unidentified foreigners are gathered under the head *lō'-'ām*, "a non-people." What we have in Hosea 1–2 is not a negation of *'ammî*, "my people," but the suffixation of the noun compound *lō'-'ām*, i.e. "my non-people." In the latter case ownership is still claimed, but Israel is no better than the heathen.

Ehyeh. An ancient synonym or alternative form of the divine name Yahweh (Exod 3:14). The formula of Lev 26:12 is not reproduced here; the second part does not contain the expected "I am not your God." At 2:1 we have the remarkable title, *bĕnê 'ēl-ḥāy*, "children of the living God," instead of the expected "my people," which has been displaced to the end of the unit (2:3). Here, instead of "your God," the text has the seemingly unintelligible "and I not I-will-be for-you." To resolve this difficulty a word for "god" is sometimes added, or the text is rewritten, replacing *'hyh lkm* by *'lhykm*, "your god" (so BH³). MT should be retained; it is fully supported by LXX, *kai egō ouk eimi hymōn*, "and I am not yours." Because *Ehyeh* is a proper noun, it cannot take a possessive pronoun suffix, and has to be modified less directly by *lākem*.

The balanced syntax supports the integrity of the text as it stands. The pronouns *'attem,* "you," and *'ānōkî,* "I," are in contrastive positions (Andersen 1974:150–153). Although *'ehyeh,* "I am/will be," is in form a verb, it is clearly used as a name in Exod 3:14. When Moses asked God to disclose his name, he said, "Ehyeh is who I am; you will tell the Israelites, 'Ehyeh sent me to you.' " This assumes that the people will recognize and acknowledge this name, perhaps a secret name, as opposed to the public Yahweh, and that Moses' use of it will lead to his acceptance by the Israelites. Here it matches the title *'ammî,* as if it were a complementary covenant synonym for Yahweh.

The etymology and meaning of this variant are another matter. In some Hebrew nouns prosthetic *'alep* is purely phonological. In some areas of Semitic it is elative (Wehr 1952). In view of the affinities with Yahweh, one might look for an *'Ap'el,* parallel to *Hip'il* (Blommerde 1969). The name *'hyh,* whatever its pronunciation, history, and meaning, is sometimes a first-person form corresponding to third-person *yhwh;* it is used as a name, as the subject of the verb *šĕlāḥanî,* "he sent me," in the critical passages in Exod 3:14–15. See further Freedman and O'Connor (forthcoming).

Wolff (1974:10) well remarks that the three name oracles become "more comprehensive, more severe, and more direct." Each oracle has the same form; the name is followed by a *kî* clause which explains the meaning of the name. Remarks about the state of society to which the oracle is addressed are lacking. Yahweh does not say clearly what the house of Jehu has done that requires judgment. He does not say what Israel and Judah have done to extinguish his love. He does not say what act of covenant violation required the decision to make them "Not my people."

2:1. *Then it will happen.* The abrupt change of mood between Hos 1:9 and 2:1–3 has startled some commentators, who have either excised the latter passage as a later addition, or else removed it to another place where it harmonizes better with the context. Wolff thinks Hos 2:1–3 originally belonged with 2:23–25, but was moved quite early to its present position by an editor who was Hosea's personal disciple (1974:26). *NAB* shunts Hos 2:1–3 to the end of c 3, though Hos 2:3 makes a lame ending to the section, whereas the present ending is effective.

While there are difficulties with the present order of the text, there are also problems with each of the proposed rearrangements. Until convincing arguments are presented against the traditional order and in favor of another, we prefer to work with what we have, and attempt to analyze the given structural patterns. In favor of the authenticity of the passage and its compatibility with Hosean authorship, we observe that Hosea often sets the most opposite ideas side by side in striking contrast. Total despair alternates with unbounded hope. It is part of Yahweh's sovereign power that he can completely reverse anything. He can change "my people" into "not my people," and he can reverse the direction too. The name and relationship can be changed back again. This is Hosea's essential theology, and Hos 2:1–2 (or 3) predicts such a future switch in the name and status of the covenant people.

The main points made are the greatness of the coming day (v 2b), clearly a day of exultation; the great increase in population (v 1a); the reversal of one of the negative names (v 1b); and the reunion of the separated kingdoms under a single ruler (v 2a). All this will be a fulfillment of ancient promises.

Hos 2:1–3 is closely related to Hosea 1. Only after the climactic naming of the third child is it possible to proceed to the total reversal supplied in 2:1–3, which picks up all three names. The reversal of all that was announced in the names of the children has a great impact because the dreadful threats in c 1 are given without comfort. The horror of the devastation will eventually be relieved by a word of hope, a new word of creation spoken to total chaos. Our recognition of the organic connections which exist within Hos 1:2–2:3 as a finished literary composition does not mean that we think that it was all done at once. We note, however, that many eschatological predictions are scattered throughout Hosea 1–3, and some of them might well have been present in the earliest stages of literary growth.

The crisis that Hosea had to interpret was different from any that had occurred in Israel's previous history. There had already been occasions in Israel's past when God made threats that he did not carry out. His impending judgments were staved off, either by the intervention of a prophet who made effective intercession (Genesis 18; Exodus 32; Amos 7; Psalm 106; etc.), or by repentance (I Kings 8), or out of sheer compassion. Not so now (Hos 1:6): Hosea makes no intercession on behalf of Israel. The people produce no change of heart. Yahweh's hand falls; Israel is discarded (Hos 1:9). Hos 2:1–3 follows, describing the steps that Yahweh will take only after he has completed his judgment. As such, Hos 2:1–3 lies in the future, a more remote future than the one viewed in Hos 1:5. According to Hos 3:4–5, this "end of days" will come only after "many days." The scope of Hos 2:1–3 points to a future that history cannot contain; the eschatological dimension is remote, not in the sense of being far distant in time, but as something beyond historical possibility without the direct intervention of God. These remote possibilities are always at hand, and all time perspective is lost in talking about them. They reverse history, canceling its evil, not by denying it or moving away from it into some transcendental realm. The realities of this remote future are still Israelites and Judahites. The day is the day of Jezreel. This gathering up, this salvaging of history is not its negation, but its fulfillment. This kind of eschatological thinking in an eighth-century prophet should be distinguished sharply from the fantastic, remythologized eschatology that came after the Exile. The superficial resemblances between the two should not mislead us into eliminating the authentic eschatological elements from Hosea by confusing them with later apocalypses. Vriezen (1953), among others, is emphatic that the note of hope in Hosea is authentic.

The particulars of Hosea's vision are seen in the verbal links between 2:1–2 and c 1. The name Jezreel is given a positive meaning. The negative names "Not-Pitied" and "Not-My-People" are themselves negated. The listing of all three names at the end (Hos 2:2b–3), with chiasm of the last two, is another reason for including Hos 2:3 in this oracle, and for regarding 2:1–3 as the response to 1:2–9. The actual pattern is as follows:

Name	Association	Name
1:4 Jezreel	Jezreel (1:4)	
	Jezreel (1:5)	Jezreel (2:2)
1:6 Lo-Ruhāma	[l'] 'rḥm (1:6)	
	[l'] 'rḥm (1:7)	Ammi (2:3)
1:9 Lo-Ammi	Lo Ammi (1:9)	
	Lo Ammi (2:1)	Ruhama (2:3)

In the first unit the names of the three children occur in 1:4,6,9. In each case there is a following interpretation or association in which the name or a play on the name occurs twice: Jezreel (1:4,5), [l'] 'rḥm (1:6,7), Lo-Ammi (1:9; 2:1). The reversal of fortunes or change of names (the two younger ones) or meaning (Jezreel) occurs at the end of the unit: 2:2–3, with chiasm of Ammi and Ruhama.

In 2:24–25 the names recur. The three names in their original form are repeated, and then the reversal is noted, either in verbal play or in the change of name. In Jezreel we have wzr'tyh, "and I will sow her," and for Lo-Ruhama wrḥmty, "and I will show pity"; for Lo-Ammi, the negative is dropped, as in 2:3, and we have Ammi.

There are further reasons for recognizing continuity between 1:9 and 2:1. The argument from syntax is strong, since 2:1–3 shares features of the three oracles about the children, especially the first. Admittedly Hos 2:1 lacks the phrase bayyôm hahû' of 1:5, but the form used is a common variant of the eschatological preface; note the reverse situation in 2:20 where bayyôm hahû' occurs, but wĕhāyâ is omitted. The two passages 1:5 and 2:1 thus complement each other; they are linked in other ways.

The eschatological formula is lacking in 1:7, but the future vision is present there without it. Furthermore, wĕhāyâ is used twice in 2:1. The pattern of 1:5, 2:18, and 2:23 makes excision of the eschatological portions impossible without serious mutilation of the overall structure.

Hosea's oracles have three points of time in view: (a) the present situation; (b) the impending situation; (c) a more remote and final state of affairs. Even if the latter is not seen explicitly as the end (3:5), his vision does not extend beyond this era. The use of wĕhāyâ to introduce the end of an oracle prevents us from regarding 2:1 as beginning a new section.

There are other connections between 1:2–9 and 2:1–3. For instance, the removal of the kingship (1:4), the impending action, will be matched by the restoration of the "one head" (2:2, cf. David in 3:5) of the tribes reunited into one people. The devastation of both Israel and Judah (1:6–7) is matched by their joint resurrection (2:2). Furthermore, the names Judah and Israel appear in 2:2 in a rare order which produces a chiasm binding 2:2 to 1:6–7, and conforms to the reversal of the names of the younger children in 2:3. The distinctive and carefully used name "Israelites" (2:1) matches the general term "the land" used in the opening accusation (1:2). This association of "the land" and "the Israelites" is appropriate because both are connected in the covenant promises hinted at in 2:1 and 2:20.

the number of the Israelites. Here bĕnê yiśrā'ēl means the entire nation. In 1:6–7 and in 2:2 Israel and Judah are distinguished, but the pronouns in those verses refer to both together.

sands. Although the simile is a cliché, it conveyed memories of the promises made to Abraham, the first and greatest ancestor of Israel (Gen 22:17). The abbreviated expression used by Hosea implies such larger constructions as 'im-tûkal lispōr 'ōtām, "if you can count them" (Gen 15:5) or wĕlō' yissāpēr mērōb, "and it is not counted because of size" (Gen 16:10; 32:13). Hosea, in using the stylistic feature of two verbs in parallel, links his vision with the idealized reign of Solomon:

'am rāb 'ăšer lō'-yimmāneh
wĕlō' yissāpēr mērōb.
I Kings 3:8; cf. I Kings 8:5 = II Chron 5:6

Similar parallelism is found also in the Oracles of Balaam, in Num 23:10.

The people are both numerous and united. Note the motif of 'am rāb in Gen 50:20. The patriarchal comparison with the sand is found in I Kings 4:20, which links Judah and Israel together, under one king. More is involved here than a dream of political unification under Jerusalem, more than propaganda (like that of the author of Kings) for the claims of the Davidic line against the rulers of the north. Hosea's solution is not just a reversal of the disruption that took place after Solomon's death. The glorified past provides only a model for a transcendent future. Both parts of the nation are equally doomed, Jerusalem no less than Samaria (5:9–14). The future king David represents, not the vindication of Judah, but the restoration of all Israel.

This promise thus has considerable historical depth, going back through Solomon to Abraham. In using the verb *mdd* rather than *mny* (Gen 13:16; Num 23:10; I Kings 3:8), Hosea seems to have a variant tradition.

in the place where. Literally "in the place of" (construct). Although *bimqôm 'ăšer* may be no more than the locative relative adverb ("where"), there may be significance in the mention of a "place." The place where the name was originally given may be the place where the name is changed; the place of renunciation may be the place of reinstatement: "the land" (1:2 and 2:25) as the "house of Yahweh" (cf. 9:3–4). Hosea has a doctrine of redemption by recapitulation. God will take Israel back into the desert, and begin all over again (2:5,16). There can be no doubt that Hosea has in mind the tradition that during the Exodus it was first said to Israel, "You are offspring for Yahweh your God" (Deut 14:1). This passage has in parallel another covenant title, "holy people," and a warning about following heathen practices. While *māqôm* can be simply a location, such as the desert, it is also used in a technical sense for a recognized sacral assembly place such as an open-air shrine. Even though there was also divine anger and rejection of Israel in the wilderness, there was also effective intercession and renewed if reluctant acceptance of the errant people. The paradox emerged early in the covenant that Yahweh had committed himself to have a people, and even their worst sins could not dissolve the relationship.

So far as Hosea's actual child is concerned, the place of naming could have been the place where a public announcement of the name was made; a shrine where the boy was circumcised or the mother purified may be meant. The plural "you" used in the third naming ceremony strongly suggests the presence of "the people" on such occasions. In the precincts of such shrines, the people would also have heard the covenant words, "I am your God: you are my people," uttered in ceremonies of covenant renewal. Hosea would have declared there his countermessages — "Jezreel, . . . Lo-Ruhama, . . . Lo-Ammi." These are now the names of Yahweh's people. However, even if a shrine were the locus of such declarations, the context need not have been a naming liturgy for the newborn. And it certainly does not follow from this that Hosea, as a prophet, was a cult officer of such a shrine. If he were, his startling names would have cut across familiar ones; if he were not an official, we imagine him interrupting and contradicting the conventional litanies, an interloper like Amos.

There are biblical incidents in which a child is named immediately on birth. The name celebrates something that happens in connection with the birth, taken as a portent of the child's destiny. In Hosea 1 the word of Yahweh came to Hosea after each child's birth — at least the events are so recorded. There is no hint of a time interval between birth and naming and no indication where the name was bestowed. The child is the message to Israel. The child will be a new message, and have a new name (2:25). If the *māqôm* is the place where the child was born, then this is to be compared with the Exodus as the time of national birth (2:5). We shall see in Hos 11:1 that this prophet views the Exodus as an adoption rather than as a birth, but this incongruity of metaphors is no problem, since he speaks of Israel equally as Yahweh's spouse and Yahweh's child.

it was said. The translator is forced to render the same verb form, *yē'āmēr,* by two difficult tenses in its two occurrences in the verse. This may be correct since the imperfect can be iterative past ("it was said," aorist, as in the first occurrence in LXX, or, better, "it used to be said") as well as future ("it will be said," as in LXX at the second occurrence). If a specific act of addressing were involved, one might have expected a perfect verb; however, *yē'āmēr* is also the verb used to report a current saying, not a statement made once and for all.

The impersonal *yē'āmēr,* "it was said," leaves room for the fluid relationship in the names which simultaneously refer to an individual (Hosea's child) and a nation (Yahweh's child). The *Nip'al* with this impersonal meaning is generally used to report a byword, something that is habitually said, particularly in comments on names (Gen 10:9; 22:14).

In Gen 32:29, however, it is used in connection with the change of Jacob's name to Israel, and this sense is to be preferred here, where the focus is on the giving of names, not the popular interpretation of them. Compare Isa 19:18; 32:5; 61:6; 62:4; Jer 7:32, which use the same idiom for a name change. Hosea knows and uses the Jacob traditions. In the center of Israel's self-consciousness as the people who have standing with Yahweh is a historic change of name. In Hosea's perspective the Bethel and Jabbok incidents are merged (Hos 12:2–6). This momentous past event provides a model for the future. Israel's name has been changed to "Not My People," but it will be changed back again; the emphasis is probably not so much on the change of the name Lo-Ammi but on the *place* where it was said.

An objection to the theory that a naming ceremony lies behind Hos 2:1 arises from the observation that what is said does not constitute two names. Thus the sentence, "You are not my people," is not a name, but a statement, based on the name of the third child. Nor is what replaces it — "children of the Living God" — a personal name, although it could be a title for a group or a nation. This shows how imperceptibly the "allegory" slides from Hosea's family to Yahweh's people. We note that the name

"My delight is in her" (Isa 62:4) is a clause. In Jer 4:11; 16:14; Zeph 3:16, in similar eschatological contexts, a similar idiom is used to affirm the new eschatological reality of the end time; cf. Ezek 13:12; Ps 87:5.

You are not my people. There are grammatical subtleties in the sequence of words used here, in contrast to Hos 1:9, with the sequence *'attem lō' 'ammî,* "You (subject) (are) not my people (predicate)." The latter is the normal sequence when Lo-Ammi is a name, whereas the inverse sequence (predicate plus subject), used in Hos 2:1, makes "not my people" designate status (Andersen 1970a). The arrangement secures chiasm between 1:9 and 2:1.

children of the Living God. That Yahweh is the sole giver of life is a constant theme of the Hebrew Bible. In creation, God breathed life into the first person, who was only inert soil from the ground; God *created* a living being. Similar language is used, particularly in psalms of lament or thanksgiving, to describe the activity of God in restoring liveliness to the sick: God *heals.* The imagery of raising the sufferer from the bed of illness is not much different from the language that is used to describe the resuscitation of the dead, who stand up out of their graves. The last two images are used as figures for each other. Death is a sickness for which resurrection is the cure; or unexpected recovery from disease is a miracle of returning from the gates of Sheol. In many texts it is impossible to decide whether to take the death/resurrection and sickness/recovery language literally or figuratively; see the NOTES on 6:1–2. *Resurrection* resembles creation quite closely, since it is the dry bones lying in the earth that are clothed with new flesh and animated by God's own breath (Ezekiel 37). It is not clear which of these focal points supplies the connotation of the title used here.

The unexpectedness of this title makes it climactic. It completes the oracle on the third child (1:8 – 2:1). In the context, "Children of the Living God" could be a new name, but it is not suitable for an individual. More likely it is the predicate of the incomplete clause "(You are) children of the Living God," paralleling the previous clause, the one *'attem* being in effect the subject of both predicates. In the same way the balancing affirmations of Hos 2:25 match: *'ammî 'attâ,* "You are my people," is followed by *'ĕlōhāy,* "(You are) my God," without repeating the pronoun. As a predicate, the phrase defines the status of the person addressed, leaving the meaning of "children" unclear. In c 1, the bad names were given along with their meanings. Here the meaning of the new name is divulged, but not the name itself. When the new name does eventually emerge (Hos 2:25), it will prove to be a positive form of the old name, *'Ammî,* "my people."

The name for God, *'ēl ḥay,* "the Living God," is itself rare (Josh 3:10; Pss 42:3; 84:3; cf. "my living God," Ps 42:9). More frequent is the prosaic *'ĕlōhîm ḥayyîm* (e.g. Deut 5:23). The mixed *'ĕlōhîm ḥay* is found in Isa 37:4,17. The parallelism in Ps 56:14 shows that *haḥayyîm* "the Living (one)" can be a name for God. By contrast with the familiar phrases, Hosea's expression (with its use of the singular for both noun and adjective, and lack of the article) has an ancient ring. As a title for the Living God, it is connected with the doctrine of God/El the life-giver, found in the ancient name *mĕḥiyyā'el/mē/ĕḥûyā'ēl* (Gen 4:18; cf. I Sam 2:6 and Deut 32:39). The generic use of El is common to all ancient Syro-Palestinian nations — the national gods are both specifically named, e.g. Qaus, Milkom, Chemosh, Dagon, etc., and generically named El. El-names can reflect any deity and in Israel are associated with Yahweh. Although Canaanite El was repudiated just as Canaanite Baal was, whereas the name Baal could be avoided, the word God/El could not. There is the further complication of Patriarchal El, in particular El Shadday.

The phrase *bĕnê 'ēl* is the ancient name for all divine beings ("gods") in Canaanite polytheism, members of the heavenly community over which the supreme god El presided. The original *banu 'ilima* survives in Ps 29:1 (*bĕnê 'ēlîm*), but the more common equivalent in Hebrew is *bĕnê (hā)'ĕlōhîm*. This phrase was never used of human beings, but continued to be used in passages with mythological roots (Gen 6:2,4; Job 1:6; 2:1; 38:7). The closely related "assembly" of gods, *'ădat 'ēl* (Ps 82:1), is the Canaanite equivalent of Babylonian *puḫur ilāni*. In early Israelite covenant thinking this concept was radically demythologized and the *'idatu-'ili(ma)*, consisting of gods, became *'ădat-yhwh* (Num 27:17; Josh 22:16; etc.), consisting of Israelites. Its historicization is seen in the common designation of the covenant community as *'ădat (bĕnê) yiśrā'ēl* or simply *hā'edâ*. Furthermore, *'ădat yhwh* is equivalent to *'am yhwh,* so the juxtaposition of *lō' 'ammî* with *bĕnê 'ēl-ḥay* is not incongruous and the El of the myths becomes the Yahweh of history.

If the procession up from Sheol described in 2:2 has first claim as the clue to 2:1, then resurrection as a new creation by the Living God is in mind. If the sexual imagery of 2:25 predicates the act of God, then "children of the Living God" is the new name of the formerly rejected people. The covenant associations of 2:1 should not be overlooked; 11:1 has the same background. There it is clear that the title "child" is conferred by adoption. In general, the Israelites rarely called themselves "children" of Yahweh. They abhorred the idea of people as the offspring of God, not to belittle people, but to protect Yahweh from any suggestion of sexuality. At the same time Hosea must insist that all children are the gift and creation of Yahweh, not Baal. Yahweh's role in conception was a "natural" one; he opened the womb when a man had sex with a woman.

Occasionally, as in Deut 14:1, Israelites called themselves "children of Yahweh," and Hosea's generally primitive language suggests that he is reviving an old expression here. In any case, the historical entity Israel is remythologized and cast into the future as the eschatological community. Not that it is detached from history. These "children of the Living God" are all the Israelites, including those who came up from Egypt, the rejected ones addressed now by Hosea, those who will "return" in the end time, revived and reassembled (Hos 2:2). The use of the epithet "living" affirms that God's final word to Israel is life, and prepares for the promise of general resurrection in v 2.

Not until 2:5 does Yahweh say he will "kill" Israel; cf. 6:5. The old covenant name Ammi will be restored (2:25), but the new name is also needed to bring out the fact that "in that day" Yahweh will bring life from death in a manner more dramatic than anything in the old stories.

2. *The Judahites and the Israelites.* It is impossible to remove the reference to Judah without destroying the structure of the unit. These names occur in a sequence chiastic with that in 1:6b–7a, where the reference is to the "states of Israel and Judah," a signal of the connection between the two passages.

The two kingdoms are distinguished in 2:2 in order to herald their future union under one head. Since the promises in 2:1 go back to the one ancestor Abram and the one king Solomon, *běnê-Yiśrā'ēl* there means the whole nation, like *běnê-Yiśrā'ēl* in 3:5. But when *běnê-Yěhûdâ* and *běnê-Yiśrā'ēl* are mentioned in Hos 2:2a, the two parts of the divided kingdom are recognized. Since Lo-Ruhama and Lo-Ammi are paired in both Hos 2:3 and 2:25, while Jezreel stands apart, it is possible that, here at least, the siblings are Israel and Judah, while Jezreel stands for the original and future nation of united tribes. In this connection it is worth noting that both Jeremiah (3:6–10) and Ezekiel (c 23) looked upon the nation in partition as two sisters.

Although the terminology, "Judahites and Israelites," comes from the divided monarchy, the language of convocation resembles that in Gen 49:1–2 and Deut 33:5, both of which have their setting in premonarchical tribal assemblies.

In Hos 2:2a, the initial verb ("will gather") and the final adverb ("together") belong to both the coordinated subjects, so there is only one gathering together. Neither part is given priority. Since the sequence Judah-Israel is designed to secure chiasm with the sequence Israel-Judah in Hos 1:6–7, Judah cannot be regarded as taking the lead, as though Israel must rejoin Judah.

will gather. The placement of *gather* and *together* invites search for closer synonymous parallelism, which could be achieved by reading a verb *yěḥādû,* which would fit the poetic and grammatical patterns nicely. The sequence of consecutive future (perfect) followed by an imperfect verb is good. If, however, *yḥdw* is to be read as a *Nip'al* of *yḥd*, "unite," there are morphological difficulties. The same problem is presented by this verb in Gen 49:6; Isa 14:20; and Ps 86:11. In Isa 9:20 *yḥdw* might be read **yēḥādû*, "they united"; in Pss 31:14 and 41:8 *yḥd* could be a verb— "they unite against me." By reading *yēḥādû*, "will be united," Kuhnigk (1974:6–8) makes the lines parallel, but thinks each refers to the unification of Israel and Judah separately, while the following pair of clauses describes the unification of Israel and Judah into "one host." It is better to retain the MT and see the appointment of one head as another indication of that national unity.

they will appoint. The same idiom is used in I Sam 8:5 for the selection of a monarch, which makes it possible that the "one head" is a king.

one head. As a token of reunification, this head must be modeled on a leader in the days before Israel was divided. This could be Moses (or a second Moses), especially if "coming up from the land" is thought of as a new exodus, as in 2:17. Since Hosea makes extensive use of the traditions of the Wilderness period, he may have in mind the insurrection described in Numbers 14, where the people reject Moses and try to appoint another leader ("head," Num 14:4) to lead a return to Egypt. Since the action described here is clearly constructive, it could be the antidote for the wilderness insubordination.

"Head" can be the title for a chief of military, judicial, or liturgical operations. The present context does not supply the connotation needed to pinpoint one of these. In the early days it was used for tribal chiefs (Num 1:16) or magistrates (Exod 18:25). The structural relationships between Hos 2:1–3 and 3:1–5 raise the question of whether the "one head" will be like David, or even David himself. The king was not called the "Head," except in Ps 18:44, "You appointed [same verb as in Hos 2:2] me as head of nations." In Job 29:25 the parallelism of *rō'š* and *melek* is quite clear.

The word "one" stands in association with the word "together" in the preceding clause. Hence it probably means "common" (that is, joint) rather than "single." The phrases *ḥuqqâ 'aḥat* (Num 9:14), *tôrâ 'aḥat, mišpāṭ 'eḥād* (Lev 24:22; Num 15:16) emphasize that all follow the *same* rule.

they will come up. The common verb "to ascend," used here, has so many meanings that it is hard to determine what nuance it bears in the present context. When the subject is an army, the verb means to mount a campaign or invade; but the country or city the aggressor "goes up" against is usually specified. The preposition "*from* the earth" is fatal to Wolff's proposal that it means "take possession of the land" (1974:28).

In a context where life is the answer to death, the radical rejection in the name "Not-my-people" calls for an equally radical remedy. At the very least, the language describes a political reconstitution of Israel by a return from Exile resembling the original Exodus. The verb here is generally used for the movement from Egypt to the promised land (Hos 2:17; cf. Exod 1:10). It is also the verb that describes the ascent from death (Sheol) to new life (cf. I Sam 2:6; Ps 30:4). If this sense is also present here, then the original coming up from the land of Egypt provides a basic model for this act. When the Exile became a fact, later prophets were able to bring the theology of a second exodus to full flower. With a knowledge of Jeremiah, Ezekiel, and Deutero-Isaiah, we tend to read this development back into earlier prophets. It is present in embryo in Hosea, but it has not yet acquired the historical realism found in later treatment. We therefore find it difficult to decide the sense in which Hosea is using the language of exodus here, especially given the brevity of statement.

The land is not identified. It could be Egypt; but Egypt is rarely called "the land." It could be Assyria, thought of as the Egypt of a new slavery (Hos 8:13). Elsewhere in Hosea "the land" means either the people (1:2), equivalent to "the inhabitants of the land" (4:1), or else the country itself (2:20–25). These meanings do not fit the present passage. Recent study has established that "the land" in ancient Israel was a name for the Underworld, the realm of the dead (Holladay 1969; Tromp 1969:23–46; Kuhnigk 1974:8–10). This meaning makes sense here. Compare Gen 2:6 (Speiser 1967:22). Recognizing Hosea's capacity for using language with more than one level of meaning, we suggest that the statement "and they will come up from the land" has two senses, one historical (the Exodus), one eschatological (resurrection). Whichever is primary, it carries a definite and intentional connotation of the other. As Moses led the united tribes from slavery, so a "single leader" will lead the reunited nation, both Judah and Israel (2:2a), out of the destruction into which Yahweh has hurled them. The destroyed nation will have to be brought back from *the Underworld* in order to become Yahweh's people again. The historical blends into the eschatological, and no dividing line can be drawn between them. The emphasis on Yahweh as the Living God (2:1) thus continues.

In 5:8 – 6:6, an oracle about resurrection is embedded in two passages about death. Here the message about the great day (2:1–3) is flanked by oracles about the children's symbolic names. In spite of the abrupt changes in mood, the passage is not intrusive, but integral to the total structure.

How great. The particle *kî* here cannot be rendered "for, because"; a logical connection between v 2a and v 2b is hard to find. The intensification of a predicative adjective by means of *kî*, "how (very)!" is now widely accepted, in view of steadily accumulating attestation (Muilenburg

1961:143). "The time of trouble for Jacob" (Jer 30:7) is called "great" in the sense of unique ("there is nothing like it"), incomparable for desolation and misery, incomparable also for restoration and joy. (There are other affinities between Jeremiah 30 and Hosea 2.) The term here is an exclamation of wonder at the marvels of the great day of national resurrection (cf. Ezek 37:1–14).

the day, O Jezreel. According to the MT, the great day is "the day of Jezreel," which has been linked to "the blood of Jezreel" (Hos 1:4). The day of Jezreel is the time when Yahweh punishes the house of Jehu for the Jezreel massacres. Such a reference to wholesale extermination is out of the question in the present context, in view of the exultant positive note that is struck throughout 2:1–2a. The elimination of Jehu's dynasty was only one in a climactic series of events which culminated in the total rejection of the nation. Now it is Yahweh's day to restore them. The greatness of Yahweh's day is celebrated in a magnificent incantation in Zeph 1:14–16, where it is called *yôm yhwh, hayyôm,* or simply *yôm.* If *yôm* in Hos 2:2b is another laconic equivalent of *yôm yhwh,* then what becomes of the phrase "day of Jezreel"? We follow *BH³,* which breaks up the phrase, detaching Jezreel from the clause and making it a vocative.

In MT, Jezreel (2:2) makes an inclusion with 1:3 to complete a section. If the day of Jezreel is a time of judgment (Isa 9:3) or disaster (Ps 137:7), Jezreel is the object of punishment, and the day is the time when the blood of Jezreel will be visited upon the house of Jehu, in line with 1:4. Such a note clashes with the tenor of 2:1–3.

The reference to Jezreel in 2:2 continues an extended pattern of inversion from 1:2 which is completed in 2:3. The names of the two younger children are reversed in 2:3 simply by removing the initial negative particle, *l':* thus Lo-Ammi becomes Ammi (the switch is anticipated in 2:1) and Lo-Ruhama becomes Ruhama. Since Jezreel is juxtaposed with the other two, it is reasonable to infer that although the name does not change, the import of it is transformed from a sign of judgment (1:4) to one of restoration and renewal, in conformity with its actual meaning "Let God sow" (cf. 2:25). This fits well with promises of national revival. Note also that Jer 31:27, which promises to repopulate the land by sowing it with people and animals, is directed to Israel and Judah together.

3. *you will say.* So far as content is concerned, 2:3 provides a fitting climax to the dramatic transformation from judgment and destruction proclaimed in c 1 to the restoration and renewal promised in 2:1–2. The reversal of the names of the two younger children brings the whole process to a conclusion.

If 2:3 completes a schematic presentation of judgment and death on the one hand, and redemption and new life on the other, it also serves as a transition to 2:4, which resumes the story of Hosea and his family (and Yahweh and his) at a particularly dramatic moment, and ultimately carries it through to a point which matches the climax in 2:3. Verses 24–25 bring together the three children in a manner reminiscent of and equivalent to 2:2–3. We may speak therefore of two major parts of cc 1–2: the division is between 2:3 and 2:4. Both parts are elaborations and explanations of the difficult but decisive verse 1:2 which initiated and summarized the prophet's call, commission, and career. Section one (1:3– 2:3) explains the matter in terms of the names of the children and their symbolic significance for the history of Israel in the immediate future and for the end time, through judgment to restoration, from death to resurrection. Section two (2:4–25) tells the same story in terms of the failed marriage, of Hosea and Gomer on the one hand, and of God and Israel on the other. Here the meaning, in personal and familial terms, of the ominous words of 1:2 is explicated in shocking detail; a scene of depravity and defection is adumbrated which is exceeded only by Ezekiel's presentation of the same experience in cc 16 and 23 of his book. In Hos 2:4–15 we have a vivid description of the private life of the prophet, as opposed to the public performance in 1:3–9. Here are the realities of a broken marriage and home, as against the formalities of a message symbolized by the names of the children of that marriage. That is followed by an account of the transformation indicated in 2:1–3, with the restoration of the people of Israel as the centerpiece of a universal renewal. Family and nation are joined through the children, whose names and fortunes are changed at the end to symbolize the transformation of nature and history, as in 2:1–3.

Section two presupposes section one, at least to the extent of establishing the cast of characters and the critical moment in the family life of the prophet when the implications of the ominous statement in 1:2 have become present reality. In 2:4, the wife, having already broken the compact of marriage, has now taken the seemingly irreversible and irremediable step of deserting her husband's bed to go after her lovers. At this moment the prophet makes a dramatic plea to their children to intervene, to carry his case to the absent mother. Here 2:3 provides a transition from section one to section two since the children are the subject of the climactic statement in 2:3. Almost instantly the picture of renewal is dissolved in a flashback, a return to a less happy occasion involving the children, when their names were as yet unchanged and they were cast in the somber role of accusers of an errant mother in behalf of a distraught father. From the great day of resurrection when the three children are united in joy, they are reminded and brought back to that other day, when the disruption and destruction of the family had been experienced and the bottom of the slide had been reached, when all the worst fears and expectations about the nations were in the process of being realized historically. It is from that point that 2:4–25 first fills in the picture of what happened to fulfill the words of 1:2 (in 2:4–15), and then goes on to describe the ultimate hope and renewal of family and national life (2:16–25).

The themes in 2:1–3 may be summarized.

2:1a The Israelites will be numerous
2:1b The designation or description will be changed
2:2a The Israelites will be united
2:2b The day is great
2:3   The names will be changed

The order of events is reversed chronologically: it is only when the favor of Yahweh is restored (the names are changed) (v 3) that all Israel can be united (v 2). It is only when they all come up from the land under one head (v 2) that the Israelites will be like the sands of the seashore (v 1). It is only at the end of the process that the children of Israel will become the children of the Living God.

The MT has an imperative verb in 2:3. The speaker is not identified, but the immediate antecedent is Jezreel, who alone is qualified by blood ties to call the other children brother and sister. The use of the plural form of the verb seems odd, especially if the subject is the oldest child, Jezreel, but this is consistent with the use of plural pronominal suffixes with the nouns, and the plural form of the nouns themselves: "Your brothers" and "your sisters." The consistent usage throughout the sentence confirms its correctness and probably means that the author wished to emphasize the social aspect; these symbolic names and persons are enlarged to encompass the whole nation, with all its people, innumerable as the sands on the seashore. Thus the plural forms also encompass the plural pronouns and nouns scattered throughout vv 1–2.

brothers . . . sisters. The singular nouns are found in some translations which derive from LXX, which has harmonized the text with c 1 by directing the reference to Hosea's individual children. The apparatus in BH³ makes everything singular by transferring the m of the plural pronoun suffix "your" to the following word, to make mēʿammî, "(one) of my people," as the name of "your brother" and *měruḥāmâ, "pitied" (Puʿal participle), as the name of "your sister." It caps the emendation by changing the first word to 'emōr, "say" (s). Every word in the verse is rewritten! MT should be retained as more difficult. The plurals are not likely to have developed from singulars; even LXX has plural pronouns. The plural verb can be explained if Jezreel represents a group, as do the others. The nation is now more obviously addressed.

The plural number is used throughout 2:1–3, continuing from 'attem in

1:9. "Brothers" and "sisters" in v 3 are congruent with the children of Judah and of Israel in v 2 and the several plurals in v 1. We hesitate to equate them, because each child seems to stand for the nation as a whole (both Judah and Israel together) in successive stages of their deteriorating relationship with Yahweh. Only the first oracle (1:4–5), with its reference to the house of Jehu, applies more narrowly to the northern kingdom. The second name is explained in terms of both kingdoms (Israel and Judah are specified in 1:6–7), and the third applies to all Israel because "my people" could hardly be used to refer to only part of the nation. The brothers to whom the new name "Ammi" is given in v 3 and the sisters who are now called "Ruhama" equally represent the whole nation. There is no easy solution to the problem posed by these near matches and we are reluctant even to be firmly vague.

II. DEFECTION AND RETRIBUTION: RECONCILIATION AND RENEWAL (2:4–25)

Desertion and discipline

The dissolute behavior of the wife

2:4 "Argue with your mother, argue
— for she is not my wife
and I am not her husband —
so that she remove her promiscuity from her face
and her adultery from between her breasts
5 lest I strip her naked,
and set her out as on the day of her birth,
lest I treat her as in the wilderness,
and deal with her as in the arid land
by killing her with thirst."
6 To her children I shall not show pity
because they are children of promiscuity.
7 Indeed, their mother was promiscuous,
the one who conceived them behaved shamefully
for she said, "Let me go after my lovers
who provide me with my bread and my water,
my wool and my flax,
my oil and my liquor."

The hoped-for repentance

8 Therefore, behold, I will hedge in your way with thornbushes,
and I will wall (her) in with its wall,
so that she cannot find her pathways.
9 When she pursues her lovers,
she will not overtake them.
When she seeks them,
she will not find (them).
Then she may say,

> "Let me go and return to my first husband,
> because it was better for me then than it is now."

The punishment and consequences

10 As for her, she didn't know
  that it was I who provided her
  with grain and must and oil,
  that I lavished silver upon her,
  and gold which they made into a Baal.

11 Therefore I will reverse myself
  and take back my grain in its time
  and my must in its season;
  and I will rescue my wool and my flax
  to uncover her nakedness.

12 Now I will expose her lewdness in the sight of her lovers
  but no one will rescue her from my power.

13 I shall put an end to all her merriment —
  her annual, monthly, and weekly celebrations —
  all her assemblies.

14 I shall lay waste her vines and her fig trees.
  Those of whom she said,
    "They are my wages, which my lovers paid me,"
    I shall consign them to the jungle,
    and wild animals of the countryside will devour them.

15 So shall I punish her for the time of the Baals
  to whom she burns incense
  when she decked herself with nose ring and necklace
  and went after her lovers — but me she forgot.
  Oracle of Yahweh.

Renewal and restoration

The new exodus

16 Therefore, behold, I am going to entice her.
  I will lead her through the wilderness
  and speak intimately to her.

17 Then I will assign to her there her vineyards
  and the Valley of Achor as a doorway of hope.
  May she respond there as in the time of her youth,
  as on the day she came up from the land of Egypt.

The end of Baal worship

18   It will happen on that day — Oracle of Yahweh —
you will call me Ishi[a]
and you will never again call me Baali.[b]

19   I shall remove the names of the Baals from her mouth;
never again will they be mentioned by their names.

Covenant and betrothal

20   I shall make for them a covenant on that day
with the wild animals of the countryside
and with the birds of the sky
and the reptiles of the ground.
Bow and sword and weapons of war
I shall destroy from the land.
I shall make them lie down in safety.

21   I shall betroth you to me forever.
I shall betroth you to me
with righteousness and with justice,
and with mercy and with pity.

22   I shall betroth you to me in faithfulness.
Then you shall know Yahweh.

Consummation: the great chorus

23   It will happen on that day
I will respond — Oracle of Yahweh —
I will respond to the skies
and they will indeed respond to the earth.

24   The earth will respond to the grain and must and oil
and they themselves will respond to Jezreel.

25   Then I shall sow her to me in the land
and I will have pity on Lo-Ruhama
and I will say to Lo-Ammi, "You are my people,"
and he will say, "My God."

[a] My man, viz. husband.
[b] My master/owner/lord/Baal. Cf. 2:25.

NOTES

2:4–5. The passage from 2:4 to the end of the chapter is a piece of sustained discourse, more prophetic in character than the blocks of narrative (Hos 1:2–2:3 and 3:1–5) in which it is set. The speech which begins in v 4 continues through v 5, a small unit within the larger structure. Its onset is marked by the abrupt change of mood between v 3 and v 4 and its end is marked by the change in personal reference between v 5 and v 6. The unit vv 4–5 has an internal design. It opens with a command to dispute with the mother (v 4aA), presuming her desertion (v 4aB). She is urged to renounce her adulterous behavior (v 4b). If she does not, the consequences described in v 5 will ensue. The structure in more detail is shown below.

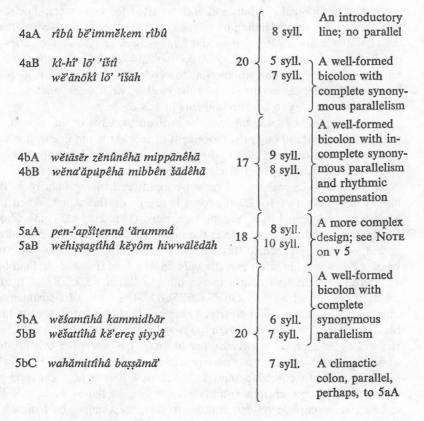

4aA	rîbû bĕ'immĕkem rîbû		8 syll.	An introductory line; no parallel
4aB	kî-hî' lō' 'ištî	20	5 syll.	A well-formed bicolon with complete synonymous parallelism
	wĕ'ānōkî lō' 'îšāh		7 syll.	
4bA	wĕtāsēr zĕnûnêhā mippānêhā	17	9 syll.	A well-formed bicolon with incomplete synonymous parallelism and rhythmic compensation
4bB	wĕna'ăpûpêhā mibbên šādêhā		8 syll.	
5aA	pen-'apšîṭennâ 'ărummâ	18	8 syll.	A more complex design; see NOTE on v 5
5aB	wĕhiṣṣagtîhâ kĕyôm hiwwālĕdāh		10 syll.	
5bA	wĕśamtîhâ kammidbār		6 syll.	A well-formed bicolon with complete synonymous parallelism
5bB	wĕšattîhâ kĕ'ereṣ ṣiyyâ	20	7 syll.	
5bC	wahămittîhâ baṣṣāmā'		7 syll.	A climactic colon, parallel, perhaps, to 5aA

218 HOSEA § II

The passage has the syntax of poetry rather than prose, for it does not use *'ēt*, and it has the suffixed pronoun object five times in v 5, where it might have used *'ōtāh*. But it is not classical poetry. The string of verb-initial clauses, with *waw*-consecutive, indicates prose discourse.

The poetic features realized by means of typical parallelism are not matched by regularities in rhythm. The lines in each of the four bicola, however, are of comparable length; length is measured above by syllables rather than by stresses or words. The major constituents are also arranged in an impressive symmetry. The opening line is followed in v 4 by two bicola making a five-colon unit equivalent to v 5, which also contains five cola. Line length varies but the totals of the two units are almost identical.

The first major section of the book (1:3 – 2:3) presents a formal aspect of Hosea's message, bound up with the symbolic names of his children, first in a threatening sense and then as signifying the final redemption of Israel. The second section (2:4–25) presents realities behind formalities, i.e. an account of Hosea's family experience interwoven with the experience of Yahweh and his people. It begins at a critical time, after the wife has finally abandoned her husband and departed for her lovers. The section reviews the events leading up to the crisis and then looks beyond it to the repentance and restoration of the family-community and the renewal of all things. Thus the opening of section 2:4–25 has the effect of a reprise, going back to the situation at the end of c 1. Hos 2:4 also goes back to 1:2 and picks up the story of the mother, who is not mentioned in 2:1–3, and who plays a background role in 1:3–9.

In trying to find our way through the intricate patterns of this discourse, we must note that although the movement of thought is not linear, it is not haphazard. The central figure is the mother; so far, no details have been given of her behavior. Her fall and restoration must now be described in detail. Verses 4–15 make sense on a personal level, not primarily as the history of Israel; in vv 16–25, the focus is mainly on the nation. When the woman is transformed by a "second" marriage (Hos 2:21–22), the whole family is renewed. Jezreel reverses the names of the two younger children in 2:3, and the response to this comes in 2:24b. In conclusion, the husband (Yahweh) himself sows his wife in the land for a new firstborn (2:25aA), assigns new names to the other children (2:25aB, bA), and finally is acclaimed as "my God" (2:25bB). The form of reinstatement implied by 2:4–25 is rather elusive. There is a hint of divorce, yet the husband continues to treat her as a wayward wife. Hos 2:9 suggests that she will come back home because her husband has made her evil life too harsh for her by the severe measures described in 2:5–15. Hos 2:16 speaks of a fresh courtship, and 2:21–22 describes a new engagement. These three images are not entirely compatible, so the ideas in the discourse resist complete systematization; further, they cannot be handled in the legal categories of Israelite family law, even though marriage customs provide the background.

2:4. *Argue.* The command to argue is addressed to Hosea's children. Since they "represent" Israel, and their mother also "represents" Israel, we have here a dialogue going on within the covenant community, one part reproaching another. We do not have to identify a "faithful remnant" rebuking an apostate segment. The children are in jeopardy along with their mother (2:6). They speak on behalf of their father, but their own interests are at stake in the fate of the mother.

The common translation "plead with your mother" (*KJV, RSV,* etc.) presents difficulties. The verb *rîb* never describes an appeal or call to repentance, but always a hostile confrontation, an accusation. It refers to an angry quarrel or altercation, in any situation, with more formal application to disputation in a court of law (Gemser 1955). The verb can mean to lay charges, denounce, bring evidence, argue a case, viz. the actions of the *aggrieved* party. The situation here is atypical: the children have a grievance, but it is their father's complaint, not their own, that is lodged. This throws even more suspicion on the unusual use of the preposition *b* "with (your mother)." In juridical contexts, *rîb* is used with several prepositions, relating the *dramatis personae* of the situation. You argue your case (object marked by *'et, nota accusativi*) before (*'el*) a judge, concerning (*'al*) some issue, on behalf of (*l*) some third party, against (*'et* or *'im*) some miscreant. The preposition *b* is used with *rîb* only here and in Judg 6:32 (Baal versus Gideon) and Gen 31:36 (Jacob versus Laban), both hostile encounters. The children are not brought into the picture to arouse their mother's better feelings; there is no appeal to motherly instincts. They symbolize the fact that relationships have broken down, but they are not merely agents to deliver the message. They are involved.

We need not suppose that any trial was held. There is no invocation of adjudicators, as in Isa 1:2; Mic 6:1, etc. unless they appear in 2:23. There is no summons to witnesses, no invitation to defend the charge, no appeal to a vindicator. The husband takes the law into his own hands, it would seem. A legal note is certainly present, but the juridical framework is neither rigid nor realistic. (Note the form-critical difficulties encountered by Gemser 1955:129.) A wrong has been done, a penalty incurred. The speech is full of recriminations, and punishments are threatened. But the way remains open for forgiveness, a possibility beyond law. We remember that death was the penalty for adultery. The laws of marriage are intersected here by the provisions of the covenant between Yahweh and Israel. The broken covenant could be mended because Yahweh's love was stronger than his wrath. It is this theological reality that transforms the message of doom in 2:4–15 into the message of salvation in 2:16–25. But since, for Hosea, salvation comes through punishment, the negative and positive actions (rejection and acceptance as contradictory attitudes existing simultaneously in the mind of the husband) are closely interwoven. The language of litigation is used to bring out the contractual and inviolable relationship between husband and wife. Hosea's marriage was grounded in both law and love, and so was Yahweh's covenant with Israel. The relationships cannot be reduced to either category alone. Both pervade 2:4–25 in a way that resists analysis. Heartbreak and moral outrage are mingled in Hosea's and Yahweh's feelings. But while marriage and covenant overlap in both love and law, the analogy does not consist in a complete set of perfect correspondences. Some of the ideas apply mainly to Hosea and Gomer; some apply best to Yahweh and Israel; many make good sense in both sets. But the limitations restrain us from pushing analogies to explain difficult passages. The demand to renounce adulterous behavior (v 4b) applies literally to the woman, figuratively to the nation. The threat to strip the recalcitrant woman naked applies to Gomer, but also, in a sense to the nation, especially if it describes the denudation of the countryside. The threat to kill with thirst could apply to both wife and nation, expulsion from the home matching ejection from the land of promise. This double meaning continues all through 2:4–25, now one side, now the other, being uppermost.

Why doesn't the husband take up the dispute himself in 2:4–15? The indirect approach adopted resembles the detachment of Yahweh, who speaks to his people only through prophets. Only once (in v 8) do we hear a fleeting word of direct address by the husband to the wife. Otherwise the husband speaks about her, obliquely, reflecting the physical fact of their separation. Hos 3:3 is the only report we have of a conversation between Hosea and Gomer. This suits the public importance of the prophet's marriage as a paradigm of the covenant. Hos 2:4–25 makes sense if Hosea is describing to the people what he will do; but it is also an oracle of Yahweh. If Hosea spoke personally to his wife, it would be difficult to see the whole speech as applying equally to his Israelite listeners. The technique of indirect communication is similar to that in Isa 5:1–7. The fact that the speech is almost a soliloquy removes it from the formal court setting.

If something more realistic is required, the task assigned to the children could arise from the fact that the parents are separated. Hos 2:7 coupled with 2:15 indicates that the wife has left the husband. In these circumstances the statement "She is not my wife and I am not her husband" could be an acknowledgment of this fact, although it is not a divorce formula. It means, "We are no longer living together as husband and wife." Thus the children must take up the matter with their mother. In purely human terms, the violent language used in v 5 discloses a state of mind in which a personal meeting between the man and his wife would be unendurable. This is not the calm reasoning in which a person would state his case to a court; in fact, there is an element of fantasy in much of 2:4–25. The wife should understand that there can be no further dealings with her husband until she can show convincing proof of a change of conduct and of heart.

The repetition of the verb makes the passage more emotional, less forensic (cf. Isa 40:1 for a similar construction). Apart from the verb, which can bear a technical meaning, the ensuing discourse does not reflect courtroom language. This word alone is not enough to shape the rest of the speech. Hence we do not translate "to accuse" or "to bring to the bar," for what follows is a bid for reconciliation, not the enforcement of criminal law.

your mother. This shows that the children are being addressed. The pronoun is plural, as in v 3. It is curious that Hosea, if he is the speaker, does not call her "my wife." This highlights the indissoluble relationship between mother and children, in contrast with that of husband and wife.

not my wife. The negatives *lō' 'ištî* and *lō' îšāh* put wife and husband on the same footing as the second and third child with their negative names. The formulation is balanced. There is a reciprocal severance of the relationship, which seems to be final, just as "Not-My-People" (1:9) seems to dissolve the covenant. But this cannot be so. The prime fact is the wife's desertion and adultery, a combination worse than either alone. Divorce is no solution. Since a close analogy is drawn between Hosea's relationship to Gomer, and Yahweh's relationship to Israel, the doubly negative couplet in 2:4 and the doubly negative couplet in 1:9 must be interpreted along similar lines. In a formal grammatical sense their structures are identical. Hos 1:9 cannot simply be an announcement by Yahweh of formal dissolution of the covenant comparable to a divorce. The covenant nowhere makes provision for such an eventuality. Covenant-breaking on the part of Israel (unilateral withdrawal) calls for severe punishment. Israel cannot opt out by no longer acknowledging Yahweh. The punishment is not an expression of a broken relationship. On the contrary, it is enforced within the relationship; punishment maintains the covenant. Similarly Hosea's threats of punishment are proof that his marriage continues. The corrective discipline expresses his authority over his wife, and his continuing claim upon her. The husband does not take any initiative to dissolve the marriage. That, rather, is what the wife has already done by her conduct. This could explain why Hosea does not take the initiative himself in argument; he is not engaged in litigation against his wife. (But note that in 4:1, Yahweh does have a suit against Israel.) This helps us to see how complex is the answer to the related questions, "Was there a divorce or not? Was the covenant dissolved or not?" From the wife's side (Israel's) the relationship was severed; from Hosea's (Yahweh's) it was not. In 2:4–25 the woman is treated as not his wife in practice and yet still his wife in principle.

It is not possible to fit the clean break of a divorce in with the other things that are happening in this discourse. The expectation of a new courtship, engagement, and marriage outlined in 2:16–22 certainly suggests that Hosea (Yahweh) will begin all over again. But neither the mending of a broken relationship within marriage nor remarriage after divorce could ever be spoken of in such terms. Hos 2:16–22 requires miraculous transformation into a first marriage "as in the time of her youth" (v 17). Here we go beyond historical realities.

Remarriage after divorce does not provide any basis for the continued dealings of the husband with the wife which occupy the greater part of c 2. It is as a husband who still has claims on his wife that he applies the various disciplines and makes the appeals. Adultery was a capital crime (*zimmâ*, Job 31:11, Pope 1973:231–232), both guilty parties to be executed (Lev 20:10; Deut 22:22). Death is threatened here (v 5). Divorce is not ruled out by the fact that remarriage to the same man after divorce was illegal according to Deut 24:1–4, since that applied only when there was an intervening marriage by the woman. That regulation was designed to discourage casual temporary alliances under the guise of marriage, but this does not apply to Gomer's situation. Jeremiah 3:1–14 shows that Yahweh saw no difficulty in overriding such legalities in order to remarry his divorced Israel. Since Jeremiah 3 shows the influence of Hosea, its clear statement that Yahweh divorced Israel (Jer 3:8), the northern kingdom, could be used as evidence that Hos 2:4 is the declaration embodied in the bill of divorce (Hendriks n.d.). Isaiah 50:1 contains another tradition; it implies that there never was a divorce. The phrase "my first husband" (Hos 2:9) does not necessarily mean that the woman now had a second husband. If she had remarried, her relationships would no longer be adultery against Hosea. The original husband would have no grounds for disciplining her or for unmasking her lovers. This is the main obstacle in the way of identifying the statement in 2:4a as an act of divorce. That would be the end of the story. There would be no basis for all that follows. But in 2:6–15 the lovers remain "lovers." Hos 2:9 suggests that the "first husband" was still her husband. She had deserted him, but he had not renounced her. Her amours continue to be adultery against him; 2:4–15 treats her as an adulterous *wife*, not simply as a promiscuous woman.

Our inability to fit the events of 2:4–25 into what we know of Israel's marriage laws is a further reason for doubting that v 4 records a court action, let alone a divorce. It remains a personal matter between the hus-

I. Middle Bronze Age Limestone Stele of a Syrian Weather God, the so-called Baal of the Lightning. The god holds a club over his head and rests his lightning-lance on the ground. There is a tiny worshipper to the right of the god, who is one manifestation of the Syrian Baal, Hadad. Ugarit (Syria). Dated MB I (Schaeffer); MB II (Albright).

II. Eighth century Basalt Stele of a
Syrian Weather God. The god stands
upon a bull with lightning-forks in
both hands; his headdress has horns.
The deity is a form of the Syrian Baal,
Hadad. Arslan Tash (Turkey). Dated
to the reign of Tiglath-pileser III
(744–727).

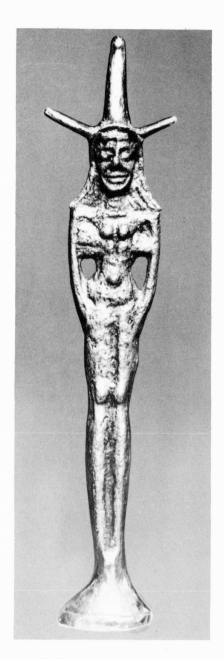 

III. *Left:* Casting from a Middle Bronze Age Figurine Mold of a Canaanite Goddess. The deity may be Asherah; the headdress is horned. Nahariya (Israel). Associated with a Middle Bronze II A-B cultic complex.

IV. *Right:* Late Bronze Age Terra-cotta Figurine of a Syrian Goddess. The deity may be Astarte. Syria. Dated to the Late Bronze Age (1500–1200).

V. Neo-Assyrian Relief of a Lion and Lioness below a Vine-twined Tree, near a Lily. Nineveh (modern Kuyunjik, Iraq) from the North Palace of Ashurbanipal (668–627).

VI. Modern Drawing of a Neo-Assyrian Relief of Gods Being Removed as Booty. The first two statues represent goddesses on high chairs; the third shows a god in a box and the fourth a weather deity with ax and thunderbolt, wearing a horned headdress. Kalḫu (biblical Calah, modern Nimrud, Iraq) from the Southwest Palace of Esarhaddon. The original may have been transferred to Esarhaddon's Palace from the Central Palace of Tiglath-pileser III to whose reign (744–727) it dates. The relief has been severely damaged in modern times, but survives in part (as two pieces in the British Museum).

band and wife, even though the contact between them is indirect. As in later parts of the prophecy, there is an ambivalence in Yahweh's feelings toward Israel. On the one hand, anger and revulsion move against her depravity with the severest penalties; on the other hand, there is compassion and undiminished desire to have and to love. The power of Hosea's theology is felt in this incandescent experience. It cannot be put into a formula; the forms of legal discourse cannot convey it. The speech must not be forced into the straitjacket of form criticism. Wolff (1974:31–33) thinks that court proceedings provide the setting for all the sayings in 2:4–17, although he calls it a "kerygmatic unit." He attributes the confusion to the changing roles of Yahweh as "plaintiff, judge, executioner of punishment and arbitrator all in one person" (p. 32). This misses the point. Yahweh's role is the same as Hosea's — husband.

A further difficulty in Hos 2:4a is the involvement of the children, if these are divorce proceedings. Note, however, that in Isa 50:1 it is the children who are asked about their mother's marital status. Wolff suggests that "the deceived husband brings his children forward to confirm his accusation" (p. 32). But, if *rîbû* means "accuse," as he says, their part is more direct, and the husband does not himself accuse. And why should the children be specially qualified to bear out the charges? Were they eyewitnesses of their mother's adulteries?

Verse 4b proceeds with exhortations as if every effort will be made to preserve and repair the marriage. It is inconceivable that such words would be addressed to a woman who has just been divorced. The energetic measures to be taken against the woman are all based on the assumption that the man still has a claim on her as her husband, and that he has a right to do these things to her as his wife. If there is something legal in the declarations in v 4a, it could be an assertion that they are truly husband and wife. If *kî* is correctly translated "for" and not "that," then it gives the reason *why* the children are to argue with their mother; it does not say *what* they are to say when they argue with her. As such it is not an announcement of a decision the husband has reached, that is, to divorce her, but a statement of the facts on which action must be based.

With respect to the assertions of 2:4a there are two possibilities. If the particle *lō'* is negative, as we believe, then the statement is realistic in the sense that the marriage is broken, because the wife has not only engaged in adulterous relations, but has abandoned her husband for one or more lovers. Legally the two remain husband and wife.

On the other hand, if the *lō'* is positive or asseverative, then the statement is an emphatic affirmation that in spite of the wife's misbehavior and desertion, they are still married, and that the husband continues to insist upon his rights, responsibilities, and claims in the situation. The woman's actions are so serious as to preclude divorce as a method of resolving the crisis. What she has done is criminal and subject to trial and determination of guilt: the penalty for adultery under the Mosaic Code is not divorce but death.

Whichever way we interpret the particle *lō'*, these points seem certain: there have been no formal proceedings and no legal divorce. The situation involves an errant wife and an offended husband; the issue and the crime between them is the adulterous behavior of the wife, compounded with desertion on her part.

promiscuity . . . adultery. The marriage bond, never relinquished by Hosea (the covenant bond never relaxed by Yahweh) provides the basis for the next step toward rebuilding the marriage. It is, in fact, an invitation, a command, to repent. Israel constantly received such messages from Yahweh, part pleading, part threatening. Gomer (Israel) is to put away her promiscuity (*zěnûnîm*). This is paralleled by the word *na'ǎpûpîm,* "adulteries," a curious word derived from the familiar root *n'p,* "to commit adultery." Verbs based on the same roots are used in parallel twice in 4:13–14, and in the same poetic sequence. Because of its derivation from the root *zny, zěnûnîm* is somewhat ambiguous; it could refer to any kind of forbidden sexual activity. In parallel with *na'ǎpûpîm,* however, it is defined as sexual misbehavior that violates the bonds of marriage: in a word, adultery. Hos 2:4 is the only occurrence of the form with the duplication of *p,* evidently an imitation of the doubling of *n* in *zěnûnîm.* The word could be a coinage of Hosea. A somewhat similar word, *ni'ûpîm,* occurs in Jer 13:27 and Ezek 23:43. Both passages have affinities with the Hosea tradition, and may be more directly related.

The removal of promiscuities from the woman's face and adulteries from between her breasts could be a dramatic and vivid way of advising her to abandon her conduct. But the references to body parts suggest something more physical, something which identified her as available, and whose removal would signify her rejection of such a status. It is not likely that the *na'ǎpûpîm* between her breasts refer to lovers as such. Since prostitutes painted their faces (Jer 4:30; Ezek 23:40) such adornment might explain the reference to her face. A bunch of myrrh between the breasts (Cant 1:13) suggests an aphrodisiac. More specific information about the dress and ornaments is hard to find. In the present case, marks of devotion to Baal are more likely than the signs of a common woman of the streets, although Gomer is never called a *qědēšâ* (cf. 4:14). The *NEB* translation "forswear those wanton looks" suggests that it is the face itself that is sinful. The following reference to her breasts would then refer to profanation of sacred sexual intimacies. The whole matter should be taken more literally — she is to set aside the badges of her profession, something on her face, something between her breasts. The usual translation of Gen 38:15

("He thought she was a prostitute *because* her face was covered") suggests that an ordinary woman would not wear a veil. The *kî* could be concessive ("even though"), i.e. a prostitute did not wear the veil usual for a married woman in public. In Assyria prostitutes were not to be veiled (*ANET* 183). But customs varied and the matter is complicated by the existence of several classes of sacred women, and differing customs connected with marriage. A hint that some kind of adornment is intended in 2:4a is given by 2:15. She wore a nose ring and a pendant. These were put on in connection with going off after lovers, and they are described with so much disapproval that they can hardly be the usual attire of a good woman. The *JB* suggests tattooing as well as amulets. Cosmetics would be easier to remove than tattoo marks. The threat in v 5 strengthens our suspicion that Hosea has material adornments in mind. If she does not voluntarily remove the shameful tokens, then her irate husband will himself tear them off.

5. *lest*. The conjunction governs five clauses, threatening the wife with punishments of mounting severity. There is one imperfect verb followed by four consecutive future (perfect) verbs. The parallelism is so marked that the usual meaning of actions in sequence is neutralized. The first pair of clauses threatens the woman with public stripping, the next pair describes leaving her naked in the desert. The fifth is unpaired and climactic. The husband will leave her to die, helpless and exposed as in her natal condition, a reversion to the state described in Ezekiel 16, a closely related passage.

strip. The parallel verb *hiṣṣagtî* has a general meaning of "to set, place," but in Job 17:6 it means to expose to ridicule. This meaning is not parallel to "to strip," but it explains the purpose of this action (Greengus 1969). She will be stripped so as to exhibit her in shame. The last phrase of v 5a is a delayed modifier of "naked." The bicolon means, "I shall strip her and display her in public, as naked as the day she was born"; cf. Ezek 16:1–5. The parallel references to shameful nakedness in vv 11b and 12a make it clear that more is involved here than just indecent exposure. Wolff sees the undressing of the wife as part of a supposed divorce ceremonial. There is a great deal about stripping bare in Ezekiel 16 and 23, yet there is no question of divorce in those chapters.

day. Most of Hos 2:5a applies best to the woman, while 2:5b applies best to the people. "The day of her birth" could apply to both and represent the point where the language changes focus. The "day" of the nation's birth then matches the day of coming up from Egypt (Hos 2:17). In Ezekiel 16, the story begins on the natal day of the girl whom Yahweh found and made his wife.

as in the wilderness. Literally, "like the wilderness." The comparison of a fertile wife with a fruitful field is widespread in the ancient Near East; in complementary fashion, the penis is sometimes likened to a plow and the word "seed" is used for all kinds of planting. A desolate wife could be compared with land that has reverted to desert. Hence many interpreters translate "And I will turn her into desert" (Ginsberg 1971:1011). But this does not provide the proper setting for the imagery of the Exodus. It is better to explain the text as referring to putting the woman back into the condition in which she lived during the desert experience; cf. Ps 95:8; Hos 2:16–17. See the further discussion of *šm* in the NOTES on v 14b. The reference to the desert in 2:16 paints the same picture — taking Israel back into the desert of the ancient wanderings, not to kill her with thirst, but to court and woo her. The desert had two aspects. It was a place of discipline and a stage on the way to the promised land.

deal with her as in the arid land. *Št* is a synonym of *šm.* In an Ugaritic text (*UT* 68:27–28) the total destruction of an enemy is described by three verbs of mounting intensity; *št* is the second of the series.

There are several reasons for believing that this is not a simile for large-scale destruction. The *'ereṣ ṣiyyâ* is not just any arid tract, but *the* desert of Israel's memory, the locus of Yahweh's definitive dealings with them. The phrase itself occurs not in the Pentateuch, but in the poetic traditions which survive in the Psalter and were used by the prophets. Of fifteen occurrences of *ṣiyyâ,* all in poetry, nine occur in the phrase *'ereṣ ṣiyyâ.* Jeremiah, who of all the prophets generally stands closest to Hosea, uses *'ereṣ ṣiyyâ* unmistakably as a name for the scene of the wilderness journey (Jer 2:6). The words occur in the poetic context of Ezek 19:13. The phrase is not a symbol of desolation as such, but of discipline. In the present context to be put back into the desert (or to revert to the desert phase of national history) is to be expelled from the promised land.

The target of Hosea's threats is not so much the land as the people. In his vocabulary *hā'āreṣ* means *yōšĕbê hā'āreṣ.* Wolff (1974:34) finds a close connection between Hosea's allegory and Canaanite mythology by equating the wife with the land and the children with its inhabitants (offspring of union between the god of heaven and the earth mother). The distinction can hardly be maintained with any consistency in the text of Hosea, however. Hos 2:16 makes it clear that Israel is to be taken back to the desert, to recapitulate the Exodus. It is not because she is *like* the desert, but because she is *in* the desert, that she will die of thirst. Here again Hosea and Jeremiah use the same idioms — the *Hip'il* of *hlk* (Hos 2:16; Jer 2:6).

killing her. The experience of thirst in the desert wanderings left a deep mark in Israel's memories. Some of the most severe times of testing and rebellious murmurings against Yahweh were associated with this dire lack of water. There are two stories of Yahweh's miraculous provision (Exod 17:1–7; Num 20:2–13), and later poets often referred to these acts as signal proofs of Yahweh's capacity for responsive love. The threat to kill with thirst applies to a person or a people, not a land, and evokes memories of Exod 17:3 and 32:12. On the first of these occasions Israel accused Yahweh of bringing them up from Egypt "to *kill* me and my children and my animals *with thirst*," exactly the words used here. Compared with this, the measures threatened against the wife in the ensuing verses are less severe, dealing only with her possessions and circumstances. A climax is reached in v 5.

6–7. These verses comprise another unit dealing with the children and the mother together, with its own symmetrical structure, exhibiting that blending of poetry and prose which characterizes the composition of this chapter.

6a	*wĕ'et-bānêhā lō' 'ăraḥēm*	9 syllables	
6b	*kî-bĕnê zĕnûnîm hēmmâ*	8 syllables	
7aA	*kî zānĕtâ 'immām*	6 syllables	A well-formed bicolon,
7aB	*hōbîšâ hôrātām*	6 syllables	complete synonymous
7bA	*kî 'āmĕrâ*	4 syllables	parallelism
7bB	*'ēlĕkâ 'aḥărê mĕ'ahăbay*	9 syllables	
	nōtĕnê laḥmî ûmêmay	8 syllables	
	*ṣamrî *ûpištay*	5 syllables	
	šamnî wĕšiqqûyāy	6 syllables	

Verse 7b is prosaic, although the arrangement of six items in three pairs has parallelism, rhythm, and rhyme; this half-verse has a key function because of its thematic connections with other parts of the discourse. The unit falls into two parts: vv 6–7a, a third-person discussion of the woman and her children, and v 7b, a first-person soliloquy by the woman about her lovers and their gifts. If *kî 'āmĕrâ* is taken as transitional, the remainder of v 7b is roughly the same length (twenty-eight syllables) as the preceding material in vv 6 and 7a (twenty-nine syllables).

The use of *bānîm* for "children" rather than *yĕlādîm* is scarcely significant; daughters would be included in either case. In contrast to 2:1–3, where the children are given good names, and to 2:4, where they are ranged on their father's side against their mother, the children are here once more denied love, as in 1:7. The use of the same word (*'ăraḥēm*) shows that the theme of 1:6–7 reappears here.

In 2:6–7, mother and children are dealt with together. Although the children are mentioned first in v 6, there are several indications that they come into the picture only in relation to her: (1) In general the mother is more prominent than the children in 2:4–25. (2) The designation "her children" rather than "my children" links them with her. (3) The clause pattern in 2:6a, with the object preceding the verb, joins this clause more closely to the preceding text, and places "her children" in a concomitant relationship with a preceding object, obviously the mother. The identity of

the subject "I" of the verbs is another continuity between v 5 and v 6a.
(4) The reason given for this denial of love is that they are children of
promiscuity (v 6b). They are not themselves promiscuous but are "disgraced . . . by a mother who has become morally degraded" (Waterman
1955:102). Wolff, however, thinks that v 6 proves that the children were
equally "guilty of whoredom" (1974:34). (5) The word *zĕnûnîm,* which
occurs twice in 1:2, turns up twice here also. In v 4 it refers to the
mother; in v 6 to the children. (6) The minor role of the children and the
indirectness of the label referring to them are shown also by the fact that
no exhortation or threat is directed to them, as to the mother in vv 4 and
5. From v 7 onward attention is directed wholly to the mother. This
makes it clear that even in 1:7 the daughter was given the name "not
loved," not to describe her personal relationship to her father, but because
of Israel's (her mother's) forfeiture of love. Birth names often record the
parents' experience rather than characteristics of the child; later on the
person could take up a new experience name.

Because the mother is to blame, not the children, the reproaches and
pleas of 2:4–15 are directed solely to her. The children are mentioned in
v 6 only to carry the focus back to her in v 7. She has sinned not only
against her husband but against her children as well, and they will bear
the consequences of her conduct.

Another connection between vv 5 and 6 is supplied by the desert motif.
The parents died for the desert rebellions, but the children were spared
(Deut 1:39–40). Now the children are also rejected. Note "me and my
children" in Exod 17:3.

6. *they.* The third party to the proceedings is identified by the pronoun
hmh. Just as the wife is identified by *hy'* (the Not-Wife) and the husband
by *'nky* (the Not-Husband), so the children are identified by *hmh.*

The three pronouns are repeated later in the section, and in each case
the connection and the identification with the earlier usage is significant:
hy' and *'nky* in v 10, and *hmh* in v 14.

7. *their mother.* There is no hint in 1:2–9 as to when Gomer began
to be unfaithful. Because she is identified as promiscuous from the
outset (1:2), she could have been such literally, but we have shown that
this is not the meaning of the phrase, that it is not likely on general
grounds, and that other passages are better understood if the misbehavior
began after marriage. The statement that "their mother" (not "my wife")
became promiscuous, seems to connect her motherhood with promiscuity,
as if she became a mother in that fashion and this could be why the children are called children of promiscuity. We have, however, found no
proof of the former, and have advanced an alternative explanation of the
latter. Her belief that the children were her lovers' payment to her for her
sexual services (2:14) could suggest that they were the product of her

promiscuity. Even if we associate her sexual activity with the fertility cult and the worship of Baal, it does not follow that the children were born of copulating at the pagan shrines, or that the connection between fertility in marriage and devotion to the god was understood in that fashion. There is no reason to doubt that Canaanites who were wholehearted worshipers of Baal enjoyed normal marital relationships. It is often assumed that the "holy" prostitutes (compare qĕdēšôt in 4:14) dedicated their sexuality exclusively to the gods; but we are talking here about the people at large. Baal worship was intended to enhance all sex life. Children conceived in wedlock were his gifts. The cult was intended to foster fertile *marriages,* not to turn the country into a *brothel.* The cult equally promoted abundant crops, through normal farming (2:7b). Waterman (1955:103), working from the case of Hannah (I Sam 1:22–28), suggests that a nursing mother stayed away from the shrines, so that if the pregnancies followed weanings, Gomer was not involved in the cult until after the third child was weaned.

The question remains obscure, but apart from the possible bearing of the names themselves, there is no suggestion of impropriety or illegitimacy in connection with the birth of the children. On the contrary, the implication of 2:6–7 is that promiscuity came later.

shamefully. The vocabulary of vv 6 and 7 is in chiasm: no *pity* . . . *promiscuity . . . promiscuous . . . shame.* The woman became an object of shame (Klopfenstein 1972), although there is no indication that the woman felt ashamed. The *Hip'il* verb does not make sense here in either of its usual meanings — causative ("to put to shame"), for it has no object, or stative ("to be ashamed"). The verb here must have active force and is best rendered: "she did something shameful," or possibly "she became (utterly) shameful" (elative *Hip'il*). While the *Hip'il* in Jer 8:12 is used with the meaning "to feel ashamed of oneself," in Jer 50:12 the *Qal* is used in a parallel that suggests ignominy. The latter has *'immĕkem* in parallel with *yōladtĕkem.* Wisdom literature has much to say about the ill repute of prostitutes. Just as a son of shame (*ben-mēbîš*), one who does something shameful, contrasts with a proficient son (*ben-maśkîl*) (Prov 10:5), so a wife of shame (who is like rot in her husband's bones) is the opposite of the *'ēšet-ḥayil,* the "virtuous woman" (Prov 12:4), who is chiefly celebrated for the public honor she brings to her husband (Prov 31:10–29). In the context of Hos 2:6–7 the implication is that the promiscuous mother has disgraced her children along with herself. Hosea's complaint on behalf of Yahweh is not simply that Israel has become ignominious; worse, she has profaned him by her conduct.

for she said. The scope and motivation of the promiscuity is set forth in narrative material found in 2:7b–15. The end of v 15a forms an inclusion with v 7b, embracing the material in vv 8–15a, which explains and elaborates the terse statement in 7b + 15a: "For she said, 'Let me go after my lovers,' . . . and she went after her lovers." The perfect verb *'āmĕrâ*, "she said," in v 7b suggests a definite resolution, carried out in v 15a, rather than continuous or habitual action.

There is no need to force the allegory at this point by trying to find some catastrophic event in Israel's history to correspond to this radical breach of the covenant relationship. The story of Hosea and Gomer has its own reality, which does not match the story of Yahweh and Israel in every detail. Because the language "Let me go after my lovers" implies permanent desertion, it could mean irrevocable enlistment in the cult, making it impossible for her to go on living with Hosea, a faithful Yahwist. Fleming James (1947:242) suggests that her desertion depicted "Israel's coming exile," but Israel did not go into exile as an act of desertion; she was forced out by Yahweh. No such ejection by Hosea figures in this story. Her act was voluntary, corresponding to (and, indeed, manifesting) Israel's apostasy in the land. Until we reach c 3 no action of the husband is recorded; c 2 records only threats. According to 2:7b, it was not only her action, but her rationale that infuriated her husband. "She said" to herself; she thought it out. Her moral fault is the result of a theological error, of considered preference for another.

after. The preposition used here is the counterpart of "being promiscuous away from Yahweh" (1:2). Elsewhere other prepositions are used — "from under" (4:12), "from beside" (9:1).

my lovers. The Pi'el *mĕ'ahăbîm*, used here for the lovers of an adulteress, is found almost exclusively in Hosea and in passages (mainly in Jeremiah and Ezekiel) influenced by Hosea. It always occurs in the plural, which suggests a multiplicity of liaisons, promiscuity. The singular term of 3:1 notwithstanding, the consistent plural seems to suggest other plurals — the Baals of 2:15,19, the idols of 4:17. These plurals resemble the standard plural word for God (*'ĕlōhîm*), and so are an imitating name for Baal himself as the anti-Yahweh. In 3:1 the single figure is connected with the "other gods" of apostate Israelites (May 1931–32).

On the human level the woman probably had relations with many men. These acts were inseparable from involvement in the Baal cult, but how the lovers were related to Baal is not explained. The impression is gained that, however conscientiously the worshipers believed in the seriousness and importance of what they were doing, the availability of women for intercourse could not be protected by the sanctities of the cult from degenerating into unbridled licentiousness; cf. Jer 2:20–28.

who provide me. Literally "the givers," a participle in apposition with "lovers." This line reveals the motive for Baal worship and the fundamental misunderstanding that Baal was the great benefactor. The motive was cupidity, the desire for material goods (Gen 28:20). Canaanite religion offered people more apparent control over their own well-being, for the provision of food and clothing was guaranteed by manipulation of divine powers through quasi-magical fertility rites. We find repeatedly a connection between sexual activity and sorcery; that is how Canaanite religion worked. The remedy for this faulty thinking is a deep conviction that Yahweh has sole power over life and death, and over all natural productivity. The chastisements described in 2:7–15 are intended to bring this truth home to those who have "forgotten" Yahweh (2:15b). The verb *ntn*, "to give," often means "to pay," and we could have translated it that way here because, in the context, a reward for sexual services is more likely to be in mind than any thought that Baal gives out of pure generosity, without requiring services in return. Here is another basic difference between the two religions. Service to Yahweh is an expression of gratitude for his free gifts, not an attempt to coerce him into giving.

The use of the participle has another effect. Hymns of praise to Yahweh recited his mighty acts and characteristic deeds. They often consisted of a list of achievements, almost like titles, in the form of participle constructions; I Sam 2:6–8 and Ps 103:3–5 are examples. One such ascription, which goes back to the Wilderness period (Exod 16:29; cf. Deut 8:18), calls Yahweh *nōtēn leḥem*, "giver of bread" (Pss 136:25; 146:7; etc.). The countercreed here cited thus involved a denial of one of the most basic articles of Israel's faith.

In one of the few statements about the prices charged by prostitutes, Prov 6:26 cites "a loaf of bread," with the suggestion that it is less than the going rate. The verb *ntn* is met in Tamar's question to Judah, "What will you pay (give) me, when you have intercourse with me?" (Gen 38:16), a rare glimpse of a man and a prostitute discussing terms. His prompt offer and her ready acceptance suggest that "a kid from the flock" was the standard price, and that Judah acted from knowledge. It illustrates, furthermore, payment in kind, as in Hosea.

my. The participle *ntny* governs a long list of nouns with 1 cg s suffixes. The construct relationship shows they mean "my givers of bread," etc., or rather, "givers of bread so that it becomes mine," etc.

The possessive pronoun, repeated with each noun, brings out the woman's acquisitiveness. In other occurrences of *ntn* in this discourse (2:10,14,17), the receiver is indicated in the usual way by means of the preposition *l.* Kuhnigk (1974:10–13) reasonably suggests that the suffixes with the nouns here serve the same purpose, and describes them as "dative." This solves the problem of ownership, since the real donor refers to "my wool and my flax," etc. in v 11. Another explanation is possible, however. The error in the statement made by the woman in v 7b is twofold. Yahweh is the sole giver of everything, but he never ceases to be the owner of everything (I Chron 29:14). It was a mistake for her to consider Baal the giver; equally a mistake for her to consider herself the owner.

The items chosen for this list are not as conventional as the grain, must, and oil of 2:10,24; cf. Deut 32:13–14; Hab 3:17. The products are not obviously connected with sexual activity; the opening of the wombs of women and beasts is not mentioned. The products are agricultural and pastoral. This deflects attention away from the mechanism of fertility rites as sympathetic magic, and a different connection is hinted at. It is greed, not lasciviousness, that drives her. Deut 28:1–14 makes it clear that what Canaanites tried to get by rituals, Israel was able to get by obedience to Yahweh's commands; cf. Hos 4:6.

Whether the pronouns in "my bread," etc. are possessive or dative, the advantages of sexual activity are seen in a personal way. Unless these staples are to be identified quite literally as payment in kind, we must suppose that they represent the earning of one's livelihood, even if the fee took some other form. There is no indication that Hosea had to struggle with poverty, so that desperation, not greed, drove her to secure income by such means. We do not know how private or theological the statement in v 7b is intended to be. If her activities were part of widespread policy, then national well-being depended on the general productivity granted by the god. While Hosea does not speak of Israel's lasciviousness in the tough language used by Jeremiah (but see Hos 4:13), he does hint here at base motives, rather than conversion to a rival theology that could be stated in sophisticated terms. The prophets in general found nothing whatever in Canaanite religion that could be considered so reasonable or attractive as to make the choice between Yahweh and Baal a difficult one. They suggest rather that Canaanite religion appealed to everything that was vile in human beings.

my bread and my water, my wool and my flax, my oil and my liquor. The basic commodities of life are listed. Bread and water are the simplest necessities of diet. These words might have been chosen here because Baal was the storm god whose chief benefaction was rain, and his father Dagan was the god of grain. The fallacy of believing that Baal controls water will be demonstrated when Yahweh kills her "with thirst" (v 5).

The list is rhythmic to the point of being poetic. There is symmetry in the placing of two items of clothing in the middle of two pairs of food items. Freedman (1955b) has argued that the fourth item should read *pištay*, because the word is usually plural and the plural secures an intricate rhyming scheme: the odd words all end in *-î*, the even words all end in *-ay*.

Wool and flax are constantly associated as the two main fibers for Israelite textiles, in spite of their differing origin, pastoral and agricultural

(Dalman 1928–42, Forbes 1956, Talmon 1963). In the present context, this gives Baal jurisdiction over both animal husbandry and farming.

The term used for oil, *šemen*, is the most general one; the more specific word for olive oil is used in vv 10 and 24. Olive oil is probably intended here also. Its use as an item of diet was only one out of many, but a most important one. *Šemen* was also used for anointing, and for cult ceremonies.

There does not seem to be any reason for changing the last word in the list to *nišqî*, "perfumes" (*NEB*). Hos 4:11 complains about the abuse of intoxicating beverages in the cult. Elsewhere Hosea uses more common terms for wine or "new wine." His preference for the rare word *šiqqûy* here is unexplained, but its authenticity need not be doubted. It is derived from the common root *šqy*, "to give to drink." We do not know whether the word means beverage in the most general sense, or whether it is specialized. Prov 3:8 indicates that it is a healthy drink, especially good for bones. When we contrast this meager attestation with, say, the dozens of words for different kinds of beer found in cuneiform sources (Hartman and Oppenheim 1950), we have to be content with ignorance.

The Lipit-Ishtar law code stipulates that a man with a childless wife who secures offspring from a common harlot must provide the harlot with grain, oil, and clothing (*ANET* 160). Other references show that these were considered standard rations.

The unit in 2:6–7 is another remarkable example of the author's practice of listing events in a sequence that is the opposite of their actual occurrence (cf. 2:1–3). Here the stages in Israel's apostasy are traced in reverse:

7bB She entertains the wrong belief about the source of life's necessities.
7bA She resolves to go off after her lovers.
7a She disgraces herself.
6aB Her children become "children of promiscuity."
6aA Her children will not be pitied.

There is no need to insist that each line represents a distinct moment in the unfolding action.

8–9. These verses constitute a clearly marked unit of discourse:

8a   *lākēn hinĕnî-śāk 'et-darkēk bassîrîm*
8bA   *wĕgādartî 'et-gĕdērāh*
8bB   *ûnĕtîbôtêhā lō' timṣā'*
9aA   *wĕriddĕpâ 'et-mĕ'ahăbêhā*
      wĕlō'-taśśîg 'ōtām
9aB   *ûbiqšātam*
      wĕlō' timṣā'

9bA *wĕ'āmĕrâ 'ēlĕkâ wĕ'āšûbâ 'el-'îšî hārī'šôn*
9bB *kî ṭôb lî 'āz mē'āttâ*

While there is some parallelism, especially in v 9a, there is no metrical
balance or rhythmic regularity. On the contrary, all the normal indicators
point to prose composition: literary, even oratorical prose, but prose,
nonetheless. The repeated use of *'et* with nouns and pronouns confirms the
impression. Verses 8b–9a fall into lines that are grammatically defined;
but they are of uneven length. We have noticed sometimes a tendency for
progressive shortening, and this would seem to be deliberate in v 9a,
where the successive objects are (1) a noun; (2) pronoun with *nota accusativi;* (3) pronoun suffix; (4) zero — all with the same referent
(Rudolph 1966:63); cf. 5:6.

Many scholars are not satisfied with the present position of 2:8–9. This
unit seems to interrupt the continuity between vv 6–7 and 10–11, which
balance nicely. The claims made in v 7 about the lovers and their payments or gifts are contradicted by the denial and affirmations in v 10, with
the threatened consequences in v 11.

Nevertheless, a case can be made for the present position of vv 8–9 if it
is recognized that the argument is not developed in logical or chronological order, and that the literary construction, as noted in the Introduction to Part I, favors a circular or enveloping pattern in which the
climactic point is reached in the center rather than at the end. Thus the circumstances described in vv 6–7 and 10–11 reach a hypothetical conclusion or hoped-for resolution in v 9b, to which vv 8–9a are the necessary
precedent link. Thus the sequence may be established in this fashion: vv
6–7 find their logical complement in vv 10–11, followed by vv 8–9a, leading to the climax in 9b; another line of development is posited in vv 12*ff*.
The threads are brought together in a summary statement, v 15, with a
resumptive echo of v 7.

It is clear that v 9b states the goal. In the introductory analysis of
cc 1–3 we saw that 2:9b occupies a pivotal position in the structure of
2:4–15. It is climactic and sounds final; yet it is right in the middle of the
speech. It is a possible end for the story; but it is not certain that it is the
actual end. Chapter 3 suggests otherwise. Hos 2:9b, a voluntary return
to the deserted husband, is only the anticipated outcome of the interference described in 2:8–9a. The impression is conveyed that such
remedies were insufficient. The motivation is still rather superficial and
selfish; the basic error stated in credal form in v 7b still needs to be eradicated from her mind. So vv 10*ff* return to this, first stating the wrong opinion again in negative form (v 10), and then applying the correction (v
11). (The position of vv 8–9 between v 7 and v 10 is much like the position of vv 12–13 between v 11 and v 14; see below.)

The transference of vv 8–9 to another place creates fresh problems. A favorite place to relocate them is after v 15. In support of this is the sequence in classical Hebrew prophecy, where a description of some fault is followed by an announcement of Yahweh's intended response, beginning "therefore." It is true that the indictment is not complete until v 15b. But v 16 already supplies the usual "therefore" clause. The three uses of "therefore" in Hosea 2 (vv 8,11,16) do not depart from the classical pattern; each is preceded by an accusation. They announce responses of different kinds to what is essentially the same situation.

vv 7–8: She said her lovers were the givers, therefore . . .
vv 10–11: She didn't realize that I was the giver, therefore . . .
vv 15–16: She forgot me, therefore . . .

But the response is altogether constructive from v 16 onward, i.e. after the full indictment. This change in mood between vv 15 and 16 would be spoiled if vv 8–9, which continue to sound the threatening note, were inserted at this point. Compare the result in the *Jerusalem Bible,* where the placing of v 9 between vv 15 and 16 creates a completely different impression of the dynamics of the relationship. Following immediately after v 9b, in which the woman resolves to return, the initiative taken by the husband in v 16 is less impressive than when it follows "me she forgot." As things stand, the new policy reflected in 2:16–17 comes after 2:4–15, with *no recorded* repentance on the part of the woman. The last word ("me she forgot") is the worst. The renewed lovemaking of v 16 comes after all the attempts described in 2:4–15 have failed, or because 2:4–15 reports the deliberation on possible remedies, all of which are considered and rejected in favor of the different approach described in v 16. By putting in a statement that the woman has decided to return to her husband at this point, the idea is expressed that Yahweh's new attitude is the result of Israel's change of heart. It is more consistent with Hosea's position in the remainder of the book to see that any change of heart (none is reported!) comes as a result of Yahweh's forgiving love, not of his punitive justice.

The use of *lākēn,* "therefore," as an introduction to a more formal declaration of divine intention is common in the great prophets. It occurs only four times in Hosea (2:8,11,16; 13:3). Hos 2:8, the first of the formal threats (there has already been a conditional threat in v 5), matches 2:16, the first of the promises, in using *hinnēh.* Hos 2:11 starts off with an imperfect verb, resembling the *wĕ'attâ* clause in 2:12 in this regard. The threats continue with consecutive future (perfect) verbs, just like the paragraph governed by *pen* in v 5. In spite of their emphatic character, the "therefore" clauses probably still have a conditional element, but it would be going too far to make them merely hypothetical — "If I should block her way . . . then she might pursue . . . and she might say." So far as the prophet himself is concerned, there is a certain lack of realism about these remarks, as if they were already tipped symbolically toward the similitude of Yahweh and Israel. On Hosea's part, they are baffled ruminations; on Yahweh's part they are regrets that he had not dealt more severely with Israel earlier in its history. The succession of threats cannot be lined up with a series of historical crises. The deprivations threatened in vv 8 and 11 are actions intended to drive the woman to carry out the action described in v 4b. There is mounting severity, with *wĕ'attâ* (v 12) as a climax. In v 8 the wife is hampered; in v 11 she is deprived; in v 12 she is humiliated and disillusioned. The climax of v 5 (killing her) is evidently not reached. This suggests that the deprivations are only contemplated.

The logic of such a series of threats of mounting severity is that, as each one fails in turn to have the desired effect, the next one is applied. Lev 26:14–45 contains a much longer list, which resembles Hosea 2 in being not punitive but remedial, intended to break Israel's stubborn pride.

Viewed in this light, the speech in Hos 2:6–15 might be taken as a soliloquy. Hos 11:8 is another instance of Yahweh struggling in his own mind to work out what to do. Here the prophet contemplates possible courses of action, starting with the extreme of putting the offender to death, and finally rejects them all in favor of the redemptive scheme described in 2:16–17. So far as Yahweh and Israel are concerned, the threats are very serious. According to Amos 4:4–12, such drastic measures were unavailing. So far as Hosea and Gomer are concerned, there is no indication that the desired outcome ever emerged.

8. *behold.* The construction *hinĕnî* followed by a participle is used 125 times in the Hebrew Bible. In all but seven occurrences the speaker is God (Humbert 1934), in an urgent announcement of ominous intention. Since the announcement serves as a warning there is still a chance that the threatened punishment might be averted by a last-minute response. Hence we do not have to look for historical events as the exact fulfillment of v 8. It is fanciful to connect the possible reference to thornbushes with the ruination of the countryside (Wolff 1974:36; cf. Isa 34:13).

hedge. A barrier of thorns along a road or a fence of stones around a field has a twofold purpose: to keep animals in or out. What is the analogy in the husband's actions to curb his errant wife? Is she penned in, so that she cannot find the way to her lovers? Or is she locked out, so that she cannot find her way home? In Job the same meanings are met, using the verb *śwk:* in Job 1:10 God protects Job from harm; in Job 3:23 the same verb describes the infuriating restrictions imposed by God upon human existence. The frustration described in Hos 2:9a suggests that, like an animal on the loose, she is prevented from straying into forbidden pastures. This means that by hedging her in Hosea will prevent his wife from reaching her lovers, or, analogously, God will prevent his apostate people from making their usual pilgrimages to the Baal shrines. The immediate picture seems to be one of abandoned and overgrown paths rendered impassable by thorns and briers, an impression confirmed by v 8b since the roads are inaccessible. The implication of v 9a is that even if she is able to overcome the hazards described (and the added one of a fence), and pursues her lovers, she will still not be able to find or overtake them.

Kuhnigk (1974:17) has suggested that the "thorns" are part of the scenery in Sheol, in line with the threat of death in v 5; cf. 9:6. But the desert is the scene of the killing in v 5, and the means is thirst. The situation is realistic. In 9:6 the reversion of farmland to waste is sufficient to explain the reference to thorns. The allegory, in order to be effective, should also be conceivable on the level of a man and his wife.

your way. Since the rest of the passage is in the third person, emendation to "her way" is an obvious possibility, and it is not surprising that the versions have already taken it up. Comparison of "her path" with "her wall" in the next line would seem to clinch this. But the more difficult reading calls for explanation. Kuhnigk (1974:14) suggests reading "emphatic" *kî* for the *k* suffix. Since the double preposition *k-b* is attested, the simple transfer of the *k* to the next word would also yield sense: "as with thorns." We think, however, that the MT can be taken literally. Second-person suffixes appear again in 2:21–22. Fluctuation in person (first-third, second-third, even first-second) is not unknown in biblical literature. The inconcinnity of "she-you" is not sufficient grounds for changing the text. This obtrusive second-person pronoun shows that the husband's message is intended for his wife.

There should be no need to defend the authenticity of this phenomenon of changing persons in midstream of discourse. The matter was thoroughly studied in biblical texts long ago by König (1900); see also J. Sperber (1918). Cassuto (1973:64–65) insists on the authenticity of a similar transition from third to second person within the "Blessings" of Moses (Deut 33:19,23,24–25,27–29). It is a feature of Jeremiah 2 (a discourse akin to Hosea 2). For Ugaritic examples see Oldenburg (1969:128).

thorn. This word is used only a few times in Hebrew. Nah 1:10 and Qoh 7:6 show that flammability was an associated idea. In Isa 34:13 thorns are a sign of desolation. Neither of these ideas seem to be present in Hos 2:8.

its wall. Literally, "her wall." It is not clear whether the pronoun refers to the roadway or to the wife. The wall along the road would parallel the barrier of thorns, but a *gādēr* is normally a fence of field stones. If it is her wall, this can only be interpreted as a wall "against" her. The same problem is met with "its (her) pathways." The description may be of a stone wall with thorns on the top. An arresting parallel to this verse is to be

found in Lam 3:7–9, especially v 9, where the same terms are used in a
similar context; the judgment of God against his people was fulfilled in
this fashion: "He has walled me about so that I cannot escape . . . he has
blocked my ways with hewn stones; he has twisted my paths."

find. The verb is clearly 3 f s, "she will find." Wolff (1974:36) identifies
the verb as jussive, and interprets the negated jussive as an indication of
purpose, leading to the translation, "so that she cannot find her paths."
There is little difference in the net effect, and since the verb can equally
well be identified as indicative, the point is academic. Wolff translates a
similar expression in v 9b as future indicative. It is possible that the implied object of "she will not find" is not "her paths" but "her lovers," as in
the next verse, in which case "her paths" would be an object of *gdrty,* "I
will wall in."

In a study of Hosea's language in vv 7–9, van Selms (1964–65) has
compared the vocabulary with that in the Song of Songs, describing
wholesome love, and that in Proverbs, dealing with prostitution. He finds
no fewer than five features in which the language of Hos 2:7–9 is erotic,
and makes the intriguing suggestion that snatches of love songs might un-
derlie some of the rhythms found here.

pathways. The nouns *nātîb* and *nĕtîbâ* are synonyms of *derek* and *'ōraḥ*
and occur in parallelism with both. They all share the ethical connotation
of conduct, good or bad. There is no indication of what kind of paths
Hosea had in mind, or what is achieved by her not finding them. Job
38:20 speaks of "the paths of her house," the well-beaten tracks that lead
to a person's home. Is it too far-fetched to say that the familiar pathways
will be altered by changing the layout of thorn hedges and stone walls?
The political counterpart of this would be a breakdown in the Israelite
communication system by setting up barriers — new regional boundaries?
— so that the people can no longer move freely to the customary festivals
at the Baal shrines. The sequel in 2:9a suggests that paths to the lovers
are meant; perhaps the plural is used to highlight the abundance and diversity of her amours.

One point, however, is reinforced. She is not a prostitute sought by cli-
ents, but an adulteress who goes after her lovers. The Book of Proverbs
uses the pair "way/path" in good and bad senses. Proverbs 7:25–27 indicates that the words refer to a prostitute's habits rather than her haunts,
and a warning is given against their deadliness. Applied to Hos 2:8, this
suggests not so much physical restrictions on her movement as a restraint
on her sexual activity by some means.

9. *pursues.* There is sustained emphasis on the initiative of the woman.
No initiative is ascribed to the lovers; no mitigating circumstances indicate
that she had been seduced. In c 2 no actions of the lovers are described.
Nor is any explanation given as to why she cannot find them. It is almost
as if they did not exist. They never appear on stage.

The root *rdp,* here *Pi'el,* is rare, and used mainly in poetry. To keep v 9 close to v 8, it may be that the verb should be taken as inchoative; because her husband has shut her in, she will desire to pursue her lovers. But the language implies futile search. The idea that the Baals are inconstant and that she has been deserted is not expressed. In v 12, the speaker boasts that no one will be able to rescue the woman, indicating that the Baals are unwilling, or unable, to help her. It is certainly her husband's intention to discredit them in her eyes.

seeks. In Hos 5:6,15, the same language is used about access to Yahweh: he is inaccessible because he has withdrawn himself. *Biqqēš* is frequently used in connection with attendance at religious gatherings, in search of some token of divine favor. In the sense of "inquire," it discloses a desire for an oracle. The failure to find any response then corresponds to the silence of an indifferent, incompetent, or absent deity (I Kings 18:27). If, by this exposure of the emptiness of Canaanite religion, Hosea is presenting a polemic against some aspects of Canaanite belief that people of his day would recognize, we are no longer in a position to appreciate his allusions. The motif of searching everywhere for a missing god and failing to find him is found in the Hittite Telepinus Myth (Goetze 1957:143–144); only indirectly could this be compared with searching for a lover in order to carry on an illicit relationship.

find. It may be that Hebrew *māṣā'* can mean "to reach" rather than "to find" (Dahood and Penar 1972:268–269) — such a meaning here would improve the parallelism with *taśśîg* — but "find" is a better correlate of *bqš,* and this seems to be the meaning of the word in v 8.

she may say. Van Selms (1964–65) has pointed out the use of the same verb in vv 7 and 9, meaning "she said to herself," to describe erotic fantasies. If the verb here describes a thought and not a decision, then it does not mean "she (certainly) will say," but only "she might say."

go and return. By hendiadys, "go back." Comparison with 6:1 shows that a larger idea of repentance is hinted at. It indicates a new motivation, the reverse of the one cited in v 7.

my first husband. This is a literal translation. In Deut 24:4 "her first husband" is *ba'lāh hārī'šôn,* mentioned in connection with divorce and remarriage. Returning to a deserted husband was illegal in Israel after divorce and remarriage to another man. Hos 2:18–19 indicates why Hosea prefers to use *'îš;* 2:9 already anticipates that change in terminology. Since there was no divorce in Hosea's case, there was no second husband; the lovers were only pseudo-husbands, surrogates for the divine husband.

then . . . now. These adverbs suggest that *rī'šôn,* in "first husband," means "as at first" or "at an earlier time." In Job 8:8 "the first generation" means "the olden days." Prophecies of restoration predict that things will be *kĕbārī'šōnâ,* "as they were in the beginning" (Isa 1:26; Jer 33:7,11). In Hosea's vision, the picture of this ideal time is drawn from the past, but not from the time of creation. The United Monarchy dominates the picture, but features of the Confederacy and the Mosaic era are also compressed into it. This reflection in the mind of the wife makes it clear that there must have been a stage in the marriage when things went well, attractive in contrast with what the life of promiscuity has turned out to be. This is a further reason for believing that Hosea's marriage was originally good, and that his wife had not misbehaved at least in its early years. Verse 9b is a climax at the center of 2:4–15. The desertion, described in vv 7 and 15a, is reversed by the return hoped for in v 9b. Verse 9b is the only clause in Hos 2:4–15 which describes the hoped-for effect of the chastisements upon the woman: their goal was to have her acknowledge Hosea (Yahweh) as her true husband.

10–11. These verses compose another unit in the discourse, an accusation (v 10) and a threat (v 11): *lākēn,* "therefore," marks the transition. There is a correspondence between the parts. The fault exposed in v 10 is ignorance (or denial) of the fact that Yahweh is the source of every good. The way to correct this fault is to take back the gifts.

This unit has prose rhythms like the ones met already in the preceding units, but there are some genuinely poetic lines.

> 10aA *wĕhî' lō' yādĕ'â*
> 10aB *kî 'ānōkî nātattî lāh*
>   *haddāgān wĕhattîrôš wĕhayyišhār*
> 10bA *wĕkesep hirbêtî lāh*
>   *wĕzāhāb 'āśû labbā'al*
>
> 11aA *lākēn 'āšûb wĕlāqahtî*
> 11aB *dĕgānî bĕ'ittô*
>   *wĕtîrôšî bĕmô'ădô*
> 11bA *wĕhiṣṣaltî ṣamrî ûpištay* (*MT ûpištî*)
>   *lĕkassôt 'et-'erwātāh*

Although many of the lines are similar in length, there is not much parallelism. There are examples of conventional coordination of traditional pairs, such as "silver and gold" (v 10b), but even in that case the remainder of the bicolon has no synonymy; in v 11aB, *dĕgānî bĕ'ittô // wĕtîrôšî bĕmô'ădô,* the parallelism is precise, and the double pairings are symmetrical. The sentence in v 10aB on the other hand can and probably should be interpreted as ordinary prose. While the verbal objects are both definite and direct, the particle *'t* is not used (contrast the usage in v 24 where the same words occur as definite objects, and *'t* is used). The variation between v 10 and v 24 cannot easily be explained, although it must reflect selection on the part of the author; the internal consistency in each case, as well as the number of items, confirms this. In general, the three particles (*'t, h, 'šr*) are good indicators of prose composition, while their omission is characteristic of poetry; but there is a good deal of local fluctuation, and in particular cases judgments may be difficult. Both vv 10 and 24 seem to be prosaic, but they differ in this respect.

This unit is linked primarily with v 7, taking up again the question of who is the giver of nature's bounty. By contrast, the break between v 9 and v 10 is quite abrupt; it seems to involve an outright contradiction: if the woman has come to realize that "it was better for me then than it is now" (v 9bB), such a frame of mind is the opposite of not realizing that it was her husband, rather than her lover, who gave her everything (v 10a). These contiguous statements must belong to different stages in the story. Either v 9b comes well after v 10a, for it supplies the corrective to the erroneous opinions expressed in v 10a or it represents a stage in the action never reached — it expresses only the husband's hopes and intentions, not a change of heart. The latter seems more likely since there are no other indications that the woman was disillusioned, realized her folly, found her husband desirable once more, and voluntarily returned.

The course of correlative action proposed, or threatened, in v 11 to counteract the false notions exposed in v 10 differs from what was proposed in v 8. It is not directed against the woman's person, it is intended to make her life more uncomfortable. The removal of wool and flax will bring about the nakedness already cited in v 5 as the first threat. In fact, this action is threatened three times, indicating its centrality to the issue, and its appropriateness for this woman.

In vv 10–11, as in other units in this discourse, there are substantial connections with the immediate context, both forward and backward. Features which do not correspond to material in the immediate environment have contacts with terms and phrases in other places, so that a network of connections extends over the whole discourse. The only link with vv 8–9 is the verb "to return."

The way in which the author uses various names for the gifts is typical of his verbal art, and provides threads for his tapestry. Six gifts, in three pairs, are listed in v 7. Five gifts are listed in v 10, none of which appears in v 7, even though v 10 is intended to counteract v 7. One might have expected exactly the same words to be used, to make the contradiction clear. Verse 11 lists four gifts which are to be taken back. Two of the items come from the list in v 10, two from the list in v 7. The sequence

> wool and flax (v 7)
> grain and must (v 10)
>
> grain and must (v 11a)
> wool and flax (v 11b)

is chiastic. In this way the two parts are brought together and unified.

10. *she didn't know*. The prominent independent pronouns *hî'* and *'ānōkî* in this verse serve to evoke v 4 where the same pronouns occur; here the primary identification is with Israel and Yahweh, whereas in v 4 it is with Gomer and Hosea, although there are crosscurrents which interlock the two pairs represented by the pronouns.

Setting "she said" (v 7) against "she didn't know" confirms our impression that the first means "thought." Israel had fallen into the error of ascribing to Baal the generous benefactions which are Yahweh's sole prerogative. There was a choice between "two different opinions" (I Kings 18:21). This destructive "lack of knowledge" (Hos 4:6) is the result of "rejecting" knowledge, not just of ignorance. Similarly, "forgetting" (v 15) is a sin, not just a mental weakness. Verse 10 implies a deliberate rejection of Yahweh in preferring Baal. This decision was not based on the abstract question, "Who is God?" but on the question, "Who gives grain, must, and oil?" So long as she continues to think it is Baal, she will never consider that it would be better to go back to her "first husband" (v 9).

provided. The meanings of the verb *ntn* are noticed s.v. v 7; in the context of sexual service, it could mean "to pay." No such meaning is possible here, for there is no hint of services rendered. In v 7 *ntn* governs six commodities (three pairs); in v 10 it has three nouns as object. The verb, and the list that follows as its object, are typically Deuteronomic.

grain and must and oil. This is a conventional list of the basic products of Israelite agriculture and the staples of the people's diet. It differs from the longer list in v 7 in that the latter could be regarded as the gifts of a husband to his wife, while the former are more obviously the gifts of the God of nature. We are close to the claim of Yahweh to be *the* fertility god. The allegory breaks down at this point. Even if the passage applies directly to Gomer, contending that what she erroneously ascribed to Baal was nevertheless all the time a gift from no one but Yahweh, this can have no counterpart on the human level.

lavished. The perfect verb continues from the previous "I gave." Guided by the correlative pair "silver . . . and gold," a holistic analysis of v 10b shows that both metals were lavished on her, and both metals were used to make idols: "The silver and gold which I gave her in abundance, they used to make images of Baal." The reign of Jeroboam II was a time of affluence and both Hosea and Amos find connections between the nation's wealth and its idolatry. Since v 10a lists natural products, it is likely that silver and gold are used not to mean money in the narrow sense, but to refer to the husband's gifts. The fundamental parallel elsewhere in prophetic thought is Ezek 16:17.

> And you took your beautiful jewelry from my gold and my silver, which I had given you, and you made for yourself male images and you were promiscuous by means of them.

silver . . . gold. Israel did not mine silver or gold. The names for the metals, unlike the three products that precede them, do not have the definite article, suggesting that they do not simply continue the list; v 10b is poetic and laconic. The sequence "silver and gold" occurs twice as often as "gold and silver" in the Bible. The former is more characteristic of early texts, the latter of later passages. The shift may reflect the change in the relative value of silver and gold from the late second to the first millennium B.C.E. The ordering may tell against Wolff's inference that gold "is placed at the end to emphasize it as the most precious of all" (1974:37). The order comes from Deuteronomy, where the expression *wĕkesep wĕzāhāb yirbeh-lak* (Deut 8:13; 17:17) is found. This, however, is no reason for removing the last two words as a gloss; the phrase has been broken up in the interests of parallelism and the balance of the bicolon invites acceptance, even though the parallelism is incomplete.

they made into a Baal. The last two words in v 10 are difficult; they do not fit smoothly with the rest of the discourse. We have already remarked on the lack of any matching passage in Hosea 1–3, which contrasts with the prevailing pattern that most things are mentioned twice in this composition. The use of "the Baals" elsewhere in the chapter, in vv 15 and 19, provides the double occurrence and leaves the singular here unexplained. The plural verb "they made" is also a difficulty, since the antecedent is not clearly defined.

We think, however, that the phrase can be defended, along with the rest of the bicolon. As for the uniqueness of "Baal," we have already noticed the departure from the neat and the expected, especially at climactic places. The unusual names for God, Ehyeh and the Living God, illustrate this.

If the author suddenly says that the metals given by Yahweh were made into a Baal, this is at once a shocking profanation and also an absurdity that debunks Baalism (Hos 8:6). Deluded into thinking that Baal is generous, his worshipers have to supply the metals to make him. Up to this point innuendos about the nationalization of a pagan cult have been hidden under the story of Hosea and his wife. Now they break into the open.

In the relative clause in v 10bB, "gold (which) they made into a Baal," we have both omission of the relative and use of an antecedent, *zhb*, without the article. It is possible that these two phenomena go together as marks of indefiniteness; but that would be strange after the definite nouns in v 10a.

The two problems with the verb are (1) who did the making and (2) what was involved? The statement in Hos 8:4–6 is so similar to that used here, that it should supply the needed key. That passage refers to the calf at Samaria, made by a craftsman out of silver and gold. In the present passage, the same identification is appropriate, except that the idol-makers are plural.

Hos 8:4 points to the meaning "made into a Baal," rather than "used (as an offering) for (a) Baal," and mentions specifically silver and gold; we can infer that 2:10b does not mean that all these gifts were given as oblations. Only the agricultural products were so used: Deut 14:23 mentions the tithe of grain and wine and oil to be eaten in festivity before Yahweh, and later Hosea will talk about eating in a cult setting. It is likely that the Baal and Yahweh cults in Israel were similar, having borrowed from each other. Hos 2:18 hints that Israel had called Yahweh himself "My Baal." On *'śy l,* see Exod 32:4; Deut 9:14; Isa 44:17; Ezek 4:9; II Chron 28:2.

In view of this evidence that Hosea is speaking quite realistically here about the use of gold to make a Baal image, the suggestion that *lb'l* means "not Baal" (Kuhnigk 1974:19) does not have much appeal. The idiom *'āśâ l* as used elsewhere confirms that *l* is the preposition. Additional arguments are needed to explain *'āśû* as infinitive; and for "not Baal," one might have expected **wĕlō' ba'al;* see Gen 27:12; Num 24:17; Deut 32:6; Isa 30:1; 31:3; Jer 2:27; Ezek 16:17, etc., and especially Hos 6:6.

11. *Therefore.* On *lākēn,* see the NOTES on v 8.

I will reverse myself. The verb *šûb* can describe the movement of returning, which implies a prior movement away. It can also serve as an auxiliary, meaning to do something again; cf. *hôsîp,* "to add," *šānâ,* "to repeat." Normally, an auxiliary is followed by an infinitive (Hos 11:9), but two finite verbs in sequence can have the same effect, by hendiadys (Hos 1:6; 3:5; 14:8). The basic meaning of "turn" implies resumption of an activity that has been suspended, and "turning around" has developed more abstractly to describe a turnabout or change of attitude, "repentance"; in Hebrew this refers to a change of behavior as well as a change of mind. In the case of the woman, it would be right for her to "return," for she has deserted her husband. As in Hos 5:4,15; 6:1; 7:10; 14:3, such a returning also involves turning around just as the original departure was described as turning aside (Hos 3:1). Hosea plays on the word in 8:13; 11:5, where the alternatives are return to Yahweh or return to Egypt. The former action involves repenting, a change in conduct; the latter involves going back, a movement in space (Hos 11:5). It would not be fitting for the husband to "return," because he has never abandoned his wife. The verb is used of movement in v 9, and the goal is indicated; cf. Hos 7:10; 9:3. The wife's *'āśûbâ* (v 9) and the husband's *'āśûb* (v 11) throw their activities into contrast, but the latter has no goal of motion. The meaning "to repeat" does not fit either.

Without implying that the action had been done before, *'āśûb* as an auxiliary could impart to the verb "to take" the meaning "to take back" (what is mine, what I gave) rather than "to take away." The point is not that Yahweh will remove what Baal gave, as, for example, Mot (Death) in the Canaanite myth causes famine by overcoming Baal, the rain god. There is no confrontation or trial of strength between Yahweh and Baal. Baal is entirely in the background, a shadow. No capability whatever is ascribed to the rival god. Hos 2:12 will stress Baal's complete helplessness; Yahweh is the only one who can do anything. Here Yahweh retrieves what he gave in the first place and what has remained his all along.

In the play between *'ašûbâ* (v 9) and *'āšûb* (v 11), it is the twist in meaning that gives the wordplay its impact. The wife will not *return,* so the husband will *change* his attitude. Hitherto he has been lavishing gifts on her, but she chose not to recognize their origin (v 10). Now she will be forced to do so. He will change his policy, and take them all back.

take. This verb is the antithesis of *ntn* "to give" in v 10. The polarity of the verbs *ntn* and *lqḥ* expresses a variety of nuances, depending on the circumstances, e.g. when *ntn* means "to pay," *lqḥ* means "to receive by payment, buy." Yahweh's insistence that the grain and wine are his excludes that idea but shows that recovery or retrieval is the meaning intended. According to Israelite law, a husband was obliged to provide his wife with three things — food, clothing, and sexual satisfaction (Exod 21:10–11). If he failed to do so, she could leave him without penalty. On the other hand, in case of adultery, the woman forfeits these rights, and in the ancient Near East generally the husband was entitled to recover everything from his wife as part of her punishment. The legal basis for this was the claim that these things (as distinct from a dowry) had never become the woman's personal property.

my grain . . . my must . . . my wool . . . my flax. In correlation with "to take," the pronouns could be dative/ventive: "I will take back the grain to/for myself." The emphasis, however, is on Yahweh's ownership of such things. The bestowal in v 10 should not permit the woman to think that such things ever become her own, as she does in v 7. Because the question of ownership lies at the heart of the theological dispute, the possessive meaning of the suffixes should be retained in both vv 7 and 11. Yahweh never ceases to own his gifts. This is why he can take them back without doing wrong (Job 1:21). In Hosea's case, where the woman wrongfully claims ownership (doubly, for she attributes the items first to Baal and then to herself) it is also a question of recovering stolen property.

in its time . . . in its season. Among the covenanted blessings is a promise to send rain on the land "in its time" (Deut 11:13–17; 28:12). To withhold it would mean drought and famine. To do so three months before harvest (Amos 4:7–8) would be bad enough. What is threatened in Hos 2:11 is more dramatic and much worse — the destruction of crops right at the point of harvest, the means to be used not indicated. Such a giving of grain and then taking it back would exhibit the power of Yahweh, whereas failure of the rain to come or failure of the grain to germinate could be interpreted as evidence of his limited control of the world. In Ps 1:3 *bĕ'ittô* means "every harvest time." In a number of passages, especially in the priestly writings, *mô'ēd,* "season," refers to a seasonal festival, and the same meaning is found in Hos 2:13. The harvest and vintage celebrations, now wrongfully directed to Baal, will be sabotaged if Yahweh destroys the fields and vineyards.

I will rescue. This vigorous action makes it clear that stolen property is being recovered. Just as *hirbêtî,* "I lavished," is more emphatic than *nātattî,* "I gave," in Hos 2:10, so here *hiṣṣaltî* is more forceful than the preceding *lāqaḥtî,* "I will take back." The repetition of the word in the next verse contrasts Yahweh's capacity in this regard with the incapacity of "her lovers."

to uncover. Literally "to cover (her nakedness)." The Syriac shrewdly supposes ellipsis: "which I gave her to cover her nakedness." The similar *RSV* "which were to cover her nakedness" is rather lame. LXX sees "to cover her nakedness" not as the purpose of the gift, but supplies a negative to make uncovering her nakedness the purpose of the stripping. The literal meaning of the Hebrew text could stand if the situation is similar to that described in Ezek 16:15–18. There the wife takes her husband's gifts — gorgeous clothing, silver, gold, bread, etc. — and gives them all to the idols. Hos 2:10 may accuse Hosea's wife of doing the same kind of thing. This proposal sustains the emphasis on giving and permits the literal meaning of the text to be retained. But it clashes with another theme of 2:4–15. The stripping of the wife is a major threat (2:5,12), so it is better to see here an example of the privative *Pi'el,* as already proposed by Dahood (Kuhnigk 1974:21–23). An analogy to the process is supplied by the cursing texts, if we follow Hillers' interpretation of Sefire I A 40–41 — "(And just as a prostitute is stripped naked) so may the wives of Matti'el . . . be stripped naked" (Hillers 1964a:59, cf. *ANET* 660).

nakedness. It is clear from Gen 9:22–23 that *'erwâ* is a euphemism for genitals. In Leviticus 18 the reference is even more directly to sexual intercourse. In Lev 20:17–18 it is used to refer to sexual relations within the forbidden degrees. Gen 42:9,12 present the nuance of something taboo, too sacred to be viewed. See the discussion of *nablût* in v 12.

12–14. The unit is prosaic; a comparison of v 12b with its poetic equivalent in 5:14 shows the difference (cf. Deut 32:39). The unit has three main clauses, the opening one (v 12a) with an imperfect verb, and two others with consecutive perfect verbs (vv 13 and 14a); v 12b contrasts with all of these. The variation in the length of these clauses shows that the unit is not poetry; at the same time it is not ordinary prose, but a rhetorical form of oratory, similar in some respects to the oratorical style of the prose sermons of Deuteronomy and Jeremiah.

The threatened punishment has three aspects — denudation (v 12), ruination of the crops (v 14a, which is like v 11, though they deal with different objects), and abolition of the festivals (v 13).

The combination wĕ'attâ, "and now," often marks a major transition in prophetic discourse, a switch from description (indicative mood) to command (imperative); Amos 7:16 is the only instance of this construction in the eighth-century minor prophets. In Mic 4:11 it is used to continue description, and the same applies to its other occurrence in Hosea (13:2). Only here is it followed by a resolution, but it does not mark a transition, because threats in a similar vein have already been made several times. Apparently, v 12 continues the speech in v 11, with nakedness as the connecting link, and the use of *nṣl*, "to rescue," as a further parallel. However, the introverted structure of 2:4–15 restrains us from finding the prime connection of v 12 with v 11. There are more verbal ties between 2:12–15 and 2:4–6. The particular climactic force of the opening of v 12 can be felt if it completes the series of three threats, the first two of which are introduced by *lākēn* (vv 8, 11). Verse 8 is preceded by the accusation in v 7, and v 11 is preceded by the accusation in v 10, whereas v 12 is not immediately preceded by an accusation. We suggest that the implicit accusations in vv 4–6 are those to which v 12 is the response. Many of the links between the opening and closing portions of the complete speech have already been pointed out in the introduction to Part I.

There is a major break in v 14 after the first three words. At this point attention changes from the devastation of the country back to the children, who were last mentioned in v 6. Verse 14aA completes the set of three related threats, all expressed in first person singular verbs, with the usual sequence of imperfect (*'ăgalleh*) followed by two consecutive perfects.

The climactic function of v 12 is seen in the way it gathers up themes from earlier parts of the discourse — the threat of stripping the woman (v 5), the reference to "the lovers" (v 7), and the motif of rescue (v 11). The three threats in vv 12–14a do not seem to be connected; for this reason it might be better not to speak of a single unit. There is some parallelism in v 12, whereas v 13 has a complex arrangement of a long clause. Verse 14aA ends the unit, a colon without a parallel. If v 12 is a bicolon, the lines are of uneven length; the second half has a note of finality about it (cf. Hos 5:14). The situation in v 13 seems to be quite different, and v 14a is different again. The three threats are unified, nevertheless, by their repeated impact on the woman (the pronoun "her" occurs ten times) as well as by their resemblance to threats already made in 2:4–11.

It may be that v 12 is best taken simply as the conclusion of vv 10–11 and that vv 13 and 14 are distinct from it and each other, though both follow from either v 12b or v 5; "lest" is implied before all of them if the latter sequence of consecutive future verbs is the operative one.

12. *expose.* In spite of the common theme of nakedness, v 12 is not identical in import to v 11, in which the lesson enforced is that Yahweh owns everything; he takes back the various commodities in order to reassert his ownership. The removal of the woman's clothing in v 12 serves different purposes, exposure of the woman to public shame, and testing her lovers' power to protect her. In v 11 the removal of the woman's food and clothing implies her abandonment by the husband; in v 12, by contrast, the challenge to the lovers to rescue her implies that the husband now has the woman indisputably in his grasp. We conclude that the imagery in v 12 is largely independent of the imagery in v 11. We are entitled to see in "Now" the usual effect of moving to something new.

There remains, however, the possibility that the phrases to "(un)cover her nakedness" (v 11) and to "expose her lewdness" (v 12) should be kept closely together. This has a bearing on the meaning of the words in both places. The relatedness of the expressions would seem to be proved by the use of *'erwâ,* "nakedness" (v 11), with *gillâ,* "to expose" (v 12), to describe sexual intercourse in Leviticus 18 and 20; the verb is used elsewhere to describe sexual intimacies (Ruth 3:4,7), including apparently indecent public exposure (II Sam 6:20).

lewdness. The CAD (B:142–144, cf. 65–66) does not bear out the claim of Wolff (1974:37) that Akkadian *baštu/baltu* means genitalia or sexual power. Since *nablût* occurs only here in the Hebrew Bible, we derive no help from other usages in settling its precise meaning. Derivation from the root *nbl* is most likely; a *nābāl,* "fool," is a slob, a person devoid of moral sensibilities or social niceties, and at the same time arrogant and contumacious. Socially deviant sexual activity can be involved. In Judg 19:23 *nĕbālâ* may refer to homosexual rape (cf. Boling 1975:276). In II Sam 13:12 it refers to incest. It refers to other forms of sexual activity as well (Gen 34:7; Deut 22:21), but often has no sexual connotations. Achan's crime was a *nĕbālâ* (Josh 7:15), a breach of covenant. At its weakest, the word means bad manners, especially truculent speech (I Sam 25:25; Isa 9:16; 32:6). It is nearly always the behavior of a man (Gerleman 1974).

Since the verb *'ăgalleh* means "reveal" in a variety of senses, it cannot be relied on to define the precise meaning of its correlate *nablût.* In v 11 the use of *lqḥ* makes it more likely that something concrete ("display your nudity") rather than abstract ("expose your folly") is intended. Our translation *lewdness* is intended as a compromise between these possibilities. Since the lovers are to view this action, it is more likely that the woman is to have her naked body put on display as obscene. There is a poignancy in this. Israelite society had strict taboos against public nakedness. The circumstances of Jacob's wedding suggest that even husbands might not normally have viewed their wives in the nude. There are many passages in the Song of Songs, on the other hand, which show that every detail of the woman's naked body was an object of enjoyment for the gaze of her lover. Why the husband should now deliberately share this privilege with his rivals is not clear, although in view of the context of the former's outrage and legitimate demand for retribution (cf. v 5), it is to be seen as a form of punishment appropriate to the crime. Just as in the past the errant wife has sought out her lovers and eagerly disrobed in their presence for the purposes of sexual gratification, so now she will be forcibly exposed in the same situation, and publicly humiliated. The subtlety of the talion here is essentially that what she did secretly and for pleasure will now be done to her openly and for her disgrace. (Note a similar theme in the story of David and Bathsheba; cf. II Sam 12:11–12 and 16:21–22). At the same time, it may be the husband's aim to demonstrate the helplessness and futility of her lovers in contrast with his own power and authority.

her lovers. See the NOTE on v 7. If behind the plural we have the god Baal, then this concedes his existence and his presence as an observer. This is difficult to accept, in view of Hosea's opinion elsewhere that Baal is a "no god" (Hos 8:6). If the human lovers are intended, we must suppose some situation in which they are assembled and where the irate husband takes this drastic step.

rescue her. The boast that no one can rescue someone from Yahweh is made several times in the Hebrew Bible. The usual reason is that there is no other god (Deut 32:39), not that the competitors lack the strength to do so. Since the existence of the lovers is recognized, and, indeed, the boast is made good in their sight, the aim of humiliating the woman is to prove their ineffectualness, perhaps simply to her. Since there is no hint of a trial of strength between the rivals, the unresponsiveness of the lovers must be because they do not dare, or because they do not care. If the immediate parallel is the failure of the god Baal to protect his worshipers, on a larger political stage the king of Assyria will be unable to protect his subjects who have preferred him to Yahweh (Hos 5:12–14). We hesitate to give the word "lovers" too many meanings. In the immediate context it refers to the human lovers active in the Canaanite liturgy, and to the god(s) they represented. To apply it as well to the international political dimension takes us on to different ground. But the statement in Hos 8:9, that Ephraim hired lovers, is made in the area of international politics, and it would be appropriate to say that a power like Assyria would not be able to interfere with Yahweh's judgments.

That Hos 2:12 has political overtones, jeering at the helplessness of Assyria to protect her vassals, becomes more plausible when we compare it with 7:11–12. The simile of birds caught in a cage, that no one can release, is used by Rib-Addi of Byblos in his frantic appeal to the Pharaoh, who has proved equally unreliable in Rib-Addi's time of need. Twice he expresses his very great fear (*pālḫati danniš danniš, EA* 74:43) that there is no one who can rescue him from the hand of the enemy (*ianu amēlim^lim ša ušizibuni ištu qati . . . EA* 74:32f, also lines 44f, cf. v 12b.) Like birds caught in a cage, so is he in the city of Byblos *kima iṣṣurāti ša ina libbi^bi ḫuḫari (kilubi) šaknāt kišuma anaku ina ^uruGubla* (lines 45–48).

13. *put an end to.* The meaning of the verb has been discussed in connection with 1:4. Here there is a play on the root *šbt* in the verb and in the noun for "weekly celebrations."

her merriment. The grouping of the five objects of the verb makes it clear that there are two sets. The middle three constitute a series. The last two of these, literally "sabbath" and "month," are to be taken as collectives, referring to weekly and monthly religious celebrations. The first of the three, *ḥag,* refers to annual festivals. In Israelite religion such festivities were closely geared to the agricultural and pastoral year. The last word, "assembly," is a general term for all three. The list of the three kinds of festive assemblies — annual, monthly, weekly — is inserted between the words "merriment" and "assembly"; these sundered words constitute a discontinuous hendiadys — "her merry carnivals." This conjunction is confirmed by the fact that only these two nouns have the word "all" in front of them.

Joy, and especially joy in worship, was a hallmark of Israelite religion. The words *śāśôn* and *māśôś* describe the duty of Yahweh's people to rejoice in his presence, with dancing and music, singing and cheering; the abolition of *māśôś* does not imply disapproval of such enjoyment. The way in which these ceremonies are called "her" festivals implies that Yahweh does not countenance them as his.

No hint is given as to what means are to be used to cause the cessation of such activities. The ruination of crops (v 11) and of fruit trees (v 14) would certainly take the enthusiasm out of the harvest festivals; but they would not immobilize the cult. On the contrary, in Canaanite religion it was precisely disasters of this kind that the rituals, especially the fertility rituals, were designed to cope with. Their total suspension would mean that society had ceased to function.

In this verse Hosea's wife and Yahweh's Israel are indistinguishable. The feminine suffix "her," which occurs five times and so is very prominent, could refer either to the woman or to the land. The two-sided reference is congruent because Gomer was an Israelite, and her adultery was an epitome and also a specific instance of national involvement in the cult.

The location of her sin in the great religious meetings shows that it is not just a matter of private misbehavior.

14. This verse picks up several motifs from the preceding material. The devastation of the orchards resembles the desolation of the desert (v 5b), and prepares for v 16. Her statement that "they" (her children) are the fee which her lovers "gave" her resembles the belief that the lovers gave her the necessities of life (v 7b). The designation of the children (*hēmmâ*) as the wages matches the description of them in v 6 as "children of promiscuity." The description of the lovers as benefactors contrasts with the statement about Yahweh in v 10. The action of putting *them* to the jungle corresponds to treating *her* as in the wilderness (v 5b). The eating of the children by animals matches killing the mother with thirst (v 5b). While v 14aA is directed against the mother, and follows on from v 13, the rest of the verse refers to the children and implements the threat to show them no compassion (v 6a).

I shall lay waste. The verb *šmm*, "to devastate," is used abundantly by later prophets, notably Jeremiah and Ezekiel, along with its cognate nouns *šammâ* and *šĕmāmâ*, both meaning "desolation." The verb is found only here in Hosea, the first noun in Hos 5:9. This sparse use is no reason for doubting the authenticity of the occurrences, for both Amos and Micah use this vocabulary. The devastation of vines and fig trees is more than the failure of seasonal crops. Something on the scale of Isa 7:23–25 is required, in which the land reverts to wilderness. In Jeremiah 4 the scale is even more colossal, the whole earth resembling pre-creation chaos. In what follows, as already noted, we recognize two levels of discourse. On the surface, the imagery of the orchards is continued and the reversion of cultivated areas to jungle is described (cf. 14b). Less apparent is the shift in focus from vineyards and orchards to the children of the marriage and their foreordained fate.

vines . . . fig trees. The Hebrew has singular nouns, but, as with the nouns in v 13, collectives are doubtless intended, and, as in v 13, LXX rightly leads the way for other versions by using plurals. In v 17, vineyards are bestowed on the bride. In herself, Gomer could be regarded as the proprietor of vineyards and orchards. The vine and fig were popular symbols of Israel as Yahweh's plantation, and Hosea uses them elsewhere in this traditional sense to refer to the idyllic Wilderness period (9:10; 10:1; 14:8). The ruination of the fruit trees is more catastrophic than the spoilage of the crops; we are nearer to the devastation of the land threatened in v 5b.

Those of whom she said. If we are correct in seeing a shift after the first line of v 14, then vv 14aB–15 constitute another unit in the prophetic discourse. The concluding "Oracle of Yahweh," if original, is a clear signal that a speech, or a major portion of it, has ended. Even without that, the finality of the closing words — "me she forgot" — is quite enough. If a scribe added the rubric, he did not spoil anything. The shift in v 14 is less obvious, and requires rather sophisticated arguments to defend it. These arguments have little weight unless the principles of composition of this discourse are correspondingly sophisticated. It has generally been supposed that "they," the wages, refers to the vine and fig tree, and that it is the vineyards and fig orchards that will turn into jungle and be eaten by wild animals. The basic idea of divine judgment resulting in the reversion of settled and cultivated areas to wilderness or forest is common in the prophetic literature (cf. Mic 3:12 and, on a more drastic scale, Jer 4:23–26), but the details here are different. It is certainly to be expected that the antecedent of the relative "pronoun" *'ăšer* in v 14aB will be the immediately preceding nouns. The trees are then identified as the payment made to the woman for her prostitute services, an idea in line with the opinion she expressed in v 7b, that bread and water and the rest were gifts (or payments) from her lovers. But it is precisely this development of the ideas of vv 6–7 in vv 14aB–15 that invites us to find a more profound (and alarming) connection of vv 14aB–15 with this earlier material than with the contiguous v 14aA.

There are several severe difficulties with an attempt to preserve the integrity of v 14. First, the clash in gender is notable if not intolerable, unless we change the pronouns or suppose that the words "vine" and "fig tree" had abnormal gender in Hosea's dialect. While both *gepen* and *tĕ'ēnâ* are normally feminine, it must be admitted that *gepen* seems to be masculine in II Kings 4:39 (the text may not be sound), and possibly in Hos 10:1, though the syntax of the latter, and hence the gender of *gepen* there, are problematic. The normal assumption that the following *bōqēq* modifies *gepen,* thus establishing its gender, is questionable. It is hard to believe that these two common words *gepen* and *tĕ'ēnâ* were ever considered masculine; but the independent pronoun (*hēmmâ*) and the two pronoun suffixes (*-m*) are masculine and can hardly be a scribal mistake. Even if we allow the possibility of a connection with pronominal forms later in the verse, which are clearly masculine, we would nevertheless be justified in looking for a more distant, but also more congruent, antecedent, namely a true m pl noun. Verse 14 would be nearer to v 7 if it were the fruit, rather than the trees, that was considered a token of favor from a fertility god. The tree itself, without a bountiful crop, would not be satisfactory. While it would make some sense if the fruit groves were turned into jungle (v 14bA), the picture is more strained if we suppose that they will also become food for wild animals. This is anticlimactic, quite apart from the question of which wild beasts would enjoy eating grapes, figs, or the leaves of these trees. Certainly frightful predators are more likely to be carnivores.

We have already pointed out the connection between v 7 and v 14 through the idea of the lovers' gifts. An additional link is that in each place this idea is something she said to herself (*'āmĕrâ*). If the "lovers" are the "givers," what are the things they gave which she calls her *'etnâ*, "fee"? A number of arguments point to the conclusion that "they" are the children.

(1) The pronoun *hēmmâ* in its occurrence in 2:6 refers to the children, correlative with *hî'* referring to their mother. (2) Mother and children are linked by the common opprobrium *zĕnûnîm* (1:2; 2:6 — the latter the last occurrence of *hēmmâ* before v 14). From v 6 through v 13 all attention has been on the mother or "the land." A comparably drastic threat is directed against the children in v 14. (3) That the mother and the children are to receive similar treatment is shown by comparing the verbs in vv 5b and 14b: *wĕśamtîhâ . . . wĕśamtîm,* "I will set her . . . I will set them." The wilderness and the jungle also make a pair, and the two passages are developed along similar lines. If, as we have tried to show, v 5b means "I shall treat her as in the wilderness," rather than "I will turn her (the land) into a wilderness," then v 14b means "I shall consign them (the children) to jungle," not "and I shall turn them (the orchards) into a jungle," although the latter remains possible. (4) The prospect of wild animals eating grapes and figs is not very frightening; it is a different story when they start eating children, and this is precisely what is threatened in cursing texts in the Bible as well as in similar liturgies from the ancient Near East (Fensham 1966b; Hillers 1964a:54–56). While in some passages, such as Hos 5:14; 13:7–8, it is Yahweh who acts like a ravenous carnivore, in other places (Jer 5:6; Ps 79:2; Ezek 29:5) the eating is to be taken literally; cf. I Kings 14:11; 16:4. This point is clinched by Lev 26:22, where Yahweh threatens to send wild animals (same phrase as in Hos 2:14) which will "bereave you of your children" (cf. II Macc 9:15). (5) The ultimate purpose of her adultery is now revealed. Whatever benefit might be found in being given "bread and water" (v 7), greater importance attaches to the gift of children; and greater error results when they are attributed to Baal rather than to Yahweh. (6) The statement begun in v 6a ("To her children I shall not show pity") is now explained. We are otherwise left with no statement of how Yahweh will withdraw love from the children, unless we have it in v 14. (7) If "her vines and her fig trees" is the antecedent of the clause "They are my wages," then the verb of speaking ("she said") is awkwardly used. It is unusual in Hebrew to have such a verb inserted parenthetically; Gen 3:2 is a rare example. For a better construction we would expect *'mrh 'lyhm/lhm,* "she said

concerning them." (8) If the location of the antecedent as far away as v 6 ("her children") is thought to put too much of a strain on the language, then such an analysis is not essential for our general results. The *'šr* clause would be *casus pendens,* resumed by the object pronoun suffixes on the verbs in v 14b — (as for those of) whom she said, "They are my wages . . ." (and) I shall put them. Even better may be the recognition that *'ăšer* does not need an antecedent; the use of *'ăšer* as a conjunction is well attested and the meaning "in that she said" is acceptable.

wages. The word *'etnâ* is found only here. The related word *'etnān,* which occurs in the phrase "a prostitute's fee" (Deut 23:19; Mic 1:7), which establishes its meaning, is known also to Hosea (9:1). The fact that Hosea avoids the regular term for a prostitute's fee, as well as the term for prostitute in speaking of the woman, indicates that she did not fill that role, at least professionally. In a relationship between lovers the exchange of gifts and services often takes place without a technical transaction. As previously argued, the opprobrium consists centrally in the violation of marriage vows and the liaison with lovers, quite apart from the exchange of gifts and services. If the unique variant used here is a coinage of Hosea's, it reverses a pattern we have already seen in *na'ăpûpîm* (Hos 2:4), of doubling the final consonant of the root (cf. Hos 4:12). Wolff (1974:38) suggests that the word *'etnâ* might have been invented or chosen to play on the sound of *tĕ'ēnâ.*

In calling her children her "wages," there is no indication that her "lovers" were fathers of the children, although such a possibility exists. Since we lack an accurate chronicle, we cannot settle this point; we have argued that Hosea was the father of them all. The aim of Baal worship was to secure the fertility necessary for offspring in marriage, not to supply an alternative to marriage. The idea of payment would be satisfied better by success in having legitimate children (Ps 127:3).

my (wages). Literally "to/for me." The construction "a payment to/for me" has a nuance which would not be achieved if a possessive pronoun suffix had been used, which would imply "my fee" (which I charge) or emphasize ownership after reception. The repeated (*'etnâ* . . .) *lî,* (*nātěnû*) *lî,* retains the idea of a donation or reward that could be separated from the transaction of hiring a prostitute. If, however, the meaning is like that in v 7, it would support the conclusion of Kuhnigk (1974:10) that the pronoun suffixes there are dative. Here, on the other hand, a benefactive ("for me") is in order. If "her children" (v 6) is the antecedent, as we advocate, then v 14aB gives the reason why they are called children of promiscuity. It is not that they themselves are promiscuous and not that they were conceived in promiscuity; it is because their mother said that they were an *'etnâ* for her in return for sexual activities.

paid. This translation is preferred to the more literal "gave" to fit the object "wages," and for reasons already discussed in the NOTES on 2:7.

I shall consign. The same construction as in 2:5b. There the object is the mother; here the object is the children. The translation recommended here is supported by Ps 85:14 (cf. Deut 22:14; Judg 1:28; II Kings 4:10; Job 29:9; 40:4).

jungle. While *ya'ar* can mean "forest" in various aspects, it is often a place of foreboding, infested by beasts of prey, notably the lion (Jer 5:6; 12:8; Amos 3:4; Mic 5:7; Ps 104:20–21).

wild animals of the countryside. LXX has added birds and reptiles, as v 20. In Ezek 14:21 the four agents of God's punishment are famine, wild animals, war, and pestilence; beasts are missing from the lists in Jer 27:8 and II Sam 24:13. The animals in question are probably the bear (Hos 13:8; cf. II Kings 2:24) and the lion (II Kings 17:25–26); these two predators are linked in I Sam 17:34–36 and Amos 5:19. The leopard (Hos 13:7) and the wolf (Jer 5:6) are also identified. In Gen 37:33, Jacob says "an evil beast" has eaten Joseph (cf. "the evil" in Gen 19:19). Jacob's terror as well as grief is explained if such a fate was a sign of a curse on the parent.

There are places in the Hebrew Bible where we are told about untamed animals foraging in the abandoned orchards. In the allegory of the vine developed in Psalm 80, a boar ravages it (vv 13–14); in Exod 23:11, wild animals eat the leftover harvest in the sabbatical year. In the present context, however, there is reason to believe that what the wild beasts will eat is human, more precisely the children. To the arguments already given above, several more may be added.

First, note the cancellation of this curse in 2:20, where a covenant is made with the wild animals; this is intended to secure the safety of human beings (cf. Exod 23:29), not just the safety of trees. Hence it is human beings who are in danger in v 14.

In the present context the threat is especially horrible, because the victims are children. Just as she said her material supplies are gifts of her lovers (v 7) and her husband will take them back (v 11), so she said her children are her lovers' payment (v 14a), and her husband will take them away (v 14b). Mother and children are linked (Hos 1:2; 2:6), and they must come to a similar end; parents and children are to share the common fate of being eaten by wild animals, according to II Macc 9:15. There are several places in the Hebrew Bible where the destruction of children, but not their parents, is the most terrible way of punishing *parents,* more terrible because the parents survive (Jer 31:15; Ps 137:9). (To be sure, when someone dies bereaved she or he is guaranteed a more miserable afterlife.) The divine punishment of parental bereavement is used notably in cases of adultery: David's child, not David, dies because of his adultery.

The penalty prescribed in Lev 20:20 for adultery with an aunt is a childless death. This does not mean simply that the parents shall be executed
quickly before they have time to have children. If they already have children, these will be killed first, so that the offenders are childless when they
die. In line with this, the prophet Ahijah warns the wife of Jeroboam I that
wild creatures will eat their children's corpses (I Kings 14:11). The punishment of recalcitrant parents by sending wild animals to tear their children to pieces is threatened in the great commination of Lev 26:22, a text
decisive for our interpretation of Hos 2:14. Mother and children are
treated as an indivisible life unit in this kind of justice, as is recognized in
Job 31:9–12, where a husband's adultery brings disaster to his wife and
children. By poetic justice, his wife is used by other men; his children are
burned (cf. Gen 38:24 and Lev 21:9, where burning is the punishment
for adultery); in Job 31:12b, *tĕbû'â* means "progeny," and not "increase"
or "income."

Finally we point out that it is this drastic threat against the children that
gives urgency to the task they are given in Hos 2:4. They must plead with
their mother, for their own survival depends on her repentance.

15. *So shall I punish her.* The same idiom is used in Hos 1:4b; see the
NOTE there. Since the Baals are unmasked in this verse, we note a distant
connection with the first crisis of this kind, the apostasy at Horeb (Exodus
32): on that occasion Moses was able to restrain Yahweh's anger, but not
to quench it. It was held in reserve until some unspecified time. "In the
day that I punish, I will punish them for their sin" (Exod 32:34). This
perspective makes it likely that, on the level of the story of Yahweh and
Israel, the "Baal days" represent the long period of time from that incident to the present.

the Baals. The term *bĕ'ālîm* is strictly speaking the m pl form of *ba'al,*
but reflects a variety of uses and meanings. Since Hosea uses both singular
and plural forms, and both are found in the present passage (cf. *bā'al* in v
10), we must review the range of meaning and reference of these terms,
in both Hosea and the other books of the Bible. The term itself, singular
or plural, is a common noun meaning "master, owner" or the like. In connection with divinities, the singular refers to a specific deity, and serves as
his title. In the Bible, as also in the Canaanite mythological literature, one
god is singled out by the title Baal, and he is meant when the term is used
by itself, or where there is no other specification that another god is
meant. As we know from the Ugaritic tablets and other sources, the Baal
par excellence, a chief god of Canaan, is Hadad the storm god (the
name Hadad is apparently derived from a common noun meaning
"thunder, storm"). Except where otherwise specified or indicated, this is
the god meant when Baal is used in the Bible and Canaanite texts; in some
cases it is likely that the plural form *b'lym* is not a plural at all but simply

the singular form with a suffixed enclitic *mem*. In other instances, orthographically the same in Biblical Hebrew, we may be dealing with a plural of majesty as in the case of Elohim, the common term for God in the Hebrew Bible. In other cases we probably have a true plural, like *'ĕlohîm* when used as a numerical plural. Baal-Hadad is in all likelihood the god designated in the contest between Elijah the prophet of Yahweh and the 450 prophets of Baal at Mount Carmel (I Kings 18). It may be argued, however, that the Baal in that story is to be identified with the chief god of Tyre (Jezebel's city of origin and hence the source of her particular form of Baal-worship). This god is commonly called Melkart (itself a compound designation—king of the city, i.e. the underworld) and thought to be a chthonic deity, like Dis or Pluto in Greco-Roman religion, and perhaps related to Reshep, known from the Bible and the Canaanite texts as a divinity of pestilence. Since, however, the story turns on the rain-making capability of the competing deities, and the contest is decided by a bolt of lightning dispatched from the heavens, followed a little later by a great rain storm, there can be little doubt that the Baal of I Kings 18 is the storm god, who must have been acknowledged in Tyre as in Samaria and Jezreel, and in fact everywhere that Canaanite religion was practiced.

Where the word *ba'al* is used in the singular as part of a construct chain, the reference may well be and often is to another deity; the phrase serves as an epithet. Thus the title Baal Shamem, literally "Master of the Heavens," which appears in the Bible only in the distorted form *šiqqûṣîm měšomēm* (Dan 9:27, cf. 11:31; 12:11), is applied to Zeus Olympios, the king of the gods, who may be equated in Daniel with Hadad, or possibly with El, the creator of heaven and earth. Similarly terms like Baal Peor, "Master of Peor" (Num 25:3,5) refer to the deity worshiped in a particular locality; the specific character or role of the deity can only be determined on the basis of additional data, often lacking. The use of the term Baal, then, does not automatically identify the deity in question as Hadad.

The plural *b'lym* in the Bible may refer to the different gods all bearing the title *b'l*, "Master," of which a number are attested; or it may refer to the different shrines at which the same god was worshiped. Given the variety of special practices and characteristics, the original deity may have been dissolved in a multiplicity of manifestations localized at the many shrines. Thus the Baal of this locality and the Baal of that locality may originally have been the same deity, but the process of localizing the deity in a separate temple, with statue and priestly entourage, would tend to differentiate this particular manifestation of the godhead from others with their own distinctive features.

In particular cases one or more of these elements might be present: originally different gods become assimilated to each other and equated under identical titles (cf. v 18); manifestations or representations of the same deity become autonomous entities distinguished by special features, especially their geographic localization.

the time of the Baals. Literally, "the days/seasons of Baalim." Gomer's own Baal days would be her time of adultery with her lovers, a time of devotion to Baal. On the national level, Israel's Baal days could go back to the first apostasy in the desert. The similarity between 2:15 and 1:4b points to a parallel between "the blood of Jezreel" and "the days of Baal." If a defined epoch is in mind in the use of the word *yāmîm* (see the NOTES on 1:1), then the "days of Jezreel" define the epoch of Jehu's dynasty, now coming to its close. The days of Jezreel will come again. Yahweh will now do to Jeroboam II's regime what the latter's progenitor, Jehu, did to Ahab's, and for exactly the same reason—for Baal devotions. In Wolff's opinion (1974:40), the Baal days are more technically the "Canaanite cultic feasts," connected with the festivals in v 13.

to whom. The word "time" is usually taken as the antecedent of the relative, yielding the translation "during which she burned. . . ." The word *bĕ'ālîm* is a better candidate, and thus our translation.

Although the plural pronoun stands in grammatical agreement with "Baalim," it does not necessarily denote a plurality of divinities. In the case of *'ĕlōhîm,* referring to Yahweh, grammar is superficially violated, since most often referent pronouns, nouns, adjectives and verbs are in the singular. Nevertheless, *b'lym* was understood as a plural form.

she burns (incense). The verb *qṭr* is used in both *Pi'el* and *Hip'il* forms, the latter being more frequent. Both forms are distributed throughout the Hebrew Bible, and both are found in Hosea, the *Hip'il* here and *Pi'el* in 4:13 and 11:2. The idea of creating an odor pleasing to deity by burning things is present in both forms. The object is not always identified, and when this is so, as here, incense is assumed, and here supplied as object. The use of the *Hip'il* here shows that the supposed rule that *Pi'el* is used for pagan worship, *Hip'il* for Yahwistic, is not strictly followed. Apart from its exact meaning, which cannot be determined as the object is not mentioned, the verb presents two other problems. The first is its tense; the form is imperfect, but because future reference does not fit, past is often assumed. If the word "Baals" is the antecedent, then a present-tense translation may be more in keeping with the verb—"the Baals to whom she burns incense." The second problem is the extent of the woman's active participation in the cult; any worshiper can be said to offer sacrifice, even if a religious functionary does it on his behalf. We cannot assume that the woman became a member of the staff of some shrine—dedicated to rituals which included the burning of incense. Since in this context the woman also symbolizes Israel, it is even less certain that the "wife" was an officiant in the Baal cult.

she decked herself. The verb is used only once of a man, Job 40:10, ironically, when God invites Job to show himself dressed as a god. Otherwise it describes the adornment of a woman for some special occasion, usually a joyful festivity (Isa 61:10; Jer 31:4). While no items of dress are consistently specified, the verb seems to be applied to jewelry of gold and silver, especially bridal adornment (Isa 61:10), the husband's gifts (Ezek 16:11). Jeremiah and Ezekiel both describe the unendurable situation in which the wife uses these precious things to beautify herself when she turns to adultery (Jer 4:30; Ezek 16:13; 23:40), a picture they may have derived from this passage.

The *waw*-consecutive construction ("and she adorned herself . . .") seems inappropriate here, after *taqṭîr* with a present-tense reference. The lack of a smooth transition between the clauses is an indication that there is another shift at this point. We have changed from the threat (future tense—"and I shall punish") to past narration ("and she decked herself . . ."). Apart from the tense, the aspects are incongruous. The time of burning incense to the Baalim was a period of continued activity, whereas the phrases "she decked herself . . . and went after . . ." point to definite, completed acts in the past. This conclusion is reinforced by the tense of the final verb—"she forgot." We cannot agree with Wolff (1974:40) that the verb here describes taking part in cult processions. With the change from ongoing activity to decisive action, the scene has changed from the cult where she was burning incense to the involvement in adultery. The clue is provided by v 7b. After a statement of resolution — "Let me go off after my lovers . . . ," we expect a statement of fulfillment — "and [she] went after her lovers . . . ," which is precisely what we have here. The narrative begun in v 7 continues, and takes us back to the beginning, the decision to run away from her husband. Such an act of renunciation is "to forget Yahweh," a deliberate, responsible decision, not a fading of memory with the passage of time.

nose ring . . . necklace. The sacred bridal gifts could be defiled by being put to evil use. If this jewelry served for more than ornamentation, deliberately to identify the wearer as a prostitute, a further attempt to establish its appearance and symbolism is called for. The author's technique in composition, profusely illustrated through cc 1–2, suggests that Hos 2:4b and 2:15a are connected:

> zĕnûnêhā mippānêhā   nizmāh
> na'ăpûpêhā mibbên šādêhā   ḥelyātāh

If *ḥălî* is the masculine of *ḥelyātâ,* as seems likely, the same ornaments occur in the same sequence in Prov 25:12. This passage provides two useful pieces of information: the ornaments are made of gold; and their associations could be wholesome.

The *nezem* is mentioned more often; and, when the material is specified, it is always gold (Gen 24:22; Exod 32:2,3; Judg 8:24–26; Job 42:11). Gen 24:47 and Isa 3:21 indicate that a *nezem* could be worn on the nose, whereas Gen 35:4 and Exod 32:2–3 show that it could be worn in the ears; the plural is used in the latter case. When the same person has jewelry for both nose and ears (Ezek 16:12), the *nezem* is for the nose. Prov 11:22 paints a ludicrous picture of such a gold ring in a pig's nose. The *nezem* could also be used to generate a pleasing simile for a well-spoken word (Prov 25:12). As an engagement gift to a young girl, the *nezem* was an honorable adornment (Gen 24:22,30,47; Ezek 16:12). In Job 42:11 it is a present to a man, but the purpose is not indicated. Judg 8:24–26 confirms that men in Transjordan wore the *nezem*, and there is an archaeological note which suggests that this was the standard adornment of Ishmaelites. Another side of the story is revealed by comparing Gen 35:4 with Gen 35:2. The removal of such "rings" could be a purification from the contaminating worship of "foreign gods," apparently associated with wearing them, rather than direct use in the cult (i.e. donation as ornaments for statues or in the casting and plating of images); the only thing to do with them was to bury them. In other situations such jewelry could be dedicated either to pagan (Exod 32:2,3; Judg 8:24–26) or proper (Exod 35:22) religious use.

On at least two occasions the gold from *nezem*s was used to make a pagan idol (Exod 32:2–3; Judg 8:24–26), most likely as gold leaf to cover a statue of some other material; Hos 2:10 indicates that the bride's silver and gold, the lavish gift of her husband, were similarly used "for Baal." Hos 2:4b and 2:15a together suggest that the bride's gifts were defiled by her using them in the pursuit of adulterous love. Proof of her reform will be given when she removes them. The apparent contradiction in saying that the bridal jewelry was used to adorn the adulteress, and also to make the idol, should not distress us. In Ezekiel 16, the same themes are mingled profusely.

The nature of the *ḥelyātâ* is less clear, for the word appears only here. The masculine form also occurs once (Prov 25:12); this passage confirms that it, too, could be made of gold. The association with *nezem* suggests that the *ḥălî/ḥelyātâ* was also a piece of jewelry. In Cant 7:2, *ḥălāʾîm* (perhaps an Aramaizing formation) has powerfully erotic associations. In a context of lovemaking, the description of the beloved proceeds from the feet to the head, and includes "the curves of your thighs," to which these jewels are compared (Pope 1977:615–616). Combining the information from Hosea and the Song of Songs, we have an association of breasts and thighs which suggests identification of *ḥelyātâ* with the thoracic bands which adorn nude female goddesses like Ishtar and Anat of the Semitic world and Atargatis and the Winged Victory of Greek antiquity. Pertinent features are the crossing over of the bands below the naked breasts, which are thereby brought into prominence. It is not certain if the attachment at this strategic point serves to join the bands, or whether the bands are worn in order to secure an amulet at just the right spot. In many representations the bands are not straight, like a solder's saltire, but have a downward curve to the xiphisternum which matches the downward curves of the groin to the vulva. The navel is emphasized as an erotogenous zone in Cant 7:2. While we cannot prove that the *ḥelyātâ* worn by Gomer was a similar article of dress, the circumstantial evidence points in that direction. One obstacle to certainty on this point is the fact that the significance of these chest bands on the naked goddesses has never been explained. Detailed studies suggest several possibilities. Du Mesnil du Buisson (1947) found connections with the symbol for Venus. From a thorough examination of the evidence, Dales (1963) found hints that the pectoral pendant had a magical function. Pope (1970, cf. 1977:171, 210) has drawn attention to the similar chest harness of warriors, including the warrior goddesses. There is not always a medallion at the crossover point. Since Anat's passion for blood and her insatiable sexual drives are aspects of her violent character, an erotic meaning for the straps is not excluded by their usefulness as part of a soldier's equipment for holding weapons. The goddess wears them even when she stands nude and unarmed. An adornment at once magical, military, and venereal would be in keeping with the character of the great warrior-virgin-mother-sorceress, and equally fitting as a badge on one of her devotees. Such ornamentation is met in the iconography of Anat at Ugarit, and the decoration of her breasts with jewels comes in for special mention when she is preparing herself for seductive lovemaking. At least this would seem to be the situation in UT *'nt* III:1–3 and RS 24.245 rev 6–8 (Virolleaud 1968:557–559), in which Anat puts *ri'mt,* "a kind of jewels," on or at her breasts. (Compare the dedication of jewelry for the goddess's breasts in the Mari economic text ARM 7.10, Bottéro 1957:5.) The erotic context is clearer in the latter Ugaritic text. The obverse has an incomplete description of Baal, whose attractions are described in a style like that of the Song of Songs. On the reverse Anat is preparing herself with oils and perfumes, and takes a lyre to accompany her singing. A portrayal of a goddess called Qudshu-Astarte-Anath shows her naked except for bracelets, collar, and bands across the chest connecting with a girdle around the waist (Edwards 1955). It may be that the female devotees of Baal dressed like his divine consort, and that the worship of some Canaanite goddess, still detectable in the biblical texts, persisted side by side with Baal worship.

That devotees of an idol might wear badges of some kind on face (forehead) and chest is shown by Ezek 14:3,7, whose language should be taken literally. These men have put their *gillulîm* "upon their heart" and they put "the stumbling-block of their iniquity" "in front of their face."

but me she forgot. The interruption of the consecutive sequence of verbs by placing the pronoun object first is not required by any rules of narrative composition, but is the result of deliberate choice and achieves two rhetorical effects. Putting a perfect verb at the end of a clause is a mark of paragraph termination, and here defers the effect of this verb until last. The object "me" is immediately next to "her lovers." This makes the two actions simultaneous (the pattern is chiastic, the last clause circumstantial to the preceding), and at the same time secures a contrast.

In the Hebrew Bible, especially in the Deuteronomic tradition, remembering, knowing, and obeying are aspects of covenant-keeping. Hosea's emphasis on "knowing" Yahweh (4:6; 6:3–6; 13:4–6) shows that forgetting, being treacherous (5:7; 6:7), and rebelling are the opposite. Forgetting is willful and culpable.

Oracle of Yahweh. This formula, used so abundantly by some prophets, notably Jeremiah, is found only four times in Hosea. Here it comes after the climactic statement that concludes the unit 2:4–15. The tone changes from this point on. In 2:18 the formula serves to introduce an oracle within larger discourse, and in 2:23 it is actually embedded in a speech. At Hos 11:11 it seems to mark another major division: see the NOTE there.

Except to mark a transition, this parenthetical statement is not integral to the composition; so its removal would not imperil any structures. It does not matter whether it comes from the prophet himself or was inserted by a compiler or editor. At this point is sounded once more the sacred Name, which has not been used since c 1, where it occurs six times. The heartbroken words "but me she forgot" could have been spoken by a human husband; the language could have been taken as imagery of human marriage. Now there can be no mistake. It is Yahweh himself who has been saying all this in the life and through the words of the prophet.

16–25. The attitude of the husband (Yahweh) in this subsection is altogether different from that in vv 4–15. There he was full of threats; here his proposals are conciliatory and constructive. There is no simple statement of the broad connection between the two major sections of 2:4–25; interpretation all the way through has had to be left open to more than one possibility. The first problem is how much realism can be ascribed to the language on the level of human husband and wife, and the level of Yahweh and his people. It is possible that a measure of realism is present in each level. Stripping the wife naked could be taken quite literally, as could stripping the country bare. But each could be a figurative way of talking about the other, and both could be symbolic of other disasters — total crop failure, military conquest, etc. There is a limit to the usefulness of 2:4–15 in reconstructing either Hosea's private life or Israel's national history.

A second general problem is to determine the extent to which 2:4–15 is documentary, whether of Gomer's personal life or of Israel's national experience, or reflective. We have noticed an absence of debate, of interaction: the passage could be a soliloquy or a reverie, in which the speaker contemplates possibilities. The erratic development of conditions and threats could reflect turbulence in the mind of a person who cannot decide what to do. Hos 6:4 and 11:8 reveal a mind tormented by such indecision, torn by the conflict between the urge to exact justified vengeance, and the contrary urge to show mercy and to forgive. This is in part the conflict between 2:4–15 and 2:16–25. If the ultimate reality of Yahweh is that he is "a gracious and merciful God" (Exod 34:6), then grace and compassion are at the springs of his being, and will ultimately overcome his anger (cf. Mic 7:18).

The exhortations in 2:4–15 do not refer to promises of what the husband will do if the wife changes her ways, but to punishments to be meted out if she does not change. By contrast, the promises in 2:16–25 are not attached to conditions of reform. In 2:16–25 the woman (Israel) does nothing and is not asked to do anything; it is anticipated that she "will respond." There is no indication that the amazing transformation between v 15 and v 16 is brought about by a dramatic alteration in the woman's (Israel's) conduct. Our impression is that none of the exhortations addressed to the woman in 2:4–15 were obeyed and none of the threats carried out. The former is more certain than the latter, if we are to be guided by the rest of the Book of Hosea, particularly passages which speak of savage assaults by Yahweh upon his people, which correspond to political events of the period. If these attacks correspond to the measures predicted in 2:4–15, then restoration comes after justice has been satisfied, making the renewal in 2:16–25 even more stupendous. But this correspondence should not be carried too far since the actions of the husband in 2:4–15 are clearly intended to be remedial and educative, corrective, not destructive. While none of the redemptive acts which follow in 2:16–25 necessarily presuppose repentance on the part of the woman, they may be linked to it through vv 8–9. The bold reversal of the sequence of repentance, reconciliation, redemption, and restoration is not as clearly expressed here as in the later prophets: the classic statement is to be found in Ezek 36:22–32, where the prophet affirms that it is the goodness of God and his redemptive activity, rooted entirely in divine grace, which lead to repentance on the part of the people.

Hos 2:4–15 is thrown into a completely different perspective if vv 8–9 are transposed to provide the transition between v 15 and v 16, as is done in some versions, e.g. *JB*. The woman's repentance and return to her husband then become the first and vital act in the process of rehabilitation. Hosea, however, contends that the initiative always remains with the husband (Yahweh), though it is only effective when there is a response (v 17b). The text does not have to be shuffled around to reach this conclusion. Hos 2:16–25 is dominated and unified by the numerous first-person verbs — sixteen in all — and these sustain its positive thrust.

The contrast between 2:4–15 and 2:16–25 can be seen in the fact that promises in the latter cancel or reverse threats in the former. Instead of taking her into the desert to kill her with thirst (v 5), the husband will take her into the desert to make love to her (v 16). Instead of exposing her children to be killed by wild animals (v 14), he will make a covenant with the animals so that all may live in security (v 20). Instead of taking away the grain and must (v 11), he will supply them (v 24). Jezreel will not be a place of blood, but a place where new life springs (vv 24–25). The Valley of Achor, where a criminal and his family were executed, will become a doorway to hope (v 17). The odious name "my baal" will be replaced by the noble title "my husband" (v 18). The negative element in the names "Not-pitied" and "Not-my-people," will be removed. The entire history of Israel will be reenacted, and this time the covenant promises will be kept.

The mother and her children remain in view in 2:16–25, although the primary focus is on Yahweh and Israel. Marriage symbolism is the unifying factor. The treatment of the mother can be traced through vv 16,17, 24a,21–22,18–19 in a development corresponding roughly to courtship, engagement, marriage. The children figure alone in v 20 and vv 23–24, while the whole family is seen together in v 25.

While the eschatological formula (*whyh bywm hhw'*) does not occur at the beginning of the unit, but is placed strategically at different places in the discourse (vv 18,20 without *whyh,* 23), there can be little doubt that the entire subsection shares an eschatological mood.

There are abrupt shifts within 2:16–25, signaled by changes in the pronouns, as the speaker ranges over the scene, focusing attention on different aspects of the restoration of all things, and talking to or about various principals. The woman is addressed directly in vv 18,21–22, and talked about in vv 16–17,19,25. More obscure are the 3 m pl forms which occur in vv 20 and 23–25, but in the final revelation "they" are identified as the children reunited with their mother in ultimate bliss. The stages in the subsection are these.

I. Restored relationships between husband and wife (vv 16–17,19); the wife addressed as "you" and "her."

II. Covenant of peace established between "them" and the animals on one hand and human beings on the other (v 20).

III. Betrothal (vv 21–22) culminating in (re)marriage (v 18); all in second-person singular.

IV. Antiphonal litany celebrating the restoration of harmony, including heaven and earth, and earth's produce; the final chorus includes Jezreel and leads to the conclusion of the subsection (vv 23–24).

V. The mother and children are reunited with the husband and father; peace and unity are restored as the names of the two younger children are reversed (v 25).

Changes in the pronouns serve as a guide to these units. The pattern of the pronouns reveals an overall symmetrical structure, and points to the unity of the whole. It also suggests affinities between the several paragraphs, I with V, II with IV, highlighting III as the centerpiece of a symmetrical arrangement. Content, as well as common pronominal references, bears this out. Each stage has elements of resolution or climax.

It is easy to understand why some scholars can divide the whole passage into several small oracles, each with its own integrity. The unit involving direct address moves from betrothal (solemnly affirmed three times, vv 21–22) and consummation of the marriage, "Then you shall know Yahweh" (v 22b), to the words "my husband" (v 18). The 3 f s forms are spread from vv 16–17 through vv 19 and 25, offering a consistent picture of fulfillment, but with differences in detail and shading: the courtship in the wilderness (vv 16–17), accompanied by the permanent abandonment of Baal worship (v 19), culminating in the reunion of the family, symbolically expressed in what approaches a rebirth of the oldest child and the renaming of the younger ones (v 25). The 3 m pl unit (reflecting the experience of Israel represented symbolically by the children) describes the new covenant of peace between people and nature, among people, and in the cosmos (vv 20,23–24), and leads directly into the denouement in v 25, a multiple climax which completes the discourse that began with v 16 and also gathers in material from the larger unit vv 4–25.

It is not easy to trace the unfolding of the drama, stage by stage, through vv 16–25. If a logical sequence is to be sought, then the betrothal, which comes in the middle (III) should come first. If the betrothal and the marriage (I) are to be separated in time, as seems to be the case in vv 16–17, then it would be helpful if we could work out where the covenant-making (II) and the answering litany (IV) fit in; perhaps they were part of the ceremonies of betrothal or marriage. We must not, however, go too far in imposing rational order on an artistic composition. Each of these five scenes is a vignette of the end time; each portrays a different aspect of what will be accomplished then, or, rather, each presents that event in the guise of five different transactions.

There is something final about each of these paragraphs, and for this reason developments parallel to Israel's historical experience are not to be sought. If the Sinai covenant corresponds to the engagement, then II and III together might be dealing with that event in recapitulation. If entering the promised land is the marriage, then I and V have these themes. IV could go with either. The abundant references to animals, plants, and cosmic powers take us beyond the historical, or at least back to the creation stories, rather than to the Exodus traditions, for the imagery being used.

Another way of coming to grips with the literary organization of this subsection is to study the use of the verb system. Classical Hebrew discourse has three verbal constructions available for the description of situations, events, and states, in future time: (1) *hinnēh* + pronoun + participle; (2) a clause with an imperfect verb; (3) a clause beginning with the consecutive perfect construction. The first describes an impending activity. It is used in v 8 and in v 16, but not thereafter. When a prediction takes on narrative form, the sequence of events is described most clearly by a chain of consecutive perfect clauses; the perfective aspect of the verb form suggests that each action is completed before the next one happens. Such a chain can be broken in several ways. (1) At paragraph boundaries a break in the narrative, especially the onset of a new episode, can be indicated by a clause that begins with an imperfect verb. (2) Transition to a new paragraph can be made even more unmistakable by using a high-level connective such as *lākēn* (vv 8,11,16), *wĕʿattâ* (v 12), or *wĕhāyâ* (*bayyôm habhûʾ*) (vv 18,23). (3) The chain within a paragraph can be interrupted temporarily by the use of a coordinated clause with an imperfect verb in which the verb does not come first but rather some other element intervenes between conjunction and verb, to form a circumstantial clause. Such a clause describes some situation or event contemporaneous with an event in the mainstream of narration.

Leaving out the high-level connectives, the clause types used in Hos 2:16–25 are as follows; initial here means clause-initial.

I.	16aA	I will entice: initial pronoun + participle
	16aB	and I will lead: consecutive perfect
	16b	and I will speak: consecutive perfect
	17a	and I will assign: consecutive perfect
	17b	and she will respond: consecutive perfect
III.	18a	you will call: initial imperfect
	18b	and you will not call: conj. + neg. + imperfect
I.	19a	and I shall remove: consecutive perfect
	19b	and they will not be mentioned: conj. + neg. + imperfect

II. 20a   and I shall make: consecutive perfect
20bA   and bow . . . I shall destroy: conj. + object + imperfect
20bB   and I shall make lie down: consecutive perfect
III. 21a   and I shall betroth: consecutive perfect
21b   and I shall betroth: consecutive perfect
22a   and I shall betroth: consecutive perfect
22b   and you shall know: consecutive perfect
IV. 23aA   I will respond: initial imperfect
23aB   (I will respond: initial imperfect)
23b   and they will respond: conj. + subject + imperfect
24a   and the earth will respond: conj. + subject + imperfect
24b   and they will respond: conj. + subject + imperfect
V. 25aA   and I shall sow: consecutive perfect
25aB   and I will have pity: consecutive perfect
25bA   and I will say: consecutive perfect
25bB   and he will say: conj. + subject + imperfect

These twenty-five clauses include the three main types of paragraph-level clauses in future indicative discourse, along with the initial participial clause, to be discussed below. (A) Clauses with initial imperfect verb, whose normal function is to open a paragraph (v 18a, v 23aA and v 23aB). The first two follow immediately the eschatological preface; the second 'e'ĕneh, in v 23aB, resumes discourse interrupted by the title "Oracle of Yahweh." (B) There are fourteen consecutive perfect clauses, which are used generally to advance the narrative from one time point to the next. If a consecutive perfect clause is used to begin a paragraph, paragraph onset is not clearly marked. If a consecutive perfect clause is used to indicate a simultaneous action, then the sequence of events is not clearly marked. (C) There are seven coordinated clauses with an imperfect verb and with some other grammatical element between the conjunction and the verb. In the case of the two negated clauses (vv 18b and 19b) this word order is unavoidable. In the case of the others, this word order is deliberate, i.e. the clause is circumstantial. In three of such clauses, this inserted element is a subject pronoun (vv 23b, 24b, and 25bB). Since this pronoun is redundant, its function as a contrivance for making a special clause type is manifest. In normal prose, the function of such a clause is to indicate an event circumstantial to the main chain of narration, i.e. an event simultaneous with an event described by a consecutive perfect clause. This relationship is clearly realized in the well-formed constructions in vv 18b, 19b, 20bA, 25bB. The other three instances, however, in vv 23b, 24a, and 24b, would seem to be used anomalously, especially if the actors are to answer each other in turn and not all at once. A corresponding anomaly is encountered in the use of consecutive perfect clauses. Quite apart from the fact that they begin new paragraphs in vv 20a, 21a, and 25aA, they clearly depart from their normal function of portraying consecutive events in vv 21b and 22a, since there is only one act of betrothal, not three. In view of this, we have to ask whether other consecutive perfect clauses, such as v 22b, and those in v 25, portray, not consecutive events in a chain, but simultaneous events in a cluster.

The usage of the three clause types in 2:16–25 is shown in the following chart.

	Clause-initial imperfect *or* pronoun + participle	Consecutive perfect	Coordinated imperfect, not initial
Paragraph opener	16aA, 18a, 23aA, 23aB	20a, 21a, 25aA	
Consecutive act		16b, 22b?	23b, 24a, 24b
Contemporaneous activity		16aB, 17a, 17b, 19a, 20bB, 21b, 22a, 22b?, 25aB, 25bA	18b, 19b, 20bA, 25bB

This shows the extent that the usage of clause types in 2:16–25 departs from the classical norms, assuming that we have correctly identified the paragraph boundaries through the pronouns. For paragraph opening, clause-initial imperfect constructions are normal; here there is abnormal use of three consecutive perfect clauses to achieve this result. For consecutive acts, the normal consecutive perfect is used only once or twice whereas three coordinated imperfect clauses are used abnormally to achieve this result (vv 23–24). Contemporaneous activity is expressed four times by the normal use of coordinated imperfect clauses; but most of the consecutive perfect clauses in the unit seem to be used abnormally, to express simultaneous rather than consecutive action. This is the most anomalous feature of the verb use, by textbook norms, which require that the consecutive perfect be sequential future tense.

The coordinated clauses vv 18b, 19b, 20bA, 25bB come nearest to standard syntax. Verses 18a and 18b are contemporary, positive and negative sides of the same act. The same goes for vv 19a and 19b. Breaking the armaments in v 20bA could be seen as a correlate of making peace with the animals (v 20a). Verse 20bB has equivocal status; the establishment of security could be the outcome of controlling wild animals and warlike men, and so follow the rest of v 20, or it could be a third approach to pacification. In v 25bB, the response of Lo-Ammi to his new name, which we might have expected to be subsequent to the change, is expressed in a coordinated imperfect clause as if it were simultaneous, as if he says "My God!" at the same time as he is called "My people."

Leaving out vv 16–17 and 23aB, twelve of the remaining nineteen clauses in 2:16–25 have abnormal paragraph functions by classical standards. We seem rather to be dealing with a literary or linguistic tradition in which different norms operate, and thus classical norms should not be taken for granted in literary analysis or exegesis. The issues in this regard are the following: (1) The paragraph boundaries are blurred by using consecutive perfects, rather than imperfect clauses, for paragraph onset; transition to new paragraphs has to be judged solely by content. (2) The action sequence is not well realized if consecutive perfect clauses are used to describe simultaneous events. This is certainly the case in vv 21–22, where there is only one act of betrothal, and even v 22b may be part of the same act. It is also possibly the case in v 25, although there a sequence of events is also conceivable. (3) The action sequence is also not well realized if coordinated imperfect clauses are used to describe events in sequence, rather than events coinciding in time; in vv 23 and 24 we cannot tell if there is one moment of responding in which all join at once, or whether these responses are made one after the other. The former is indicated by the syntax, but the latter seems more likely.

This divergence from the canons of classical composition calls for a study of Hosea's verb system. The only safe inference to be made here is a negative one: clause types cannot be used as a dependable guide to the temporal relationships among the events reported. We are further restrained from attempting any schematization by remembering that 2:16–25 has a complex structure, in which there may be only three points of time, betrothal, covenant, and marriage. Even if this sequence is accepted as corresponding to both life and history, the fact remains that the development of distinguishable events is hard to trace.

16. *Therefore.* On *lākēn* in Hosea, see the Notes on 2:8. The typical sequence is indictment + *lākēn* + penalty, and thus "therefore" is often the first word in a judgment oracle. Here, however, it begins a salvation oracle. That the ultimate sin of forgetting Yahweh (v 15) should be the reason for a mighty act of salvation (v 16) is startling, and the use of "therefore" to make the connection flouts all logic. The leading of Israel into the wilderness could mean either that the enterprise of making a special people had failed and they are to be sent back to where they were first found; or that there will be a new beginning, with the slate wiped clean of guilt and wrongdoing. In vv 16–17 Yahweh has in mind nothing less than a *recapitulatio* of the Exodus, Wandering, and Settlement. The references

to "the land of Egypt" and "the Valley of Achor" in v 17 suggest the time span, though they appear in reverse historical order.

The conjunction at the beginning of v 16 and the use of the eschatological formula in v 18 isolate vv 16–17 as a unit in discourse. The references to the age of Moses and Joshua are clearest in this passage.

16aA	lākēn hinnēh 'ānōkî mĕpattêhā
16aB	wĕhōlaktîhā hammidbār
16b	wĕdibbartî 'al-libbāh
17aA	wĕnātattî lāh 'et-kĕrāmêhā miššām
17aB	wĕ'et-'ēmeq 'ākôr lĕpetaḥ tiqwâ
17bA	wĕ'ānĕtā šammâ kîmê nĕ'ûrêhā
17bB	ûkĕyôm 'ălōtāh mē'ereṣ-miṣrāyim

The main moments in this episode are indicated by the opening clause and the consecutive clauses which follow it. There are five actions, four done by the man (allures, conducts, speaks, gives) and one by the woman (she responds). It seems impossible to give the verbs their usual tense values. If the woman's response is the last event, then Egypt is the reference point (v 17b). If the gift of vineyards has something to do with the Valley of Achor (v 17a), then we are in the land of promise; certainly it would be better to locate vineyards in Palestine than in the wilderness (but cf. Hos 9:10).

The grammatical constructions suggest that v 17a refers to one moment and that v 17b refers to another; we assume that the days of her youth and the day when she came up from the land of Egypt are the same. The similarities in thought between v 16aA and v 16b invite linking them as poetic parallels, which would reduce the action to four moments — the seduction (vv 16aA and 16b), the journey (v 16aB), the endowment (v 17a), and the response (v 17b). Except for reading v 16b out of sequence, the ordering is roughly historical. The design of the paragraph is not fully displayed by linking the lines together in pairs to make possible bicola; apart from v 17b and 16aA plus 16b, there is not much parallelism of the usual kind. There is some unity in v 17a, if only syntactic; but the Valley of Achor is not an obvious parallel to "her vineyards." There are verbal signals and recurring motifs that unify the seven lines; the whole is not just a pasticcio of "Exodus" motifs.

The reference to the Valley of Achor is obscure. The original incident (Joshua 7) is well known. Tradition attaches importance to the name of the valley (Josh 7:26), in an etymological play on the verb 'kr, "to trouble." The unit's structure would be clearer if we could work out what the adverb "there" refers to in its two occurrences in vv 17aA and 17bA. If it is simply anaphoric, then she will be given vineyards in the desert (v 17aA referring back to v 16aB) and she will respond in the Valley of

Achor (v 17bA referring to v 17aB). Neither equation seems appropriate. If a favorable response comes early in the story, then Egypt or the desert would be the best place for it. The unity we have already observed in v 17a suggests that the promised land would be the best place to be given the vineyards (v 17aA). These observations lead to a different pairing of the lines:

16aB   A   I will lead her through the wilderness
17bB   A'   As on the day she came up from the land of Egypt
16b   B   And I will speak intimately to her
17bA   B'   And may she respond there as in the time of her youth
17aA   C   And I will assign to her there her vineyards
17aB   C'   And the Valley of Achor as a doorway of hope.

The overall structure is then seen to be A B C C' B' A', after v 16aA, which is the opening statement. There are two locations, the desert (AA') and the land (CC') and two moments, the courtship (in the desert) and the marriage (in the land); the lines dealing with the desert are wrapped around the lines which describe the later phase. Once more we encounter a pattern in which the lines in the middle represent the climax and final outcome of what is happening in the entire paragraph. The importance of the verb *ntty* "to give/assign" in this climax should not be overlooked. The new gift of the land is the culmination of the historical covenant and is theologically all-important. It was because Israel no longer acknowledged Yahweh as the sole giver of everything (2:10), but rather ascribed natural products to Baal (2:7), that Yahweh would take back his gifts (2:11), and then restore them (2:17). This pattern of deprivation before renewal, trouble before hope, is the key to Hosea's thought. In the end Israel will say, reversing Job, "Yahweh took away, Yahweh gave back; blessed be Yahweh's name" (cf. Job 1:21).

I am going to entice her. This verse varies the common *hinnĕnî* plus participle formula for imminent action in using the long personal pronoun *'ānōkî*, which focuses attention on the speaker, and points a powerful contrast. Another pronoun in a similarly prominent grammatical position is expected; the contrast goes back to the preceding verse: "She forgot *me*, but *I*, for my part, will allure her."

The idea of deception is present in other Hebrew occurrences of the verb *pty*, especially 7:11; cf. Jer 20:7. In its one occurrence in Ugaritic literature (*UT* 52:39), it describes the sex act, or at least the overtures preceding intercourse. If the word has such associations here, as in Job 31:9 and Exod 22:15, then we have a very bitter irony indeed. The husband's only chance is to play upon his wife's depravity. Such an idea is jarring in the present context; it conflicts with the tenderness of v 16b. To make such language sound right in the mouth of the disillusioned husband, it must be given the connotation of the artful wooing of a simple girl. It must be admitted, however, that in its typical use, the verb indicates deception for sinister purposes, whether by sexual wiles (Judg 14:15; 16:5) or by other means (I Kings 22:20–22).

I will lead her through the wilderness. The *Hip'il* of *hlk* is not a common verb. In several occurrences it describes the trek of the Israelites through the desert under Yahweh's leadership — Deut 8:2,15; 29:4 (cf. Amos 2:10); Jer 2:6,17; Pss 106:9; 136:16 (Fritz 1970). The absence of a preposition with "wilderness" gives the construction an archaic flavor, but leaves us unsure as to the exact force of the phrase, though it is unmistakable that a recapitulation of the Exodus is intended. The story begins here with the escape from Egypt; how the latter-day Israel got back there is not explained although later passages in Hosea clearly contemplate such a return (7:16; 8:13; 9:3,6; 11:5).

speak intimately to her. The reference is to speaking endearingly, in courtship (Gen 34:3; Ruth 2:13; Isa 40:2).

17. *I will assign.* A further answer to the erroneous opinions expressed in 2:7 and 10, not corrected by the deprivation described in v 11. When the gifts are renewed the power and the generosity of the donor are proved. Since we have had only partial success in tracing the narrative thread through these lines, we cannot be sure of the socioeconomic framework of this gesture, i.e. we cannot tell whether this gift is gratuitous, albeit motivated by love, or part of the formal proceedings of marriage. Further, if the latter is true, then it is not certain whether this is the bridegroom's gift as such (Burrows 1938:46–48; cf. Josh 15:16–19).

to her. The indirect object is shown by the pronoun. The pronominal suffix with the noun ("her vineyards") must therefore be possessive. This tells against Kuhnigk's interpretation of the similar construction in v 7b as dative (1974:10–13).

there. Literally "from there." The force of the preposition is not clear; it is hard to give the phrase a temporal reference — "after that." The wilderness is unlikely as the location of the vineyards, which are more suitably placed in the promised land. It is often difficult to detect any difference in the meaning of *šām, miššām,* and *šammâ.*

vineyards. The choice of this word requires some explanation. It has not appeared in the long list of things identified as gifts in 2:4–15, although there were references to liquor (v 7), must (vv 10,11), and the vine (v 14). With so much here that reminds us of the Deuteronomic tradition, we recall the frequent use of *ntn,* "to give," to describe the fulfillment of the promise of a land, but *krmym,* "vineyards," are rarely cited in that connection. In Deut 6:11, vineyards are only one feature of the total gift. In Num 16:14 the phrase "field and vineyard" is the nearest we have to a description of the land as a plantation of trees.

A text which might offer some clues to the situation in Hos 2:17 is *UT* 77, "Nikkal and the Moon." Although the *Sitz-im-Leben* of this piece has not been determined with certainty, it clearly centers around marriage. The pertinent lines are:

17	*tn nkl*	Give (me) Nikkal
18	*yrḫ ytrḫ ib*	Let Moon marry Ib
19	*t'rbm bbhth*	Let her enter his house
20	*watn mhrh labh*	And I shall pay her bride-price to her father
	alp ksp	one thousand [pieces of] silver
21	*wrbt ḫrṣ*	ten thousand [pieces of] gold
22	*išlḫ ẓhrm iqnm*	I shall send lapis lazuli
	atn šdh krmm	I shall give vineyards as her field
23	*šd ddh ḥrnqm*	as the field of her love *ḥrnqm*

The text presents several points of comparison with Hosea. The silver and gold reminds us of 2:10. Gordon renders *atn,* "I will give/pay" in its second occurrence, in line 22, as "I'll make her field into a vineyard" (1949:64); this obscures the possibility that two distinct "gifts" are involved. The first is the *mhr* "bride-price" for the father, who is expressly identified as the recipient; it consists of silver, gold, and gems. The second is mentioned in line 22; the recipient is not identified, but if *šdh* means "her field," then the inference is that this is a *pretium pudicitiae* for the bride. The parallel *šd ddh,* "field of her love," points in the same direction. The conjunction of field and vineyard invites comparison with Num 16:14, but more significant is the request made by Achsah, at the time of her marriage, that she be given "a field" (*śādeh*) (Josh 15:15–19 and Judg 1:11–15). The details of this incident are important. Although it is her father, Caleb, who gives the gift, so that it seems to be a dowry, it is her husband Othniel who is urged to make the request for her. The special circumstances of this request are worth noting, since we cannot assume that what is reported here happened at every marriage. On the contrary, the fact that these details are recorded probably points to their exceptional character. Othniel had qualified for Achsah's hand by capturing Kiriath-sepher, thereby becoming a propertied man. Does this imply that, formerly landless, he could not have aspired to such an alliance? Caleb became the ruler of Debir and Hebron (Judg 1:20), whereas Othniel and Achsah settled in the Negeb, by her father's arrangement (Josh 15:16–19; Judg 1:12–15). The extraordinary circumstance is that Othniel, having acquired Kiriath-sepher in behalf of Caleb, is still without "the field" to which his wife is entitled as a bride-gift. By abandoning the MT and following the versions which read "he nagged her," Boling (1975:56–57) misses the point. The article in Judg 1:14 ("the field"), though lacking in the Joshua version of the story, points to a technical usage. There is no particular field in mind; at least, it is not a field that is given in response to the request. The occasion should also be noted: it was at the point of marriage. Caleb has already given her to Othniel as wife (Judg 1:13). It was when "she came" that she urged him to request "the field" from her father. Because it is she, not he, who follows through on the matter, we can see why the versions have changed the original text to "he nagged her." This is transparent harmonizing. "The field" (Judg 1:14), to be secured by the groom, is probably the same as "her field" or "the field of her (marriage-)love" in *UT* 77, to be given to Nikkal by Moon at their marriage. In each case it is not a field as such that is actually given. Achsah receives much needed supplies of water; Nikkal receives "vineyards," a gift which appears to be a lavish one and is called "her field" in *UT* 77. We suggest that "her vineyards" in 2:17 is a similar gift. The fact that the plural is used in both *UT* 77 and here supports this view.

This interpretation of "her vineyards" as a bridal gift seems to be better than taking the pronoun suffix as evidence that the vineyards were already hers in some sense, now to be given back after being taken away (v 11).

Verse 17aA thus covers the same ground as the marriage of Othniel and Achsah, and of Yariḫ (Moon) and Nikkal. This is shown in the following table:

	Verb	Giver	Recipient	Name	Gift
Joshua 15	*ntn*	father/ groom	bride	*śādeh* (*běrākâ*)	*gullōt*
Judges 1	*ntn*	father/ groom	bride	*haśśādeh* (*běrākâ*)	*gullōt*
UT 77	*ytn*	groom	bride	*šdh // šd ddh*	*krmm*
Hos 2:17	*ntn*	groom	bride	_____	*krmyh*

Although *ntn // ytn* is a common root, its prominence in all these texts should be appreciated. Although the name for the gift is lacking in v 17, we identify "the field" as a special gift from the groom to the bride at the time of the wedding, distinct from both the bride-price, paid by the groom to the bride's father at the time of the engagement, and the dowry, which the father gave to the bride. This present is called *běrākâ*, "blessing" (not *běrēkâ*, "pool"!), in Josh 15:19 and Judg 1:15, although in Gen 33:11; I Sam 25:27; 30:26; II Kings 5:15, such a gift has nothing to do with marriage. If a distinction is made between *mōhar* (bride-price for the father) and *mattān* (wedding present for the bride) in Gen 34:12, then *mattān* in a wedding context is another synonym. Some scholars interpret the phrase *mōhar ûmattān* as a hendiadys, but *mattān* invites comparison, if not equation, with Akkadian *nudunnū*, a special and apparently optional settlement of a husband on his wife (Code of Hammurapi ※※171–172, cf. *ANET* 173), although there is no reason to expect marriage arrangements to be constant in either space or time, and thus cross-cultural identifications cannot be regarded as definitive. The similarities are striking, nevertheless. The Code of Hammurapi shows that such provision could make a significant difference in a wife's financial security. The technical term "the field" identifies a piece of real property. The alternate name "the field of her love" suggests that the field is linked with the institution of marriage. Our analysis of vv 16–17 indicates that the gift of the vineyards comes at the moment of marriage. So far as Yahweh's marriage to Israel is concerned, a wedding present from the groom to the bride is the only gift possible. There can be no bride-price or dowry, for Yahweh has no father-in-law.

The events connected with Achsah's marriage can now be reconstructed in detail. In order to win Achsah's hand in marriage, Othniel had to accept Caleb's challenge and conditions and capture Kiriath-sepher, which became part of Caleb's domain. This was the bride-price given to Caleb by Othniel. Caleb has *given* Achsah the land of the Negeb: this is the dowry, which provides the couple with an estate. At the time of the marriage Achsah expects an additional gift, from her husband, "the field." This, it would seem, her husband was unable to supply, just as he had no bride-price before he captured Kiriath-sepher. He is in a humiliating situation, and she has to nag him to ask his father-in-law for it. What happens from this point on is unclear. The roles of Achsah and Othniel in securing the gift, and the roles of Caleb and Othniel as giver, are mixed up; it would seem that the two Hebrew recensions, to say nothing of the versions or later commentators, have forgotten both the procedures involved and the circumstances of this case. An unusual initiative is taken by the bride, and this is what makes the incident memorable. She has to travel on a donkey from the Negeb to Hebron, to ask her father for a "blessing": "Although you have (already) given me the land of the Negeb, I would also like some water stores" (Josh 15:19 = Judg 1:15). She knows what she wants, nominates what form the "field" should take, and Caleb proceeds to meet her need.

the Valley of Achor. In Joshua 7 the valley was the scene of the execution of Achan. The reason for its choice as the site of Yahweh's new marriage to Israel is not clear; somehow this sinister place is to become a symbol of renewal. This agrees with Hosea's basic theology that new life is found beyond and through judgment and death. When sin was eradicated in Achan's death, Israel's fortunes turned, and they went on to conquer the land. The valley which formerly had blocked the way to successful entry now becomes the highway to it. A similar allusion is met in Isa 65:10, where Achor becomes a rich pastureland in the end time. The word "valley" suggests that there is some connection with the Valley of Jezreel (Hos 1:5); both Jezreel and Achor carry a double meaning — death under Yahweh's judgment, new life under his mercy.

a doorway of hope. We do not know what this phrase means, nor did the earliest versions. The thought is unusually abstract. The old traditions fail to provide the needed clue, for *tiqwâ* occurs nowhere in the Penta- teuch. Two-thirds of its occurrences are in Proverbs and Job. The same word in Josh 2:18,21 is a homonym meaning "thread"; the former verse contains the only biblical occurrence of *tiqwâ* as *nomen rectum,* that is, as attribute. In Joshua, the *tiqwâ* is the scarlet cord placed by Rahab in the window of her house; this story is near enough to the Achan incident to suggest that Hosea has deliberately connected them. Achan was a rene- gade Israelite who succumbed to the enticement of pagan ways. Rahab was a heathen harlot who became a devout Yahwist, and, if Matt 1:5 refers to the same woman, rose to the honor of being an ancestress of no less a person than David. (The rabbis do not seem to know this tradition, but they esteem Rahab in other ways.) The creed she recites in Josh 2:9–11 is impeccably orthodox. If Israel's history in the land began with the drastic punishment of a person like Achan in the Valley of Achor, it also included a story about the radical conversion of a Canaanite woman, who found refuge and respectability through faith in Yahweh. This implies a great deal of homiletical development on Hosea's part, too much, per- haps, to extract from a stray reference; and the sort of punning or am- biguity involved is rare in the Bible, though common in later Hebrew texts.

The analogy involved is germane. Now that Israel herself has practically become a promiscuous Canaanite, a way remains open for her return into a similar covenant of safety (2:20). It remains to add that "hope" is often connected with death (Ezek 19:5) or childlessness (Ruth 1:12), pre- sented in its extreme form in the question of whether the people can be brought back from death (Ezek 37:11). The phrase "doorway of hope" may include the promise that the new marriage will be fruitful; cf. v 25.

respond. This is the most relevant sense of the verb, especially if we are correct in seeing it as the consequence of the husband's speaking. But there are some difficulties; the usual idiom for this verb is not completely realized, and there are alternative possibilities. When the verb *'ānâ* means "to reply," it usually continues with what is said; otherwise it can indicate a non-verbal response (Hos 14:9). Here there is no speech by the woman, unless in v 18, which is separated by the eschatological preface. If v 18 does contain the response, this would fit the marriage setting we have found in v 17; but v 17 is in the third person and v 18 in the second per- son. It may be that the wife says "My husband" in v 18, while the child says "My God" in v 25. Yet even this does not cohere entirely, for the for- mer is on the human level (Yahweh being a husband only in figure), while the latter is entirely in the sphere of the divine (Hosea's children could never have called him "my God").

Another possibility is that the verb means "to testify" as in Hos 5:5; 7:10. The discourse is not juridical, and although the term could be used in connection with a marriage oath, even that seems too formal for the ardent and private relationships that are being developed in these verses. LXX renders *'nth, tapeinōthēsetai,* "she will be humbled," which would require a passive or reflexive form of a homonymous root. LXX is otherwise accurate and literal at this point, so the reading should be considered. A point in its favor is that it echoes the language of Deut 8:2, with which Hos 2:16–17 has some vocabulary in common. A more remote possibility is that the verb is connected with the rare word *'ōnâ,* a hapax legomenon found in Exod 21:10, where it refers to a married woman's legal right to sexual intercourse with her husband.

All in all, "respond" seems to be the most suitable meaning. Testimony is not needed, although some kind of ceremonial response may be in mind, and this may be the first response in the covenant-making that ensues. In this, however, the initiative is taken by Yahweh, who says, "I will respond" in v 23. "She will be humbled" also seems out of place. The time for that has passed; we are now in the time when joy is to be restored. LXX probably reflects the error of a translator who had not caught the change of mood after v 15.

there. The character of the response depends in part on the location, whether Egypt, the desert, or the Valley of Achor. It may be that this has been left somewhat vague intentionally; this verse is a prediction, perhaps only a hope, and not a description of an accomplished event. The important thing is that she will respond "as in the time of her youth," identified with the time when she came up from the land of Egypt. With this historical reference, it is clear that Israel now occupies the stage. We can only suppose that it is the good side of her conduct in the desert, not the murmurings and apostasies, that provides the standard. Her response contrasts with the ones described in 2:4–15, which were sought, but not, apparently, evoked; in any case they do not compare with the responsive love that begins to develop in v 17. The directional meaning of *šāmmâ* then implies entry into the land corresponding to the consummation of the marriage.

18–25. The eschatological formula, "and it will happen on that day" (vv 18 and 23), and the title, "Oracle of Yahweh" (vv 18 and 23), introduce further predictions (vv 18–25). The repetition of the formula in vv 20 (partial) and 23 emphasizes the simultaneous interaction of the different classes of participants in this "little apocalypse." The vision of the transformation of nature and achievement of universal harmony is unified by the eschatological frame of reference and the use of verbs in the first person throughout, so that there is no change of speaker.

18–19. The unit in vv 18–19 contains two balancing statements. Each has a positive and a negative part.

18aA	wĕhāyâ bayyôm hahû’	7 syllables
	nĕ’ūm yhwh	4
18aB	tiqrĕ’î ’îšî	5
18b	wĕlō’-tiqrĕ’î-lî ‘ôd ba‘lî	9
19a	wahăsîrōtî ’et-šĕmôt habbĕ‘ālîm mippîhā	15
19b	wĕlō’-yizzākĕrû ‘ôd bišmām	9

It is understandable that the versions have supplied lî, "to me," in v 18aB since grammatically the line is incomplete and poetically it is short. The similarity in rhythm and length between vv 18b and 19b can hardly be a coincidence, especially when we observe the repeated lō’ . . . ‘ôd, which contrast strikingly with lō’ . . . ‘ôd as used in 1:6. But this only leaves the disparity between vv 18aB and 19a more unaccountable. The whole can be called poetic only in a loose sense of that word, although there is no question that the style is quite elevated.

18. on that day. The eschatological day in Hosea is not distant, but decisive. It fixes the end of the old order of things and initiates the new age, in which all things work together for good, and after which there will be neither ending nor beginning, no future decisive moment. The prophet betrays no curiosity as to what will occur after the Day of the Lord. In 2:18 the eschaton is the marriage day, obviously not the end of the story, but certainly the end of the troubles between Yahweh and Israel. It is implied that this time the covenant vows will be spoken in truth, and that the marriage will endure.

you will call. The verb qr’, "to name," is used also in Hosea 1, though not in 2:1. The theme of name changing, which began at 2:1, is here resumed; it is completed in v 25. The wife is the only member of the family who is not given a new name. In 2:18 the wife gives her husband a new title; it could not be simpler — "my husband." With its activation goes the abolition of its odious competitor — "my Baal." This is never to be used again. While the contrast in usage seems to arise out of an ordinary domestic situation, the force of the prohibition is to banish the use of the title Baal from the religious vocabulary of Israel forever. The command is dramatized by setting it in the framework of address by a wife to her husband, but in this case the wife is Israel and the husband is God. To what extent Yahweh was called Baal is not clear, though there are indications that the title was used, and in some instances there may have been a mingling of attributes between Yahweh and the great storm god of Syria-Palestine, if not a merging of identities. The dangers of such assimilation were so great that nothing less than the total abandonment of the term itself was necessary in all religious connections (though it survived in secular usage, as attested in the Bible). The following verse shows that by abolishing the name Baal from the Israelite vocabulary, the prophet intended to eliminate both the worship of all other gods who might bear that title, and the false worship of the only true God, Yahweh.

In the tradition that enshrines the Ten Commandments at the heart of the Mosaic-Sinai covenant, any use of the names of alien gods was illicit from Israel's beginnings. Exod 23:23–33 shows how thorough and uncompromising the crackdown should be. The fact that the rules were frequently violated does not mean that they did not exist. Hosea accuses Israel of forgetting and rejecting such instruction. Hosea's ban was not a revolution but a reformation.

19. *I shall remove.* We saw above that the use of the consecutive perfect clause does not necessarily point to a later moment in time, so it does not follow that v 19 is subsequent to vv 16–17 or 18. It is more likely that they are concomitant. LXX has normalized the text by reading third person throughout; but the MT should be retained.

never again will they be mentioned by their names. This solemn phrase makes it clear that something more serious is at stake than merely calling one's husband "my Baal." In correlation with "her mouth" (v 19a), this memorializing of the Baals by their names suggests the liturgical recitation of the names of Baal in formal worship. Compare the recitation of the fifty names of Marduk in *Enuma Elish* (*ANET* 69–72). Although Baal was known under many names at Ugarit (van Zijl 1972), no litany in which they were systematically recited has come down to us. Although *zkr* can mean "remember," its cult associations indicate that the renown of the god was kept alive by both invocation and recital (Childs 1962; Schottroff 1964). The verb *zkr* is used in connection with the invocation of pagan gods by their names in Josh 23:7; for Yahweh, see Isa 48:1; Amos 6:10; Ps 20:8 (cf. Hos 1:7). When Israel occupied the promised land the people were specifically commanded to destroy the names of the Canaanite gods (Deut 12:3). This includes the use of their names in oaths as well as prayers, placing severe restrictions on trade relationships with neighboring peoples, a prohibition quite impracticable from the political point of view (cf. Exod 23:32). Logically the greater act is the complete removal of names of the Baals "from her mouth" by Yahweh. Only after such purification will the woman's vocabulary be cleansed from using the word itself, even in common everyday use.

20. In this oracular prediction the phrase "on that day" introduces a new section of the larger unit vv 16–25 which is characterized by use of the 3 m pl pronoun and pronominal suffix. As already noted, this passage is linked with vv 23–24, which in turn lead into v 25. At this point the language becomes more formal, the vocabulary of covenant-making more evident, the frame of reference more universal. The beneficiaries of the

covenant are not identified. We are no longer in the context of marriage, for the discussion has moved from "her" to "them." In the larger context of 2:4–25, the reference can only be to the children, who represent Israel. The covenant has three aspects. The animals are to be restrained (v 20a), war is to be abolished (v 20bA), and security established (v 20bB); the last is the outcome of the first two.

The structure of this oracle can be seen below.

20aA	wĕkārattî lāhem bĕrît bayyôm hahû'
20aB	'im-ḥayyat haśśādeh
	wĕ'im-'ôp haššāmayim
	wĕ- remeś hā'ădāmâ
20bA	wĕqešet
	wĕḥereb
	ûmilḥāmâ 'ešbôr min-hā'āreṣ
20bB	wĕhiškabtîm lābeṭaḥ

The pronoun "them" occurs in association with the opening and closing verbs. The clause in v 20bA stands in a chiastic relationship with the preceding clause. Each has a list of three things, the objects of pacification — three kinds of creatures (made by God), three kinds of weapons (made by people). Ground and earth also balance, as do the skies and earth here and again in v 23. The pattern of "threes" in this verse and in vv 21–22 (the threefold repetition of the verb 'rśtyk with a total of six modifiers), as well as v 24 (the three products of the soil) may reflect the three children of the marriage.

make. Literally "cut." To "cut" a covenant is the commonest expression used in the Hebrew Bible to describe this transaction. Details preserved in Genesis 15 and Jeremiah 34 suggest that cutting might have been part of a sacrificial or oath-taking ritual that went with covenant-making. The free interchangeability of "cut" with verbs designating establish, give, issue, enter, etc. shows that the literal denotation of the word was not considered essential in the idiom during the historical period.

The initiative of Yahweh in making the covenant should be noted in line with his complete command of the situation here. The person who makes the covenant is the author and imposer of the entire arrangement, and its guarantor. There are no negotiations, since the lord establishes everything by right. In 2:20 there are three parties — Yahweh, the animals, and "them." The covenant is not between Yahweh and Israel, so we do not have here a renewal of the Sinai covenant, or any such early model. Nor is the covenant between "them" and the animals, mediated by Yahweh. It is between Yahweh and the animals for the benefit of "them." Yahweh asserts his power over all creation.

There are two aspects of the covenant. One creates safety for the children by controlling the animals, while the other abolishes the threat of human warfare — the reversal of what was done by God himself in 1:5 and 7. Both these provisions culminate in the safety described by the last words of v 20.

for them. The beneficiaries are the children, and the pacification of the animals reverses the threat made in v 14, where the wild beasts were likely to eat them. The mother, who has been the center of attention in vv 16–19, seems to be left out here; this is characteristic of cc 1–3: mother and children are rarely dealt with at the same time; only in the climactic v 25 are they all together.

covenant. Hosea uses this word five times, here and in 6:7; 8:1; 10:4; 12:2. In the other occurrences Israel is one of the parties. The specific covenants are not identified. Hos 6:7 and 8:1 accuse the people of breach of covenant with Yahweh, but this could be a general indictment for any kind of treachery. In the other two places they are accused of making unauthorized covenants with alien powers. The use of the word here is unusual in its orientation to the creation traditions.

with the wild animals. The countryside here is not cultivated land but the untamed wild. These are savage animals, outside human control, and often dangerous to people. The listing of wild beasts, birds, and reptiles is like that in Genesis 1, in sequence and in vocabulary. In the present construction the omission of the preposition from the third noun phrase is a phenomenon to which no special significance can be attached.

The nearest thing in Scripture to a threeway covenant involving God, people, and animals is found in Gen 9:8–11, where, after the Flood, Yahweh gives a covenant never again to destroy the world by such means. Such does not seem to be the tradition behind this verse; the language of Gen 9:8–11 is different from that used here. There, people and beasts stand together as living things endangered by the flood, and now promised safety in the future. In Hos 2:20 it is people who are promised safety from the animals, who are restrained by bringing them under the authority of God. The idea of restoring to people primal dominion over the creatures, lost by human disobedience, is not present. In spite of this incomplete use of the Genesis traditions, however, the cosmic scope of Hos 2:16–25 is unmistakable; it includes an eschatological vision not unlike that of Isaiah (11:6–9; 35:9) (Kötting 1964). Wolff (1974:51) acutely points out that here is the first appearance of the idea of a new covenant for the end time, which will reach a climax in Jer 31:31–34; cf. Ezek 36:24–32.

Bow and sword and weapons of war. The same three words occur in the same sequence in 1:7, where the list, however, includes five items.

destroy. Literally "break." The verb is so widely used that the action described here cannot be precisely determined. It could mean to break the threat of a foreign invader, and so give the nation safety. But the achievement seems to be more complete, more permanent, than such an act of deliverance. The promise of living in safety, immune from the threat of invasion by men or beasts, was included in the ancient covenant blessings (Lev 25:19; 26:6, contrast 22). If *h'rṣ* means *the land* of Israel, rather than the earth, then the divine action would involve the enemy, whose weapons will be shattered in their defeat. The land will be free of threats, and there will be no further need of armaments, a vision of a nation at peace with its neighbors. If the term has the wider reference, we might be approaching the vision of Isa 2:4 = Mic 4:3.

There is a significant connection between 1:5 and 2:20. Not only is the eschatological formula *bayyôm hahû'*, "in that day," used in both passages, showing that the time frame is the same, but the phrase *šbr qšt*, "to break the bow," also appears. The balancing of perfect and imperfect forms of *šbr* (*wšbrty* in 1:5 and *'šbwr* in 2:20) and the chiastic structure (*wšbrty 't-qšt . . . wqšt . . . 'šbwr*) indicates the bonding of the two passages. In 1:5 the "breaking of the bow of Israel" represents a final defeat and destruction of the army of Israel in the Jezreel Valley, whereas in 2:20 the breaking of the bow and other implements of war ushers in the new age of security and bliss. The passages are complementary: first the judgment against Israel results in the end of its armed forces; then the enforced disarmament of the rest of the peoples makes possible an era of peace and reconciliation, and the renewal of all things.

lie down. The picture of sleeping without fear here invites comparison with the promises made in Job 5:17–27 (Andersen 1976a:121–126). There it is promised that the wild animals will be allies of people, not a threat. "You won't be frightened of the wild animals; yes, your treaty will be with the sons of the field [*'abnê* is a byform of *bĕnê,* with prosthetic *'alep*]; and the wild animals will make peace with you." The key words of the Job passage, *bryt* and *šlwm,* "covenant" and "peace," match Hosea's usage of *bryt* and *bṭḥ,* "safety." The common thought is peace between people and animals, imposed by the common reign of God. Freedom from other plagues, including war, is also promised to Job. Note also Lev 26:3–13. Conscious safety means freedom from worry, expressed by the word "to know" (Hos 2:22; Job 5:25).

21. *betroth.* The repetition of the same verb for the same act is unusual for consecutive perfect clauses and has an almost incantational effect; the design is poetic. The repetition of *lî,* "to me," emphasizes the personal relationship.

21a   *wě'ēraśtîk lî lě'ôlām*   8 syllables
21b   *wě'ēraśtîk lî   běṣidq ûběmišpāṭ*   5+6
             ûběḥasd ûběraḥămîm   8
22a   *wě'ēraśtîk lî be'ěmûnâ*   9
22b   *wěyāda'at 'et-yhwh*   6

This unit is structurally symmetrical. The first and last occurrences of "betroth" have one noun adjunct, which together form a pair ("eternal faithfulness"). The middle clause has four objects, arranged in two pairs: "righteous justice" and "compassionate lovingkindness" (following the analysis of Gordis 1971:81). The four interior qualities explicate the enclosing pair. Taken together, they constitute a profound theological statement describing the foundational components of the marriage relationship, which derive from the character of Yahweh himself. The balanced enclosed structure of vv 21 and 22a sets off v 22b, which serves as a climax to the betrothal. The betrothal comes chronologically before the response of v 18 and the renewal of the family in v 25.

The verb *'rś*, "betroth," refers to an engagement, preliminary to marriage and separated from it by a space of time (Deut 20:7; 28:30). It is a relationship established by the payment of the bride-price (II Sam 3:14). Because the idiom in II Sam 3:14 uses *b* to mark the price, it has been suggested that the preposition has the same meaning here; this is unlikely. Righteousness, justice, loyalty, and love are four of the greatest of Yahweh's attributes. In the marriage to come, the bride will receive the fruits of these qualities, and will share in them eternally. They constitute at once what the groom contributes to and expects from the relationship. The attributes are promises for the marriage, and not once-for-all payments at the time of engagement. The emphasis on the betrothal, rather than the marriage, makes the situation more dramatic, highlighting the thoroughgoing rehabilitation secured in this miraculous re-creation of all relationships. The hopes expressed in 2:4–15, especially in v 9b, were that the woman would come to her senses and go back to her husband. The marriage would be salvaged. In 2:21–22 the idea is more daring: a new courtship to be followed by a new wedding will take place. Everything is now as it was "in the time of her youth" (v 17), and she is as a potential bride.

22. *you shall know Yahweh.* This reverses "me she forgot" in v 15. A number of Hebrew manuscripts read, "And you will know that I am (*kî 'ănî*) Yahweh," a change to a familiar formula which makes the text refer to the giving of assent to a theological proposition. To know Yahweh is more personal and intimate (cf. 4:1; 6:3). This verse describes the renewed relationship, seen at its best in marriage. The idiom does not

describe sexual intercourse, although the verb is so used elsewhere in the Bible, since in that usage the subject is male.

Hosea, although he is daring in his use of imagery to describe Yahweh's relationship to Israel, generally cloaks it within a metaphor in which the primary application is to Hosea and Gomer. The cloak is thrown off at the end of v 22. In a surprise change, the focus suddenly shifts from a man and a woman in love, to Yahweh, who speaks of himself here and elsewhere in the third person. It is clear that it is Israel and Yahweh who are to be united in marriage. This arresting turn explains why scribes fell back on the formula, "You will know that I am Yahweh." Although sexual connotations are not indicated, except insofar as the context of betrothal hints at them, the word "to know" is rich with intimate personal overtones. It is Yahweh himself who will be known, in all the attributes he has just listed. Verse 22 cancels the *lō' yādě'â* of 2:10, where it is clear that what she did not know was that Yahweh is the giver of everything, and her only good.

The verb "to know" also has covenant connotations, and in this passage the betrothal is a covenant. The attributes in vv 21–22 are the attributes of Yahweh in covenant-keeping. To live in the covenant is to know Yahweh. The verb "to know" in 2:22 is as climactic as it is in 6:3, where it is the end result of returning to Yahweh. The knowing of Yahweh, which is the climax of the betrothal, is matched by the titles which the husband receives in marriage in v 18, in which the wife calls the husband *'îšî* (the first title in 2:1–25).

23–25. The two stories of Hosea and Gomer, and of Yahweh and Israel, are told as if they are one. Hosea 1–3 is not a simple allegory in which a story told on one level (the human) has a meaning on another level (the divine). Gomer's story is Israel's story, and although Hosea and Yahweh cannot be identified in the same way, the prophet and his God are faced with similar problems. If Hosea's behavior does not follow human custom, it is because he has been admitted to the mind of Yahweh, and treats his own wife the way Yahweh treats his people (1:2). Hosea's domestic tragedy is not only a paradigm but a part of Yahweh's historical crisis. The two sides of this single story occasionally are exposed separately and in turn to the viewer, but much of the time they are both seen at once. What begins on the human level as Hosea's problem in 2:4 is turned imperceptibly until the final "Oracle of Yahweh" in v 15 shows that now the focus is on the nation. The same thing happens in vv 16–25; all that is said in vv 16–22 applies in part to Gomer as an individual and Israel as a nation, and never completely to both. The repetition of "Oracle of Yahweh" in vv 18 and 23 mounts from climax to climax, bringing Yahweh rather than Hosea center stage.

23. *It will happen.* The eschatological preface shows that these last two paragraphs reach a finale. Verses 23–25 gather up all that precedes. Verses 24b–25 are the cancellation of 1:2–9. The connections of vv 23–24a are less clear, because the roles of the sky, the earth, and the grain and wine and oil are not defined.

I will respond. As in v 17, the woman responds to the man. The verb can refer to replies in conversation. When it is God who "answers," the verb often indicates a favorable response, in deed or word, to a plea for help, so that the verb implies salvation (Jonah 2:3). In vv 23 and 24 the verb seems to describe some kind of liturgical response (Andersen 1966c), but it is not easy to reconstruct the situation. One problem, already discussed above, is the use of the verb forms: the use of imperfects rather than consecutive perfects (as in v 17) suggests that the responses are concurrent, and not in sequence, like a greeting handed on from one to the next. Yet the chiastic patterns of objects and subjects create a chain, suggesting sequence.

23aA		*wĕhāyâ bayyôm hahû'*
		'e'ĕneh nĕ'ūm yhwh
23aB		*'e'ĕneh 'et-haššāmāyim*
23b	*wĕhēm*	*ya'ănû 'et-hā'āreṣ*
24a	*wĕhā'āreṣ*	*ta'ăneh 'et-haddāgān wĕ'et-hattîrôš wĕ'et-hayyiṣhār*
24b	*wĕhēm*	*ya'ănû 'et-yizrĕ'e'l*

There is much that is obscure here, and translators have taken great liberties with it. The *JB,* for instance, translates:

> When that day comes—it is Yahweh who speaks—
> the heavens will have their answer from me,
> the earth its answer from them,
> the grain, the wine, the oil, their answer from the earth,
> and Jezreel his answer from them.

In a note, the editors trace the movement backwards. "Jezreel pleads, as it were, with the produce of the soil, which plea is passed to earth and sky and finally to God who grants it." Though fanciful, this does give dramatic coherence to the passage. The difficulty remains that nothing is known of a plea or request relayed from Jezreel to Yahweh through nature. More promising is the recognition that these responses are part of a covenant-making rite, begun in v 20. In the ever-expanding scope of the covenant the animals are joined by sky and land and plants.

The responses in the covenant ceremony are given in the presence of witnesses. Yahweh responds in the presence of heaven. "They" (the children) respond in the presence of the earth, perhaps Underworld. The earth, perhaps land, responds in the presence of the grain and must and oil.

On the face of it, the *hēm* in v 23b refers to "the skies" and the *hēm* in v 24b refers to the three products. The repetition of *hā'āreṣ* in v 24aA points to a different pattern. If repetition had been used consistently to make the speakers' identity certain, then "heaven" would be repeated in v 23b and "grain," etc. in v 24b. In the absence of such repetition, it seems that *hēm* refers to the children responding to the covenant. Verses 23–24 are closely connected with v 20, in which the children are beneficiaries of the covenant. The repetition of *hēm* shows that the four responses come in two pairs. The repetition of *hā'āreṣ* marks a new beginning.

The roles of Yahweh and the children as parties to the covenant are clear from v 20. In v 23 the skies and the earth (Underworld) have their familiar role as witnesses to the covenant. The covenant is sealed by means of new covenant names, which are pronounced in v 25. Compare also the response of the woman (v 17b) who utters the new marriage name (v 18).

The earth and its three products correspond to the mother and her three children in v 24, so that the chain of salutations and the paean of joy involve both nature and people, the cosmic powers and the human family, with God as initiator of the eschatological age.

The key role of Yahweh is clear from the repetition of the opening verb "I will respond." The first "I will respond," although grammatically incomplete, helps both the rhythm and the rhetoric, and should by all means be retained, although the versions delete it. As the favorable, saving response of Yahweh, it need not suppose some prior petition. It is unlikely that Yahweh's response is an answer to prayer (Gen 41:16; I Kings 18:37). The cosmic powers are more likely to be responding with oaths than giving testimony (Gen 30:33; Deut 31:21) to Yahweh's faithfulness (Pss 50:6; 97:6). Even when these covenant connotations are allowed full weight, the connections with v 20 are not clear, for the cosmic powers do not appear there, and the habitat of the land creatures is not *'ereṣ* but *śādeh* and *'ădāmâ*. If we refrain from trying to fit vv 23–24 into too rigid a framework, then it might be enough to think of a grand eschatological chorus — Yahweh and the whole world. Since the verb *'ānâ* can mean "to sing" in Hebrew, Yahweh is the precentor (cf. Ps 50:4), and the chorale spreads through all creation (Ps 96:11). There are parallels elsewhere. In Isa 44:23 and 49:13 the skies and the earth sing in celebration of the downfall of Babylon and Israel's redemption. Isa 51:16 has the sequence of fixing the skies, forming the earth, and saying to Zion, "You are my people"; cf. 2:25.

There is a passage in *UT 'nt* (III:10–28) which displays some affinities with this passage. Lines 10–14 record a decree of Aliyan Baal to banish war from the earth (*qryy barṣ mlḥmt*) and pour out peace over the earth (*sk šlm lkbd arṣ*). Later there is a celebration of Baal's settlement in his inheritance, Mount Ṣapon. In between is a passage in which the powers of nature seem to be exchanging greetings:

> The word of a tree,
> The whisper of a stone
> The conversation of heaven with earth
>> of the deeps with the stars
>> Stones of thunder which heaven knows well
> The word which people know well
>> and which the denizens of the underworld know well.

(Read the *l* in the last three lines as assertative.) Identifying *arṣ*, "the earth," as Underworld, we have a three-storied universe over all of which Baal is lord. The word here is his decree of peace, love, and victory.

they. As already noted, it is not likely that this pronoun refers back to "the heavens." In 2:6 and 14 *hēmmâ*, "they," refers to the children; and *hēm* in 2:23 and 24 probably is the same. The variant forms are used consistently here: *hēmmâ* is the subject in a verbless clause after the predicate; *hēm* is the subject in a verbal clause before the predicate.

the earth. In the context of creation language and in correlation with "the skies," *hā'āreṣ* can mean "the world," rather than "the land," as usual in Hosea, or "the Underworld" as in 2:2. The same word in the next verse may have a different referent.

24. *the grain and must and oil.* These products as tokens of God's approbation represent the paradisiacal plenty promised in traditional blessings. They were also to be a feature of the end time (Jer 31:12; cf. Hos 14:8; Amos 9:13–14; I Enoch 10:19; II Baruch 29:5). The same list appears in v 10, where these natural products may stand in a slight contrast to some of the manufactured goods listed in v 7.

The list in v 24 might not be the object of the immediately preceding verb but the delayed object of the verb "I shall give" in 2:17. Note that the words of 2:10 *'nky ntty lh hdgn whtyrwš whyṣhr* are repeated verbatim in vv 16 (*'nky*), 17 (*ntty lh*) and 24 (*'t-hdgn w't-htyrwš w't-hyṣhr*), a curiously scattered pattern.

Although *dāgān*, "grain," is strictly the only one of these crops grown by "sowing" (v 25), the conventional list is not out of place here. In v 11 Yahweh threatened to take back grain and wine; in v 14 he threatened to devastate vine and fig tree. The restoration of fruitfulness is part of the total picture.

they. This could refer to the preceding phrase of three nouns, but probably harks back to the two younger children, who are responding to their elder brother. This balances the situation in 2:3, where Jezreel gives his "brothers" and "sisters" their new names.

25. *I shall sow her.* The suggestion that the pronoun be changed to "him" is unwarranted, since it supposes that the reference is to the place Jezreel, and that "sow" has its primary, agricultural meaning. This misses the sexual reference (Num 5:28). The insemination of a woman is like the sowing of a field. The object is not "the land," for it happens "in the land," but rather Israel, restored to "the land." In normal usage, the verb *zr'* can mean either "to seed" or "to sow." The close resemblance of "I shall sow her to me (*lî*)" (v 25) and "I shall betroth you to me (*lî*)" (vv 21–22), especially the prominent first-person pronoun in both places, shows that the imagery is consistent, with close links between the two stages of the marriage — betrothal and consummation. In the single picture, the union of Gomer and Hosea, of Israel and Yahweh, is one.

The comparison of a fertile wife with a cultivated field is an old one. A famous simile in the Amarna correspondence says: *eqliya aššata ša la muta māšil aššum bali errēšim,* "My field is the proverbial 'wife without a husband,' because it lacks a cultivator" (*EA* 74:17–19; 75:15–17; 90:42–44; cf. 81:37–38, all from Rib-Addi of Byblos; cf. *ANET* 426). A similar proverb compares unsupervised people with a field that has no plowman (Lambert 1960:229, 232). The circumstances described by Rib-Addi are that the wars have caused the people to take refuge in the cities "like birds in a cage." It is not that the fields have no cultivators but that the farmers cannot go to work.

have pity. This cancels 1:6 and 2:6, fulfilling the promise of 2:3.

"You are my people." This cancels 1:9, fulfilling the promise of 2:3. In the reversal of the names at 2:1, "Not-my-People" was changed to "Children of the Living God." Verse 2:25bA returns to the title drawn from the covenant vows.

he will say. In 2:1 the pronouns are plural. By using the singular here, the individual members of the family are highlighted. In the immediate context the speaker is the former Lo-Ammi, whose name in the previous clause has been changed to Ammi: "You are Ammi = my people." It is appropriate that Ammi should respond by affirming the matching title "My God." The balancing pronouns, *'th,* "you," and *hw',* "he," support the connection.

The symbolic equations are not maintained consistently; the mother, or any of the children, can represent Israel in general terms. Attempts to sharpen the equations by distinguishing the northern and southern kingdoms are probably oversubtle. Such a scheme does, nevertheless, have some plausibility: the mother is "the land"; Jezreel all Israel; (Lo)-Ruhama Ephraim; and (Lo)-Ammi Judah. In 2:2 Judah and Israel are reunited to become Jezreel. Jezreel, reinstated, renames the other children. The two children respond to Jezreel (2:24b), because he gave them their new names in 2:3.

"My God." This affirmation matches the name *'ĭ̃lî* in 2:18.

The various rituals and pronouncements connected with adoption, marriage, and covenant-making in general, show that a dual affirmation like this one was usually made by one person, not antiphonally. Such an exchange is not met elsewhere in accounts of Yahweh's covenant with Israel. This exchange of similar statements matches the reciprocal affirmations made in vv 23–24, whose content was not specified.

The discourse is characterized throughout by changing the focus on Yahweh/Israel and Hosea/Gomer. Both are always present, but at some points the prime reference is to Yahweh, while at others the human situation is more to the fore. Yahweh is the primary speaker in vv 16–17; but it is more appropriate for the human husband to be called "my *'ĭ̃š*" (v 18). Verse 19 is a suitable speech for God, whereas the betrothal makes more sense on the human level (vv 21–22). The covenant (vv 20, 23–24) is an activity of God. In general, address in the second person is more suited to a human wife, while third-person address comes from God to Israel. Verse 25 mixes both of these inextricably. The prophet speaks in the name of God, though their identities are never confused. On the other hand, the wife and Israel have much in common, and there is less need to distinguish their identity. While nearly all of the text can refer to God, there are some historical and theological remarks which cannot refer to Hosea. "You (pl) are not my people" (1:9) can be spoken only by God; cf. 2:25. The 2 f s forms reflect the intimacy of the husband-wife relationship at the point where divine and human dimensions of life are completely fused.

We have repeatedly pointed out that the themes of Hosea 1–2 do not move along a straight line to a single climax. The problem and its solution are brought into focus again and again so that there are many climaxes. In particular, 2:16–25 sum up the resolution with courtship, betrothal, covenant-making, exchange of vows, and the giving of new names. Each of these moments has a key expression that strikes a note of finality — "the doorway of hope," "my husband," "I will make them lie down in safety," "You will know Yahweh," "(You are) my God."

Notwithstanding, v 25 is the final climax in which many threads in the preceding discourse are gathered into a single knot.

I will sow. The root *zrʿ* is the last echo of the all-important name Jezreel; the first-person verb is one of three in this verse which match the threefold "I will betroth" in vv 21–22. *Her.* The suffixed object "her" echoes "her" in vv 16–17, 19 and matches "you" in vv 21–22;

compare the three verbs in 2:5b, all with the same object. *To me*. This repeats the threefold *lî* of the husband in vv 21, 22; cf. *lî* in v 18 (the husband) and in vv 9, 14 (the wife), and in 3:2,3. *In the land*. This goes back to the opening statement about "the land" in 1:2, and completes the movement in 2:16–17, showing that a return to the promised land means a renewal of the marriage in the husband's home. *And I will have pity*. This cancels 1:6–7 and 2:6, repeats 2:3, and reaffirms the quality of the covenant (2:21). *And I will say*. Cf. 2:1,3,18. *"You are my people."* This cancels 1:9 and completes a development that began in 2:1. *And he*. The personal pronoun probably refers to Ammi, the last child, and the last speaker. *"My God."* This completes the series "my husband" (2:18) and "Yahweh" (2:22).

III. HOSEA AND THE WOMAN
(3:1–5)

The recovery of Hosea's wife

3 ¹Then Yahweh said to me once more: "Go love the woman who is beloved of another and an adulteress, just as Yahweh loves the Israelites, although they are turning to other gods and are lovers of raisin cakes." ²So I procured her for myself with fifteen shekels of silver, and a homer of barley, and a letek of barley. ³Then I said to her: "For many days you will wait for me. You will not be promiscuous and you shall not belong to a man. Then indeed I will be yours."

Israel: repentance and restoration

⁴For many days the Israelites will wait, without king and without prince, without sacrifices and without cult pillars, without ephod and teraphim. ⁵Afterwards, the Israelites will return and seek Yahweh their God and David their king. And they will come trembling to Yahweh and his goodness at the end of the age.

NOTES

3:1–5. This chapter is one of the most vital in the prophecy; it is also one of the most problematical: the text presents some insoluble problems and some phrases have dubious authenticity. A basic question is the realism with which it describes events in Hosea's life. If factual, what does the account mean? As allegory, how does it correspond to Israel's historical experience?

The relation of c 3 and cc 1–2 is complex. Chapter 3 stands complete in itself: there is a fresh beginning of narrative at v 1, a note of finality at v 5, and no continuity with c 4. Chapter 3 differs from cc 1–2 in being a description in the first person, as opposed to third-person description and first-person prediction in the earlier chapters. Chapter 3 presupposes much that is in cc 1–2. The two situations are at least similar, if not, as we argue, the same: they center on a man whose wife has become adulterous. Some of the terminology of cc 1–2 is used, and while several new terms are introduced, the difference between biographical (c 1) and autobiographical (c 3) writing is not great. The two sections share a common literary technique. The comparison between the woman and Israel is explicitly made in 3:1, as it was in 1:2. As in cc 1–2, both levels of the story are dealt with here at once, though they are more clearly distinguished. In vv 2–3 the human level is foremost; vv 4–5 apply the similitude to Israel's historical experience.

While cc 1–2 provide the best aid available for the interpretation of c 3, not all problems can be solved therewith, and on the whole it is better to deal with c 3 as an independent unit. The problems of c 3 are not solved by taking it out of the realm of the personal or historical and calling it a vision or a parable. Its prophetic purpose is served by the symbolic character of the actions performed, but this does not make them any less concrete. Whether a spoken parable, or an acted one, the intelligibility of the story depends on its recognition by listeners or observers. Even as vision or parable, its terms correspond to familiar social customs and relationships. Because the meaning of what is done must have been evident to Hosea's contemporaries, requiring no exposition, it is obscure to us.

The simplest approach is to suppose that this account corresponds to actual events in Hosea's life. There are then two ways to tie cc 1–2 and c 3 together. One supposes that c 3 is a variant account of the events reported in cc 1–2. Being autobiographical, it must come directly from the prophet; cc 1–2 provide a more ample and theological interpretation drafted by his disciples. The second explanation is that c 3 describes events which happened after cc 1–2. The measures threatened in 2:4–15 were not carried out; what was actually done is described in c 3. Yet c 3 diverges from cc 1–2, not only in its silence concerning the children, but also in the complete absence of the tenderness and vigorous lovemaking described in 2:16–25.

There are more drastic solutions, such as that of Batten (1929:271–272), who concludes "that Hosea had no hand in the composition of the passage; that it has nothing whatever to do with his life or message, that it was one of those innumerable scraps produced in the late days of Israel which the compilers of the prophetic books incorporated according to their convictions of suitability, not always critically sound, and that the compiler inserted the passage in Hosea, quite in the wrong place, because its contents were sexual in character." With this and similar approaches we shall not be concerned.

That c 3 is not a variant of cc 1–2 but rather presupposes the earlier material is indicated by the following points. (1) In c 3 the woman is already an adulteress; this point is underscored by what is said about her lovers. In 1:2, if we are correct in interpreting "promiscuous wife" as an anticipatory retroflection from a later point in time, we have there the beginning of marriage. (2) The word 'ôd, "again, further," in 3:1, no matter which verb it is attached to, suggests continuity. (3) Development is implied in the contrasting terms used. The first command was to acquire a wife, that is, to get married; the second command was to "love" a wife already wayward. (4) The discipline enforced in 3:3 is not the training of a bride, but the subjection and purgation of a fallen wife. (5) Although 3:3 could correspond to the incarceration supposed to be described in 2:8, and represent the implementation of that threat, we have proposed a somewhat different interpretation of 2:8, and caution once more against accommodating the two sections to each other. There is a separation between husband and wife in 2:8, whereas in 3:3 they are close to each other.

While c 3 seems to come after 1:2–9, in spite of its failure to notice any children, 3:5 in some ways parallels 2:1–3. Both reflect the end time, which is described again in another way in 2:16–25. The relationship of 3:1–4 to 2:16–17 is less clear: what is done in 3:1–3 is rigorous compared with the kindness shown in 2:16–17 and logically 3:3 could well come between 2:15 and 2:16; some scholars so rearrange the text. The harsh measures described in 3:3, while not going so far as the first part of c 2, certainly leave no room for the constructive activities intended by the husband in the second part of c 2. The opening command of c 3, to "love" a woman, is not fulfilled in the chapter: 3:3 is altogether obstructive and negative, and what it achieves is not described, at least on the human level. Nowhere in cc 1–3 is a penitent response by the woman described, except by way of prediction of a possibility (2:9b), or as a hope (2:18). What Gomer actually did we are never told. The focus switches completely from the woman to Israel before this point in the story is reached, that is, in moving from 3:3 to 3:4. Here, at last, there is anticipation of some initiative to be taken by Israel in "returning" (cf. the similar act of the woman in 2:9, using the same verb); in 2:16–25 the initiative is all Yahweh's. The command to love a woman might well be carried out along the lines of 2:16–17, and then 3:4–5 (which resembles 2:18–25 in its eschatological color, if not in detail) would follow. To this extent, c 3 and cc 1–2 are complementary: 3:3 would supply a transition between 2:15 and 2:16, as 2:16–17 would supply a transition between 3:3 and 3:4. We do not advise such an actual conflation; rather we seek to observe the several motifs in their present artistic arrangement without imposing an artificial schematization.

To sum up. What is described in 3:1–3 seems to come after the events of 1:2–9; 2:7,15b. It could be related to the rest of 2:4–15 in one of three ways. (1) The threats made in 2:4–15 were unavailing and remained simply threats. The woman did not return as hoped for in 2:9b. So the husband had to adopt the measures recorded in 3:2–3 to bring her back to his home forcibly. The children recede from the picture in c 3 because their efforts to persuade their mother did not succeed. (2) On the other hand, 2:4–15 could describe the steps taken by the husband during the period of rehabilitation mentioned in 3:3, which would then precede in time the situation of 2:4–15. This does match to some extent Yahweh's historical treatment of Israel, described in 3:4. If Gomer has already been brought back home (3:2–3) when 2:4–15 transpires, then the family are all together, and this accounts for the use of the pronouns. Hosea can speak *to* the children (2 m pl) or *about* them (3 m pl) to his wife. He can speak *to* her directly (2 f s) or *about* her (3 f s) to her children. (3) If the statements in Hos 2:4–15 are considered to be in chronological order, so that v 15b comes last, then that passage could describe an early attempt to keep the family together (between the woman's first adultery and her final desertion); c 3 would come well after that. Since we have maintained that 2:15 comes early in the story, this third reconstruction seems quite improbable.

In all this the anonymity of Gomer is remarkable. There is no direct description of anything that she did or said. The facts about her opinions, motives, actions have to be gleaned from oblique references. So far as Hosea himself is concerned, there is no indication that he ever regained his wife's affection, and that they lived happily ever after. There is no ending to assert that love conquers all. The story ends abruptly and unsatisfactorily at 3:3, perhaps because the hoped-for reconciliation was no more than a hope, a hope grounded in unquenchable love, like Yahweh's love for Israel.

3:1. *Yahweh said.* The narrative here resembles 1:2b. The reclaiming of the adulterous wife is like starting the marriage all over again, treating the defiled woman as a pure girl.

once more. Because of its position in between "said" and "go," '*ôd*, "again, further, once more," could be attached to either. The Masoretic punctuation joins it to the preceding verb and it is more common for '*ôd* to follow the verb it modifies; Zech 1:17, however, shows that '*ôd* may precede. Our rendering, which follows the Masoretes, involves some strain, for the adverb is separated from the verb by the subject and indirect object. Since '*ôd* is unusual before, rather than after, the verb it modifies, for "Go again," we would expect *lek* '*ôd*. The statement "he said . . . once more" apparently continues the series of speeches described in 1:2–9; Yahweh had spoken to Hosea there, but the prophet had not been commanded to "love" before. This may be splitting a hair, since he had been told to "go" before, and the difference between "take a woman" (1:2) and "love a woman" (3:1) is probably slight; the second time he is not told to marry her, for he is already married to her. The thing to be done now is to love a woman who is already his wife.

It may be sufficient to have the adverb modify both verbs rather than choosing one. If extended to "love" as well, it would indicate that the marriage was grounded in love at the start, not that love had to be brought in first at this late stage. This would also correspond to Yahweh and Israel. As Fleming James (1947:242) says, "There is always an 'again' with love."

Gordon (1967:21) has suggested that the similarities between 1:2 and 3:1 and the use of the adverb "again" point to a second marriage; not the remarriage of a divorced wife, but the taking of a second wife (cf. Toy 1913:77; Ginsberg 1960; Hendriks n.d.:162). Guided by the analogy of Ezekiel 23 and the Ugaritic text *UT* 52, Gordon considers that Hosea took two different women as wives to represent the two kingdoms of Israel and, by the same token, suggests that this motif betrays the poetic use of an old mythological theme, to be taken as allegory, not fact. We cannot accept this: the indications are that the events here are real, however unclear. There is no internal evidence that each supposed wife represents only half of Israel. The bigamy of Ezekiel 23 arises from the historical facts, not from old myths and is a later development of Hosea's theme. Elsewhere Yahweh's marriage to Israel is monogamous. Israelite marriages were commonly monogamous (although royal harems seem to have been the rule) apart from those of the patriarchs, whose multiple marriages reflect special circumstances; otherwise bigamy is rare, e.g. Elkanah the father of Samuel, who had two wives, one of whom, Hannah, was sterile; this factor may have provided the reason for a second marriage. Plural marriages and questions of inheritance are dealt with in the legal codes, signifying that such marriages existed in Israel. None of the known factors seems to have been present in this case (de Vaux 1961b:24–26).

love. In view of the use of the root *'hb* throughout these chapters, the command to love probably does not mean "to court," that is, to try to elicit a response of love, the action of 2:16, nor does it mean simply "to declare the love you feel." It is more general. Hosea is urged to reaffirm his marriage, by words and acts of love. The love of Hosea and the love of God alternate with the perverse love of the adulterer and the idolator. Ginsberg (1971:1012) weakens the force of this word by arguing that it means no more than "befriend." The four occurrences of the root *'hb* in 3:1 are stylistically like the four occurrences of the root *zny* in 1:2; it would be going too far to search for a distinct meaning for each of these (Buber and Rosenzweig 1934).

the woman. That is, "your wife." The choice of words is deliberate. In
1:2, instead of the conventional "take a wife," there is the startling command to take a promiscuous wife. Here, the ordinary word for "woman/
wife" is used. It is as his wife, as one on whom he has legitimate, inalien-
able claims, that Hosea must love the woman again. That a definite
woman is meant, and not just any woman who is an adulteress, is shown
by the pronoun in v 2 — "and I procured *her.*" In contrast to Ginsberg's
(1960:51 n 3) peremptory dismissal of the definiteness, Schmidt
(1924:262) is equally emphatic that the suffix in v 2 refers to "an entirely
distinct person."

beloved of another. LXX takes the participle as active and the following
noun as a homograph, *r*', "evil," — "she who loves wickedness." This interpretation is in line with the active use of the verb *'hb* in its other occurrences, and parallel to the active participle *mĕnā'āpet,* "one who commits
adultery," although the reading of *r*' cannot be correct. When a passive
participle stands in construct relationship with a noun, the noun refers to
the performer of the action. Consistent with this construction is the
repeated designation of her lovers as *mĕ'ahăbîm,* the active participle.
The point is a fine one; but the balance of evidence favors the MT. In its
occurrences in the Bible, the active participles of this root are regularly
masculine; the passive participles are commonly feminine, though there
are exceptions in both categories; see e.g. Gen 25:28 for an active feminine form; Neh 13:26 for the passive masculine. The relationship is reflected in the comparison stressing Yahweh's love for Israel, conceived as
the feminine partner in 3:1b.

The active reading of *'hbt* in LXX may be favored by the chiastic structure.

> she loves another
> she commits adultery
> they turn aside after other gods
> they love raisin cakes

Turning aside to other gods could be equated with committing adultery,
and raisin cakes with the other beloved. The chiasm remains, however,
even if we read *'hbt* as passive.

another. Literally "friend, neighbor, someone else." This is the first time
that *rēa'* has been used for the person with whom the wife commits adultery. In Jer 3:20, *rēa'* means "husband" (cf. *RV* margin and Gordis
1954:24). It does not, as such, ever mean paramour, unless here and at
Jer 3:1 (cf. Lam 1:2), which could be derived from Hosea. In Cant 5:16
rē'î, parallel to *dôdî,* means "my lover." A technical meaning has been
suspected for some uses. The clearest is the use of *rēa'* to describe a
bridegroom's best man. This applies to the wedding situation the idea of

"best friend." Thus the god Erra is designated Hammurapi's "companion" (*rûšu*, cognate with Hebrew *rēaʿ*, cf. *ANET* 165). Tushingham (1953) has conjectured that a king or priest, the "best man" of a god, is described here. He surmises further that the priest, in his capacity as best man, could substitute for the god in the performance of sexual intercourse as a sacral rite, and that the *rēaʿ* of 3:1 is the priest referred to in c 4 (cf. Schmidt 1924:264–268). Although there seems to be no doubt that Gomer was involved in adultery in the context of Baal worship, to identify her lover as a priest requires several links in a chain of inference which are not firmly joined. We could only reach certainty on this point if we could find out whether she was a member of the officiating personnel at such a shrine or whether she participated more generally as a worshiper. Unfortunately the situation from which she is removed in v 2 is unknown.

Used as it is with the root *nʾp*, "commit adultery," *rēaʿ* may be used in its legal sense, "fellow man" ("neighbor" in traditional English versions), or better "fellow citizen," not any person, but a member of the same community. The Law forbids a person from coveting his "neighbor's" wife (Exod 20:17; Deut 5:18); a person who commits adultery with "his neighbor's wife" (Lev 20:10; Deut 22:24) incurs the death penalty. The most general sense, however, is "another person" and we prefer it here.

Yahweh loves. The comparison is with the husband's love for his adulterous wife, not with her love for her "friend," and thus we translate the conjunction in the next clause as concessive. Yahweh loves Israel — to whom he is married — in spite of the fact that Israel loves other gods. Hosea is to love his wife the way Yahweh loves Israel. This close comparison between God's love for his people and a man's love for his wife sums up the story of Hosea's marriage. Commentators have indulged in sentimental fabulation in dealing with this verse. The more romantic among them see Hosea brooding on the alienation that prevents his love's fulfillment until he comes to the insight, "Yahweh's love is just like mine!" This is not the way 3:1 puts it. If this were the thought, then the comparison would be the other way — Yahweh loves Israel the way Hosea loves Gomer. Rather, Hosea is commanded to love, an instruction which people who think that love is the spontaneous expression of feeling find impossible. In scripture love is always a command; love is action in obedience to the word of Yahweh. "At the discovery of God's love he (Hosea) perceives how he must act towards his wife" (Wolff 1974:60). The love of God is not "natural"; nor is human love. It is unreasonable.

Once more Yahweh uses his own name when referring to himself, rather than using the first person.

they. The pronoun is used emphatically. It would seem that all Israelites are turning aside. The use of the present participle makes the clause circumstantial: while they are in the very act of turning aside after other gods, Yahweh keeps on loving them. The verb "to turn aside" figures in Deuteronomic vocabulary, where it designates apostasy: Deut 29:17; 30:17; 31:18,20.

other gods. This phrase is also characteristic of Deuteronomy, which uses it fifteen times, in contrast to, e.g., Josh 24:23, which has *'ĕlōhê hannēkār,* "foreign gods." The rival deities are not named here; the Baals are clearly intended, although insofar as the phrase stands for all other gods, female deities could also be included.

lovers of raisin cakes. It is not certain whether the phrase refers to the other gods or the Israelites. If the former, then the preposition "(turn) to" governs the whole of the coordinated phrase, an unusual construction. If the latter, as we believe, then *hēm,* "they," is the subject of a clause whose predicate is two coordinated participles, the first absolute and verb-like, the second in construct and noun-like. Although there are grammatical incongruities in either interpretation, the first can be ruled out because neither Hosea nor any prophet would acknowledge that other gods were capable of any word or deed. They were literally nonentities. The Israelites, then, are the fruit-eaters here.

While the exact recipe for raisin cakes is no longer known, it would seem that they were made out of crushed dried grapes (Pope 1977:378–380). According to II Sam 6:19, they could be used in the legitimate cult of Yahweh as refreshment for the worshipers. Since there was nothing reprehensible about that use, the cultic setting does not explain why Hosea should single out a love of cakes as the epitome of Israel's apostasy. In Isa 16:7, crop failure means that this commodity is not available, but again there are no reprehensible associations (Driver 1958:43). The context of the other occurrence of the word, in Cant 2:5, is suggestive; the cakes seem to be an aphrodisiac. Their use in the Baal cult would then be different from their use in the Yahweh cult. If the cakes are offerings to the gods, then they might be compared with the *kawwānîm,* dough cakes made for the Queen of Heaven (Jer 7:18).

2. *I procured.* The unique form *wā'ekkĕrehā* can be derived from *kārâ,* "to buy," though the morphology is difficult. The root with this meaning has dubious attestation in Deut 2:6; Job 6:27; 40:30. In these the *k* is *raphe,* as expected; the dagesh in the *k* here is inexplicable. If it is called *dagesh forte dirimens* (GKC §20h), to make sure that the shewa is pronounced, then we have two problems. First, if it comes from *kārâ* the shewa should be silent; secondly, this would seem to be the only occurrence of such a dagesh in a *k,* and no phonetic explanation is in sight. Gesenius' suggestion that the dagesh makes the *k* a stop is unconvincing, unless the consonant is doubled. The textual support for the dagesh is unswerving. The supposed nuance of *kārâ,* "to get by trade," is preferred by

Th. H. Robinson; but the problem is not simply hitting on the right English word. The connotation is what matters, for it raises such questions as the status of the woman at the start of the transaction; the nature of the payment — why it is silver plus barley, and who gets it — and the specific proprietary rights of the new "owner." Nyberg (p. 23) preferred the nuance "to hire" since the Arabic cognate means "to hire a beast." This would imply that Hosea took over the management of a prostitute, but did not put her to work. (The Arabic cognate also means "to sleep.") This etymon *kry* must be reluctantly accepted.

All this is so unsatisfactory that many scholars prefer an alternative derivation from *nkr*, "to purchase (for marriage)" (Gordis 1954:25). The use in I Sam 23:7 of *nikkar* is quoted to support this, because LXX has "sold," but LXX probably read *mkr*, "to sell" (cf. Judg 2:14; 4:9). There is no proof that *nkr* means "to purchase," and Ginsberg (1960:57) dismisses the supposed sense as "mythical." Tushingham (1953:153) tries to develop the meaning "to acquire possession" from the juridical meaning of *nkr*, "to acknowledge or recognize as a possession." There are other explanations which emend the text (1) to a form of *śkr*, *wā'eśkěrehā*, "I hired her," after LXX (Ehrlich 1912:171); (2) to a form of *krr*, "I caused her to turn back to me" (Waterman 1918:203). Waterman subsequently (1955:106), following Tushingham (1953), accepted the meaning "So I acknowledged her as mine," but eliminated the idea of purchase altogether by explaining the following words as banning the woman from using silver and barley in playing the harlot. We note the occurrence of the word *mōkeret*, a title given to Nineveh in Nah 3:4, a passage cited earlier because of its affinities with Hosea. Dahood (1971) has improved our understanding of Nah 3:4 by pointing out the causal meaning of *b*, and repointing the participle as *mukkeret* from *nkr*. Analogous constructions (such as *'ăhubat rēa'* in v 1) support analysis of passive followed by agent. His identification of the root *nkr* as "to know" is not entirely satisfying. The point is not simply the fame of Nineveh among the nations, but her notorious promiscuity and sorcery. Like Babylon of the Apocalypse, "the kings of the earth committed fornication with her" (Rev 18:3,9). Nah 3:4 and Hos 3:2 have a common context of adultery.

The carefully recorded silver and barley in Hosea are best explained as a payment; the preposition is the *b* of price. This gives firm grounds for explaining *'ekkěrehā* as containing a verb meaning "to buy." There is a similarity between *wě'ēraśtîk lî bě* (2:21–22) and *wā'ekkěrehā lî bě*, though the nouns in the former that are governed by *b* can only be construed in a symbolic and figurative sense, and it seems unlikely that 3:2 records a betrothal. A more popular suggestion is that the husband had to redeem his wife from slavery, both in view of the price and also because the actual price suggests bargaining, as Wolff suggests (1974:61).

It is hard to see why, if Hosea was determined to get his wife back, he would haggle over the payment and try for a bargain. It is more likely that the charges were paid partly in metal and partly in kind. Certainly the care with which the price is recorded suggests a formal agreement, properly documented. There is no hint anywhere else that the woman had become a slave. Even if she were destitute, she could not sell herself; and there is no suggestion that the husband sold her, and later bought her back. This idea has given rise to a lot of romantic exposition, which lacks foundation in the text. A connection between some kind of bondage and prostitution might be supposed if Gomer had become a temple prostitute. But, quite apart from the legal question of whether this could have been done without her husband's consent, there is the further question of whether a temple would sell its personnel to a private buyer. Unfortunately the verse gives no hint as to whom such a payment might have been made.

with fifteen shekels. The construction is abnormal grammatically in that the preposition is used only once with the three coordinated nouns. The Hebrew says simply "silver," but the shekel is implied as the unit. The price itself does not give us much help in understanding the nature of the transaction. It is unique in combining money and food. For comparison we note that fifty shekels of silver was the bride-price in the case of compulsory marriage after forcible rape (Deut 22:29); thirty shekels of silver was the value of a slave (Exod 21:32; Lev 27:4). Joseph was sold for twenty shekels (Gen 37:28).

Since the value of the payment approximates that of a person or slave as recorded in other places in the Bible, it may be that purchase of the person is involved rather than the hiring of services. Hosea has secured complete proprietary rights to the woman, and can restrict her activities and direct her behavior.

homer. This common volume measure is probably related to the Hebrew word for donkey. The other measure, the *letek,* is mentioned only here in the Bible; the word is used at Ugarit, but its size there is not known. Tradition has it that the *letek* was half a homer. Further, we do not know the market value of either unit.

barley. This did not appear as one of the several products listed in c 2. The uniqueness of the word *letek* points to the general authenticity of the MT, but LXX preserves a reading with high claims. It reads "a nebel of wine" as the third item, instead of "a letek of barley." This could be original, since "barley" could hardly be read as wine, whereas the second "barley" could have come in as a repetition of the first.

3. It is regrettable that this crucial verse is so difficult. All the words are familiar, simple, and clear. But the syntax, the idioms, the arrangement of the parts, the frame of reference, the life situation — all are opaque. The text has been rewritten extensively by moderns in order to make it intelli-

gible, a course we are reluctant to follow. We suspect that the trouble arises from the use of vernacular laconisms, highly abbreviated expressions current in living speech, clear enough to contemporaries in the context. We know neither the context nor the fuller forms. Some illumination comes from vv 4–5. The phrase "many days" makes it clear that the two situations are similar. Israel's experience is well known: they were to be deprived of the familiar furnishings of worship and denied a close relationship with Yahweh, for a considerable period, after which the old relationship would be restored. So, in the same general way, the wife will be deprived, and her freedom will be restricted for a long period.

I said to her. This is the only recorded direct speech of Hosea to his wife. The verse falls into four unequal parts:

> 3aA *yāmîm rabbîm tēšĕbî lî*
> 3aB *lō' tiznî*
> 3bA *wĕlō' tihyî lĕ'îš*
> 3bB *wĕgam-'ănî 'ēlāyik*

Comparison with the opening words of v 4, which repeats *yāmîm rabbîm yēšĕbû,* suggests that the verb is used absolutely, that is, without specifying the location of the activity; in such cases, *yšb* does not mean "to sit, dwell," but "to remain, wait"; cf. Deut 9:9. The Masoretic punctuation links *lî* with the verb *tšby.* If this construction is to be retained, it must mean "you will wait for me for a long time," as in Gen 22:5; 44:33; Exod 24:14; Lev 12:4; I Sam 1:23. Traditional translations, such as "Live with me," have no support. The pronominal balance in vv 3aA and 3bB, and the repetition of the negative particle in vv 3aB and 3bA suggest that we are dealing with an envelope construction. Verses 3aA and 3bB then describe her relationship to her husband; vv 3aB and 3bA describe her relationship to everyone else. The syntax of the conjunctions points in the same direction, especially since there is no conjunction between vv 3aA and 3aB. The two parts of v 3b are not related consecutively; we need not try to explain each line in terms of the other. Rather we must explain v 3bA as parallel to v 3aB. The categorical prohibitions make it clear that she must not be sexually active, that she must have nothing to do with any other man. (LXX actually supplies *heterō,* "other," in v 3bA.) The usual interpretation, "thou shalt not be any man's wife" (*RV*), is to be rejected; the idiom *hyy l* can indicate all variety of possession. It can refer to belonging to a man in marriage (cf. Ezek 23:4), but this simply does not fit the situation. Such a prohibition is scarcely required unless marriage is a real possibility which has to be blocked. But Gomer is married to Hosea and we have found on his part no intention of divorcing her. If he has done so, what is he doing with her now? She would be free to marry any man except her former husband. We must ask if the clause *wĕlō' tihyî lĕ'îš* might refer to something other than marriage.

While *hyy l* is used in the most general way to refer to any kind of ownership, when the subject is a woman, and the complement is *lĕ'îš* or the like, then it describes the marriage relationship in general, with no particular emphasis on getting married (I Kings 4:11), and in other contexts, it seems to be a way of talking about sexual intercourse. When no details are given, i.e. when the process of getting married is not broken up into separate stages, then *hyy l* covers the whole (e.g. I Sam 25:42). When the process is broken up into stages, *wattĕhî lĕ'îš* can refer to more than one of these stages. The possibilities are:

1) Becoming engaged
2) Getting married (the formal ceremony)
3) Being married (the continuing state)
4) Having sex with a man
5) Marrying for a second time

1) Lev 21:3 (cf. Ezek 44:25) describes a person's "sister," a close relative, as a "virgin who has never belonged to a man." As in the parallel passage about Rebekah in Gen 24:16, it doubtless means "who has never had intercourse," but it may also signify a virgin who is not yet engaged, and is therefore free of marriage commitments. If Lev 21:3 can bear this interpretation, then *hyy l* refers to the first step toward marriage. Comparison of Lev 21:3 with Gen 24:16 shows that the word *bĕtûlâ* by itself meant a marriageable woman, while the following clause specifies her premarital virginity. If Lev 21:3 is similarly constructed, then it may mean that she was a betrothed virgin whose marriage had not yet been consummated. So long as she remained a virgin, she continued to be a member of her father's household and they were responsible for her mourning rituals.

2) The marriage ceremony, as distinct from consummation in intercourse, may be described with *hyy l* in Ruth 4:13, if the three clauses are in sequence: "And Boaz took Ruth; [*wattĕhî-lô lĕ'iššâ*] and she became his wife; and he went in to her." Intercourse took place after she had become his wife.

3) A complex procedure is reported in Deut 21:10–14. It contains quite a bit of vocabulary met also in Hos 3:3, suggesting that a comparable routine is being followed there.

A man sees a good-looking prisoner of war.
He falls in love with her.
He takes her as his wife — *lqḥ lô lĕ'iššâ* (cf. v 3bA).
He takes her into his house.
She shaves her head, cuts her nails, removes her prisoner clothes.

She remains in his house — *yšb běbêtô* (cf. v 3aA).
She mourns her parents one month — *yeraḥ yāmîm* (cf. v 3aA).
After that — *'aḥar kēn* (cf. *'aḥar* in v 5),
    he goes in to her — *bā' 'ēlêhā* (cf. v 3bB).
He becomes her husband—*ûbě'altāh*.
She becomes his wife — *wěhāyětâ lěkā lě'iššâ*

The last clauses then refer to the continuing state of marriage. Compare the sequence in Gen 24:67. The expression *hyy l* in II Sam 11:27 has this sense; some time after David and Bathsheba have had intercourse and she is pregnant, it describes the formalization of their relationship when they begin living together.

4) Naomi's remark in Ruth 1:12 probably refers to having sex. Her reference to "tonight" and her hope of children highlights belonging to a man in intercourse. In Ezek 16:15 *lô-yěhî*, although it is a difficult construction, describes the act in which a prostitute gives herself to a client.

5) If *lě'îš* in v 3bA is an abbreviation of *lě'îš-'aḥēr* (Deut 24:2; Jer 3:1), then legitimate marriage of a divorced woman is meant. Hosea is saying, "You will never marry another man" (because I will never divorce you?). Cf. Judg 14:20, where the deserted bride is given to another man.

Without trying to pinpint the meaning more exactly, it would seem that vv 3aB–3bA impose a total ban on all sexual activity, inside marriage as well as outside it. At least it is better to take the middle two lines together than to take the first two together, which leads to incongruities. If v 3a means "You will remain with me for a long time (and) you won't be promiscuous," does this mean that after the "many days" are up, she will be able to be promiscuous again?

The nearest analogy to the total suspension of Israel's cultic life (v 4) would be the total suspension of the woman's sexual life (v 3). Verse 4 does not make it clear whether the items listed are used in the worship of Baal or of Yahweh. The list is mixed, and could represent both intentionally (cf. cc 8–9). The Israelites will worship formally neither their true god (Yahweh) nor the false ones (the Baals). The wife will have no sexual relations, neither with her husband nor with her lovers. Since, however, the situation of husband and wife is not the same as that of God and Israel, it may be better to regard *wl' thyy l'yš* as the complement of *l' tzny,* "you shall not be promiscuous, i.e. you shall not have relations with any (other) man." The relation with the husband is to be defined by other words and will follow a different course. For "these many days" she cannot have intercourse with her husband (v 3aB) because she has been unfaithful; she cannot have intercourse with anyone else (v 3bA) because she is a married woman.

There is no resolution of the tension between husband and wife as there

is between Yahweh and Israel (in v 5). There is nothing in v 3 to correspond to the "afterwards" of v 5. If Hosea is to love Gomer the way Yahweh loves Israel, then this will require a period of effective isolation until
there is a change of heart. Israel's restoration must wait until the "end of
the age." There is no indication of what finally happened in Hosea's
dealings with his wife.

Then indeed I. In parallel with v 3bA, v 3bB is usually taken to mean
"You won't have sexual relations with any man, and I similarly won't
have relations with you." But why should Hosea avoid his wife when he
has just been told to "love" her? The answer surely lies in v 4 — Hosea's
extended continence is to be a prophetic act, symbolic of the long arrest
of Yahweh's relationship with Israel. And since v 4 shares the phrase
"remain (or wait) for many days" with v 3aA, we link v 3bB with
this also. Hence our translation. The interval of inaction has sometimes
been compared with a woman's period of purification, since Israelites
refrained from intercourse when women were "unclean." Otherwise the
husband is waiting for a change of heart.

There may be a parallel situation elsewhere. David segregated the concubines that Absalom had taken in a guardhouse. He provided them with
sustenance, but he did not have sex with them. They were incarcerated
until the day they died, *'almĕnût ḥayyût* (II Sam 20:3). This unique
phrase has been declared impossible, and either or both words emended to
something more familiar; *ḥayyût* is a hapax legomenon, and *'almĕnût* occurs four times. In Gen 38:14,19 and Isa 54:4, *'almĕnût* means "widowhood"; *ḥayyût* corresponds to the period until the women's deaths, i.e. the
phrase means "widowhood for life," the state of a widow who may not
remarry. These concubines were Absalom's "widows," although they had
not been his "wives" in a formal sense. There was no ban on marrying
widows; Absalom's own action was part of a pattern (II Sam 3:7; I Kings
2:22). In reclaiming kingship, David took them back, but did not visit
them. (The rule of Deut 24:4 hardly applies, for the women were not
wives, and they had not been divorced.)

Verse 3bB as it stands could mean almost anything. Rowley
(1956:203 n 2) lists a number of quite divergent and highly improbable
solutions. The only remedy is to supply or understand some verb. If the
speech is laconic, the words do not have to be literally supplied. It would be
intelligible, however, only if the abbreviated idiom were easily recognized,
or if one of the preceding verbs carried on into the following elliptical
clause. Although all three verbs in the speech in v 3 are attested in combination with the preposition *'el,* different prepositions (*lĕ* in the case of *yšb*
and *ḥyy*) or none at all (*zny*) are used in v 3. The change of preposition
in v 3bB would imply either that none of the three is intended, or that
there is a shift in meaning or nuance. At the same time the use of *gam* in

wĕgam-'ănî, "and I also," points to a similarity between the man's action and the woman's. "You will act in a certain way, and I also will act in the same way." It would be possible to conclude that the husband will wait, just as the wife does, in spite of the fact that the idiom *yšb 'el* is attested only once in a doubtful case (I Sam 28:23; LXX reflects *'l* for MT's *'l*).

Many scholars, as we noted above, wish to continue the negatives in vv 3aB and 3bA into v 3bB. In the Middle Ages, Ibn Ezra and David Kimḥi understood the words *lō' 'ābô',* "I will not come (in) to you," to be implied. Wellhausen restored them to the text. But if v 3bB is parallel to v 3aA, rather than to v 3aB or 3bA, the negative should not be read — "You will wait a long time . . . and then I shall come to you." The resumption of normal relations then corresponds to the restoration of Israel's relations with Yahweh and David; v 3bB corresponds to v 5.

In any case, v 3 seems to encompass both the disciplinary treatment of the errant wife and the expected reconciliation in parallel with vv 4–5. It is perhaps best to read the text as it stands, without presupposing or supplying any verb. The relationship between the two principals ("I and thou") is defined by the preposition *'el,* which goes beyond possessive *l* (i.e. I will belong to you) to convey the idea of action or motion (i.e. *hyy l* means "to belong to," while *hyy 'el* means "to come to"). The effect is much the same as though the verb *bw'* were inserted, but its omission may be due to the fact that the idiom *bw' 'el* has been preempted in the Bible for sexual congress, whereas the meaning here transcends, while including, that aspect of reunion.

4. *many days.* The period is long, but indeterminate; although the same phrase is used in v 3, here its duration must be seen in Israel's long history. The concluding phrase of v 5 ("at the end of the age") opens up a perspective that reaches into the future.

without. The negative existential predicator *'ên* is used before each of the six nouns except the last, underscoring the scope of the deprivation. The six items are grouped in three pairs. They are restricted to the institutions of political life and the equipment of cult life. Doubtless they stand for national existence, and their disappearance signals the end of the state. At the same time, it is clear that the people, in some recognizable corporate form, will survive; this remained a possibility even in the face of conquest and captivity in the eighth century B.C.E.

The two things that Hosea constantly assails have already been marked out in the preceding discourse — the monarchy (1:4) and false worship (2:15); 3:4 combines and summarizes these themes, although it does not assert that these institutions of national life are to be expunged permanently. On the contrary, deprivation of them is the punishment, and rehabilitation will involve their return, as v 5 makes clear: the monarchy will be restored with its rightful king, David, as will the legitimate worship of the true God, Yahweh.

king and *prince*. These words are frequent parallels in Hosea. A *śar*, traditionally "prince," is an administrative official, not necessarily royal. Hosea shares with other prophets an ambivalent attitude toward the monarchy. Hos 8:4 gives the impression that Yahweh did not recognize the monarchy at all, but it could mean that he did not recognize kings who were appointed without his approval.

cult pillars. The standing stones in shrines were esteemed differently in Israel at various times. In patriarchal times they were set up without censure. Later, because of their association with Canaanite worship, orders were given to abolish them. At this stage it is likely that they were considered illicit by stricter Yahwists. If the other items also belong to pagan cults, what is being done here fulfills the promise made in 2:19. But if Baal religion is to be banned, there is less impression of deprivation. If all religion ceases to function, the loss is complete. This fits in with v 3: the woman has no sex life, neither with her lovers (the Baals) nor with her husband (Yahweh).

ephod. Ephods were used in both legitimate Yahweh worship and pagan cults, as part of the priest's vestments, and in divination, perhaps because the Urim and Thummim were carried in their pouch. As a garment for an image, made of gold and precious stones, Gideon's ephod (Judg 8:24–28) is a good example of the paganizing of Yahweh worship.

The use of the ephod for divination in the early days seems to have passed out of vogue with the rise of prophetism, and its continued use degenerated into magic and superstition.

teraphim. As noted earlier, the negative particle '*yn* is omitted with the sixth and final term, though it occur with the other five. This probably indicates that *ephod* and *teraphim* are combined into a single unit, more closely than is the case with the other pairs. *Teraphim* are images of some kind, usually understood as household gods, and regularly condemned in the strongest possible language; the case of Rachel and the *teraphim* of her father, Laban, is exceptional. They are, however, rigorously excluded from Israel's worship, so in this case we must suppose that the deprivation will be permanent, and that the reference is to pagan or paganizing worship in Israel. The association of *teraphim* with the *ephod* is attested elsewhere (Judg 17:5; 18:14,17,18,20), along with other terms for idols. It would appear therefore that no purified and revived religion could include these contaminating features even if they were once part of an acceptable cult.

5. Commonly deleted as a gloss (Harper 205, 223).

will return. When this verb is followed by another verb, and does not have an adverb of place, it can serve as an auxiliary; cf. 2:11. Here we would have, "The Israelites will seek Yahweh again." The idiom *šwb 'el* (Hos 6:1) can be recognized here, broken over the verse — "they will return . . . to Yahweh," as in 6:1. Since the roots *šwb* and *yšb* sound alike, and some forms are similar, it is possible that there is a play involving *yĕšĕbû* in v 4 and *yāšūbû* in v 5.

There is no indication of the means that Yahweh will use to bring about this return. The whole chapter emphasizes the inactivity of Yahweh, in contrast to c 2. In other prophetic writings the return of Israel to Yahweh is matched by Yahweh's turning back to his people (Zech 1:3; Mal 3:7). There are two biblical traditions on this point. One is illustrated by Deut 30:1–10 and I Kings 8:4–5: the people's repentance in exile is the turning point for recovery of their lost relation with their God. The other tradition copes more drastically with the inability of the people to turn, and ascribes all the initiative to God; this is illustrated by Ezek 36:24–31. Here the people are brought back, unrepentant, by God himself; they are cleansed, spiritually transformed, called "my people," given grain and all good things (cf. 2:24), and reestablished in the land. Only then do they come to loathe their filthy practices. Repentance is the result, not the condition, of Yahweh's love. Hosea's cryptic remarks cannot be tied to either tradition.

seek. And undoubtedly find, unlike the frustrating experiences described in 2:9 (seeking the lovers in vain) and 5:6 (seeking Yahweh in vain).

David. The close linkage of David and Yahweh is unacceptable to many scholars. The reference to the king is commonly deleted as a late Judahite interpolation. There is no need for this, as the thought is not inconsistent with prophetic views generally, and there is need for a suitable conclusion to the section. We hardly know enough of Hosea's political thinking to rule out the restoration of the Davidic kingdom as an eschatological expectation (Crüsemann 1978:88–94).

The passage's structure suggests an integral design.

5aA   *'aḥar yāšūbû bĕnê yiśrā'ēl*
5aB   *ûbiqšû 'et-yhwh 'ĕlōhêhem wĕ'ēt dāwīd malkām*
5bA   *ûpāḥădû 'el-yhwh wĕ'el-ṭûbô*
5bB   *bĕ'aḥărît hayyāmîm.*

The two activities, seeking (5aB) and fearing (5bA), are encompassed by two time references (5aA, 5bB), both involving the root *'ḥr*. The name Yahweh is prominent as the goal of this return. In v 5aB Yahweh is linked with David; in v 5bA with "his goodness."

Ps 2:2 and Jer 30:9 illustrate the close association possible between Yahweh and his anointed. It is appropriate that the king, removed in v 4, be restored in v 5. Compare Ezekiel 34.

come trembling to. The idiom *pḥd 'el,* "to fear to," is awkward, if the preposition governs the object of the verb. It does, however, occur in Mic 7:17; the idiom in Jer 36:16 is different. Given the unusual construction with *phd* and the lack of a complement for *yāšūbû, 'el yhwh* may specify the goal of both verbs, "return" and "fear."

goodness. The idea of trembling in fear before the "goodness" of God shows that this is the reverence of admiration and appreciation, not terror. The distinction between the nouns *ṭûb* and *ṭôb* (the latter identical with the adjective "good") is a fine one. The difference in vocalization is so minimal that we cannot be certain that the Masoretes always preserved it correctly. The rarer of the two, *ṭûb,* occurs about thirty times. It is more concrete than *ṭôb,* and refers to tokens of material prosperity — wealth (Gen 24:10; Deut 6:11; II Kings 8:9) or the produce of the soil (Gen 45:18,20,23; Isa 1:19; Jer 2:7; Ezra 9:12). The phrase *ṭûb yhwh,* which might be present in Hos 3:5 by hendiadys, is found in Ps 27:13 and Jer 31:12 (cf. Jer 31:14). The last occurrences are interesting because "the goodness of Yahweh" (in an eschatological setting which has not a few affinities with Hosea) is identified as "grain and must and oil"; cf. Hos 2:24. "The goodness of Yahweh" is associated with satisfaction and joy on the part of his people.

at the end of the age. This phrase occupies a strategic place at the very end of the section — the end of Part I, consisting of Hosea 1–3. While the word *'aḥărît* sometimes has a spatial reference, it is best known in its meaning of "end time," with the stress on fulfillment rather than on termination (Carmignac 1969). "The end of the year" (Deut 11:12) is the time of harvest. The association of *'aḥărît* with *tiqwâ* in Jer 29:11; 31:17, Prov 23:18; 24:14 (in hendiadys) is important in view of the occurrence of the latter in Hos 2:17. Compare the *'aḥărît . . . šālôm* which is the destiny of the perfect and upright man (Ps 37:37; contrast Prov 24:20). The associations of *'aḥărît* are almost entirely positive. It is the good time in the future when everything is put right (Job 42:12). Sometimes the corresponding destiny of the wicked is an *'aḥărît* of death. The moral contrast drawn in Psalms and Proverbs suggests a judgment, a confirmation of people in their acquired characters.

It is often argued that the technical phrase "the end of days" is a product of later eschatological thought — "characteristic of a post-exilic interpolation" (Harper 1905:224). On the contrary, of the dozen occurrences of this phrase in the Hebrew Bible, none occurs in a passage demonstrably postexilic and typically eschatological. In Gen 49:1 and Num 24:14 it simply refers to a future portentous time. In Jeremiah (23:20; 30:24; 48:47, 49:39) and Ezekiel (38:16; cf. 38:8) eschatological ideas are taking shape around this phrase, but we are still a long way from the conceptualities which emerge in Daniel and in the Qumran texts. In this development, Isa 2:2 (= Mic 4:1) occupies a key position, since its authenticity as an eighth-century oracle (contemporary with Hosea!) can hardly be doubted. Although more mythological ("the mountain") and more universalistic ("all nations") than Hosea, it shares the theme of movement toward Yahweh. None of the usual translations ("the latter days"; "the end of days"; "the last days") does justice to the meaning given to this phrase by the things that happen then. The term "many days" in v 4 implies that this will happen after a considerable, but indeterminate, period of time. There is no hint that this is the end of the story or of history; or, if there is a continuation, that it now moves into a transcendent mode of being "beyond history." The events of "the end of the age" grow out of current events, and the historical realities are the same — Israel and the nations. If, however, we take the reference to David literally, there is a hint that the characters of the "end time" are gathered up from past history. What is unmistakable is the note of finality, not in a cessation of time, but in the achievement of a state of affairs after which no new decisive events will occur.

PART II

Hosea's Prophecies

(Chapters 4–14)

INTRODUCTION

The Gathering of Hosea's Prophecies

Part I of Hosea (cc 1–3) is biographical; Part II (cc 4–14) is more like traditional prophecy.* Its oracular character is shown by the opening exhortation to "hear the word of Yahweh" (4:1), and many similar commands are addressed to Israel and others. The speaker is usually Yahweh (even when he refers to himself in the third person), although the voice of the prophet can be heard occasionally.

There is little that can be identified with confidence as editorial commentary, and there is no narrative. Any references to contemporary events are incidental to the oracular message; and they are so oblique that no part of the text can be attached with certainty to known happenings. This problem is compounded by the sparse documentation of Israel's history during this period. Hence it is impossible to date any parts of the discourse, and organization of the material along historical lines involves too much guesswork to lead to firm interpretation. The rule that a passage can be understood only in the light of its historical setting can be used to a limited degree; and the desire for certainty in this matter has produced many arbitrary and strained hypotheses. None of the persons discussed in cc 4–14 is given a name, a circumstance which underscores the interpreter's plight.

In cc 4–14 a high degree of continuity is secured by the regular appearance of the same themes. The literary technique is essentially the same throughout. From the philological point of view, this is the most archaic of biblical prophecies of any scope. By contrast, even the nearly contemporary prophecy of Amos is written in a manner more like classical poetry and prose.

A major problem for any interpreter is the determination of overall structure, that is, the identification of the constituent literary units and

---

* The commentary is keyed to the numeration of the translation, not the Hebrew text. Thus, in cases in which the Masoretic verse division is regarded as wrong, there is no special external marking, although the redivision is always noted in the comments. Similarly, the division of each verse into a and b segments does not always agree with the position of the athnach in the MT; the a and b segments are, however, always marked in the translation. The further subdivisions into A and B components are ad sensum.

their connections with one another. Is Hosea 4–14 made up of unrelated oracles, or does it consist of paragraphs joined together in continuous discourse? Except for the familiar "Oracle of Yahweh" (11:11), it lacks the rubrics which are often used to mark the onset of a new unit. Nor are there many grammatical clues which show the beginning or the ending of a self-contained composition. The dramatic command in 8:1 probably marks a new section, especially since 7:16 sounds a note of finality. Hos 9:17 is similar in this regard, and the historical reminiscences become deeper from 10:1 onwards. Hos 11:11 may mark the end of a piece of discourse that begins at 4:1. Even so, it must be admitted that, if the "Oracle of Yahweh" formula were not present, a clear break at this point would not be obvious, for the discourse continues in characteristic fashion. No logical development can be traced from section to section, but the emergence of a clearer note of hope in 14:2 makes it appropriate to take 14:2–9 as the concluding section.

In rough outline, Part II includes three divisions. The first division, cc 4–7, outlines the state of the nation. The second, cc 8–11, rehearses the spiritual history of Israel, while the last, cc 12–14, presents both retrospect and prospect. The themes in each of these divisions are so numerous and so diverse that it is misleading to give a title to any of them. When attention is paid to the numerous topics and the abrupt transitions from one to the next, it is easy to conclude that the whole is a congeries of brief oracles, assembled without any recognizable principles of order. Probably a majority of scholars hold such an opinion. When some measure of coherence is detected, it is possible to recognize a dozen or so "diatribes" (so Eissfeldt 1965), some of which correspond to the present chapter divisions. This is not satisfactory, however. The recurrence of the same theme, often with further development in an ensuing section, shows that these compositions are not self-contained. At least they belong to the same cycle, if not to a single long composition. Hos 6:4 and 11:8 are obviously on the same wavelength, and some kind of connection exists between them. Numerous examples of such phenomena in Hebrew verse could be given.

In broader fashion *NEB* recognizes two major sections: cc 4–9 ("God's case against Israel") and cc 10–13 ("God's judgment on Israel"), followed by "Repentance, forgiveness, and restoration" in c 14. These titles are not very helpful, as they emphasize certain features to the exclusion of others. The distinction is too neat; there are threats of judgment in cc 4–9, and accusations continue in cc 10–13. Furthermore, the call to repentance is sounded from time to time, and God's anxious concern for his people is evident throughout. In fact, these ingredients are scattered over the whole of Part II, and critics who are not willing to recognize mixed forms, because each prophetic message is supposed to sound only one note, finish up with an assemblage of small or even fragmentary oracles.

We can ask whether Hosea 4–14 is a compilation of brief spoken messages or a sustained literary composition, but the truth of the matter probably lies somewhere between these extremes. A related problem, no matter what the typical size of a unit is considered to be, is to establish what kind of composition each unit is. This task is obviously inseparable from that of settling the identity of each unit. In the twentieth century research in these matters has been dominated by the axiom, laid down by Gunkel (Hayes 1974), that the classical prophets were not writers, but messengers who delivered brief oracles orally. Mays (p. 5), for example, says that Hosea 4–14 consists of "sayings originally prepared for oral delivery to an audience." Even so, the thirty units he finds in cc 4–14 are too lengthy to fit Gunkel's formula. They are, to all intents, literary pieces.

If the essential material in Hosea consists of brief spoken messages, delivered on a specific occasion to a particular audience in a specific community institution with customary ceremonial, then their interpretation requires that all these features of the original setting be discovered as the key to their interpretation. To judge from the small measure of agreement achieved by modern research on this first step, form criticism has not demonstrated its capability. Hardly any of the "forms" in Hosea match the models in the inventory of modern form criticism. This raises a fundamental doubt about the premises of this approach. Further, even granted that prophecy did begin as spoken messages, this material is now presented to us as literature — whether this was begun or done by the prophet himself, or whether it was the work of later redactors is not the first question; we are trying to come to terms with the form of the material as we have it.

This is not to belittle the insights of form criticism. A determined scholar whose hermeneutical routine demands that the form must be established before anything else can be done will do his best to attach a label to each unit. If the unit does not fit the pattern (and it rarely does in Hosea), then the temptation is to save the theory at the expense of the text. This can be done in several ways. The text can be repaired by emendation or trimmed by removing unsuitable parts as editorial or scribal additions. Abnormal ingredients can be squeezed into the mold by strained interpretations. An incomplete form can be explained as a fragment. Or, when even these solutions are beyond the scholar's ingenuity, or when he halts at rewriting the text too drastically, the abnormality of the form can be attributed to Hosea's peculiar style, or else considerable transformation of the original beyond recovery can be blamed on those who collected and transmitted the raw oral material.

The difficulty of arriving at a consensus on even such rudimentary questions as the "forms" of Hosea's sayings can be illustrated by the opinions of two recent commentators. Mays (pp. 5–6) says: "Hosea was not given to following the structures of speech types." Brueggemann (1968:56) says: "It seems clear that the prophet did indeed follow a fairly fixed pattern of speech." Even so, he makes a substantial concession: "We will most often find only fragments of form," and does not make it clear whether he means by this that Hosea himself produced these fragments; the impression is rather that the original sayings, which were probably well-formed, survive only in fragments. He finds numerous examples of the standard forms of prophetic speech — the speech of judgment, the oracle of promise, the summons to repentance. In spite of their fragmentary character, Brueggemann sees these forms as appropriate parts of speeches made by the prophet as "prosecuting attorney" (p. 87) in a covenant lawsuit. The situation is formal. In explaining the coordination of these diverse forms into a speech of formal indictment made in a solemn assembly (p. 86), he gives them a forensic rather than a homiletical character. We have already pointed out the limitations of strictly legal categories as the key to the speech in c 2.

Even if fragments of the primal oral ingredients can still be perceived in the extant text of Hosea, this does not mean that the material has deteriorated. On the contrary, the recognition that numerous rhetorical devices have been cleverly used to knit the material together has forced us to the opposite conclusion. And, without denying that Gunkel could be correct about the presentation of oracles as brief spoken messages, Hosea 4–14 has been preserved as a literary composition, and it is all of a piece.

We do not insist that our approach is inherent in the material. Rather, we are trying to describe the material as we have it and consciously avoiding the apparently unattainable goals of critics who concern themselves with origins and developments in a way we find impossible. We assume in general the fewer hands the better, though that point is immaterial to our premises about observing unities of form and composition. Ours is an approach, not a provable conclusion. It is essentially a statement that most biblical criticism has not proved successful and that more can be gained by looking to other, more truly literary approaches to texts.

The continuities in theme and in literary texture, which we shall point out in detail in the NOTES that follow, make it impossible to analyze cc 4–14 into discrete sections. The appreciation of Hosea 4–14 as a sophisticated literary composition is more important than the recovery of the process of its literary genesis. We have no way of telling who was responsible, but we can describe the finished product. If it bears the stamp of one creative mind, the best candidate for author is the prophet himself. If we explain its production as the preservation of the prophet's message by a close disciple, there need not have been much drift or distortion. So long as we are not bound to a rule that Judean or apocalyptic materials could not have originated with Hosea (a rule that is far from self-evident), there is little or nothing in the present text that requires its completion later than the end of the eighth century.

The Texture and Themes of the Prophecies

Each of the twenty sections into which we have divided the text of cc 4–14 presents its own problems of internal structure and external relations. We will begin by considering two groups of three sections each, both in poetic and thematic terms, to broach questions of approach and hint at some of the features that link the various sections. These groups are Sections IV–VI (4:1 – 5:7) and Section VIII–X (5:12 – 6:6). Section VII poses extraordinary problems, and we leave it to be treated separately.

The sections marked off vary tremendously in size, between three and sixteen verses, though verse divisions are hardly a reliable guide to size. Half the sections are between six and nine verses (Sections VI, XI, XIII, XIV, XV, XVI, XVII, XVIII, XIX, XXIII). Four are longer (Sections V, XX, XXI, XXII); and half-a-dozen shorter (Sections IV, VII, VIII, IX, X, XII). The first group of three sections treated here includes one section of each size range, twenty-six verses in total; the second group, only ten verses long, includes three short sections.

The consistency of texture in the first group (4:1 – 5:7), and complexity of dramatic flow in the second (5:12 – 6:6) are rare in Hosea, though similar aspects of other sections are discussed elsewhere in the commentary. These examples, then, are no more representative than could be expected in a piece of writing as diverse as Part II of Hosea.

Sections IV–VI (4:1 – 5:7)

Hosea 4:1 – 5:7 is a large unit, composed of three sections and integrated by rhetorical devices similar to those already observed in cc 1–3. On the whole, it is more poetic than cc 1–3, although bits of prose are embedded in what is otherwise a rhythmic composition. Perhaps more pertinent for analysis and interpretation is the arrangement of the whole in extended structural patterns.

There are some standard bicola, with non-chiastic synonymous parallelism; the following are examples.

4:3a	'al-kēn te'ēbal hā'āreṣ	8/6 syllables
	wě'umlal kol-yôšēb bāh	7
4:13a	'al-rā'šê hehārîm yězabbēḥû	10
	wě'al-haggěbā 'ôt yěqaṭṭērû	10

4:14b   *kî hēm 'im-hazzōnôt yĕpārēdû*   10
        wĕ'im-haqqĕdēšôt yĕzabbēḥû   10

4:15a   *'im-zōneh 'attâ yiśrā'ēl*   8
        'al-ye'šam yĕhûdâ   6

Note also 4:17b–18a, 18bA, 18bB–19a; 5:1bB, 3b, 4b, 5b, and 7a.
The following are examples of synonymous parallelism with some chiasm.

4:4a   *'ak 'îš 'al-yārēb*   5 syllables
       wĕ'al-yôkaḥ 'îš   5
4:5a   *wĕkāšaltā hayyôm*   6
       wĕkāšal gam-nābî' 'immĕkā lāylâ   11/10
4:8   *ḥaṭṭa't 'ammî yō'kēlû*   7
       wĕ'el-'ăwōnām yiś'û napšô   9
4:9b   *ûpāqadtî 'ālāyw dĕrākāyw*   9
       ûma'ălālāyw 'āšîb lô   8/7
4:10a   *wĕ'ākĕlû wĕlō' yiśbā'û*   9
       hiznû wĕlō' yiprōṣû   7
4:12a   *bĕ'ēṣô yiš'āl*   5
       ûmaqlô yaggîd lô   6
4:13b   *'al-kēn tiznênâ bĕnôtêkem*   9
       wĕkallôtêkem tĕnā'apnâ   9
4:14a   *lō'-'epqôd 'al-bĕnôtêkem kî tiznênâ*   12
       wĕ'al-kallôtêkem kî tĕnā'apnâ   11

Note also 4:7, 11, 12b; 5:3a. Some of these bicola have a third line connected with them; e.g. 4:4b (with 4:4a), 4:5b (with 4:5a), 4:19b (with 4:18bB–19a), and 5:1bA (with 5:1bB). As observed, the first two clauses of 4:15 constitute a bicolon, and the remaining clauses form a tricolon in 4:15b.

4:15b   *wĕ'al tābō'û haggilgāl*   8 syllables
       wĕ'al ta'ălû bêt 'āwen   8/6
       wĕ'al tiššābĕ'û ḥay-yhwh   9

These lines in v 15b have as their subject the two nations mentioned in 15a. Another tricolon may occur in 4:16a–16bA. A clearer case is 5:1a.
Hos 4:6aB–6b is a complex four-line unit.

4:6aB   *kî-'attâ hadda'at mā'astā*   9/7 syllables
       wĕ'em'āsĕ'kā mikkahēn lî   9/8
4:6b   *wattiškaḥ tôrat 'ĕlōhêkā*   9/8
       'eškaḥ bānêkā gam-'ānî   8/7

This has an intricate and beautifully balanced design. The pronouns at the beginning and end (*kî-'attâ // gam-'ānî*) constitute an inclusion that sets the actions of the priest and the actions of Yahweh side by side. Four different verb forms are used. In the first bicolon a perfect verb "you have rejected" (the priest's completed action) is followed by the threatened response of Yahweh. Instead of using the standard judgment formula, introduced by "therefore," or the consecutive future (perfect), the second line has "and" plus the imperfect ("I will reject you"). In the second bicolon a second accusation is made — "you have forgotten." For perfect symmetry one might have expected *kî šākaḥtā*. Instead, the narrative resumes with the *waw*-consecutive construction. In classical prose this would imply a sequence of actions, but here the parallelism and other interconnections between the bicola suggest that we have two aspects of the same activity, or two concomitant activities. The single use of *kî* embraces both ("Because you renounced . . . and forgot . . ."). The fourth line uses an imperfect verb to predict the punishment, but does not use the conjunction. This is surprising; for "I shall renounce . . . (and) I shall forget . . ." would have the conjunction the other way round. Yet this tiny feature is not without significance. Hosea often uses two verbs with the same tense and the same subject in sequence without a conjunction. The effect is to represent them as two aspects of a single activity. It is necessary to read the parallel lines together — first with third, second with fourth — to get the complete picture. Neither bicolon is complete. What is lacking in one must be supplied by the other. The use of an item which occurs but once in a bicolon to do double duty in both lines of the bicolon is a familiar feature of Hebrew verse. In these four lines some items do double duty between the two neighboring bicola. Comparison with 4:1 shows that the "knowledge" rejected by the priest is knowledge of God. So *hadda'at* parallels *tôrat 'ĕlōhêkā*, the definite article linking *da'at* with "your God." Since the next line says "I will reject *you*," this implies "you have rejected and forgotten me," not just knowledge in general (cf. 2:15). In a similar fashion the priest's children as well as the priest are to be rejected from priesthood and forgotten, so *mikkahēn lî* serves both bicola.

While there are many bicola, tricola, etc., in the lines which resemble poetry, there are also some single lines. These often have parallels elsewhere, pointing to more remote correlations in larger structures. Such pairs are discontinuous bicola. In 4:9–10 there are six lines. Verse 9b is a well-formed bicolon, with the singular pronoun "him." Verse 10a is another well-formed bicolon with plural "they." Verse 9b is best referred to the priest; v 10a seems to deal with a larger group. All this is introduced by a single line (v 9a) which says that priest and people are alike. The concluding single line (v 10b) says that "they" have deserted Yahweh. This should refer to all those involved. The delay in the completion of the statement begun in v 9a inverts the logic. In a prophetic message the accusation (v 10b) usually precedes the predicted punishment (vv 9b–10a), so logically v 10b should precede v 9b.

This group of sections (Hos 4:1 – 5:7) substantiates Hosea's predilection for ordered lists, noted above.

4:1b   integrity, mercy, knowledge of God
4:2a   swearing, lying, murdering, stealing, adultery
4:3b   animals, birds, fish
4:13b   oak, poplar, terebinth

Sometimes a single word serves as an inclusion, as in 4:6–8, a unit that begins and ends with "my people." Sometimes a word is repeated as a link between neighboring units. *Nidmû* (4:6a) picks up *dāmîtî* (4:5). *Haddā'at* (4:6aA) is continued by *hadda'at* (4:6aB). As a result of this twofold repetition, 4:6aA, which is otherwise a line without proximate structural parallel, links the preceding text (in which the word *dāmîtî* is climactic in the denunciation of the priest) to the following (in which the theme of knowledge is pursued, and the people as well as the priest are denounced). Further, 4:6a has a long-range link with 4:14bB.

Hos 4:1 – 5:7 is unified by the intertwining of two themes. The key is in 4:9 — "like the people, like the priest." Similar things are said about them both. The children of the chief priest constitute a third focus of attention. This resembles the parallel treatment of mother and children in cc 1–3. The priest is addressed, for the most part, in second person singular; the people are referred to in third person plural, e.g. *'ĕlōhêkā* (4:6) // *'ĕlōhêhem* (4:12). But the priest is sometimes referred to in the third person (4:12), while the people are addressed in the second person (4:13b). In 4:12a "he" is the priest, while in v 12b "they" are his children, a transition like that between vv 9b and 10a. Hos 4:9a does not make it clear where the primary responsibility rests, with priest or with people; both will perish together. The priest has rejected the knowledge of God (4:6b); the people are ruined for lack of knowledge (v 6a; cf. 4:1b).

A similar alternation between singular and plural, and between second and third person, was observed in cc 1–3. Here Hos 4:4–6 has second person, and this reappears in 4:15. Hos 4:7–13a is in the third person. The change to second person *plural* after *'al-kēn* in 4:13b is striking, but the unit is small, and v 14b reverts to the third person in a way that sets "they" in contrast with "you." It is hard to keep track of the referents in 4:15–19, although all are in the third person, except for the tricolon in 4:15b. The alternation of singular and plural is made all the more bewildering by the appearance of feminine pronouns in 4:18–19.

We shall not attempt to clear up this confusion by emending the text. The apparatus of BH³ records many such proposals. The versions already betray embarrassment in this regard. Their occasional variant readings are more likely to reflect efforts to cope with the problem than a more original text. The ancient scribes and translators felt the jarring effect of these sudden transitions, and found ways to soften them. Even though all the details of the pattern are not yet understood, we are reluctant to smooth away such features, except as a last resort. The changes in number, person, and gender are closely woven into the fabric, and this happens too often in Hosea to be explained as corruption in copying.

The imperative verb *šim'û,* "Hear," shows that 4:1 begins a new section; and the same verb in 5:1 marks another beginning. Whether c 4 is a single composition or a gathering of several distinct oracles is not immediately evident. The Israelites and the land are addressed in vv 1–3, and Israel, Judah, and Ephraim appear in vv 15–19. People and priest are introduced at v 4, and most of the material in vv 4–14 can be referred to the priest, his children, or the people. These are nearly always distinguishable by the use of singular pronouns for the priest (except in v 15aA) and plural (you or they) for the children and the people (except in v 14b). People and priest appear together in v 9a. For the most part, however, priest, children, and people are dealt with serially. Statements about them are found in units of between two and ten lines, leaving a few single lines at places which are pivotal in the total structure.

Two kinds of things are said about priest, children, and people. Wrongdoings are listed, and appropriate punishments are threatened. This is not done systematically or logically. The usual development of judgment oracles, in which an accusation is made and then the punishment proclaimed, is not followed. For example, v 5 announces that the priest will stumble, but his delinquency is not explained until v 6. The basic theme is "Like the people, like the priest" (v 9a); this, however, is not asserted at the beginning or end, but partway through. A logical arrangement would be to take the priest first, list his failings, and declare his penalty, and then do the same for the people. But the faults and penalties of all are intermingled.

Verse 6aA and v 14bB constitute a well-formed discontinuous bicolon:

> *nidmû 'ammî mibbĕlî haddā'at*
> *wĕ'ām lō'-yābîn yillābēṭ*

Here is synonymous parallelism with chiasm. The chiasm makes the complete text of vv 6–14 begin and end with a verb in an inclusion. The sequence of perfect and imperfect verbs is classical. The exact correspondence shows that just as *lō'-yābîn* is an attribute of *'ām,* and not a modifier of the verb, so the synonymous *mibbĕlî haddā'at* modifies *'ammî,* "my ignorant people." This ignorance is willful, not accidental, and hence culpable; it is the cause of the people's ruin. There is a discrepancy between the verbs in number, as if *'am* were plural in v 6 and singular in v 14, but *'am* is a collective noun and may be used with either number. The difference in tense is the same as that in v 6b and v 10a. This disarticulated bicolon is like a vast pincers grasping vv 6–14. The accusation beginning *kî-'attâ* is the first statement in this block of discourse, just after v 6a; and this fits; the accusation *kî-hēm* in v 14bA is the last statement in the block, and seems out of order. What is logically the first statement about the children comes structurally last; the symmetry of this arrangement must be intentional; it constitutes a framework for the discourse.

Another symmetrical pattern within the passage can be observed: 4:4–15 begins with a prohibition (v 4a) using *'al* twice. It ends with a prohibition (v 15) using *'al* four times. At the same time, v 4a is a well-formed bicolon, whereas v 15 is quite heterogeneous. It begins with second person singular, changes to third person singular, and then to second person plural. The last gives a tricolon, indicating that the clauses in v 15a about Israel and Judah form a bicolon, with parallel and complementary elements. The heart of the discourse consists of the following material.

6aA	Ignorant people (one line)
6aB–6b	The priest (four lines)
7–8	His children (four lines)
9	Theme: LIKE THE PEOPLE LIKE THE PRIEST (three lines)
10	The children (three lines)
11–12	The priest (six lines)
13–14bA	The children (ten lines)
14bB	Ignorant people (one line)

Of these thirty-two lines, over half (seventeen) are devoted to the high priest's children. Ten focus on the priest. The remaining five comprise the framing bicolon and the core assertion. Not all features are equally clear, but the guiding principles of composition are evident. Besides the material dealing with the priest and the children separately, their relationship to the people is also stated. The priest has deprived the people of the knowledge (v 6a); therefore the ignorant people will be ruined (v 14b); the priest has misled the people (v 12bA); they have misbehaved sexually in defiance of their God (v 12bB); priest and people will be judged alike (v 9a).

The particular sins of the priest, the priestly cabal, and of the people, and their corresponding punishments may be summarized. The priest has rejected the knowledge of God; he has forgotten the torah (v 6b). Instead, he makes inquiry by means of his staff, and his stick gives him messages (v 12a). By means of wine and must, the priest has captured the mind ·of the people (v 11), and corrupted them by the spirit of promiscuity (v 12bA). So the priest will be punished for his ways and for his doings (v 9b). He himself will stumble (v 5). He will be removed from the priesthood (v 6aB) along with his children (v 6bB). Even his mother will be ruined (v 5b).

Because of the priest, the people do not know God (v 6a). His children have deserted Yahweh (v 10b), and committed sexual crimes in defiance of their God (v 12bB). They have sinned against him (v 7a) by consorting with prostitutes (v 14aB) under the trees (v 13bA). They have sacrificed and burned incense (v 13a) with feasting. Therefore the people will perish in ignorance (v 14b), and the priestly children will eat without satisfaction and indulge in sex without reproduction (v 10a).

In cc 1–3, the prophet deals with two matters at once — his wife's infidelity and the nation's apostasy. The two are virtually indistinguishable because Gomer's activity is more than a paradigm of Israel's disloyalty; it was a specific instance of the heresy. It was not just that promiscuity was a sin against Yahweh as well as a wrong done to her husband; the form of her promiscuity involved her in the Baal cult. The same activity was at once promiscuity and idolatry. There was also an ingredient of sorcery. The same themes continue in Hos 4:1 – 5:7, and many of the key words of cc 1–3 continue to be used. Although the remainder of the book is in a different mode from it, these chapters are the seed bed of the exposition that follows. Hos 4:1 – 5:7 is dominated by a cluster of words based on the root zny, which occurs twelve times. It is almost as though the passage were a commentary on Yahweh's first word to Hosea (1:2), in which this root appears four times. The references to mother and children in c 4 also seem to have a connection with Hos 1:2.

Hos 4:1 – 5:7 greatly enlarges the number of sins with which Israel is charged. In the preface, 4:2 gives a rather conventional inventory; the application of the Decalogue is unmistakable. The complaint that they have rejected "knowledge" and forgotten tôrâ (4:6) is fairly general, but points to the same tradition. The real concern continues to be matters bound up with the cult. This involves sacrifices (4:8,13,14; 5:6) and the burning of incense (4:13); resort to hill shrines (4:13), Mizpah and Tabor (5:1), as well as such regional centers as Gilgal and Bethel (4:15); oracular inquiry from an idol, contemptuously called "Wood" (4:12); and the orgiastic use of intoxicants (4:11,18). Worst of all, it involves sexual activities which were at the heart of this cult. To these Hosea turns again and again.

His preoccupation with this theme is seen, not only in his constant use of words based on zny, but in the many synonyms he uses to describe or evoke these unholy sex acts. Note nā'ōp, "adultery" (4:2, cf. 14); qālôn, "ignominy" (4:7,18); ḥaṭṭa't, "sin?" (4:8); 'āwōn, "iniquity?" (4:8; 5:5); 'zb, "to desert" (4:10); śṭy, "to deviate" (5:2); t'y, "to stray" (4:12); srr, "to rebel" (4:16); 'hb(hb), "to love" (4:18); bgd, "to cheat" (5:7), and others which less directly suggest sexual immorality.

The first part of Hosea deals with the woman's situation by bringing an accusation against a wife and mother (2:4). In the next sections (4:1–5:7), the high priest (4:4) and other priests (5:1) are condemned. The people come into it also, because they are like the priest (4:9a). The priest's children (4:6) and even his mother (4:5) are connected with him, and so, too, is a prophet (4:5) who is mentioned only in passing. The bewildering changes in the pronouns—singular and plural, masculine and feminine—show that now an individual, now a group, now men, now women, are being assailed by the word of Yahweh (6:5). The referents of these pronouns are not always clear. A collective noun such as "Israel" can be used as singular or plural, but sometimes the plural points to the two kingdoms. Although words like "priest" and "prophet" can be generic and collective, 5:1 distinguishes "priests" from the individual "priest" who is denounced in c 4; the plural pronouns do not always refer to the people. "Your daughters" and "your daughters-in-law" (4:13b,14a)—the pronouns are plural also—could be all the young women in Israel, but probably they are the priest's daughters. The priest's sons are dealt with in 4:6. Lev 19:29, using the same language as Hos 1:2, forbids Israelites from giving their daughters to promiscuity in a context that suggests a pagan practice; and Lev 21:9 imposes the death penalty on a priest's daughter guilty of fornication, as if it were more heinous in her case than in that of other people.

Although females are mentioned in 4:13–14, the main emphasis seems to be on the sins of Israelite men committed in the cult. Exod 34:15–16 shows that both men and women were culpable in the first crisis of Israel's covenant faith. This distinguishes the Horeb apostasy from the Baal-Peor incident, for in the latter it was precisely "the daughters of Moab" who invited the Israelite men to their ceremonies (Num 25:1–3). What made the matter so much more serious in Hosea's time was the fact that either the people were following the priest's lead or the priests had conformed to popular practice. In cc 1–3 the wife is promiscuous with "lovers" (masculine), clearly surrogates for Baal. In Hos 4:1–5:7, on the other hand, the daughters and daughters-in-law are promiscuous, while the men engage in liaisons with female prostitutes (4:14), presumably surrogates for some corresponding goddess, although she is never named. Her identity can only be guessed. There is reason to believe that some of the plurals, *bĕ'ālîm*, *mĕ'ahăbîm*, *'ăṣabbîm*, are imitations of *'ĕlōhîm*, "God," and mean simply "Baal." The plural *'ăgālîm*, "calves" (13:2), although there was more than one calf idol, is probably the same as "the calf of Samaria" (8:5,6). Hence we do not know whether the plurals *zōnôt* and *qĕdēšôt* (4:14) represent the goddess herself, so that the language of 4:14 is figurative for worshiping (committing "spiritual" fornication with) the goddess, or as seems more likely, whether they indicate access to her powers through her human devotees and female surrogates. This unnamed goddess seems to be called *rûaḥ zĕnûnîm* (4:12; 5:4), a phrase comparable to *'ēšet zĕnûnîm* in 1:2. In 4:19 this "wind" is evidently feminine, and the word *zĕnût* in 4:11 could be another name for her. Perhaps she is also the "Sin" (feminine) in 4:8. Remembering that this goddess, whatever her current name in Israel in Hosea's time, has a reputation for sorcery as well as sex, we suspect that it is owing to her baleful influence that the Israelites are "made to go astray" (4:12 — the verb is masculine; entanglement with magic, however, is certain) under a magical spell (4:17) which deprives them of their judgment and discernment (4:14b; cf. 4:11). That an actual deity is involved, and not just a "spirit" of promiscuity, is seen in the contrast between her false claims and the claims of Yahweh from whom she has seduced them. In 5:4, the Spirit is said to be in their midst, a perversion of the standing theological assertion — "Yahweh is in your midst" — substituting the rival title in a bitter parody. The same contrast occurs in 4:12, where being led astray by "the spirit of promiscuity" is the same as committing "sexual sins in defiance of their God." The feminine gender here and in 4:19 refers to a goddess.

It is surprising that names of pagan deities are rarely mentioned in the Bible. The word "goddess" is never used. Baal is almost the only one whose name is used openly, and even that was often replaced with insulting substitutes and parodies, of which several are found in Hosea. This was doubtless due to conscientious revulsion (2:19). The Canaanite goddesses most commonly associated with Baal in biblical times were Asherah and Astarte (Ashtaroth). Originally El's consort, Asherah was assimilated to Astarte, Baal's wife, and the names are virtually interchangeable in our period (Albright 1969:73–77). In the older Canaanite theology, as we have it from Ugarit, the goddess most commonly associated with Baal is Anat. The Bible preserves no explicit memory of this goddess, who was in time fused with Astarte. Perhaps it is she, not Asherah, who is "the Queen of Heaven" (Jer 44:17). The Beth-Shan stele shows a goddess "Antit, the queen of heaven, the mistress of all the gods" (Vincent 1937:645). Several goddesses have been given such a title, but the Egyptian background, coupled with the evidence of an Anat cult in the Jewish colony at Elephantine, constitutes good circumstantial evidence.

Place names in the Bible preserve traces of the Anat cult in Canaan proper. If the Elephantine colony was of North Israelite origin, then the Anat-Yahu cult attested there could be derivative of the apostasy attacked in Hosea. We have little more than the names to go on, but it seems that a community of Jews in Elephantine, who considered themselves sufficiently orthodox to communicate with the priests in Jerusalem, assimilated Yahweh to Baal to the extent of giving him a consort called

Anat. Among the inscriptions from Quntillet Ajrud dating from about 800 B.C.E., there are religious texts containing the divine appellatives Yahweh and Baal, both used in a positive and constructive fashion. In addition we have the expression *lyhwh . . . wl'šrth* which must be rendered "to Yahweh . . . and to his *'ăšērâ.*" The last word looks suspiciously like the biblical Asherah, a symbol of the pagan goddess usually in the form of a wooden pole or tree.

In Israel, at least as expressed in Proverbs 1–9, personified Wisdom was set up as an anti-Anat. Antit of Beth-shan has an *'ankh* sign in her right hand, a *was* scepter in her left, whereas Wisdom has "long life" in her right hand and "riches and honor" in her left (Prov 3:16). This identification is not contradicted by other evidence that Anat is the naked goddess who rides on horseback with sword and shield, for in the Ugaritic texts she is also described as playing love songs on a lyre, and even holding a spindle as the patron of the gentler crafts of domestic women. Anat was celebrated for her violence, as well as for her sexual prowess. As the heifer (cf. 10:5) her amatory achievements with the bull Baal are described in the Ras Shamrah texts with tremendous gusto (van Zijl 1972).

Sections VIII–X (5:12–6:6)

The poetic texture of these sections is as finely woven as that of any passage in Hosea. There are hardly any lines which could be called prose. The familiar synonymous parallelism is consistently used.

There is one bicolon with complete synonymous parallelism and extensive repetition.

6:4a	*mâ 'e'ĕśeh-llĕkā 'eprayim*	7/6 syllables
	mâ 'e'ĕśeh-llĕkā yĕhûdâ	8/7

There is one bicolon with complete synonymous parallelism and chiasm.

6:2a	*yĕḥayyēnû miyyōmāyim*	8/7
	bayyôm haššĕlîšî yĕqîmēnû	10

The most favored form is incomplete synonymous parallelism.

5:12	*wa'ănî kā'āš lĕ'eprāyim*	9/8
	wĕ- kārāqāb lĕbêt yĕhûdâ	9
5:13aA	*wayyar' 'eprayim 'et-ḥolyô*	8/7
	w- -îhûdâ 'et-mĕzōrô	7
5:13aB	*wayyēlek 'eprayim 'el-'aššûr*	9/8
	wayyišlaḥ 'el-melek yārēb	8/7
5:13b	*wĕhû' lō' yûkal lirpō' lākem*	9
	wĕ- lō'-yigheh mikkem māzôr	8
5:14a	*kî 'ānōkî kaššaḥal lĕ'eprayim*	11/9
	wĕ- kakkĕpîr lĕbêt yĕhûdâ	9

6:1b	kî hû' ṭārap wĕyirpā'ēnû	9
	yak wĕyaḥbĕšēnû	6
6:3b	wĕyābô' kaggešem lānû	8/7
	kĕmalqôš yôreh 'āreṣ	7/6
6:4b	wĕḥasdĕkem ka'ănan-bōqer	9/7
wĕ-	kaṭṭal maškîm hōlēk	7
6:5a	'al-kēn ḥāṣabtî bannĕbî'îm	9
	hăragtîm bĕ'imrê-pî	7
6:6	kî ḥesed ḥāpaṣtî welō'-zābaḥ	10/8
	wĕda'at 'ĕlōhîm mē'ōlôt	9/8

There are two bicola whose parallel lines are separated in the text to serve structural ends.

| 6:1a | lĕkû wĕnāšûbâ 'el-yhwh |
| 2b | wĕniḥyeh lĕpānāyw wĕnēdĕ'â |

| 6:3aB | kĕšaḥar nākôn môṣā'ô |
| 5b | ûmišpāṭî kā'ôr yēṣē' |

The second of these discontinuous bicola shows synonymous parallelism with chiasm: A : B : C :: C' : A' : B'. There is also a cross relationship between C (môṣā'ô) and B' (yēṣē'), which have a common root. A discontinuous bicolon often serves as an envelope around a complete unit, or otherwise fits into an introverted structure. Hos 6:3aB and 6:5b are not like that. Each line comes near the end of a smaller unit and is followed by one concluding bicolon (6:3b and 6:6).

The only lines in 5:12–6:6 not listed above as poetry are 5:14b–15 and 6:3a. These have a less clearly defined poetic structure. See the NOTES on these verses.

To understand the overall structure, it is important to see the connections between 5:14–15 and 6:4–6 (spoken by Yahweh). A basic decision for interpretation is to discover the climax, the outcome, of the entire piece. The facts of punishment reach a dreadful crescendo in 5:14–15, where the lion imagery is as savage as anything in the book. The language of 6:4–6 is equally violent; it speaks of killing in unqualified terms. By contrast 6:1–3 sounds a strikingly different note of life and hope. Where does it all end? We suggest that a step-by-step linear analysis will yield a wrong result. If the last word comes at the end, it is a word of death. But when it is seen that 6:1–3 is flanked by balancing passages (5:14–15 and 6:4–6), then the climactic word is in the middle, in the promise of new life. The sustained speech of Yahweh, dominated by first person pronouns and verbs, continues into c 7. Embedded in this speech is the eventual response of repentant Israel (6:1–3).

From another perspective the last word does come at the end, and it comes from Yahweh. Logically this affirmation is the basis of the whole pericope, a statement whose centrality has always been appreciated. Yahweh's ultimate passion is for *ḥesed.* He has an unswerving commitment to covenant obligations. The curses and blessings of the covenant work out in two contradictory directions — destruction and re-creation. The crisis in the mind of Yahweh is forced by the fact, heartbreaking for him, that Israel's *ḥesed* is so ephemeral — like morning mist, like clouds, insubstantial and speedily dissipated. In contrast to this, Yahweh's declaration is as certain as daybreak. In his *ḥesed* Yahweh is unalterably committed to two things: he will have a people of his own; and he will relentlessly punish the covenant violator. These commitments collide and the collision leads to an impossible situation because the drive to punish and the drive to accept his people unconditionally are equally manifestations of his *ḥesed,* his determination to keep the promises he has made *in both these areas.* He looked above all for a *ḥesed* in Israel to match his own (6:6), but Israel's *ḥesed* was like vapor (6:4a). Hence Yahweh's question to himself: "What shall I do?" (6:4).

For hundreds of years this question had grown in intensity. The answer had been put off. Yahweh was "slow to anger." He often relented and restrained himself. According to the analysis of Israel's prophetic historians, toward the middle of the eighth century even the patience of Yahweh was exhausted. At last the will for justice overcame the compassion which had hitherto restrained the divine anger. The covenant curses are to be put into operation. The punishment is described in passages of unexampled horror. They are made the more frightening because all secondary agents disappear, and the acts are ascribed to Yahweh himself. He will rip, injure, hack and kill (5:14; 6:1,5; cf. 11:9).

At this point in the interpretation a crucial decision has to be made as to how to take this language, couched as it is in figures about lions and other animals. The language of sickness and healing is used; also the language of death and resurrection. It could be an exaggerated way of talking about national calamities, disastrous, but not amounting to annihilation. They will be battered, chastened, but not obliterated.

If something less drastic than national destruction is supposed, then Yahweh continues to have a people. If, however, the statements are taken at their face value, he no longer has a people; Israel is "not my people" (1:9). The earlier history of Israel never reached this point. Earlier solutions to the problem of Israel's apostasy included a proposal, which Yahweh himself made, to wipe out Israel and start all over again with Moses, as he had done with Abraham earlier (Exod 32:10). With daring arguments, Moses dissuaded Yahweh from this drastic step. The suggestion that Yahweh might try again with another people was never seriously entertained. That would bypass the historical-theological fact that Yahweh had committed himself to Abraham, Isaac, and Jacob, and thus to Moses' people, Israel. It would be in Abraham's seed that all nations of the world would find their blessing (Gen 12:3).

In Hosea we meet for the first time the clear statement of an astounding solution to this problem — Yahweh's problem. This solution satisfies both sides of his *ḥesed*. Guilty Israel will be executed; that will satisfy covenant justice. Then the people of Yahweh will be reconstituted through resurrection (see the NOTES on 2:2a). This totally different future is acclaimed in the central section (6:1–3).

> He will cure us,
> He will heal us,
> He will restore us to life,
> He will resurrect us.

The judgment passages that surround these lines (5:12–15; 6:4–6) come logically before it. Unless this is seen, there is no way of explaining why, after the impressive return to Yahweh in 6:1–3, Yahweh should still be pondering what to do (6:4a), reproaching them for their inconstant *ḥesed* (6:4b), and giving this as his reason for chopping them up and slaying them (6:5). But once 6:4–6 is seen as a mirror image of 5:12–15, the centrality of 6:1–3 can be affirmed, and the last word of restoration is "We shall live by his will" (6:2bB). This corresponds to the new name for the covenant people, "Children of the Living God," already announced in 2:1.

The central passage (6:1–3) is locked into the encompassing material by various rhetorical signals. In 6:1b,

> *kî hû' ṭārap wĕyirpā'ēnû*
> *yak wĕyaḥbĕšēnû*

the first line describes the action of 5:14b and the second the action of 6:5. We have already met this kind of backward arrangement of the movement of thought in Hosea. Thus 6:6 comes logically before 6:5 — it is because I desire *ḥesed* and the knowledge of God more than sacrifices and burnt offerings that I have smitten them by prophets and slain them by the words of my mouth. Hos 6:6 also comes logically before 6:4a — I desire *ḥesed,* but your *ḥesed* does not last. This situation is altered fundamentally in 6:3a, where the people show a complete change of heart by diligently pursuing the knowledge of Yahweh (the word "know" is used twice — contrast 4:1,6). This cancels 5:4.

In order to find a linear and logical connection of thought from 5:14 through 6:6, commentators have to denigrate the expressions of contrition and faith in 6:1–3. Yahweh is said to be distrustful of such words (v 4). He is still unconvinced that the *ḥesed* has the desired constancy. Thus Wolff: "It must be that her confession of guilt is deficient and that her confidence rests too much on the laws of nature, resulting in the confusion of Yahweh with Baal" (1974:119). This interpretation goes back to Alt's 1919 paper. There is no trace of such notions in 6:1–3. In point of fact there is not even an acknowledgment of guilt. There is only the most unqualified affirmation, not only that the hand of Yahweh (his alone) has struck the people down, but also that his hand will raise them up. The presence of Yahweh completely fills their mind; they express complete confidence in his reliability; they have now but one desire — to know him. This must be the climax of the story. Nevertheless 6:1–3 remains a statement of faith. It remains in the mouth of Israel. It is not confirmed as an oracle of Yahweh at this stage. That comes in 13:10–14.

Looking more closely at the texture of 5:14 – 6:6, we see that the repetitious vocabulary and the structural symmetry bind the various elements together, even though, from the form critical point of view, the compositions are completely different. The most vivid vocabulary items are the verbs — *ṭrp, rp':* they occur together in 6:1. But since *ṭrp* occurs in 5:14 and *rp'* in 5:13, their linkage in 6:1 is a further reason for keeping 5:12–13 and 5:14–15 together, even though in other ways they contrast. Hos 5:12–15 has four similes for Yahweh, in two pairs, and Hos 6:1–6 has another four similes. In addition there are two similes describing the people's fickleness (6:4).

We note in conclusion that the parallelism of Ephraim and Judah in 6:4 matches once more their frequent occurrence in parallelism in c 5.

In the preceding discussion we have passed over vv 12–13 of c 5. This passage belongs now with what precedes it, now with what follows. We often observed the same pattern in the material in cc 1–3; various passages in c 4 also have links in two directions, some with cc 1–3, some with c 5. The double orientation of 5:12–13 is a further indication that there is no single structure which we must try to identify to the exclusion of all others. More than one pattern can exist in the same material.

The similarity between 5:12 and 5:14a is obvious because of the pronouns. Verses 12 and 13 together balance vv 14–15. Each can be viewed as a sequence of smaller units.

Syllable count

12	$8 + 9 = 17$	14a	$9 + 9$	$= 18$
13aA	$7 + 8 = 15$	14b	$6 + 5 + 4 = 15$	
13aB	$8 + 7 = 15$	15a	$9 + 6$	$= 15$
13b	$9 + 8 = \overline{17}$	15b	$6 + 4 + 6 = \overline{16}$	
Total	64			64

In spite of the *zāqēf qāṭōn* of the Masoretic punctuation in v 14b, the recognition of Hosea's two-verb phrase *'ēlēk 'eśśā'* permits a better analysis. Verses 14 and 15 contain an introversion but the parallelism is not well developed. Verse 14b is a tricolon with lines of 6, 5, and 4 syllables; it matches 15b, a tricolon with lines of 6, 4, and 6 syllables.

IV. THE STATE OF THE NATION: PREFACE
(4:1–3)

Hosea addresses all Israel

4:1a Hear the word of Yahweh, Israelites.[a]
  1b Indeed Yahweh has a dispute with the inhabitants of the land
    For there is no integrity and no mercy and no knowledge of
        God in the land.
  2a Swearing, lying, murdering, stealing, committing adultery,
  2b They break out — blood everywhere — and they strike down.
  3a Therefore the land dries up
        and all its inhabitants are enfeebled.
  3b Along with the wild animals and birds of the sky and even
        fish of the sea, they are swept away.

NOTES

4:1–3. We have called this a general preface to cc 4–7 rather than a
fragment of a lawsuit between Yahweh and Israel. Since the discourse
continues through c 11, "The Word of Yahweh" could also be the title
for this entire piece, whose end seems to be marked by the colophon
"Oracle of Yahweh" (11:11bB). "Word of Yahweh" and "Oracle of
Yahweh" would then constitute an inclusion around the heart of the book
(cc 4–11), and the concluding chapters, 12–14, which have no title of
their own, would balance cc 1–3. At the same time each oracle is a

---

[a] The commentary is keyed to the numeration of the translation, not the Hebrew
text. Thus, in cases in which the Masoretic verse division is regarded as wrong,
there is no special external marking, although the redivision is always noted in the
comments. Similarly, the division of each verse into a and b segments does not
always agree with the position of the *athnach* in the MT; the a and b segments
are, however, always marked in the translation. The further division into A and B
segments are *ad sensum*.

distinct "word of Yahweh" so this phrase could refer immediately to 4:1–3.

Attention switches to the priest at v 4, but the indictment of "the inhabitants of the land" (4:1b) is general and comprehensive. It includes all sectors of the community which appear in cc 4–11 — priest, prophet, king, prince, people, man, woman, child, and even beasts, birds, and fish, it would seem (4:3). Furthermore, the opening accusation that there is no knowledge of God in the land is reiterated elsewhere. The list of crimes in v 2 is examined in what follows, and the general threat in v 3 is developed.

The isolation of 4:1–3 from the rest, or its integration with what follows cannot be proved; the same is true for all the other units we shall identify, and we will not need to repeat the point. If common vocabulary links 4:1–3 to the rest, there are also peculiarities that set the passage apart. There is a certain completeness in it that befits a formal declaration, whether as initial or summary statement. It contains more of the features of classical prophecy than most sections of Hosea, and some of these uncommon elements have been ascribed to a redactor. After an opening address ("Hear the word of Yahweh . . ."), the speech is identified as the indictment in a lawsuit (cf. Mic 6:1–8). The accusation refers to both sins of omission (v 1bB) and sins of commission (v 2). The final part, the threat of punishment, follows. On closer examination, however, the design of 4:1–3 will be seen to be more intricate than this simple outline of invocation (v 1a–1bA), accusation (vv 1bB–2), and punishment (v 3).

The pericope presents eight distinct units.

A	1a	šim'û děbar-yhwh běnê yiśrā'ēl	11 syllables
B	1bA	kî rîb lyhwh 'im-yôšěbê hā'āreṣ	11
C	1bB	kî 'ên-'ĕmet wě'ên-ḥesed wě'ên-da'at 'ĕlōhîm bā'āreṣ	15
D	2a	'ālōh wěkaḥēš wěrāṣōaḥ wěgānōb wěnā'ōp	14
E	2b	pārāṣû wědāmîm bědāmîm nāgā'û	12
F	3a	'al-kēn te'ěbal hā'āreṣ wě'umlal kol-yôšēb bāh	13
G	3bA	běḥayyat haśśādeh ûbě'ôp haššāmāyim	12
H	3bB	wěgam-děgê hayyām yē'āsēpû	10

The balance of the outermost units, and of the alternating pairs of inner units, can be seen in the counts.

A + B	22 syllables	} 49
C + E	27 syllables	
D + F	27 syllables	} 49
G + H	22 syllables	

Prevailing interpretation of the unit is based on several questionable assumptions. We can approach them by trying to identify the participants in the scene. The dramatis personae are Yahweh; the Israelites, the inhabitants of the land; the creatures in v 3b; and also possibly the (unidentified) persons accused of the crimes in v 2. Because of parallelism, we can say that the Israelites and the inhabitants of the land are the same. It is often assumed that, because there is a *rîb* with the inhabitants of the land (v 1bA), these are the ones accused of the crimes in vv 1bB–2, and that all these crimes are charged against the same defendant.

If vv 1bB–2 are the indictment, the apparent discord in the three lines constitutes a serious obstacle to interpretation. Verse 1bB says that there is no integrity, mercy, or knowledge of God in the land. Verse 2a lists five crimes, using infinitive absolutes. Verse 2b changes gears, using two perfect verbs, which are plural. Verse 2b is a line with one noun repeated twice between two verbs. Verse 3a is a well-formed bicolon, but v 3b presents difficulties. Structurally it is a continuous statement, not a bicolon. On the basis of common usage elsewhere, it can be assumed that beasts, birds and fish constitute a single group, but the grammar of the coordination phrase is unusual. The first two nouns are governed by the preposition *b;* the last noun lacks it, but has instead the particle *wĕgam* which is hardly equivalent, but serves as a novel variant.

There is no reason to believe that the text has suffered any damage in transmission. Every word is familiar. The lines all have commensurate length. The shorter lines come at the beginning and at the end, and the identical length of vv 1a–1bA and 3b (twenty-two syllables each) gives the passage symmetry. The problem is to find a structural pattern which will harmonize the inconcinnities. In the case of the indictment (vv 1bB–2; lines C, D, E) we can assume either that the grammatical confusion is the result of careless composition or patchwork editorial work; or that it is the result of deliberate planning. We assume the latter and contend that we should pay close attention to fine details and use them as clues for discovering the structure. Often we find that lines which are not contiguous are related in some other way.

The connection between D and E can be discovered by asking which of the lines is best qualified to be called "the word of Yahweh." In Jeremiah 7 an indictment entitled "the word of Yahweh" asks, *hăgānōb rāṣōaḥ wĕnā'ōp,* "Will you steal, murder, and commit adultery?" (Jer 7:9). The use of the infinitive absolutes is the same as in Hos 4:2a, and much of the vocabulary is the same. The speech in Jeremiah is addressed to the people of Judah in the second person, and begins *šim'û dĕbar yhwh* (Jer 7:2), just like Hos 4:1. The striking resemblance of Hosea 4 and Jeremiah 7 renders superfluous the arguments of Wolff (1974:65) that "the series of infinitive absolutes as subject requires a predicate" in the verb *pārāṣû* leading to the translation "Cursing, cheating, murdering, stealing, and adultery break out." The occurrence of *pārīṣîm,* "bandits," in Jer 7:11 suggests that *pārāṣû* describes criminal activity in Hos 4:2, although there it seems to be less concrete.

The *kî*'s at the beginning of v 1bA and v 1bB mark new beginnings in the discourse. Whereas v 1a is second person, v 1bA is third. Verse 2b is also third person, and together they spell out the *rîb,* "controversy," which Yahweh has with the inhabitants of the land. The inhabitants of the land are the ones who have broken all bounds and committed murder, and crimes of violence involving grievous assault.

The link between vv 1bB and 3bA is provided by the preposition *b.* This preposition is the principal problem in v 3, and no satisfactory explanation has been proposed for it. *Beth essentiae* would place the animals and birds in opposition with "all who live in it," making the inhabitants of the land creatures rather than human beings (Joüon 1947:404–405). Wolff (1974:65) prefers to give the preposition the meaning "sharing with," so that the animals and birds are coordinated with "all who live in it" as the subject of *'umlal.* We also recognize here the *beth comitatus,* but disagree with Wolff's recognition of a break between v 3bA and v 3bB. The beasts and birds are far more important in this situation than has hitherto been realized. The wild animals and birds are mentioned together in 2:20, where they are distinguished from reptiles in being governed by the same preposition, which the phrase for reptiles lacks. In 2:20, Yahweh makes a covenant, in the end time, with the beasts and birds, to prevent them from killing and devouring the children. Until they are restrained, they are likely to do this as agents of Yahweh's judgments. When the covenant virtues — integrity, mercy, and knowledge of God — are lacking in the earth, even the animals behave outside the bounds of acknowledgment of God. When the world is destroyed, they are destroyed along with it. But when Yahweh includes animals in his merciful salvation, he makes a covenant with Noah that provides for their safety (Gen 6:18–22); renewed after the flood in Genesis 9 it features the animals prominently. The linkage of vv 1bB and 3bA then represents an inclusion of the creatures in the domain of the covenant, as in 2:20. Their rapacity, which makes human existence so precarious, results from a breakdown of the good order of a universe in covenant with Yahweh. It is not farfetched to say that there is no knowledge of God among the beasts and birds. In contrast to this present state of the world, when "the earth will be filled with *the knowledge of Yahweh,* as the waters cover the sea," the dangerous animals "will not hurt or destroy (the children) in all my holy mountain" (Isa 11:9). In Isaiah 11, it is emphasized that it is the children who will be safe when the animals are tamed (esp. Isa 11:8).

The setting of Hos 4:1–3 is in a sense cosmic. In Amos 7:4, Yahweh's call for a *rîb* with fire threatens the primal elements, the great deep and the land. There are other places which use the language of Hos 4:3a, notably Amos 8:8 and 9:5. Jer 5:19–28 speaks of the devastation of the whole world, so that it mourns. "The land" in Hos 4:1–3, while it suggests Israel in the first place, suggests also universal destruction. Note the use of *hā'āreṣ* eight times in Gen 6:5,6,11–13.

The three prongs of this oracle in Hos 4:1–3 can now be identified. While addressed primarily to Israel, it can include all people and even the beasts, birds and fish. There is no knowledge of God among any of them. The comprehensive threat in v 3 embraces the two orders of being, the fish representing the lower animals.

The analysis does not mean that several fragments have been loosely assembled. The eight units, connected together in four pairs, are woven together in a complex pattern. If one ignores superficial breaks in grammar, and the strange use of conjunctions and prepositions, it is possible to derive sense from a continuous reading from beginning to end.

A basic division of the passage into two parts will indicate the principal links, while observing the grammatical peculiarities. The sequence of the elements and the corresponding matchings can be shown in the following pattern.

1a	Hear, Israelites	they are swept away	3b
1bA	... dispute with the *inhabitants* of the *land*	the *land* dries up / its *inhabitants* are enfeebled	3aA
1bB	no integrity / mercy / knowledge	they break out / they strike down	2b
2aA	swearing / lying	committing adultery / stealing / murdering	2aB

4:1a. *the word of Yahweh.* Cf. 1:2a. The use of the conventional opening of the "messenger" formula is the nearest we have to a traditional prophetic form of speech. Hosea's private life, so prominent earlier, has receded into the background. Here he speaks in public about community matters. This and 1:1 are the only places where Hosea uses the phrase "the word of Yahweh." In both places it could serve a dual purpose, as title to the whole book in 1:1, or to a large middle section in 4:1; and as referring to the word of Yahweh that immediately follows — the command to Hosea in 1:2, here the charge against Israel.

Israelites. This phrase occurs five times in cc 1–3, and not again after 4:1. For this reason Wolff (1974:66) thinks that this verse is redactional, and influenced by the preceding text. We have already pointed out that there are numerous connecting threads between the first part of the book and the middle section, many in Hos 4:1–3.

1b. *dispute.* As in 2:4, so here a form of the root *ryb* is used near the opening of a section. Its position here is often taken as a sign that vv 1–3 (or even more of the text) is a transcript of a formal lawsuit. Since the forms of that supposed genre of prophetic speech have never been defined with adequate precision, we may prescind from explaining the absence of a true judicial interchange.

integrity . . . mercy . . . knowledge of God. The three words designate representative elements of the covenant faith. All three or related words appear in 2:21–22, where the covenant takes the form of a betrothal. Words like *'ĕmet, ḥesed, da'at* are guiding stars of prophetic thought. They are defined by the covenant within which they are used. *'Ēmet* is genuineness, integrity, reliability. *Ḥesed* includes the essential ingredients of kindness and mercy; it transcends the formal requirements of a covenant, adding that basic requirement of generous and forgiving treatment that makes coexistence with other people possible and qualifies judgment with mercy, producing a blend of retribution and forgiveness which constitutes *mišpāṭ,* "justice." *Knowledge* or *recognition of God* means the understanding of his ways as revealed in the covenant. Hosea's use of God rather than Yahweh here gives this knowledge a wide connotation. Knowledge of Yahweh is Israel's special privilege in the covenant. To the world, including animals, he is the creator, Elohim.

Because these virtues overlap, they should not be defined narrowly; but they should not be merged into one semantic lump. These qualities are expressed in personal relationships. In Yahweh's covenant, they are shown by loving obedience to his ways; but his "ways" are his own treatment of his creatures — he is good to them. Obedience to his ways means keeping the commandments he has given concerning human conduct in all the relationships of life. Hence when the three covenant virtues fail, the crimes listed in v 2 follow. They are all crimes against humanity. The integrity, mercy, and knowledge of God mentioned in v 1 are qualities of people whose dedication to God finds expression in relations with their neighbors. The crimes committed against people in v 2 are seen to be even worse because they are acts of rebellion against God. There are ten items in vv 1bB–2 as in the Ten Commandments, although there is no constant one-to-one correlation.

2a. *Swearing . . .* The list of sins in v 2 is in two parts, each of which uses different grammatical forms. The first part uses five infinitive absolutes; in the second part two perfect verbs are used. The first list reads like an excerpt from the Decalogue. The Masoretic placement of *zāqēf qāṭōn* separates the first two sins from the rest, to reflect the fact that the third, fourth, and fifth transgressions are based directly on Exod 20:13–15 (= Deut 5:17–19), whereas connections between the first two and specific commandments of the tradition are harder to trace. If the first pair is a hendiadys, it would mean lying under oath, and would be the same as taking Yahweh's name with intent to evade the law in a false oath of self-exculpation (Exod 20:7). But it is more likely that *'ālōh* breaks the third commandment (false asseveration with the name of Yahweh) and *kaḥēš* the ninth (false witness not under oath). The other three, which are used in exactly the same way in Jer 7:9, come from the sixth, seventh, and eighth commandments. Hosea uses the Sinai/Horeb covenant to test Israel's performance. The fourth sin in Jeremiah's list (*hiššābēaʻ laššeqer*) uses a verb not in either Exodus 20 or Hosea 4, although *laššeqer* is similar to *laššāw'* in the Decalogue, and the phrase could mean swearing by a false god. Jeremiah's fourth accusation could correspond to either the third or the ninth commandment. All the lists have a common core, and fasten on the sins that do most harm to other people. The sequence within this group differs in each case.

Exodus 20	Jeremiah 7	Hosea 4
rṣḥ	gnb	rṣḥ
n'p	rṣḥ	gnb
gnb	n'p	n'p

The use of the same verbs for robbery (or kidnapping, in the first instance), murder, and adultery points to a common tradition. The variable selection and sequence, and the different ways of talking about false oaths and deception suggest that the tradition, although partly fixed, nevertheless could be expanded and adapted by the prophet as occasion required (Cazelles 1969:14–19). Jeremiah augments his list by adding a specific, contemporary reference to burning incense to Baal and turning aside to other gods. Hosea's specific addition has something to do with violence and bloodshed. This might seem at first to be repetitious, since v 2a mentions murder, but a special form of bloodletting seems to be meant, one that was sanctioned by the state, and in particular the priesthood.

2b. *They break out.* While the word *pārāṣû* is isolated from its context according to grammar and syntax, nevertheless its form is comparable to *nāgāʻû*. The verbs are not synonymous, but complementary. *Prṣ* describes a violent action by God, people, or animals. God can break out of his holy confines in angry destruction (Exod 19:22,24; II Sam 5:20 = I Chron 14:11; II Sam 6:8 = I Chron 13:11; I Chron 15:13; Ps 60:3). *Prṣ* describes the action of a man breaking into a house (II Chron 24:7), or a baby bursting from the womb (Gen 38:29; Hos 4:10). It describes an animal breaking through a stone wall (Mic 2:13; Neh 3:35; Ps 80:13; cf. Qoh 10:8). The verb can also denote other kinds of breaking, such as the bursting out of water (II Sam 5:20), mining operations (Job 28:4), shipwreck (II Chron 20:37), or the breach of defense works (Ps 89:41). In a psychological sense it describes forceful insistence without physical violence (II Sam 13:25,27; II Kings 5:23). The verb is used also to describe the increase of human or animal population, which bursts out in all directions (Isa 54:3; Job 1:10; Gen 28:14; 30:30,43; Exod 1:12, etc.).

None of these settles the connotation of *pārāṣû* here. Other possibilities for translation can be mentioned. Destructive entry to burglarize could be meant and if *dāmîm* is taken simply as bloodshed, then robbery with murderous assault would fit. Human beings can be the object of the verb *prṣ*, but this seems to be restricted to the divine outbreak — II Sam 5:20 (= I Chron 14:11) where Yahweh breaks David's enemies, and Ps 60:3, where the pronoun is probably the indirect object — not "you have broken us," but "you have broken out upon us." In Job 16:14 the verb describes God's savage assault on Job.

Although the Masoretic punctuation, which we follow, isolates *pārāṣû* as a complete clause, the structure invites search for a more integral connection.

> *pārāṣû wĕdāmîm*   6 syllables
> *bĕdāmîm nāgā'û*   6

If it were not for the powerful emphasis on "blood," the connotation of the second verb "to touch" (here, to get to the point of murder after murder), would also be obscure. As it is the phrase *dāmîm bĕdāmîm* is quite unclear (cf. Jer 46:12). Given the arrangement of two pairs of rhyming words, it could be suggested that the verbs are near synonyms (cf. Job 16:14 and Ezek 18:10), together meaning "they have wounded fatally." It is also possible that *dāmîm* is used by metonymy for *'anšê (had)dāmîm*, "murderers"; Ps 51:16 makes more sense if it means "Deliver me from murderers" (murderers would be the normal agents of Yahweh's vengeance on David as a murderer; that is, since he had murdered, he would be murdered), rather than "Deliver me from bloods."

The term *dāmîm*, we propose, however, probably refers to the shedding of innocent blood by official action, and the crime charged against the nation here, as elsewhere, is the formal sacrifice of human beings, in particular children who are innocent and unblemished, so as to meet sacrificial requirements. The combination of verbs may suggest that armed parties under the authority of the priesthood broke into households to seize victims for sacrifice, leaving a trail of blood from the beginning of the process until its end. In any event, the shedding of innocent blood (cf. Ps 106:38) is an ultimate crime in the eyes of the great pre-exilic prophets, all of whom use the same or similar language; it symbolizes the ultimate rebellion against ‟God in the destruction of human beings who are made in his image and represent him on earth. If therefore the term *rāṣōaḥ* covers murder generally, then this phrase relates specifically to the ritual sacrifice of human beings, especially children, and hence involves both leadership and people in a common and universal guilt.

Kuhnigk (1974:26–28) has offered a solution to *dāmîm bĕdāmîm* in 4:2, based on Dahood's suggestion that *dāmîm* sometimes means "idols" (from *dmy*, "to resemble"). This meaning does not quite fit, but the arguments which support the proposal are nonetheless worthy of careful attention. (1) In Jer 7:9, idolatry is added to a list of sins based on the Decalogue. (2) In the following text Hosea talks more about idolatry than the other sins in 4:2, although most of them come up again somewhere; but it would be surprising if he did not include idolatry in his list of capital sins. (3) Murder has already been covered by *rāṣōaḥ;* but this hardly counts against the overwhelming evidence that *dāmîm* means some sort of "murder."

3a. *the land.* It could mean no more than the land of Israel, devastated by drought. Or it could mean "the earth," that is, the entire world.

dries up. There are two problems to be solved with this verb, its meaning and its tense. There can be no doubt that the common meaning of the verb *'ābal* is "to mourn," i.e. to perform mourning rites. If it is considered that it is fanciful for "the land" to mourn, we note that "the land" can refer to "its inhabitants." If there is evidence of a drought, mourning in time of drought would be a familiar exercise. In Canaanite religion, the drought was believed to be caused by the death of Baal, who must be mourned in order to revive him in due course and restore fertility.

Driver (1936) has proposed that *'bl* can mean "to dry up." (1) The verb *abālu* in Akkadian has the meaning "to dry out" when applied to canals, fields, plants, etc. (2) In Amos 1:2; Jer 12:4; 23:10, the verb parallel to *'bl* is *yābēš*, "to be dry"; so arguments from poetic parallelism require a similar meaning here. (3) The parallelism of *'umlal* in Hos 4:3 points to the same result (Wolff 1974:65). Joel 1:10–12a has these verbs in parallel, along with *šdd*.

10a	*šuddad śādeh*	Field is devastated.
	'ābĕlâ 'ădāmâ	The ground is dried out.
10b	*kî šuddad dāgān*	Grain is devastated.
	hôbîš tîrôš	Must has dried up completely.
	'umlal yiṣhār	Oil has languished.
11a	*hōbîšû 'ikkārîm*	Farmers are ashamed.
	hêlîlû kōrĕmîm	Vinedressers wail
	'al-ḥiṭṭâ wĕ'al-śĕ'ōrâ	over wheat and barley.

11b *kî 'ābad qĕṣîr śādeh* The harvest of the field has perished.
12a *haggepen hôbîšâ*   The vine has dried up.
  wĕhattĕ'ēnâ 'umlālâ The fig tree has withered.

This poem shows wordplay, e.g. in the use of *ybš,* "to be dry" (vv 10bB, 12aA), and *bwš* "to be ashamed" (v 11aA). In general, when there is mourning for drought, the verbs that have human subjects mean "to wail," etc., while verbs with plants as subject mean "to wither," etc. Verbs with "land" as subject could go either way. The use of *'umlal* in parallel with *hôbîš,* "dry," is a good argument for taking *'ābal* as "to dry out" in Hos 4:3.

The second problem is the time reference. If it describes the present state of affairs, the prophet is explaining the prevailing drought as the result of wickedness exposed in v 2. No remedy is proposed. If the verb is future, then the construction follows a judgment oracle. Because of the sins just enumerated, there will be punishment. The imperfect verb points to a threatened judgment. But an actual drought is not excluded, a warning and foretaste of more severe punishment to come. Note that Joel uses perfect verbs to describe a present drought.

all its inhabitants. This includes animals as well as humans. In 2:20 the animals were given a prominent role in the covenant. In Gen 9:5, beasts and humans are included in the law about murder (cf. Josh 7:24). In Egypt, the firstborn of animals were killed with the firstborn of humans. The list of animals in Gen 9:2 is like the one here, and they are all in the renewed covenant of Genesis 9.

enfeebled. The form of the verb *'umlal* is unusual. In the present construction it is a consecutive perfect (future), which cannot have its normal sequential meaning, since the two situations are obviously concomitant. The root *'ml,* considered the base of the verb used here, has no active forms, and no imperfect tense; the root *mll* is considered the base of the *Polel* and *Hitpolel,* which occur only as imperfects; thus the morphology is curious. The verb can have plants or people as subject. The translation "to wither" suits the former, "to languish" the latter.

3b. *are swept away.* The most obvious subject of the verb is either the long phrase listing three orders of creatures, or the last phrase, "fish of the sea." Since the three groups make up the animal kingdom, it is likely that they should be taken together. The prepositions show that there is a link between this passage and v 1bB with the threefold repetition and the use of the preposition. We believe that *dgy hym* is governed by the preposition of the preceding phrases (the preposition is not repeated to avoid particle overload), and that the subject of the verb is the inhabitants of the land. As to the meaning of the verb, it must be determined from its context. The verse has a cosmic ring about it, with overtones of the creation story. It resembles Jer 4:23–28, which describes the ruination of all nature in the last judgments of God. In Jer 4:28, "the land is dried up" after the reversion of the universe to primeval chaos and the depopulation of the world. The implicit agent here is God, who has gathered in all living things through death (cf. *UT* Krt 18–19; Isa 16:10; Jer 48:33). The order of creatures could be significant: the listing of fish after beasts and birds (unlike the reptiles in 2:20) resembles the lists in Genesis 1, and emphasizes the denizens of the three great regions of the universe — land, air, water; cf. Exod 20:4.

V. THE STATE OF THE NATION:
PRIEST AND PEOPLE
(4:4–19)

A chief priest rebukes Hosea

4:4a   Let no one dispute,
　　　　　let no one debate.

Hosea replies. The word of Yahweh to the priest

4b   My contention is indeed with you, priest.
5a   You will stumble by day
　　　　　and the prophet will stumble with you by night
5b　　　　and I will ruin your mother.
6a   My people are ruined for lack of the knowledge.
　　　　Because you have rejected the knowledge,
　　　　　I will reject you from being priest to me.
6b   You have forgotten your God's instruction —
　　　　　I will forget your children.

The actions of the chief priest's children

7a   As they grew proud, so they sinned against me.
7b   Their Glory they exchanged for Ignominy.
8a   The sin-offering of my people they devour
8b　　　　and toward their iniquity-offering they lift their throats.

Yahweh's principle

9a   It shall be: Like the people, like the priest.
9b   I shall punish each for his conduct,
　　　　　I shall requite each for his deeds.

The fate of the chief priest's children

10a   They have eaten, but will not be satisfied.
　　　　They have been promiscuous, but will not increase.

The actions of the chief priest

10b	For they have deserted Yahweh.
11a	He holds to promiscuity through wine.
11b	Through must he takes away my people's heart.
12a	He makes inquiry of his Wood
	And his Staff reports to him.
12b	By a promiscuous spirit he has led them astray.
	They act promiscuously in defiance of their God.

The actions of the chief priest's children

Male

13a   On mountain tops they make sacrifice
      and on high peaks they burn incense.

Female

13b   Under oaks, poplars, and terebinths, whose shade is good,
      Because your daughters are promiscuous
         and your daughters-in-law commit adultery
14a   I will punish your daughters because they are promiscuous
         and your daughters-in-law because they commit
            adultery.

Male

14b   They segregate themselves with sacred prostitutes
         and make sacrifices with sacred prostitutes.
      A people without discernment will be ruined.

Oaths and actions forbidden the people

The forbidden oaths

15a   "You, Israel, are not a prostitute."
      "Let Judah not be held guilty."

The prohibitions

15b   Don't go to Gilgal.
      Don't go up to Beth Awen.
      Don't swear "As Yahweh lives!"

The results of the chief priest's action: Israel & Ephraim in apostasy

16a Indeed like a rebellious cow
     Israel has rebelled.
16b Now Yahweh will shepherd them.
     Like lambs in a wide pasture
17a   Ephraim has been joined to idols.
17b He has abandoned them for himself.
18a   He has turned aside from their drunkenness.

The actions of the chief priest's children

18b They have been promiscuous,
          they have made love continually.
     He has constrained the Ignominy, with its shields,
19a   her lustful spirit, with its wings.
19b They have behaved shamefully at their altars.

NOTES

4:4–19. The divisions of the text marked above are intended as a guide to the shifts in reference and address; these are clearer in Hebrew, which is inflected for gender and number. The focus in this long passage is the family of a chief priest, either of the northern kingdom or one of its major shrines. His mother is mentioned, and his sons and daughters are treated at length. Also cited is a major associate of his, the prophet, who is evidently a correspondingly high-ranking cult official. The people are largely peripheral here, victims of the greed and deception of the chief priest's family (vv 8,11b,12b,14b,15a); they have, however, followed the priest's lead and are consequently lost (vv 9,16–19).

4–5. These verses have a certain measure of coherence, notwithstanding some textual problems.

4aA	'ak 'îš 'al-yārēb	5 syllables
4aB	wĕ'al-yôkaḥ 'îš	5
4b	wĕ'immĕkā kîm(ā) rîbî kōhēn	9/8
5aA	wĕkāšaltā hayyôm	6/5
5aB	wĕkāšal gam-nābî' 'immĕkā lāylâ	11/10
5b	wĕdāmîtî 'immekā	7/6

The change from the long lines of vv 1–3 to the short lines dominant here is striking. Because v 4a is a well-formed bicolon, and because v 5a exhibits parallelism, despite the unequal length of the lines, vv 4b and 5b might go together.

The protagonists can be identified by inference from the text. The speaker, who threatens to ruin "your mother" and presumably also to bring about the stumbling of priest and prophet, is Yahweh. The person addressed in v 5 (2 m s) is clearly the chief priest of v 4b. The identity of the person referred to in v 4a, if there is one, is less evident. If the speaker is prohibiting all argument, as we contend, then the word *'yš,* "man," is virtually a pronoun ("any one"). Gordis argues that v 4a is a hostile response to vv 1–3, and that the priest means to forbid the prophet in particular from continuing the *rîb* begun in vv 1–3.

4a. The particle *'ak* marks the transition to a new section. The text of v 4a is not in doubt, but the meaning is not obvious despite the perfect parallelism of the bicolon and its identical line lengths. The verbs are synonymous; the bicolon is repetitious, the chiasm purely artistic. If Yahweh is the speaker, as is often supposed, it is not obvious why he should launch a *rîb* (v 1) and promptly ban all disputation. In Isa 1:18, he invites such debate. The *rîb* of v 1 was wide in scope. It might include the whole world, but at least involves all Israel. If, suddenly, the *rîb* is narrowed down to one priest, then v 4 could be taken as saying, "Let nobody else interfere in this quarrel, because my dispute is exclusively with you, O priest!" We could also suppose that the situation has changed completely from vv 1–3, and that the two units have been put together because both contain the root *ryb,* and not because there is any organic connection between them. We have suggested, on the contrary, that vv 1–3 are a kind of preface to the ensuing discourse, and that v 4 marks a new beginning.

The solution proposed by Gordis, and adopted by us in part, may seem overly ingenious, but it contains points to be considered seriously. He argues that often in biblical literature quotations are introduced without being labeled as such, and conversation is reported without any indication of the change of speaker; and that 4:4a is an example. It is spoken, he contends, by the people in response to vv 1–3, and expresses their "stubborn refusal to accept instruction" (Gordis 1971:113). It is not the prophet's statement, but a quotation of the point of view he proceeds to attack in the following lines.

This makes sense, but the picture needs to be brought into sharper focus. The weakness in Gordis's theory is the ascription of obduracy to *the people,* since the prophet does not aim his rebuttal at them, but directs his riposte against a particular priest, and a prophet associated with him. The passage becomes clearer if we take v 4a as a direct attack on Hosea, not by the people, but by an officer of the cult, not unlike the confrontation between Amaziah and Amos (Amos 7:10–17). Since prophetic oracles often took the form of a *rîb* against Israel in Yahweh's name, the negative response in both instances was a ban on prophesying as such. We have Hosea's report of his spirited interchange with a priest. The utterance-initial *'ak* is a modal (emotional) modifier rather than a conjunction; some of its adversative, contradictory force is retained.

no one. Literally "(may) a man not (contend)." If this refers to an individual, rather than being generic (i.e. *nobody*), it could be a contemptuous reference to Hosea. This could also be true if the term *'yš* is an abbreviation for *'îš hā'ĕlōhîm,* "the man of God," an early title for "prophet." Amaziah addresses Amos as *ḥōzeh,* "seer," in a sarcastic manner (Amos 7:12), and Hos 9:7 records similar insults hurled apparently at Hosea.

dispute . . . debate. More than argumentation or remonstration is implied by the verbs, which are the terminology of formal litigation. Accusation is implied. From a grammatical point of view, the construction *'îš 'al* + jussive means "let nobody . . . ," imposing a total ban (cf. Exod 34:3 bis).

If it were Yahweh, through his prophet, who was taking this initiative, it is not easy to see why everybody should be banned from disputation. When the *rîb* of the law courts supplies the model for Yahweh's moral evaluation of Israel, reply is always permitted, indeed encouraged; for then it is made clear that Israel is guilty and has no excuse. Because we cannot imagine Yahweh prohibiting such a response to his charges, a more organic connection has been sought between v 4a and v 4b. Wolff (1974:70) has translated:

> No, not just anyone should be accused,
> nor should just anyone be reproved!

It is necessary then to read both verbs in v 4a as passive, with Budde (1926:284). Since this explanation of v 4a leans heavily on the interpretation of v 4b, we turn to the latter.

4b. *My contention is indeed with you.* MT reads "your people" instead of "with you." Verse 4b is notoriously difficult, although MT is reasonably well attested. Two of its three words are familiar, although one of these requires the slight emendation noted: *kimrîbê* is more problematical. It seems to contain a plural noun in the construct state, preceded by the preposition *k,* "like." The noun **mĕrībîm,* while not impossible, does not have much support. If it is based on the root *ryb,* which is used in vv 1 and 4a, then it could be the *Hip'il* participle or simply a noun with preformative *mem.* The *Hip'il* of the verb is not used as such; the participle may occur in I Sam 2:10, where it means "those who contend against him (Yahweh)"; this is slender support. The putative noun is not known else-

where. The most literal translation of MT would be either "and your people are like the contentions of a priest," or "and your people are like those
who strive with a priest." A noun *mĕrîbâ,* "contention," is found in Gen
13:8; Num 27:14, but it could owe its existence to etymologizing on the
place name Meribah (Exod 17:7; etc.). LXX confirms MT in the main; it
reads "my people," and seems to have read *mryby* as a singular adjective
antilegomenos, "(like an) accused (priest)." This comparison of people
and priest could have been influenced by 4:9a.

Numerous solutions have been proposed. Not all of them can be examined here. They vary in the degree to which they rewrite MT. Their
claim for acceptance diminishes as the changes made become more substantial. Most desirable is a reading that involves changes in the vowel
points only, without touching the consonants. Almost as good is a reading
that rearranges word boundaries without changing the consonants or their
order. Less attractive are emendations that involve the deletion or addition of consonants. More drastic measures, which require the replacement
of consonants as well as changes in sequence, deletion, addition, redivision, and revocalization, are so desperate that it would be better to abandon the text as incorrigible than to resort to them. Suggested readings are
shown in the following.

MT	w'mk	kmryby	khn
	and-your-people	like-disputations-of(?)	priest
LXX	w'my	kmryb	khn
	and-my-people	like-accused	priest
BHS	w'mk	ryby	hkhn
	and-with-you	my-lawsuit	O-Priest
Wolff	w'mk	ryby	khn
(1974:70)	and-with-you	my-lawsuit	Priest
van	w'mkm	ryby	khn
Hoonacker	and-with-you	my-lawsuit	priest(s) (col.)
Lohfink	w'mk	mryby	khn
(1961)	and-with-you	my-contention	priest
BH[3]	w'my	kkmrw bny	kkhnw
	and-my-people	like-its- my-son	like-his-priest
		idol-priest	
BH[3]	w'm	kkmr wnby'	kkhn
	and-people	like-idol- and-prophet	like-priest
		priest	
BH[3]	'my	kmwk	hkhn
	my-people	like-you	O-Priest

BHS	w ' m k	' n y r b	(h) k h n
	and-with-you	I contend	O-Priest

Kuhnigk	w ' m k	k m r y b y	k h n
Andersen &	and-with-you	indeed is-my-contention	O-Priest
Freedman

There does not seem to be any good reason for discarding the initial *w-* of MT, though the connection between v 4b and v 4a is not easy to find. If the prophet speaks in v 4a, it could mean that the groundless complaints of the people against God are disqualified. By calling them "your people," not "my people," Yahweh sees their contentions against him as inexcusable, like the rebellions of Israel in the desert. In the Horeb incident (Exodus 32), Moses calls Israel "your people" when talking to Yahweh and Yahweh refers to "your people" while addressing Moses.

There is some basis for retaining the MT reading of *'am,* "people," rather than changing to the preposition *'im.* The conjunction of "people" and "priest" in v 9a, and the occurrence of "people" in v 6, encourage the retention of the word in v 4b. It is, however, going too far to bring v 4b as closely in line with v 9a as some proposals do. The arguments for *'imměkā,* "with you," are strong. The idiom *ryb 'm* occurs in v 1. The quarrel is with a priest, whose punishment is described in v 5 and whose sin is described in v 6. The pronoun suffix with *'m* is "you" (m s), either "your people," or "with you." If a priest is being addressed, "your people" is certainly an unusual designation, and "with you" relieves that difficulty. It is understandable that some modern scholars wish to follow LXX in reading "my people," as in vv 6 and 12. Such an emendation is unwarranted, however, and it is better to read the preposition *'im* with the 2 m s suffix, "with you," as in v 5a. The correlation of "day" and "night" in the same context supports this analysis; see below.

The addition of the word *'ănî,* "I," is too substantial a change to be entertained seriously.

The real trouble lies with the consonants *kmryby* of MT. One suggestion is to attach *km* as the suffix on the preceding *'m,* eliminating one *k* as a dittograph. Since the pronoun "you" (m s) occurs three times in v 5, this change to plural seems to make things worse. It also requires *kōhēn* to be taken as collective (plural). If this word is divided *k-mryby, k* could be the preposition "like"; a similar outcome is arrived at if prepositional *km* is recognized, the *mem* being enclitic. In spite of the comparison made in v 9a, it is hard to see what the comparison is here, especially if we retain "the contentions of a priest."

An admirable solution was proposed by Gordis, who recognized asseverative *kaph,* and read *wě'amměkā kiměrîbay kōhēn,* "and your people are surely my foes, O priest" (Gordis 1971:113). The statement that the people *are* adversaries is better than a mere comparison. But the reference to *"your* people" is unexampled in this chapter, where the noun either stands alone or has the suffix (referring to Yahweh, not the priest).

The possibility that the consonants *kmr* are the word *kōmer,* "idol-priest," has considerable appeal, especially in view of the fact that Hosea (at 10:5) contains one of the three biblical occurrences of this word. The other two are II Kings 23:5 (where they burn incense to Baal, among other gods) and Zeph 1:4 (where they are Baal worshipers). But this creates problems. The residue of the word — *yby* — is difficult. The consonants *'mk kmr* [*r*]*yby* can yield "With you, O idol-priest, is my quarrel"; the second *r* reflects the single writing of a double consonant, or a haplography. This leaves the following *khn* stranded, unless it is joined to what follows.

Because the word **mārîb* is so poorly attested, the *m* has been eliminated in several of the reconstructions listed above. An explanation that makes provision for the *m* is to be preferred. If the root *ryb,* "to contend," is to be retained, then some meaning has to be found for the phrase embodied in the Masoretic pointing. Neither of the obvious possibilities — "contentions of a priest," or "those who contend against a priest" — seems to fit. There is no litigation conducted by any priest nor is there any sign of the people disputing with a priest. If there is any dispute, it is against Yahweh, or by Yahweh. It is possible to read **měrîbay,* "those who argue with me," and take *kōhēn* as a vocative in agreement with the pronoun on *w'mk.*

The word *rîb* can be defended because it has already occurred in v 1 and the verb is used in v 4a. "My contention is with you, O Priest," is an attractive reading, requiring minimal changes. Those who advocate it have to delete *km* or explain it in some other way. Wolff (1974:70), for instance, suggests that *kōmer* was originally present; that *kōhēn* was added as its gloss, then *kmr* became *km* by haplography. This is rather tortuous. It could be argued equally well that it is precisely the presence of *rîb* in v 1 that has led to the misreading of (*mě*)*rîb-* in v 4b. Close in meaning to *měrîbay,* "those who contend with me," is **mōrê bî,* "those who rebel against me." The word is often used to describe the contumacity of the Israelites (cf. Hos 14:1). The construction in which a participle in the construct state governs its object through a preposition is grammatical.

The last word is to be retained as in MT, but *kōhēn* is vocative (the article need not be added). The *km* in the middle word is best. read as asseverative, although the preposition "like" is still possible.

The consonants *kmryby* can be read as emphatic *k* with *měrîbay,* "those disputing with me"; or with *mōrê bî,* "those rebelling against me"; or as emphatic *kim*(*a*) *rîbî,* "my quarrel." The last has the advantage of changing the focus from people (who are not clearly in view here) to the priest (who certainly is). A further advantage of the last solution is that it fits the context, since vv 5–6 contain accusations of the priest and sentences against him. Its disadvantage is the need to invoke the long form of the asseverative particle *kim(a)*. The other two proposals have the advantage of including the people with the priest in the indictment from the outset. In what follows both defendants are dealt with in alternation.

There is a difference in the way priest and people are treated, however. The people are like the priest in following his lead and hence in ending up like him. They will also suffer the consequences of his evil direction. But theirs are sins of ignorance and omission, his of deliberation and initiation. They are more to be pitied and he is more to be scorned. And nowhere in this chapter are they called "your people," whether the pronoun is referred to Yahweh or to the priest. In fact, they are Yahweh's people, not the priest's.

indeed. Adopting Gordis's suggestion that the *kaph* is asseverative, and is to be read with enclitic *mem* (= *kîm[a]*). Alternatively we may read *kammâ* "how much, how often," understood assertively rather than interrogatively. The line would then be linked more directly with *hywm* and *lylh,* and would refer to the controversy between Yahweh and priest rather than the stumbling of priest and prophet.

5. This verse issues a threat against some unnamed individuals. There are three lines; one deals with a priest, one with a prophet, and the third with someone's mother, presumably the priest's, as the priest seems to be addressed throughout. Verse 5a exhibits good parallelism in spite of the inequality in the length of the lines. It is hard to see how a prophet and the priest's mother come into the picture. The parallelism in v 5a could account for the "prophet" as a companion of the "priest." The conjunction of "the day" and "by night" is poetic. It does not specify the exact times when each will stumble: both priest and prophet will stumble all the time, by day and by night. There are two reasons for not equating the priest and the prophet. The conjunction *gam* indicates that the prophet will stumble as well as someone else. The phrase "with you" in v 5aB, which would refer to the priest, makes it clear that two persons are stumbling together (cf. 5:5). It would seem, then, that while the main focus is on one priest, he will not be alone in his punishment.

The passage vv 4b–5a can be construed as a unit, since the parallel expressions are distributed over the two parts, which divide as follows.

w'mk km ryby khn
wkšlt hywm
wkšl gm-nby' 'mk lylh
wdmyty 'mk

Some of the less obvious correlations can best be brought out in a paraphrase.

And with you indeed is my contention by day
with you (is my contention) by night
(And you shall stumble, O priest
and the prophet also shall stumble)
And I will destroy your mother.

If the reading '*mk*, "with you," is correct in v 4b, then the repetition in v 5a must share its force and context. The association with "day" and "night" may refer to Yahweh's contention or controversy with the priest rather than the consequence — stumbling — as indicated in the paraphrase. This is not to deny the sense of a consecutive reading. Typically the parallelism is not synonymous in either case, but combinatory and complementary: You and the prophet shall stumble together continually.

The reference to the priest's mother is enigmatic, but presumably she exerted an important and baleful influence on the life and career of her son, as was the case with some notorious queen mothers in the history of Israel and Judah (e.g. Jezebel). In any case, the priest's family will share in his destiny (cf. v 6); compare this passage with Amos's fierce denunciation of Amaziah the priest of Bethel (7:10–17). In the latter passage, Amaziah's wife and children are singled out for condign punishment, while here it is the priest's mother and his children. It is not impossible that Hosea has in mind the same person, although more than one wicked priest could flourish in the same period, as we know from the Dead Sea scrolls where we are embarrassed by the number of candidates for the role. The prophet mentioned here is presumably a major cultic functionary, associated with the chief priest.

5a. *stumble*. When this word is used again in Hos 5:5 (cf. 14:2), it is clear that a serious, even fatal downfall is in mind, and not just some passing discomfiture. In some occurrences (Ps 31:11; Neh 4:4), to be sure, the verb has its plain meaning; here it seems to be figurative. The fitness of the punishment is not indicated. In other places in this context a close connection is shown between crime and punishment, e.g. the people are ruined, so I will ruin your mother (vv 5b,6a); you have forgotten the torah, so I will forget your children; you have rejected me, so I will reject you (v 6). A matching fault would be causing the people to stumble, a charge not explicitly made until c 5.

by day. Because *hayyôm* does not exactly match *lāylâ*, Gordis (1971:151 n 33) transfers the *h* to the verb. This seems unnecessary: *yôm*, *yômām*, and *hayyôm* can all be used with the meaning "by day," whereas *lāylâ* receives the article less commonly. Although the spelling *wkšlth* is not impossible, the final *he* is mainly added to verbs with biconsonantal roots.

prophet. There is no other place in Hosea where prophets are attacked, whereas the priests are denounced again and again. Jer 2:4–13, which has several affinities with this part of Hosea, also mentions priests and prophets in parallel (2:8).

5b. *ruin*. Verse 5b presents several problems. The sudden change to the first person shows that Yahweh is judging, which continues through v 9. Presumably he is responsible for the stumbling in v 5. In his study of this passage, Lohfink (1961) gathered evidence of a scheme of three generations in ancient curses, which embrace a culprit's living forebears and his children. The whole family collapses under the sin of one member. Samuel's decree that Agag's mother will be childless among women (I Sam 15:33) is punishment for his atrocities of killing women and children together, particularly mutilating pregnant women. Cf. Ps 109:14. In spite of Jer 31:29, Jeremiah pronounced the threefold sentence on Jehoiachin — he will be expelled to a foreign land and die there; so will his mother; he will be childless (Jer 22:25–30). The priest's father is not mentioned here because the person addressed is a chief priest who would have succeeded on his father's death, a privilege to be denied his children (v 6b).

There are two roots *dāmâ* used in the *Qal,* as here. One means "to resemble," the other "to cease, be at rest." The former does not suit here for an act of God with a person as its object, although LXX tried to use it; the result is hardly intelligible. The *Nip'al* of the second root (cf. v 6) is more common, meaning "to be dumbfounded." It describes the silence of a ruined city (Isa 15:1; Jer 47:5). In this sense it is used in Hosea at 10:7,15. The *Qal* of this root is here used, as in Jer 6:2, as a transitive verb in a context describing ruination. The parallelism in Jer 6:2 with *šdd* suggests a meaning like "to destroy."

Kuhnigk (1974:30–35) has proposed a solution which eliminates the reference to the mother completely; he reads *wdmyt 'mh* (*ky*), "and you will perish fearfully." This proposal is ingenious but unconvincing.

6. A new stage of discourse begins here. It is unlikely that it is a threat. The cause (lack of knowledge) suggests moral ruin rather than physical devastation. The priest is blamed for abandoning "the knowledge," knowledge of God.

6a. *My people*. This most affectionate term on Yahweh's lips, in spite of the absolute renunciation expressed in cc 1–2 in the symbolic name of Hosea's third child ("Not-my-people"), gives the statement a particular pathos. Wolff hears v 6a as a "lament over personal loss," especially with the verb coming first in the clause (1974:79). In 7:9, the prophet describes the nation as suffering deterioration without being aware of it; here, however, the phrase *mibbělî hadda'at* probably does not mean that the people are ruined without realizing it. *"The* knowledge" referred to here is the knowledge of God in the torah for which the priest is responsible. The parallel in v 14b shows that the people are deprived of understanding, not simply that they are unaware. While it is true that *mibbĕlî* can sometimes indicate a result (S. R. Driver 1885–86), here it is either descriptive (my ignorant people) or causal (because they lack knowledge). The first line is isolated but has verbal links with the preceding (*dmy*) and following (*d't*) discourse.

rejected. The attitude of the priest to "the knowledge" is expressed with the verb *mā'as,* which implies rejection as a result of disagreement or disesteem. The Israelites forfeited their chance of entering the promised land because they "despised" it (Num 14:31; Ps 106:24). While the verb sometimes describes rejection on good grounds (Isa 7:15–16), and with deserved contempt (Jer 4:30), the frequency with which this verb refers to the disdainful rejection of God, his word, or his covenant, gives it the meaning of perverse refusal to value a thing at its true worth, so that the renunciation insults the generous donor and hurts the one who refuses. Such a spurning of the knowledge of Yahweh on the part of a priest is much more serious than disobedience to the word on the part of the people. As custodian of this revelation, the priest is responsible not only to honor it, but to spread it and to regulate national life by means of it. When this knowledge is not merely neglected, but despised, God himself is brought into disrepute, and the priest forfeits all claim to continue in his holy office. The same verb is used in I Sam 15:23,26 to describe Saul's rejection from office for rejecting Yahweh's word.

I will reject. The placement of the first object ("the knowledge") before the verb in the previous clause brings the two clauses into a chiastic pattern. Unlike v 5 and v 9b, a consecutive perfect (future) verb is not used here to proclaim the punishment; the imperfect is simply a variation from the norm. The use of the conjunction before "I will reject" but not before its parallel "I will forget" is unusual.

The spelling of the verb with an extra *'alep* at the end is unaccountable as a scribal error, and inexplicable in terms of pre-exilic orthographic practice. It seems to represent medial short *a* between the stem and the suffix. Cf. Kimron (1974–75), Freedman and Ritterspach (1967).

from being priest to me. While no special title is given, it is clear that Hosea is speaking of a high priest or chief priest at a central shrine. The seriousness of the charges, and the singling out of *one* priest for accusation, makes it clear that he is held responsible for the state of the entire nation. Amaziah, "the priest of Bethel" (Amos 7:10) springs to mind, although neither his name nor his shrine's is supplied by Hosea. From the activities described in the remainder of the chapter it is clear that Yahweh worship had been converted into blatant paganism as a result of radical apostasy on the part of the leading ecclesiastical functionary.

6b. *forgotten.* The importance of *škḥ* against the background of the

Deuteronomic tradition has been pointed out in the NOTES on 2:15. It implies more than a lapse of memory; it implies deliberate rejection.

your children. While the rejection of the children seems to reflect family solidarity, there is reason to believe that they deserved their condemnation as in the case of Eli and his sons. When Yahweh "forgets" the priest's children, he does not simply overlook them, he expels them. The sons of Eli were at fault (I Sam 2:12–17,22–25), and their sins included having sex with women in the shrine (v 22) as well as general cupidity (v 16). Eli is blamed for not restraining them, and they are to be excluded from office (I Sam 2:27–36) by a continuing curse on Eli's male descendants.

7–8. This unit, which employs plural verbs and pronominal suffixes, reflects a shift in focus from the chief priest alone to a group. While "people" is construed as plural in v 6a (note that the versions render the verb there singular), it is singular in v 14b (*yillābēṭ*). In the occurrences of "people" in a verbal clause, it is either the subject of a passive form (vv 6, 14) or the object of an active one (vv 8,12). Verses 6a and 14b are isolated lines next to good bicola; together they make a fine discontinuous bicolon. There are thematic connections between v 8 and v 12. In v 9 the comparison between "priest" and "people" stresses the sameness of their fate rather than of their behavior. The crimes are those of the priest, the consequences involve both priest and people. In the present instance, we look for the antecedent of the plural forms in the preceding verse and find it in *bānêkā*, "your children." While the sins described in vv 7–8,10, and 14b are not sufficiently specific to establish the distinction between priests and people as the culprits, they are consistent with the proposed identification. More decisive is the reading of v 8a, where according to the usual analysis the subject of the verb *yō'kēlû* must be a plural other than *'ammî*, "my people." If this is correct, then the subject must be "priests" since, according to the applicable law (Lev 6:18–19), they alone were entitled to eat the remains of this offering.

7a. *grew proud.* The construction resembles 11:2 in part; note also Jeremiah's complaint that Israel had as many gods as towns (Jer 2:28). Then the reference is to their pride rather than their numbers.

they sinned. The perfect verb describes the accomplished act. The preposition *l* can refer to the one sinned against (Gen 40:1). The following imperfect verbs are in poetic parallelism and expound the details of the sins. The threatened punishment is in v 10, in the consecutive perfect (future). A connection between the sin and its punishment should be sought; it is likely that the sin in question is exchanging Yahweh (the Glory of Israel) for Baal, Ignominy, and calling Baal *Kābôd*. It is possible that the acclamation *Kābôd* in Ps 29:9 was present in the original Baal poem, on which the Hebrew poem is based. The plural here shows that the children of the priest are meant.

7b. *Glory.* That is, Yahweh. Note the assonance of *kĕrubbām* and *kĕbôdām.* Each line in the bicolon of v 7 has exactly eight syllables; there is not much parallelism in the bicolon. In Ps 106:19–20 there is a report of Israel's first calamitous excursion into idolatry.

> They made a calf at Horeb,
> And bowed down to a casting,
> And they exchanged (*wayyāmîrû*) their Glory
> For a statue of a bull, an eater of grass.

The use of the same idiom in Hos 4:7 suggests that this incident is meant. *Qālôn,* "Ignominy," is the opposite of *Kābôd,* "Glory," in Isa 22:18; Prov 3:35; 13:18. In Ps 106:20 "their Glory" is Yahweh; so in the MT of Hos 4:7 "their Glory" seems to be a sarcastic name for the anti-Yahweh, Baal. But this is awkward and the reverse of what we have in Psalm 106 and Jeremiah 2. Jeremiah, who is so often close to Hosea in thought and vocabulary, is straightforward. Yahweh is aghast at Israel's unheard-of action: "My people exchanged (*hēmîr*) its Glory for Unprofitable" (Jer 2:11). Jeremiah's name for the substitute god (*bĕlô' yô'îl*) is a play on the name Baal. In Hos 4:7 *qālôn* is a name for Baal expressing disgust. The illicit name "Glory" (9:11; 10:5) will be removed from Baal and he will be given his true name, "Shame."

they exchanged. MT reads "I exchanged." Some versions bear witness to the alternative reading used here: *kĕbôdî bĕqālôn hēmîrû,* "they exchanged my Glory for Ignominy." This is so close to Jer 2:11 and Ps 106:20 that it is hard to see why it was considered objectionable. In these parallel texts, "their Glory" refers to Yahweh, who is replaced by a false god, variously styled.

If MT's *'āmîr,* "I will exchange" is retained, since Yahweh would not replace *himself* with Shame, *kĕbôdām* could not have the same meaning here as in Jer 2:11 and Ps 106:20. But it seems better to interpret v 7 in line with the other passages and read *hēmîrû* for *'āmîr.*

Kuhnigk (1974:39–45) normalizes the second line to the first, to yield "they exchanged," by proposing to read *'myr* as an *Ap'el* alternative to the *Hip'il.* This is possible.

The contrast of *kābôd* and *qālôn* is met with in Prov 3:35.

> *kābôd ḥăkāmîm yinḥālû*
> *ûkĕsîlîm mērîm qālôn*

A traditional translation is: "The wise will inherit honor, but fools exalt disgrace." If *mērîm* is *Hip'il* participle of *rm,* it does not agree with the plural subject; and the meaning is not parallel to "inherit." Attempts to make it fit are not satisfactory (Scott 1965:46). Emendation to *môrîšîm* solves both these problems, for *yrš* is a semantic parallel to *nḥl*. But considerable changes are needed in the text, and the parallelism is still not good since *yrš* means "to dispossess, forcibly possess," and this is not comparable to *nḥl*, "to inherit (legally)."

Gordis (1970:102) tried to solve the problem by reading *mērîm* as the *Qal* plural participle of *mwr*, the verb used here in Hos 4:7. He has probably hit on the right root, but his arguments are weak, and his translation is still unsatisfactory, "But fools acquire shame." This makes *qālôn* the only object of *mērîm*, and the exact nature of the transaction remains undefined, unless by the Aramaic parallel "to purchase." The meaning of the Aramaic (or Arabic) cognate should not be permitted to impose the result unless other occurrences in Hebrew attest the existence of that meaning in that language.

Morphology in Gordis's solution is problematic. There are no *Qal* forms of this root recognized by philologists; this is not an objection, only a caution. By analogy *mērîm* is like *mētîm*, so the parsing is not impossible. Gordis may be right in recognizing a *Qal* in Isa 38:17, *mār*, "changed," but Gordis loses as much as he gains from this excursion. Paradigmatic analogy suggests that *mērîm* should be stative, like *mētîm*, and the vocalization of *mār* is different, if MT be retained. So the existence of a *Qal* of *mwr* remains speculative.

If emendation is permitted, the reconstruction of *Hip'il* of *mwr* is not as drastic as the *Hip'il* of *yrš*: *mēmīrîm* can be recovered simply by reading the preceding *m* twice.

The syntactic difficulties in the way of Gordis's interpretation are more formidable. The *Hip'il* of *m(w/y)r* is used typically as a ditransitive verb; its first object is the thing given away (with *'ēt* as *nota accusativi*, if a marker is used), and the second object is the thing acquired (with *b* as *nota accusativi* if a marker is used).

The grammar excludes acquisition by purchase, for then the original possession would have the *b* of price. Ps 106:20 realizes this syntax fully, and may be taken as normative. This text also makes it clear that "Glory" as the object of *hēmîr* is a byword, as is confirmed by Jer 2:11. Hos 4:7 does not contain the *nota accusativi*, but the idiom is similar. Lev 27:10,33 describes the replacement of one intended gift by another; cf. Ps 15:4; the Levitical rules refer to the *tĕmûrâ*, something put in the place previously occupied by something else.

There is no thought of purchase with *mwr*, for there is no second party in any of these transactions, and there is no hint that one object is the price of the other. In Job 15:31; 20:18; 28:17, however, *tĕmûrâ* does have connotations of exchange, and could be abstract. The negotiation in Ruth 4:7 is in line with Leviticus 27, contra Campbell (1976:139). As we have already seen, the connotations of the root *mwr* do not suggest that *tĕmûrâ* refers to the acquisition of land by purchase, or even by redemption (= exchange), and in Ruth there is no hint of the payment of a price. The land is *inherited* by the man who, in a posthumous pseudo-adoption by the deceased Elimelech, becomes his heir, because his marriage to Elimelech's widowed daughter-in-law is tantamount to this. It should not be implied that the ceremony of the sandals served to ratify "exchange transactions" in general. It is highly specific and symbolizes the replacement of one *gō'ēl* by another; *kol-dābār* here means "the whole matter." The phrase *"gĕ'ûlâ* and *tĕmûrâ"* is a hendiadys, meaning "an interchange of the right of redemption," or rather the replacement of one redeemer by another. In the ceremony of the sandals, Boaz and the first *gō'ēl* swapped sandals to symbolize this exchange of roles.

If, as Gordis suggests, *hēmîr* describes the bartering of one object for another, then *hēmîr* would mean "to sell." But there is never a hint of a buyer; the action is entirely carried out by one party. Ezek 48:14 carefully distinguishes between sale and replacement. In the restoration, the best land will be holy for Yahweh, *wĕlō'-yimkĕrû mimmennû wĕlō' yāmēr wĕlō' ya'ăbîr,* "and they will not sell any of it, and he (!) will not replace [any of it] and he will not make [any of it] pass over." The Qere/Kethib reading of the third verb (Qere — Hip'il; Kethib — Qal) shows that its exact meaning was unclear. It refers either to a third way of getting rid of property, or is meant to cover all processes of alienation; the distinction between selling and replacing is clearly made. It is misleading to say that *yāmēr* in Ezek 48:14 has no object: the first two verbs have a common object, and this confirms that the first object of the verb is the original possession, which is replaced. Most of the clear cases of *mwr* show that the action is one of replacing this original object by an inferior one: replacing the true God by an idol (Ps 106:20; Hos 4:7; Jer 2:11); or replacing one votive offering by another (Lev 27:10,33; Ezek 48:14). Even the opposite case envisioned by Lev 27:10 (replacing an original gift by a "better" one) can be understood as plugging a casuistic hole in the primary rule: you must not replace your promised gift by a worse one, or indeed by anything, even if you claim it is better.

It is possible that the verb might describe an act of relinquishment when there is no replacement. It has been difficult to take *hāmîr* as intransitive in Ps 46:3; it could mean "when he relinquishes the earth," but the parallel suggests that here God replaces the land by sea in a reversion to precreation chaos. Similarly Mic 2:4 could mean "My people have given up (their) patrimonial land." We can summarize the recorded interchanges.

	first object	replaced by
Ps 106:20	kĕbôdām	bĕtabnît
Jer 2:11	kĕbôdô	bĕlō' yôʻîl
Hos 4:7	kĕbôdām	bĕqālôn
Prov 3:35	kābôd	qālôn
Lev 27:10	ṭôb	bĕraʻ
(cf. 27:33; Ps 15:4)		
Ps 46:3	'ereṣ	yām?
Mic 2:4	ḥēleq	?
Ezek 48:14	rē'šît hā'āreṣ	?

To sum up: The biblical evidence affords no basis whatever for the existence of a *Qal mwr* "to acquire." The root occurs only in the *Hipʻil* (except for the *Nipʻal* in Jer 48:11), and it has no meaning other than "to replace." It is better to try to make "to replace" fit the obscure passages than to resort to unattested meanings in an attempt to resolve the obscurity. The word-field of Prov 3:35 fits the dominant usage, showing that "glory" is the object of both verbs in the verse. The wise preserve honor as a heritage; fools replace it with disgrace. The similarities of Hos 4:7, Ps 106:20, and Jer 2:11 show that the theme in each is idolatry, replacing Yahweh by an idol which can only be called "Ignominy."

8a. *The sin-offering of my people.* Questions of translation and interpretation of this verse have exercised scholars and produced a great deal of discussion, but a straightforward rendering would seem to be best. The passage describes in more detail the sin of the priest's children, who apparently were greedy and avaricious about seizing and devouring their share of the sin-offerings of the people. While v 8a on the face of it only mentions a practice authorized by biblical custom (Lev 6:17–23; 10:19), in the present context we must suppose that the priests abused their privilege by taking more than they were entitled to, and infringed on the rights of the deity or the people, probably both. That desire or greed was involved is implied in v 8b by the phrase *nś' npš* (Deut 24:15; Pss 24:4; 25:1; 86:4; 143:8; cf. Lam 3:41). It is a vivid expression of gluttony — literally, lifting the throat. We must interpret *'wnm* as a synonym of *ḥṭ't*, "sin-offering," although there is no direct warrant for this equation in the ritual literature. Since we are dealing with prophetic literature of the eighth century and not the Priestly Code or the priestly prophet Ezekiel, the usage may not be as unthinkable as earlier scholars believed. What we have is a sequence of charges against the priests to explain and justify the condemnation pronounced in v 6. The children of the chief priest are guilty of a multitude of sins and have earned their just punishment quite apart from sharing in the consequences of their father's misdeeds. They have exchanged their Glory (Yahweh) for Ignominy (Baal), devoured the sin-offerings of the people, and greedily consumed their sacrifices for guilt.

It is possible to understand the MT of v 7b as a form of punishment for the sins of v 7a (i.e. "I will change their Glory into Ignominy"), and if that is correct, we should also interpret v 8b as a description of punishment to come rather than of crime committed. In this regard, it may be noted that while the expression *nś' npš* is well attested, the idiom *nś' 'wn* is even more common, and its basic meaning, "to bear guilt, punishment," would be entirely appropriate here. That leaves initial *'l* and final *npšw* to be explained; we may treat these words as a separated prepositional phrase: *'el — napšô,* meaning "to life itself," i.e. to death; *napšam* can mean "fatally," as in the penalty for a capital crime. This regrouping would also solve the problem of the anomalous suffixes: the 3 m pl suffix on *'wn* would refer to the sons of the priests, the plural subject of the different verbs, while the 3 m s suffix on *nepeš* would be the equivalent of the definite article, providing desired emphasis. We would render the clause as follows: "And they will bear their guilt (= punishment) to the point of death (= at the cost of life itself)." The two possibilities for this quatrain (vv 7–8) would be as follows; the first follows the versions of v 7b, the second the MT.

A. As they grew proud, so they sinned against me.
   Their Glory they exchanged for Ignominy.
The sin-offering of my people they devour
   And toward their iniquity-offerings they lift
      their throats.
B. As they grew proud, so they sinned against me.
   (So) I will change their Glory into Ignominy.
   (As) they devoured the sin-offerings of my people,
   So they will bear their guilt (= punishment) at the
      cost of life itself.

8b. *their throats.* Literally MT reads "his throat"; the reading is an abbreviation of the distributive construction *yiś'û* ('*îš*) *napšô,* "each person lifts his throat." Kuhnigk (1974:46) identifies the suffix as an old accusative ending (as in Phoenician). The sporadic survival of such a fossil is highly doubtful. If the Hebrew *-ô* found in archaic forms that derives from the old case ending survives, it probably has determinative meaning — "the soul," meaning "their soul(s)" — when the possessor of a body part is the subject of the verb of which the name for the body part is the object.

9a. *It shall be.* The proverb "Like people, like priest" is one of the best known of Hosea's sayings; but it is doubtful if it has been rightly understood. In the first place, the opening *wĕhāyâ,* whenever Hosea uses it (it occurs elsewhere only in 1:5; 2:1 bis, 18, 23) is always future, if not es-

chatological. Here it states the principle of Yahweh's intended judgments
— "Like the people, like the priest."

The second problem is what is being compared to what. The construction "Like X, like Y" occurs several times in the Hebrew Bible.
Which item serves as the standard of comparison for the other? There are
three possibilities. (1) X is like Y; Y sets the standard. X is likened to Y;
the people, dependent on the priest, become like him. The people are just
as bad as the priest, and are corrupt because the priest has shown the way.
One would expect the priest to be better than the people. (2) Y is like X;
X sets the standard. Y is likened to X. The priest, conforming to the low
standards of the people, has become as bad as they are, instead of maintaining a superior level of holiness. (3) X and Y are alike, neither is the
starting point. Similarity as such is asserted. Priest and people are indis-
tinguishably guilty of the crimes listed.

The point is a fine one, but it is important. The context does not settle
the point, but v 4b, as we read it, indicates that the priest was the prime
target for Yahweh's *rîb*. The passive verb in v 6a indicates that the people
have been ruined by the priest who rejected "the knowledge," not that the
priest has been corrupted by the people. As a forecast of future judgment,
is the prophet saying that (1) the people will be judged in the same manner as the priest; or (2) that the priest will be judged in the same manner
as the people; or (3) that both will be judged alike? Harper (p. 258)
takes Hos 4:9 to refer to the fall of the priest to the level of the people
(2). His main argument is that the whole passage deals with the degenera-
tion of the priests. The neutral interpretation (3) is preferred by G. A.
Smith. The community as a whole is in the same condition, people and
priest alike. Wolff makes the important observation that in Hosea's
numerous similes, "the thing being compared more often precedes the
image of comparison that follows it" (1974:83).

Other occurrences of the same construction do not settle the question
either way, for both sequences are found. (1) X is like Y. *Kāmôkā
kĕpar'ōh* (Gen 44:18), "You are like Pharaoh." Pharaoh is the measure
of power, but Joseph is just as powerful, in Judah's opinion. *Kaṣṣaddîq
kārāšā'* (Gen 18:25), "The righteous will be like the wicked." The wicked
are the model of retributive judgment. If the righteous perish with them,
God is treating the good as if they were evil. *Kaqqāṭōn kaggādōl* (Deut
1:17): while this could mean that rich and poor are to be treated alike, it
probably means that magistrates are to show as much respect to the
socially inferior as to the superior, and treat the poor as if they were rich.
Hălō' kāmōhû kĕ'ayin bĕ'ênêkem (Hag 2:3): the new temple is like
nothing compared with the old. In I Kings 22:4, Jehoshaphat invites
Ahab to regard himself and his army as his own — *kāmônî kāmôkā
kĕ'ammî kĕ'ammekā kĕsûsay kēsûsêkā.*

Consider *kĕśākîr kĕtôšāb yihyeh 'immāk* (Lev 25:40): this statement has been interpreted as meaning that an Israelite who sells himself into debt slavery will not be treated like a foreign slave, but will retain a status like that of wage laborers or resident aliens who, while not full citizens, were nevertheless free men. This improbably supposes that *kĕśākîr kĕtôšāb* is a coordinate phrase in spite of the absence of "and" in Hebrew; hence *NAB*, "Let him be like a hired servant or like your tenant." Rather it means: "The rule among you will be this: Like hireling, like alien," i.e. the hireling is the Israelite who must not be given worse treatment than a free resident alien. The statement is like *kākem kaggēr yihyeh lipnê yhwh* (Num 15:15), viz. the alien is to be under the same regulations as the Israelites — Y is like X (construction 2). Other examples of type (2) are: *kekōhî 'āz ûkĕkōhî 'attâ* (Josh 14:11), "I am just as strong now as I was then," the standard for comparison coming first. *Kahaṭṭā't kā'āšām* (Lev 7:7; Sam reads this at Lev 14:13): the comparison is made in rubrics about the guilt offering, which is to be the same as the sin offering. *Kāmôkā kĕmôhem* (Judg 8:18): "They looked just like you." *Kĕḥēleq hayyōrēd bammilḥāmâ ûkĕḥēleq hayyōšēb 'al-hakkēlîm* (I Sam 30:24): while there is an emphasis on equality (a half-share is mentioned), the principle to be established is that support personnel are to be treated just like combat troops.

Isa 24:2 has a list of six such comparisons, beginning with the one we have in Hos 4:9. If a lender is superior to a borrower, then the inferior person does not always come first (as with slave — master). In any event, the total effect is to emphasize the equality of treatment that all will receive, irrespective of rank, in the day of judgment. These are best classified as type (3). If Lev 25:40 is compared with Exod 12:45, it appears that *tôšāb* and *śākîr* have the same status: both are banned from the Passover rites, since both are non-Israelites. In Josh 8:33 *kaggēr kā'ezrāḥ* means that the resident alien is under the same obligation as the native-born Israelite to participate in the commination ritual. Lev 24:22 specifically says that both follow "the same rule."

The comparative evidence is indecisive. Hos 4:9a seems to be neutral (3), emphasizing equality. In the context, however, it moves toward the sense that the people will be judged in the same manner as the priest. Verse 9a does not necessarily mean that the people and priest will receive the same punishment. It means that both will be punished by applying the same rule (Lev 24:22); the harvest of punishment is like the seed of sin. Although the priest dominates this section, the people are not marginal: their appearance in v 9 is central, balanced by references to their folly (vv 6 and 14) and misguidance (vv 8 and 11).

9b. The bicolon in 4:9b, expounding v 9a, is elegantly constructed, with complete synonymous parallelism and chiasmus. A similar bicolon appears at 12:3; the use of the preposition *k* there shows the flexibility in Hosea's use of the particles, and suggests that their omission is often a feature of his poetry. The text is literally "I shall punish him/it (priest *or* people) for his/its (priest's/people's) ways // I shall requite him/it for his/its deeds." We represent the four-way ambiguity by omitting some pronouns in the translation.

I shall punish each. Compare Hos 1:4; 2:15; Amos 3:14; Zeph 1:8,9,12. The preposition is always *'al.*

requite. With this use of *'āšîb* in parallel with *pqd,* compare its occurrence eight times in Amos 1–2 (1:3,6,9,11,13; 2:1,4,6).

deeds. Hosea often uses the word *ma'ălālîm* (5:4; 7:2; 9:15; 12:3), as does Micah (2:7; 3:4; 7:13).

10a. *They have eaten.* The plural verbs in this verse correspond to those in vv 7–8 (note *y'klw* in v 8 and *w'klw* in v 10) and presumably the subject is the same, the children of the priest, or perhaps the priests generally. So far, in talking about sins and penalties, the verbs have been used for the most part in accordance with classical norms. The things the priest has done are described with perfect forms (*m'st*) or *waw*-consecutive with imperfect forms (*wtškḥ*). The penalties are announced using imperfect forms (*'škḥ*) or *waw*-consecutive with perfect forms (*wpqdty*). In v 10, the negated imperfects are evidently penalties, but the verb *hiznû* is formally past tense while *wě'ākělû* is ambiguous. It is precisely because of this ambiguity that *wě-* plus perfect is usually future, rarely past, as it is here.

In v 8 we suggested that gluttonous and sacrilegious eating on the part of the priests corrupted public worship. Here the consequences of such eating, joined to sexual activity of a cultic nature, are described. The quasi-magical character of contemporary Israelite religion is apparent here. Ceremonial eating was intended to secure abundance of food, but it will have an opposite effect. Ritual intercourse was intended to secure fertility, but won't succeed. Compare 9:14.

Ginsberg (1967:73–74) achieves closer parallelism by translating:

> They shall eat and not be satisfied,
> guzzle and not be slaked.

He finds *zny* "to drink heavily" in v 18b also. It seems better to keep the meaning of the root *zny* constant, in view of its repeated use, and to explain the *Hip'il* (which occurs again in 5:3) as elative rather than causative. Ginsberg does not bend any of the *Qal* forms to this meaning. Prov 3:10 supports our rendering, in the parallelism of *śb'* and *prṣ,* but the roots are used in different senses here.

increase. Literally "break (out)." The meaning of the verb *pāraṣ* was discussed at v 2. When Judah resorted to a prostitute (Gen 38:15), there was "breaking out" in childbirth (Gen 38:29). This meaning, the bursting of the child from the womb, could apply here, or the reference may be to the spreading out of increased population.

10b. *they have deserted Yahweh.* This line and v 12bB may constitute a discontinuous bicolon, with parallelism and chiasm in the positions of verbs and objects, forming an envelope around a unit (vv 11–12bA) which shows how the priest entangled the people in drink, magic, and sex. Note the inverted position of *kî* on the last internal rather than on the opening line of this unit; cf. v 14aB. To desert Yahweh (or his Torah or his covenant) is a common accusation; Elijah's complaint (I Kings 19:10, 14) is typical. In contrast Yahweh does not abandon his covenant-loyalty (Gen 24:27; Ruth 2:20).

The verb *'zbw* is plural, in continuity with the verbs of vv 10a and 7–8. Being perfect, it describes some accomplished sin; vv 10b and 12bB provide the reason and basis for the judgment pronounced in v 10a. The accusation is energetic and climactic. The use of *kî* is significant: as a subordinate conjunction, it links v 10b with the preceding clauses. In addition, it offers a balancing term for *ky* in v 12bA. We notice that, apart from *kî ṭôb ṣillāh* (v 13aB), in which it functions differently, *kî* is used four times at pivotal points in this passage: *kî-'attā* (v 6b) balances *kî-hēm* (v 14b); and v 10b balances v 12bA, which has a singular perfect verb to compare with the plural perfect in the present clause. The intertwined themes of priest and priests continue: v 10b refers to the group, and v 12bA refers to the individual priest.

10b–11a. The end of v 10b is difficult. In MT the verse ends with an infinitive, *lšmr,* "to watch, hold to"; some kind of object seems necessary to complete the meaning. *BH³* and *BHS,* following LXX and many scholars, attach the first word of v 11 ("promiscuity") to the end of v 10. This produces the construction "to keep *zĕnût.*" Since any continuity between *'zbw* and *lšmr* is debatable, it is better to read *lšmr* as the perfect form of the verb, 3 m s, with the emphatic *l* (Dahood and Penar 1970:406). The combination *šmr znwt* does not occur anywhere else, but could be correct, if Hosea is being deliberately bitter. In the Deuteronomic tradition, the usual object of the verb *šmr* is the word or commandment of Yahweh. The "knowledge of God," his Torah (v 6b), has been rejected by the priest, who prefers to observe *zĕnût,* the covenant code of Baal. Thus *lšmr znwt* is similar to *rwḥ znwnym* in v 12b. The spirit of *zĕnûnîm* may be a rival god of Yahweh, and v 12bA is a parallel for v 11a; if a participle of *šmr* is read, then *šmr zĕnût* might be a pejorative name for a god. If we then relate these phrases to the idols mentioned in v 12a, we may have both a male (*šmr znwt = mqlw*) and a female (*rwḥ znwnym = 'ṣw*) deity represented in the passage. The proposed treatment of *šmr,* "he holds to," is supported by the language of Ps 31:7, where "those who keep worthless idols" (Dahood 1966:185, 151) are the opposite of those who trust in Yahweh. See a similar expression, using *Pi'el,* in Jonah 2:9, which, like Hos 4:10, sets "keeping worthless idols" as the counterpart of "deserting their *ḥesed.*" An abstract object of *šmr* is used in Hos 12:7 as well, where deserting Yahweh is matched by returning to Yahweh. Amos 2:4 covers the same range of ideas as Hos 4:6–10. It uses the verbs *m's, šmr,* and *ht'ḥ.* The faithful have integrity (*'ĕmet*), which is lacking in the land. To "keep" *zĕnût* is the principle of disloyalty.

Translating "to practice" or "to revere" would be suitable. If *zĕnût* is not accepted as the object of *lišmōr,* then we must fall back on the MT, and attempt to interpret *'āzĕbû lišmōr* as a compound verb with *'et-yhwh* as object. The awkwardness is apparent in *ASV:* "Because they have left off taking heed to Yahweh." It may be noted, however, that *šmr* is used without an object in Hos 12:13 (cf. Gen 30:31).

11–12. In finding our way through this uncertain terrain there are a few firm footholds. The entire discourse describes the misconduct of the priest and his children. This misconduct in the religious domain involves drunkenness, sexual activity, and divination. We have observed that v 10b (up through *'zbw*) is linked effectively with v 12bB to form an envelope around vv 11–12bA. The subject is evidently the same as for vv 7–8, namely the children of the priest (v 6), or priests generally, represented by the 3 m pl pronominal forms. The intervening material itself forms a block in which there are four verbs which clearly have 3 m s subjects, and a fifth, if *lšmr* is parsed as a *Qal* perfect form with emphatic *l.* In our opinion, the subject of the singular verbs is the priest himself, particularly in vv 11 and 12.

Within this unit, we can detect a pair of parallel cola, v 12a (without *'my,* which belongs with the preceding line): *b'ṣw yš'l // wmqlw ygyd lw.* Moving outward from this pair we find the phrase *yqḥ lb* (*'my*) parallel in sense to *ht'ḥ:*

11b   He takes away my people's heart.
12bA   By a promiscuous spirit he has led them astray.

The pair *wyyn wtyrwš* should be divided between contiguous cola.

In exploring the poetic organization of these lines, a clue is supplied by a principle already established in other parts of this discourse. Singular verbs have "the priest" as their subject, while plural verbs have "the priests." It is "the priest" who makes inquiry by means of his stick and whose staff speaks to him. The priest also is the subject of the singular verbs *yiqqaḥ* and *hit'â.* There is another grammatical principle to be borne in mind: the sparing use of prepositions, with the result that some nouns are to be understood as governed by prepositions, or better, to have adver-

bial functions. So, instead of the usual "must takes away the understanding" (which is sententious and banal), we have "He (the priest)
takes away my people's heart (by means of) must."

The extent of the clause in v 11 is indeterminate. The MT seems to
mean "Prostitution and wine and must (he) will take to heart." The incompleteness of this statement can be remedied by detaching the first
word of the next verse ("my people") to make "the heart of my people"
the object of the verb in v 11 (so LXX). Verse 12 is improved by this ad-
justment of clause boundaries. As we have seen, the first word of v 11 belongs with the end of v 10. This leaves "wine and must" as the apparent
subject of v 11. The verb, however, is singular, but a phrase of two (or
three) coordinated nouns is plural, raising doubts that it is the subject. We
have seen that the change from singular to plural verbs and pronouns consistently marks the change from the priest to the priests as topic. So, in v
11 it is the priest, not wine, that captures the mind of the people. The
priest has gained control of their "heart" by various means. He has kept
them in ignorance, ruining them (v 6), with wine (v 11; cf. 7:5), and by
means of "the spirit of promiscuity" (v 12). The combined use of sex,
magic, and intoxicants in the Baal cult has debauched and degraded the
people, and the priest is responsible for it all (cf. 7:14 and 9:1–2).
Verses 11b and v 12bA are thus closely parallel.

Verse 11 is not a text against alcoholic drinks. To capture the heart is
an act of deception; compare *gnb lb* in Gen 31:20. In Hos 7:11, *lēb* is intelligence, good sense. If v 11 charges the priest with seizing control of the
people's thoughts, it strengthens the case for identifying the priest also as
the implied agent of the passive verb *nidmû* in v 6a. His devices are ignorance (v 6a), sex (vv 10a, 11a, 12b), and magic (v 12a).

12a. *makes inquiry*. The verb *šā'al* with the preposition *b* is used to
describe the search for guidance. In the early days Yahweh himself was
the legitimate object of such inquiry (Judg 1:1; II Sam 2:1). How it was
done is no longer known, but there is evidence that yes/no questions
could be answered by manipulating the ephod, perhaps using the Urim
and Thummim for casting lots (I Sam 14:38–42). In Hos 4:12 someone
is accused of doing this with his Wood or Tree. Since "my people" is attached to v 11, the subject of the verb "inquires" is not stated; since the
verb is singular, it must be the priest.

his Wood. In parallel with the word *maqqēl*, "staff," *'ēṣ* probably refers
to a staff of some kind (Gen 32:11; Num 22:27; I Sam 17:40; Zech
11:7). Any connection with Aaron's rod (Numbers 17) is doubtful, since
the latter is a *maṭṭeh*, a symbol of office for a tribal head. It is unlikely
that Hosea is here accusing a high priest of misusing this sacred object for
magical purposes.

At first sight the bicolon in v 12a is not perfect: *bĕ'ēṣ* is apparently instrumental, but its parallel *maqlô* has no preposition, so it seems to be the subject. Hence the traditional rendering, which we adopt in part: "My people ask counsel at their stock, and their staff declareth unto them" (*ASV*). LXX has already brought the two cola into line, translating both nouns as plural dative of instrument: "by their staffs . . . by their staves. . . ." If this is correct, no change in the text is called for; the preposition does double duty. The traditional reading makes sense, if *bĕ'ēṣô* is the object, not the instrument of the verb. The preposition indicates an instrument in Ezek 21:26, but the god or spirit that makes the reply in Judg 18:5; 20:18; I Sam 14:37; I Chron 10:13: "He asks his Stick, and his Staff reports to him." The usual object of *šā'al* is a god; the usual subject of *higgîd* is a speaker; thus *'ēṣ // maqqēl* is the symbol of a deity. If Ginsberg (1967:74) is correct in his suggestion that the parallel nouns here mean penis, then either the idol was a phallus — or the term is a contemptuous name for a wooden idol. Hosea uses many words for the Canaanite gods, and it seems that the gods of magic are the gods of sex. The form of divination practiced here is not rhabdomancy, or casting of lots with (magic) wands, or listening to the sounds in a tree. The "pole" is the wooden statue of the god; how it might have been supposed to speak we can only guess. Psalm 115 contains a polemic against idols in which their dumbness is given special prominence; statements that they are inarticulate come as an envelope around the list of their deficiencies (vv 5–7). This and Isa 58:1 show that *gārôn* is an organ of speech, "voice box" rather than "gullet." The central issue in Elijah's experiment on Mount Carmel was his disproof of Canaanite belief that Baal could answer with a voice (I Kings 18:26,29). Dussaud connects this belief with the iconographic feature of showing the Adam's apple prominently on statues of the Heliopolitan Jupiter (1920:6), a mythographic descendant of Baal. The oracle may have been uttered as a thunderclap, interpreted by the priest. In Hab 2:11,19, idols are called *'ēṣ* and *'eben,* and the combination of genders suggests male and female deities (cf. Deut 29:16; 32:16), although if the pole is the Asherah and the standing stone is a phallic symbol of Baal, the genders of the names of the materials do not correspond to the genders of the deities.

12b. *spirit.* Hebrew *rûaḥ* is usually feminine, but it is not uncommon for it to be masculine. In v 19 the feminine pronoun ("her wings") refers to a "spirit" which is not otherwise identified; it is probable that these two spirits are the same, to be equated further with *zĕnût* in v 11; *rûaḥ* in v 19 and *zĕnût* in v 11 make the complete phrase. We have already noted that *zĕnût* is best explained as a description of a female deity. But since the verb *hit'â* is masculine ("he caused them to err"), the promiscuous spirit (cf. 5:4) is not its subject unless "spirit" is abnormally masculine, in discord with v 19, or unless two quite different spirits are involved. Isa

19:11–17 throws light on this. The princes of Egypt cause the people to err, "like a drunken man staggering in his vomit." The reason is that Yahweh has sent *rûaḥ 'iw'îm,* "a spirit of vacillation," into their midst. It is not the spirit itself that causes the error; it is the leaders who are possessed by this spirit. The verb in Hos 4:12bA has no object, and LXX has taken it as passive, with "spirit" as an instrumental dative. A few Hebrew MSS add an object "them" in anticipation of v 12bB (see *BHS*). But the true object, in view of the parallelism between v 11 and v 12bA (as pointed out above, the expressions *yqḥ lb* and *ht'h* are equivalent), is "my people," with *rûaḥ zěnûnîm* the instrument. Cf. Ps 95:10; Mic 3:5. It is probable that *tō'ê-rûaḥ* in Isa 29:24, usually taken to mean "those who err in spirit," means "those deluded by a spirit." The phrase matches *'ēšet zěnûnîm* (Hos 1:2), "a promiscuous wife," and points to a spirit that incites or encourages promiscuity.

led . . . astray. The root *t'y* occurs as *Qal* (intransitive) and *Hip'il* (causative). The former means "to go astray, wander aimlessly"; the latter "to lead someone astray." Since a root with an intransitive *Qal* can hardly have a passive *Nip'al,* according to the usual rules, the *Nip'al,* which occurs only twice (Isa 19:14; Job 15:31), is a passive of the *Hip'il,* and has a meaning indistinguishable from *Qal.*

While the verb lends itself to an abstract meaning, describing ethical aberration (Ps 58:4; Prov 7:25; 14:22), in the literal sense it is most commonly associated with drunkenness (Isa 19:14; 21:4; 28:7; Job 12:25). The meanings overlap, and they fit the present context. The verb describes the senseless wanderings of a drunk. The use of this verb to describe straying animals (Exod 23:4; Isa 53:6; Job 38:41; Ps 119:176) suggests that a person who is lost (Gen 21:14; 37:15; Ps 107:4; Isa 47:15) or inebriated (Isa 28:7) is like a mindless beast. The cause is in the loss of the mind ("heart" in Hos 4:11; cf. Isa 47:15). It is possible that the *Hip'il* is an intensive intransitive form in some of its occurrences (Prov 10:17). But it is more likely here, at least, that "the people" is the unspecified object, for the figure of the people straying (Ezek 14:11) or being led astray "like sheep" is described with this verb (Isa 53:6; Jer 50:6). That "the priest" is the subject of *hit'â* is confirmed by widespread evidence that the prophets held the priesthood responsible for the state of the nation (Amos 2:4; Ezek 44:10,15; 48:11; along with prophets, Isa 28:7).

act promiscuously. The verb is masculine, and as such should perhaps be repointed as *Hip'il* in line with v 10aB. Hosea uses several prepositions with the verb *zny.* The idiom *zny mittaḥat,* literally "to behave promiscuously out from under," is strange, but is found also in Ezek 23:5 (cf. Num 5:19). Wolff (1974:85) compares it with *pš' mittaḥat,* "to rebel out from under," and sees in the choice of the preposition here "the rebellious betrayal of an obligatory relationship of obedience and submission," something much stronger than "from behind" in Hos 1:2. The preposition could be used here in anticipation of v 13.

13a. *make sacrifice . . . burn incense.* It is not clear whether this verse describes "the practice of the fertility rites of the Baal cult in the worship of Yahweh" (Waterman 1955:103), or the Baal cult itself, with conscious repudiation of Yahweh. The verbs used here occur in the same sequence in 11:2, where idols of Baal are the objects of worship. In 2:15, the burning of incense is the only act of worship directed to the Baals; 4:14b completes the picture, citing "sacrifice" in the company of cult prostitutes. A detailed study of the stock phrases used here has been made by Holladay (1961). The plurals show that these are the activities of the priests and, following v 12bB, they are the result of deserting Yahweh. In this we agree with Wolff, who, however, thinks that vv 13b–14a apply to Israelite fathers in general (1974:85). We hold that the plural subject is the same throughout, namely the children of the high priest, perhaps extended here and elsewhere to the entire Israelite priesthood.

13b. *Under oaks, poplars, and terebinths.* Another list of three items. The singular nouns are collective. While a location under various green trees is commonly connected with pagan worship on mountain tops, two distinct activities were involved. Amos 2:8 suggests that ritual sex could take place "beside the altar," but the offering of sacrifices and incense seems to be distinct from ceremonial intercourse, which took place under trees. Hence v 13bA goes better with v 14a than with v 13a, as it is usually taken. The preposition points to prostitution rather than sacrifice as the activity in the arboreta. The anomalous order, with the location (v 13aB) before the activity (v 14aB), is not unusual in Hosea.

whose shade. Literally "her shade," the pronoun taking its gender from that of the last noun. It is true that oak, poplar, and terebinth are among the best shade trees in Palestine, but this would be a banal, if practical, reason for having ritual sex there. Does this reference to shade show that the rites were performed on hot sunny days, rather than at night, as is sometimes suggested? The image of worshipers going off into thickets around the sanctuaries, as if the attendant measure of privacy showed the preservation of a little dignity, is dubious. We do not know the details, or the reasons for them.

13bB–14a. This unit of two well-formed and closely interconnected bicola stands apart from the rest of the discourse. It contains the only 2 m pl pronouns in the chapter, and the only references to daughters and brides. The lines are long compared with the remainder of the chapter (forty-one syllables rather than the thirty-two common in other four-line units in Hosea 4). It interrupts the development of the theme. Whether v 13bA is connected with v 13a or with v 14a, vv 13a and 14bA describe the activities of men, and vv 13b–14a, which refer to the activities of women, come in the middle of that description. Furthermore, the conjunction "therefore" does not adequately join v 13a and v 13b. The involvement of the men in the cult is not the reason why the daughters and brides commit adultery, unless these women are the same as the "harlots" and "cult prostitutes" mentioned in v 14b. This is possible: the cult provided the means for Israelite men and women to be promiscuous together. But the terminology of vv 13 and 14 suggests that the men resort to the female prostitutes of the cult shrines and the women commit adultery with male counterparts. In recognizing vv 13b–14a as a distinct and self-contained block, dealing with two groups not dealt with elsewhere in c 4 (the daughters and brides and their fathers and fathers-in-law, called "you"), we do not mean to suggest that it does not belong there and should be removed. Its distinctiveness should not be blurred by normalizing the second-person suffixes to third person (Ginsberg 1967:74).

The apparent meaning of MT, which excuses the women from punishment (v 14a) because the men are entirely to blame (v 14b), is hard to fit into context. In fact, the apparent negative at the beginning of v 14 is unaccountable. The verb *pqd* is always used by Hosea to announce divine punishment (1:4b; 2:15; 4:9b). It is inconceivable that the women could be exculpated, even if the men were primarily responsible. The problem could be solved by taking v 14aA as a rhetorical question — "Shall I not punish . . . ?" The preceding word ends in -*h* which could be supplied also before *lō'*, either by repairing a haplography, or by *scriptio continua*. Alternatively the *l'* could be asseverative, a solution which we prefer; the particle may be *l* here, if the ' is a dittograph.

13b. *daughters-in-law*. A *kallâ* is strictly a bride, but, in parallel with "daughters," it is more likely to be sons' brides. No distinction should be made between "daughters" (who are promiscuous) and "daughters-in-law" (who commit adultery). The parallels are mutually defining; the *zĕnût* // *zĕnûnîm* that is going on here is the kind of promiscuity that involves a married woman in adultery. The imperfect verbs used in vv 13 and 14 point to habitual activity on the part of both men and women. Wolff (1974:86–87) suggests that the supposed negative in v 14a ("I shall not punish") shows that the women were exempt because they were forced by custom to do this, and then only once in a lifetime. The indirect way in which the sin of these women is condemned gives a further clue. They are not directly accused or threatened; the remarks are addressed to their fathers. It is because they are the daughters of a particular person that their activities are so wicked. The concern of the entire chapter is the wickedness of the priest and his corruption of his sons, and how he and they lead the people astray and ruin them. In warning Israel against pagan cults, Lev 19:29 warns against profaning one's daughter by making her a prostitute, "lest the land be promiscuous" (cf. Hos 1:2). The peril would seem to have been greatest in the case of a priest's daughter, suggesting that this warning was directed against Canaanite custom. Lev 21:9 not only prescribes the penalty of burning for a priest's daughter who is a prostitute; it gives as a reason that she "profanes her father" by doing so. The attention given to the behavior of daughters and daughters-in-law in vv 13b–14aA can be seen as more serious if they are all priests' relatives. The marriage patterns within priestly families meant that there was less likelihood that a married woman moved out of her father's authority into her husband's family.

14b. *They.* The words *kî hēm* match the *kî 'attâ* of v 6b. Verse 14b resumes discourse about the priests, confirming that vv 13b–14a are parenthetical. After the interlude of the priest's daughters, v 14b returns to the behavior of the men, already partly described in v 13a. The language of v 14b makes it clear that promiscuity and sacrifice were part of a full-scale cult. The form *yĕpārēdû* is the only *Pi'el* of its root (there is a *Pu'al* in Esth 3:8). The *Pi'el* is preferred because of parallelism with *qṭr*. The action involved is somewhat obscure (cf. Weider 1965). The terms *zōnôt* and *qĕdēšôt* are mutually defining; they refer to cult prostitutes, women who participate fully in the cult. The articles with the nouns make them almost titles. *Prd,* in parallel with *zbḥ,* could refer to some technicality of the cult. The *Nip'al* of the verb usually means "to separate one from the other," while the *Hitpa'el* describes the dismembering of a slaughtered animal. The sacrificial act may involve dismembering (the bones of) the slaughtered victim (cf. Pss 22:15; 92:10; Job 4:11; 41:9). In II Sam 1:23, *niprādû* means that Saul and Jonathan were not separated in life or death (cf. Ruth 1:17); a similar meaning here would be that men separate from their wives to cohabit with prostitutes. But the *Nip'al* does not settle the meaning of the *Pi'el*. The usual interpretation is that the men go off by themselves in the company of prostitutes, which suggests a more private activity than would occur if the coupling was ceremonial in the context of a public liturgy. In Hos 11:2, some of the verbs used in 4:13 describe the worship of idols.

Keeping in mind the way plural nouns are used to refer to false gods, and noting that the feminine plural "heifers" (Hos 10:5) could refer to the female deity, we can ask whether the language of 4:14 connotes the worship of Baal's female counterpart, called *zōnôt // qĕdēšôt*. The use of the preposition *'im* suggests, however, that they are fellow worshipers.

A people without discernment. The use of *'am,* "people," here joins several references to "my people" (4:6,12), and "the people" (9a). The noun has no article or suffix because it is modified by the following clause "does not discern." The use of the singular of *ylbṭ* and *l'-ybyn* is a deviation from *ndmw* in v 6, but this reflects the ambiguity of the noun *'am* which is collective, and therefore can be construed with either singular or plural verbs. Deut 4:6 boasts that Israel is the wisest and most discerning of people, and the envy of the entire world, because they possess the statutes of Yahweh. When this knowledge is rejected, the people will come to ruin. Ruin is the fate of the foolish talker in the two other places where the verb *ylbṭ* occurs (Prov 10:8,10). This proverb does not make the meaning of the verb any clearer, but it suggests that this line, which is rhythmical and alliterative, is part of a Wisdom saying; this might account for the singular number of the verb, as "people," usually without the article, always has a singular verb in Proverbs. Note especially *'am lō'-'āz* (Prov 30:25) and *'am lō'-'āṣûm* (Prov 30:26).

15. None of the reported attempts to improve this verse by excising or rewriting troublesome words is convincing. One expedient comes from LXX, which translated vv 14b–15aA as "and the people, which does not understand, has entangled itself with a prostitute," reading *'im* rather than *'im*, "if," at the beginning of v 15. LXX read the continuation of v 15 differently also, redistributing the verbs and subjects. It confirms the existence in the text of "Judah," the word which causes most trouble to modern critics, especially if they consider favorable references to the southern kingdom to be the work of later redactors. The abrupt change from second person for Israel to third person for Judah, while grammatically difficult, has a precedent in the opening lines of Deuteronomy 32, which has many affinities with Hosea; v 2 reads *ha'ăzînû haššāmáyim . . . wĕtišma' hā'āreṣ,* "Give ear, heavens . . . and let the earth listen."

In spite of the changes in person and number, v 15 does display some coherence, in the parallelism of the nations and of the cities. The entire nation is the people of God, and northern and southern kingdoms are usually together in Hosea's mind. The two cult sites he names were ancient national (not just tribal) shrines, conveniently situated in the middle of the country where people in both kingdoms would have access to them. Gilgal was the first important campsite west of Jordan (Josh 5:9). Hosea regards it as an evil place (9:15; 12:12), as does Amos (4:4; 5:5). The importance of Bethel goes back to the Jacob traditions, which Hosea knows and uses. Pilgrimage festivals are involved, since it is going (up) to these places that is forbidden. It was at these assemblies (2:13) that the activities of vv 13–14 took place.

15a. *"You . . . are not a prostitute."* This line, introduced by the oath particle *'m,* is the first of two oaths forbidden in v 15b; it would have been spoken by the priest's children. This is the only place where Israel as such is called a prostitute (or perhaps pimp); the rare masculine participle agrees with the gender of the pronoun.

be held guilty. Often when Hosea uses this verb (here and in 10:2; 13:1; 14:1), it carries with it a threat of punishment. Here it is part of a judgment of Judah's innocence which the priest's sons are forbidden to make. The sins enumerated in v 2 were crimes against people; *'āšām* is guilt in relation to God, especially in cult matters. To go to Bethel or Gilgal was to incur such guilt; to refrain from going would remove it.

15b. *Beth Awen.* Literally, "House of Wickedness"; probably a surrogate for Bethel, "House of God." The persons called *pō'ălê-'āwen,* "doers of iniquity," referred to fifteen times in the Psalter, and several times elsewhere, were probably "idol manufacturers," who violated the second commandment by making an image. Many scholars have seen in the phrase a reference to magicians casting spells. This meaning is not incompatible with idolatry, since magical power would be attributed to such objects, especially the figurines of the naked goddess that were produced in such quantity as talismans of the religions of the ancient Near East. Abstract names like *'āwen* are often used for concrete objects, and so the name may mean "House of (the) Idol(s)." It is possible that Amos was originally responsible for this change in an ancient and honorable name, for he warned that "Bethel shall become *Awen"* (5:5). Bethel was one of the places where Jeroboam I had set up the golden calves, causing all Israel to sin (I Kings 12), a constant target of prophetic assault (I Kings 13). By the time of Amos it had become the major center for the kind of worship which the prophet disapproved (Amos 3:14; 4:4; 5:5 bis,6; 7:10,13). It competed with the political capitals as a national center, and had acquired the status of "the king's sanctuary," that is, it was the location of the royal chapel which wedded the monarchy to the priesthood and gave the royal family the legitimation of religion (Amos 7:13). Hence speech against this shrine was both blasphemy and treason (Amos 7:10). Hosea shares with Amos outrage at what has happened to this place; he calls the place Bethel twice (10:15; 12:5), and Beth Awen three times (4:15; 5:8; 10:5).

swear. Although the last line has no parallel, it rounds out the two preceding bicola. Just as v 15bA warns against going to either of the popular shrines, so v 15bB prohibits the making of the specified oaths using the formula "Life of Yahweh" or "(as) Yahweh lives." There is no categorical ban on oaths (Jer 4:2; 38:16). The right use of the name of Yahweh in making legitimate and honest oaths was one of the privileges of the faithful Israelite (Deut 6:13; 10:20). Here we must suppose that false use of the formal oath is involved (cf. Jer 7:9 and Hos 4:2). "By the life of Yahweh" is not the oath itself, but the protective invocation of deity as guardian of the oath. The oath proper traditionally begins with *'im,* an emphatic negative. Jer 4:2; 12:16; Isa 45:23; 48:1 show how seriously other prophets regarded perjury in the name of Yahweh. Compare I Sam 24:22; I Kings 1:51; I Sam 17:55 (a denial); after "by the life of Yahweh" (I Kings 18:10).

False use of the oath of clearance, denying guilt, is the opposite of repentance. It is stubbornness (4:16), the false swearing denounced in 4:2.

16–19. This difficult unit may be analyzed into subsections in the following manner:

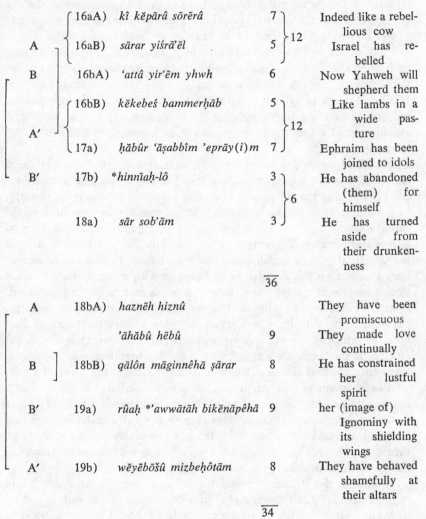

A	16aA)	kî kĕpārâ sōrērâ	7 ⎱ 12	Indeed like a rebellious cow
	16aB)	sārar yiśrā'ēl	5 ⎰	Israel has rebelled
B	16bA)	'attâ yir'ēm yhwh	6	Now Yahweh will shepherd them
A'	16bB)	kĕkebeś bammerḥāb	5 ⎱ 12	Like lambs in a wide pasture
	17a)	ḥābûr 'ăṣabbîm 'eprāy(i)m	7 ⎰	Ephraim has been joined to idols
B'	17b)	*hinnīaḥ-lô	3 ⎱ 6	He has abandoned (them) for himself
	18a)	sār sob'ām	3 ⎰	He has turned aside from their drunkenness

                                                  36

A	18bA)	haznēh hiznû		They have been promiscuous
		'āhăbû hēbû	9	They made love continually
B	18bB)	qālôn māginnêhā ṣārar	8	He has constrained her lustful spirit
B'	19a)	rûaḥ *'awwātāh bikĕnāpêhā	9	her (image of) Ignominy with its shielding wings
A'	19b)	wĕyēbōšû mizbeḥôtām	8	They have behaved shamefully at their altars

                                                  34

In spite of the best efforts of many scholars, this passage remains obscure and difficult. To date the only way to make sense of the unit has been to engage in extensive emendations, which are a tribute to scholarly ingenuity but leave serious questions about the validity of the changes and the intention of the original author. On the other hand, efforts to retain the MT, or at least the consonantal Hebrew text, result in strained and dubious renderings and interpretations. Trapped between these undesirable alternatives, we have kept alterations at a minimum and at the same time have attempted to indicate the lines along which progress may be achieved. We have pointed to linkages of different kinds, structural patterns and other details which tend to support the transmitted text, and encourage us to examine existing possibilities with renewed attention.

The unit as a whole may be divided as above into two major parts: vv 16–18a, and vv 18b–19. These are about equal in length, and each may be further analyzed into four subsections, organized along familiar lines. Part I reflects an interlocking sequence in which the A sections (vv 16a, 16bB–17a, each 12 syllables, divided 7 + 5 and 5 + 7) describe the behavior of Israel and Ephraim, while the B sections (vv 16bA,17b–18a, 6 syllables each) reflect the response, actual or expected, of Yahweh to this behavior.

Essentially the A units describe the character and activity of the sinful nation in terms of a pair of similes: Israel is rebellious, like a rebellious cow; Ephraim is associated with idols like a flock of lambs in the country. In the former example, the equation is established by the repetition of the verbal root *srr* "to be stubborn, rebellious." In the latter case, the comparison is less obvious. The argument for the proposed analysis is based on the structural pattern and the inherent parallelism. If Israel is compared with a cow, then the association of Ephraim with a lamb, more likely a flock, seems reasonable. Then, too, if Israel is in rebellion against God, Ephraim's involvement with idols seems apposite. In what way, however, can association with idols be compared with lambs in the country? Perhaps the principal point of contact, and generally only one is needed or indicated, is that both are examples of collective brainlessness: idolatry is often characterized as essentially stupid, and idolators are mocked as devoid of common as well as theological sense. Similarly sheep without a shepherd, like a stubborn cow, mill around aimlessly; cf. Jer 2:23. There is another reason for linking the two phrases (vv 16bB and 17a) and that is the apparent wordplay of *bmrḥb* and *ḥbwr* involving the use of the same three consonants in the roots of both words. Such a device would alert the hearer to the connection between the parts.

Turning to the B lines, we find the initial clause, "Now Yahweh will shepherd them," fairly clear, though the exact force of the verb is subject to debate. Here it must be minatory (as in Mic 5:5), since a mood of judgment pervades the entire unit. When we attempt to link this clause with the closing bicolon, vv 17b–18a, difficulties emerge. If we correctly understand the 3 m pl suffix attached to *yr'm* to refer to Israel/Ephraim, then we may interpret the suffix with *sb'm* in the same way. This would help to establish Yahweh as the subject of the verbal form *sār* and also of *hnh* in the parallel clause. The latter, *hnh-lw*, is so brief that any attempt at interpretation must be tentative and to a certain extent guesswork. The

MT pointing of the verb as imperative hardly seems in place since other-wise all verb forms throughout the passage are in the third person. If we read it as a 3 m s perfect form, *hinnîah,* it would conform to the other verbs. In view of *sr* "to turn aside," *hnh* can then be understood as "to leave, abandon." The accompanying *lw* presumably serves as an ethical dative, referring back to the subject; the 3 m pl suffixes are used for the two nations. The syntax of *sr sb'm* is not clear, but since the *Qal* form of *swr* is not transitive, we must suppose that *(sb')m* is an indirect object. The implied preposition is *min.* There is a tension between the theme of abandonment in the second unit, and the emphasis on "shepherding" in the first *(yr'm)*; we retain the pastoral nuance only because of the similes involving domestic animals. In this case, the shepherd is going to attack and destroy his recalcitrant flock. Nevertheless, the resulting picture is not entirely satisfactory.

When we advance to the second half of the section, vv 18b–19, we note a shift to 3 m pl verb forms. The immediate antecedent would be the two nations mentioned in vv 16–17, but there is reason to believe that the poet has rather in mind the priests who have figured prominently in the chapter thus far.

The opening words (*hznh hznw*) not only define the nature of the love mentioned next (*'hbw hbw*) as sexual and cultic, but evoke major emphases of the preceding units (vv 10–15), and point to the priests as subject, without exculpating the nation as a whole. Part A (v 18bA) is connected with A' (v 19b), which closes the unit, by the common 3 m pl verb forms and the content: the shameful behavior at the altars is the ac-tivity stressed in v 18bA, cultic sex under the auspices of the ecclesiastical establishment. A literal rendering of the MT of v 19b yields: "And they will be (*or* let them be) ashamed of their sacrifices"; but the supposed f pl of *zebah* can hardly be justified. It is more likely that future repentance is not in view here, but present indictment — namely that verb *ybšw* refers not to "being ashamed" but "committing shameful acts." Normally the lat-ter sense is expressed by the *Hip'il* form (cf. Hos 2:7), while the former is expressed by the *Qal.* That would require repointing of MT to *wayyābîšû,* but it may be that the *Qal* also can sustain this sense. The following word is much more likely to be the normal f pl of *mizbēah* "altar" than a unique f pl of *zebah* "sacrifice." The missing preposition *min* before the word can be explained in one of two ways: (1) scribal error, haplography of initial *mem;* or (2) the deliberate omission of the preposition, a charac-teristic feature of Hosea's prophecy. This propensity of the poet compli-cates analysis and interpretation but must be acknowledged.

The remaining segment, B–B' (vv 18bB,19a), is one of the most ob-scure and difficult passages in Hosea. The introduction of 3 f s forms is un-usual, the meaning and connection between "shields" and "wings" are un-certain at best, the verb *srr* has a variety of possible meanings, none of which seems entirely suitable in the context; in fact, even the general sense is elusive, and the relation of *rwḥ* and *'wth* to each other and the rest of the sentence is not at all clear.

The subject of the 3 m s verb *ṣārar* is Yahweh (cf. v 16bA); the action threatened is a punishment of the nation, including its priests, for the misbehavior described particularly in v 17 (the association with idols). The word *qālôn*, "ignominy, shame," is used not only to describe the shame and ignominy which will befall the nation but has clearly defined sexual connotations and is used in Nah 3:5 and Jer 13:26 of the exposed genitals of the disgraced woman who symbolizes the nation through its capital city (respectively Nineveh, Jerusalem). We assume that the *qālôn* is related to the *rwḥ 'wth;* we interpret the latter as *rûaḥ 'awwātāh* "her spirit of desire, her lustful appetite." The reading *'awwātāh,* based on the consonantal text, is to be preferred to MT *'ôtāh,* "herself," because the sign of the definite direct object with pronouns is not common in Hebrew poetry and is rare in the poetic parts of Hosea. In addition, the full spelling *'wt* is also unusual, and is limited for the most part to later sections of the Bible. (In the pre-exilic minor prophets, *'ōt* occurs seven times and *'ôt* four times.) The remaining words, *mgnyh,* "her shield," and *bknpyh,* "with her wings (skirts)," are linked by the common 3 f s suffix, and form a combination, "with her shielding wings." The pronominal suffix seems to refer to *rwḥ,* the only feminine noun anywhere nearby, which we have linked with *qālôn* as descriptive of a statue or image of a goddess (cf. *sml hqn'h* in Ezek 8:3,5). We visualize such an image as combining armorial and sexual features; representations of the goddess Anat include such aspects in a variety of combinations (see the examples in Pope 1977). Whether the image had wings or flowing robes in not clear. We may render vv 18bB–19a: "The (image of) Ignominy (with) its shields, / He has restrained the spirit of its appetites with its wings (or skirts)." We may put them together in a more tolerable fashion: "He has constrained the lustful spirit of Ignominy with its shielding wings."

In the 3 f s forms in this verse there may be a distant echo of the condemnation of the mother of the high priest in 4:5. Perhaps she was seen as the guiding evil genius behind the corruption of the priest and the nation, much as in an earlier period Jezebel in the north and Athaliah in the south were seen in such roles.

16a. *like a rebellious cow.* Ephraim is called an *'eglâ,* "heifer," in 10:11. The choice of *pārâ* seems to have been influenced by a desire to secure assonance; the consonant *r* occurs six times in the line. The simple animal comparison, typical of Hosea, shows that he is close to the Wisdom tradition; see the NOTE on v 14b. The repeated root *srr,* "stubborn," recalls the *bēn sôrēr* of Deut 21:18, who is to be stoned. Compare *'am sôrēr* (Isa 65:2), *dôr sôrēr* (Ps 78:8).

16b. (*shepherd*) *them*. The plural pronoun is not inconsistent with the suffixes preceding. The singular suffixes refer to Israel or Ephraim separately, while the plural identify both of them together. It is also possible to retain the *mem* as part of the verb, and look for another root. This becomes part of a wider question, since the kindly meaning that "to shepherd" usually has does not fit the judgmental mood of this passage, or of Mic 5:5, in which the future rulers of Israel "will shepherd Assyria with the sword." While "to shepherd" could mean "to rule" in this passage, some more hostile action may be required; hence the traditional interpretation "to graze bare" in judgment. In Jer 6:3, shepherds make destructive inroads on a desolated countryside, and in Ps 80:14 judgment turns the land into pasture for wild beasts (cf. Isa 7:23–25; Hos 2:14). Since the usual object of *rāʿâ* is the flock, not the pasture, we must ask if Hosea is concealing some sinister second meaning beneath this familiar verb. It is only in a metaphorical sense that *rāʿâ*, "to graze," can mean "to shave bare" in Jer 2:16 (cf. Gen 3:15b). Wolff (1974:72) seeks to reverse the pleasantness of v 16b by reading it as a question to which the answer is No; this has been followed by *NAB*. Quite apart from the lack of explicit interrogation in the clause, the usual precative function of ʿattâ would seem to rule out a question.

The root presents other possibilities: (a) **yarʿēm*, "he will thunder," a hostile action of the storm god, root *rʿm;* (b) *yārîʿēm*, "he will raise a shout of war (or triumph) against them," root *rwʿ;* (c) *yrʿm*, "he will harm them," root *rʿʿ;* (d) *yĕrōʿēm*, "he will smash them (on the skull with a mace)," root *rʿʿ;* as in Ps 2:9. If the word was originally one of these, it has been attracted to the "shepherd" of the MT by the animal husbandry images used in the context. Hosea may have intended a play on words, but there is no firm evidence for it. All in all, the meaning "to shepherd" with sinister connotation is preferred.

wide pasture. This traditional rendering, which fits in with "shepherd" and "lamb," has been questioned. Kuhnigk (1974:50–53), following Dahood (1966:111), gives *merḥab* the meaning of "vast territory" (of the netherworld); as such it has no necessary connotation of pasture. In Hab 1:6 (cf. Job 38:18), the word means simply an unconfined space. But it seems to us that the idea that Yahweh will "shepherd them like a lamb" in the pastures of Sheol is somewhat farfetched.

17a. *joined to idols*. The traditional rendering used here supposes a meaning such as "to associate" for *ḥbr*. This interpretation must solve several problems. Why is the familiar *ḥābēr*, "associate," not used? The variant could be dialectal; cf. *ḥubura*, a West Semitic loanword into Egyptian, the designation of a flotilla of ships banded together for mutual protection (Albright 1965:482–483 n 80; cf. Malamat 1962). Why is the passive participle used? Or, if the identification of *ḥābûr* as passive participle is not accepted, could it be a noun in the construct state? The *nomen rectum* of a passive participle in the construct state is normally the subject of the verbal activity. Hos 4:17 is the only occurrence of this passive participle. Any connection with Hebrew *ḥeber-ḥābēr* would seem unusual, for these words emphasize the identity in status of the companions (cf. Akkadian *ibru*, "peer"). The existence in Ugaritic of two roots, *ḥbr* and *ḫbr*, opens other possibilities (Finkelstein 1956). In Hebrew itself a word like *ḥabbûrâ*, "wound," and the association of *ḥbr* with weaving point to further possibilities, including the weaving of sounds in speech or music (Pope 1973:122). In Deut 18:11 and Ps 58:6, the verb describes the binding of people by the weaving of spells, or the tying of magic knots. Note that Isa 1:23 associates *sōrĕrîm* (cf. *sōrērâ* in Hos 4:16) with *ḥabrê gannābîm*. Ephraim has been captivated by idols, a statement similar to those in vv 11 and 12; those who meddle with magic are trapped by it. The spirit of harlotry, of magic, of idolatry is seen in various guises throughout c 4 (cf. once more Isa 47:9–11). In v 12, the object of idolatry is the female principle; here it is the male, *'ăṣabbîm*, Baal.

idols. The singular is used only in Jer 22:28, where it refers to (Je-) Coniah ben Jehoiakim. Otherwise the plural is used (I Sam 31:9; II Sam 5:21). Like other plurals in Hosea, *bĕ'ālîm, mĕ'ahăbîm, 'ăgālôt*, which refer to heathen deities, the word imitates *'ĕlōhîm*, "God," and may mean just one pagan god, namely Baal. In Hos 13:2 *'ăṣabbîm* and *'ăgālîm*, "calves," occur (cf. 8:4); the reference is to the bull calf (8:5,6).

18a. *He has turned aside.* The words *sār sob'ām* are difficult. Since the rest of the verse is a little clearer, the Masoretes isolated the first two words as if they were a complete clause. *BH³* joins them to v 17, but the suffixes "him" and "them" collide unless, as we contend, *lô* is an ethical dative rather than a direct object. All translations betray guesswork. Some kind of reference to intoxication seems to be involved, because the noun *sōbe'*, "drink," perhaps "beer," seems to be present. This could be a reference to the notorious drunkenness of Ephraim/Samaria at this time, portrayed so vividly by Isaiah 28. The participle of *sābā'*, "to drink to excess," is used in Ezek 23:42 to describe the men who resort to the harlot-wife Oholibah; the orthography is a problem. The participle is attested in Prov 23:20,21, where it describes the habitual drunkard. The suffixed form occurs only here and in Nah 1:10. It makes textual scholars unhappy at both places. Nah 1:10 also has an apparent passive participle. Isa 56:12 contains the only occurrence of the verb proper. Deut 21:20 offers the clearest parallels to Hos 4:18. Isa 1:22–23 and 11:13 have much of the same vocabulary, with similar wordplay.

We have seen already that Hosea continually uses phrases which we find in Deuteronomy. Israel is Yahweh's "son" (Hos 11:1). Israel is *sōrēr,* "stubborn" (Hos 4:16). The charge in Deut 21:20 reads:

běnēnû zeh sōrēr ûmōreh	This our son is stubborn and a rebel
'ênennû šōmēaʿ běqōlēnû	(he doesn't heed our voice),
zôlēl wěsōbē'	a glutton and a drunk.

It may be that *sr sb'm* contains an accusation echoing this. Compare *sar wězāʿēp,* "sullen and resentful" (I Kings 20:43; 21:4), and *sārê sôrěrîm,* "the most stubborn of the stubborn" (Jer 6:28), for evidence of the shorter form of *srr.* The root here, however, is probably *swr,* "to turn aside." There does not seem to be any basis for the traditional "to sour," and little for "to come to an end."

18b. *They have been promiscuous.* The *Hipʿil* is preferred for masculine subjects. The plurals take us back to the priests in vv 6–14, especially vv 13a and 14a. The combination of drunkenness and sexual licentiousness is present in Genesis 9 and Ezekiel 23, where many associated ideas and some of the same vocabulary are met.

they have made love. Hosea uses the root *'hb* in a good sense to describe the divine love (Hos 11:1; see NOTES on 3:1), and also for immoral sexual activity. The unique *'hbw hbw* is not readily explained, since *hb* as a biconsonantal byform of *'hb* is not otherwise known, and prima-*'alep* verbs do not develop in this way. Note also, however, that the root *'mr,* "see," in Ugaritic has developed an alloform *mr,* so *hb* from Hebrew *'hb* would be both reasonable and appropriate. *Sār sobʿām* and *haznēh hiznû* provide rhythmic parallels. The grammatical analogies are less evident. It is possible that a single word should be read, a coinage of Hosea's made by reduplicating the last two consonants (*Peʿalʿal*) along the lines of *naʿăpûpîm* (Hos 2:4). In any case, an elative meaning is probably intended. Compare *yopyāpîtā* in Ps 45:3 (Dahood 1966:271).

VI. THE STATE OF THE NATION: THE LEADERS' PROFANITY
(5:1–7)

An address to the leaders
5:1a Hear this, priests!
        Pay attention, house of Israel!
        House of the king, give heed!
  1b This verdict applies to you.
        You have become a trap for Mizpah
        and a net spread on Tabor.
  2a The rebels are deep in slaughter.
  2b I am a chastisement to them all.

The effects of their sins
  3a I know you, Ephraim.
        Israel cannot hide from me.
  3b Now you, Ephraim, have been promiscuous.
        You, Israel, are defiled.

A description of the leaders
  4a Their deeds do not permit them to return to their God.
  4b A promiscuous spirit is in their midst
        and Yahweh they do not know.

Further effects of their sins
  5a Israel's pride will testify against it.
  5b Israel and Ephraim will stumble in their iniquity.
        Judah will stumble with them.
  6a With their flocks and herds they will go to seek Yahweh.
  6b But they will not find him. He has withdrawn from them.
  7a Against Yahweh they have been traitorous.
        They have engendered foreign children.
  7b Now he will eat their property at the New Moon.

NOTES

5:1–7. Chapter 5 grows out of c 4 and continues most of its themes. Its opening invocation (5:1) is typical of the commencement of a confrontation in legal dispute, like 4:1–3. Accusations are made, punishments are threatened. In c 4, attention is largely focused on one priest and his family. In c 5, as in 4:16–19, the whole nation comes into view. The northern kingdom is in the center of the picture, but "house of Israel" (5:1) could mean all Israel. The priests and "house of the king" (5:1) are probably those of the northern kingdom; but the reference to Judah in v 5 should not be deleted.

The vocabulary of cc 1–4 continues to be used. Chapter 4 and 5:1–7 have much in common: "the spirit of promiscuity," the verb *hiznâ*, "to act promiscuously," and the verb *kšl*, "to stumble." The forbidden oath of 4:15 finds a counterpart in *ky 'th hznyt 'prym*, "Now you have been promiscuous, Ephraim" (5:3). The sequence *yhwh . . . 'lhyhm* in 4:10–12 is balanced by the same terms in chiastic order: *'lhyhm . . . yhwh* in 5:4.

The situation in 5:1–7 seems to be later than that in c 4, though neither can be dated specifically. According to v 6 "they" continue to do what was prohibited in 4:15, to seek Yahweh in the festivals (5:6). The charge that they do not know Yahweh (4:1,6) is extended: they have behaved treacherously (5:7). The word *ma'ălālîm*, "deeds," is used in both 4:9 and 5:4; in the latter, they prevent the leaders from returning to their God (cf. 3:5). The imperative *šim'û* in 5:1 (as in 4:1) begins a new oracle, the termination of which at v 7 is shown by the imperative verb that begins v 8.

The changes in the use of the pronouns in 5:1–7 seem bewildering. They create an impression of such incoherence that continuous discourse cannot be recognized. The verses are often taken as a congeries of prophetic utterances, many of them authentic, but related only loosely by general themes. Without denying that there are serious difficulties, we suggest that some measure of integrity can be discerned once we recognize Hosea's characteristic procedures. In c 2, his speech alternated between mother and children, with corresponding changes in the pronouns. It also fluctuated between second and third person, while Yahweh as speaker used first or third person to refer to himself. The same fluctuation occurs in c 4: Yahweh is "I" or "he"; the priest is addressed as "you" or "he"; the sons of the priest or priests generally are "you" or "they." The use of singular and plural is generally consistent, in a pattern in which two strands of discourse are woven together.

The opening address to the priests, house of Israel, and house of the king, all as "you" (pl) is sustained in the accusation of v 1b, but no further. In vv 2 and 3 Yahweh speaks as "I," whereas in vv 4–7 he is "Yahweh," or "their God," and the verbs are third person. It is therefore possible that vv 4–7 are not the direct speech of Yahweh, but the prophet's exposition; in the mode of prophetic discourse, this could be a distinction without a difference. Although vv 2 and 3 have the first-person speaker in common, they differ in other pronouns. The shift from second to third person suggests that Yahweh is speaking about the leaders, rather than to them, in v 2. Since he addresses Ephraim in v 3, the same audience may be assumed for v 2; so, then, he is talking *to* the people *about* the priests and the royal family. In vv 5–7, all the pronouns are third person, the people being referred to mostly as "they." There do not seem to be any remarks about the priests or the royal family in this portion. But v 5a refers to Israel as "he" and Judah is "he" in v 5bB. This agrees with the singular forms in v 3. Otherwise the plurals in vv 5–7 refer to the whole people, or to be more precise, the kingdoms. If "Israel," "Ephraim," and "Judah" are generally singular alone, and plural only in combination, we need to ask if the plural verb *yikkāšĕlû* in v 5 is plural because Israel and Ephraim are synonyms, and each is plural, or because Israel and Ephraim are different, and the coordination phrase is plural. The latter, which is far more likely, would reflect a time when the northern kingdom had been divided into two political entities — Israel and Ephraim; Judah (v 5bB) is a third part "with them." In v 3 also Ephraim and Israel would not be synonymous parallels, but complementary political units. Israel designates the east bank of the Jordan, the Gileadite area which was first annexed by Assyria; and Ephraim refers to the west bank area which remained under Samaria's control.

The independent pronouns, which were so useful as guides through the structure of cc 2–4, are little used in 5:1–7. In fact, only *'ny,* "I," occurs, twice (vv 2 and 3). Hos 5:1–7 consists of:

1a   Invocation, addressed to priests, people, and royal family.
1b   Accusation, confined to the authorities.
2–3   Past conduct of the leaders.
4   Moral paralysis of the leaders.
5–6   Consequences for the people.
7a   Final accusation.
7b   Final threat.

There is no reason to believe that the thought develops along a straight line. The main idea seems to be that Israel's present indulgence in promiscuity (vv 3b,4b) is rampant throughout the country with the encouragement of the rulers, political and religious (v 1). As a result of their rejection of Yahweh (vv 4b,7a), they will all stumble (v 5b). The leaders cannot repent (v 4a), and even if the people sought Yahweh (v 6a) they would not find him, because he has withdrawn (v 6b). Their properties will be eaten up (v 7b).

5:1a. *Hear.* This opening command is characteristic of the early prophets and continues into Jeremiah and Ezekiel. When *šim'û* is used in similar fashion in 4:1, the following reference to a *rîb* shows that the speech is to be a quasi-legal pronouncement; that speech is further identified as "the word of Yahweh." In 5:1 there are no such clues. The three synonymous verbs available for a call to attention—"hear this," "pay attention," "give heed"—are used here. The same three are used in Isa 28:23 in only two lines; pairs made up from these terms appear often in poetic passages.

It is possible that there are only two groups addressed—priestly and royal, and that the middle term "house of Israel" goes with both— "priests of the house of Israel," "royal family of the house of Israel," although that involves a little awkwardness in the repetition of *bêt*. "House of the king" includes more than the monarch. Since the accusations become increasingly political from this point onward, the priests recede from view. The entities are Ephraim and Judah, as well as Israel, which is both a separate state and the inclusive name for all of them together.

The verbs used here do not determine the nature of the ensuing discourse. In the prophets an invocation like this one sometimes begins a dispute involving accusations of covenant-breaking (Hos 4:1; Isa 1:2,10); these texts resemble the ancient poem of covenant ratification and exhortation (Deut 32:1), and later recitations of the Torah (Isa 51:4). Similar usage can preface more general prophetic proclamation (Isa 32:9; 49:1; Jer 13:15; Joel 1:2), and it can introduce a theophany (Mic 1:2). This is how poets begin a hymn of victory (Judg 5:3) or a boasting song (Gen 4:23). A parent or teacher would begin moral instruction by asking the pupil to pay attention, with such words (Prov 4:1; 7:24; cf. Ps 49:2; Job 34:2; Isa 28:23). Such a request gives an earnest tone to a debate (Job 13:6; 33:31) when it comes in the middle or even toward the end of a speech. There are accusations here, and warnings, and at least predictions of consequences. There are no exhortations, teachings, or promises of forgiveness and deliverance. In the absence of clear pointers to the dramatic situation, the tools of form criticism are not sufficient to identify the forms of speech, or to cast Yahweh in the role of wisdom teacher, judge, or sovereign. Verse 2b could provide a clue, for the word *mûsār,* which has to do with discipline, belongs with Wisdom vocabulary; the speech itself, however, does not contain moral advice.

priests. The noun "priest" and the singular pronouns in c 4 make it clear that a chief priest has been singled out for accusation. The plural forms in the same chapter show the priest's children, both literally and by extension representing the whole priesthood, are also on target. In c 5 priests generally are addressed.

house of Israel. Hos 4:1 begins with an address to the "Israelites," an expression confined to 1:1 – 4:1. "House of Israel" occurs five times, here and in Hos 1:4,6; 6:10; 12:1. In c 1, it seems to be restricted to the realm of the house of Jehu, but since both Israel and Ephraim are used in what follows, and Judah also is mentioned, the house of Israel in 5:1 could mean the entire nation. But the reference to "the house of *the* king" suggests only one royal family, so the northern kingdom is more likely. As usual the spotlight is on Israel-Ephraim-Samaria, even though Judah is not left out (5:5). Compare Micah's call to the "rulers" of the house of Israel (Mic 3:1,9).

House of the king. Isaiah seemingly addressed Ahaz as "House of David" (Isa 7:13); however, not only the king, but his entire family, and perhaps his administrative officials, are covered by the term "the house of the king." Elsewhere in Hosea the "princes" are mentioned in association with the king.

With two or three groups distinguished at the outset, the question arises as to whether everything that follows is addressed to all of them together (note "to them all" in v 2b) or whether each group has a distinctive message addressed to it. Because of the names mentioned in them, vv 3 and 5 are clearly addressed to the nation; 5:6 could also apply to the people. In the light of c 4, 5:4 would make sense as an accusation of the priest or leaders generally. This leaves vv 1b–2a and perhaps v 6 to apply to the royal family. The failure to find Yahweh was the last horror of reprobation in the career of Saul (I Sam 28:6), and Hos 5:6 could be saying something similar about the last kings of Israel. This assigns two tetracola to each of the three groups. The analysis of vv 1 and 2 is uncertain. The conjunction *kî* occurs five times in vv 1–7, but perhaps it should not occur twice in the same paragraph (v 1); v 1bA might then go with the rest of v 1a as part of the opening invocation, applying to them all. But v 2b does not fit well with vv 1b–2a, whereas it might go with the first three lines of v 1a, in spite of the change of person from second to third, to complete the exordium.

1b. *This verdict.* If the first clause here gives the reason for something, then we must find out what it goes with. Hosea does not always use the sequences *Principal Clause — "because" — Subordinate Clause* and *Subordinate Clause — "therefore" — Principal Clause.* He may have *"Because" — Subordinate Clause — Principal Clause* (without "therefore," using a *waw*-consecutive construction instead). He places *kî* clauses in unusual positions. Accordingly, the reference to judgment could go with what precedes, as is usually supposed, giving the reason for the call to attention, "Listen . . . because this verdict applies to you"; *lākem* would thus refer to all three groups mentioned in v 1. *L* in a verbless clause of this kind would normally indicate possession; hence Wolff's translation, "For you are responsible for justice" (1974:94). This could be true of priests and royal family. It can hardly be true of the house of Israel. Wolff gets around this objection by arguing that "house of Israel" means "heads of the house of Israel," shortened for the sake of rhythm. The syntactic parallels he adduces (Deut 1:17; Jer 32:7; Ezek 21:32) are not close to the present passage. The emendation of *bêt* to *nĕbî'ê*, "prophets of Israel" (*BH³*), relies on the parallelism of priest and prophet in other places (cf. 4:5), but has no textual support. In Jer 21:11; 22:6, the king is addressed as *bêt-melek yĕhûdâ*. We notice that the second and third lines of 5:1 have "the house of Israel" and "the house of the king" in chiasm, which implies that they might be more closely connected than the priests. This may give a warrant for conflating the two phrases to mean "the house of the king of Israel." According to I Kings 12:31, northern priests were royal appointees. But it may be going too far to see all of v 1aA as addressed to a single group — the priests of the house of the king of Israel. Despite these objections, Wolff's rendering may be correct, or the line may be intentionally ambiguous.

The interpretation we propose tries to get over these difficulties: "Listen . . . because the judgment (that is, the one I am about to pronounce) concerns you." If what follows is the judgment, and it is pronounced against all of them, then we should not try to divide vv 2–7 among the three groups.

have become. The perfect verb probably indicates that a particular event is meant.

trap. See also Hos 9:8. A trap was a device placed on the ground to catch birds (Amos 3:5; Prov 7:23; Ps 124:7); cf. Driver (1954b).

Mizpah. Since the place name elsewhere occurs with the article, the Masoretic pointing without the article is unexpected. It may be that *mṣph* should be read as the common *miṣpeh*, "watchtower," and linked with *'al-tābôr*, "at the watchtower on Mount Tabor." At the same time, it may be noted that the phrase *ršt prwš* defines or illustrates the parallel term *paḥ*, "snare," which in this case is an outspread net, used to trap an unwary bird. The entire line, v 1b, could then be rendered "Indeed you have become a trap (i.e. an outspread net) at the watchtower on Mount Tabor." If, however, *mṣph* is the proper noun, then a number of possible sites must be considered. The one referred to here is probably the site in Gilead or the old assembly point of the federation, in Benjamin, mentioned in Judges 20–21 and elsewhere. It appears in I Samuel 7 as an assize town on Samuel's itinerary. These associations fit the present context, with its reference to judgment.

Tabor. If this imposing mountain was a cult center, it would qualify as a good site for the sacrifices described in 4:13. None of the associations of Tabor throw light on the mention here (cf. Dahood 1968:314).

2a. *The rebels are deep in slaughter.* Verse 2a is largely unintelligible in its present form. Harper (pp. 267–268) lists an extraordinary number of emendations. Because of the change to third person, it does not fit well with the preceding. Verse 2b is not promising as a parallel. A popular solution in v 2a is to change *šḥṭh* to *šḥṭ,* "a pit used to catch wild animals." This makes the line continue the imagery of v 1b. The word *šēṭîm* is commonly changed to the toponym *šiṭṭîm.* The last word also has been changed. The situation is desperate if every word has to be altered before the text can be read. The first change receives some support from Hos 9:9, which has *he'mîqû-šiḥētû* "they have deeply corrupted themselves," but there the root *'mq* has a different meaning (cf. Isa 31:6; Ps 92:6; cf. Dahood 1968:336). The change to Shittim takes us to the location of the Baal-Peor apostasy (Hos 9:10) reported in Numbers 25. It also gives us another place name to line up with Tabor and possibly Mizpah. In Mic 6:5, Shittim is linked with Gilgal (cf. Hos 4:15).

The feminine abstract noun *šaḥăṭâ* of the MT is unique and unexplained but that difficulty is no reason for abandoning it. The verb *šāḥaṭ* means "to slaughter, sacrifice," particularly in pagan cults. The occurrence of the word in Ezek 16:21 and 23:39 deserves close attention: there the harlot mother offers her own children to the *gillûlîm,* "stinking idols," in the house of Yahweh. This usage is sufficient reason for retaining it in Hosea. In the light of these passages, the use of the same verb to describe Abraham's sacrifice of Isaac (Gen 22:10) takes on a more dreadful significance. Isaiah 57 is even more outspokenly addressed to "the sons of a sorceress, the seed of an adulterer" (v 3), the *šōḥăṭê haylādîm,* "those who sacrifice children" (v 5). The whole passage is reminiscent of Hosea.

The word *šēṭîm* is also suggestive. Here we must look at the account of the apostasy preserved in Psalm 106 (cf. the NOTES on 4:7):

36 They worshiped their idols (*'ăṣabbîm*).
  They became a snare for them (*môqēš,* elsewhere parallel to *paḥ*).
37 They sacrificed (*zbḥ*) their sons
  and their daughters to demons (*laššēdîm; cf. šēṭîm*).
38 They poured out innocent blood,
  the blood of their sons and their daughters,
    whom they sacrificed (*zbḥ*) to the idols (*'ăṣabbîm*) of Canaan.
  They polluted the land with blood (*dāmîm; Hos 4:2*).

39 They did foul things with their artifacts (*ma'ăśîm;* Hos 13:2; 14:4).
They were promiscuous (*zny*) in their deeds (*ma'ălālîm*).

(On *môqēš,* note especially Exod 23:33; 34:12–17; Deut 7:16; Judg 2:3; 8:27.) Psalm 106 has other affinities with Hosea — "they forgot" (vv 13, 21; cf. Hos 2:15); they made a cast bull (v 19; cf. Hos 13:2); they exchanged their glory for a bull (v 20; cf. Hos 4:7); they rebelled (vv 7, 43; cf. Hos 4:4); they spurned (*m's,* v 24; cf. Hos 4:6); and finally, they ate (*'kl,* v 28), at the same cult feast as in Hos 4:8, "human sacrifices," cf. Hos 13:2. Some of the ideas in Psalm 106 are found in Hosea, but expressed in different words. "They intermingled with the nations" (v 35) is like Hos 7:8. Ps 106:28 preserves the idiom of Num 25:3,5 for "linking themselves to Baal Peor," *niṣmad,* which may correspond to Hosea's *prd* (4:14) and *ḥbr* (4:17). Another version of a primeval apostasy is supplied in Deuteronomy 32 (cf. Kuhnigk 1974:35–39); specific details are not given, so we cannot be sure whether the Horeb, Baal-Peor, or some later incident is meant. That it is the Baal-Peor affair is suggested by the fact that both Deut 32:17 and Ps 106:37 state that sacrifices were made "to the demons," although only the Psalm makes it clear that the sacrifices were children. Most of the vocabulary of Deuteronomy 32 is otherwise quite different from the Psalm; the idols e.g. are not called *'ăṣabbîm,* but Foreigners and Abominations (v 16); but note "they forgot El" (v 18) and compare the use of El in Hos 12:1. The divine response (v 20), hiding the face, resembles the withdrawal of Hos 5:6. More pertinent is v 19: "And Yahweh saw (it) and condemned (them) because of (*min*) the provocation (*ka'as*) of his sons and his daughters." The phrase "the provocation of his sons and his daughters" matches *ka'as qorbānām,* "the provocation of their offering" (Ezek 20:28), which Ezek 20:31 makes clear was sacrificial burning of children, by which the people became foul with their *gillûlîm.* The construction in Deut 32:19 is an objective, not a subjective, genitive. It was not that the sons and daughters provoked Yahweh; he was provoked by (the offering of) his (Yahweh's!) sons and daughters to the demons. That the children are considered to belong to Yahweh is indicated by the contrast of "his" to the surrounding plurals, and also by the designation of God as "the Rock who gave birth (*yld*) to you" in the preceding verse, 32:18.

The Phoenician god *Šdrp',* "the demon has healed," was probably a god of both disease and healing (Levi della Vida 1942). While Hosea took the Baal of Peor as the great Canaanite god Baal, originally he was probably the baal (master) of the place (Mendenhall 1973:105–121). The twin themes of disease and healing are prominent in the Baal-Peor story, and Hosea makes a special point, in denouncing that idolatry in 11:2, that Israel is to blame for not realizing that "I healed them" (v 3). Yahweh's competence in this field is contrasted with the futility of resorting to other healers in 5:13; 6:1.

There are five possibilities for the word *šēṭîm:* (1) to leave it as it is, as we do, and read a noun meaning revolters or corrupt ones from the root *śwṭ;* note also *śṭy,* which describes the defection of a faithless wife, resulting in "defilement" (Num 5:12), a word which follows in Hos 5:3, and *śṭm,* whence *maśṭēmâ,* "hostility," used in 9:7,8; (2) to see it as a variant of *šēdîm* (note the *t* in *Satrapes,* the later form of *šdrp'*), influenced, perhaps, by assonance with the preceding word; (3) to read it as *Šiṭṭîm* (Num 25:1), which Mic 6:5 connects with Gilgal. If the latter were original, it is hard to understand how it could ever have been changed to the rare word of MT. While a place name would link v 2a more closely with v 1, the change from second to third person still marks a discontinuity, and the text is not clear with only that change from MT; (4) to find a noun derived from the root *śṭm,* meaning a hostile person, parallel to *mûsār,* referring to Yahweh; (5) to suppose that the letter *ḥ* has been lost from the second word, and that originally we had a cognate pair. We choose the simplest of these solutions.

From Hos 9:9 it is clear that the verb *'mq* can describe profound corruption. This would apply to child sacrifice, the ultimate religious horror. The first word, designating sacrificial slaughter, is in agreement with this. The picture is supplemented by the traditions in Numbers 25, Deuteronomy 32, and Psalm 106. The position of the verb at the end of v 2a connects the line with those preceding, as the conclusion of the paragraph. Verse 1b is addressed to the royal family; v 2a describes the resulting depravity. What the Moabites did originally at Peor, the kings of later Israel did at Mizpah and Tabor, and the rebellious leaders deeply corrupted themselves by offering child sacrifices at those places.

2b. *chastisement.* The phrase *mûsar yhwh,* "Yahweh's training," embodies one of the most important ideas in the Wisdom tradition. The word *mûsār* describes the corrective disciplining of children, and can include the educational task of curbing undesirable tendencies in sinners; the idea of punishment is not present here unless it means "I (decreed) chastisement for all of them." The term is rather surprising in the present context, where we would have expected something more rigorous; although the person who applies *mûsār* is generally kind, *mûsār* is severe in Jer 30:14. The abstract noun is used in a way that makes it seem a title of Yahweh — "I am *mûsār* for all of them," although an active participle would fit the syntax and could be another item in Hosea's peculiar vocabulary. Note the strange form of the *Qal* of *ysr* in 10:10 and the *Pi'el* in 7:15. In view of the morphology of this root at Ugarit, where Proto-

Semitic *w- persists in the *Pi'el,* a *Pi'el* participle would not be out of the question here — *mĕwassēr* (cf. Deut 8:5).

Since the clause is circumstantial and has no tense, its connection with the context is not clear. The fresh beginning of v 3 without a conjunction requires that v 2b be attached to the preceding. But we have already observed that the position of the verb at the end of v 2a marks it as the end of a paragraph, and vv 1bA–2a make a four-line unit of a kind used throughout this pericope. On this analysis, with v 1bA joined to the rest of v 1b and v 2a, v 2b could be added to v 1a to complete the four-line unit of the proem. The change from second to third person is still a problem, as is the mild tone of v 2b in contrast to the seriousness of the crimes alleged.

The interpretation of *mûsār* is problematic in several ways. The third-person modifier (*lĕkullām*) makes it difficult to connect it with v 1, and the role of educator is different from that of prosecutor (v 1). Furthermore, the extreme iniquity exposed in v 2a calls for stronger measures than chastisement, which always has a kindly ingredient. If the following text is a development of the same theme, the breakdown in relationship between Yahweh and Israel is complete. They have passed the point where repentance is possible (v 4a). They no longer know Yahweh (v 4bB). Any attempt to seek him by the usual cultic means will fail because he has withdrawn from them (v 6b). Instead of Yahweh being "in their midst," "a promiscuous spirit is in their midst."

It would be in keeping with this if v 2b meant "And I have turned aside (or, have been removed) from them." Such a withdrawal would be Yahweh's reaction to the defilement of the land, which makes it impossible for him to remain (Num 35:34; Isa 1:15). Is it possible to support this philologically by deriving *mwsr* from *swr*? The passive (*Hop'al*) participle (Isa 17:1) is possible, although there is a theological difficulty with Yahweh in a passive role. It could mean that the people have explicitly renounced Yahweh, who has been deposed "by all of them." It corresponds to the renunciation of pagan gods by converts to Yahwism (Gen 35:2; Josh 24:14,23); cf. Hos 8:12. Such rejection took place at Baal Peor, and the same kind of rejection has taken place in Hosea's time. It is a reversal of I Sam 7:4, and corresponds to the rejection described in Hos 4:6 and 2:15; cf. Num 11:20; I Sam 8:7. The active participle *sār* is used to describe Yahweh's departure from a reprobate (Judg 16:20; I Sam 28:16). In view of the difficulties, we retain the MT.

to them all. LXX reads "to all of you." This was probably influenced by the second person in v 1, but clashes with the third person of v 2a. The expression balances *to you* in v 1, although the comprehensive "all" may refer to the people, not just the leaders.

3a. *I know* (*you*). The pronoun *'ănî,* "I," is repeated from v 2, and occurs again in v 14. Because Ephraim is addressed as "you" in v 3b, it is
likely that this is also true in v 3a, and that Israel is also addressed, which
requires reading *nikḥad* and *niṭmā'* as participles, not perfect verbs. It is
possible that Ephraim alone is addressed, that the statements about Israel
are in third person, and that all the verbs can be treated as perfects. The
translation would then be, "I know you, Ephraim . . . and you, Israel, are
defiled." For a similar use of a verb without an object, when it is obvious,
see *yimṣā'û* (v 6).

In v 3 Ephraim and Israel are each treated as grammatically singular.
Israel is singular in v 5a as well, and so is Judah in v 5bB; hence the plurals in v 5bA, as well as the pronoun in v 5bB, refer to Ephraim and Israel together, again treated as distinct entities. If v 4, which is plural
throughout, refers to the countries mentioned in the verses that precede
and follow it, so that vv 3–5 as a whole talk to or about Ephraim, Israel,
and Judah, then v 4 applies to the whole nation. We think, however, that v
4 should be referred to the leaders of v 1aA, as noted above.

The patterns of the two bicola of v 3 are not the same. Verse 3a has
chiasm; in v 3b Ephraim and Israel end their respective lines. Verse 3bB
has no conjunction; compare 4:6, where the last line similarly begins with
the verb without a conjunction. The parallelism in v 3 can be seen in two
ways. Gordis (1971:79) argues that there is a statement about Ephraim
(vv 3aA, 3bA) in two lines, and one about Israel (vv 3aB, 3bB) in two
lines. The parallelism is alternating. The syllable count supports this;
Ephraim has fifteen syllables, Israel fifteen, even though the lines differ
considerably in length. On the other hand, the internal parallelism is
closer if the bicola are taken in sequence. Ephraim is known // Israel is
not concealed; Ephraim has been promiscuous // Israel is defiled. Perhaps
it is not necessary to decide between these two possibilities, since each is
based on features of the text. Taken together, both Ephraim and Judah
are known to be defiled by promiscuity.

cannot hide. The *Nipʿal* can be passive (II Sam 18:13); but when it is
negated and the observer is God, a middle voice is indicated (Pss 69:6;
139:15). The same applies to *niṭmā'* in v 3b, where a stative or reflexive
meaning is appropriate. In Ezekiel 16,20,23, defilement with idols and
through prostitution are one and the same thing. Verses 3bA and 3bB are
parallel; a subordinate relationship need not be sought. Hos 6:10 similarly
parallels prostitution in Ephraim with defilement in Israel.

3b. *Now.* The use of *kî ʿattâ* here is puzzling. In 2:9 *ʿattâ* is used as an
adverb of time. Otherwise it begins clauses in a manner that suggests it is
a signal of transition or even a kind of conjunction. In 5:4, discourse
switches to third person for both Yahweh and Israel. Usually *wĕʿattâ*
marks a change in discourse from description to resolution or command;

2:12 and 13:2 are the examples. Constructions without wĕ- (4:16; 5:7; 8:10,13; 10:2) or even with kî could have the same effect (10:3). The use of 'attâ, "now," with a perfect verb would seem to be impossible, unless the verb describes the continuing result of a past act. This would fit 7:2 and 8:8, as well as 5:3; but why the adverb should be used in v 3b, in the middle of the four lines about Ephraim and Israel, is unclear. Kî could be asseverative; compare v 7a.

you . . . have been promiscuous. The causative sense of the Hip'il of zny, appropriate elsewhere (Exod 34:16; Lev 19:29; II Chron 21:11,13) does not fit here. Hosea's usage is, however, consistent (cf. 4:10,18; for the masculine, cf. 4:15).

defiled. Compare 6:10; 9:4; in 4:15 the verb parallel to zny is 'šm.

4. This verse refers to the leaders, especially the priests. (1) "Their deeds" corresponds to the priest's deeds in 4:9, and 5:2 also. (2) The spirit of promiscuity in their midst is the spirit active with the priest in 4:12. (3) The priest is charged with ignorance of "the knowledge" in 4:6, and with rejecting Yahweh (cf. 5:2b). Hos 5:4 applies to all priests (v 1) what was applied to a particular priest in the preceding chapter. There is a difference, however. Hos 4:9 says that "his doings" will be returned to him; he will be punished in a manner corresponding to his crimes. Returning to Yahweh is a prospect often held in hope (3:5; 6:1). Here it is said to be impossible because their deeds will not allow it. Verse 4b implies that the spirit of promiscuity in their midst has completely displaced Yahweh. He has been forgotten (2:15); they are totally ignorant of him; the idea of returning to him no longer enters their mind. Cf. 4:14, where the only prospect for a people devoid of discernment is to perish.

The immense weight of the final statement of v 4 can be felt when we observe that its syntactic arrangement achieves three effects. First, the placement of the verb at the end marks the end of a paragraph, justifying our recognition of a new beginning of discourse with v 5. The negated verbs lō' yittĕnû and lō' yādā'û constitute an inclusion for the four-line unit in v 4. There is a larger inclusion with vv 3 and 4: "I know Ephraim . . . but they don't know me." Note the same effect in 4:10.

The reason for this ignorance of Yahweh is made clear in v 3bA. He has been displaced by a rival deity, a spirit of promiscuity. That a god is intended here is clear from the mockery of creedal language: the affirmation that Yahweh was "in the midst" of Israel was central to covenant thought. Holiness (qdš) and defilement (ṭm') are opposites, and the presence of defilement, to which Hosea often alludes, means the absence of God: he has withdrawn (v 6).

4a. permit. The suggested emendation to yittĕnûm is acceptable, because one mem could have been lost by haplography, or one could serve to represent two at the word juncture. However, *ntn* does not need an explicit object when followed by an infinitive (Exod 16:3; II Sam 19:1).

5a. *pride*. Presumption, trust in one's own splendor. The phrase is devastating after the statement that Israel is vile. Its total lack of foundation makes Israel's pride self-condemning.

will testify. The language of legal disputation is used. The *waw*-consecutive construction does not follow well from v 4, unless it means that Israel's pretensions to knowledge are expressions of ignorance, and self-condemning. Since the speech has returned to Ephraim and Israel (to which Judah is added), a link with v 3 is possible, especially if v 4 is correctly referred to the leaders. Verse 3 is the accusation, v 5b is the punishment. Since the idiom *'ānâ b* means "to testify against" (cf. Deut 31:21), the line is not likely to refer to Yahweh. Verse 5a has no poetic parallel. As in Mic 6:3, *'ānâ* describes the response of a defendant to an accusation. The sentence follows in v 5b. In 2:17–24, *'ānâ* is used in an eschatological setting; the same note of finality is present here. The noun *gā'ôn* has been taken to refer in a good sense to Yahweh as Israel's pride, but this is not correct. In no case does it refer to Yahweh. Here *gā'ôn* is parallel to *'āwôn;* both could be other names for the rival god — Pride, Insolence, Arrogance; note "the pride of Israel" in Nah 2:3, and "the pride of Jacob" in Amos 6:8; 8:7 ("Yahweh has taken an oath against the pride of Israel"); and Nah 2:3 (cf. Ps 47:5).

Pride is the sin, and stumbling, the punishment. There is justice in this (Prov 4:19; 24:16). The sequence *gā'ôn,* "pride," and *kiššālôn,* "downfall" occurs in Prov 16:18. Isaiah speaks of the drunken arrogance of Samaria (*gē'ût*) at this time (Isa 28:1,3). There is nothing in the present context to explain what constitutes this "pride." It can hardly be false trust in ritual; it is more likely the belief that there is no need for repentance.

Hos 5:5 is closely parallel to 7:10. If both are constructed according to a similar plan, then a closer connection between v 4 and v 5 should be sought. In both places the identical clause (5:5a = 7:10a) is preceded by a statement "And he does (or: they do) not know (Yahweh)." This makes it possible that "Yahweh" is the elliptical object in 7:9, not "it." In both places it is emphasized that the people do not or cannot return to Yahweh. In 5:4 this comes before 5:5; it follows 7:10. The idea of "seeking" Yahweh is also found in both passages (5:6; 7:10). In each the title "Yahweh their God" is used; in Hos 5:4 the phrase is split up.

against it. Literally, "to/in his face." Cf. Job 16:8; Deut 31:21.

5b. Verse 5a is an individual line wih no parallel; v 5b achieves a measure of parallelism, in spite of the top-heavy effect of "Israel and Ephraim." It repeats the patterns of 4:5; compare *gam-yĕhûdâ* with *gam-nābî'.* The imperfect // perfect sequence is poetic, and the subjects and verbs are in chiasm.

Israel. The repetition of Israel in v 5bA shows again that Israel and Ephraim are distinct. It is easy enough to drop the second "Israel," and leave Ephraim and Israel in parallel (reversing the order in which they occur twice in v 3); this improves the rhythm but is tampering. With the three names — Israel, Ephraim, Judah — in sequence, the picture is not clear. Are the first two in synonymous parallelism? The name pattern in v 3 alternates Ephraim and (Gileadite) Israel; after the initial reference to (all) Israel (or perhaps only northern Israel) in v 5, the names (Gileadite) Israel and Ephraim appear in the opposite order. The clash between the plural and singular in the verbs remains. The plural verb in v 5bA indicates that Israel and Ephraim are distinct entities.

(Judah will) stumble. For the sake of congruency, *kāšal* must be future, even though it lacks the customary *waw*-consecutive conjunction. LXX has "and" with the future; Wellhausen normalizes to *yikkāšēl.* The *Qal* is used twice in 4:5, and again in 14:2 (where the verb occurs in conjunction with a call to repentance that shows that the downfall is not irreversible). The use of *Nip'al* and *Qal* in parallel with identical meaning in 5:5 is no cause for alarm. It is a peculiarity of this root to use *Qal* for perfect and *Nip'al* for imperfect, as the statistics show:

	Perfect	Imperfect
Qal	22 times	Only in Prov 4:16, which has difficulties
Nip'al	3 times (all in Daniel)	17 times

There is accordingly no need to change the *Nip'al,* or seek a passive, middle or reflexive meaning for it. In 4:5, where the same verb is used in repetitive parallelism, the constructions are classical. The two passages are connected: there it was a priest and a prophet who will stumble together; here it is Israel, Ephraim, and Judah. "Like the people, like the priest" (4:9) is the pivot. The priest stumbles in 4:5; the people in 5:5. Verse 5bB is often removed as a gloss, because of the reference to Judah, but the reference is not favorable, and it balances the reference to Judah in 4:15. A predicted disaster, like stumbling, is usually threatened as fit punishment for a similar sin. Stumbling could be connected with falling into a trap (v 1).

6a. Often in Hosea, there is a pseudo-sorites, a train of thought which does not seem logical as it moves from step to step, e.g. "I will hamper her so that she will not find her paths; but even if she does, and pursues her lovers, she won't find them; but even if she does find them, they will spurn her, because her folly will be exposed in front of them" (2:4–15). In 9:11–12 a similar series is condensed: "There will be no conception; but even if there is, there will be no gestation; but even if there is, there will

be no delivery; but even if there is, the parents won't raise the children;
but even if they do, I will bereave them." Similarly the argument in 8:7
can be expanded: "If they sow seed, it won't germinate; even if it does, it
won't grow; even if it does, it won't produce grain; even if it does, they
won't make flour; even if they do, they won't cook it; even if they do,
strangers will eat it." A similar line of "reasoning" resolves the apparent
discrepancy between v 4 (which says that they are not able to return to
Yahweh) and v 6 (which says that they will go seeking Yahweh). Although their doings will not let them return to Yahweh, even if they try,
they will not find him. It is not that the spirit of promiscuity restrains
them. Yahweh decides whether they will find him or not, and he has withdrawn. On the sequence "seek" // "find" see Hos 2:9; Jer 2:24.

  flocks and herds. This conjures up a picture of wanderers moving with
property to a shrine for a seasonal celebration more ancient than the pilgrimage of settled Israelites with a few sacrificial animals to a temple. The
pilgrimages retained a typological touch of the Exodus trek, so both
meanings are present in this anti-Exodus. The language of Exod 10:24
used here arouses memories of Israel's first search for Yahweh in the desert; but cc 4–5 contain no hint that that is where they will look for him.
The references to contemporary festivals in 2:13, and to shrines in 4:15
and 5:1 suggest sacrifices of the kind described in 4:13–14, at the altars
of 4:19, which are to be desecrated. Here, as in 4:15, it is clear that Yahweh worship is involved, presumably at traditional Yahweh shrines. A
journey to the desert would be more hopeful, for this is the place where
good relations will be restored (2:5,16; 9:10; 12:5). But this will take
place only at Yahweh's initiative, and in his time, not because of Israel's
change of heart. There is a nostalgic touch in "their flocks and herds"; agricultural produce is not mentioned. If v 6 is a threat, it could predict
reversion to pastoral pursuits because agriculture has been ruined (Isa
7:21–25). "To seek Yahweh" normally means to seek him through the institutions of the cult. To do it with flocks and herds indicates that
sacrifices of sheep and cattle will be used. If they do not find him, that
means he is no longer "in the midst," that is, at the shrine. The evidence
of this would be the failure of the usual token of the divine presence — the
giving of oracles.

  6b. *withdrawn.* This translation is not certain, as this is the only example of an intransitive or reflexive use of the verb. *Ḥālaṣ* in the *Qal* normally denotes the removal of clothing (Deut 25:9; Isa 20:2). In the more
common *Pi'el,* which is used mainly in poetry, the stem means to
withdraw someone from danger. The Phoenician personal name *ḥlṣb'l*
shows that it is an activity or appellative of deity, and in such a name,
could hardly have a negative connotation. The usual interpretation of the
final clause is that it gives a reason: "They will not find (him) (because)

he has withdrawn from them." This is possible, although comparison with v 5bB suggests that the verb could be future.

7. This is another part of the indictment, followed, after 'attâ, by the threatened punishment, a pattern used throughout 4:4–5:7.

7a. *they have been traitorous.* While *bāgad* can describe any kind of treachery, involving deception, it applies as appropriately here to the deception of a husband by a wife outwardly loyal, secretly unfaithful (cf. Exod 21:8). Jer 3:20 makes the meaning plain: *'ākēn bāgĕdâ 'iššâ mērē'āh kēn bĕgadtem bî bêt yiśrā'ēl,* "Surely as a wife deceives her husband, so you have deceived me, house of Israel." We are dealing with hypocritical Yahweh worship: the depravity that makes repentance impossible is not renunciation of Yahweh, but complacent religiosity. The children, who seem to be the husband's, are really *bānîm zārîm,* "foreign children," illegitimate in the sense of being conceived during the adultery of a married woman.

The adjective *zārîm* can mean "foreign" in the ethnic sense also: the children are "foreign" in that they take the nationality of their fathers; this seems unlikely. If "children of foreign fathers (viz. gods)" is meant, *bĕnêma zārîm,* construct with enclitic *mem,* can be read (cf. Ps 44:21). Jeremiah 2, which uses many of Hosea's terms, points to this possibility: the woman goes off after "the Baals"; she loves "foreigners."

have engendered. Since the verb often describes the female part in childbearing, the feminine reference here would continue the discussion of the conduct of the priests' daughters, though they may be representative of the whole population. A priest's daughter who marries an *'îš zār* (Lev 22:12) is to be excommunicated. (This was not as serious as prostitution — Lev 21:9.) Bearing "foreign children" is treachery against Yahweh, so it must be more than marrying a foreigner. Dahood (1968:59) suggests that *zwr* here means "to be loathsome," which does not receive support from the context, since it is the foreignness, not the nastiness, of the liaisons that is condemned. The suggestion misses Hosea's consistent argument. The people have not proved faithless to Yahweh because they were born loathsome children. On the contrary, Yahweh has withdrawn from them because they have been treacherous against him, and their treachery is that they have given birth to foreign children.

7b. *Now.* In 4:16b 'attâ is followed by a jussive; 5:7b could be the counterpart of that imprecation. This would fit with other places where "eating" is a destructive act of God. In Amos 7:4, fire eats the *ḥēleq* in this way. If the reference to farmlands is to be taken literally, compare 4:3.

eat. The verb seems to have two objects, a pronoun *-ēm,* "them," and a noun. A similar problem is presented by Gen 6:13 — *wĕhinĕnî mašḥîtām 'et-hā'āreṣ,* apparently, "and behold I am destroying them the earth." In neither case is the translation of *'et-* as "with" desirable. In both cases, the *mem* is enclitic; the noun is the only object. (Another possibility is that the suffix anticipates the following noun object; cf. Exod 2:6; it is also conceivable that the prophet claims that Yahweh will consume the Israelites.) The verb could be literal, implying the destruction of farmlands, or technical, referring to the usufruct of them.

property. In Gen 14:24 *ḥēleq* is "rations," but this is not likely to apply here. The idiom "to eat a portion" is found in Deut 18:8, where it refers to the equal share in the people's offering to which every Levite is entitled (Deut 14:29), because the Levites did not have a regular *ḥēleq wĕnaḥălâ,* "inherited allotment," of land. "The oblations of Yahweh" were the portion of Levi. Since Hosea has just spoken of the journey of the Israelites with their flocks and herds to seek Yahweh, it may be that these offerings, including the priests' rations, instead of being rightly used in Yahweh worship, are devoted to pagan gods in a new moon festival (cf. 2:13). If *ḥōdeš* is the festival of a false god, then the devouring of sacrifices (Deut 32:38) with no return for the worshipers is the fraudulence of paganism.

Another side of the problem is put in focus by Lev 22:12, a verse already cited. A priest's daughter who married a *zār* was specifically forbidden to eat the priests' rations, since no *zār* could eat holy food. This threat is similar to that in 4:6 — exclusion of the priest's sons from the priesthood because they are *bānîm zārîm.*

New Moon. The word *ḥōdeš* seems to be the subject, but no one has ever explained how the new moon could eat fields. Harper (p. 271) explained it as a reference to a time interval; "within a month ruin may overtake them." The nearest antecedent is "Yahweh" in v 7a. A simple solution is to change the word to *ḥsl,* "locusts" (so LXX and Wolff 1974:95). Although this could be right, and the MT simply in error, it is hard to see how such an error could have been perpetrated. A corrupt text is more likely to arise by confusion in an obscure text than by material change in a clear text. Note that Hosea includes considerable play on the word "eat." For instance, in 7:7 the people "eat" their judges, and in divine retribution "foreigners" eat their strength (7:9). In the latter instance, *kōaḥ* could mean "produce," bringing that verse closer to 5:7. The purpose of the ritual eating described in 4:8,10 was to secure a bountiful harvest by fertility rites. These efforts will be thwarted; "they will not be satisfied" (4:10), and 5:7 may give the reason — their fields will be consumed. Isa 1:7 says that *zārîm* devour the land; cf. Ezek 11:9; 28:7; 30:12. Since *bānîm zārîm* have just been mentioned, it is possible that they are the subject of the verb here also, though that is not likely, because the number conflicts. Rather, Yahweh is the subject and *ḥōdeš* is an adverb. New moon festivals were important in Canaanite religion, and it would be appropriate if some kind of disaster were to take place at that sacred time.

It is possible that *ḥdš* is not to be vocalized "new moon." It requires no change of consonants to read *ḥādāš*, "(someone) else." This is what is threatened in 8:7: they will prepare their food, but *zārîm* will gobble it down. This could be the old threat of Yahweh to give up on Israel and to fulfill his purpose with a new people (Exod 32:10). The use of the word *ḥēleq* evokes the central theme of inheriting the patrimony. If the children are "foreign children," they are disinherited, and a new people will eat their heritage. In Deut 32:16–17 the previously unknown or unacknowledged gods (note *yd'* there and in Hos 5:4) are called variously *zārîm*, "foreigners," *tô'ēbôt*, "abominations," *šēdîm*, "demons," *lō' 'ēlōah*, "non-god," *ḥădāšîm*, "novelties." The collocation of *zr* and *ḥdš* is striking. (The Deuteronomic *'lhym 'ḥrym*, "other gods," occurs in Hosea only at 3:1.) We have already noticed that Jer 2:25 has *zārîm* with the same associations as Hos 5:7a; there also, the unfaithful wife says, "I will go off after them" (cf. Hos 2:7 and 2:15), saying to "the pole" (cf. Hos 4:12) "You are my father," and to the stone (feminine), "You gave birth to me" (Jer 2:27 — Ketib). The apostate in Deut 32:18 denied that the Rock gave birth to him. Jer 3:13 has similar language. Ezek 16:32 also speaks of an adulterous woman receiving *zārîm* (or according to the versions, a harlot's pay from foreigners). All these are versions of the apostasy to the *'ēl zār* of the Psalter (Pss 44:21; 81:10), called simply *zār* in Isa 43:12. Since Hosea uses several plural names for Baal, modeled on *'ēlōhîm*, perhaps *zārîm* means simply Baal, and *ḥdš* is the *ḥdšym* of Deut 32:17, the new gods. Jer 2:30 provides another link in using the word *mûsār*, "correction"; cf. Hos 5:2. In Jeremiah, the acclamation of the wooden pole as father and the standing stone as mother is quite incongruent with the imagery that the false gods are "lovers." The statement corresponds to the genders of the words ("wood" masculine, "stone" feminine) but it is the opposite of the symbolism (tree is Asherah, stone is Baal). We have switched to the relationships of Hos 11:1. The children now acclaim Baal, not Yahweh, as their parent. Whether as offspring of the pagan god, or simply by allegiance to him, the people are no longer "the children of Yahweh" (Deut 32:18–19), but "foreign children," with no inheritance in Yahweh's land. Their inheritance will be taken over by *zārîm* (Lam 5:2), the curse of Deut 28:33. Foreigners will intrude on the priests' privileges, and usurp the priests' role, as threatened in Hos 4:6. Just as the priests permitted their daughters to prostitute themselves with *zārîm* (whether men or gods, 4:13b), so *zārîm* will eat the food (7:9; 8:7) which the priests' daughters are denied (Lev 22:12). The *'îš zār*, forbidden by Torah from drawing near the *sancta* (Num 17:5), and forbidden to eat the consecrated foods (Exod 29:33), will draw near and eat. In the end "the foreigners moved into the sanctuaries of the house of Yahweh" (Jer 51:51), when Yahweh confirmed the desecration of his own cult, doing what his own people had already done. This fulfills the biblical principle that Yahweh punishes people by the means with which they sinned (Wis 11:16).

Despite the fact that foreigners are crucial here, it is likely that *ḥdš* refers to the new moon festival. The focus is on members of the priestly families (without excluding the people in general), whose "portions" are the offerings eaten in the cult. *Ḥēleq* can also describe the share of the sacrifice to be eaten by the worshipers. The text portrays a destruction of the cult and its officers.

VII. THE STATE OF THE NATION: THE NATION'S POLITICS
(5:8–11)

The alarums of war

5:8a Blow horns in Gibeah,
    trumpets in Ramah!

8b Rouse alarms in Beth Awen:
   "We are behind you, Benjamin!"

The background of the war and its effects

9a Ephraim, you will be a desolation on the day of
   accusation.

9b Among the tribes of Israel I have made that known with
   certainty.

10a The princes of Judah are like those who move boundary
   stones.

10b Over them I will pour my fury like the waters of the flood.

11a Ephraim will be oppressed. He will be crushed in judgment.

11b He has persistently gone off after Filth.

NOTES

5:8–11. Because of the similarity of the similes in vv 12 and 14, the major break in the second half of c 5 should be put before the former. In vv 8–11 the topic is the local political activity of Ephraim and Judah; the international scene appears in v 13. In vv 12, 14–15, more attention is paid to Yahweh's dealings with his people. Verse 13 has some connection with what follows, e.g. in the theme of healing. The crisis reported in v 13 could account for the drastic measures adopted in vv 14–15. Verse 12 could then be a companion to v 14, even though the events on which these responses are based are not reported until v 13; in other words the two

sets of two parallel similes in vv 12 and 14 form an envelope around the
history in v 13.

Except for vv 8 and 11, the speech in 5:8–11 is in the first person. The
opening speech is a twofold command to blow the horn and sound the
alarm. It is in the plural, and the most likely persons to receive such a
command are priests. After that, the text refers to Ephraim, with Judah
nearly always in parallel. When each is referred to alone, the verbs and
pronouns are singular. Plurals refer to both together, i.e. to the entire nation. In vv 9b and 10a "the tribes of Israel" and "the princes of Judah"
seem to be parallel. In vv 12–14a every line begins with w, "and," except
for kî in v 14aA, while the simple conjunction does not occur once in vv
8–11.

The placement of the verb at the end of v 15 is a sign that a major unit
ends there. This is confirmed by the fact that there is a change to first-person plural (the first in Hosea) at 6:1. In the remainder of 5:8–15, several
kinds of clause are used, most of which follow the norms of classical
prose. Two imperative clauses begin with the verb in v 8. In two clauses
with an imperfect verb (vv 9a and 10b), the verb is not clause-initial. The
position of the perfect verbs in the clauses in vv 9b, 10a, and 11b varies.
The commencement of v 10a with hāyû is startling; one would have expected that either the subject would precede the verb or wayyihyû would
have been used. The verbless clause in v 11a is normal; the position of the
pronoun subject in the verbless clauses in vv 12 and 14 shows them to be
circumstantial. The 1 cg s verbs in vv 14b and 15 begin their clauses, contrasting in this respect with the pattern of v 10b. With the use of the consecutive in v 13, vv 11–15 are nearer to classical norms than vv 8–10; this
is a third contrastive feature between these two sections.

The general effect is that vv 8–10 do not seem to be as coherent as the
rest, and their analysis is correspondingly difficult. After the initial alarm
is sounded (v 8), the discourse develops as a series of accusations and
corresponding threats. What is happening in vv 9–11 is far from clear.
Since the clause beginning with the passive participle has the familiar form
of a curse in v 11a, while v 11b states a fact, using perfect verbs, it would
seem that we have the accusation (v 11b) after the threat (v 11a). The
threats seem to mount in seriousness, suggesting that the corresponding
sins (which we do not understand until we reach v 13) are increasingly
grave.

From the point of view of poetic structure, 5:8–15 shows a mixture of
lines which are, in effect, prose, and lines which fall into well-formed
bicola. There are no tricola or more complex units. There are no bicola
with complete synonymous parallelism. The most common form is incomplete synonymous parallelism with rhythmic compensation: vv 8a, 12,
13aA, 13aB, 13b (cf. 14a); also apparently, v 8b. Verses 9–11 are prose.

It has generally been recognized that vv 8–11 have a certain unity. The style contrasts with what comes before and after; the absence of prose particles is striking. The historical situation involves Ephraim and Judah in military and political maneuvers. The call to arms focused on the main towns in the territory of Benjamin suggests a war (threatened or actual) between Ephraim and Judah, both of which are mentioned in this chapter. Both states are later said to be sick (v 13); and both resort to Assyria, each apparently seeking favorable alliance against the other. All to no advantage, as the remainder of the chapter shows.

Substantial progress in the interpretation of 5:8–11 was made by Alt (1919), who set the whole of Hos 5:8 – 6:6 against the background of the anti-Judah alliance of Ephraim and Syria reported in II Kings 16 and Isaiah 7. To work out his hypothesis, Alt had to reconstruct the history from meager data. His main point is that Judah invaded Ephraim from the south. In addition, Alt was obliged to make a considerable number of alterations in the text. A few emendations are undoubtedly called for on any theory; but when there are so many, they become cumulatively dubious, and erode the credibility of the scheme that requires them.

From the literary point of view, Alt discovers five oracles in 5:8 – 6:6, a series of comments on successive events, moving through a rapidly changing situation and representing the prophet's interpretation and assessment of the events as they occurred. The unity in the series is supplied by the thread of history, and the variety among the oracles, which could give the impression that they have little to do with each other, is due to the changing situation.

It is not our intention to give a detailed reevaluation of Alt's work. This has already been done by Good (1966b), whose results show that a different approach can throw the material into a different focus. He sees Hos 5:8 – 6:6 as a poem with a liturgical function, although he recognizes the diversity of elements within the "poem." These include a setting in an autumnal festival, elements of a covenant-lawsuit, theophanic imagery, and oracles which are part of cultic activity. It is hard to see how it all hangs together.

The term "poem" is altogether unsuitable. Quite apart from begging the question of lyrical unity, on the purely formal level the poetic art is so poorly developed that liturgical use must be ruled out. The mixture of oratorical prose discourse with brief patches of poetry is characteristic of prophetic speech. Without trying to enumerate oracles or identify speeches, we can attribute the continuity within 5:8 – 6:6 to secondary literary organization along schematic lines. The distinctiveness of prophetic discourse, with so much originality and inventiveness in the handling of conventional forms, makes it futile to seek a specific institutional setting (such as an autumnal festival) or precise functional (or literary) forms (such as a covenant lawsuit). Good has not succeeded in reconstructing either a ceremony or a literary piece of known genre. His analysis — "The prophet states the charge and Yahweh decrees the sentence" (1966b:278) — is quite artificial, and we have no other instance of such "a dialogue in litigation form."

We do not pretend to be able to solve the problems. We suspect that the heuristic questions of both Alt (What is the historical setting that explains the text?) and Good (What is the cult setting that explains the text?) are not capable of handling the material. Alt's extensive emendations betray one kind of inadequacy; Good's silence on many details and strained enforcement of form-critical expectations betray another.

Our moral is not to be too ambitious, not to claim too much. One could not force the material into a specific historical situation (even if we could be sure what it is), because Hosea has made literary use of certain archaic motifs which go back to disputation in the old tribal league and which no longer reflect political realities of his day. "The tribes of Israel" is a blatant anachronism; "the princes of Judah" (not the king) are accursed; and so on. Nor should one force the material into oral-institutional forms (festival liturgy, lawsuit, etc.). Finally, one should not insist on tracing a logical-chronological development through the passage. This would require the interpreter to show how 6:1–3 (1 cg pl) could follow c 5, and how 6:4–6 could follow after 6:1–3. But, as we hope to show, 6:4–6 goes with 5:12–15, and 6:1–3 is embedded in between as the climax and outcome of the whole discourse. In a similar way the accusations and threats in 5:10–15 should not be oversimplified into a series in which a specific accusation is followed immediately by the corresponding threat. To give only two examples: an accusation of Ephraim (in v 11) is followed by a threat against both Ephraim and Judah in v 12; and it can hardly be maintained that Ephraim's sin of walking after *ṣāw* (v 11b) was later than Judah's sin of changing the boundaries (v 10a).

Alt did show that 5:8–15 could fit into the historical circumstances of the Syro-Ephraimite War and Judah's political entanglement with Assyria around 733 B.C.E., for the most part. The text of Hosea should not be changed to bring it closer to the realities of that time; the details of the text cannot be used with certainty to supply historical information. Thus, we still do not know whether Ephraim had annexed Benjamin, and Judah later recaptured Benjamin; or whether Judah invaded Ephraim from Benjamin. The merit of Good's work is to draw attention to features which fit better in ceremonial contexts than amid concrete political realities. Yet the text cannot be moved entirely into the realm of cult generalities suitable for seasonal repetition. Whether the threats were realized concretely is another matter. As it is, they are couched in rather extravagant similes, as Good points out. To translate the activity of Yahweh described in v 14 into a specific historical event would be pure speculation. Alt's aim of "a complete historical understanding" of everything in the text is asking for too much.

Hos 5:8–11, and to a lesser extent 5:8–15, is unified by various literary, thematic, and structural devices. (We shall discuss below the possibility that 5:8 – 6:6 is a single composition.) A helpful observation for finding our way through the composition is the recurrence of speeches made by Yahweh in the first person, without any of the usual introductory formulas. These include the revelation cited in 5:9b, and the threats in 5:10b, 12, 14–15. These threats (when names are mentioned) are directed against both Ephraim and Judah; and pronouns (when they are used) are plural. The threats are interspersed with accusations. These are indirect, i.e. they are spoken about Judah (v 10a), Ephraim (v 11), and both (v 13a), not to them. Yet both are addressed jointly in v 13b, and v 9a seems to be a threat spoken to Ephraim by God.

The fact that such oracles were spoken by the prophet on behalf of God does not help us to recover the situation in which this was done. Verse 9b provides the important information that Yahweh (presumably) laid firm charges on the tribes of Israel "on the day of accusation." Such a tribal assembly is imaginary: historically speaking, it is unlikely that a national gathering of Israel took place to provide the setting for Hosea's denunciations. Nor are we to suppose that "the princes of Judah" were formally arraigned (v 10a).

The most obvious historical interpretation of the charge that the princes of Judah are like those who remove border markers is that Judah had invaded Ephraimite territory. This charge would not be germane if 5:8 refers to an incident in which Judah recovered (or tried to reclaim) Benjaminite territory previously annexed by Ephraim in the combined attack of the Samaria-Damascus axis on Jerusalem in 733 B.C.E. Judah would have been justified in retrieving her rightful territory. But v 10 shows that Judah was considered guilty of transgression. Hence v 8 refers to an invasion (projected or actual) of Ephraim proper, launched from Benjaminite territory with the muster in three main Benjaminite cities. It is also a reasonable historical inference from v 13 that Ephraim and Judah had each recently sustained injuries resulting from military defeat, perhaps inflicted on each other. As a consequence each country sought the aid of Assyria. Although each nation is spoken of in similar terms, and both are denounced together in v 13b, these were doubtless independent political maneuvers to secure the support of Assyria against the other. The folly of this must have been evident to the prophet. The ills of the nation as a whole would never be cured by setting one part against the other.

We ought to distinguish between the state of the nation as a result of punishment — the injuries to be described in v 13 — and the sins for which they are punished. The nature of Judah's sin is evident from v 10a. Ephraim's pitiful state (v 11a) is explained as the result of persistently walking after ṣāw. In spite of the verb, this is probably not the same activity as walking to Assyria in v 13, but another way of talking about Ephraim's idolatry.

One possible course of events can be reconstructed as follows. (The setting of the reconstruction is another matter. The Syro-Ephraimite War remains possible, but Assyria in Hosea is remote and at least a potential ally, i.e. the Assyria of Tiglath Pileser's early years, rather than an immediate threatening presence; perhaps Judah intervened in the civil war between Menahem and Shallum.) The moment which gives the whole account its perspective is the Judean call to arms for an attack on Ephraim (5:8). From this point the prophet analyzes prior events and looks forward to the response of Yahweh. The prospective view (vv 14–15) does not take the concrete form of a prediction of the devastation of either country by Assyria. Verse 14 describes a great devastation and v 15 looks to the future consequences. It is Yahweh himself who has inflicted the wounds. Events are not recounted along a straight time line. Theological interpretation is implied in this arrangement. All destructions are seen as judgments of God; this is why no innocent victims are identified. Here is a provisional reconstruction.

A. The discourse begins with a quotation (not identified as such) of Judah's war cry, mustering troops in Benjamin for an assault on Ephraim (v 8). Verse 9aA could be a taunt, made in connection with this— "Ephraim, you will become a desolation."

B. The response of Yahweh to this internecine strife is to arraign the culprits "among the tribes of Israel" (9b). Yahweh announces the true bill. Such a convention of the old tribal league must be considered a projection, imaginative but pertinent. A recognizable quotation from the Song of Deborah (Judges 5) makes the point.

The initiative lies with Judah, who is guilty of aggression. There would be less point in the condemnation if this were a counterattack, and Ephraim is not accused of invading Judah. We note in passing that Aram is nowhere in view.

C. The threat against Ephraim (v 9aA) is interpreted as a just punishment because he persistently walked after ṣāw (v 11).

D. Even though Judah was Yahweh's agent for carrying out Ephraim's punishment, Judah is not necessarily in the right. On the contrary, Judah is guilty of a crime similar to a serious offense in the old covenant league of tribes — moving a boundary (v 10a), in this case, intertribal. For this Judah too will be punished (v 10b).

It is possible that the plural (ʿălêhem) in v 10b refers to both Ephraim and Judah, and that v 11 completes the dispute in the assembly of tribes.

We suspect that Good is wrong in seeing v 12 as the threat following the accusation in v 11. On the contrary, v 10b may be the threat flanked by the accusations of Judah (v 10a) and Ephraim (v 11).

5:8a. *Blow horns*. The plural verb does not require a plural object; *šôpār*, "horn," and its parallel are collective. *Šôpār* occurs in both singular and plural forms, the latter confined to Joshua 6, Judges 7, and II Chron 15:14. In many of its occurrences, the singular of the noun is collective. The *šôpār* was the horn of an animal, generally the ram, sometimes the ibex, used in battle and worship. It was blown as a public signal for several purposes — to assemble, to warn, to announce war (Jer 51:27), to give battle orders (for advance, Joshua 6; or retreat, II Sam 2:28; 18:16; 20:22); to add to the noise and confusion of battle (Judg 7:18); to arouse valor (Job 39:24,25); to induce panic (Amos 3:6); to celebrate victory. In the present passage an alarm is being sounded. While the immediate focus is on some places in Benjamin, the opening words evoke wider associations. They are reminiscent of the warnings sounded at Sinai against the destructive presence of Yahweh (Exod 19:16). As with other great historical theophanies, this language is projected into the great future outbreak of divine retribution (Isa 18:3; Joel 2:1; Zeph 1:16), when Yahweh himself will blow the horn (Zech 9:14). Compare "the last trumpet" of Christian apocalypses. Hos 5:8 suggests no more than the call to arms sounded when an enemy is approaching, and the local place names lack the cosmic dimension. But the historical and the eschatological are often intermingled in prophetic visions, e.g. Jer 4:5–31. The words of Hosea here, like those of Jeremiah (6:1), probably echo the orders issued to the army chaplains, the levitical *šōṭĕrîm*, whose prerogative it was to arouse the country. As a priestly act, its mention here is the more pungent after a passage (4:4 – 5:7) that blames the priests for the state of the nation. Now it is they who must sound the last call to arms.

trumpets. This is the only occurrence of the singular of *ḥăṣōṣĕrâ*. Otherwise the plural is used, mostly in the Priestly History (twenty-eight occurrences), which suggests that it was not used as a solo instrument. To judge from Num 10:2, where Moses is instructed to make a pair of silver trumpets, and the illustrations of the trumpets looted from Herod's temple shown on Titus's arch, as well as representations on Jewish coins, these instruments were long, thin, and straight. It seems certain that they were played in pairs, but whether in unison, for harmony, or antiphonally, is not known. Musical performance on a single trumpet is attested from Egypt, but Israelite use is ceremonial, not for entertainment. If there was no solo use in Israel, the singular noun here must be collective (Sellers 1941).

8b. *Rouse alarms*. Literally "shout." In Josh 6:5 the shout is the response of the troops to the call of the trumpets. Although the activities are split up in the poetic design, we must suppose all the activities took place at all three places.

Beth Awen. The preposition *b* which is used with the two place names in v 8a operates here also. It is not unusual for Hosea to omit a preposition. Further, when a noun begins with a labial consonant, as here, phonetic influences frequently cause the dissimilation of the homorganic *b* to zero. Once more *Bêt 'āwen* is a pejorative name for Bethel.

The three towns mentioned are probably old mustering centers. If a foreign invader from the north had reached these hill strongholds, little of the northern kingdom would remain. They lie on the ridge road that leads from Jerusalem into Ephraim, through Benjaminite territory. They are, in fact, the first centers that an invader *from Judah* would meet: Gibeah is only three miles from Jerusalem, Ramah five, and Bethel eleven. The south-north orientation is seen by Alt as evidence of an invasion from the south, but the historical circumstances of such intervention and its political motivation are less clear. Alt interprets vv 8–9 as a warning given to Israel by the prophet. Hosea seems almost to welcome the disaster as confirmation of his prophecies.

Noth (1960:259) sees the towns as a recent acquisition in the course of the Syrian-Ephraimite attack on Jerusalem in 733 B.C.E. In that case 5:8 would be the muster for invasion, not for defense, but v 9 indicates that Ephraim, which is distinguished from Benjamin, is to be devastated.

"We are behind you, Benjamin." Literally, "after you, Benjamin." Judg 5:14 has the same expression, and its meaning should be sought there, since Hosea is apparently repeating an ancient and hallowed watchword, to be shouted in Beth Awen. Boling (1975:111–112) translates the Judges line, "Behind you, Benjamin," and thinks that Hosea's use is sarcastic. He adds, "It may have something to do with an obscure technical military term for 'bringing up the rear.'" In Judg 5:14, Benjamin is mentioned along with other tribes; here, along with three cities. Judg 5:14 describes the muster of the tribes; Hos 5:8 seems to describe the spreading of news or the advance of an army from town to town. Even if Beth Awen is not the same as Bethel but another place farther east (Josh 7:2; 8:12 Ketib; 18:12; I Sam 14:23), the towns are important in the tribal territory of Benjamin; Gibeah and Ramah have ancient associations, particularly with Saul and Samuel. Compare Mizpah and Tabor in 5:1.

It is important to assess the relationship of Benjamin in v 8 to Ephraim, Israel, and Judah, whose names follow in vv 9 and 10. Ephraim (a Joseph tribe; Hosea does not use the name Joseph as Amos does, 5:6,15; 6:6) and Benjamin are prominent in the northern confederation, even though historically Benjamin is often linked with Judah. The prominence of Benjamin here may reflect, not some local incident, but a time when this tribe had a position of leadership in the national army (cf. Ps 68:28). This would belong to the tradition about the youngest son, or an unexpected son of old age being superior to the older brothers. This is not the marching order of Numbers 10, and may come from the time of the Judges.

The mention of "the princes of Judah" in 5:10 suggests that the whole nation is in the picture here. The series in Judg 5:14–15 — *śrśm, 'ḥryk, mḥqqym, mśkym, śry* — suggests that the several detachments of the tribes, with their distinctive names, were "followers of Benjamin." The phrase *'ḥryk bnymyn* could be a construct, the first part a participle or noun, and *k,* a construct marker (Andersen 1969b). A participle ("following") finds support in the apparent verbal use of *'ḥr* in Ps 68:26. In I Kings 1:7 *'ḥry 'dnyh* probably means "(they helped) as followers of Adonijah." In I Kings 21:21, *'ḥryk* means "your progeny," elliptical for "your seed after you," as the idiom in I Kings 14:10 and 16:3 makes clear. On this analogy, *'ḥryk bnymym* means "your successors, O Benjamin." For the use of *'ḥr* with the meaning "tarry" see Judg 5:28, and compare Ugaritic. These meanings would not seem to be applicable to Hos 5:8. If those who come behind are those who follow, rather than those who succeed or delay, then the whole nation, not just Benjamin, is being called together after the manner of the tribal muster in the days of the Judges.

Given that such a solution is problematic, the preposition of MT is to be preferred; "behind you, Benjamin" can be construed in two ways. Either it is a verbless clause — "Behind you was Benjamin" (Judg 5:14, *NAB*), which leaves "you" unidentified; or the prepositional phrase is used as an imperative — "Look behind you, O Benjamin" (Hos 5:8, *NAB*), or "We are behind you, Benjamin," a rallying cry. The latter would be the object of the verb "shout." The difficulty of MT was felt in antiquity. LXX reads *eksestē* and this has been used to emend the text to something like *haḥărîdû,* "Terrify Benjamin." This parallels *harî'û;* but implies that Benjamin is a victim.

If the phrase is nominal ("followers of Benjamin") then it would be the subject of the verb "to rouse alarms"; the soldiers utter the battle cry. It is relevant to record that the accepted meaning of *'aḥar,* "after, behind," has been rejected in favor of "with" in some of its occurrences (Dahood and Penar 1970:390); note also Exod 11:5 (pointed out by Alan Friend, in a letter); Gen 16:13; 22:13; 24:67.

9a. *will be.* Verses 9 and 10 should probably be treated as a unit. The term "the tribes of Israel" covers the whole nation. The preposition *b* could mean "among" or "against"; since Ephraim is being singled out for special accusation in the presence of the assembled tribes (cf. Judges 19–21, where Mizpah, Gibeah, and Bethel are prominent, along with Shiloh), "among" is preferable. In any case the perfect verb asserts that Yahweh has made known Ephraim's fate with certainty. Since Ephraim

and Judah are common parallels, vv 9a and 10a may belong together as a
discontinuous bicolon if *hāyû* at the beginning of the latter is future consecutive, in spite of the absence of the *wāw;* see the NOTES on v 5. Each
line would then refer to the threatened punishment, and both be summed
up in v 10b, where "them" would refer to the whole nation, and not just
the princes of Judah mentioned in v 10a. The reference to the "day of accusation" in v 9a agrees with the picture of a general assize in the assembly of tribes, where the performance of each tribe is under scrutiny. The
movement of thought through vv 9 and 10 can then be traced to v 11b.
Verse 11 contains the accusation made "on the day of dispute."

accusation. Because what precedes it is a complete clause, it is possible
that the phrase "on the day of accusation" goes with v 9b. The feminine
participle, "(with) certainty," may go with the noun *tôkēḥâ,* "a valid accusation, a faithful reproof," cf. *běrîtî ne'ĕmenet,* "my confirmed covenant" (Ps 89:29), *hā'ēl hanne'ĕmān,* "the trustworthy god" (Deut 7:9).

10a. *princes.* The king is not mentioned because the terminology is
drawn from the period of the Judges (Ps 68:28), and refers to the tribe
as such.

Judah. This is the only place in the entire book where Ginsberg
(1971:1017) thinks that "Judah" is authentic.

move. Those who move boundary markers are criminals. Assuming that
hāyû is past tense, and believing that a simile is not appropriate, Gordis
(1943:177) has identified the *k* as asseverative — "the princes of Judah
are indeed those who remove landmarks." Since the crime in the legal tradition is domestic, while the one here is international, we retain the simple
sense of *k.* The heinous domestic offense (Deut 19:14) is appropriately
cursed in Deut 27:17. This and Hos 5:10 are the only places where the
participle *mśyg* is used. This is further evidence for Hosea's dependence
on the Deuteronomic tradition, but it does not explain why he should seize
on this particular crime to characterize the princes of Judah. The crime
here is not a case of social injustice with regard to personal property; the
vocabulary has been extended to the relationships between the nations
who were formerly members of the tribal league. Thus the annexation of
territory may be described as moving the intertribal boundary marker.

like the waters of the flood. Literally, "like the waters." The Masoretes
have pointed this with the article; the phrase refers to the waters of the
sea which Yahweh will pour out over the surface of the earth (Amos
5:8; 9:6). The imagery is derived from the flood tradition, and suggests
judgment on a cosmic scale; cf. Hos 4:3.

10b. *fury.* This noun usually occurs in parallel with *'ap* (Hos 13:11;
Amos 1:11; Hab 3:8).

11a. *oppressed . . . crushed.* The passive participles identified by the
Masoretes make this verse hard to interpret, since there is no mark of fu-

ture reference. The text seems to say that Ephraim is oppressed and crushed by judgment, because he preferred to walk after *ṣāw*, viz., judgment for this aberration has already taken place. How this happened is not explained, unless the sickness to be described in v 13 is the result of Yahweh's destructive activity described in v 12. No identification of this calamity with any known historical event has proved convincing. The future orientation must be supposed from the context, especially v 9a.

As noted, Hos 5:7 contains an echo of Deut 28:27–33, part of a long and terrifying commination, which says that "you will be nothing but *'āsûq wĕrāṣûṣ* every day," when a nation whom you did not know eats up the fruit of your land and all your exertion (v 33). Hos 5:11a could be a similar curse. The parallelism of the same verbs in Amos 4:1 refers to social injustice of a vicious and ruthless kind; it refers to those "who oppress the poor / and crush the destitute."

The phrase "crushed (in) judgment" presents difficulties. This is the only place where *rṣṣ* is used with *mišpāṭ*. The coupling of a noun for justice with a verb for injustice seems incongruous, but *mišpāṭ* could be a legal verdict or a covenant curse, applied to Ephraim. Verse 11b describes the particular sin (walking after Filth) for which Ephraim will be "oppressed," though usual connectives are lacking.

NAB makes the argument oversubtle and rhetorical: "Is Ephraim maltreated, his rights violated? / No, he has willingly gone after filth." There is no indication that v 11a is a question; and it is better to see *kî* at the beginning of v 11b as introducing the reason for the adverse verdict of v 11a.

11b. *persistently.* Quite apart from Hosea's propensity for two-verb phrases, *y'l* followed by a finite verb is not uncommon, and there is no need to normalize *hālak* to an infinitive, as in I Sam 17:39. There seem to be two roots *y'l.* *Y'l* I, which occurs only as *Nip'al*, means "to be foolish," because of ignorance (Jer 5:4). (Ginsberg 1967:77 suggests that the *Hip'il* here has the same meaning, citing the analogous case of *hiskîl/niskal.*) The parallel with *ḥṭ'* in Num 12:11 suggests wickedness, not just stupidity. *Y'l* II occurs only in the *Hip'il*, "to be persistent," and does not imply that the action is sinful, merely tenacious; it often implies repeated but unsuccessful attempts. The *Hip'il* used here agrees with the statement about Israel's stubbornness in 4:16, but a charge of folly would also fit the case. A *Hip'il* of *y'l* I could be elative—"they reached the limit of folly."

gone off. The idiom of "walking behind" is used to describe loyalty to Yahweh (1:2; 11:10) or deflection to a rival (2:7,15). This strongly suggests that *ṣaw* here refers to an alien god.

Filth. For MT's *ṣw*, perhaps read *ṣw'*, the ' lost by the failure to record the sequence *w'* twice. A four-letter word is needed to bring out the asso-

ciations of this term (however read) with human excrement. The spelling
ṣāw occurs only here, if correct, and in Isa 28:10,13, where it occurs in
the drunkards' mocking jingle:

> ṣaw lāṣāw ṣaw lāṣāw
> qaw lāqāw qaw lāqāw

This has been subject to many different interpretations. The familiar version, "Precept upon precept, precept upon precept, / Line upon line, line
upon line," finds real words, tracing ṣaw to the root ṣwy, "to command."
Others have found it a meaningless ditty, the monosyllables being non-
sense words, suitable for the mouths of drunks. Perhaps they were intended to mock Isaiah's prophetic messages as unintelligible gibberish
(Hos 9:7), or infants' babble. Driver (1954a:89–90, 168) has pointed
out that ṣaw and qaw come in the sequence of the letters ṣ and q in the alphabet, suggesting that this is a schoolroom jingle. Whatever they meant
by the taunt, Isaiah throws it back at them, comparing it with the unintelligible speech of foreigners by whom Yahweh will now speak to
Ephraim.

Ṣāw in Hos 5:11 and in Isa 28:10,13 should be explained similarly, as
the passages have much in common. In Isaiah 28 the drunkenness of
Ephraim is the main theme; here it is marginal (cf. Hos 4:18), but it
reappears in full force in c 7. Isaiah portrays both priest and prophet staggering in their intoxication (Isa 28:7); cf. Hos 4:5. Isaiah's disgusting description of the tables covered with filthy vomit (qî' ṣō'â) (Isa 28:8) is a
sickening picture of a helpless drunk. The word ṣ'h means "excrement,"
and is derived from the root ṣw', "to stink." In Hos 5:11 traditional renderings like "he walked behind a commandment" are not suitable (contra
Good 1966b:277). The filth of drunkenness is meant. The complete
idiom means to join a cult by following a detestable god, called "Shit." In
Deut 4:3, a similar idiom describes Israel's perversion to Baal Peor. Jer
2:5 describes apostasy as "walking behind" hahebel, "the empty thing,"
(= habba'al, as the play on sounds suggests). LXX renders tōn mataiōn,
"the vanities," which could be a guess, but probably indicates another
Vorlage which read šāw', another term for a false god (Hos 10:4; 12:12).
Other suggestions have been made. Alt, for example, emended to ṣārô,
"his enemy," with the explanation that Ephraim had followed Damascus
as an ally although traditionally they had been enemies.

VIII. THE STATE OF THE NATION: ASSYRIA AND YAHWEH'S SENTENCE (5:12–15)

Yahweh as the vermin of the people's open sores
5:12a   I am like larvae in Ephraim
12b   and like decay in the house of Judah.
13a   Ephraim saw his wound
          and Judah his oozing infection.
          Ephraim went to Assyria
          and (Judah) sent to the Great King.
13b   But he cannot heal you,
          and he cannot cure the infection of either of you.

Yahweh as the ravisher of his people
14a   I am like a lion for Ephraim
          and like a young lion for the house of Judah.
14b   I, yes I, will rip them to pieces.
          I will go and carry them off.
          No one will rescue them.
15a   I will go and return to my lair.
15b   When they realize they are guilty
          they will seek my favor.
          When they are distressed,
          they will search hard for me.

NOTES

5:12–15. The alternate speakers in the exchange that stretches from 5:12 to 6:6 are not overtly identified. It is clear, however, that God speaks in 5:12–15, and that Israel or some Israelites speak in 6:1–3, while God resumes speech in 6:4–6.

The consistent parallelism here casts Ephraim and Judah in similar roles with similar fates. In vv 8–11, Judah's sin is political and Ephraim's cultic; in vv 12–15, however, both states have the same faults and Yahweh deals with them in the same way. The historical outcome was otherwise: Assyria conquered Israel and deported the population; Judah survived. No hint of this distinction is given in c 5. In fact, Hos 1:6–7 is the only passage in the prophecy that could be read as asserting that Judah will be favored and spared, and we have already shown that this interpretation is not certain. Everywhere else Judah and Israel/Ephraim are together, in sin and under threat. Hosea clearly did not anticipate the discrimination that would send Ephraim and Judah along different paths. Hosea's messages must have been fixed before it became evident that history would not confirm them. By the seventh century the survival of Judah would have required drastic revision in Hosea if a Judean editor felt obligated to bring the book into line with the facts by adding to it prophecies after the events.

5:12. *larvae . . . decay.* The same words occur in Job 13:28, but in reverse order (Pope 1973:106). The parallelism in Hos 5:12 would suggest either that "rottenness" is abstract for concrete, or more likely, that '*š* and *rqb* form a single phrase. *Rāqāb* usually describes the rottenness in wood or bones (Hab 3:16; Prov 12:4; 14:30; cf. Job 41:19; Isa 40:20) or clothes (Job 13:28), caused by a grub of some kind; and '*āš* refers to the maggots that already have infested open wounds, and begun to devour the flesh, whether of the living or the dead. The phrase '*āš . . . rāqāb* means "the larvae (that cause) rottenness." The definite articles of the MT do not have a high claim for acceptance; if authentic, they would point to *the* larvae of proverbial speech. The unification of the phrase points to the wholeness of the bicolon and the structure of the passage. Both Judah and Israel are suffering from injuries as a result of conflict (vv 8–11); they appeal to Assyria (v 13a), in vain (v 13b), because it is Yahweh who has done the damage (vv 12,14). Only when they seek him (v 15b) will they be healed (6:1). It is not as though Yahweh were larvae only for Ephraim and rottenness for Judah. He is the same for both; each will be treated alike. Since the image of sores dominates v 13, and larvae (rather than moths) grow in open sores, we so render '*š*.

The two clauses in this bicolon have no verbs, so the time is left indeterminate; most likely it is not future. Hos 6:1 makes it clear that Yahweh caused the sickness. A connection between v 12 and v 13 might be traced through the pronouns. "I" is prominent in v 12a. In this position it usually contrasts with some other agent also referred to by a pronoun. The nearest instance is "he" in v 13b. Yahweh's power to inflict injury is then contrasted with the Assyrian inability to cure it, precisely because Yahweh has caused it.

13a. *wound . . . oozing infection.* Ḥŏlî is generic; *māzôr* is more specific, and indicates an ulcer or a boil. In Isa 1:6 the verb *zwr* describes the squeezing out of pus. A holistic approach to poetic parallelism recognizes that no sharp distinction between the affliction of the two states can be insisted on. Together the words indicate an infected, running wound. Each group is suffering in the same way, and each resorts to the same remedy — Assyria.

Ephraim . . . (Judah). Ephraim and Judah are closely paralleled through 5:8–15. The references to Israel are less clear, and the mention of Benjamin in v 8 complicates the picture. We cannot be sure that the entire passage is built around the same historical moment. The parallelism is maintained throughout the five bicola in vv 12–14a. This unit is enclosed by the closely similar bicola, vv 12 and 14a. The use of synonyms for "lion" in the latter shows clearly that Ephraim and Judah are on the same footing, and the same is true in v 12 as well. The name Ephraim occurs in the first line in four of these five bicola. The name Judah occurs in parallel with it in three of the five — twice as "the house of Judah." The alteration of Judah to Israel by various scholars (Harper 1905:277; Batten 1929:259) is completely unjustified. In v 13a the verbs and pronouns in concord with Ephraim and Judah are singular and third person. In v 13b the address switches to second person, and the number changes to plural; the states are addressed jointly. If Judah as well as Ephraim cannot be healed by Assyria, Judah must, like Ephraim, have appealed to Assyria for aid. We suggest, therefore, that Judah is the subject of the last clause in v 13a. The name is omitted for the sake of the rhythm, as the symmetry of vv 12 and 13 shows.

12	*waʾănî kāʿāš lĕʾeprāyim*		8/9 syllables
	wĕkārāqāb lĕbêt yĕhûdâ		9
13a	*wayyarʾ ʾeprayim ʾet-ḥolyô*		7/8
	wîhûdâ ʾet-mĕzōrô		7/8
	wayyēlek ʾeprayim ʾel-ʾaššûr		8/9
	wayyišlaḥ	*ʾel-melek yārēb*	7/8
	. . . .		
14a	*kî ʾānōkî kaššaḥal lĕʾeprayim*		9/11
	wĕkakkĕpîr lĕbêt yĕhûdâ		9

The close parallelism of the second bicolon in v 13a is seen in the sequence "went . . . sent." Hosea uses the verb *hlk* as the first member of a two-verb phrase in 1:6; 3:1; 5:14,15; 6:1. Hence "Ephraim (and Judah) went-and-sent (an embassage) to Malki-Rab, of Assyria." Note the plural "they walked (to) Assyria" in 7:11b. In any case *hlk* has nothing to do with exile; it is used as an auxiliary verb which may describe eager or repeated activity.

Great King. LXX *Iarim* or *Iareib* confirms the MT *yārēb*, which must

have been identified as the personal name of an Assyrian king, in spite of
the unusual position of the (indefinite) title "king" before the name. This
doubtless arose from misdivision of *malkî rāb*. The title *mlk rb* is found
on the Sefire I inscription (Fitzymer 1967:61) and represents the common Assyrian honorific *šarru rabū*. The first word has been translated into
Hebrew, while the second is common to both branches of Semitic, and has
the same meaning in Hebrew. The original *malkirab* probably introduced
the vowel *-i-* after the analogy of Hebrew names which have *malki-* as
their first element. Since only the title is used, we cannot identify the Assyrian monarch. One of the weak predecessors of Tiglath Pileser III is
probably intended. Good (1966b:277–278) retains *yārēb,* as does Ginsberg (1971), who says it means "patron king." Cf. Isa 51:22.

13b. *he.* The prominent pronoun at the beginning of v 13b contrasts
with "I" in vv 12 (and 14b). The same emphasis is placed on *hû'* (Yahweh) in 6:1, which makes the contrary assertion that Yahweh *can* heal.

cannot. Hosea constantly asserts the impotence of heathen idols and
foreign powers, a point developed in v 14b.

While Assyria could hardly be accused of having an altruistic concern
in the well-being of any other nation, it had a strong interest in dominating all the nations in the region. Its characteristic policy was to prevent the
formation of alliances and coalitions among the nation states, by exploit-
ing local rivalries and hostility, and by reducing some of them to vassalage
and attacking the recalcitrant remainder. The context of this Assyrian
contact is unknown but it must predate Ahaz's embassy to Assyria about
734.

cure. Yigheh is a hapax legomenon. The translation is based on poetic
parallelism. If *māzôr* is taken as a flowing wound, perhaps "to staunch" is
the meaning. The verb has two objects, unlike the preceding *lirpō',* which
seems to have none. Since *rāpā'* can have either the patient or the disease
as its grammatical object, its elliptical object must be *ḥŏlî // māzôr* while
the benefactive *lākem* matches the partitive *mikkem,* "either of you," here.
The etymology of *gāhâ* suggests an intransitive verb, with sickness as the
subject — "the sore did not remove from you." This spoils the symmetry
of the bicolon, and takes the attention away from the failure of the Assyrians to cure Israel's ills. It is not necessary, however, to bring the lines
into grammatical congruence; that is, the implied object of the first verb
(illness) can be the subject of the second verb; cf. 4:12a. A *Hip'il*
(*yagheh*) would be transitive and has been suggested as an emendation,
but the point is not material.

14a. *lion.* Hebrew has at least six words for "lion"; five of them occur in
Job 4:10–11. The precise denotation of each is not known. The lion was
the most fearsome of all predators known to ancient inhabitants of Palestine; it is referred to as such dozens of times in the Bible. According to

proverb, it is the mightiest animal (Prov 30:30); there is nothing stronger than it (Judg 14:18). A man who can overcome one in single combat is the greatest of heroes. This is how Samson (Judg 14:5), David (I Sam 17:34–37), and Benaiah (II Sam 23:20) made their fame. Saul and Jonathan were stronger than lions (II Sam 1:23). The lion was dangerous because it attacked human beings (I Kings 13:24; II Kings 17:25–26; Amos 5:19; Prov 22:13; 26:13) as well as livestock (Amos 3:12). A predatory ruler (Prov 28:15) or an aggressive nation (Jer 50:17) could be compared with a lion. Nahum's description of Assyria is classic. An individual under extreme distress might blame his condition on the hostility of God, who like a lion is breaking all his bones (Isa 38:13; cf. Lam 3:4; Job 7:15). In keeping with this there are several speeches in which Yahweh talks about himself, or is referred to, in similar terms, using one or another of the words for "lion": 'ărî (Lam 3:10); 'aryeh (Isa 31:4; Hos 11:10; Amos 3:8); šaḥal (Hos 5:14; 13:7); kĕpîr (Hos 5:14; Isa 31:4; Jer 25:38); lābî' (Hos 13:8). The thought is quite prominent in Hosea, who uses four of the lion words. Hosea, like the other prophets, depicts Yahweh as behaving violently. Hosea adorns with the lion similes language from the old boasting poem of Deut 32:39, echoed in Ps 50:22 and Mic 5:7. The verbs in v 14b are not given objects, but v 14a makes it clear that the statements are not generalized; Ephraim and Judah are the victims.

14b. *No one will rescue them.* The verb *nṣl* may mean "to take away" rather than "to rescue"; see Gen 31:9; Exod 12:36; cf. *1QapGn* 22:10,19 (Fitzmyer 1971:72, 74). The usual phrase "from my hand" (Deut 32:39; Isa 43:13; Hos 2:12) is lacking, as at Mic 5:7. The statement that "there is no rescuer" is the final tribute to Yahweh's incontestable power. Verse 14 may describe the mauling Ephraim and Judah have received. Attempts have been made to connect v 14 historically with an event such as the Assyrian devastation of Gilead and Galilee. Such a warning, in traditional language, does not require a specific fulfillment.

15a. *I will go and return.* The phrase '*ēlēk* '*ăšûbâ* in v 15 is like several others in Hosea; cf. 2:9 and 6:3–4. The Masoretic punctuation of '*ēlēk* with *zāqēf qāṭōn* in v 14 should be revised to restore the phrase '*ēlēk* '*eśśā*'. The effect is seen in the similar phrasing of these double verbs, where *hlk* is an expression of resolve.

lair. Literally "place." Since this is a general word, its connotation in each occurrence can be judged only by the circumstances. It can scarcely bear the weight that Good (1966b:279) places on it. He points out, quite appropriately, that Yahweh's "place" in many instances is a shrine. It "is also found in two theophanic contexts as the place from which Yahweh comes forth (*yṣ*') to execute his judgment (Isa 26:21; Mic 1:3)." Verse

15 speaks of a decisive withdrawal, and provides no basis for locating the poem in "cultic sites in which theophanic liturgies take place."

There is a paradox in this language. Sometimes Yahweh is inaccessible because he has withdrawn (5:6). There is no use looking for him; you won't find him even if you try. On the other hand, he is waiting to be sought; and people will do this when they are in distress (v 15b).

15b. *When.* For the same idiom see Gen 27:44–45. Yahweh will absent himself only until the following conditions are satisfied.

guilty. Ye'šĕmû can mean "they will be guilty"; cf. 4:15; this meaning does not do justice to the present context. They are obviously guilty; what is needed is confession and contrition. This will come through distress (v 15b), and be expressed by turning back to Yahweh (6:1). But there is no acknowledgment of guilt in the liturgical form. Because of this difficulty, an emendation to yāšōmmû, "they will be devastated," following LXX, has been accepted by some scholars. Either the verb 'šm here is subjective, or it refers to the guilt sacrifice; certainly the associations of the word are as often cultic as juridical. Here the reference is to recognizing guilt. The futile search for Yahweh "with their flocks and herds" (5:6) can be changed into effective discovery. In the light of Deut 32:39, this penance should include acknowledgment that it was Yahweh who made them sick, and he alone who can heal. This is the form of confession in 6:1. The tokens of admitting guilt are returning to Yahweh and seeking him.

seek . . . search. Šiḥēr is a synonym of biqqēš, and this parallelism serves as a guide to the compact structure of v 15b. The phrase baṣṣar lāhem is parallel to the acknowledgment of guilt. The speech that follows immediately in c 6 is what they will say when they return. The similarity of the root šḥr to the word for "dawn" scarcely warrants the identification of a dawn liturgy (Good 1966b:280).

distressed. There is a parallelism between alternating expressions:

> When they realize they are guilty
> they will seek my favor.
> When they are distressed
> they will search hard for me.

The state of distress brings on renunciation of the arrogance that prevents contrition. The intention of the punishment is not to destroy the people permanently, but to bring them to a different mind. In terms of poetic arrangement being distressed and admitting guilt are complementary, but logically the sequence is the other way around.

IX. THE STATE OF THE NATION:
ISRAEL'S REPENTANCE
(6:1–3)

The people speak

6:1a Come, let us return to Yahweh.

1b   Although he tore us apart, he will heal us.

       Although he smashed us, he will bandage us.

2a   He will revive us after two days,

       and on the third day he will raise us up.

2b   We will live in his presence so that we know him.

3a   We will pursue knowledge of Yahweh.

       His utterance is as certain as sunrise.

3b   He will come like rain for us.

       Like spring rain he will water the earth.

NOTES

6:1–3. This unframed speech by the people is a highly rhythmic piece, though the lines are not of uniform length. Only v 2a and v 3b constitute bicola of a canonical kind, i.e. lines with a high degree of parallelism. Verse 1b also has parallelism, but of a different kind, which is complicated by the use of four verbs, one of which is monosyllabic. In this bicolon, condensation is achieved by double-duty items: (*kî*) *hû'* goes with *yak* as well as *ṭārāp;* the object *-nû* goes also with the preceding verb in each case.

There is only one line which lacks close connections with the rest, v 3aB; its parallel is v 5b. Together they constitute a bicolon which goes with v 3b — each has a double simile describing the beneficent response of Yahweh. The speech made by Yahweh in vv 4–6 matches the speech made by Ephraim and Judah in vv 1–3. The statements of what "we" will do (v 1a and v 3aA) go together, and encompass the main statement of what Yahweh will do (v 1b–2).

The most remarkable feature of the composition is the highly concen-
trated use of verbs. Of twenty-two words in vv 1–3aA, twelve are verbs.
The situation in c 6 is one of suspense. Yahweh has beaten the people
severely (v 5a) because their *hesed* is so ephemeral. They are dead
through their sins, and he is waiting for them to repent. The question of
what to do next (v 4a) will be answered on the basis of v 6. This is the
platform for the future relationship, just as it has always been the basis of
the covenant. The response in 6:1–3 remains a possibility. If this acknowledgment is made, then Yahweh will come like the rain, and his word
will go forth like sunlight.

The interchange between Yahweh and his people in 6:1–6 is part of a
larger poem which begins at 5:12, and has four stanzas of comparable
size. Stanza I (5:12–13) has sixty-four syllables. Stanza II (5:14–15) has
sixty-four syllables. Stanza III is less clearly defined, because of the floating line in v 3aB; but the "we" passage continues to the end of v 3, so we
can say that Stanza III is 6:1–3 (eighty syllables). Stanza IV (6:4–6) is
another of Yahweh's speeches, which is partly retrospective and partly de-
liberative; it has sixty-eight syllables. Stanzas II and III have affinities, and
so have I and II. Each stanza has a bicolon with a double simile, and a
fifth pair of similes is distributed over Stanzas III and IV. The slight
difference between I + IV and II + III can be traced to the unique line (v
2b), which is the climax of the unit.

6:1a. *Come.* The plural cohortative *nēlēk* or *nēlĕkâ* is not used. The imperative *lĕkû*, which is preferred here, is an exclamation, often used to
command attention at the beginning of a speech.

let us return. In sequence with an imperative, the long form of the
prefixed verb (*nāšûbâ*) may be subjunctive, indicating purpose — "that
we may return" (Dahood 1968:8). Here, however, the preceding verb is
probably not a command for motion. Both verbs do have full force in
5:15, and their repetition puts Yahweh's action and the people's action in
counterpoise.

1b. *Although.* The *kî* is usually translated "for," making v 1b a clause
subordinate to the opening exhortation, which gives the reason for returning to Yahweh; but the fact that Yahweh had ripped them is no reason for
returning. As so often in Hosea, the dependent clause comes at the end of
the pericope; see e.g. the discussion of 4:14b. Verse 1a and v 3b present
the two sides of the movement into reconciliation. When Yahweh comes
like the rain, the healing in v 1 will take place, and it is because he will
come like the rain that the people return to him. Verse 3b comes logically
and chronologically before vv 1b and 2. It is also possible that v 3a, with
its repetition of "Yahweh," is parallel to v 1a; but it is more likely that it
describes the pursuit of Yahweh by the revived people after restoration,

not by the repentant people before revival. Verse 1b then marks a new beginning, and *kî* must be concessive. For examples of concessive *kî* in similar syntax, see Gen 3:5; 4:12; 8:21; etc. and Vriezen (1958). Here the conjunction governs the next pair of clauses as well. The absence of a conjunction before *yak* is startling, if we expected a *waw*-consecutive (**wayyak*) after the perfect *ṭārāp;* but the sequence *qtl/yqtl* with past reference is thoroughly poetic (Dahood and Penar 1970:420–422); the omission of the conjunction brings *yk* into tandem with *ṭrp*. By the same device the next two verbs, *yĕḥayyēnû* and *yĕqīmēnû*, whose clauses have no conjunctions, are brought into line with *yaḥbĕšēnû*, which they define and amplify. Whereas each of these four verbs has the same object *-nû*, "us," neither *ṭārāp* nor *yak* has an expressed object; the sort of reciprocal brachylogy shown here is not as common as ellipsis of a suffix with the *second* of two verbs which have the same object.

　　tore . . . heal . . . smashed . . . bandage. These verbs, describing the activity of Yahweh, are paralleled with other statements made nearby. That Yahweh can tear to pieces without interference (5:14b), and heal without rival (5:13b) has been asserted. He can both destroy and recreate; cf. Isa 19:22. How metaphorical is the language of sickness-healing and death-revival in 5:12 – 6:6? In reference to the nation as an entity, and not its individual members severally, the language is of necessity figurative. The question is one of degree. Do references to sickness indicate a serious mishap, from which the people might recover; does the language of death indicate annihilation?

　　The imagery is mixed: *ṭārāp*, "to rip, rend, tear apart," is the act of a beast of prey, especially a lion, as in 5:14; rending can be done with claws (Deut 33:20) or teeth (Job 16:9; 18:4). The emphasis here is on the mutilation and eating of the victim, presumably after it is killed. It is not a mild but a fatal injury that Yahweh inflicts; compare the killing in 2:5: 6:5 is equally explicit, although with a different figure.

　　The understanding of the language of resurrection in v 2 will depend on the evaluation of the references to sickness and death in v 1. Only recognition of death itself will do justice to the passage. Note the following points: (1) Yahweh's assault in the guise of a lion represents a remarkable assimilation of the role of Mot (Death) in Canaanite theology, and of other, similar gods of the Underworld, in the ancient Near East (H. O. Thompson 1970). (2) In 5:14 such an attack is clearly fatal. (3) This language stands directly in the tradition of Deut 32:39 and I Sam 2:6, which state bluntly that Yahweh kills. (4) The verb *nky* generally describes a murderous blow. In Gen 14:15 it implies serious defeat, not merely attack; see also Gen 32:9; 34:30. The sequence *hikkâ*, "to strike," and *hārag*, "to slay," in Exod 2:12–14 makes the point; cf. *hrg* in Hos 6:5. (5) The fact that Yahweh slew them is stated clearly in Hos 6:5, and our structural analysis has shown that this passage goes with 5:14, both preceding 6:1–3 in time.

The matching verbs *heal* and *bandage* are preparatory for the stronger and climactic language of v 2. The parallelism of *rp'* and *ḥbš* is used in a similar passage in Job 5:18, as well as in Ezek 30:21; 34:4; and Isa 30:26, where the eschatological reference is more explicit.

2a. *revive . . . raise (us) up.* The repeated pronoun suffix object on four verbs in vv 1b and 2a has a forceful, chant-like effect, and form critics have sought to recognize a penitential song. Simply because similar language is found in the Psalter, there is no need to identify its use here as insincere, "words which Hosea's contemporaries, perhaps the priests, uttered in opposition to him" (Wolff 1974:109). Hos 13:14 contains a similar affirmation embedded in a context of reproach. Verse 2 opens and closes with the statements that he will make us live and we shall live. Explicit hope for resurrection of the body can hardly be denied in this passage, but commentators have been reluctant to admit it. The sequence "two days . . . on the third day" is an artistic turn, not a time schedule, though it may reflect the widespread belief that there was a three-day period after death before the final separation of the soul from the body. Such evidence is no warrant for finding here a reflex of the myth of the god who dies and is restored to life. In the Canaanite religion this is Baal, but this motif is not as prominent in the Ugaritic myths as is sometimes supposed, and not until the Tammuz cult comes in do we find this idea in Israel. In any case the death and resurrection of the people has nothing in common with a myth in which *a god* dies and comes back to life.

The death and resurrection descriptions are comparable to those of Ezekiel 37, although not as graphic or detailed. Hosea reflects the adaptation of individual physical death and resurrection to the experience of the nation, and thus is figurative. The underlying picture, while deriving from the realm of sickness and severe injury, and associated with it, must also embrace the notion of real death and real revivification. Most scholars find a doctrine of death and resurrection of people at this stage in Israel's thought altogether too advanced. Recent research on the belief of early Israelites in personal survival after physical death has weakened this approach (Tromp 1969).

Unconvinced that resurrection is intended, finding the reduction of this strong language to the level of illness unsatisfactory, and finding further that there is no trace of the myth of the dying and rising god, Wijngaards (1967) has proposed for 6:2 a *Sitz-im-Leben* in Israel's covenant thinking. He brings comparative evidence from ancient treaty-making to show that the formal dethronement of a disloyal vassal was described as "killing" him, and his reinstatement as bringing him back to life. We have petitions from a suppliant, beseeching his lord to raise him to life. There must be a sense in which the people speaking in 6:1–3 are not wholly dead, for they make an exhortation to return to Yahweh. Full acceptance of Wijngaards' hypothesis is made difficult by the absence in 5:12 – 6:6 of supporting forms of covenant formulation. This is not to deny that covenant thinking is present in a general way; note e.g. *ḥesed* in 6:4,6. Nonetheless, the language of resurrection is not used by Hosea in the places where covenant renewal is to the fore, notably c 2. Other instances of the same usage in the Hebrew Bible are not clear enough to lend the support needed to prove the theory.

The *Pi'el* of *ḥāyâ* normally has a factitive meaning, "to make alive"; the permissive meaning "to let live" (Exod 1:22; Num 31:15; Josh 9:15) is secondary. The sequence in I Sam 2:6 is decisive: *yhwh mēmît ûměḥayyeh*, with its continuation *môrîd šě'ôl wayyā'al*, "he brings down to Sheol and he brings up" (cf. Deut 32:39; Dahood 1968:72). So *hôrîd* also means "to kill" and *he'ělâ* means "to resurrect." The *Hip'il* of *qûm* means "to raise up, make to stand up"; in the present context it does not refer simply to reinstatement, but to rising from the grave after lying down in it. Cf. Ps 88:11; II Kings 13:21; Isa 26:14.

The frequent expressions of hope for personal resurrection in the Psalter have been amply displayed by Dahood (1966, 1968, 1970) and Tromp (1969). For example, the verbs *he'ělâ* and *ḥiyyâ* are parallel in Pss 30:4 and 71:20. In Isa 26:19 the statives *ḥāyâ* and *qām* are parallel, as in Hos 6:2; the idea of "waking up" is added to "getting up" and "coming up" to complete the description; cf. Dan 12:2 (Hartman and Di Lella 1978:273, 307–309). Job 14:12 uses the same word-field, adding *'wr*, "to be aroused."

The language of resurrection can be used dramatically to describe the recovery of a sick person from illness as rescue from the gates of Sheol (Johnson 1949:93–107; Mowinckel 1962 I:241; Hempel 1926:196–233), but it does not follow that such language was exclusively metaphorical, and even if so, it must have been grounded in a certain type of expectation about the future life. Its currency testifies to the fact that the idea of resurrection *after* death was entertained. Behind similar metaphorical uses of the language with regard to covenant restoration or the recovery of Israel from a national disaster (Dahl 1962), there lies a picture of death and resurrection which was widely accepted, though not a part of the major dogmatic traditions.

after two days. The use of the series x, x + 1 to achieve a climax is common in ancient literature, especially in the Canaanite tradition (Roth 1962, 1965). Here the sequence "two days" . . . "on the third day" is a little out of the ordinary, since in early narrative "the third day" conventionally marks a short interval (Gen 22:4; 34:25; 40:20; 42:18; Exod 19:11,16; etc.).

For *min̦*, "after," the sense preferred here, see *miyyāmîm*, "after some time" (Judg 11:4). The day *after* two days coincides with the third day, the day of the resurrection. In counting days, the first is "day one," or "one day," not "the first day" (Gen 1:5); the second day (*yôm šēnî*) would then count as "two days." This usage is found in Exod 21:21: *'ak 'im-yôm 'ô yômayim ya'ămōd*, "But if he gets up on the first or second day"; the case is analogous to that in Exod 21:19, and a special meaning, "to survive," for *'md* is not needed. Note also that *pa'ămāyim* means "a second time," not "twice," in Gen 41:32; Nah 1:9; *bištayim* means "a second time" in I Sam 18:21 and Job 33:14 ("another way"), and perhaps in Ps 62:12.

The attempt of Good (1966b:281) to find a "liturgical-festival" background to the two-three day period on the basis of Exod 19:11–16 is not convincing. It is more likely that the interval corresponds to the time during which it was urgent to revive the dead (Jonah 2:1) before bodily decay was irreparable (John 11:39).

2b. *in his presence*. The sense "in his presence" is quite suitable for the context, and agrees with 5:15; to enjoy life in the presence of Yahweh himself is the remedy for his withdrawal.

In Gen 17:18 Abraham prays, "O that Ishmael might live before you," according to the common understanding. Speiser has shown (1964:LXVIII) that contemporary idiom points to the meaning there "by your will," and that sense may be apposite here.

we know him. The suffix of *lpnyw* does double duty; Gordis (1971:151) claims the support of most moderns for the unnecessary emendation to **wĕnēdā'ēhû*, "and we shall know him." Correctly transferring the word to the preceding verse, he translates: "That we may live in His presence and know Him" (p. 115). This makes a climax rather like that in 2:22. Gordis gives two reasons for the move: (1) Instead of two beats in v 2b, and four beats in v 3aA, this rearrangement gives three beats in each. (2) It avoids the repetition of "know" in v 3. The redivision of the cola is appealing and results in improved line balance.

3a. *We will pursue knowledge of Yahweh*. The lack of a conjunction before *nirdĕpâ* marks the onset of a new clause, and secures the compound idea of the assiduous pursuit of the knowledge of Yahweh. In 4:6 *hadda'at* is despised by the priest. Here Israel pursues it. In 2:9 the woman vainly pursued her lovers; here Yahweh is the object of pursuit. This prominent personal dimension carries with it the idea of "love" and "fear" as ingredients in the "knowledge" of Yahweh.

Rādap, "pursue," usually means to chase with hostile intentions, but is used in a good sense in such constructions as *rōdĕpê ṣedeq* (Isa 51:1); the root *rdp* occurs again in 12:2.

His utterance. Literally "his going forth." We suggest that *môṣā'* is laconic for *môṣā' šĕpātayim* (Num 30:13; Deut 23:24; Jer 17:16; Ps 89:35) or *môṣā' pî-yhwh* (Deut 8:3), referring to a solemn vow or promise. Compare *hayyōṣē' mippeh,* a vow "that comes out of the mouth" (Num 30:3; 32:24), and *myhwh yāṣā' haddābār,* "the matter came forth from Yahweh" (Gen 24:50). The certainty of Yahweh's word encourages those who here renew their devotion. The imagery is common. Mic 7:9 speaks of vindication by God's justice as coming out into the light; Sir 24:3 uses the same simile of the brightness (or perhaps the regularity) of dawn. As a presage of coming day, so the word heralded by the prophet is the inauguration of Yahweh's "day." In Isa 2:3 the torah and the word of Yahweh "go out . . . from" (perhaps "at") Jerusalem, that is, they are issued or uttered by Yahweh from his headquarters there (cf. Amos 1:2). Since Isa 55:10 says that the word of Yahweh which goes out from his mouth is like rain (*gešem*), it may not be coincidence that the same image follows in Hos 6:3b. Our conclusions respecting v 3aB are confirmed by the parallelism of v 5b; we do not infer from this, however, that this discontinuous bicolon should be reassembled by moving one of the lines into contiguity with the other.

The difficulty of v 3aB is reflected in LXX, which reads, "As sure as the morning we shall find him," carrying on the idea of pursuing Yahweh from v 3aA, and completing it with the verb of 2:9. There are several possible explanations: (1) the Greek translator found the Hebrew unintelligible, and did his best to make sense, guided by the general context; or (2) he had a text in which the emendation had already been made; we are then obliged to retain the MT as the more difficult; or (3) the *Vorlage* implied by LXX could be genuine, the MT a corruption of it. Gordis offers *kĕšaḥărēnû kēn nimṣā'ēhû,* "As we seek Him, we shall surely find Him." The reading follows a proposal of F. Giesebrecht, based on LXX (Gordis 1971:114–115, 151). It is lucid and ingenious, and harmonizes with the context, but requires considerable alteration of the consonantal text. A further reason for not accepting this emendation is that the existing text, for all its difficulty, does offer a parallel for v 5b. With Giesebrecht's reading both vv 3aB and 5b are left as orphans.

In favor of the theory that *môṣā'ô* refers to Yahweh's personal appearance ("his coming out") are the following: (1) the next verse may say "and he will come like rain"; (2) such a return corresponds in reverse to the action of going off to his place (5:15a), as described in Isa 26:21 and Mic 1:3, where he comes down onto the earth in judgment from his heavenly headquarters; (3) *môṣā'* could have such a meaning in a few places; but the examples usually cited (II Sam 3:25; Ps 19:7) are further instances of the locative meaning — the place where one comes out. Against it are (1) the availability of ṣē'tô, "his going out" (Ps 121:8); (2) the parallelism with v 5b.

Is this coming forth of Yahweh, or of his word, like the light of dawn, beneficial or destructive? This is not easy to decide, and it is made more complicated by the insertion of the two lines of this bicolon (v 3aB and v 5b) like prongs into two different places in the discourse. One line is spoken by the people in a mood of hope; the other is spoken by Yahweh in a mixed setting. The image of light is certainly positive, for darkness is the symbol of judgment (Amos 5:20). The statement that his utterance is certain contrasts with Israel's fickleness (v 4b). His shining decree (mišpāṭ) is a determination to secure ḥesed and the knowledge of God in his people (v 6).

certain. This is the attribute of a decree which Yahweh has firmly established (Gen 41:32), and it is also an attribute of God himself, reading 'ēl nākôn at I Sam 23:23.

as sunrise. The translation of v 3aB is not secured by settling the basic meaning of each word: "like/as dawn (more exactly, sunrise or predawn twilight), certain is his going out." Like the simple natural similes about rain of v 3b, "like dawn" probably continues the eschatological evocations of the preceding verses.

Since môṣā', "going out," can mean "sunrise" (Ps 19:7) or the east — the place where the sun emerges (Ps 75:7) — one is tempted to sustain the imagery of the word "dawn" and see here a description of the great theophany as the rising of the sun (Mal 3:20), bringing light to the dead (Isa 26:19). Furthermore there is another comparison with light in v 5 echoing v 3aB, and suggesting that these be interpreted in a similar way. The covenant promise is as fixed as "the sun for light by day" (Jer 31:35).

As the predawn twilight, the glow of šaḥar is the first token that darkness is to be dispelled. This distinction is important for understanding the sequence of events in Gen 32:22–32, where the sun ('ôr) rises later than šaḥar. This predawn was the mystical moment when prayers were answered (Dahood 1968:54–55).

3b. rain . . . spring rain. The syntax of these lines is not clear; the most likely subject is Yahweh (as probably in Psalm 72), but it is possible, in the light of Deuteronomy 32 and Isaiah 55, that it is môṣā'ô, "his utterance." The difference is slight. The use of l, rather than 'el which is usual with bw', as well as the abnormal position of lānû at the end of the clause (ordinarily it would follow the verb), suggest that lānû is benefactive rather than locative. The second colon has no corresponding phrase, unless 'āreṣ is the parallel, with l in lānû doing double duty. Comparison with Jer 5:24 suggests that three words for "rain" are present in v 3b, but the sequence of the last two is usually m/yôreh ûmalqôš (Deut 11:14; Jer

5:24; Joel 2:23). *Yôreh* is the early rain of autumn; *malqôš* is the late rain of spring. Hos 10:12 matches 6:3b rather closely: *'ad-yābô' wĕyōreh,* "until he comes and he rains." *Ywrh* is also a verb in 6:3; if three kinds of rain were in the simile, we would have expected **whywrh.* Rather, *ywrh* parallels *yābô;* the pattern is chiastic.

> He will come (A) like the rain (B) for us (C).
> Like spring rain (B') he will water (A') the earth (C').

The mood is altogether benign; it is not the terrifying theophany of the thunderstorm, it is the bounty of the good king (II Sam 23:4; Ps 72:6).

earth. Deut 11:14 has *mĕṭar-'arṣĕkem,* "the rain of your land," the "genitive" of the construct being benefactive. This phrase comes in parallel with *yôreh umalqôš.* This leaves open the slight possibility that *ywrh 'rṣ* is a construct phrase, "rain (for the) land."

The motif of rain does not seem to have any connection with special prayers in time of drought, or with a seasonal liturgy, which places all talk about death and resurrection in the context of a fertility cult. It is a simile; and the other similes so abundant in these chapters cannot be used as pointers to cult events.

X. THE STATE OF THE NATION: YAHWEH'S SENTENCE (6:4–6)

Yahweh speaks

6:4a   How shall I deal with you, Ephraim?
         How shall I deal with you, Judah?

   4b   Your mercy passes away like a morning cloud,
         and like early dew it passes away.

   5a   That is why I hacked them with my prophets;
         I killed them with the words of my mouth.

   5b   My judgment goes forth like the sun.

   6a   For I desire mercy rather than sacrifice

   6b   and the knowledge of God rather than offerings.

NOTES

6:4a. *How shall I deal with you.* We have rejected the prevailing view that this anguished outburst is a direct response to 6:1–3, which is thereby shown to be unacceptable to Yahweh, the inference being that it was half-hearted or hypocritical. Nothing in 6:1–3 itself gives such an impression. Rather 6:4–6 goes with 5:12–15 in mood, and 5:12–15 and 6:4–6 together come before 6:1–3 logically, and in time. We note in particular that what Yahweh requires is knowledge (v 6), and this is what Israel will diligently seek (v 3).

Ephraim and Judah are on the same footing, so far as Yahweh is concerned. The use of the pronouns is precise and consistent. In 6:4a each is addressed singly in the singular; in v 4b both are addressed together in the plural.

Yahweh reveals a similar agony of indecision at 11:8. There it would seem that he is torn between unleashing his wrath (5:10b) and continuing to manifest his long-suffering compassion. The indecision of v 4a matches the openness of the situation at this point. The people have been ruined, and Yahweh is waiting for them to repent. There is no positive affirmation from Yahweh himself that he will fulfill the aspirations expressed by the people in vv 1–3.

4b. This is the only accusation in the speech. It points to failure at the heart of the relationship with Yahweh, a failure of ḥesed.

passes away. In v 3b the similes refer to the verbs and not the subject: Yahweh will come "like the rain"; it is not asserted that *he* is like rain. In 5:12 and 14, on the other hand, Yahweh is directly compared with larvae and lion, etc. In v 4b it is generally assumed that "like a morning cloud" and "like dew" go with "your mercy" in direct comparison and the participle *hlk,* "goes, passes away," then modifies "like dew" as relative clause. So *RSV:*

> Your love is like a morning cloud,
> like the dew that goes early away.

Current interpretation, then, supposes that *maškîm hōlēk* is a phrase in which "early" modifies "goes." This is dubious. A virtually identical expression occurs in Hos 13:3: "Therefore they will be like the morning mist / and like the dew *maškîm hōlēk.*" This variant shows that the similes modify the verb.

The verb that describes the evanescence of the morning cloud is *hlk* (Job 7:9). Growing out of v 3, there is a striking contrast between Yahweh's *ḥesed* and Israel's: his is like the rising sun, which increases in strength as day advances; theirs is like the morning cloud which vanishes quickly. *Hālak,* "to walk," sometimes has connotations of death, being laconic for *hālak lĕmôt.* Gen 25:32 should be taken literally, and Gen 15:2 means "I am about to die childless." Cf. Dahood (1968:62).

The images are congruent, and may be integrated. Even though *hlk* is postponed until the end, the participle goes with both nouns. Only one phenomenon, in fact, is meant: the early morning ground fog, a "cloud" associated with the formation of dew. (The Bible speaks of dew as falling, not as condensing directly from cloudless air on to a cold surface.) In any case, the idiom *hškym bbqr,* "to be busy early in the morning," supports a close linkage between the two lines of the bicolon. There is an irony in the use of such a word as *hškym* with its connotations of diligence to describe the efficiency with which the morning mist evaporates. This ground fog is both unsubstantial and transient and of little benefit – not like the *gešem* and *malqôš* of Yahweh's coming (v 3b).

The closely woven poetic texture suggests that *maškîm* is parallel to *bōqer.* By making *ṭal* definite, the Masoretes left *maškîm* detached from it, and by their punctuation, linked it with *hōlēk;* hence "going away early." The absence of articles on both participles, however, tells strongly against the identification of them as modifiers of "the dew." The lack of

articles with the participles fits in with their verbal functions, set out
above. The parallelism points to the following:

> like morning cloud
> And your loyalty   goes (away).
> and like early dew

Gordis (1971:151) supports this result, and points out that *maškîm* has
the meaning "early" in the Damascus Document and in Mishnaic Hebrew,
where it denotes the time for getting up in the morning.

5a. *That is why.* As in its other occurrences in Hosea, *'al-kēn* does not
link adjacent clauses as it does in classical Hebrew prose: v 5 is not necessarily the logical consequence of v 4. There is an abrupt change from second person to third; note elsewhere the same juxtaposition of second person (5:13a) with third (5:14–15). The perfect verbs in v 5 could be
precative, making it a threat; but the verse is more likely to be a review of
past history, earlier, therefore, than any other reference nearby, because
the plural "prophets" conjures up long succession, which could go back as
far as Moses.

hacked them. The object of the verbs turns up in v 5aB (retroactive
double-duty suffix). The object "them" on *hrgtym* can be taken as a continuation of the plural of v 4b, applying to both Ephraim and Judah. The
third person goes back to 5:15.

Hewing as an act of divine judgment describes the victory over Rahab
in Isa 51:9; the verb usually describes an action performed on stone, chip-
ping out a cistern or a sepulcher. The work can be done with an ax (Isa
10:15), normally used to chop wood (Deut 19:5; 20:19). Since the assault on Rahab, described as chopping and stabbing in Isa 51:9, is elsewhere described as crushing (Ps 89:11), one wonders if a mace rather
than an ax is the weapon implied. In Ugaritic the cognate verb, *ḥṣb,* is
used to describe an assault, agreeing with the parallel "to slay" in 6:5aB.
Similar verbal violence is described in Isa 11:4.

prophets . . . words. It is tantalizing that Hosea does not tell us whom
he means by "the prophets" (v 5aA). Two distinct prophets are referred
to in 12:14, perhaps Moses and Samuel. On Hosea's knowledge of Elijah
and Elisha traditions, see the NOTES on 1:4. One wonders how much he
was aware of the ministry of his contemporaries Amos, Micah, and
Isaiah. Hosea's thought seems to be, for the most part, original and independent, despite his abundant use of the community traditions. In any
case, he does not doubt the validity of the ministry of his precursors, and
sees his own activity as a continuation of what Yahweh did through earlier
prophets. He is vividly aware of the instrumental power of the prophetic
utterance, the words of Yahweh put in a man's mouth (Jer 1:9). In Isa
55:11, the word of Yahweh is almost autonomous in its effectiveness. That

word is life-giving; here "the words of my mouth" are deadly (cf. Isa 11:4). If we try to identify these death-dealing words more exactly, we have to choose between the covenant curses, which set death before the people as one of the alternatives (Deut 30:15), and the later pronouncements of doom made against a disobedient people. The parallelism suggests that the words are a message of judgment delivered by a prophet.

5b. If 6:5b has an integral place in 6:4–6, it states the certainty of the adverse judgment executed in v 5a; if v 5b is nearer to its poetic parallel, v 3aB, then the *mišpāṭîm* that are uttered forth like sunshine are decrees of deliverance, not destruction. The "judgments" in v 5b are parallel to "words" in v 5aB, making them ominous of death; as a transition to the hopeful note of v 6, with its change of tense and simile, v 5b promises a verdict of acquittal as Yahweh's final word. Correspondingly, the sentiment of vv 1–3 is what God still hopes to find in his people; and its absence (v 4b) causes heartbreak (v 4a) deeper than rage (v 5a). He overcomes his anger and pardons them because he delights in *ḥesed* (v 6; Mic 7:18).

My judgment. When *k* is tranferred to the next word, *-y* can be identified as a first-person suffix, appropriate in the context of first-person statements (Kuhnigk 1974:81).

goes forth. The singular verb suggests that *'ôr*, "light, sun," is the subject; this is possible, because *yṣ'* can describe the emergence of the sun. It is also possible that *yēṣē'* modifies *'ôr*, "like the sun when it rises." See the NOTE on v 3 for evidence that *môṣā'* and the verb *yṣ'* describe the utterance (i.e. issuing) of speech. The Servant announces (*yôṣî'*) to the nations the message (*mišpāṭ*) of salvation (Isa 42:1). When the day of Yahweh is light, not darkness, that is a time of deliverance (Amos 5:18–20). The same word-field of verbs and nouns is met in Ps 37:6, where a favorable verdict is brought out like "the light." The imagery in Judg 5:31 and Hab 3:4 makes it likely that *'ôr* here means "sun," linking v 5b quite closely with v 3aB. When vv 3aB and 5b are recognized as a bicolon, the parallelism helps to define the meanings of the words more exactly. Thus "his utterance" // "my judgments." The collocation of *mišpāṭ* and *nākôn* occurs in Prov 19:29.

There are additional associations of the light of the rising sun with the dawn of the day of resurrection, set against the darkness that pervades the abode of the dead. (Eph 5:14 seems to be a later development of this tradition.) In Hos 5:14, Yahweh boasts that no one can rescue when he, like a raging lion, rends and carries off the living. In Ps 56:14, the counterclaim is made, in language reminiscent of Hos 6:1–6, that Yahweh can rescue from Death, so that one may walk around (that is, live out one's life) in the presence of God in the light (*'ôr*) of the land of the living (*ḥayyîm* = the resurrected).

We have already observed a balance between the attack described in 5:14b and the assault in 6:5. Our analysis of 5:12–15 and 6:4–6 as matching blocks embracing 6:1–3 suggests that each is describing the same, or a similar, event.

6. This verse makes a basic statement which is the foundation of all that precedes. As the rhetorical climax of the entire section, it is also the final truth. Verse 7 begins a new discourse.

I desire mercy. Ḥesed is a matter of ultimate concern for Yahweh. The use of this emotional word, rather than one which emphasizes formal authority or power, matches the expressions of disappointment and anguish at the people's inconstancy (v 4). The use of the perfect form of the verb raises the question of its time reference. The usual translation as present ("I desire") makes it a timeless truth, a general motto. Hosea here repeats two of the three qualities listed in 4:1; this shows that 6:6 rounds off, to some extent at least, the discourse that began with c 4. The same virtues are highlighted throughout — "mercy" and "knowledge of God." While it is true that Yahweh is always pleased when his people have these qualities, the reproach in v 6 is directed against their distorted values, esteeming sacrifices and offerings as more important. In the past, Yahweh has made his wishes known, so that the people have no excuse for doing the less important thing, to the neglect of the more important; the Decalogue, of which we have a summary in 4:2, does not include rules for the offering of sacrifices.

rather than. The negative in v 6a is paralleled by *min* in v 6b. It is possible either that the *min* is negative — "I desire knowledge of God *and not* burnt offerings" — or that the comparative *min* makes the preceding negation comparative also — "I desire mercy *more than* sacrifice." The idiom "rather than" is the convergence of the two particles' senses.

This verse has been often quoted as proof that the prophets, or Hosea at least, made a radical break with the cult, maintaining that it was never part of Yahweh's purpose for his people. They were to serve him solely by loyalty and knowledge, by obedience to the ethical provisions of the covenant. It is a plea for inwardness and morality as the sum of religion. The point at issue is whether the prophets in the eighth century came to think of the cult as extraneous or even deleterious to Israel's relationship with Yahweh. It seems rather that sacrifice is not denigrated; it is simply put in second place.

It needs to be emphasized that, since the sacrifices mentioned here were intended to please Yahweh, the verse has nothing to do with Israelite involvement in Baal worship. There was no doubt about condemning that. The worship mentioned in 4:15 is Yahweh worship, because they swear "by the life of Yahweh." The worship in 5:6 is sacrifice for purposes of seeking Yahweh. In both instances Hosea declares such worship void and useless; cf. 3:4. These sayings could be directed to the situation at that time, and not be intended to give a blanket appraisal of Israel's worshiping of Yahweh. Hos 6:6 gives the reason for 5:6. They will not find Yahweh when they come with flocks and herds, because he desires mercy, not sacrifice.

It seems certain that Hosea has in mind the oracle of Samuel in I Sam 15:22–23.

22a Does Yahweh delight in offerings and sacrifices
    As much as in obedience to the voice of Yahweh?
22b Obedience is better than sacrifice,
    Paying attention is better than rams' fat.
23a The sin of soothsaying is rebellion.
    The iniquity of household gods is arrogance.
23b Just as you [Saul] rejected Yahweh's word,
    So Yahweh rejects you from being king.

(The *w* on *wtrpym* in v 23a is emphatic; read *mimlōk* in v 23b with manuscript and versional support.) The oracle is replete with the language of Hosea 4–6; I Sam 15:23b is largely reproduced in Hos 4:6, except that Hosea is dealing with rejection from priesthood, rather than kingship. The verbs of I Sam 15:22b are used in 5:1. In view of repeated indications that Hosea is attacking sorcery, the references to soothsaying and *teraphim* (household gods) in I Sam 15:23 are significant. Most pertinent is the fact that the language of I Sam 15:22a turns up in 6:6, showing that *šĕmōaʻ*, "obedience," corresponds to *ḥesed* in Hosea. The verb *ḥpṣ* occupies a key position in both texts, and *min* is used in the same way.

The conclusion of the discourse in 6:6, in spite of the strength of this statement, leaves everything up in the air. Yahweh's response is not nearly as negative as some exegetes claim. He does not spurn the people's expectations expressed in vv 1–3. What is lacking is a strong affirmation by Yahweh of what he will do. It is one of the merits of Good's study that he is puzzled by the ambiguity of the text in this matter. The truth is that at this point everything is open. There are no predictions. Who knows whether the people will repent? Is it possible that Yahweh himself does not know what to do (cf. 6:4a with 11:8)? A positive statement of intention by Yahweh does not come until 6:11b – 7:1a, which is a largely isolated oracle.

XI. THE STATE OF THE NATION: THE PRIESTS' CRIMES
(6:7 – 7:2)

Priestly crime in open country

6:7a   They, as at Adam, broke the covenant;

7b   there they practiced deception against me.

8a   In Gilead is the city of evildoers,

8b   a deceitful city, because of bloodshed.

9a   Those who lay in wait, bands of men,
        gangs of priests,

9b   Committed murder on the Shechem road.
        They have perpetrated enormities.

National defilement

10a   In the house of Israel I have seen disgusting things.

10b   There Ephraim has promiscuity,
        Israel is defiled.

11a   Judah also—he set a harvest for you.

11b   When I restore the fortunes of my people,

7:1a   when I bring healing to Israel,
        Then Ephraim's iniquity will be uncovered
        and Samaria's wicked acts.
        They have manufactured an idol.

Priestly crime in the city

1b   A gang of thieves will come,
        A gang of thieves will mug (people) in the streets.

2a   They do not speak honestly
        but all their wickedness I have remembered.

2b   Now their deeds surround them.
        They are right in front of me.

NOTES

6:7 – 7:2. This section resumes the theme of the malfeasance of the priesthood. In c 4 an individual is addressed; in cc 5 and 6 "priests" are addressed. In c 5 the emphasis is on the neglect of justice and the fostering of idolatry. Here the priests are charged with public crimes of robbery and murder.

A new stage in the discourse clearly begins with 6:7, after the decisive verse 6:6. This demarcation does not overlook the fact that wĕhēmmâ is linked backwards to some group that has already been introduced. The repetition of bāgā/ĕdû (5:7; 6:7) supplies a link which suggests that 5:1–7 and 6:7 – 7:2 need to be examined together. Hos 5:1–7 begins with an address to the leaders, especially the priests, but shifts attention to the people. Hos 6:7 turns again to the priests. The two passages continue the exposition of the proposition in 4:9a.

The speech which begins at 6:7 could extend as far as 7:7 or even 8:1, but there seems to be a major break after 7:2. In addition to formal, grammatical signals, the general context is a guide to delimiting constituent speeches. Hos 7:8–16 focuses on Ephraim, and Judah is not mentioned in parallel; otherwise the political situation is not unlike that in 5:3–15; note the repetition of 5:5a in 7:10a. Hos 6:7 – 7:2 exposes crimes committed by priests, although 6:10–11 shows that the whole nation is implicated. It may be appropriate to note here that there is no component of international politics in this material, except for the resort to Assyria for healing. Hos 7:8 may mark a change in this respect — there Egypt and the nations enter the picture. Everything through 7:7 can be explained against the background of the transition from Jeroboam II to Menahem, so long as we recognize that Hosea supplies the historical information, not found elsewhere: (a) that Judah intervened; (b) that the priests were active; and (c) that Assyria was already seen as a possible savior, its only role in the book.

Besides changes in thematic focus in 6:7 – 7:2, there are grammatical and structural signals which confirm this analysis. There are three units: 6:7–9; 6:10 – 7:1a; 7:1b–2. Each begins with the topic before the verb, and each ends with a verb in the 3 m pl perfect; there are chiasms of the pattern in vv 6:9b and 7:1a. The break between 6:9 and 6:10 is marked by the decisive clause kî zimmâ 'āśû, which ends the first stanza; and the switch to first person in v 10. The middle stanza contains more direct address. In the opening and closing strophes the criminals are spoken of in the third person.

The terminations of the second and third strophes are marked by clauses of the same kind—*kî pā'ălû šāqer* and *neged pānay hāyû*. The strophe-terminal lines are part of a pattern which unifies the entire scheme of three stanzas. A fourth line of the same kind comes near the beginning of the first strophe: *šām bāgĕdû bî*. Not one of these four lines is part of a standard bicolon in the place where it occurs; together they constitute a discontinuous tetracolon of intricate design:

6:7b	*šām bāgĕdû bî*
6:9b	*kî zimmâ 'āśû*
7:1a	*kî pā'ălû šāqer*
7:2b	*neged pānay hāyû*

Each line consists of three words, including a perfect verb. Each has five syllables, in a symmetrical pattern:

$$
\begin{array}{ccc}
1 & 3 & 1 \\
1 & 2 & 2 \\
1 & 3 & 1 \\
1 & 2 & 2 \\
\end{array}
$$

The first and last lines have locatives, and refer to the speaker, Yahweh, in chiastic prepositional phrases. The second and third lines begin with *kî*, making a chiastic pattern. The second and third lines identify the idolatrous sins which are declared to be treachery in the first line. These are *zimmâ* and *šāqer*. The verbs *'śy* and *p'l* are poetic parallels. The pattern of verbs and objects in the middle lines is chiastic. The postponement of the perfect verb to the end of the second and fourth lines is particularly dramatic, and achieves a rhyming effect. A recognition of the integral connections among these scattered lines enables each to be used to clarify the others. The subject of *hayû* is *zimmâ* and *šâqer*. Foulness and deceit were "in front of my face" (7:2b).

Judged by traditional canons, the poetry in 6:7–7:2 is not well developed; it is hard to find a single well-formed bicolon. The following come closest to classical norms.

6:11b–7:1a	*bĕšûbî šĕbût 'ammî*
	kĕrop'î lĕyiśrā'ēl
7:1a	*wĕniglâ 'ăwōn 'eprayim*
	wĕ- rā'ôt šōmĕrôn
7:1b	*wĕgannāb yābô'*
	pāšaṭ gĕdûd bahûṣ

Hos 6:7–7:2 is not a typical judgment oracle. It is a long tirade against all kinds of wickedness, using a remarkable profusion of vocabulary items

which reflect the sordid state of affairs. Some of the words are generic; their meaning here is defined by the more specific terms.

6:7a	covenant violation	*'brw bryt*
7b	deception	*bgdw*
8a	idolatry/evil	*'wn*
8b	deceit	*'qbh*
9a	banditry	*gdwdym*
	conspiracy	*ḥbr*
9b	murder	*yrṣḥw*
	foulness	*zmh*
10a	abomination	*š'ryryh*
10b	promiscuity	*znwt*
	uncleanness	*nṭm'*
7:1a	iniquity	*'wn*
	wickedness	*r'wt*
	idolatry	*šqr*
1b	theft	*gnb*
	banditry	*pšṭ*
	mugging	*gdwd*
2a	insincerity	*bl-y'mrw*
	wicked deeds	*kl-r'tm*
2b	(evil) practices	*m'llyhm*

From this long indictment there is only the terse sentence—"A harvest / limit is set for you" (v 11a). In the middle of it all, there is a bicolon which sounds a positive note of renewal and healing (6:11b + 7:1aA). This is not explained or connected logically with the remainder of the speech. The attention of the speaker is otherwise absorbed by the wickedness of the people, which he describes in manifold ways. Punishment and hope are hardly mentioned.

6:7–9. On first reading, this unit gives the impression that it is a heap of *membra disjecta*. With more patient attention, however, a single picture emerges. Previous study of v 9b has yielded an important and widely accepted result. The sense can only be "They murder on the way to Shechem" (*RSV*). The breaking of the bound pair *derek . . . šekmâ*, by the insertion of a verb, shows how innovative structurally and unconventional grammatically our author is. Furthermore, this is the most concrete and specific statement in the entire strophe, and serves to interpret the more abstract and general statements that accompany it. It is better to suppose that all the references to wickedness are related to this same crime rather than to a whole collection of different criminal acts. Considerable progress can be made by supposing that the passage is about one act of unexampled wickedness, done by one group of people at one time and place. We suggest that that crime was murder, done at or near Adam by a gang of priests; the victim (or victims) was on the way to Shechem.

This involves the identification of Adam as the town at the Jordan crossing on the main road linking Shechem to the Israelite centers in Transjordan, notably Succoth and Mahanaim. This identification, which restricts the activity to one place and one time, is a key to the interpretation which can be demonstrated with more certainty than has been possible hitherto. It has been usual to suppose that there are two or even three different places mentioned in the strophe — Adam, Gilead, and Shechem. Note, however, that v 9b does not locate anything at Shechem as such; it says that people committed murder on the road that leads to Shechem, and this could be the east-west road that crosses the Jordan at Adam. The murder could have been committed in Adam itself or elsewhere on the road. Further, Gilead is not a city, but a district. If it were not for the apparent meaning of 6:8, the identification of Gilead as a city would not have appeared in the lexicons. Gilead refers to individual towns only in the double names Jabesh-Gilead and Ramoth-Gilead, where "Gilead" is attributive. Since Adam is a town in Gilead, the name "Adam-Gilead" may have existed to distinguish the city from an Adam in another district; this name, we suggest, is broken up and distributed between v 7 and v 8; it is the same town that is further designated "the city of evildoers." This supports the hypothesis that Adam was the scene of terrible crime. The statement that Gilead is a city of evildoers is eliminated.

If we search for the identity of the evildoers, the clearest designation is "gangs of priests" in v 9a. Complete sense can be made of vv 7–9 on the hypothesis that this is the subject of all the 3 m pl verbs in the strophe. No objection can be raised on the grounds that the subject is strictly *ḥeber,* a singular noun, since it is collective, and in any case the number would be attracted to the "priests." This gang of priests broke the covenant and deceived Yahweh there, at Adam; they are evildoers, who have committed murder on the Shechem road, and they are guilty of *zimmâ.* This gang of priests is apparently also called a band of robbers — '*îš gĕdûdîm.* The parallelism supports this, but the identification is not inevitable. We need more details about the crime to settle this question. The murder(s) on the road to Shechem, at Adam, could have been perpetrated by persons on their way from Transjordan to Shechem, or priests from Adam could have murdered travelers going to Shechem. Since *gĕdûd* can mean a raiding band of outlaws, either the priests are considered no different from thugs or they made use of gangsters in some kind of political conspiracy involving murder. Both meanings converge if a gang of renegade priests from Gilead (= Gad, the land of the *gĕdûd,* Gen 49:19) crossed the Jordan at Adam on their way to participate in some insurrection on the west side (perhaps the episode of 7:3–7), committing murder on the way. But a once-only event need not be insisted upon.

Murder is the only crime clearly identified in vv 7–9. All the other terms for wickedness are more general, and could refer to a variety of crimes. At the same time they indicate that this was no ordinary murder. It was a serious breach of covenant, involving deception, wickedness, and treachery and adding up to the worst possible crime.

7a. *They.* The obvious meaning of *hēmmâ*, "they," a personal pronoun, is acceptable. A suggestion has been made that *whmh* should be recognized here as an isogloss of *whnh*, "and behold" (Kuhnigk 1974:82–85; cf. de Moor 1969), but this is not necessary. Hosea has a marked propensity for the free 3 m pl pronouns: *hēm* (2:23,24; 3:1; 4:14; 8:4; 13:2) and *hēmmâ* (2:6,14; 6:7; 7:13; 8:9,13; 9:10). The syntax here presents some difficulty. A new unit begins at this point and there is no antecedent for the pronoun; and the structure of the clause as circumstantial does not fit in well with what follows. If v 6 begins a new strophe, then v 7 could be adversative—"I desired loyalty . . . but they . . . violated the covenant . . ."; the crimes which follow, especially idol-making and murder, are blatant violations of the covenant stipulations in the Decalogue. However, the structural arguments given above for regarding 5:12–6:6 as a unit require a new beginning at v 7. The preceding section, for the most part, is an address in which the identity of the speaker (Yahweh) is disclosed by use of the pronoun "I." The Israelite states were addressed as "you" in v 4, and referred to as "they" in v 5. A hint as to Yahweh's stance and audience might be gained from the double use of "there" (vv 7,10). Its repetition links the two verses and brackets vv 7–9 as a unit within the larger discourse. The list of faults echoes the opening indictment in 4:1–3, but here it is not a charge made only against the people in a formal *rîb*. The trial is apparently held in the absence of the criminal, as inquiry is made as to what to do about the crimes reported. This reflective discourse of Yahweh, probably in the form of a soliloquy, partakes of a common Hosean form. Even when the nation is apparently addressed, God is talking to himself (2:4–25; 5:12–15; 6:4; 11:8–9), although God could be talking privately to the prophet, or else going over the matter in the divine assembly with the prophet present as reporter.

Ephraim, Israel, and *Judah* are all in the picture. The same list of three states was met in 5:5, and the occurrence of *gam-yĕhûdâ* in both places is a further indication that the two passages should be studied side by side. Hos 5:3b is almost identical with 6:10b. So, if 5:3–7 is balanced by 6:7–7:2 (and the structure of the intervening materials supports this), then the opening *'ănî*, "I" (5:3), is the lead to which *wĕhēmmâ* in 6:7 is the counterpoise. In that 5:3–7 grows out of the call to hear charges in

5:1–2, 6:7 might be the continuation. Hosea supplies little information about the setting or circumstances of these speeches, either in historical events, or in his own experience. Furthermore, Hosea, unlike his contemporaries, does not use the mise-en-scène of his revelations.

as at Adam. Hosea has an amazing stock of similes, including historical ones. He compares Israel's fate to that of Admah (*k'dmh*) and Zeboiim (11:8) and refers also to Shalman's destruction of Beth Arbel (10:14). The simile he is using in 6:7 is obscure. There are three explanations offered.

1) Taking up Dahood's suggestion that *'ādām* is sometimes equivalent to *'ădāmâ,* McCarthy (1972b) translates: "Behold, they have walked over the covenant like dirt; lo, they have betrayed me"; cf. Kuhnig (1974:82–83). There is no biblical evidence that *'dm(h)*, "ground," was regarded as contemptible, and thus could supply such a simile for disdain; furthermore *'br* means "to cross over, pass by," not "to trample on (with scorn)."

2) A widely accepted proposal, followed here, is that Adam is a place name. The translation "in Adam" (Wolff 1974:105) requires a change in the preposition, which has no support from texts or versions. (The further change to "in/against Aram," so *BH³*, is gratuitous; Hosea never mentions *'ărām.*) The arguments for "in Adam" are based on the fact that reference to the Adam of the creation story is problematic; even if it is supposed that the prophets did know that tradition, Genesis does not represent Adam as standing in covenant with Yahweh. A locative is required in 6:7a by *šām,* "there," which otherwise does not have an antecedent.

The only important city named Adam is mentioned in Josh 3:16. Equation with Admah in 11:8 is out of the question; *NEB,* however, so renders. The Cities of the Plain could hardly be meant, as they were symbols of inescapable divine judgment, destroyed in dim antiquity, and never rebuilt (cf. Isa 1:10 on the identification of Israel with Sodom and Gomorrah). There is a pass in Naphtali called Adami (Josh 19:33). Adam by the Jordan was the place where the waters of the river dammed up so that the Israelites could cross over downstream, near Jericho. Hosea refers to several places involved in that history, including Peor and Achor. Nothing reprehensible is known about Israel's past conduct at Adam. If the covenant-breaking is contemporary rather than historic, the only detail given is the crime of murder described here. Mays (p. 100) suggests that Hosea is alluding to some contemporary "breach of a specific requirement of the covenant" known to his immediate hearers, but now quite forgotten. This is possible; we know little of the historical background of Hosea's oracles and our identification of that specific breach as murder arises from the passage itself.

3) The traditional interpretation of the text is that Israel is compared to "Adam," the model sinner (Genesis 3), or with people at large, all covenant breakers. In view of the prominence given to Adam in later theology, at least in the Christian tradition (Jewish thinking paid more attention to Gen 6:1–4 as a record of the first serious corruption of the race), it is surprising that so little use is made of this tradition in the Hebrew Bible. The scarcity does not mean that the story was never used, however. The J corpus was settled long before Hosea wrote, and there seems to be no reason why Hosea should not have known and used it, in some form. The objection that traditions do not say that Yahweh made a covenant with Adam is significant. Since, however, it is a commonplace of prophetic thought that Israel kept on acting like their unfaithful ancestors, the covenant-breaking theme could easily have been extended back to the beginnings of humanity. The pattern of obligations followed by curses for rebellion found in Genesis 2–3 suggests covenant without using the word. If v 9 provides a clue, we note that Adam did not break the covenant by committing murder. Although Masoretic practice varied enormously (see the discussion on the use of Lebanon in c 14), the reference to Adam without the article differs from the terminology of Genesis, which mentions "the man" when the primordial individual is meant.

On the possibility that '*ādām* is derived from an Amorite divine name, see Buccellati (1966:130).

The best conclusion, we believe, is that Adam is a place and *kĕ'ādām* means "as in/at Adam," although Adam is not the only place where such things occur. For the same syntax, see *kmdbr*, "as in the wilderness" (2:5), although the *k* could also be explained as asseverative.

broke the covenant. There is a similar accusation in 8:1, which has "my covenant"; "my torah" is the parallel, pointing to the Mosaic covenant; cf. 4:6 and 2:20. It has often wrongly been said that Hosea makes little use of the covenant idea, which was mainly developed in Deuteronomistic circles after Hosea's time. The lack of a suffix on the noun here does not make the word "covenant" general, as if it could refer to other agreements, such as political treaties. The parallel, "they deceived *me*," shows that Yahweh's covenant is meant.

This is the general indictment; the particular crime of murder at Adam on the way to Shechem provides a vivid illustration.

7b. *there.* *K'dm* provides an antecedent for this adverb; it could also be an advance reference to the following place name, "Gilead." The adverb here is balanced by a second, *šām* in v 10. Hosea's use of *šām* is difficult; see the discussion of 2:17.

they practiced deception against me. Most of the verbs in this unit are perfect, but since three are imperfect (6:9b; 7:1b,2a), we cannot readily determine whether we have a historical retrospect or an account of cur-

rent events. The accomplished fact implied by the use of the perfect need
not refer to the remote past. The verb *bgd* here does not itself identify a
particular deception. A similar accusation was made in 5:7, where the deception leads to the birth of "foreign children." This suggests marital
infidelity, and the renewed reference to promiscuity in v 10 supports this.
This staccato, five-syllable line is typical of Hosea; cf. *kî zimmâ 'āśû* (v
9bB), which is the parallel to v 7b.

Elsewhere the Bible derides the self-deception of those who fancy that
God does not observe their furtive sins. The statements "Israel is not hidden from me" and "I have seen . . ." (5:3; 6:10) as well as "They are
right in front of me" (7:2) are sufficient commentary. If the priests (v 9)
are supremely guilty of this deception, it would seem that they maintain
the outward shows of orthodox Yahwism while secretly using their position in society for purposes contrary to Yahweh's covenant.

8–9. The difficulties we have encountered in finding the structure in
6:7 – 7:2 can be resolved in part in this smaller unit, which seems to have
an elaborate pattern of introversion.

8a	crime	*qiryat pō'ălê 'āwen*	a city of evildoers
8b	murder	*'ăqubbâ middām*	deceitful, with blood
9a	robbery	*ûkĕḥakkê 'îš gĕdûdîm*	liers-in-wait, bands of men
	robbery	*ḥeber kōhănîm*	gangs of priests
9b	murder	*derek yĕraṣṣĕḥû-šekmâ*	they murdered on the Shechem road
	crime	*kî zimmâ 'āśû*	they perpetrated enormities

Some parts of the text remain enigmatic. While *zimmâ,* which occurs only
here in Hosea, commonly refers to the worst vices, it would be not unsuitable to apply it to idolatry. The only clear statement is v 9bA — murder
on the Shechem road. It is probable that the reference to "blood" in v 8b
is a parallel statement about murder. Verse 9a is regrettably obscure, except for the indication that the priests are deeply involved in criminality.
The crimes of murder (v 9), theft (7:1), and adultery (7:4) are listed in
the same sequence as in 4:2, using the same roots as there.

8b. *a deceitful (city), because of bloodshed.* The meaning of *'qbh mdm*
remains almost entirely obscure. The most likely grammatical construction
is to see it in apposition with the preceding, i.e. as another designation of
Adam in Gilead. The use of feminine singular is agreeable to this. The
story of Jacob focuses on two senses of the root *'qb,* "to deceive" and
"heel." The meaning of the word *dām* in this context is not clear enough
to help with the other words, and they do not clarify the meaning of *dām.*
LXX diverges widely from the Hebrew; its rendering "the one who troubles water" points to *mym* rather than *mdm,* but the rest is obscure, and
does not help us recover a better Hebrew text. It would seem that the
Greek translators were already struggling with the problems we have.

The verb *'āqab* is used in 12:4 in connection with the Jacob tradition. The meaning of treachery is uppermost here and we have in 6:8 an adjective modifying the city; the treachery was expressed in murder. As a passive, or better, stative adjective, *'qbh* is similar to *('îr) šōpeket (dām)*, "(a city,) a shedder (of blood)" (Ezek 22:3), where, however, the participle is active. Compare *'îr dāmîm*, "murderous (or murderess) city" (Nah 3:1; Ezek 22:2; 24:6,9). Another comparison is afforded by Hab 2:12:

> *hôy bōneh 'îr bĕdāmîm* Woe to the one building a city with blood,
> *wĕkônēn qiryâ bĕ'awlâ* and establishing a city with iniquity!

9a. *lay in wait.* The phrase *kĕḥakkê* is difficult. The chaos of the versions reflects either ancient disorder in Hebrew manuscripts, or crude attempts to emend the incomprehensible reading we still have. Since we know from 6:9b that murder was involved, lying in wait to murder people fits the context, even though it is largely guesswork. *Ḥakkê* looks like a *Pi'el* infinitive construct of the root *ḥky,* "to lie in wait"; the form is closer to the infinitive absolute (*ḥkwt* would be the construct) and the orthography is archaic, for the absolute would usually be written *ḥkh*. Further confusion is created by the use of this form before *'îš gĕdûdîm,* which may be an inverted plural (*gĕdûd 'ānāšîm,* "a troop of men"), or simply the plural of *'îš gĕdûd,* "gangster."

The verb *ḥky* normally means to wait upon God in a good sense, not lying in ambush with evil intent. It can mean to wait in expectation, with patience as a virtue (Ps 106:13; Hab 2:3), or with longing, especially for or of God (Ps 33:20; Isa 30:18). It can mean "to wait one's turn" (Job 32:4); and it can refer to irresponsible dillydallying. In Hab 1:15 the enslavement of the world by Babylon is described as catching men with nets and hooks (*ḥakkâ*). In II Kings 5:2 the marauding bands who dragged off the Israelite girl as a slave are called *gĕdûdîm.* This could be a significant clue, for the *gĕdûdîm* are generally associated with Aram, Moab, or Ammon, which fits in with the Transjordan locale of Gilead. To this evidence may be joined the use of *gannāb,* "thief," in parallel with *gĕdûd* in 7:1; cf. 4:2, where the background of the Decalogue identifies the crime as capturing people to sell as slaves. These gangs were not involved in common brigandage but kidnapping, and the priests were hand in glove with them.

gangs. See the discussion of *ḥābûr* at 4:17. *Ḥeber kōhănîm* is the subject of *yĕraṣṣĕḥû,* "they murder." The connection of the root with magical arts should not be overlooked. The singular *ḥeber* is regarded as collective.

9b. *Committed murder.* Murder is the one crime on which Hosea focuses; all the other terms are generic. The same root is used in 4:2. Cf.

Ps 62:4. Although it can describe any kind of homicide, involuntary and premeditated (Numbers 35), its use in Ps 94:6 (where it parallels *hrg*) and in Isa 1:21 suggests willful assassination of defenseless people for spoil.

Shechem road. An example of a discontinuous phrase (Freedman 1972c). Compare the normal *derek timnātâ* (Gen 38:14), *derek ṣāpônâ* (Ezek 8:5), and *derek têmānâ* (Ezek 21:2); the directional *-â* shows that it is the road *to* Shechem.

enormities. Zimmâ is among the strongest words for human depravity, rich as Hebrew is in the vocabulary of sin. It sometimes refers to infringements of Israel's sexual taboos, though, except for *zĕnût* in v 10, there is no reference to sexual immorality here. Since cc 4–7 are a large unit, and the crimes in 6:7 – 7:2, murder, robbery, and idolatry cover most of the items in the list in 4:2, some mention of sexual vice is to be expected. If more details are sought, perhaps they are to be found in 4:13; why are the fathers and fathers-in-law accused, and not, say, their husbands, or the women themselves? If the priests were guilty of using their own female relatives sexually, they would only be following the customs of their neighbors, and this would certainly be called *zimmâ* in Israel. Closely related is *nĕbālâ*, "disgraceful folly," a root used by Hosea only in the hapax legomenon *nablūt* (2:12), which describes wantonness and hence covenant violation.

The structure presented above suggests that *zimmâ* refers to idolatry; in Hosea this would still be fornication, though not literally. In 7:1a there is a line that resembles 6:9bB: *kî pāʿalû šāqer*. Since *pʿl* is a rather infrequent biblical parallel to *ʿśy*, the juxtaposition of *pʿly ʾwn* in 6:8a and *pʿlw šqr* in 7:1b, together with the likelihood that *šāqer* also means "idol(s)," strengthens the circumstantial case for *zimmâ* having the same referent.

10a. *house of Israel.* Here, as in 5:1, Hosea is referring to the whole nation; cf. "tribes of Israel" (5:9). The parts are then itemized, so that Ephraim and Israel are the parts of the divided northern kingdom, and Judah is a third part of the nation (cf. 5:5). Each of the four lines in this unit contains the name of one of the Israelite states: "house of Israel, Ephraim, Israel, Judah"; an arrangement in four lines is possible. The lines are of uneven length, and there is little parallelism apart from the names.

I have seen. In view of other similarities between 6:10 and 5:3, this statement is similar to "I know Ephraim" at 5:3.

disgusting things. The unique word *šʿryryh* cannot be connected with most of the other words which have the root *šʿr*. The extension of the root by repeating the last consonant resembles *naʾăpûpîm* (2:4) and both could be coinages of Hosea. Tradition assigns the term a meaning that continues the idea of *zimmâ* from v 9. Jeremiah has some apparently related forms: *ša'ărûrâ* (Jer 5:30; 23:14) and *ša'ărûrît* (Jer 18:13, cf. the Qere in Hos 6:10), as well as the "rotten figs" (*kattĕ'ēnîm haššō'ārîm,* Jer 29:17). This context in Hosea suggests that the rotten thing is *zĕnût,* also called *zimmâ* and *šeqer.*

10b. *There.* Compare *šām* in v 7. If the whole composition is integrated, this might refer to Shechem or Adam. Otherwise its antecedent is "the house of Israel."

11a. The great difficulty of this verse speaks against its being a conventional gloss. The address to Judah breaks with the context; *gam-yĕhûdâ* resembles 5:5, where the same cluster of names occurs. The subject of the verb *šāt,* "he set," is not identified but it is probably Yahweh. If it is Judah, then "for you" refers to another party, quite obscure; and what would it mean for Judah to appoint a harvest for someone? The introduction of the imagery of harvest is abrupt, and it is not developed. Amos (8:2) has used the image of fruit harvest to illustrate God's judgment, and Hosea also speaks of reaping (10:13 — same root as here), but it is doubtful if a final judgment is yet in mind. This association appears in Jer 51:33, and later in the apocalypses. If v 11a contains a threat of retribution, it contrasts with the hope of restoration expressed in v 11b. The use of *gam* suggests that Judah *as well as* the other countries will experience something — and *gam* would link Judah back with some preceding name. (On the *šām . . . gam* sequence, cf. Ps 137:1.) Since Ephraim is charged with prostitution, and Israel with uncleanness, a similar statement about Judah should accuse her of something, but v 11a is not an accusation. Judah usually comes after Ephraim, and in parallel with it. Here Ephraim is in parallel with Israel in a balanced bicolon, within a tricolon, with Judah in the third line. The political situation is based on three entities — Israel, Ephraim, Judah. *Niṭmā'* resulting from *zĕnût* is charged against all three, and the judgment (*qāṣîr*) is a disaster for all three. The integration is implied, not developed, except that *gam* points to similarity among them, as in 5:5. The following *'ammî,* "my people," should be referred to the entire nation, balancing "house of Israel" (everybody) in v 10a.

harvest. Qāṣîr can mean both harvesttime and what is harvested. The former would supply the idea of a day of accounting. The root also has connotations of impatience or short temper, the opposite of God's quality of "long-suffering."

If *qāṣîr* is the subject and *št* is passive, then the parallel idea of "return" as a reversal of fortune (v 11b) suggests a favorable oracle, making harvest a time of joyous celebration. This continues into the following statement about healing (7:1a), but the negative note in 7:1b suggests that such a hope is not likely to be realized. In 10:12 the harvest is good, but in 10:13 it is bad. The neutrality of "harvest" as an image requires its connotation to be determined by context. Here it is a harvest of judgment for all.

Hos 6:11–7:1aA describes the favorable outcome of the corruption described in the surrounding text, through restoration and healing, and it occupies in 6:7–7:2 a pivotal position in regard to the contrasting passages before and after it, just as 6:1–3 is pivotal within 5:14–6:6. Hos 6:7 and 6:10 are general accusations enclosing the specific charges of 6:8–9. Hos 7:1aB and 7:2 are more general charges enclosing the more specific charge of 7:1b, which resembles 6:8–9.

11b. *When I restore.* Infinitival constructions like this one do not generally constitute a complete utterance. They usually begin a paragraph, and supply a time reference for what follows. If this construction ends the paragraph, going with what precedes, then it gives the circumstances under which Yahweh has appointed a harvest for Judah, that is, when he returns the returning of his people. Hos 7:1aA is another infinitival construction, in *k* rather than *b;* the parallelism is not complete, but the 1 cg s suffix is a strong indication of continuity in the discourse. The two infinitival constructions then stand before the next clause.

The expression here need not imply that the people are captives or exiles. In general terms it can mean to reverse the fortune; cf. Job 42:10. While *šûb* is not usually transitive, it seems to be so here, with the cognate object.

7:1. As in 2:16, and generally in Ezekiel, the repentance of the people seems to be the result — not the precondition — of divine restoration. It is Yahweh's generosity, not his severity, that makes them ashamed of themselves. The question of sequence remains, since the order of the clauses is not necessarily chronological.

1a. *healing.* Compare 6:1. The verb usually has an accusative object, but *l* with the person healed occurs e.g. in Num 12:13; II Kings 20:5, 8.

uncovered. The same verb is used in 2:12 for the exposure of the wayward wife. Here the "iniquity of Ephraim" (as in 4:8) and the "wicked acts" of Samaria are in full view. Compare *rā'îtî* (6:10) and *neged pānay* (7:2).

wicked acts. The feminine noun *rā'â* occurs three times in this chapter (*rā'ātām* in 7:2,3); perhaps the plural in v 1 is equivalent to *kol-rā'ātām*, and should not be given a special meaning. We suggest that *'āwōn* is sometimes concrete (a god called Iniquity), not abstract, and the same could be true here. If so, the plural *rā'ôt* could match the many other plurals used to refer to the gods: in this instance feminine, suggesting again that a female deity is involved. The "calf" (*'ēgel*) of Samaria (8:5,6) is similarly matched by the "heifers" (*'eglôt*) of Beth Awen (10:5).

1b. *thieves.* Stealing was one of the crimes listed in 4:2. "Come" here may mean "he will come inside," that is, burglarize. The sequence imperfect-perfect settles nothing as to the time reference. The chiastic arrangement of the verbs, and the lack of a coordinating conjunction within the bicolon, are typical of Hosea. Dahood (1976) reads for the MT's *pšṭ,* "he/it will mug," the sequence *pa,* the conjunction, and *šāṭ,* "he/it will roam"; the change is not necessary.

mug. The verb means technically "to despoil" at war. Here it describes the stripping of the victims of assault or murder, in a further detail of the crime already mentioned.

2. The interpretation of this verse depends to a considerable extent on the treatment of the adverb '*th* at the beginning of v 2b. It could be simply a designation of time — "at this very moment." It could be a mark of transition within speech; in this case v 2b could round off the entire unit, so that it is not necessarily connected closely with v 1a. If it is the last word, then the situation ends with the people surrounded by their wicked deeds. The solution of the problem of '*th* depends in part on what is decided about the tenses of the verbs. Since the imperfect in v 2a describes habitual action, "they say," the perfect verbs would seem to be eligible for translation in the present tense — "I remember," "they surround" "they are." Remembering that Hosea often fails to use *wĕ-,* "and," where it occurs in normal prose, the lack of conjunctions between the verbs leaves us with no guide to the connection between the clauses. If '*attâ* is equivalent to "and now," a transition to precative speech is possible, making v 2b a judgment sentence — "And now, let their deeds surround them." Since the lack of conjunctions is not evidence that the clauses within v 2 are interconnected, parallelism between "all their wickedness" and "their deeds" is possible; "I have remembered" and "They are right in front of me" could also be parallels, especially if "their deeds" is the subject of both "surround" and "they are" in v 2b. Otherwise, "I have remembered" finds its counterpart in "I have seen" (6:10).

Most of the verbs in this unit are plural. The singular verbs in v 1b interrupt the connection between "they have manufactured an idol" (v 1a) and "they do not speak" (v 2a). There could be a connection between these two statements, since resorting to idols (v 1a) goes with a low opinion of Yahweh's capabilities. The singular verbs can be brought into line if the nouns *gannāb* and *gĕdûd* are collective.

The negative *bal* is rare, but could be used here to distinguish an indicative use of the verb from a precative use; the verse is a statement of fact, not a warning. In 7:14 the people are accused of not crying out to God with their heart, using the preposition *b.* This makes the use of the preposition *l* in 7:2 hard to explain.

Although we recognize a major division between vv 2 and 3, we note that the word *rā'ātām* is repeated, and could be a link between them.

Verse 2 may be transitional; vv 3–7 describe in detail the evil deeds that surround them, and which they think Yahweh does not remember. Even if we recognize vv 3–7 as dealing with a distinct situation or episode, we recall that all of cc 4–7 is an extended discourse with persistent themes.

2a. It is best to take v 2aA as absolute, since v 2aB is not a suitable object. The two statements are in contrast in a bicolon with typical features. The first line has the conjunction and an imperfect verb; the second has no conjunction and a perfect verb.

honestly. Literally "to their hearts."

XII. THE STATE OF THE NATION:
DOMESTIC POLICIES
(7:3–7)

A priestly attack on the court

7:3a In their wickedness they made the king rejoice,

3b   and in their wily schemes, the princes.

4a All of them are adulterers;

        they are like a burning oven.

4b The baker ceases to be alert,

        to knead the dough until it's leavened.

5a By day they made our king ill,

        the princes, with poisoned wine.

5b He stretched out his hand with scoffers.

6a When they drew near,

        their heart was like an oven.

During their ambush all night long

6b   their baker slept until morning.

It was burning like a blazing flame.

7a All of them became heated like an oven.

        Then they devoured their judges.

7b   All their kings fell down.

Not one of them calls on me.

NOTES

7:3–7. While many problems remain, the basic pattern and plot-line may be analyzed. The plural subject throughout is an unidentified group, presumably of priestly background, which schemes against and is responsible for some malevolent action against the king and princes of Israel. The episode involves a drunken feast among the foremost leaders, possibly including drugged or poisoned wine, culminating in an ambush and presumably the assassination of the king and his courtiers. Tentatively we may identify the plotters and schemers with the leading priests since they are the constant target of the prophet's accusations. A similar episode involving the aristocracy of Ephraim is recounted by Isaiah (c 28), using much the same vocabulary, and it is possible that a single event triggered both prophetic diatribes.

The king and the princes are linked in the passage as targets of the plotting and victims of the assault. Thus in v 3, the plotters instigate a festal celebration for king and princes in their malicious scheme to ruin them. In v 5a the plot is brought to fruition, when the evildoers make both king and princes sick with poisoned wine. A comparison of vv 3 and 5a reveals a common interlocking structure:

> 3a *br'tm yśmḥw mlk* // 5aA *ywm mlknw hḥlw*
>
> 3b *wbkḥšyhm śrym* // 5aB *śrym ḥmt myyn*

In both cases a single verb governs both parts of the bicolon: imperfect in v 3, perfect in v 5a, a well-known pattern. The verbs, while not obviously parallel, do balance each other, as the true meaning of the deceptive *yśmḥw* is brought out by *hḥlw*. The purpose of the drinking bout was to render the king and princes helpless, and put them at the mercy of the ambush prepared for them. In both bicola chiasm is in evidence: *yśmḥw mlk // mlknw hḥlw* and *wbkḥšyhm śrym // śrym ḥmt myyn*. The ultimate fate of king and princes presumably is reflected in vv 7aB–bA, which, however, is a more general statement of the prevailing anarchy, as well as a structural counterpart of v 3. So vv 3, 5a, and 7aB–bA constitute the primary unit or framework dealing with the king and princes as targeted victims of the plot.

The plotters are further described and evaluated in vv 4a, 5b, 6a, and 6bB–7aA. Two vivid epithets are applied to them: *mn'pym,* "adulterers," and *lṣṣym,* "scoffers." The exact relevance and force of these terms are not clear, especially with regard to the immediate context, but the charges are typical of the prophetic diatribes against those who cynically abuse offices of trust and responsibility. In three passages they (or their hearts) are compared with an oven, which blazes out of control, vv 4a, 6b, and 7a. A pair of bicola form the envelope around the body of the pericope and exhibit a striking chiastic structure:

> 4aA *klm mn'pym* // 7aA *klm yḥmw ktnwr*
> 4aB *kmw tnwr b'r hm* // 6bB *hw' b'r k'š lhbh*

Note that the opening line of v 4a is matched with the closing line of vv 6bB–7aA (*klm* is common), while the internal lines, vv 4aB and 6bB, balance (*b'r* is common). The pronouns *hm,* "they," and *hw',* "he/it," likewise match in opposite positions, and the comparative phrases balance, at opposite ends of the lines. In keeping with the chiastic pattern, the order of clauses in vv 6bB–7aA is effectively reversed, and the pronoun *hw'* is kataphoric, representing *tnwr* in the following line (the oven burns like a blazing fire); in v 4, the pronoun *hm* picks up the preceding *mn'pym*. The repetition of three key words ensures the linkage between the two passages. The occurrence of the phrase *ktnwr* in v 6 makes it clear that plotters and ambushers belong to the same larger group, separated only by roles in the nefarious scheme.

The remaining member of the cast of dramatis personae is the mysterious baker, whose activity or lack thereof is described in detail; just what his role in the transaction actually was, or was supposed to be, is obscure. It is also not clear whether he belongs to the imagery of the blazing oven, which is used to describe the plotters, or whether he was a real person who acted in the drama. It is not surprising that some scholars in their bafflement have eliminated the baker from the text entirely, but this hardly conforms to acceptable methodology. Our provisional view is that the material should be taken at face value, especially since the baker is mentioned in two passages which, while separated in the text, are nevertheless symmetrically placed in the overall structure; it is not likely that such a pattern resulted from accidental errors in two different passages. The basic information about the baker in vv 4b and 6bA is that he did not perform his duty to knead the dough properly. This failure would hardly call for prophetic denunciation, but it seems to have occurred at a critical time, namely when the plot to do away with king and princes reached its culmination. The baker seems to have slept through the action, and not to have awakened before morning. He could be accused of negligence, even gross malfeasance, only if his assignment also included keeping watch through the night (though one might wonder at the rather informal bodyguard arrangements if the baker turned out to be the key person).

The pivotal passage on which the role and importance of the baker to the narrative turn is v 5b, which seems to stand by itself at the center of the oracle: "He stretched out his hand with scoffers." If we are right in identifying the *lṣṣym* with the plotters, and the baker as the subject of *mšk,* then it appears that his failure to be awake and alert, and to sound the alarm, was not inadvertent but deliberate and malicious, i.e. that he was in league with the conspirators. The only other possible subject of the verb (which is 3 m s) is the king (v 5a), but this hardly seems possible. In the passage as a whole, the king is regularly linked with the princes, and throughout he and they are the targets and victims of the plot, not doing anything on their own. It seems more likely therefore that it is the baker who put his hand in with the mischief planners and who helped, by a convenient slumber, to betray king and princes into the hands of the plotters.

The structure of the unit is complex and a variety of analyses is possible. The intricate pattern of repetitions and echoes reflects careful design, but it is not always clear where metrical and strophic boundaries lie. The parallels in wording and meaning between the opening and closing suggest the familiar envelope construction, and details of word order, including chiasm and the location of pronouns, confirm the basic impression.

As is usual with Hosea, the composition of this unit has a texture which is neither poetry nor prose, nor a mixture of the two. It is poetic prose in which the achievement of classical rhythms varies in degree from lines which are indistinguishable from prose to bicola which attain the strictest canons of regularity. This variation, however, is not central. Of more importance is the weaving together of such lines into a unified fabric.

Among the well-formed bicola is v 7aB–7bA, which shows complete synonymous parallelism with chiasm. The throwing of the perfect verb to the end of the clause in v 7bA, besides achieving chiasm, suggests that a unit ends here. This leaves the connections of v 7bB as a distinct question, discussed below. Within the bicolon the parallelism is not realized grammatically, since "judges" is the object of the first verb whereas "kings" is the subject of the second verb. Another bicolon is v 3, which has incomplete synonymous parallelism, with no chiasm. These two well-formed bicola, with their common theme, embrace the whole unit and clearly mark its boundaries.

In the reconstruction of the unit, the following preliminary points may be noted:

1) Verse 3 is a bicolon which matches v 7aB–bA:

| 3a | br'tm yśmhw-mlk | 9 syll. | 7aB | w'klw 't-šptyhm | 9 syll. |
| 3b | wbkhšyhm śrym | 7 syll. | 7bA | kl-mlkyhm nplw | 7 syll. |

The parallel sequences *mlk-śrym* // *šptyhm-mlkyhm* establish the relationship, while the verbs summarize the narrative, which begins with the plotting of the unnamed conspirators and ends with the downfall of kings.

2) Verse 4a corresponds to vv 6bB–7aA:

| 4aA | klm mn'pym | 6 syll. | 6bB | hw' b'r k'š lhbh | 8 syll. |
| 4aB | kmw tnwr b'r hm | 7 syll. | 7aA | klm yhmw ktnwr | 8 syll. |

3) Verse 4b corresponds to v 6bA, but there is an apparent imbalance, since v 4b is a bicolon, while v 6bA is a single line. There are three candidates for the missing line: (a) v 7bB, (b) v 5b, and (c) v 6aB. Let us consider each in turn. (A) Verse 7bB may be the missing element to complete the bicolon in vv 6b–7 and match v 4b. This produces a minor enve-

lope structure for vv 6b–7, and reflects adequately the balance between
the opening unit vv 3–4 and the closing unit vv 6b–7.

4bA	*'ph yšbwt m'yr*	6 syll.	6bA	*yšn 'phm bqr*	6 syll.
4bB	*mlwš bṣq 'd-ḥmṣtw*	8 syll.	7bB	*'yn-qr' bhm 'ly*	7 syll.

The repetition of the term *'ph*, "baker," confirms the link between vv 4b
and 6b, while we may infer that the same mysterious figure is the subject
of the singular construction in v 7bB (i.e. *'yn qr'*). (B) Since, however, v
7bB introduces a new element ("to me") and otherwise seems to be isolated from the rest of the passage, it may be necessary to look elsewhere
for the expected complement to v 6bA. It is possible that "the baker" is
also the subject of the verb *mšk* in v 5b, which has no obvious connection
in the immediate context. The nearest noun is *malkēnû* in v 5a, but the
king seems to be the object of the plot and the victim of the actions mentioned rather than a participant. (It may be, nonetheless, that he was associated with the scoffers and this thoughtless behavior led to his downfall.) If the baker is the subject of the verb in v 5b, then his role, albeit a
relatively passive one, in connection with the conspirators becomes somewhat clearer. (C) The most likely candidate is nonetheless the line with
which v 6bA is continuous, v 6aB.

Since on other grounds it is possible to identify the 3 m pl subject
throughout this pericope as the priests, or a cabal of them, we may conclude that the baker is the chief of them (the subtle interaction of "the
priest" with "the priests" has already been explored by the prophet in
cc 4–5). There is a play on the words *mn'pym* (root *n'p*), "adulterers"
(v 4a), which is applied to the conspirators and *'ph* (root *'py*) "baker,"
which is applied to a key figure in the story. If he is also the subject of
mšk ydw in v 5b, and the term *lṣṣym* is another epithet for the conspirators,
then the picture is complete. Through some planned oversight, the baker
neglected his business, and the plot of the mischief makers succeeded
against the royal house.

What still remains a puzzle is whether the description of the baker and
his masterful inactivity is part of the actuality of the festive occasion with
its dire consequences, or an elaborate figure of speech, an analogy or metaphor for the criminal action taken against king and princes. This problem
cannot be separated from the "oven" which could be (a) a real object at
the scene of the crime or (b) a simile of rage.

The central section may be analyzed in the following manner: vv 5a–6a
are defined as a unit by the opening *ywm*, "day," and the bridging *kl-
hlylh*, "the whole night." The contrasting terms form a *merismus*, restricting action to the day of infamy on which the action described took
place. With the exception of v 5b, with its 3 m s form, which should be

linked with terms in vv 4 and 6, the material is reasonably homogeneous, relating to the conspirators (always m pl) and their behavior.

The general structure of the unit can then be described:

> Victims
> 3a   br'tm yśmḥw-mlk
> 3b   wbkḥšyhm śrym
> Conspirators
> 4aA   klm mn'pym
> 4aB   kmw tnwr b'r hm
> > Baker
> > 4bA   'ph yšbwt m'yr
> > 4bB   mlwš bṣq 'd-ḥmṣtw
> > > Victims
> > > 5aA   ywm mlknw hḥlw
> > > 5aB   śrym ḥmt myyn
> > > Baker
> > > 5b   mšk ydw 't-lṣṣym
> > Conspirators
> > 6aA   ky qrbw
> >   ktnwr lbm
> > Conspirators-Baker
> > 6aB   b'rbm kl-hlylh
> > 6bA   yšn 'phm bqr
> Conspirators
> 6bB   hw' b'r k'š lhbh
> 7aA   klm yḥmw ktnwr
> Victims
> 7aB   w'klw 't-šptyhm
> 7bA   kl-mlkyhm nplw
> 7bB   'yn-qr' bhm 'ly

The framework consists of the opening, v 3 and the closing, v 7aB–bA; v 7bB, the last line, is a coda linking this passage with others which also end with a personal reference by the deity. The main part of the unit has an envelope construction with repetitions and echoes to establish the pattern. Thus v 4aA and v 7aA both begin with *kullām*, and refer to the same group. The imagery of the burning oven is repeated in almost the same language: *kmw tnwr b'r* (v 4a) ~ *hw' b'r k'š lhbh . . . ktnwr* (vv 6b–7a). The pattern of one envelope inside another continues with the occurrence of *'ph* in v 4b and its echo, *'phm* in v 6b. The kernel of the pericope is to be found in vv 5–6a, whose limits are defined by the merismatic pair *ywm* (v 5a) and *hlylh* (v 6a). The imagery of the oven links this unit to the immediately surrounding envelope (v 6a), while the reference to king and princes ties in the opening and closing. Verses 6bB–7aA, unified by the parallel similes, may show the conspirators (*klm*) along with their leader (*hw',* unless this is kataphoric for *ktnwr* in v 7aA). While details of the passage may be obscure, and in dispute, the intricacy of the patterning argues for the integrity of the whole, and the deliberate positioning of the various elements. One can only speculate as to the reason for the confusion in meaning and understanding. It may lie either in the material itself or in the inadequacy of scholarly skills and knowledge; if the material is at fault, either accidental factors have disrupted the sense, or there was a deliberate obscuring of the details of what must have been one of the great scandals of the royal court of Israel—especially if the leading priests were mixed up in it. In other words, the pericope seems to be integrated and unified around certain key words and ideas, but at the same time maddeningly obscure in terms of an identifiable cast of characters and sequential narrative leading to a clear conclusion. A third explanation would be that the author and readers knew what was being discussed. The events had not yet become historic, requiring narrative, and the speech never came under the pen of an editor who felt the need to supply the background. Everything is concrete: time, place, actors; and points to a single event. Like the rest of cc 4–7, this text deals in a contemporary way with internal events in Palestine, perhaps with Menahem's succession. Only from 7:8 on does the setting become international.

The possibility that the baker is not meant as a historical person can be considered further. The text may have reference to a proverb about a house that burned down because a neglected oven burst into flames while the baker was asleep. Note that the oven and the fire are always introduced in similes, while the baker apparently is not. Perhaps the priests blazed like an oven while the king and his princes were off their guard under the influence of hot wine. Or again, if the adulterers in v 4 are everywhere, the entire population is aflame like an uncontrolled oven. The custodian of the oven, the king, has permitted things to get out of hand. While he slept, the anger of the people blazed up and destroyed him. This would agree with the circumstance that the last Israelite kings perished through civil insurrections rather than by foreign conquest.

We may essay another reading of the passage. The real events are presented under an elaborate simile. The assassination of the king is related in the guise of baking bread. The focus is on the baker. His role in the baking process is clear; but there seems to be negligence on his part. He stops being watchful and actually goes to sleep. The counterpart of the oven in the real events is found in the destructive rage of the conspirators. This simile is presented three times. The counterpart of the baker of the simile in the real-life situation is less clearly identified. He seems to have been an accomplice, perhaps the chief instigator. A person close to the king (someone with a high command in the military, as so often in such cases) with responsibility for his safety, aids and abets the assassins (his hand is stretched out to them). Even if his contribution to the plot was simply to signal to the waiting assassins when the time was right (when the king was good and drunk), the prophet's knowledge of such treachery against "our king" (the suffix expresses loyalty) leads to this denunciation. All are condemned.

7:3a–b. *wickedness . . . wily schemes.* In v 2 the people were accused of thinking that God had forgotten "all their wickedness." Putting another reference to "their wickedness" first in vv 3–7, the prophet introduces an account of a piece of wickedness that Yahweh certainly has not forgotten. On deceit and mendacity, see 4:2; 9:2; 10:13; and 12:1. In the bicolon these two words are fused to give the idea of "wicked schemings."

king . . . princes. The word *śrym,* "princes," is always plural in Hosea, except at 3:4, where it is generic (collective). The word always occurs in parallel with and after *melek,* or coordinated with it. The conjunction of "king" and "princes" here suggests that the whole of the court, not just the monarch, was the target of a plot. The absence of the article with both nouns makes it possible that something is being said here, not about "the king," but about "kings" in general (cf. v 7bA *mlkyhm*). The following details are so specific, however, that it is more likely that the article is omitted for poetic reasons; note especially *mlknw* in v 5a. None of the nouns in this passage has the article in the consonantal text, striking evidence that it is an ancient composition.

3a. *rejoice.* There is no need at all to emend *yśmḥw* to *ymšḥw,* "they anointed," by interchanging two consonants. While such a scribal error is common enough, there is no evidence in the Hebrew MSS or versions for such a change, nor is there any, for that matter, in the context. Hosea makes several disapproving statements about the monarchy, of which the strongest is that Yahweh gave them a king only in his anger (13:11), but v 7 makes it clear that here removal of kings, not their making, constitutes the wicked deed.

The central treatment of royalty in Hosea, at 8:4, is a blanket rejection of both kings and princes, but it is not intended to cover the whole of Israel's history and does not support the emendation to "anoint" in 7:3. Hos 8:4 does not mean that Yahweh never instituted or recognized kings or princes in Israel. The qualification "They made kings, but not from me" there suggests that, if the kings had been "from Yahweh," it would have been all right; or that kings which he set up were different from kings whom "they" set up. The ambivalence of the Bible on this question is not due simply to the contrary opinions of royalists and antiroyalists. Individual prophets display an ambiguity which alternates between disagreeable historical experience and the idealized pictures of the past or expectations for the future.

Since *šmḥ* means "to rejoice," and the *Pi'el* is factitive, v 3 could mean that the king and his officials were delighted with the wicked schemings of the priests, since they are all in it together (5:1). It is more likely, however, that making the king rejoice is itself the act of wickedness, done deceitfully. In view of v 5a, which speaks of wine, we suggest that what is going on in v 3 is a drinking party at court. In Judg 9:13 the power of wine to make gods and people merry is celebrated, but on this occasion it would seem that the wine made the court sick. Some congruence between vv 3 and 5 is possible if each is describing the same thing, namely, a party at which the priests deceitfully and deliberately encouraged the king and his princes to overindulge, so that they would have a chance to assassinate them. The subject of the verb is not identified; it is likely that the schemers are priests.

4a. *All of them are adulterers*. That is, the schemers. Since adultery took place in the cult, the term refers to the priests who fostered and practiced it. The activities described in vv 3–7 do not seem to include adultery, and there are no indications of sexual immorality in the context. The use of *n'p* here and in 4:2, where the reference is to the Decalogue, coincides with the appearance of *kḥš*, "deceit" in 4:2 and 7:3. If "adulterers" designates the priests in general, it has its secondary association of "idolaters."

The word *'ōpeh*, "baker," could have been brought in because of a play on the roots *'py* and *n'p*, though they do not seem to have any common ground semantically. It is not likely that *mn'pym*, "adulterers," has arisen by mistake from the root *'py*. The *Nip'al* of *'py* is attested (Lev 6:10; 7:9; 23:17), and the participle **ne'ĕpîm*, "baked," may have been obscured here by dittography. The noun *ma'ăpeh*, "something baked," occurs in *ma'ăpê tannûr*, "baked in an oven" (Lev 2:4), a collocation that could be significant in view of the prominence of the oven in Hos 7:3–7, though the metaphor would be mixed if the conspirators are both oven and bread. Another suggestion removes the apparent incongruity in the metaphor by reading *'ōnĕpîm*, "snorting with anger." This is congruent with the simile, but is too radical a change. We retain the MT.

they. The word division and vocalization of MT yields: "All of them are adulterers, like an oven heated by a baker." This involves several difficulties: (1) The long line of prose does not yield to structural analysis. (2) The f participle *bō'ērâ* is incongruous with the m *tannûr*. (3) The agential use of *m(n)* is difficult, especially because the participle is active, not passive. (4) An oven is heated by fire; the verb *b'r*, "to be alight," would be inappropriate unless the baker stokes the fire.

When the word boundaries are revised by reading *b'r hm 'ph*, these difficulties are overcome. The clause *kmw tnwr b'r hm*, "like a burning

oven (are) they" is grammatically excellent, and its structural relationships with the preceding line are clear; the chiasm between "all of
them" and "they" is particularly striking.

oven. The picture is not clear and the point of the simile eludes us. If
the conduct of the plotters is excessive and harmful, "like a burning
oven," then presumably the oven is malfunctioning and dangerous, blazing
out of control.

A *tannûr* is a fixed or portable earthenware stove, used especially for
baking bread. As noted above, loaves are *ma'ăpēh tannûr* (Lev 2:4; cf. Lev
7:9; 26:26); this phrase shows that a baker (*'ōpeh*) is a person who uses
a *tannûr,* and suggests that the baker in 7:3–7 may be dependent on the
oven in the picture. One kind of *tannûr* was big enough to destroy people
by putting them in it (Ps 21:10), perhaps a pottery kiln (Neh 3:11;
12:38). This destructive use of a *tannûr* as an incinerator provides a symbol of divine judgment on the Day of Yahweh blazing like an oven (*bō'ēr
kattannûr*) (Mal 3:19). In Gen 15:17 a smoking *tannûr* represents Yahweh himself.

In c 7, it seems to be people who are hot. Heat can be the result of intoxication (v 5), sexual desire (Gen 30:38,39; cf. "adulterers" in v 4), or
anger (Ps 21:10). Since v 3 speaks of the evil schemes of the priests, it is
probably they who are said to be burning in their hearts. Hebrew psychology could speak about ideas in the mind as a fire in the bones or the heart.

4b. *baker.* We cannot be certain if the lack of the article makes the
figure general, since we do not fully understand Hosea's use of the article.
A particular person seems to be intended here, as with *mlk* in v 3.

Verse 4b is probably independent of v 4a, contrary to many translations. The rendering, "A heated oven, whose baker ceases to stir the fire"
(*RSV*), is obscurantist; the point is lost, since the fire will go out and the
oven will not be hot at all, as it is in v 6bB. Verse 4b is to be detached
from v 4a; the baker's neglect concerns the dough, rather than the oven;
he did not knead the dough until it was leavened. (Strictly speaking, it is
not kneading which *leavens* the dough, but if the dough is not well
kneaded, it will not rise evenly.) The consequence of not kneading the
dough properly is not pursued in the image; it is simply that the product
will be defective. Something similar is taken up in 7:8 ("an unturned
cake"), though this describes technical incompetence at another point.
Gentle heat, carefully controlled, will assist the rising of dough. If this is
not maintained, because the baker falls asleep while the dough is rising, it
might not be ready for baking. The residual warmth of a stove whose fire
has died out would usually be sufficient for overnight rising and early
morning baking. A freshly lit stove, on the other hand, blazing rather than
glowing, will ruin bread that is rising and burn bread that is baking.

ceases. Šbt min-, "to cease from," is a common idiom.

to be alert. The root *'wr,* "to be awake," is usually transitive in the *Hip'il;* here the missing object is generally supposed to be the fire. This would be the only example of such an elliptical use; the suggestion reflects the belief that v 4b is a relative clause modifying "oven" in v 4a. The verb is not used for stirring a mixture, as if *mē'îr* were a synonym of *millûš.* Here, if *mē'îr* is absolute (elative of the *Qal*), it would mean, "he stops being as alert as he might be"; or *m'r* could be short for *mē'îr rûḥô,* "keeping himself alert," which amounts to the same thing. The root *'wr* contrasts with *yāšēn,* "to be asleep," in Ps 44:24; cf. v 6b.

to knead. Or "to stir." Gaster (1954), who eliminates the baker completely by reading *ma'ăpeh* in v 4 and *'aphem* in v 6, considers *millûš* to be simply a hypermetrical gloss on *mē'îr.* Even if he is right about the similarity of these words, and we recognize two infinitives in apposition, this is no argument against the authenticity of the text. Hosea often places two similar verbs in immediate sequence to make a two-verb phrase.

it's leavened. Ḥumṣâ, which occurs only here, seems to be a stative infinitive. It refers to the rising of the dough before, not during, baking. The connection of this process with the baker's neglect of the fire is not clear, unless the time the bread takes to rise should normally be used for getting the oven ready for the next stage, baking. If the baker does not heat the oven (the fire is actually in the oven, and is removed, to be replaced by the loaves, once the walls of the oven are hot) while the dough is rising, he may then stoke up the fire too fiercely, so that it blazes out and ruins the bread.

5a. *By day.* The preposition is not explicit. Another reading is "the day of our king." In any case, there is no indication of the identity of the speaker. "Our king" is sometimes a cult title for Yahweh (Isa 33:22; Pss 47:7; 89:19), but probably not here. "Our king" rather is human, and the pronoun implies approbation and loyalty, perhaps to Zechariah, the last of Jehu's line, recognized by Hosea as of divine appointment, though this seems to collide with 8:4. Isa 33:22 is emphatic about such titles belonging to Yahweh alone. Wolff (1974:107, 125) avoids the difficulty by following the Targum and reading "their king." He thinks the event may be the celebration of the accession of Tiglath Pileser's vassal. The situation seems to be more convivial than ceremonial, however; and, if we are right, the time is too early for that.

Day is probably the general time, followed by the more specific "night" and "morning," although it may be that the three time words mark three moments in the episode. Given that *yôm* is followed by *malkēnû,* it is possible to read a double *mem, yômām,* "by day," but this is not indicated.

made . . . ill. The *Hip'il* could be causative, as we render, or elative: "They were extremely sick with poisoned wine," except that there is no appropriate subject. The *Hip'il* is not often attested, and this is the only place where it could have an absolute sense. If we are right to look for parallelism between v 3a and v 5a, then a factitive meaning is required for both verbs. A compelling solution is handicapped by the several roots which have the consonants *ḥl*, though none suits the context as well as *ḥly*, "to be sick."

poisoned wine. Literally "heat of/from wine." Cf. Deut 32:33. See GKC ⚹130a for this and other examples of a preposition within a construct phrase. The meaning of *min*, "from," is hard to fit here, however, and we read an enclitic *mem* (Hummel 1957:99). "The heat of wine" may simply describe the psychological-physiological effect of wine on the body. This heat does not seem to be the same as the oven heat of the assassins' rage, even though the verb *ḥmm* is used in v 7. Any incongruity is of little moment, however. In Wisdom writing it is common to put more than one simile side by side for a cumulative effect; see 13:3. The oven blazes out destructively (v 7) against the princes; the victims, not the attackers, are sick. The usual sense of *ḥēmâ*, "hot rage," can be reconsidered here; with the verb *heḥĕlû*, the meaning "poison," which is well attested, suits better. Pss 58:5 and 140:4 make it clear that *ḥēmâ* can denote snake venom. The options here, "heat," or "poison," are present also in Job 6:4, where the ambiguity lies between poisoned arrows and arrows with burning materials attached. This has occasioned considerable debate as to the weapon used by Shadday in attacking Job. The verb "to drink" there points to poison, as does the association with "wine" in Hos 7:5.

5b. *He stretched out.* A clue to the force of *mšk* is supplied by Judg 20:37, where it occurs in association with *hā'ōrēb*, as in Hos 7:6; *mšk* is an activity of *hā'ōrēb*, the ambush prior to assault. In Job 21:33, *mšk* describes a processional line, and military usage, as in Judges 4, suggests that it means to form ranks. The next verb, *qrb*, also describes a tactical movement. The idiom *mšk yādô* is not used elsewhere. In military contexts, *mšk* can have a weapon as its object. If, in concert with the *lōṣĕṣîm*, the subject is doing something violent with his hand (i.e. with a weapon in his hand), *mšk yādô* could be similar to *šlḥ yādô* or *nṭy yādô*, gestures often connected with physical assault.

scoffers. Gaster (1954:79), who denies that *lōṣĕṣîm* means "scoffers," connects the root *lwṣ* with an Arabic root, "to divert"; he does not explore the consequences for 7:5. The context offers no help at all; the identity and function of this group in the situation remains quite obscure, as does the gesture cited. If "to extend the hand" means "to make common cause with," no support is gained from any other occurrences of the words in this line. In Wisdom literature the *lēṣîm* are proud mockers; in Prov 20:1, wine itself is called a *lēṣ*, making the similarity to the word-field of Hos 7:5 rather intriguing. The root does not seem to have any connotations of revelry (rather, the opposite), so "mockers" does not seem to refer to the princes as the king's companions in idle pleasure-seeking. Only in Hos 7:5 is the *Pōlēl* participle used; the meaning could be specialized.

The *lēṣîm* are more than scoffers; they are depraved. The sense of the term in Wisdom literature is not powerful enough to fit the seriousness of its use in prophetic literature, although it could be that its seriousness has not been recognized in the traditional translation "to scoff." The consequences of "scoffing" are drastic; cf. Prov 21:24. Apart from its numerous occurrences in Wisdom literature, the root is met only in Isa 28:14,22; 29:20, and here. Its parallel *'ārîṣ* (Isa 29:20), "ruthless," is a strong word.

6a. *they drew near.* If *kî* gives the time for what follows, it describes the approach of those who lay in wait all night, whose heart was like an oven: the assassins whose work is described in v 7. The *Pi'el* of *qrb* is problematic, since the *Qal* would make sense. The *Pi'el* is used only seven times, excluding Hos 7:6. It has an object in Isa 41:21; Ezek 37:17; Job 31:37; Isa 46:13; Ps 65:5. It is intransitive in Ezek 36:8, and especially in Ezek 9:1, which, like Hos 7:6, refers to violent crime. In Hos 7:6, *qērĕbû* is laconic for *qērĕbû lābô'*, as in Ezek 36:8; cf. Gen 12:11. The verb seems to be inceptive. The narrative stops at this point; the murder is not described.

their heart. Jeremiah speaks about an uncontrollable emotion as a blazing fire in the heart (Jer 20:9). With the nearby reference to the heart as the seat of secret thoughts in Hos 7:2, this suggests that their secret schemes (7:3 — note the repetition of *rā'ātām* in vv 2 and 3) are perceived by God, contrary to their self-delusion expressed in v 2. These are the murderous intentions that will blaze up destructively "in the morning." This fits in with the picture of lying in wait.

their ambush. In Judg 16:2 residents of Gaza lay in wait for Samson; the construction *wayye'erbû-lô kol-hallaylâ* is similar to this text. The night is one of debauchery (cf. II Sam 13:28).

6b. *It.* Or "he." The referent is not clear, and this is a misfortune, for the line seems to be a climax, and we need to know what or who it is that blazes like a flaming fire in the morning. There is an apparent incongruity between the statement that they (we have retrieved *hēm* from the text) are like an oven (v 4aB), "all of them" (v 7aA), and the statement in v 6bB that "it" or "he" (*hû'*) is like a flaming fire. The obvious conclusion is that it is the oven which blazes: there are close structural connections between the two lines through *bō'ēr*.

Four things are said about heat.

A. They (*hēm*) are like a *burning oven* (v 4aB).
B. Their heart was like an *oven* (v 6aB).
C. It (*hû'*) was *burning* like a blazing flame (v 6bC).
D. All of them became heated like an *oven* (v 7aA).

A, B, and D have the word "oven" in common. A and C have the word "burning." A and D have a plural reference ("they," "all of them"), while B and C are singular ("their heart," "it"). A and C have pronouns (*hēm* and *hû'*). B and D have the similar *libbām* and *kullām*. This all points to the equation of "it" with the oven.

7a. *became heated*. The use of the root *ḥmm* to describe the sting of wine and the heat of a furnace could be no more than play with sounds, or both may be combined in one picture: the conspirators struck when they were as hot as a furnace, due to wine. The heart is the locus of inebriation as well as anger; when it is on fire, self-control is lost (Jer 20:9).

devoured. This verb probably continues the image of fire. In Ps 21:10 the fire of Yahweh's anger devours his enemies "like an oven." Cf. Hos 8:14; Judg 9:15; Amos 1–2.

judges. If vv 7aB and 7bA constitute a bicolon, then "judges" // "kings" instead of the usual "king" // "princes." Cf. Pss 2:10; 148:11. We are back to 5:1: the king and his officials are reminded of their duty to secure justice. In 7:16aA "their princes" occurs with the verb *npl*, but without any obvious parallel. Hos 7:7bA and 7:16aA would make a good bicolon, with chiasm. This suggests that vv 3–7 find an echo at the end of the chapter, unifying the whole unit.

7b. *calls on me*. This is the only personal remark made by God, his only comment on the event, and it is surprisingly succinct. Although we have included this in the structure of vv 3–7, its connection with the whole is not clear. It seems to begin a new thought, and might be transitional to the following. At the same time it is a kind of coda to the story of the murder of "our king." Hos 7:14aA is similar. Whatever the artistic intention of the author, the effect of such linkages is to sustain the discourse. If v 7bB rounds off the preceding account, summing it up, it may mean that no one calls out to Yahweh against (*b*) them, i.e. nobody makes any protest to Yahweh about the violence represented by such a palace of revolution as seems to be going on in vv 3–7. Under the circumstances of the violence and chaos described in vv 3–7, it would be the final proof of the total loss of the knowledge of Yahweh (4:1) that even in such an extremity none of them calls on Yahweh. Had they done so, there would have been deliverance, even at the last minute.

Hos 7:14 says that they do cry out in protest, but not sincerely. If v

7bB is an isolated thematic statement of a more general kind, it could be an inclusion for 6:7 (note *hēmmâ* and *bāhem*), thus isolating 6:7 – 7:7 as a major unit:

> There they acted treacherously against me,
> None of them calls out to me.

(Note the matching positions of *bî* and *'ēlāy*.)

XIII. THE STATE OF THE NATION: INTERNATIONAL POLITICS
(7:8–16)

Ephraim: raw food, rotten food

7:8a   Ephraim — he is mixed up with the nations.
  8b   Ephraim has become an unturned cake.
  9a   Foreigners have eaten away his strength,
          but he has not realized it.
  9b   Mold is sprinkled upon him,
          but he has not realized it.
10a   The pride of Israel will testify against him.
10b   They have not returned to Yahweh their God.
          They have not sought him in all this.

Ephraim: a dumb dove

11a   Ephraim became like a silly brainless dove.
11b   They called to Egypt,
          they went to Assyria.
12a   As they have certainly gone to Assyria —
          I will spread my net over them.
12b   Like birds of the skies I will bring them down.
          So I will chastise them according to report of their treaties.

Ephraim wanders from Yahweh

13a   Woe to them, for they have wandered away from me.
          Destruction to them, for they have rebelled against me.
13b   Yet I was the one who redeemed them.
          They were the ones who told lies about me.
14a   They did not cry out to me from their hearts.
          They did not shriek from their beds.
14b   For grain and must they lacerate themselves.
          They have departed from me.

VII. Neo-Assyrian Relief of a Lion Being Released from Its Cage. Nineveh (modern Kuyunjik, Iraq), from the North Palace of Ashurbanipal (668–627).

VIII. Neo-Assyrian Relief of Chariot Battle Attack. Kalḫu (biblical Calah, modern Nimrud, Iraq), from the Northwest Palace of Ashurnasirpal II (883–859).

IX. Neo-Assyrian Relief of Horseback Battle Attack. Kalḫu (biblical Calah, modern Nimrud, Iraq), from the Northwest Palace of Ashurnasirpal II (883–859).

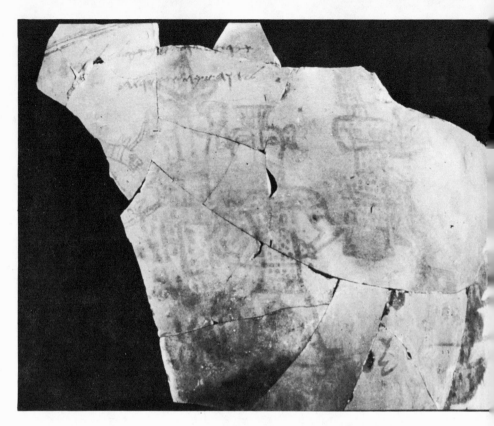

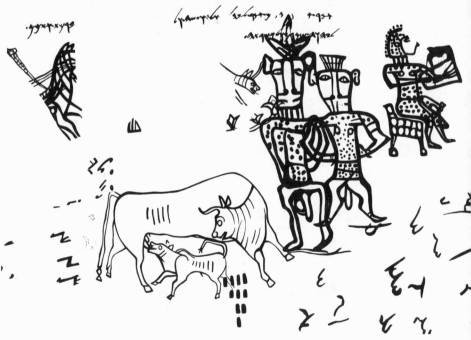

X-XI. Iron Age Pithos Jug with Drawing and Inscription, which reads in part *brkt.ʾtkm.lyhwh.šmrn.wlʾšrth*, "May you be blessed by Yahweh, our guardian, and by his Asherah."

Ephraim turns to a no-god
15a I was the one who trained them;
     I strengthened their arms;
15b But they plotted evil against me.
16a They turned to a no-god.
     They became like a slack bow.
16b Their princes fell by the sword —
     out of the rage of the tongue of the One who mocked them —
     in the land of Egypt.

NOTES

7:8–16. This passage deals with various aspects of Israel's entanglement in international politics. It is less coherent than other parts of the book. No single situation can be discerned; no one theme dominates and unifies it. From the literary point of view its texture is like that of the rest of Hosea: it is quasi-poetical. There are some well-formed poetic units, interspersed with lines which are closer to normal prose.

The bounds of 7:8–16 as a unit are marked by the closure at 7:7 (although 7:7bB could be a suture), and by the new beginning at 8:1. Furthermore, 7:8 is the onset of a new discourse, and 7:16 has the stylistic marks of a conclusion. This does not prove that everything in between is a single piece. The unit is commonly viewed as a collection of small, even fragmentary, oracles. In terms of theme and composition it divides into four parts. There are continuities, such as the themes of going to Assyria and Egypt, and the similes. Verbal signals supply connections, on the domino principle. Thus v 11 ends with *'šwr hlkw* and v 12 begins *k'šr ylkw* (Ceresko 1978:3–4). The last line of v 13 is close enough to the first line of v 14 to be considered a poetic parallel. The question is whether this organizing principle is part of the original craftsmanship of the author, or whether it is an artificial arrangement of an editor. If the former, an attempt should be made to make sense of vv 8–16 as a whole; if the latter, the interpreter is under a lighter obligation on that score, namely, to follow the path of the editor.

Verse 8 is a bicolon in which Ephraim is repeated, suspended for topicalization in its first occurrence; only in a general way is the content of the lines similar. Each is a distinct *māšāl,* linked only by the common background of cooking. Verse 11b is a well-formed bicolon:

> *miṣrayim qārā'û* 5/6 syllables
> *'aššûr hālākû* 5

Verse 12b exhibits parallelism with chiasmus.

> *kĕ'ôp haššāmayim 'ôrîdēm* 8/9 syllables
> *'aysīrēm kĕšēma' la'ădātām* 8/10

The absence of any coordinating conjunction in these bicola is noteworthy. Verse 13b has two lines of quite unequal length, but the contrastive juxtaposition of the free-form pronouns indicates antithetic parallelism.

> *wĕ'ānōkî 'epdēm* 6 syllables
> *wĕhēmmâ dibbĕrû 'ālay kĕzābîm* 6 + 5

Verse 10 is best analyzed as a tricolon. There is an introductory line followed by a bicolon which provides a more detailed exposition of the first line. With the disproportion between the parallels *'el-yhwh 'ĕlōhêhem* and *-hû*, there is room in the last line for further development, with the climactic *bĕkol-zō't*.

> *wĕ'ānâ gĕ'ôn-yiśrā'ēl bĕpānāyw* 11 syllables
> *wĕlō'-šābû 'el-yhwh 'ĕlōhêhem* 11
> *wĕlō'biqšūhû bĕkol-zō't* 8

The same kind of tricolon (an unmatched line followed by a more regular bicolon) is used in vv 11 and 12aB–b; the bicola in these verses have already been described above.

Verse 9 is a well-formed tetracolon, made up of two long sentences of identical grammatical structure. The use of the conjunctions here is interesting: *wĕ* is used for antithesis ("but"); coordination is secured by *gam*. Verse 13 contains four clauses in two compound sentences. Verse 14 is construed as four lines, although the last line, *yāsûrû-bî*, is much shorter than the other three, which have ten syllables each. Since the middle two lines are fairly close in meaning, chiastic parallelism (A B B' A') is present. Poetic patterns are much harder to trace in vv 15 and 16.

There is effective use of repetition. "Ephraim" is repeated in v 8. "But he has not realized it" is repeated in v 9. The two clauses in v 10b begin with "and not." "To them" is repeated in similar clauses in v 13.

Hos 7:8–16 contains some of Hosea's most memorable similes: Ephraim is like a silly dove (v 11); Israel is like a slack bow (v 16). Verse 8 contains a metaphor, a rarity in this book as in the entire Bible — "Ephraim has become an unturned cake." The simile in v 12 illustrates the activity of Yahweh rather than the state of the people. From our point of view, the artistry is hard to grasp. The purpose of a simile is to make something clearer by saying that it is "like" something else. But v 11 is the only simile which provides the other member of the comparison. Apart from vv 11b, 12a, and 16b, there is no allusion to any identifiable historical event or tradition. Aside from Ephraim's foolish involvement in international politics and neglect of trust in Yahweh, the faults are of a general character. "A cake unturned" is certainly a fanciful description; but what does it refer to? In what respect is Ephraim a cake not turned over? In what kind of conduct is Ephraim like a slack bow?

Ephraim dominates the passage. Unlike other places in Hosea, Judah does not appear here in parallel to Ephraim. This raises the question of the subject of the plural verbs. The use of *hû'* in vv 8 and 9 shows that Ephraim is singular. Elsewhere plural verbs and pronouns show that both parts of the nation are in view. The reference to "Israel" in v 10a is similarly singular; but in v 10b the verbs are plural. Verse 11a refers to Ephraim as singular, followed by a bicolon in v 11b in which the verbs are plural. From this it can be inferred that Ephraim and Israel are not the same. They must refer to distinct parts of the northern kingdom, individually denounced in vv 10a and 11a; and denounced together in vv 10b and 11b. After v 11a, the verbs and pronouns in vv 12–16 are plural; but neither Ephraim nor Israel is named. This inference — that Ephraim and Israel are different — agrees with 5:5. It suggests further that Ephraim and Israel might not be synonymous in other places, such as 5:3, as generally assumed.

7:8–9. These verses constitute a little poem that can be separated from the rest, although v 10 must have some climactic or connective function.

8a. *Ephraim.* Verse 8 is clearly a bicolon, its structure reinforced by the repetition of Ephraim. Yet the parallelism between vv 8a and 8b is not evident. This could be intentional: Hosea's extensive use of similes is reminiscent of the enigmas of the "wise."

The absence of a conjunction before v 8b is not a sure sign that there is a major break here. Better evidence comes from the use of the key words "Assyria" and "Egypt," and from the overall structure. If *'šr* at the beginning of v 12 is rightly read as "Assyria," then vv 12–16 are marked as a unit by the inclusion "Assyria . . . Egypt," in a sequence the inverse of that in v 11b (Lundbom 1979). If the "nations" mentioned in v 8a are not all nations, or nations in general, but specifically the two nations spoken of in vv 8–16, then there is a close link between v 8a and v 11, with two images of Ephraim, the cake and the dove.

mixed up. This is the only occurrence of the *Hitpolel* of *bll.* The *Qal* is transitive, and means "to mingle"; largely a technical term in cookery, it means to make a mixture, as of flour and oil, presumably homogeneous. As a reflexive the *Hitpolel* would then mean "Ephraim mixes himself up with the nations, so as to become indistinguishable from them." In Ps

92:11 the *Qal* has the less common meaning "to anoint a person with oil." In Gen 11:7 and 9 it describes the confusion and difficulties of communication which result from mixing together people of different languages. The image of blending in cookery might be a continuation of the baker image from 7:3–7. It would mean that Ephraim has reverted completely to paganism. Such a mixture could come about in two ways. First, Ephraim is dispersed through foreign countries, losing its national identity. Secondly, foreign manners have so penetrated the homeland that Ephraim is no longer a distinct people. The choice between these two depends on whether *yitbôlāl* is middle or reflexive. The reflexive would place the blame on Ephraim — he has mixed himself up with the nations. If middle, the statement could mean that he is all mixed up in himself; and the verb could be durative — he is continually in confusion, in parallel to vv 9aB and 9bB, "he has not realized it." Verse 9 gives the impression that Ephraim is unaware of deterioration, and strikes a note of pity.

The meaning of *bll* in Genesis 11, if applied here, would mean that Ephraim has been thrown into confusion; *b* would be instrumental, "by." With the *Qal* of *bll*, *b* marks the material that is mixed in, usually oil. If the image is meant to apply exactly, this would mean that Ephraim has mixed foreigners into himself, like oil into flour. Since the imagery of baking is present in v 8b as well, this result is preferred, although in vv 12–16 Hosea will talk about scattering Israel among the nations, or at least a return to Egypt and exile in Assyria. This does not mean, however, that the lines are synonymous or that the figures have to be congruent.

nations. Cf. 9:1; 10:10. Since Egypt and Assyria are still remote, the "nations" here could also be the smaller nations with which Ephraim was involved in alliances and wars. These experiences were generally disastrous. Alternating cooperation and conflict with Damascus, for example, was incongruous.

8b. *unturned.* The negative *bĕlî*, "not," is rarely used with a participle; see II Sam 1:21. In baking, the small cakes of bread are put on the inside walls of a heated oven. If they are not turned over they will not just be "half- (i.e. incompletely) baked"; rather they will be burnt on one side and raw on the other. This would happen if the baker suddenly left his work in the middle of the process, just as Yahweh might withdraw from Israel (5:6). A similar thought recurs in 8:8. Although *hāpak* can mean not only "to turn over" (and hence to overturn), but also to turn around or to turn something into something else, here the action is almost certainly the turning over of a piece of bread. The simile describes a defect, but does not serve to diagnose it. It seems to be general political folly. Verses 8a and 9a describe the reality; vv 8b and 9b are metaphors.

9a. *Foreigners.* The word *zārîm* occurs in 5:7, and again in 8:7, where it is also connected with eating. The perfect form suggests that this has already happened, although Ephraim does not realize it. The verb "to eat" is probably not tied to the preceding remark about a cake; cf. Isa 1:7. The "foreigners" are connected with the "nations" (v 8a) with which Ephraim has mixed himself. In the light of 5:7, where the offspring gained by adulterous connection with a rival god are called *bānîm zārîm,* the strangers who now have eaten Ephraim's strength might not be foreign invaders or overlords, but his own bastard children.

strength. The word *kōaḥ* usually means (physical) strength, including virility, but can designate the produce of the soil (Gen 4:12; cf. Job 6:22; Prov 5:10). Verse 9aA is accordingly ambiguous, but the verb "to eat" suggests that the consumption of Israel's agricultural products is literally intended. Even so, "eating produce" could be used figuratively to refer to tribute paid to a foreign ruler. In common parlance, "to eat a piece of land" means to have the usufruct of an estate, which could describe the obligations of a vassal Israelite king to Assyria, as a result of which Israel was laid waste economically. Ephraim was unaware of its plight, because it saw only the temporary advantages of survival and security.

9b. *Mold.* Verses 9a and 9b have the same grammatical structure, and the same number of syllables. The traditional picture of aged Ephraim with grey hair must be rejected. Grey hair was worn with pride and satisfaction in Israel; old age was respected, and the evening of life was a time of prestige and usefulness. Hence grey hair would be welcomed, not ignored. It would not be a matter for pity or reproach.

The verb *zāraq, Qal* transitive, means "to sprinkle," and is used mainly for blood. It cannot be applied to hair in the same sense; the usual preposition is *'al,* not *b.* The form here is probably a *Qal* passive since there is a *Pu'al* but no *Pi'el.* The difficulty in the verb has been recognized for a long time. The LXX, translating "sprang out," seems to have a reading *zārĕḥâ;* cf. the Syriac. Koehler-Baumgartner (1958:269), following G. R. Driver, suppose *zrq* II, meaning "to be bright or light." Hos 7:9 is the only case they recognize of this root with such a meaning. Blau (1955:341), drawing on Arabic cognates, proposes a verb *zrq* meaning "to creep up to stealthily." The picture of vv 8–9 can be completed if we recognize that *śêbâ* here designates, not grey human hair, but the hairs of mold on food, like Akkadian *šibu* (Paul 1968:119–20). The analogy here continues the cake reference of v 8b and the general pattern of culinary language; the Akkadian cognate is used specifically of moldy bread.

The twice repeated "but he has not realized it" is given added pathos by the prominent personal pronoun *hû';* cf. Isa 1:3. Hosea has repeatedly asserted that Israel does not know Yahweh; as a consequence they do not know their own condition. Verse 11 presents Ephraim as stupid and gullible. It all adds up to a picture of self-deception, a refusal to face the facts.

Israel was still harboring delusions about the game of international power politics; actually the nation was exhausted.

10. The poetic structure of v 10b, which is a well-formed bicolon, leaves v 10a somewhat isolated, but the whole should be viewed as a tricolon, with the first line a general statement of which the following two are an expansion. Verse 10a is the same as 5:5a, which is also followed by a bicolon. See the NOTES there. "The pride of Israel" is blind insolence, self-condemning, all the while refusing to turn to Yahweh. The remainder of the chapter gives reminders of Yahweh's benefactions (vv 13bA, 15a), set against Israel's acts of rebellion. The indictment here leads to various threats (vv 12, 13a, 16b).

10b. *returned.* The sequence "return . . . and seek" is found also in 3:5; see the NOTES there; the phrase "Yahweh their God" occurs there too (cf. 1:7; 12:10; 13:4; 14:2).

all this. That is, the distressing situation described in vv 8 and 9, capped by the accusation in v 10a. The divine call is heard in chastisements (v 9a), in the experience of rotting (v 9b), in the word of condemnation (v 10a), in the constant reminder of Yahweh's past favors (v 13b). Only in 14:3 is an explicit call to repent ("return to Yahweh") given. Otherwise the people's deeds do not allow them to return (5:4); they refuse to return (11:5); they do not return (7:10). Yahweh himself will have to bring about their return (6:11), at the end of days (3:5).

11a. *became.* Like *hāyâ* in v 8b, *wayĕhî* indicates a specific development, not just a general characteristic. It is precisely the negotiations with Egypt and Assyria (v 11b) that reveal this flaw in Ephraim's character.

brainless. Literally "without heart." The word *lēb* is used quite often in this part of Hosea. It has connotations of discernment, not simply intelligence. In Isa 1:3, where the phrase *lō' yāda'* is used, Israel's lack of sense is contrasted with the wisdom of animals who know their master's manger. The blunt phrase used here, *'ên lēb,* can be construed in several ways. It could stand in apposition with *pôtâ* as another attribute of the dove, as we render it; or it could be a complement of the clause, an attribute of Ephraim: "and Ephraim has become mindless (like a silly dove)." That the people have lost their senses has already been stated in 4:11. This is not a statement that Ephraim is like a dove which in its innocence (Matt 10:16) could be admired. The aimless activity of the dove here, flying from one place to another, suggests that it is frightened, rather than gullible; the Targum has picked up this nuance by translating *lēb* as "courage" rather than intelligence. Nonetheless something more reprehensible than timidity is present. Hosea constantly emphasizes Israel's culpable ignorance. The people have abandoned covenant knowledge and thereby perverted their knowledge of other reality. Enmeshed in theological error they misjudge the political situation and have no self-knowledge. Their stupid blindness is seen at its worst in their incomprehensible refusal to return to Yahweh or to seek him "in all this" (v 10), i.e. in spite of the severity of all the disasters that have overwhelmed them since they deserted Yahweh (Amos 4; Jeremiah 44), and in spite of the warmth and openness of his constant invitation to return (14:3). The simile is repeated more favorably in 11:11.

dove. The bird is fluttery, so simple-minded as to be easily deceived and enticed. Do the several similes of vv 8 and 11 help to interpret each other? What is the similarity between an unturned cake and a silly dove, if both images describe the same defect in Ephraim? Deut 11:16 associates the verb *pty*, "to be simple," with the "heart" in the matter of Israel's deflection to idolatry.

11b. *Egypt.* This country is mentioned thirteen times in Hosea. Five times (2:17; 11:1; 12:10,14; 13:4) the name occurs in recitations of the Exodus tradition. If we include *'šr* in 7:12 (see the NOTE there) Assyria is mentioned ten times; twice it is cited as a vain political hope for Israel (5:13; 14:4). In seven occurrences, Egypt and Assyria are mentioned, as here, in synonymous parallelism. They are the two great powers between which the little countries of Syria-Palestine lay. The sequence Egypt–Assyria is used four times (7:11; 9:3; 11:5,11). In one bicolon (12:2) the sequence Assyria–Egypt is met. In two more occurrences Assyria and Egypt, in that sequence, are mentioned in separated, and otherwise unpaired, lines, marking larger structures; these are 7:12a with 16b and 8:9a with 13b. Isolated statements that Israel will return to Egypt (9:6) and will be taken to Assyria (or at least their spoil will) (10:6) constitute another such pair whose connection should be sought in a larger structure. The politics are realistic, although Egypt and Assyria are not yet directly involved. A time of decision is being described. Hosea cannot foresee the consequences. He does not predict conquest by Assyria, for example, but he knows that the outcome will be terrible if present policy is pursued.

The absence of the usual prepositions with the verbs "called" and "went" makes the bicolon terse and tight. Both nouns should be considered the objects of both verbs. Ephraim has sent ambassadors to both countries to cry out for aid.

12. This verse presents a number of difficulties. Verse 12b is almost unintelligible. Verse 12a seems to have a close connection with v 11 in the repetition of the verb "to go" and in the continued use of bird similes.

12a. *Assyria.* In the MT, the first word is *ka'ăšer*, "like that," or "when." This is plausible, and with the verb *yēlēkû*, "they (will) walk," continuing from v 11, would mean "as they walk (to Assyria and Egypt)." There are, nevertheless, several reasons for reading emphatic *kaph* and "Assyria" instead of *k'šr*. (1) The relative *'ăšer* occurs only about six times in cc 4–14, and is unlikely to be used in a passage like

7:8–16, which is certainly not prose. (2) The text with emendation repeats the last clause of v 11. (3) The occurrence of Assyria provides a poetic partner for "Egypt" in v 16. This is needed because, as shown above, Egypt is mentioned alone by Hosea only in reference to the Exodus event, never to the contemporary situation. Furthermore, unless v 16bB is linked with v 12, it does not have any other connection with the context; such an inclusion makes the unity of vv 12–16 clearer, a further aid to interpretation. The same kind of device marks 8:9–13 as a unit. (4) This emendation makes v 11 a text for vv 12–16: the names Egypt / Assyria // Assyria / Egypt are used in chiasm so that the unit from v 11b to v 16 begins and ends with the word "Egypt." In v 16 Egypt is called "the land of Egypt" (one of five times in Hosea); Assyria is called "the land of Assyria" only once (11:11). There we have the parallels "Egypt" // "land of Assyria"; here we have "Assyria // "land of Egypt." Assyria is spelled *plene* generally, but *defective* spellings occur both in Hebrew (I Chron 5:6) and in contemporary Aramaic texts (Fitzmyer 1967:45).

net. In Ezek 19:8 a similar clause, "They threw (*yprśw*) their net (*rštm*) over him," describes the capture of a lion. Unfortunately the identity of the prey in Hos 7:12a is unknown, though a bird seems likely. Evidently, similar equipment was used in bird-catching and in snaring terrestrial animals. The historical reality which corresponds to this image is not explicated. There are no grounds for supposing that it describes the Captivity; on the contrary it gives the impression of frustrating an attempt to reach Assyria or Egypt or both.

12b. *birds.* The singular noun is collective. Hosea usually says "bird(s) of the skies" (2:20; 4:3; 7:12); only 9:11 lacks the epithet. The verse describes catching birds of the air with a net, something different from birds being ensnared by a ground trap (Amos 3:5), though it is not clear in what way. Amos 9:2 has the same verb as Hos 7:12 and the same picture of bringing a bird down from the sky. Attempts have been made to fill out the picture, by supposing that the birds are actually lured down from the sky by some kind of bait; or first brought down by a missile, before the net is cast over them. This is not necessary if the imagery permits the divine bird-catcher to fly through the air with his net, like Enlil. It is possible that Yahweh moves "like an eagle" (Hos 8:1). The sequence of events in v 12 could be as follows: (1) I will bring them down like birds of the sky [by unspecified means]; (2) I will throw my net over them [not just to catch them, but to imprison them]; (3) then I will discipline them.

chastise. '*ysrm* seems to have the root *ysr* like *ysrty,* "I trained," in v 15, and *mûsār,* "chastisement," in 5:2, which is close to *paḥ* and *rešet.* Some MSS read '*ysyrm* (cf *BH²*), which supports the MT parsing of the form as a *Hip'il* of *ysr.* The context, however, suggests the root '*sr,* "to bind," although neither *'sr* nor *ysr* has an attested *Hip'il,* unless here. An inverse problem turns up in 10:10, where *'srm* occurs; it looks as if it comes from the root *'sr,* but could be derived from *ysr.* Such variants could be copyists' errors, but it is significant that the confusion occurs in words which have roots with a weak consonant in the first position. *Yissartî* (7:15) is a stable form and its presence nearby is a powerful argument for leaving the root *ysr* intact in v 12. In **'a'asîrēm,* from *'sr,* the second *'alep* could dissimilate (palatalize) to give the form in v 12, a credible change from the phonetic point of view. Such an apparent convergence of the roots *'sr* and *ysr* would be aided both by the two consonants that the roots possess in common, and also by some semantic overlap of the roots in the idea of corrective punishment. Here it could mean "to capture," that is, imprison for punishment, combining both ideas.

The MT pointing of *'ysrm* in 7:12 is another matter. As a *Hip'il* it is difficult. The defective orthography gives no support to -*i*- as the stem vowel; the initial diphthong *'ay*- is difficult in Hebrew, especially in the northern dialect; reading a medial *šewa* cannot save the form, for such has no place in a *Hip'il.* And, as has been observed, the *Hip'il* of this root is not otherwise attested. Its presence here could be simply an imitation of the preceding *'ôrîdēm.* These are some of the reasons why other commentators prefer to read a *Pi'el* of *ysr,* **'ăyassĕrēm,* "I will chastise them," a credible form which does justice to the consonants and fits the severe tone of the passage.

according to report of their treaties. This requires reading for MT's "their congregation" (root *y'd*), *'ēdûtām,* "their oath, covenant" (root *'wd*). This line identifies the form of rebellion against Yahweh, and fits Menahem's deal with Pul (II Kings 15:17–22). The payment of his tribute is recorded in the Assyrian annals. On the etymology of roots with *'-d* and their associations with covenant ideas, see J. A. Thompson (1965), and on the type of treaties involved, see Fitzmyer (1967:23–24). Such a treaty would certainly involve submission to the Assyrian gods, and so treachery against Yahweh. According to Ezek 12:13; 17:20, it is fitting punishment for a treaty breaker to be caught in a net. On the covenants made with both Assyria (v 12) and Egypt (v 16) at the same time, see 12:1–2, where several of the ideas of c 7 are met again. If 12aB–12bA are read as a bicolon, v 12aA is left to be more closely connected to v 12bB.

13a. This can be construed as two lines with a marked caesura in each.

> *'ôy lāhem   /   kî-nādĕdû mimmennî*
> *šōd lāhem   /   kî-pāšĕ'û bî*

There is a marked increase in intensity in the second line. "Woe" means "destruction," while "wandered away" is specified as "rebelled."

Woe. Compare 9:12, where *'ôy* occurs in a different kind of clause. Of twenty-three biblical occurrences, *'ôy* is used twelve times in "woe to me" as an expression of distress (e.g. Isa 6:5); four times in "woe to you," where it sounds like a threat (e.g. Jer 13:27); and six times in "woe to him/them," as here, an indirect threat. (One occurrence is indeterminate.) The use of *'ôy* in parallel with *šōd* makes the former a noun, rather than an exclamation; these short clauses are more like curses than predictions. It remains possible, however, that a note of compassion rather than vindictiveness is present; cf. 11:8.

wandered. Not the wanderings of someone who is lost, but those of a person driven out and finding no home. See 9:17. The impression given is that the wanderer loses security and does not find another haven. There is no substitute for the security of life with Yahweh. The element of willfulness is secured more clearly by the parallel "rebelled." In Jer 4:25 and 9:9, *ndd* is used to describe the (seasonal?) disappearance of birds; cf. Isa 10:14. The idea of homeless wanderers is dominant here, as in Jer 49:5.

There is no evidence that the allegory of cc 1–3 receives any attention in cc 4–14. The picture of the errant wife who strays from her home may be in the picture, but it is doubtful.

13b. In this bicolon, a coordination of two clauses with the free form pronouns in prominent positions secures contrast. The charges of covenant-breaking (6:7) and treachery are here specified as slandering God. Yahweh's goodness in redeeming them makes more inexcusable their ingratitude not merely in forgetting him (2:15), but in slandering him. One part of the slander was to attribute his generosity to the Baals (2:7); this is the negative side of their "lies." Another slander, recorded in 7:2, is to say that God has forgotten all their evil. A connection between devastation and lying is made again in 12:2, showing that v 13b is connected with v 13a. It is also to be linked with what follows. In vv 14–16 the sin condemned is not illicit activity in international politics, as in vv 11–12, but involvement in Canaanite religion. Speaking lies against me (v 13bB) and plotting evil against me (v 15b) are similar. The rebellion is not only overt (resorting to Baal, going to Assyria), but it is also in the mind, a theological error that begins with a false opinion of Yahweh's character.

The similarity between v 13b and v 15a is shown by similar use of pronouns *'nky* and *'ny,* "I." Note also the sequence of verb forms:

> 13b Yahweh's act of redemption — imperfect verb
> Their act of rebellion — perfect verb
> 15a Yahweh's act of chastisement — two perfect verbs
> Their perverse response — imperfect verb.

Apart from the chiastic pattern, it is not possible to find any distinctions of either tense or aspect in the use of these verbs, or to decide the question of temporal subordination of the clauses.

redeemed. The verb echoes the language of the Exodus story. A past tense rendering is required; there is no need to use a subjunctive — "I would redeem them" (*RSV*). Harper (p. 305) considers other possibilities. Exodus 15 uses the verbs *qny* and *g'l* to describe redemption; *pdy,* used here, is Deuteronomic (Deut 7:8; 9:26; 13:6; 21:8; etc.; cf. Ps 78:42). Verse 15a moves on to the phase of salvation history that follows the Exodus, the discipline of the desert; here already they had begun to speak words against the Most High. Israel's reactions to Yahweh will make it appropriate for him to reverse the movement from Egypt through the desert to the promised land. The people will be defeated in their land (v 13), foreigners will possess it (v 9; 8:7); they will return to Egypt (v 16; 8:13) and die there (9:3,6).

lies. Hosea uses several other roots to describe deception, such as *bgd,* *khš.* The one used here, *kzb,* occurs again in 12:2. The preposition *'al* here is ambiguous; it could mean the lies were told "against," "concerning," or simply "to." Once again the historical realities which are branded as "lies" are not specified. The people have been accused of holding various false opinions about Yahweh; the text implies not mere ignorance or forgetfulness, but willful perversion of the truth about God. If one opinion is to be identified as the supreme "lie" about Yahweh, it is that "he cannot save" (Jer 14:9). It is this unbelief that attracts the people to Assyria and Egypt as possible saviors; and this hope must be renounced (14:4). The more immediate context suggests that the "lie" is not in the appeal to Assyria rather than Yahweh (v 11b), but in the use of pagan rites, which mean that "they have turned aside from me" (v 14), instead of calling on Yahweh "from their hearts." Verse 15 shows that the "lie" has gone so far that they plot against Yahweh. In the context of covenant-making, *dbr* has connotations of swearing forbidden oaths, not simply making false statements. This theme continues into c 8: v 1 says their rebellion (*pš'*) was breaking the covenant with Yahweh (*'br*).

14–15. These verses are unified by the similarities between v 13b and v 15 already pointed out, and by internal features. The use of *'ēlay,* "to me," in vv 14a and 15b serves as an inclusion.

In vv 12–16, the prophet denounces the political and diplomatic activities of Ephraim // Israel and links them with an attack on the people's religious defection to pagan gods and practices (vv 14,16). By wandering away from Yahweh in pursuit of other gods, they have abandoned their only true security; small wonder that they then turn to Assyria or Egypt for help. So rebellion against God and covenant violation will produce disaster in the foreign field as well.

The four lines in v 14 are quite uneven in length, and do not display the usual patterns of parallelism. Verses 14aB and 14bA make a good bicolon: the same preposition is used in each line and the imperfect verbs are in chiasm. This bicolon extends v 14aA, which may be linked in envelope fashion with v 14bB. Besides the connection with v 14bB, v 14aA has connections with other passages. It stands in parallel with v 13bB. Verse 14aA implies that there is invocation of Yahweh, but that it is insincere; the same stress on false thinking is found in 7:2. The statement in v 7bB, that "none of them call upon me," can be harmonized with the rest if the qualification "with their hearts" is understood from v 14a. Cf. Isa 29:13. The same goes for the repetition of the verb "to cry out" in 8:2, where the claim to know the God of Israel is palpably false (see the NOTE there). "Calling out to Yahweh" was what started the Exodus (I Sam 12:8,10; Exod 2:23) and stimulated other rescue acts later in their history. There is a similar appeal to God, but it is false.

The short concluding line of v 14 is like similar accusations that appear from time to time in this section, the nearest being in v 13 — "for they have wandered away from me"; "for they have rebelled against me"; cf. "they have perpetrated enormities" (6:9); "they have manufactured an idol" (7:1).

Paul diagnoses the state of the heathen by saying that when they exchanged the Good (cf. Hos 8:3) for evil (cf. Hos 7:15), they were given over to abominable practices (Rom 1:24f). This is essentially what the Israelites have done. The parallelism of z'q and yll is found in Ezek 21:17, where z'q describes a cry of distress for redress of grievances and yll describes the expression of grief in mourning rites. The source of the distress out of which they should call upon Yahweh, but don't, is the crop failure, threatened in Hos 2:11. Joel 1:10–11 illustrates the situation, using the idiom hylyl 'al.

14a. beds. What beds are used for in this situation is not clear. If they are cult furniture on which liturgical acts were performed, then this would be different from the mourning ritual; see Mic 2:1 and Isa 57:5–11, which have many elements in common with Hosea 7. They show that the "bed" is used in the cult in connection with rituals of the worst kind. Ps 149:5 has the faithful expressing exultant praise "on their couches" (Dahood 1970:357). Ps 6:7 presents a pitiful picture of a grief-stricken person watering his couch with tears; in the Ugaritic story of Keret, the bereaved king does the same (Dahood 1966:38). Compare also Enoch in the Second Book of Enoch, which begins with the patriarch weeping on his bed (cf. II Esd 3:1). The bed then can be used for proper and improper liturgical acts. If Hos 7:14 is like Mic 2:1, screaming on their beds is contrasted to calling on God with their hearts. If it is like Ps 149:5, it is a legitimate act of devotion to Yahweh, which they are neglecting, and lō' in v 14aA covers the verb of v 14aB.

14b. grain and must. Grain and related products are mentioned six times in Hosea, notably in c 2 (vv 10,11,24), where the point at issue was whether Yahweh or Baal provided these necessities of life. The provision of grain will mark the eschaton (14:8). The crisis, which stimulated resort to these pagan techniques, was a failure of cereal and grape harvests. Note that the nouns have no articles, and that the preposition is not used before the second member of this closely coordinated pair, as is normal in Hebrew.

lacerated. Emend MT's *ytgwrrw* to *ytgwddw.* Similar measures, in time of drought, are described in I Kings 18:28. It has often been suggested, but never demonstrated, that mimetic magic supplies the motivation for self-mutilation. The flow of human blood imitates the release of the fertilizing forces (or rain) by the god. This is the form that "calling upon god" takes in Canaanite religion. Jer 41:5 seems to indicate that such things could even be done for Yahweh; cf. Joel 1:10–11. Verse 16aA suggests that something worse is happening than not calling on Yahweh sincerely (v 14aA). They are not calling on Yahweh at all. Perhaps they were calling on all the gods they knew about — Yahweh and Baal being the most prominent. Jer 16:5–9 prohibits the use of pagan mourning rites for the human dead in Israel. The circumstances of this prohibition were exceptional, since all normal life was to be suspended; it could be that in better times the people would be able to mourn in this fashion without censure. But Deut 14:1 also forbids mourning rites like those of the Canaanites, without qualification, presumably because they were inextricably bound up with devotion to the gods. In these passages, forms of the root *gdd,* "to cut," are used, and many manuscripts read *yitgôdādû* here for the form *yitgôrārû* of MT. (The reverse happens in Jer 5:7b, where the text is *yitgôdādû,* and some MSS have *yitgôrārû.*) The confusion is easily explained; *r* and *d* are similar in most forms of Hebrew script and indistinguishable in some.

The form *yitgôrārû* is hard to explain in the context if derived from *gwr* I, "to sojourn," thus perhaps "they have made themselves aliens." This could be interpreted as a parallel to v 14bB. In its only other occurrence (I Kings 17:20), the *Hitpolel* means "to secure hospitality with." If the verb is derived from *gwr* II, "to stir up (a quarrel)," then it could describe hostility against Yahweh, and again the last line may be parallel; this would be the only example of this root in the *Hitpolel.* Because vv 14aB and 14bA make a good bicolon, it would be appropriate to see the two clauses as parallel. To rile oneself up for a quarrel could mean to work oneself up into a frenzy, but the emotions and motives are quite different. The *Hitpolel* of *grr* in Jer 30:23 describes a sweeping whirlwind (*sa'ar mitgôrēr*) and the similar *sa'ar mitḥôlēl* in Jer 23:19 confirms the idea of a whirling motion. Accordingly, it remains possible, although dubious, that the MT of Hos 7:14 is correct.

departed from me. This sense of *sûr* is suitable; the idiom and situation require that *bî* be interpreted as "from me." *Yāšûbû* in v 16aA is a matching word, the other side of the action: they turn from me and they turn to Baal. It has been suggested plausibly that we read **yāsōrû,* from *srr,* "to rebel"; the root occurs in 4:16. A byform *sr* is possible, and would fit in with Hosea's vocabulary (see *sār* in 4:18).

Hos 7:14 has vocabulary in common with Mic 2:1, where Israel is accused of thinking (*ḥšb*) iniquity and doing evil (*r'*) on their beds (*'al-miškĕbôtām*). As in Hos 7:6, they carry out their deeds in the morning, when the sun rises.

15a. This verse is close to v 13b in grammatical structure; both contain memories of the Exodus.

trained. The verb *ysr* describes corrective and instructive punishment; a pun may be intended between *yāsûrû* (Israel's disdainful act) and *yissartî* (Yahweh's kindly act). This is the language of Deut 8:5, where the point is made that in the desert Israel had thoroughly learned that Yahweh was training them as a man trains his son; here the contrast is between Yahweh's educational care and Israel's perverse response. "At the present, all discipline seems not to be joy, but pain" (Heb 12:11), and discipline is easily misinterpreted as a sign of God's disfavor. So Israel interpreted their bad experiences, not as a father's hand guiding them into the right way, but as evidence that Yahweh bore them ill will.

strengthened their arms. Strengthening the hands is a figure of that growth in moral strength that comes from exercise. The normal idiom refers strength (*ḥzq*) to *yād,* "hand," and extension (*nṭy*) to *zĕrôa',* "arm" (Deut 4:34, but cf. Jer 21:5).

15b. *they plotted.* There is much to be said for an only slightly less obvious rendering, "They thought me evil/The Evil One." In Canaanite religion there is no consistent belief that disasters like a crop failure were caused by moral faults of the people as a whole. In the Ugaritic legend of Aqhat, after Aqhat has been murdered, curses are pronounced on neighboring villages, out of the blight of blood-guilt. There is no accompanying doctrine in Canaan that divine favor can be restored when the people turn to righteousness as there is in Israel. The ancient Near East was haunted by the suspicion that the gods are malicious, at least willful. As against this Israel insisted that Yahweh, in his essential character, is gracious and compassionate. The afflictions he sends express his justice, and are intended to correct faults (v 15a). In v 15b Israel may be accused of projecting onto Yahweh the character of other gods, the quality of being "evil." This old slander they already used in the desert (Num 14:3), a slander more suited to Egyptian than Israelite lips (Num 14:16). Since *ra'* is the usual antonym of *ṭôb,* v 15b is completed by 8:3, where Yahweh is given the name "Good." It may be that Yahweh has been dubbed "the Evil One" (like *ho ponēros* in the New Testament, Matt 6:13), a name more suited to Baal. Dahood (1970:XLIX) suggests that "the Evil One" is an epithet of the god Mot, Death. When Amos exhorts the people to "seek good, and not evil, . . . Hate evil, and love good" (Amos 5:14–15); when Micah accuses them of hating good and loving evil (Mic 3:2); when Isaiah charges them with calling good evil, and evil good (Isa 5:20): they are using the language of religious allegiance as much as that of ethical evaluation.

The verb *ḥšb* means "to devise [evil] against someone," with the preposition *'al;* and "to consider someone to be something," with *l* (I Sam 1:13). The difficulty in Hos 7:15b lies in the use of the preposition *'el,* rather than *'ēt,* for the first object, and the lack of *l* for the complement.

16. This verse seems to be fragmentary, although most of the individual words are recognizable; it is the combinations that are apparently meaningless. The syntactic connections often seem disjointed. Thus the last phrase "in the land of Egypt" is a locational prepositional phrase modifying some verb, and forming an inclusion with "Assyria" (v 12a). In spite of these difficulties there are some clear patches. "Their princes fell/will fall by the sword" is a good line of poetry, with an abnormal word order which suggests that it fits into some larger poetic structure. Secondly, the short phrases, although enigmatic, fall into a rhythmic pattern that suggests a tightly woven passage. Thirdly, Hosea frequently uses such brief staccato lines in his verse, so we are encouraged to accept them here also.

turned. Hosea uses *šwb* geographically, for going back to some place one has previously left (8:13), and theologically, for turning back to Yahweh in repentance after sin or even apostasy (6:1). Earlier in 2:9 these meanings merge. The preposition *'l* is usual, but its absence from the immediate proximity of the verb here is not an insuperable difficulty; it is possible that the goal of the return is "the land of Egypt," which is not mentioned until the end of the verse, although the preposition *b* would go better with "they will fall" (location) than with "they will return" (goal). This might indicate that *yš(w)bw* is to be read as "they will reside," as is probably required in Hos 9:3; it is less likely here. No preposition at all is used in 8:13.

no-god. Assuming that the preposition is missing, we take the goal of their return to be *lō' 'āl,* "Not-'Al," a negative divine name. The name *'al(i)* is a variant of *'elî, 'elyôn,* "The Most High God," attested in the combination *'el-'al,* "God Most High," in 11:7 (cf. Dahood 1970; Pope 1973). Dahood in a personal communication reads a double divine name, *lē' 'ali,* "the Omnipotent Most High," recognizing the participle of *l'y,* "to be strong," here as elsewhere, as a name. He renders the line "The Omnipotent Most High withdrew," the plural verb governed by a singular subject, since the subject, God, attracts a plural of majesty.

We prefer to look for continuity with v 15; interpretation must decide where the description of Israel's perfidy ends, and the announcement of threats begins. Yahweh's goodness is described by two perfect verbs (v 15a); Israel's hostile response is described by an imperfect verb in v 15b, either iterative, or simply past. Verse 16a adds two more examples of Israel's defection, using an imperfect verb, *yšwbw,* and a perfect, *hyw.*

The most likely background for this accusation is Israel's first apostasy in the desert and a comparable apostasy in Hosea's time. Deuteronomy 32, which contains similar reproaches, fails in the same way to provide explicit identification of a known historical event. It could be talking about their behavior in the desert (Horeb or Peor), or it could be more general. In Deut 32:21 *lō' 'ēl* means "a not-god, something that is not a god," and the negative name here is similar. Perhaps *lō'-'āl* is a play on *ba'al,* and the negative divine name *lō' yô'îlû,* "the Non-Helper," mentioned in Jer 2:8. If, however, this title is intended to be a jingle that parodies the name of Baal, it is a little surprising that Hosea did not say **bal 'al,* since this negative is in his vocabulary, and, being privative, it would be an even more devastating assertion that Baal is a nonentity; cf. Hos 8:6.

In 3:1 the verb *pānâ,* "to turn away," and in 7:14 the verb *swr,* "to turn aside," are used to describe Israel's desertion of Yahweh. The use of the verb *šwb,* "to turn back," here could imply reversion to a paganism that the people had previously renounced (Josh 24:23), for Israel clearly remembered turning to Yahweh from other gods at a definite point in its past history. Since turning to the non-god appears to be the wrong alternative, it is more likely that here it describes penitential exercises (as described in v 14b) directed toward Baal in the time of drought. This is congruent with the following simile of the slack bow.

slack bow. In this verse there does not seem to be any direct connection between sword and bow, in spite of their similar sound and their association elsewhere (Hos 1:7; 2:20). The defect described by *rĕmiyyâ* is not clear. Koehler and Baumgartner (1958:894) distinguishes a word meaning slack (or applied to the soul, sluggish), and another meaning deceitful (used mostly of the tongue). Wolff (1974:128) follows Driver in taking *qešet rĕmiyyâ* as a weapon with no spring, whose arrow cannot reach its target; Ephraim is an implement to be discarded because useless. This is a colorful image, but it lacks the element of culpability that we would expect to give force to the present passage. An ill-made or worn-out bow would misfire. In Ps 78:57 (the context has Hoseanic references to turning away from Yahweh), the poet's image is a faulty bow that recoils and injures the user. Ps 11:2 contains a strange statement about shooting arrows against the righteous in the dark, generally interpreted as "from an ambush." It is possible that the arrows in question are words of slander, and the bow of deceit that shoots them is the deceptive tongue (cf. Mic

6:12 and Ps 101:7). A similar connection in Hos 7:16 would not only explain in part "their tongue" in v 16bB; it would also tie in with what has been said repeatedly: "They . . . told lies about me" (v 13b). The whole of 7:7–16 sets in contrast the various uses of speech: they didn't call on Yahweh (vv 7bB, 14); they called on Egypt (v 11b); they spoke lies (v 13b).

16b. *Their princes fell by the sword.* This line does not have connections with the immediate context; it has a remote linkage with v 7bA, with which it makes a good bicolon:

kol-malkêhem nāpālû	7 syllables
yippĕlû baḥereb śārêhem	8

We may note the chiastic structure, the alternation of perfect and imperfect of the same root, and the collocation of "kings" and "princes." The initial *kl* may govern both clauses. Verse 16 identifies the instrument of downfall, but whether by assassination or on the battlefield is not clear. Nor can we determine whether the line describes a disaster that has already happened, or a punishment about to fall. If it is coupled with a return to Egypt, then defeat in the promised land would begin the reversal of the original conquest and occupation. The syntax of the line is slightly abnormal, with the insertion of the instrument between verb and subject (but cf. Ps 78:64).

out of the rage. The four words in MT that follow "princes" constitute one of the most difficult passages in Hosea. In other parts of Hosea we have been helped out by his habit of using the same word more than once, often repeating the word in a poetic or structural pattern. Here such aid is not forthcoming; *za'am, lāšôn* and *la'ag* occur here only in the prophecy. The word *za'am* is used exclusively of divine indignation, even in Jer 15:17 where the prophet says to Yahweh, "You have filled me with *za'am,*" i.e. with Yahweh's own rage. In Isa 30:27, we are told that Yahweh's nostrils are flaming, his tongue is a devouring fire, and his lips are full of *za'am.*

of the tongue. We could also render, as Dahood points out in a personal communication, "the double blade," an Israelite dialectal dual, not a suffixed form; in our rendering, the *-m* is taken as an enclitic.

There may be a play on words here, in which *lšwn* has its basic meaning of tongue, and is linked to *zw l'gm,* "the one who mocked them," but also signifies the blade of a sword, referring back to *ḥrb* earlier in the verse. The dual ending could then signify both a forked tongue and a two-edged sword.

the One who mocked them. Read *l'g* as a participle. The exclusively divine reference of *z'm* suggests that this phrase is another allusion to Yahweh, although the mockery of an unknown foreign language could also be meant (Isa 28:11; 33:19), in describing a failed diplomatic mission. Israel remembered coming out from a country of alien speech (Ps 114:1). In Isaiah 28, Ephraimites ridicule the Word of Yahweh as so much babble, even though the prophets speak plain Hebrew. In the phrase *zw l'gm, zw* (which occurs elsewhere in this spelling only in Ps 132:12) is probably not demonstrative, marking the commencement of a new clause (so most translations), but as in Ps 132:12, determinative. The tongue with which Yahweh rages against them he uses to deride them. Derision, like rage, can be a proper activity of God (Pss 2:4; 59:9; Job 9:23).

in the land of Egypt. This phrase may go with "they fell/will fall," or "returned/will return" in v 16a, or both. This does not exclude a connection with the references to the derisive speech. The land of Egypt would be a suitable place to hear the rage of Yahweh's derisive tongue. There can be no doubt that "in the land of Egypt" is climactic. As such it could round off a number of ideas that have been developed in the preceding chapter. From the word "Assyria" at the beginning of v 12, the whole of vv 12–16 deals with the attempt to make alliances with Egypt and Assyria, first described in v 11. Hos 8:9–13 has the same arrangement; the paragraph begins with the word "Assyria" and ends with the word "Egypt." Hos 11:5 makes explicit the argument: because they refused to return to Yahweh, they will return to Egypt. The structural pattern in c 7 suggests that the main clue for the interpretation of the word "Egypt" in v 16 should come from the word "Assyria" in v 12. This seems to say that as the ambassadors are going to Assyria, they will meet with some disaster that will abort their mission; Yahweh will bring them down like birds of the air. Similarly, as they call on Egypt, instead of on Yahweh (v 7bB), their princes (ambassadors) will fall by the sword in the land of Egypt. While we cannot be certain, we think it most likely that "in the land of Egypt" has such a connection with "their princes fell by the sword."

XIV. THE SPIRITUAL HISTORY OF ISRAEL: THE CALF OF SAMARIA
(8:1–8)

Mutual rejection

8:1a   Like a horn to the mouth!
        Like an eagle over Yahweh's house!

1b   Because they transgressed my covenant
        and rebelled against my instruction,

2a   Although they cried out to me,

2b   "God of Israel, we know you!"

3a   The Good One rejects Israel.

3b   As an enemy he will pursue him.

Errors of politics and religion

4a   They made kings, but not from me.
        They made princes, but I did not acknowledge them.

4b   With their silver and gold they made
        idols for themselves.
    So that it will be cut off

5a   he rejects the calf of Samaria —
    My anger is kindled against them.

5b   How long will they be unable to be clean? —

6a   even from Israel.
    As for it, an artisan made it

6b   and it is no god.
    The calf of Samaria will become fragments.

An agricultural curse and a pseudo-sorites

7a   They will sow when it is windy.
        They will reap in a whirlwind.

7b   If it grows, there will be no sproutage on it.
        It will not make meal.
    But if it it does make (meal), foreigners will swallow it.

8a   Israel has been swallowed.
8b   Now they have become among the nations
        like a jar that gives no enjoyment.

NOTES

8:1–8. Chapter 8 is a unit in a larger discourse that extends through c 11.
The clear ending at 8:14 (which may be an editorial gloss), and the new
beginning with 9:1 suggest that a section of the speech finishes there. The
point of transition between cc 7 and 8 is hard to find, since both 7:16 and
8:1 are difficult. From 8:2 onwards, however, the composition is clearer,
although not without many difficulties. Two blocks of material can be distinguished, each of which deals with a conspicuous evil in Israel. Verses
4–6 present another assault on idolatry learned from the Canaanites; vv
9–13 contain a denunciation of alliances with foreign powers. The boundaries of the latter passage are clearly marked by the matching words "Assyria" (in the first line) and "Egypt" (in the last line). The connections of
vv 7 and 8 are less clear; they develop an agricultural image of their own.
They are joined by the word "swallow," which occurs in both. The reference in v 8 to the nations may anticipate the subject matter of vv 9–13;
and the figure of sowing and reaping in v 7 may sum up the argument in
vv 4–6. We take vv 7 and 8 as both boundary and bridge. While v 14 has
a certain independence, its logic matches that of the rest of the chapter,
especially the summaries in vv 1–2 and 7–8.

The opening complaint of the chapter is that the people have broken the
covenant. This rebellion is expressed in four activities, all forbidden by
covenant regulations, all the opposite of trust in Yahweh. First, they set
up rulers that Yahweh did not authorize (v 4a); second, they made idols
(v 4b); third, they made treaties with Assyria (and/or Egypt, vv 9–13);
fourth, they built palaces and defense works (v 14). All of these will receive appropriate penalties (v 13b). The downfall of kings and princes
has already been described in 7:3–16, so 8:4a is a colophon for that
theme. There is an incidental reference to political leaders in v 10, where,
however, it is their action in making alliances that is condemned. The sin
of idol-making will be punished by smashing the idol (v 6b). The foreign
alliances will be frustrated. The fortifications will be burned (v 14b).
Most of the subsections of c 8 end with a threat, and the threats constitute
a series that serves further to unite the whole.

Although we approach c 8 as a fairly self-contained unit, there are some
tangible links that tie it to the larger discourse of cc 4–11 and the rest of

the book. The horn of 8:1a occurs in 5:8. "Yahweh's house" (v 1a) is mentioned again in Hosea only in 9:4. The phrase "transgressed (my) covenant" (v 1b) is used in 6:7. The word "instruction," which occurs here in vv 1 and 12, also appears in 4:6, with an accusation that the priest has forgotten it. The accusation "they rebelled" (v 1b) is made in 7:13. The verb used for calling upon God in v 2a was used in 7:14. The idea of "knowing" God is frequent in Hosea, and important. The term "enemy," which is often used by the pre-exilic minor prophets, occurs only here in Hosea (v 3); the idea of pursuit is crucial in 2:9. Kings and princes (v 4) are often referred to in Hosea, and the making of silver and gold into an idol has already been described in 2:10. The word "idols" in v 4 is used four times in Hosea. This inventory could be continued, but the point is clear; for other connections see the NOTES below.

The only speaker who can be identified with certainty in c 8 is Yahweh, although the first person is not used consistently. Note the nouns "my covenant," "my instruction" (v 1), "my anger" (v 5), "my instruction" (v 12), "my loved ones" (v 13); the pronoun "me" in vv 2,4; the verbs "I acknowledge" (v 4), "I will assemble" (v 10), "I wrote" (v 12), "I will send" (v 14). Only vv 6–9 are without first-person referents. Verses 6 and 7 may contain proverbial material. The use of the third person from time to time, such as the use of the name Yahweh in vv 1 and 13, or the verbs in v 13b, does not diminish the first-person dominance.

The speech is not direct address. The "you" in v 2 is used in reported speech. The apparent second-person suffix (*'glk*) in v 5 is, we think, part of the construct chain. In v 1, the suffix *-k* is probably the preposition *k* which belongs with the following word: "like a horn" in parallel with *kn**š**r* "like an eagle." From v 1b onwards the speech is about "them." The chapter is dominated by plurals, referring in all likelihood to the people. Only where there is a similitude (v 7b), and where Israel (vv 8 and 14), Ephraim (v 11) and Judah (v 14) are mentioned do we find singular forms. Here the pronouns "they" (vv 4 and 13) indicate one major referent.

The speech in 8:1–8 and in what follows gives the impression of viewing Israel somewhat from a distance. This, and the lack of an identifiable audience, gives the speech the detachment of a soliloquy. Yahweh is deliberating his course of action; appropriate responses are considered, even decided. But to whom are they announced? There is no commission to deliver news of the decision by way of oracle. The messenger formulas, introducing an address by the prophet to the people in the name of Yahweh, are not present. This absence, a great deviation from the habits of Isaiah and Jeremiah, goes a long way to explain the failure of traditional form criticism to come up with firm conclusions identifying the *Gattung* of this speech, or its constituent parts. Results are fragmentary, often equivocal.

The most serious defect is that the congeries of supposed *Gattungen* hampers recognition of the integrity of the material in both theme and structure. If the theory that Yahweh is here reflecting in his own mind is outré, it may be suspected that the prophet is simply transcribing a speech made by Yahweh in the divine council, where the audience is not involved as a concerned party, and, indeed, is largely passive. Hosea offers little or no evidence of the mythological trappings of such a setting, so we can only guess.

Problems of analysis are met also on the level of grammar. While most of the text contains standard constructions, there is a troublesome residue of small units which have few obvious connections with their context. The most striking of these is v 1a. Among scraps which are hard to fit into the larger passage are "so that it will be cut off" (v 4bB) and "even from Israel" (v 6aA), which may be connected. The only thing to do with the text is to start with what is clear, and proceed to the obscure; much depends on finding where one clause ends and another begins. The standards of normal syntax are often not enough to settle such questions, for Hosea has his own dialectal usages and other samples of Hebrew cannot be used with safety to control them. Further, Hosea's highly original literary method plays tricks with the language for artistic effects that are not met with in normal prose. Conjunctions are prime signals of interclausal relationships, and at the same time, of clause onset. When conjunctions are used sparingly, both these grammatical features are left in doubt. A search for the clause boundaries and interclausal relationships in vv 7b–8a will show what is meant. As we have already noticed, particularly in c 2, some phrases often have close connections with distant passages.

In the literary design of c 8, especially 8:1–8, well-formed poetic units, mainly bicola with parallelism, are interspersed with single lines, or lines which read more like prose.

The bicolon in v 1b has synonymous parallelism with chiasm. There is a bicolon in v 3, with chiasm. Verse 4a contains a two-line construction similar to 7:9. In the poetic passages listed the lines tend to be short, with many of five syllables. The intervening prose-like lines tend to be longer.

8:1a. This verse is enigmatic, especially so since it begins the pericope. While the individual words are well-known, the connections and sequence are not at all clear, and the general sense is elusive. Emendation of varying kinds and degrees seems almost mandatory, but results are less than satisfactory. Under the circumstances it seems best to follow the MT, and at the same time to look for clues to the poet's intention in structural patterns. Thus vv 1b–3 form an intelligible unit charging the people with covenant violation and defection, aggravated by their apparent claim to special treatment on the basis of intimate acquaintance with and knowledge of their God. The isolation of this unit may be justified additionally on grammatical grounds. Verses 1b and 2 are united by the occurrence of 3 m pl verb forms throughout (*'brw, pš'w, yz'qw*), whereas in v 3 we are dealing with singular forms: *znḥ* and *yrdpw* (MT *yirdĕpô*, probably to be read *yirdĕpēw*). We suggest, therefore, that v 1a may be explicated in part by v 3, and that together they form an envelope around the middle section. The whole unit vv 1–3 is minatory in tone, and therefore we would expect the opening words to conform to this pattern. Verse 3 provides the basic story line of rejection and pursuit. For the transgressions mentioned in v 1b, Israel will be attacked, in spite of the people's claim of a special relationship to Yahweh. In v 1aB, there is a comparison with the eagle or vulture which may be a symbol of guidance and protection or of menaced attack; cf. Hab 1:8, of Babylon: "They swoop like an eagle, swift to devour." We suggest that the comparison here is with the pursuing enemy; cf. Lam 4:19 where the pursuers are said to be swifter than eagles, a common figure.

The opening words may then be addressed directly to the prophet: "To your palate a horn," a command to sound the alarm (cf. 5:8), a role as watchman which is properly assigned to him. The theme of prophet as watchman is developed in detail in the Book of Ezekiel, but there is no reason to suppose that it originated with him (cf. Amos 3:3–8). We, however, parse the opening line not as an apostrophe to the prophet, but as the first of two analogies for the actions of v 3; the line is read *'l-ḥk kšpr*, and understood in the plain sense "Like a horn to the palate/mouth." The unusual word order arises from the chiasm of the two lines of v 1a.

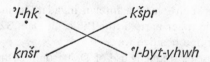

horn. It is somewhat strained to understand this, as is commonly done, as a command when no verb is present — "Put a trumpet to your mouth!" In 5:8 the command to blow the horn is clearly made; that passage has probably influenced the interpretation of 8:1. In some places the palate is associated with the tongue, usually when the tongue cleaves to the palate as the result of paralysis (Ps 137:6) or thirst (Lam 4:4; cf. Ps 22:16). Such a thought does not seem to be present here, so the word "tongue" in 7:16 does not help to solve the problem of "palate" in 8:1. The only verb ever used with *šōpār* is *tq'* (5:8); it is not present here, and no adjacent word invites emendation so as to retrieve it. This is enough to throw doubt on the word *špr*, which might not be "horn" at all. The horn is not played with the palate, but with the lips, although no body organ is actually connected with *špr* in the Bible. The spelling of the word is a bit suspicious: out of fifty-one occurrences, only nine, including this one, are defective (three of these in Exodus, four in II Samuel). Elsewhere in the minor prophets, including Hos 5:8, the spelling is full, *šwpr*. Finally, it is hard to see how the blowing of a horn can be associated with "an eagle over Yahweh's house."

The consonants *kšpr* have encouraged other scholars to look for two similes in parallel; some suggest Akkadian *šapparu*, "wild goat" or *saparu* [*sic*], the kind of net Marduk uses in the Creation Epic to ensnare Tiamat (cf. *ANET* 66, 67, 69, 502). The antiquity of the problem is reflected in the despair of the Greek translators, for the unintelligible LXX suggests a literal translation from equally unintelligible Hebrew, quite different from the present MT: *eis kolpon autōn hōs gē*, from *'el ḥēqām ke'āpār*, "unto their bosom like earth."

There are four problems here: (1) the lack of a verb, and the difficulty of interpreting a prepositional phrase as a command; (2) the problem of blowing a horn with the palate; (3) the spelling of the word "horn"; (4) the incongruity of the reference. No satisfactory solution is in sight. The Targum made a sensible paraphrase which recognized that the palate was sometimes mentioned as an organ of speech. It attached the *k* to *šōpār* to make another simile — "Speak with your palate like a horn." This solution we follow in essence. In 5:8, the horn was sounded to give the alarm for an invasion. The same imagery may be found here, with the eagle over Yahweh's house as the image of the foreign invader.

Like an eagle. Or "vulture." The Masoretic pointing with the article may be secondary, but the usage is not clear. Since there is no clear connection with what precedes, we cannot tell who is being compared to an eagle. It is either Yahweh or a foreign invader, to judge from the use of the same simile in other parts of the Bible. In Deut 32:11 the simile is applied to Yahweh in a positive way.

In view of Hosea's frequent use of Deuteronomic traditions, and his especial use of the traditions now in Deuteronomy 32, it is likely that the positive image of Yahweh as the eagle (found also in Exod 19:4) has been turned upside down by the prophet, because the covenant has been broken. Israel has spurned Yahweh as the Good One, so he has become like an Enemy, pursuing them.

Yahweh's house. Hosea never refers directly to Jerusalem, or its temple. "The house of Yahweh," here and in 9:4, probably refers to the promised land as Yahweh's realm or estate, synonymous with "the land of Yahweh" in 9:3.

1b. *Because*. This is the only place in Hosea where *ya'an*, "because," occurs. It is found over ninety times, alone or in combination with other particles, in the Hebrew Bible, including the reinforced *ya'an bĕya'an* (Ezek 36:3) and *ya'an ûbĕya'an* (Lev 26:43; Ezek 13:10). In Ezek 12:12, in combination with a negative, *ya'an* has the unique function of indicating purpose rather than cause ("so as not to . . ."). That passage probably is corrupt; the emendation *lĕma'an* has plausibly been proposed. In Isa 61:1 *ya'an* does not seem to be a conjunction for a logical relationship, but resumptive. The two occurrences of *ya'an* in Hag 1:9 are atypical; in the first it is interrogative; in the second, a preposition. This seems to be a late development, and we leave it aside. *Ya'an* is unevenly distributed in the Bible: it is found rarely in the Torah, and thirty-seven times in Ezekiel. It is lacking in hymnic writings (only once in Psalms) and Wisdom literature (only once in Proverbs).

Several variables determine the syntax of *ya'an*. While it is used alone fifty-two times, it is often followed by *'ăšer* (thirty-one times) as if it were a preposition in a compound conjunction. In several occurrences, all pre-exilic, the combination *ya'an kî* is used, as if the conjunction "because" were being repeated. As a conjunction introducing a subordinate clause, *ya'an* can be placed in various relationships to the main clause, or the clause which states the consequence. Most often (over seventy times) the consequence follows, and the *ya'an* clause opens the discourse. This is its most striking difference from *kî*, which has the same meaning, but which usually introduces a "reason" clause that *follows* the main clause. In three instances, the *ya'an* clause is followed by another *ya'an* clause before the consequence follows (Jer 29:25; Ezek 21:29; 28:2). In two places, the consequence is left unstated (I Kings 8:18; Ezek 12:12). In only a dozen occurrences does the *ya'an* clause come after the main clause, the way a *kî* clause usually does (Num 11:20; Josh 14:14; I Kings 11:33; 14:13; II Kings 21:15; Jer 29:23; 35:17; Ezek 15:8; 20:16,24; Ps 109:16; Lev 26:43; Isa 66:4). In some texts (I Kings 11:33; 14:13; II Kings 21:15) the placement of the "cause" after the "result" achieves chiasm within a paragraph which thus begins and ends with such a *ya'an* clause. In one instance (I Kings 14:15) the *ya'an* clause is embedded in two clauses which together state the consequences. It is common for *ya'an* to be used in prophecies which state some fault as the reason for an ensuing judgment.

These data make it clear that there is a downward continuity at 8:1b, and that any direct connection with v 1a is unlikely. Verse 1b does not provide the clue needed to solve the riddle of v 1a. It is usual for *ya'an* to open a speech and to be followed by a clause which states the consequences. We must therefore look for the consequences of v 1b further on in the chapter.

The syntactic linkages between a *ya'an* clause and the following clause which states the logical consequences exhibit considerable variety. *Ya'an* itself is usually followed by a perfect verb, although an infinitive construct occurs about ten times in Ezekiel, indicating a trend to prepositional status on the part of *ya'an*. The consequence clause usually has an imperfect verb or *hinnēh* followed by a participle. The *ya'an* clause describes something that has happened in past time; the consequence clause predicts something that will happen in future time. Unlike *kî, ya'an* never gives the reason for something that has already happened. This distinctive feature should help us to find the consequences of v 1b in the text that follows. The commonest continuation, found in over half the examples, uses *lākēn,* "therefore" (once *'al-kēn,* Ezek 44:12; and once *kî,* Gen 22:16, but the latter is asseverative, not a conjunction). This usage of *lākēn* is dominant in Ezekiel, so no statistical inference as to normalcy can be made. *Lākēn* occurs either alone, or followed by *hinnēh* (once *wĕlākēn hinnēh,* Isa 8:6); or by *kōh 'āmar* and an oracle (*kōh 'āmar* occurs once without *lākēn*). *Hinnēh* sometimes introduces the consequence clause by itself (never in Ezekiel). It is a remarkable fact that *wĕ,* "and," so ubiquitous in Hebrew, is never used to link a *ya'an* clause to the consequence. Nor are *'attâ,* "now," or *wĕ'attâ,* "and now," ever so used. This last fact rules out vv 8b and 13b as consequences of v 1b. In contrast to the non-use of *wĕ, gam* and *wĕgam* are used several times. None of these clues as to the consequence of v 1b operates in c 8, because neither *lākēn, hinnēh, gam,* nor any of the others occurs, except for *gam* in v 10 which is followed by *kî.* Once, the consequence of *ya'an,* although not yet accomplished, is described using a *waw*-consecutive past-tense clause (I Sam 15:23). Several times the future consequences are predicted using a *waw*-consecutive future-tense clause. None of these is found in c 8 either.

There is another feature of the syntax of *ya'an* that should be noted, because it is quite different from other Hebrew conjunctions in this regard. When several reasons are listed in a string of clauses, *ya'an* is used only once at the beginning of the first. Other subordinating conjunctions are repeated, and the subordinated clauses are coordinated with "and." Hence the sequence *kî . . . wĕkî . . . wĕkî . . .* is found. There are three places (Jer 29:25; Ezek 21:29; 28:2) where two *ya'an* clauses come in series, but they are in apposition, not coordination; they state two aspects of the same reason, not two reasons. In fact, **wĕya'an* occurs nowhere in the Hebrew Bible.

The significance of all this for 8:1b may be summed up. (A) The consequences of v 1b are more likely to be stated after it than before it. (B) Because *ya'an* is not repeated, we do not know how far the "reason" paragraph governed by *ya'an* extends. Although *ya'an* is not elsewhere followed by an imperfect verb, it may be continued into v 2. Because *ya'an* is followed normally by a perfect verb, it is possible that several of the clauses in this chapter which contain such verbs continue to assert reasons for judgment, all governed by the *ya'an* at the beginning of the speech. (C) Apart from the several formal signals of a consequence clause following *ya'an,* all of which are unfortunately lacking in c 8, there are about eight passages in which the consequence clause follows without any conjunction at all (I Sam 30:22; I Kings 11:11; etc.). Since conjunctions are sparse in Hosea, many clauses might qualify as consequences under this rubric. The best clue would be the use of an imperfect verb, though we cannot be altogether sure about this, because Hosea's use of verb forms does not follow classical norms. Further progress must be guided by the general context and by literary considerations. Firm ground is provided at the beginning by the prime reason for Yahweh's threats: "They transgressed my covenant." We have already shown that the details of this transgression are itemized in what follows, so these statements are carried by ya'an. The consequences are similarly stated in clauses interspersed through the following discourse, even though their identification is made difficult by the lack of connectives and by Hosea's atypical use of verb forms. Verses 3b, 6bB, and the threat of v 7 are the most likely candidates.

transgressed. The idiom 'br běrît was used in 6:7; see the NOTE there.

rebelled. The charge of rebellion was made at 7:13; see the NOTE there.

instruction. Torah. In 4:6 a priest was accused of forgetting the torah of his God. Rebellion against the torah is not just failure to keep the law; it is renunciation of the claims of Yahweh on his people and leads to forfeiture of the status of "my people." The specifics of this general charge are given in what follows. According to our interpretation, the acts of rebellion catalogued here include the choosing of kings without Yahweh's approval (v 4a), the making of idols (v 4b), and the contracting of foreign alliances (vv 9–13 — an expansion of 7:11b). The preposition generally used with the verb pš', "to rebel," is b, "against." This is so in 7:13, so that the use of 'al here is unsupported by other cases, and inconsistent within Hosea itself. Since Hosea tends not to use prepositions, even when the normal idiom requires them, the prepositional status of 'al in v 1bB may be questioned. There is sporadic use of 'al as a conjunction meaning "because"; here it could be coordinated with ya'an. This seems unlikely, however.

2. To call out to God, to claim to know him as God of Israel, would be an expression of loyalty. According to 7:7, none of the people call upon God. According to 7:14, they do not cry out "from their hearts," that is, sincerely. On the face of it, the statement in v 2 cannot be fitted into this state of affairs, and is almost contradicted by the accusation that precedes it in v 1b. It is sometimes said that the statement is intended to be sarcastic, describing a hypocritical continued use of old expressions of loyalty while all the time the people have deserted the covenant and rebelled against the torah. Their shouting of the liturgical formula, claiming to know Yahweh as their God, adds sin to sin. Thus NAB translates: "They have . . . sinned against my law, while to me they cry out. . . ." A simi-

lar result is obtained if v 2 is interpreted, not as circumstantial to v 1b, but as concessive and subordinate to v 3a: "(Although) they cried out to me . . . (nevertheless) the Good One rejects Israel." Wolff (1974:117, 138) interprets this text and 6:1–3 as insincere uses of a liturgical appeal, unsupported by moral reform.

The Israelites' claim to know Yahweh was the reflex of a conviction that Yahweh had chosen Israel out of all the nations of the world to be his unique and peculiar people. The confidence that the special relationship between God and Israel would always guarantee Israel's survival and success regardless of the actual behavior of the nation was apparently unshakable in the face of all the evidence to the contrary. The prophets of the eighth century all confronted the invincible self-assurance of the people and challenged this basic presupposition of their faith. Amos articulates the true state of affairs in dramatic form, when he concedes Israel's unique status, but insists that the consequences of disobedience will be the reverse of what the people imagine: "You only have I known of all the families of the earth. Therefore I will punish you for all your iniquities" (3:2).

In the present passage, the claim of the people to know Yahweh is doubtless sincere, that is, they believe it. After all, Yahweh knows them and has revealed himself to them in his mighty deeds and words. How could they not know him? But in fact they do not know him at all: who and what he has been, and will be. This is not hypocrisy — although that ingredient may be present as well — but sublime arrogant self-deception, invincible self-delusion. As long as they continue in that state, no hope for recognition of the true state of affairs or genuine repentance remains. They will continue in their ignorance until they are rudely awakened by destructive judgment when it is too late.

2b. *God of Israel*. The Masoretic pointing *'ĕlōhay*, "my God" (cf. 2:25), leads to the awkward "My god, we-know-you Israel," in which "Israel" is generally taken in apposition to the subject "we," to yield: "My God, we (Israel) know you." This is a grammatical monstrosity. If Israel is speaking, why do they not say "our God"? LXX and Syriac omit, or used a text which lacked, the word "Israel." The title "God of Israel" is suitable in this context. This construct phrase can be read without making any change in the text except the vocalization *'ĕlōhê*, since a discontinuous construct phrase is quite possible (Freedman 1972c). Perhaps the original form of the construct ending *-ay* was retained because of the following *yōd*.

3a. The word *znḥ*, "to reject," is powerful. It implies complete severance of relationships, as in the firing of an employee. It usually designates a drastic action of God, and Israel is nearly always the object. The most obvious interpretation of the text is to identify "Israel" as the subject and "good" as the object. In the context this would mean Israel's decisive rejection of Yahweh as the Good One; because of the dominant usage of *znḥ*, we read the reverse: God is the subject and Israel the object.

The Good One. There are several places in the Hebrew Bible where the noun *ṭôb* is used virtually as a personal name for God (Dahood 1970, index s.v.). A slightly more abstract rendering is possible, given the syntactic ambiguity of the line. Israel may be the subject, as we have noted; repudiating good is the same as leaving the covenant. Moran (1963) has shown that in treaty terminology the word "good" can mean amity or formalized friendship; Hillers (1964a) has added biblical parallels. This reading could be defended in the present context, for, as we shall see particularly in the discussion of vv 9–13, this chapter deals with covenants.

3b. *As an enemy.* Whether *ṭôb* in v 3a refers to Yahweh or to friendship in the covenant, and whoever acts there, the repudiation of this relationship leads to enmity. The enemy is then either Yahweh, as Israel now regards him; a foreign nation which acts as Yahweh's agent; or Israel as Yahweh now regards it. Friend ("lover") and enemy ("hater") are often opposed in treaty terminology when referring to the loyal and the disloyal (Hillers 1969:53). The Hebrew clause may be interpreted in different ways, with *'wyb* as subject or object complement. It is simplest to read it as the subject, and understand the line as a description of Yahweh or the nation which he sends against Israel. We prefer a slightly more abstract understanding: *'wyb* is a description of the capacity in which Israel has forced Yahweh to function. Comparison with 2:9 suggests that *'ôyēb* is used here as a parody of *'ōhēb,* "lover." It is out of the question that the enemy who will pursue them is some kind of demon like Mot. When the curses of the covenant are set in motion, and all kinds of terrifying things "pursue" the people, Yahweh says that he is pursuing them with sword, famine, and pestilence (Jer 29:18; cf. Lam 3:43, 66), or through the agency of a foreign power.

4a. *They.* The free form of the pronoun is emphatic, and as usual, sets the people over against Yahweh in rejection. We might have expected the new paragraph which begins with this pronoun to be balanced somewhere by a contrasting paragraph which begins *wa'ănî,* "but I. . . ." What we find instead in v 6b is *wĕhû',* "and it." The topics here are Israel and the calf, alternately:

Israel	Calf
v 4a	
	v 4b
	v 5aA
v 5aB–b	
	v 6

The forms *hēm* and *hēmmâ* generally stand in complementary distribution in Hosea. The short form is used when the verb is a participle or imperfect, except here; the long form is used as the subject of a verbless clause, or with a perfect verb (except in 8:13). This suggests that *hēmmâ* should be read here. The emendation is modest, since the initial *he* of *hmlkw* may also serve at the end of *hm*. This also brings v 4 into line with v 9.

made kings. In the historical books the *Hip'il* is used to describe the people's part in coronation ceremonies, rather than some prior act of selection. Just who was considered responsible for making kings is not clear, but from the way Israel is mentioned in this chapter, it would seem to be the people in general.

not from me. This disclaimer does not indicate how far Hosea's disapproval of the monarchy went. Did he dislike the kings of the north, for disloyalty to David and Jerusalem; or the kings of both kingdoms, including David; or only selected kings chosen by people, in contrast to the ones chosen by Yahweh; or simply the upstart kings of Israel's decline such as Shallum and Menahem? On this question, see Gelston (1974).

In v 4 the making of kings and princes is so closely linked with the making of idols (v 4b) that it is likely that much Canaanite kingship ideology had been incorporated into Israel's cultic and political life. Israel's valid king was Yahweh's anointed. If now kings had been appointed, "but not from me," the ceremonial forms involving divine sanction may have been observed, without the substance.

made princes. As usual in Hosea, kings and princes are closely associated. This suggests that it was not individual kings, but the whole method of government that went with monarchy, that is denounced. This is the only occurrence of the *Hip'il* of this root.

but I did not acknowledge them. Here *yd'*, "to know," signifies approval. Obviously Yahweh knew what was going on. When Deut 32:17 speaks about Israel's change of devotion to new gods, "which they did not know," this does not mean that they had never heard of them before; the parallel says "which your ancestors had never dreaded." Here "to know" means "to acknowledge." In some contexts, "to know" also has covenant associations of election. "I did not know" is then synonymous with "not from me," and means "I did not choose them." In Jer 1:5 *yd'* is parallel to "to consecrate," and refers to the election of a prophet.

4b–6. Analyzing the structure, content, and meaning of these verses, we suggest that the central theme is the idol-making proclivities of the people of Israel, which occasions divine rejection and wrath, with cutting down and shattering of the image(s) as the imminent consequence, itself a portent of the destruction of the nation. The principal object is the "calf of Samaria," otherwise unattested but perhaps a generic title for the bull-images at Bethel and Dan. The images made of silver and gold (v 4b) are subsumed under the title "calf of Samaria" which is emblematic of the people. This calf is the target of Yahweh's rejection and rage (v 5a); it is the work of an artificer and no true deity (v 6aB); it will be smashed to smithereens (v 6b). It will be cut off (v 4bB) from Israel (v 6aA).

4b. *their silver*. It is not clear whether this verse refers to the people, who are blamed for making idols as well as for setting up their own rulers; or whether it means that after the people had set up kings and princes, these misused their revenues (the people's wealth or the royal treasury) to make idols. As shown in 2:10, the gold and silver used in adorning the idols came ultimately from God, which adds irony to a situation full of absurdity. The same language is used in 2:10; see the NOTES there. The only difference is that there the object, the Baal image, has the preposition *l*, whereas here the object is unmarked. This could be due to the intervention of the ethical dative ("for themselves"). Comparing the two passages suggests that the metals were used for a Baal image, and that the generic word *'ăṣabbîm* here refers to Baal. See the NOTE at 4:17.

cut off. The singular verb, referring to the calf in v 5a, breaks the plural series. The versions read this verb as a plural, but they could have been influenced by "idols," the nearest preceding word to which this verb might refer. If "idols" is a plural of majesty, meaning the image of the false god, even this is not necessary. The idol and object of cutting down seem to be the calf of Samaria; v 6b says it will be smashed. If the people were to be cut off for making kings etc., the verb would be plural. Because there are so many plurals in the chapter, this singular verb should be retained. If it does not refer to the calf, it could refer back to the pronoun object of *yrdpw*, "he will pursue him," at the end of v 3, which is itself to be identified with Israel (v 3a). This connection remains possible: "As an enemy he will pursue him . . . so that he will be cut off."

The passive verb refers to an act of Yahweh, which parallels the rejection of the calf of Samaria (v 5a). Since the *Nip'al* of *krt* is used in Leviticus for excommunication, the idea may be similar to that of *znḥ;* but since the form is used to describe the chopping down of the idols in the great purges, it could be intended literally.

For a comparable use of *lm'n* with *krt,* see Obad 9, and note the connection of the same verb with "enemy" in Mic 5:8.

5a. *rejects*. For the meaning of the word, see the NOTE on v 3. The verb is not common and its use at the beginning of two verses so close together requires some connection to be found between them. The simplest relationship would be one of cause and effect, presented in the opposite order. In v 3 what is spurned is Israel; in v 5, it is "the calf of Samaria." No subject is provided for the verb, although Yahweh is most likely, as the parallel colon v 5aB shows. The same ambiguity shifting between people and the idol(s) which symbolize their attitude and activity is to be seen in this verse. The 3 m pl suffix after the preposition *b* may refer to the idols (*'ṣbym*) in v 4 or to the people who made them. Similarly the calf in v 5aA symbolizes the people who worship it, and whose emblem it is. While the shift from third person (*zānaḥ*) to first person (*'py*) is acceptable, it is possible to read the initial verb as the infinitive absolute (*zānôaḥ*) with Yahweh as first-person subject, since he is speaking.

calf of Samaria. While the traditional "your calf, O Samaria" makes sense, there is no supporting evidence that Samaria is being addressed here. Except for the suffix *k* the phrase is identical with *'ēgel šōmĕrôn* in v 6. This is an example of the use of -*k*- within a construct phrase; cf. *ḥydr-k-b'r-šb'*, "the pantheon of Beer Sheba," in Amos 8:14 (Andersen 1969b).

is kindled. The verb *ḥārâ* can be used impersonally, with the agent marked by referential *l* or else with the noun *'ap*. While the latter can be used occasionally of human anger (Job 32:2), it nearly always identifies the anger of Yahweh. The use of the idiom in places like Exod 22:23; 32:10–11; Deut 6:15; 7:4; 11:17; etc. provides the background for Hosea's use: idolatry above all things arouses Yahweh's anger. Although Hosea does not use the phrase "Yahweh's anger," it is mentioned in 11:9; 13:11; and 14:5. The perfect form of the verb reflects the accumulation of past reactions culminating in the present state of affairs.

5b. *How long*. It is hard to see how a question fits in at this point, a problem compounded by its obscurity. Verse 5b is a long line, and there is no obvious way of dividing it into two parts. There are some places where *'ad-mātay* seems to mean "forever," without being interrogative. In Jer 23:26, for example, if *'ad-mātay* is an adverb modifying the preceding verb, the line there means "I have dreamed forever." Similarly Jer 13:27 means, "Woe to you, Jerusalem! Will you never be clean?" (Bright 1965: 94–95). This thought is not unlike Hos 8:5. In II Sam 2:26, *'ad-mātay* is parallel to *hălāneṣaḥ*, "Will it be forever?" In Hab 2:6, the prophet says "Woe to him who never stops accumulating what is not his." Compare Pss 6:4; 90:13. This makes it possible to attach the phrase to v 5a, viz. "My anger will burn against them forever."

unable. The verb *ykl*, "to be able," is usually followed by an infinitive, sometimes by an imperfect verb. In the present context, *niqqāyôn* has been taken as a verbal noun meaning "to be (or become) innocent." A construction similar to this one occurs in Isa 1:13, *lō'-'ûkal 'āwen wa'ăṣārâ*, "I cannot . . . iniquity and assembly," where the missing verbal form "to endure, stand" is to be understood. The generally accepted interpretation finds support elsewhere in Hosea; cf. "Their deeds do not permit them to return to their God" (5:4). The idiom *'ad-mātay lō'* plus a verb means "how long will it be until . . . ?" So II Sam 2:26 means,

"How long will it be until you command the army to stop pursuing their brothers?" or, in simpler English, "Will you never command the army . . . ?" Zech 1:12 means, "How long will you keep on not showing compassion to Jerusalem?" If v 5b is a question, it means, "Will they never be capable of innocence?" The expected response is "Never," i.e. those who have ordained kings and princes without divine authorization, and made idols of silver and gold, will never be able to cleanse themselves of guilt or establish their innocence. This explains Yahweh's anger.

   to be clean. A common word related to the rare one used here, *nāqî,* is a forensic term, meaning "objectively exempt from punishment." The noun *niqqāyôn* occurs five times, three times in the phrase *niqqāyôn kappay* (Gen 20:5; Pss 26:6; 73:13). The fifth is in Amos 4:6, where "cleanness of teeth" is a metaphor for starvation. A corresponding adjective for personal innocence (*nĕqî kappay*) also occurs. In the Psalms "innocence" refers to the performance of an act of ritual purification, perhaps a ceremonial hand-washing (Dahood 1968:191). A paraphrase of Hos 8:5b, guided by the general themes of the chapter, might be that Israel cannot call upon Yahweh with innocence because its hands are contaminated with idol-making (cf. Isa 1:15); cf. 7:14a. Israel had long been living in a state of probationary exemption from punishment. The question is not how long before they repent, but how long before the probationary period runs out, and they can no longer be accounted innocent. The answer is, not long.

   6. Within v 6a the chiastic placement of the two uses of the pronoun *hû'* marks off a well-formed bicolon. Verse 6bB is a complete clause, more prose-like in character. The variable length of the lines affords no further assistance in recovering the poetic structure.

   It is hard to find any connection between v 6aA, *kî miyyiśrā'ēl,* and the rest of v 6, and the attachment to vv 4bB and 5a suggested here is not much better. We could read "like the day of Israel," changing no consonants; this phrase would refer to the time of reckoning for Israel; Hosea uses "the day of . . ." or "the days of . . ." in this way several times; cf. 2:5; 9:9; 10:9; cf. Isa 9:3. Perhaps *kym* is an asseverative particle with enclitic *mem.* In the Lachish Letters *kym* means "at once." The morphology of the phrase is not clear; it probably does not contain the word "day," although occurrences of the form in MT have been so identified (Torczyner 1938:106–111). Pope (1953) suggests that the first *wĕhû'* in 8:6 be read as the subject of a verbless clause, "Surely, it is only (a product) of Israel." This requires some dubious assumptions about *kî* and *min.*

   6a. *artisan.* The root *ḥrš,* used here (Ugaritic *ḥrš*), refers to craftswork of all types; it is distinct from *ḥrš,* "to plow" (Arabic and Ugaritic *ḥrṯ*); *ḥrš,* "to be silent" (Arabic *ḫrs*); **ḥrš,* "to be wooded" (Arabic *ḥrš,* with an irregular sibilant correspondence). The root here may be the same as *ḥrš*, "to work magic."

This use of *ḥrš* is the only occurrence of the word in the pre-exilic minor prophets. This unit is often regarded as a later interpolation, and is in conformity with the anti-idolatry polemics of the seventh–sixth centuries and later. The theme is elaborated in Jer 10:1–16; Isa 40:18–20; 44:9–20; 46:1–7; Ps 115:3–8; and Wisdom of Solomon 13–15. In v 14 Yahweh is called Israel's "maker." Yahweh as creator and giver of everything excludes all rival gods (2:10).

6b. *fragments.* What can be made can be destroyed, in a final proof that the calf of Samaria is not a god. Other prophets ridicule the idea that the god who is prayed to as a protector has to be protected by his worshipers, and the god who is expected to preserve them from captivity is taken captive; cf. 10:6. This is the only occurrence of *šbbym* and thus it is not clear what kind of destruction will take place. In Exod 32:20 Moses burned the calf and ground it to powder. The calf of Samaria was made of "silver and gold" (8:4) and the metals as such are not friable. Wooden idols were usually burned, suggesting that the calf at Horeb was a carving with gold leaf overlay, though Aaron's lame excuse in Exod 32:24 suggests a crude casting.

7a. The imagery changes abruptly; a piece of gnomic wisdom, a pseudo-sorites is presented. Its compact character has resulted in universal misunderstanding. Because Hosea's frequent omission of prepositions has not been recognized, "wind" and "whirlwind" have been identified as objects of the verb. Sowing and harvesting are correlative ideas; the verbs are used together several times in proverbial statements. Reaping is a time of punishment or reward, and the adage "You reap what you sow" has received many applications (II Cor 9:6; Gal 6:7). Wisdom literature uses a concrete analogy for a didactic purpose. To do something good or bad is "like" sowing seed; the consequences are "like" reaping a harvest. Hence the metaphor "to sow" righteousness (Prov 11:18), or trouble (Job 4:8), or injustice (Prov 22:8). These proverbs say either that the crop is the same (Job 4:8), or that "injustice" produces "calamity" (Prov 22:8). Sometimes the agricultural image leads to the doctrine that you reap *more* than you sow, up to seven times, either from injustice (Sir 7:3) or righteousness (II Enoch 42:11, Charles 1913:457). These examples have been taken to support the interpretation: "For they sow the wind / and they shall reap the whirlwind." This has maintained itself because the dramatic words appeal to the imagination. The greater intensity of the windstorm means that the disaster which will overtake the criminal will be much greater than his original crime. The implication is that the consequences of criminal behavior extend far beyond the original crime and criminal. This is in accord with divine, not human, justice which is restricted to equivalence between fault and penalty. In any interpretation of the passage the disproportion between action and reaction, sowing and reaping, should be retained.

The problem with the usual rendering and analysis lies in the imagery. To sow iniquity like grain is a good metaphor; to sow wind like grain is meaningless. If such an act reaps a dreadful harvest, "wind" must be a metaphor for some sin. Such a metaphor within a metaphor lacks the realism that characterizes Hebrew Wisdom sayings. Further, 8:7a does not have the form of a proverb at all. The words "sow" and "reap" used together give the false impression that it does. The opening conjunction *kî*, on which Wolff sets so much store (1974:142 n 82; 172), should not be translated "because," but, as Wolff observes, "indeed." Further, the genuine proverbs listed above use the participle *zōrēaʿ*, "sowing" or "a sower," and do not work out a causal connection using a subordinate conjunction.

The following observations place v 7 in an entirely different perspective. The two faults for which Israel is condemned in this chapter are making kings and making idols. It is not easy to see how such activities could be described as "sowing wind," but there ought to be some connection between the sin and its punishment. The purpose of idol-making was to secure good harvests, among other benefits, and it is likely that the king himself was a sacral person in the performance of the necessary rites. A fit punishment for such contempt toward Yahweh would be the removal of the kings, destruction of the idol (v 6), and ruination of agriculture. Now the whole of v 7 describes the agricultural process from sowing to eating. We suggest, accordingly, that v 7a is not a separate proverb, but an integral part of the whole verse. It is an opening statement, the first of a series of curses.

Hosea often omits prepositions in statements of this kind. "Wind" does not make a good object for "sow," but it does make a good adverb. Hence we conclude that judgment is pronounced in the form of a suitable curse: "Indeed, let them sow when it is windy / and let them harvest in a whirlwind." The farmer is to be frustrated at each major stage of his work. Sowing in the wind, he loses much of the grain at the start. Harvesting in a gale, he loses most of the yield at the end.

7b. The continuation of the image of wheat-farming in v 7b is even more compact: a series of related curses embodies the pseudo-sorites, a form of non-logical logic which we have discussed above. We can add another example here. At Mount Horeb Yahweh told Elijah to anoint three persons as instruments of his judgment — Hazael, Jehu, and Elisha. Then he says: "Him who escapes from the sword of Hazael shall Jehu slay, and him who escapes from the sword of Jehu shall Elisha slay" (I Kings 19:17). While the statements are elliptical, the logic is impeccable: one disaster is heaped upon another to ensure that there will be no final survivors. A similar series of calamities, leading to total disaster, is described in II Baruch 70:8 (Charles 1913:517):

> And it will come to pass that
>   whoever escapes from the war will die in the earthquake,
> and whoever escapes from the earthquake will be burned by the fire,
> and whoever escapes from the fire will be destroyed by the famine.

A similar line of reasoning is developed by Job when he curses his existence in Job 3 (Andersen 1976:105–106). He wishes his mother had remained a virgin (v 10a). But, since she did not, he wishes he had not been conceived (v 3). Or, if conceived, he wishes he had died in the womb (v 11). Or, if not that, he wishes he had died in childbirth or infancy. A similar series of successive disasters is found in Hos 9:11–16, although somewhat scattered; see the NOTES there.

Joel 1:4 has a different picture, but the same logic:

> What the cutting locust left, the swarming locust has eaten.
> What the swarming locust left, the hopping locust has eaten.
> And what the hopping locust left, the destroying locust has eaten.

Deprivation of grain and oil and wine (Hos 2:10) is described in Mic 6:15, beginning with the same verbs as in Hos 8:7a. That, however, is a simple picture: they will sow, but not reap. The preceding verse, Mic 6:14b, has another example of the staggered logic illustrated above:

> You will store away, but you won't keep safe;
> And what you do keep safe, I shall give to the sword.

Hos 8:7, for all its brevity, distinguishes no fewer than seven stages in the provision of food from soil to table.

1) They will sow in the wind.
2) If any grain is sown, it will not spring up (*qāmâ*).
3) If it does grow, it will not mature (*'ên-lô ṣemaḥ*).
4) And they will harvest it in a whirlwind.
5) If they do get any grain, it will not make meal (*bĕlî ya'ăśeh qemaḥ*).
6) If they do mill the grain, they will not cook it (*'ûlay ya'ăśeh*).
7) If they do cook it, foreigners will swallow it (*zārîm yiblā'ûhû*).

The last setback is the worst; the food was almost in their mouths. The change from plural verb in v 7a to non-personal singulars is only a slight inconsistency. Verse 7a has a measure of completeness in itself, with internal parallelism; it includes two moments which are not in line with the development in v 7b, since the growth described there comes between sowing and reaping.

The assonance contributes further to the density of the language. The two verbs in v 7a have each a sibilant, and a laryngeal and the same liquid. The words *qāmâ, ṣemaḥ, qemaḥ* all have consonants in common. The repetition of the verb *'śy,* "to make," links vv 7bA and 7bB. Pointing the second of the forms as *ya'ăśēhû* (or *ya'ăśūhû*) would enhance further the rhymes within the poem.

If it grows. We suggest that *qāmâ* is a complete, conditional clause, a verb, with seed as its understood subject. The noun *qāmâ* means standing grain which has reached full height; if this noun is the subject of what follows, then *lô,* "to him," will have to be altered to *lāh,* "to her," as suggested in *BH³.* According to Jer 23:5, the fully grown stalk does not have the "sproutage"; Jeremiah promises *wahăqīmōtî lĕdāwīd ṣemaḥ,* "and I will raise up for David a sprout." This shows that the sprout is for the seed, not the plant; hence *lô* in v 7bA refers to the seed, rather than to Israel. *Lô* is in the trope, not the allegorical parallel.

This compact curse also recapitulates the history of Yahweh's long-suffering treatment of Israel. He could have discarded the people early in their sinful career, letting the seed of his purpose perish in the promised land. But he planted them in it (cf. Hos 2:25; Ps 80:9–12), and let them grow. He could have ruined the crop, as he threatened (Deut 28:38); but no, he gave them grain (Hos 2:10), unrecognized and unthanked (7:14). And so it went.

sproutage. Ṣemaḥ can mean the first tender growth of grain, vine, or tree; or the foliage, the new growth of the vine and tree. It is the latter sproutage that leads directly to the putting out of fruit or ears of wheat. In Gen 41:23, the verb *ṣmḥ* describes the growth of ears of grain.

if it does. The meaning of *'ûlay* is usually "perhaps," but the word can serve as a conjunction for conditional clauses, as in Gen 18:29–32.

make (meal). Here we do not interpret *ya'ăśeh* as the action of the plant in yielding grain, although the root has that meaning. The nearest possible subject of the verb is *qāmâ,* which if it were a noun would be feminine; and there is no evidence that the plant was thought to produce the meal as such. An impersonal passive ("meal will not be made") is not a satisfactory solution to the problem, but it is not impossible. It is remarkable that the grain as such is not named. The transition from *ṣemaḥ* to *qemaḥ* may serve the interests of rhyme to the exclusion of other nouns. In any case, *'śy qmḥ* probably means "to grind (grain into) meal." In I Kings 17:12 *'śy qmḥ* means to cook porridge, and it is possible that the verb has this meaning in its occurrences here. Certainly *'āśâ* is the common verb for the preparation of food. Whether we read *ya'ăśēhû* in v 7bB or not, "meal" is the object of the verb in both its occurrences. The only question is whether *'śy* means "to grind (it) (to) meal" in v 7bA and "to cook (it)" in v 7bB.

foreigners. With the mention of *zārîm*, the political threat, which continues into v 8, becomes clear. "Israel is devoured" because "foreigners have eaten away his strength" (7:9; cf. Isa 1:7). The last clause makes it plain that v 7 is not a proverb, but a realistic comment on economic conditions in the country.

8a. *swallowed*. With the mention of Israel, it is plain that the nation is the subject of the preceding curses. The last verb of the preceding clause is repeated as the first verb of v 8, on the domino principle. Isa 28:7 contains the only other occurrence of the *Nipʻal* of *blʻ;* there a priest and a prophet are coupled as in Hos 4:5. The arguments are quite similar: the actors there overindulged in wine, so they will be devoured by wine. In keeping with the language of v 7, "swallowed" or "devoured" may be taken quite literally; *blʻ* is used of animals and occasionally of persons (Isa 28:4; Job 7:19) gulping down food.

8b. *Now*. When this adverb is used for transition, rather than specifying the time when something happens, it is usually followed by a command or exhortation, or as here, by what may be a precative. In v 6 the calf of Samaria is to be smashed to pieces; here Israel is discarded like a useless pot, broken and scattered. Jeremiah uses the same expression in connection with Moab (48:38). He uses the same idea in his parable of the potter (18:1–23). In Jer 22:28 Jeconiah is compared to an *ʻeṣeb, kĕlî ʼên ḥēpeṣ bô,* to be hurled away into an unknown land. The Jeremiah parallels permit the inference that Hosea applied the image of a useless pot either to the calf (literally) or to Israel (figuratively). Since the calf image symbolizes Israel, the difference is insignificant. At the same time the specific reference to Israel in v 8a, and the mention of the nations in v 8b, make it clear that the people as a whole are meant, and that the simile of the worthless pot is associated with them.

Verse 8 closes the first part of the chapter (vv 1–8), but it also leads into the second (vv 9–14). Mention of the nations (*bgwym*) in v 8 suggests the two nations, Assyria and Egypt, which are prominent in the next section (cf. *bgwym* in v 10). The intrigues of international diplomacy and the threatened consequences for beleaguered Israel are spelled out in an intricately patterned diatribe about the two great powers which dominate the historical scene (Assyria, v 9, and Egypt, v 13). The envelope construction is deliberate and portentous.

XV. THE SPIRITUAL HISTORY OF ISRAEL: ALLIANCES
(8:9–14)

Making alliances and the economic demands

8:9a   Indeed, they have gone up to Assyria. . . .
          Ephraim is a wild ass wandering off alone.
  9b   They have hired lovers.
 10a   Indeed, they have hired them among the nations.
          Even now, I will assemble them.
 10b   They were contorted in pain a little while ago
          King and princes, on account of the tribute.

The religious demands

 11a   Indeed, Ephraim has behaved arrogantly —
 11b   He had altars for sin offerings,
 12a   So I wrote against him altars for sin offerings.
         —With arrogance against my instruction.
 12b   They are considered pagans.
 13a   Sacrifices of my loved ones they sacrificed.
         They ate flesh.
         Yahweh does not accept them.
 13b   Now he keeps track of their iniquity.
         He will punish their sins.
         . . . They have returned to Egypt.

Closing

 14a   Israel forgot its maker.
         He built palaces.
         Judah multiplied them, in fortified cities.
 14b   So I will send fire into its cities
         and it will devour its fortifications.

NOTES

8:9–14. This unit is defined by the discontinuous bicolon (vv 9aA and 13bB) which forms an envelope around it. The two clauses would be regarded as a perfect bicolon if they were brought together, but being separated by sixteen other cola, their relationship to each other has not been recognized (Lundbom 1979). The use of the independent pronoun *hmh* in both vv 9a and 13b is sufficient to establish the connection. The association of Assyria and Egypt is amply attested in Hosea. The chiastic pattern (*'lw 'šwr // mṣrym yšwbw*) and the alternation of perfect and imperfect verb forms are characteristic of classical Hebrew poetry. The two cola are also identical in length (seven syllables). The final verse serves as a coda to the unit.

The opening and closing lines of vv 9 and 13, or rather the statement they secure when they are read together, supply the main topic for the material they enclose, and so serve as a key to interpreting the unit. We then have good reason to suppose that vv 9–13 concern political relations of Ephraim with Assyria and Egypt. The vocabulary used throughout suggests that this involved arrogant rejection of Yahweh's Torah, the making of forbidden covenants, the payment of tribute, and the erecting of sinful altars upon which illicit sacrifices were offered.

From the structural point of view, the speech is composed with a symmetry that is almost complete. By syllable count it divides almost exactly in the middle where there are two lines with extensive repetitive parallelism (vv 11b, 12aA; three of the four words in the lines are identical). The central point is also marked by the similarity between vv 11a and 12aB, with the repetition of the root *rb-*. The forms probably refer to arrogant action, the first being a verb and the second a cognate accusative, and these two lines together form a single clause: "Ephraim has behaved arrogantly, with arrogance against my instruction," repeating the thought of 8:1b.

Apart from the two lines of eight syllables each in the middle, and v 13a, the lines into which this paragraph divides are generally even in length, ranging from five to seven syllables. There is little parallelism in this unit. The language is terse and cryptic; connections are often hard to find. Verse 13bA is a well-formed bicolon, and v 13aA may also be such.

There are several patterns which serve as a guide to the connections. In lines whose parallelism cannot be disputed, the sequence of verbs is commonly perfect // imperfect, and they refer to the same situation: the first verb controls the tense of the second. So in vv 11–12 *hāyû* // *'ektôb* are both past tense. In vv 9aA and 13bB *'ālû* // *yāšûbû* are also both past tense, describing the shuttle diplomacy of princes dealing with both Assyria and Egypt; this shows that the reference to Egypt is not a threat about the future (compare the two perfect verbs used in 7:11b). In vv 9–10 *hitnû* // *yitnû* are both past tense. After *'attâ* the imperfect verb in v 10aB has a normal future meaning and records a threat.

In some instances rhyme is a guide to the grouping of lines into pairs. The ending *-îm* suggests that vv 9b and 10aA are a bicolon (cf. v 10b). The three lines of vv 12b–13aA end in *-û*, and the three lines of v 13aB–13bA end in *-ām*. The two pivotal lines in the middle end in *lô*. (This, together with the equality in length and the high level of repetition, justifies the revision of the relevant verse boundary to reconstitute a bicolon.)

There are other long-range signals within the unit. The statement "Yahweh does not accept them" (v 13aB) matches "Even now, I will assemble them" (v 10aB), in spite of the change in person. Immediately adjoining these two lines are the only two verbs in the unit with *waw*-consecutives: *wayyāḥēllû* (v 10b) . . . *wayyō'kēlû* (v 13aA). The similarities in structure and sound are obvious. The abnormal word order in v 13aA, which places the verb after the object, ensures that the block of material between vv 10b and 13aA begins and ends with similar verb forms. These matching verbs describe effect and cause: they were contorted in pain because they ate human flesh.

The first person is used only five times in the unit (vv 10, 12 bis, 13a, and 14b), but there need be no doubt that Yahweh is the speaker throughout. The three lines in v 13 which refer to Yahweh in the third person are in accord with common practice in dignified speech, where a switch to third person, especially for the sake of using the personal name, is not uncommon after a first-person opening. It is better to recognize the unity of the speech in this way than to suppose that there are two speeches, one by Yahweh and one about Yahweh. No one is directly addressed in this speech, i.e. there are no second-person forms. The third-person pronouns and verbs fluctuate between singular and plural. Consistency can be recognized if there are two distinct referents: Ephraim (always singular) and the royal establishment (king and princes — who account for all the plurals). With this distinction as a guide we can sort out the activities of these two protagonists — the country as a whole, and its emissaries. The key words (*hēmmâ* and Ephraim) occur twice each, in a chiastic pattern.

The king and princes of Israel are regarded as pagans (v 12b). They go as ambassadors to Assyria (v 9aA) and Egypt (v 13bB), bearing tribute (v 10bB). They secure allies (v 9b) among the nations (v 10aA). To make a treaty, the most radical rebellion against the covenant of Yahweh, they participate in the cult of their allies, sacrificing and eating flesh (v 13). This incurs Yahweh's displeasure against them (v 13aB): he will remember their iniquity, punish their sin, and gather them in (vv 13b, 10aB).

Ephraim is a wild ass wandering alone (v 9aB). The country has acted arrogantly (v 11a) against the torah (v 12aB); it has altars for sin offerings (v 11b). The three occurrences of *lô* (vv 9aB, 11b, 12aA) highlight the singular pronoun in contrast to the plural forms. In distinguishing between Ephraim and the royal house, we do not mean to imply that there are two threads of narrative interwoven here. The princes are acting on behalf of Ephraim in their diplomatic maneuvers. The altars attributed to Ephraim in v 11 are probably the ones on which the profane sacrifices are made (v 13).

The treatment outlined requires a reordering of the verse and clause boundaries of MT. Each such change must be justified on its own terms, and this will be done in the NOTES. In general it can be observed here that the analysis receives some support as a result of syllable counting. We have already remarked on the regularities in the lengths of the lines. Related lines and related sets of lines tend to be of equal size. Thus the first and last lines, which embrace vv 9–13, are the same length. The two lines at the midpoint are also equal. In the nine lines from v 9 to v 11, there are fifty-six syllables; in the nine lines in vv 12–13, there are fifty-eight syllables.

8:9a. *Indeed. Kî* is usually translated "for," but a logical conjunction does not fit the grammar, since there is no principal clause. The repetition of *kî* with *gam* in v 10aA supports this, and also indicates that both relevant clauses refer to the same event, as does the clause introduced by the third *kî*, in v 11. The first two belong in statements about the royal party, the third goes with Ephraim. The particles serve to mark the two topics of the unit.

they. On the importance of *hēmmâ* see the NOTE on 8:4. Here the pronoun marks the onset of the unit, and its repetition in v 13bB marks a closure.

have gone up. At 7:11 the verb *hlk* is used; it is not clear why *'ālû* should be used here. Verse 8b has said that the Israelites are among the nations like a useless implement. In relation to the Exodus and Egypt generally, verb usage is commonly "to go down" (to slavery and Egypt) and "to come up" (to freedom and from Egypt). There could be a geographical dimension in this. We note Hosea's characteristic omission of a preposition with the goal of a verb of motion.

In the light of what follows, we see this journey as the attempt of the princes to secure an alliance. We do not know what historical moment is reflected in this desperate bid. We suspect that the mission resembled that of Ahaz to Damascus (II Kings 16:10–16), but was undoubtedly of an earlier date. We know that Menahem, a usurper, secured the recognition of the Assyrians by payment of a huge tribute, and some such embassy may be meant here (cf. II Kings 15:19–20).

wild ass. The MT makes Ephraim the subject of the verb *htnw* in v 9b, wrongly, since elsewhere, especially in this unit, Ephraim is singular. By identifying Ephraim as the subject of a verbless clause, the common sequence of predicate–subject is manifested. Following on the utensil simile in v 8, the use of a metaphor at this point suggests that we are dealing with a new theme, and a parallel simile (as in 7:12 and 13:3) should not be supposed. In 7:11, which records the same sort of diplomatic activity as here, we are told that Ephraim is like a silly dove, and comparison of the two passages might be instructive. We should not take it for granted that in Israel the ass was proverbial for stupidity, as in our culture; in Ps 32:9, horse and mule (*pered*) are said to require restraints because they are senseless, but that failing is not what we mean by asinine behavior since it is also associated with equines. The use of the word *pere'* in particular is in part explained by wordplay on the name *'eprayim: pr'/'pr*. In Jer 2:24, the *pereh* is an animal willfully straying; the context implies promiscuity, using Hoseanic language (*'āhabtî zārîm*, Jer 2:25). In context *lô* probably means "alone, by himself," reflexive, not ethical or possessive. In Isa 14:31 *bôdēd* refers to a straggler in the army, and in Ps 102:8 it describes a solitary bird (cf., however, Dahood 1970:13). The general impression is that of a figure forlorn and friendless.

9b. *hired.* Ephraim is usually identified as the subject of "hired," but we propose that the opening pronoun *hēmmâ* provides a subject for *hitnû* as well as *'ālû.* Verse 9a, with its plural and singular, introduces, first of all, the two protagonists—"they" (royal party) and Ephraim. Verse 10 continues with the king and princes, and v 11 takes up Ephraim.

The verbs *hitnû* and *yitnû* constitute the only clear examples of the root *tny*, glossed "to hire"; the form in Ps 8:2 is difficult (cf. Andersen 1970b). Hos 8:9 is the only example of the *Hip'il;* and why it should be followed by the *Qal* in v 10 is not clear. Because of its collocation with the root *'hb*, it has been connected with the word *'etnâ* or *'etnān* (Hosea uses both forms—2:14; 9:1); hence the standard interpretation "to hire," by paying the harlot's fee. Although the picture is incongruous, the respective roles of Ephraim and Assyria are correctly defined by these terms. Ephraim has paid for the services of Assyria, although the relationship no doubt was described differently. It is no accident that Nahum calls Nineveh the classic prostitute (*mrb znwny zwnh*, 3:4). At the same time, Ephraim could be called a harlot, since its services were for sale to the highest bidder. On the economics of hiring Assyria in the Kilamuwa Inscription (the verb is *škr*), see O'Connor (1977).

lovers. MT does not use *'ōhăbîm*, "lovers," the *Qal* participle, but the plural of a rare word, *'ahab*. Hosea's word for the "lovers" of an adulterous wife is the *Pi'el* participle (2:7,9,12,14,15). In its only other occurrence, the word used here is an appellative of a lovable wife (Prov 5:19). In the context of c 8, the "lovers" are political allies. Ezek 16:33 records as an extreme of depravity the situation in which the prostitute pays men to make love to her. Wolff (1974:143) finds the same idea in the present verse. "Lovers" could be subject or object grammatically, but since there is a reference to Assyrian royal tribute in v 10, there is no doubt that "lovers" is the object, and the royal party is the subject of *hitnû*.

10a. *Indeed. Gam kî* is a rare combination. Here *gam* is the conjunction, and *kî* intensifies the verb.

they have hired. The Masoretes read the form *yitnû* as *Qal* because it has no apparent object. It is better to bring it in line with the preceding *hitnû*, to which it is obviously parallel, and to suppose that the same object serves for both. The MT verse boundaries are not a sure guide to discourse syntax. The *gam kî* links back to the opening *kî* of v 9 (both particles are asseverative); *'attâ* in the next line marks the transition to a new theme.

Even now, I will assemble. 'Attâ here introduces the threat of judgment. The verb *qbṣ* is used in 9:6. Its force is ambivalent. It is often used in the *Pi'el* to describe the protective action of a shepherd collecting his dispersed flock; the *Qal* is often used to describe the mustering of troops. In the context the significance of such an act of God is not clear. Again, *qbṣ* describes the activity of assembling the nations for judgment (Joel 4:11), or gathering the sheaves in harvest (Mic 4:12). Zech 10:8–10 uses it in a favorable sense to describe the gathering of his scattered peoples; such an event is distant from the setting of Hosea 8. Ezek 16:37 is nearer to Hosea's situation; there Yahweh assembles Israel's lovers in order to expose her indecency to them. In Hos 9:6, *qbṣ* points to the objective of death. This threat of judgment here, whatever its exact sense, is completed in v 13b, where the repetition of *'attâ* is a link with v 10aB.

10b. There is a problem in identifying the root in *wayyăḥēllû;* cf. the discussion at 7:5. The fact that king and princes are associated with similar verbs in two occurrences in Hosea is an argument that there is some link between the passages. On the one hand, the verbs may have the same meaning, or they may be homonyms with quite different meanings, but equally related to the dual objects. Because of the association with wine, we considered that *heḥĕlû* in 7:5 means "they became sick," from the root *ḥly*. Despite the similarity of eating here and drinking there, we prefer another explanation here.

There are some passages where a root *ḥ-l* occurs in association with *qbṣ* with the meaning "to writhe in agony," i.e. *ḥwl*.

Nah 2:11b   *weḥalḥālâ běkol-motnayim*
           ûpěnê kullām qibběṣû pā'rûr
           Writhing in all hips,
           and all faces contracted with disfigurement.

Joel 2:6   *mippānāyw yaḥîlû 'ammîm*
           kol-pānîm qibběṣû pā'rûr
           Before him peoples are in agony,
           all faces contracted with disfigurement.

These are the only uses of *pā'rûr* and its meaning is not clear. The root *p'r*, "beauty," does not seem appropriate, unless it has been polarized to an antonym. The two verses present a conventional description of the suffering brought about by calamitous war. Although the co-occurrence of the roots *ḥl* and *qbṣ* is suggestive, the verbs in 8:10 are quite laconic, and it is not certain that we should fill them out with the subjects and other modifiers used in Nahum and Joel. The sequence in 8:10 is also the inverse of the other two so it is less certain that vv 10aB and 10bA are a bicolon. The use of both imperfect and consecutive past verb tenses is a formidable barrier against uniting these clauses, but we note the same sequence in v 13; *yzbḥw . . . wy'klw,* where the tenses must be the same.

Nevertheless the metrical pattern includes a distinctive chiasm:

which supports the view that these clauses belong together and that the general sense is that of suffering occasioned by conflict and defeat. The verb in v 10aB could be rendered "I have squeezed them."

Verse 10bA may refer to the tribute paid to Tiglath Pileser by Menahem or some similar episode, and be a warning that such an expedient act, however successful in achieving legitimacy for the usurper, would result in defeat and devastation, symbolized by suffering of the kind associated with childbirth.

The problem of the verb in v 10b cannot be separated from the problem of *mě'āṭ,* which means either "a little bit," or "a little while." If the verb describes an act of wickedness, it is not likely that the prophet would say that it was only on a small scale. If the verb describes some future judg-

ment (so *RSV*), then it could be announced as coming shortly; the tense
of the verb is against this, which suggests the adverb is temporal but refers
to the past rather than the future.

King and princes. It is usual to identify a coordination phrase here, in
spite of the absence of a conjunction, because king and princes are frequently associated elsewhere in Hosea, e.g. in v 4. It is possible that *melek
śārîm* is a construct phrase (cf. *malkî rab*), "king of princes," i.e. the
king of Assyria, an attempt to translate the title *šar šarrāni*, "king of
kings."

However, it is more likely that "king (and) princes," in spite of the unusual position at the end of the clause, are the subject of *wayyāḥēllû* and
the other plural verbs in this unit.

11a. *has behaved arrogantly*. The accepted interpretation of the MT of
v 11a is that Ephraim "multiplied" altars in order to sin. *RSV* further
takes the initial *kî* as a conjunction, and makes v 11a subordinate to
v 11b; the translation is inane: "Because Ephraim has multiplied altars for
sinning, they have become to him altars for sinning." By relocating the
boundaries of vv 11–12, we have retrieved two lines with close parallelism, located in the center of the unit vv 9–14. This rearrangement apparently leaves *hrbh* without an object. There are other examples of an
absolute use. In I Sam 2:3 *tarbû* means to speak arrogantly, as the context
shows. A root different from the familiar *rby* is not needed. It is used here
of arrogance and Hosea mentions Israel's "pride" elsewhere (5:5; 7:10).

It is not likely that we have in v 11a a polemic against a multiplicity of
altars, in the interests of a policy of one central shrine, although the disen-
chantment of the prophets with the local shrines had reached the point
where centralization of the cult might appear the most logical next move.
Hosea, like Elijah, seems to accept the numerous shrines as legitimate centers of Yahweh worship. It is not the altars as such, but the use of them,
that deserves censure, as in 10:1. The form *rbw* in v 12 is a cognate accusative of the verb of v 11a. See the NOTE there.

11b. *for sin offerings*. The Masoretes recognized an infinitive indicating
the purpose of the altars, which could be correct. In the common phrase
mizbēaḥ lĕyhwh, "an altar for Yahweh," *l* introduces an attributive — "a
Yahweh altar." Here *l* introduces another purpose designation, although
this usage suggests that *ḥṭ'* could be the name of the god to whom the
altars were dedicated, perhaps *ḥēṭ'*, as in Isa 31:7, where the language is
like that of Hosea, e.g. in 8:4. In Josh 22:16, the illicit altar built by the
Israelites in Transjordan is called a *mizbēaḥ limrodkem*, "altar of your rebellion." The altars in Hosea are condemned, not because they are
numerous, but because they are used to make the sacrifices described in v
13, which were contrary to the Torah and involved breaking Yahweh's
covenant. These sacrifices belong among the ceremonies required as an act

of submission to Assyria, for the sake of political protection. If the case of Ahaz is a guide (II Kings 16:10–16), these were not altars to Canaanite Baals, but to Assyrian gods. Our rearrangement of clause and verse boundaries eliminates the difficulties of the traditional rendering.

12a. *I wrote.* The form is imperfect, but the sense requires a past tense; threatening to write something in the future is rather mild. The apparent sense of the MT, "I wrote for him myriads of my Torah," has given rise to a great deal of discussion, little of it relevant here. The difficulty does not lie in the existence of the Torah in the time of Hosea, since he has already accused the priest of forgetting the Torah (4:6) and the people of rebelling against it (8:1). We have pointed out the resemblance of 4:2 to the Decalogue, and at numerous points Hosea displays knowledge of traditions now found in the Pentateuch. The difficulty lies in the phrase "numerous things of my Torah," stipulated by the Qere *rubbê tôrātî*, which seems easier than the Ketib *rbw,* "myriad of my Torah," although not obviously meaningful. It is usual to explain the clause as hypothetical and exaggerated: so *RSV,* "Were I to write for him my laws by ten thousands." But Hos 6:5 shows that the mode of divine communication was the prophetic word, not written Torah, and the grammar of the line is even more eccentric than Hosea usually is.

By attaching "I wrote" to the preceding words, the act becomes the recording of Ephraim's guilt, not the writing of Torah. As already pointed out, the parallelism is greatly improved.

with arrogance. The sense of *rbw* is given by *hirbâ,* although the *w* remains a problem in parsing; we suggest that the form is a noun used as a cognate accusative. Verse 12aB matches v 1bB, which says that the people "rebelled against my instruction."

12b. *are considered.* The subject of the form *neḥšābû* is not obvious. The traditional interpretation is that the myriads of the Torah are regarded by Ephraim as a "strange thing." The subject of all plural verbs in this unit is "king and princes," and that seems to be the case here. Though they would not think of themselves as pagans, others would so reckon them — as the prophet does.

pagans. The clash between the plural verb and the singular complement suggests that the latter is collective, hence our translation as plural. *Kĕmô* marks a complement, not a comparison. The word *zār* is plural in its other occurrences in Hosea (5:7; 7:9; 8:7) and carries a great deal of theological freight. We use the word "pagan" rather than "foreign" because of its associations with *'ēl zār,* "alien god" (Pss 44:21; 81:10 — the latter has *'ēl nēkār* as well); *zār* (Isa 43:12) and *zārîm* (Deut 32:16) designate a male pagan deity. In Exod 30:9; Lev 10:1; Num 3:4; 26:61, *zārâ* means "unholy." The line refers to engaging in the rituals of foreign religions necessary for consummating a treaty.

13a. *my loved ones.* The word *hbhby* is a hapax legomenon, and widely suspected of being corrupt. It was probably developed by duplicating *hb,* derived from either *yhb,* "to give," or better, *'hb,* "to love." The Greek translators show awareness of both possible derivations, but the difficulties were too much for them. Either root could make sense in the present context: sacrifices of things brought, or sacrifices having to do with "love." *Zibḥê* can govern the thing sacrificed, as in *zibḥê mētîm,* "human sacrifices" (Ps 106:28); or an attribute — *zibḥê šĕlāmîm, zibḥê-ṣedeq;* and even "the sacrifices of God" (Ps 51:19). The word "love," if it lies behind *habhābay,* is connected here with the lovemaking, and the objects of devotion. Hence we identify *habhābay* as a word for beloved children. We need not decide whether the sense of lovemaking or familial love is behind the use of *'hb.* The possibility that the children are taken as gifts (from *yhb*) remains; cf. 2:14, in which the children may be identified as the *'etnâ,* "wages," of lovers.

The suffix on the form suggests that my *habhābîm* are mentioned by Yahweh in yet another reference to child sacrifice (cf. Ps 106:37; Ezek 16:20–21,36–37; 23:36–39). Since the sacrifices are eaten, the implications are barbaric, but as we know from reports of the practice, not beyond human capacity (Green 1975). Since, however, Hosea uses *śādāy* twice (10:4; 12:12) where the ending is not the pronoun suffix, but an obsolete noun ending, the same explanation may obtain here.

they sacrificed. The verb *zbḥ* occurs in the *Qal* only here in Hosea; elsewhere it is *Pi'el.* The reason for the usage is unclear.

They ate. If *wy'klw* begins a new clause, there are two nouns available as objects of the previous verb and none for *y'klw.* Current emendations confront the dilemma by recovering an extra verb from *hbhby* (see, e.g. *RSV*). We propose that each verb is preceded by its object. Deut 15:20 and 21 show that *'kl (bśr)* after *zbḥ* means to eat the flesh of a sacrificed animal. Compare Deut 27:7 and Jer 7:21. The eating of flesh was part of the sacramental meal that sealed the alliance. The resumptive *waw* has been identified by many scholars.

Yahweh does not accept. In the absence of a conjunction, it is far from certain that this clause is simply adversative to the preceding. Actually, this line is not linked directly with the preceding but expresses Yahweh's displeasure generally with his people. The shift in person is characteristic of high style. The speaker, Yahweh, is the same.

13b. Note the quotation of this verse in Jer 14:10.

Now. Compare "now" in v 10.

he keeps track. There is a similar bicolon in 9:9. Compare the parallelism of "sin" and "iniquity" in reverse sequence in 4:8.

They have returned. Because *yāšûbû* is imperfect, prevailing interpretation lines it up with the preceding imperfect verbs, translates them all as future, and sees v 13bB as the entailment of the threat to "punish their sins," i.e. "they shall return to Egypt." The reversal of the Exodus is a fit penalty for violating the covenant. Against this interpretation, there are arguments from literary structure for retrieving the discontinuous bicolon, used as an envelope. The chiasm throws the verb into clause-terminal position, a signal that we have reached the end of a unit; this leaves v 14 as a detached coda. In this unit, when an imperfect verb (*yšwbw*) follows a perfect verb (*'lw* in v 9), it shares the past tense with it. Verse 13bB may also be construed as a threat, however. The prophet might well have imagined that when the northern kingdom was conquered, it would be divided between Assyria and Egypt, with some of the people being deported to Assyria, while others were sent to Egypt. Note that when Judah was overrun by Nebuchadnezzar, many people were deported to Babylonia while others, including Jeremiah, fled to Egypt for refuge. In the eighth century, however, the same pattern is not recorded although some historians have traced the first stages of later Jewish communities in Egypt to such an early migration. It is more likely, however, that if v 13 is a threat of exile (rather than a description of diplomatic traffic, our preferred interpretation), then it is a prophecy which turned out to have been wrong. Egypt was less prominent in the fate of the northern kingdom than Hosea's symmetrical statements suggest.

14. This verse is not easily integrated with the surrounding text. It has been treated as an intrusion, mainly because of the reference to Judah, which has not been mentioned since 6:11. The verse consists of five lines of unequal length, which exhibit a measure of parallelism.

14a	*wayyiškaḥ yiśrā'ēl 'et-'ōśēhû*	10 syll.
	wayyiben hêkālôt	5/6
	wîhûdâ hirbâ 'ārîm běṣūrôt	10/11
14b	*wěšillaḥtî-'ēš bě'ārāyw*	8
	wě'ākělâ 'arměnōtêhā	9

The balance of the last two lines suggests poetry. The repetition of "cities" suggests an introversion. The *'arměnôt* are identified as "her fortifications," in contrast to "his cities." The discrepancy in the gender of the suffixes is curious, and suggests that the second referent is "city" (from *'ryw*, but understood distributively: each city), as in the frequently made threat in Amos 1 and 2.

It may well be that the scribe was unduly influenced by the repeated refrain in Amos (. . . *w'klh 'rmnwtyh*, 1:7,10,14, etc.), where the 3 f s suffix is appropriate, and inserted it here, where it does not obviously belong. Nevertheless, the text is not identical with any of the passages in Amos, so there is no reason to suppose that the whole was borrowed from that prophet. After all, the two men were roughly contemporary along with Isaiah and Micah; they shared, to a considerable degree, a common theology and drew upon a common stock of literary traditions and formulations.

The first clause, "Israel forgot its maker," makes a satisfactory close to the chapter, echoing, as it does, similar sentiments strategically located at other breaking points in the book (e.g. 2:15; 13:6). The final four lines may have been added by an editor to provide a more elaborate coda for this unit, and a bridge to the next. If so, it has been done with some skill, and the addendum cannot now be separated from what precedes, since the necessary subject for *wybn hyklwt* must be found in "Israel" in the opening clause. In the material at hand, Israel is the subject of the first two clauses, while Judah is the subject of the third. There is chiasm of subject and verb:

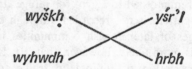

along with the alternation of imperfect (with *waw*-consecutive) and perfect forms of the verb. The sequence *yśr'l // yhwdh* shows that the editor has understood the former to refer to the northern kingdom only, and that the two together cover the whole people. In addition, we must combine them to make reasonable sense of the passage: Israel and Judah have both forgotten their maker; likewise they both build many palaces within their fortified cities. Finally, the fires of war will devour cities and citadels indiscriminately in both countries (cf. especially Amos 2:5 for his oracle on Judah — there is no corresponding one on Israel).

Some other points of contact between v 14 and other prophets may be noted. Although the title "Maker" is not used anywhere else by Hosea, it is found in both parts of Isaiah. The reference to fortified cities is characteristic of Isaiah (25:2; 27:10; 37:26), but it is also found in Deuteronomy (1:28; 9:1). The adjective *bṣrwt* refers specifically to the walls, and the fortifications (*'armĕnôt*) have similar associations.

14a. *palaces.* Or "temples"; the building of shrines would match the building of altars. Other associations in v 14 point to palaces, possibly fortified, especially if the chiasm in the last four lines links "palaces" with "strongholds."

Hosea has exposed the futility of foreign alliances. Amos spoke more pointedly, and repeatedly, about the futility of strong defense works. Israelite historians could never quite make up their minds as to how to assess the magnificent dwellings of kings. They tended to regard luxury as pretentious (Jer 22:13–16), but some of the traditions about Solomon's glory take it as a fitting mark of international prestige that impressed even the Queen of Sheba. On the other hand, the exploitation of the work force, and the infringement of citizens' rights that made Solomon's achievements possible left a great bitterness. The absurdity of trusting in such things is a common prophetic theme.

XVI. THE SPIRITUAL HISTORY OF ISRAEL: DESOLATION AND PROPHECY
(9:1–9)

Promiscuity, starvation, defilement

9:1a Don't rejoice, Israel.
> Don't exult like the peoples.
> For you have been promiscuous away from your God.

1b You made love for a fee by every threshing floor.

2a Grain —
> From threshing floor and wine vat Yahweh will not
> > nourish them.

2b — and must Yahweh will cause to fail from it.

3a They will not reside in Yahweh's land.

3b Ephraim will return to Egypt.
> In Assyria they will eat unclean food.

Deprivation, pollution, isolation

4a They will not pour out their wine as a libation for Yahweh,
> and they will not bring their sacrifices to him.
> Indeed, the food of idols is theirs.
> All who eat it become unclean.

4b Indeed, their food was for their life's preservation.
> He will not enter Yahweh's house.

5a How will you celebrate the festival day,

5b Yahweh's assembly day?

Devastation, dispossession, visitation

6a For behold, they flee from the devastation —
> Egypt will collect them.
> Memphis will bury them.

6b — with the best of their silver things.
> Weeds will dispossess them,
> thorns, from their tents.

7a The days of visitation have come.
        The days of recompense have come.

Prophecy, hostility, memory
  7b Let Israel know—
        (They say) "The prophet is a fool,
                    the man of the Spirit is insane,
                    because your iniquity is great,
                    and your hostility is great."
  8a The prophet is a watchman of Ephraim with my God,
  8b   a trap set on all his paths,
                    hostility in the house of his god.
  9a — that they have deeply defiled themselves
                    as in the days of Gibeah.
  9b He will remember their iniquity.
        He will punish their sins.

NOTES

9:1–9. Although this unit contains many different ideas, it achieves a significant unity of thought. The stimulus of cc 1–3 is once more in evidence, as the vocabulary shows. Again Israel is blamed for promiscuity (v 1). The numerous cult words — rejoice, exult, sacrifice, libation, festival, assembly — show that illicit worship is competing with the legitimate worship of Yahweh (v 5). The illicit acts are performed at threshing floors (v 1) and wine vats (v 2), indicating festivities tied to agricultural life. The theory that the donation of sexual services to the god in sacred ritual secured his benefactions on crops and herds was morally degrading and a theological disaster for Yahwism. This theory governs the acts of other nations, and is not a matter of rejoicing for Israel (v 1). On the contrary, it leads Israel to forfeit their standing in Yahweh's "land" and "house" (vv 3a, 4b). The self-deception of the followers of this religion is possible only because they have rejected Yahweh's prophets as madmen (v 7b). Things have become as bad as they were in the days of Gibeah (v 9a). Now is the time of reckoning (v 7a); sins will be dealt with (v 9b).

Accusations (unmasking sin) and condemnations (unveiling punishment) alternate throughout the passage. Justice will be done: having defiled themselves with what they have eaten in their ceremonies (v 4a), they end by eating foul things in a foreign land (v 3bB). As so often in the Hebrew Bible, the irony of turning away from Yahweh is that it has a result the opposite of what was sought. Baalism allured Israel because it seemed to have a better technique for securing fertile flocks and fruitful fields. In Yahweh's reaction, harvest and vintage fail (v 2). The response goes further than merely frustrating them, however; such acts characterize only the early stages of Yahweh's discipline. At the last, hopeless stage he acts more drastically: those who live on wickedness (v 4a) defile themselves, and must be ejected from his territory (v 3a). The gift of covenant land is annulled; the Exodus is reversed (v 3b). If they prefer the way of the nations (v 1a), then let them go off and live among the nations (v 3b). If the people prefer to eat foul food (v 4b), let them live where the diet has such staples (v 3b). They have disqualified themselves from participating in Yahweh's cult (v 4a); they no longer have anything to do with his festivals (v 5). They have fouled Yahweh's land (v 4), so he will devastate it and make it uninhabitable (v 6b). The population will take refuge in Egypt only to die there (v 6a). The people have scorned the prophet (v 7b), but he will snare them in the end (v 8b).

In this difficult passage, the focus is on Israel's rebellion in the matter of religious practice in the homeland, rather than on the disloyalty expressed by foreign alliances, the theme of 8:9–14. Even there we saw that the pagan rituals borrowed from treaty partners were among the most objectionable features of such covenants.

The themes and ideas are woven together in a complex poetic and rhetorical pattern. The several strands can be distinguished in part by pronominal usage which gives the initial impression of confusion, but rightly followed, can help the reader find a way along the intertwining threads.

First person singular — "my" (v 8a); this is most likely the prophet; unlike 8:9–13, spoken by God, this speech is indirect.

Second person singular — "you" (vv 1,7b); this is Israel in v 1, and the prophet in v 7b.

Second person plural — "you" (v 5); for lack of clearer identification, we assume that this refers to the people, although in other places in the book such plurals refer specifically to the priests or the royal party, or to Israel (Ephraim) and Judah together.

Third person singular — "he" (vv 3b,4b,8b), identified in v 3 as Ephraim; the referent of "his paths" and "his god" in v 8 is less certain: it could be Ephraim or the prophet.

Third person singular — "(it/)her" (v 2b), obscure.

Third person plural — "they" (vv 2a,3a,3b,4 seven times, 6 six times, 7b,9 four times). In general, Israel and Ephraim are referred to in the singular, and together in the plural, but the pattern does not hold firmly in this material. Confusion arises from the fact that Israel is 2 m s in v 1, possibly 2 m pl in v 5, and 3 m pl in v 7b.

The changes in the person of the pronouns is not detrimental to the unity of the passage. A speech can begin in the second person, and then switch to talking *about* the person being addressed in the third person. In the present passage vv 1–3 illustrate this pattern (from second to third person) while vv 4–5 show the reverse (third to second person). In a similar way the speeches in c 8 begin in the first person (Yahweh referring to himself as "I") and change to third (Yahweh referring to himself as "Yahweh").

The passage 9:1–9 divides evenly between vv 1–5 (125 syllables) and vv 6–9 (124 syllables). These major units also divide into subsections, as follows:

Part I.   vv 1–5   125 syllables
    A.   vv 1–3   Promiscuity (69 syllables)
    B.   vv 4–5   Deprivation (56 syllables)
Part II.   vv 6–9   124 syllables
    A.   vv 6–7a   Devastation (55 syllables)
    B.   vv 7b–9 Prophecy (69 syllables)

These observations on the themes and general structure of the passage are supported by an analysis of poetic forms. The familiar units of bicolon, tricolon, and tetracolon are worked together into a larger overall design.

There are several well-formed bicola with standard patterns of synonymous parallelism.

1aB   *kî zānîtā mē'al 'ělōhêkā*
1bA   *'āhabtā 'etnān 'al kol-gěrānôt*

"You made love for a fee" is parallel to "you have been promiscuous"; "away from (*'al*) your God" contrasts with "by (*'al*) every threshing floor," making it clear that the granaries were the locations of acts as idolatrous as they were immoral. The bicolon is synonymous at one point and has a contrast at another.

3b   *wěšāb 'eprayim miṣrayim*
     ûbě'aššûr ṭāmē' yō'kēlû

This bicolon has the same juxtaposition of singular and plural as v 2. Balance between cola is achieved by the names of the two countries: Egypt and Assyria. These are complementary rather than parallel, as are the chiastic verbs. While each unit is specific and complete in itself, the force of each extends to the other: thus the return to Egypt will involve Israel ("they" = Israel plus Ephraim) as well as Ephraim, while "eating unclean things" will take place in Egypt as well as Assyria (to which "they" will go as also to Egypt).

> 4aA   *lō'-yissĕkû lyhwh yayin*
>   *wĕlō' ye'erbû-lô zibḥêhem*

This displays complete synonymous parallelism; nothing disturbs the lexical correspondences. Even the sequence of the items is the same, although this requires the less usual sequence, in the first line, of an indirect object before an object. Only the pronoun "their" has no counterpart in the preceding line: this does double duty, modifying both "wine" and "sacrifices."

> 5a   *mah-ta'ăśû lĕyôm mô'ēd*
> 5b   *ûlĕyôm ḥag-yhwh*

The parallelism is incomplete, but rhythmic compensation makes the lines of almost equal length.

> 6aB   *miṣrayim tĕqabbĕṣēm*
>   *mōp   tĕqabbĕrēm*

Here the parallelism is enhanced by alliteration. The matching words begin and end with the same or similar sounds; the verbs differ in only one consonant.

> 1aA   *'al-tiśmaḥ yiśrā'ēl*
>   **'al-gîl kā'ammîm*

> 7a   *bā'û yĕmê happĕquddâ*
>   *bā'û yĕmê haššillūm*

> 7bA   *'ĕwîl hannābî'*
>   *mĕšuggā' 'îš hārûaḥ*

> 7bB   *'al rōb 'ăwōnĕkā*
>   *wĕrabbâ maśṭēmâ*

> 8b   *paḥ yāqôš 'al-kol-dĕrākāyw*
>   *maśṭēmâ bĕbêt 'ĕlōhāyw*

> 9b   *yizkôr 'ăwōnām*
>   *yipqôd ḥaṭṭō'wtām*

This inventory shows that many of the lines in this unit occur in bicola which are contiguous and have a fair degree of parallelism; and the lines are of regular length.

Other units are more complex, or rather compact, since the majority of the lines have only five or six syllables, and are often elliptical, not to say enigmatic. There are further complications because connected materials are separated from each other in various ways. For example, "grain and must" is a stock phrase, but the words are not contiguous in vv 2a and 2b. We do not propose to reunite them by reorganizing the text; rather we assume that the dismemberment of this phrase was a deliberate part of a sophisticated literary technique. Analysis must be guided in part by the recognition of poetic lines of reasonable length, even though these vary roughly from five to ten syllables, often much more widely. In vv 1–2, we have detached the final word of v 1, *dgn,* and connected it with the beginning of v 2, resulting in the following bicolon:

2   *dāgān   —   gōren wāyeqeb lō' yir'ēm*
    wĕtîrôš   yĕkaḥeš bāh

The present division in the MT, *'l kl-grnwt dgn,* "by every threshing floor of grain," produces an unbalanced line in v 1b. The word "threshing floor" is then a link between vv 1 and 2. Everything needed for parallelism is present in v 2, but "grain and must" is a better parallel to "threshing floor and wine vat" than "must" alone. It is possible to transpose the word "grain" into the second line, and form the phrase "grain and must." But if *dgn* is left where it is, an interesting variation of a common expression is apparent. The opening *dāgān* is held in suspense; in effect, a whole clause is inserted into the coordinate phrase *dāgān* (. . .) *wĕtîrôš.*

A different kind of complexity is met in the following bicolon.

6bB   *qimmôš yîrāšēm*
      ḥōaḥ   bĕ'ohŏlêhem

This unit has to be read holistically: "Weeds (and) thorns will dispossess them from their tents." The coordinated nouns are split between the two lines, as in v 2. If this is a complete bicolon, there is no need to ignore the pronoun object ("them") and identify the first phrase in v 6b, which is difficult in itself, as the object of "possess." Two bicola are embedded in embracing lines and the whole of v 6 is well formed. The phrase *kî-hin-nēh* introduces a poem of six lines, all of roughly the same length.

6a   *kî-hinnēh*
         hālĕkû miššōd
                      miṣrayim tĕqabbĕṣēm
                      mōp   tĕqabbĕrēm
6b   *maḥmad lĕkaspām*
                      qimmôš yîrāšēm
                      ḥōaḥ bĕ'ohŏlêhem

A rhyme scheme supports the analysis. The apparently isolated second and fifth lines are related in a third, discontinuous bicolon, without parallelism.

This leaves only a few lines unaccounted for. In v 4 the repetition of the word *leḥem* suggests that the two lines that contain the word form a discontinuous bicolon; "for them" and "for their life's preservation" are obvious parallels. The last line of v 4a has no certain companion nearby; the roots for "eat" and "unclean," however, both occur in v 3bB, in chiasm with v 4aB.

> 3bB In Assyria unclean food they will eat.
> 4aB All who eat it become unclean.

This does not mean that v 4aB is unrelated to the encompassing lines, both of which refer to food. The connections between vv 3 and 4 manifest a more complex integration of the whole, through the parallelism between single lines in each verse. These lines display parallelism to each other when taken in pairs; the exact structure of the larger configurations remains to be determined. Thus vv 3a and 4bB constitute a good bicolon:

> 3a   *lōʾ yēšĕbû bĕʾereṣ yhwh*
> 4bB *lōʾ yābôʾ bêt yhwh*

They embrace the whole passage. The syntax of the lines is identical; the verbs are similar; the repetition of "not" and "Yahweh" points to synonymy, and suggests that "Yahweh's house" and "Yahweh's land" are the same. In another light v 3 can be analyzed as a tricolon, the first line making a general statement, the next two expounding it in more detail: the people will no longer reside in Yahweh's land, but instead, in Egypt and Assyria. Similarly the first two lines of v 4a and the last line of v 4b constitute a tricolon; the more general single line comes after the bicolon in which the details are given: they will not come into Yahweh's house, viz. shrine, and they will not present offerings of either drink or food. That we have an introverted structure is shown by the unusual sequence of wine before food, which realizes a chiastic match with the "grain and must" of v 2. We have already seen that the second and third lines of v 4a and v 4bA constitute a tricolon in which the central line is general, the surrounding ones specific, while the last line of 4a has some parallelism with v 3bB. Verse 3bB faces both ways: parallel to v 3bA ("Egypt" and "Assyria" in parallelism and chiasm), and to the end of v 4a ("unclean" and "eat" repeated in chiasm). The two lines to which v 3bB is parallel are not parallel to each other.

To sum up, the nine lines in vv 3–4 constitute three tricola: Lines 1 (general), 2, 3 (bicolon); lines 4, 5 (bicolon), 9 (general); lines 6, 8

(bicolon), 7 (general). They are tied together by the relationships between lines 1 and 9; and 3 and 7, which constitute subsidiary bicola.

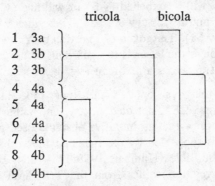

Verses 5–7a are a block of similar size. The structure of the three bicola
in v 6 has already been described. This verse is encompassed by a bicolon
(v 5) before it and one (v 7a) after it. These balance in that each has the
same word ("day" or "days") in repetitive parallelism. Instead of the joyful day of Yahweh's festival, there will be the days of retribution. Instead
of gathering in assembly, they will be scattered.

In vv 7b–9 there is a similar block of material. Eight of the lines constitute recognizable bicola, and between all of them there are additional signals as a result of repeating certain key words: "prophet" joins vv 7b and
8a, "iniquity" joins vv 7b and 9b, "hostility" joins vv 7b and 8b.

Verse 7a also faces both ways. We have included it with vv 5–6 because
of the repetition of "days," but "days" is also a link between vv 7a and 9a,
and the repetition of the root *pqd* in vv 7a and 9b constitutes an echo, or
envelope. Viewed in this perspective, v 7a is a hinge between two units, vv
5–7a, and vv 7a–9.

The first lines of v 7b and v 8a are without parallels, although the latter
has a connection with v 7b in the word "prophet." It is possible that these
lines are parallel, through the names "Israel" and "Ephraim." We have already noted that these names occur separately in the first unit (vv 1, 3),
but are linked by common themes and grammatical elements.

The themes in the entire unit are as follows: Israel is forbidden to
rejoice and celebrate like the nations (v 1a). Acting like the nations, Israel has been promiscuous (v 1b). The nation has become as deeply
defiled as in the time of the Gibeah incident (v 9a); this refers to Judges
19–21, a low point in national corruption, when sexual depravity led to
civil war and catastrophic depopulation. Now once more the days of reckoning have come (v 7a); their sin will be remembered (v 9b). The form
of the punishment will suit the fault. Because they relied on Baal for prosperity, the crops will fail (v 2); there will be nothing to bring as an offer-

ing, even if they seek Yahweh (v 5; cf. 5:6). To save their lives they will eat vile food (v 4a). The land itself will be devastated and depopulated (v 6). The people will be expelled (v 3) or will flee (v 6a), taking refuge in Assyria (v 3b) and Egypt (vv 3b, 6a). There they will eat defiled food (v 3b), and die (v 6a). The token of rejection of Yahweh is contempt for his prophet. Although the latter is the guardian of the country (v 8a), he is opposed and dismissed as a madman (vv 7b, 8b).

9:1a. In the MT this verse opens with a long, prose-like clause, with no apparent parallelism. LXX detected poetry, and either read '*al-tāgēl*, or treated the MT form *gyl* as an infinitive absolute used as a jussive, as we do. This reading is supported by the fact that the verbs *śmḥ* and *gyl* are often parallel in the Bible (Humbert 1958:111–145). Important new evidence for the correlation comes from the Tell Siran Bottle Inscription (Zayadine and Thompson 1973), where the sequence is the inverse of that here. The form *gyl* cannot be an imperative, because that form is never negated. The infinitive absolute is usually negated with *lō'*, not '*al*, even if used as an imperative. The MT pointing could be an artificial way of avoiding such complications by identifying *gyl* as a noun and '*l* as a preposition.

MT derives some support from Job 3:22, where a similar construction occurs: *haśśĕmēḥîm 'ĕlê-gîl*, "those who rejoice unto excitement," a phrase which students of Job have found difficult to accept. It is curious that, in spite of the support that Hos 9:1 and Job 3:22 give to each other, both texts are commonly emended, and in different ways! If Hos 9:1 has been adjusted to Job 3:22, it is strange that the scribes did not make a more obvious correction; the evidence of LXX is that it was made in some manuscripts.

Even if the MT were retained out of respect for that tradition, and because it represents the more difficult reading, this would not deny that the roots *śmḥ* and *gyl* have their usual connotations in association with each other. Humbert's study has shown that both are associated with the cult in the great majority of their occurrences. This agrees with what follows, for Hos 9:1–9 is saturated with the language of ceremonial religion. Here Israel is reprimanded for its joyful participation in the cult. This must be a pagan cult, and since the concern is the production of grain and wine, it is more likely to be a Canaanite fertility cult, rather than the Assyrian influences found in c 8, which were of political value on the international scene. The excitement here is the festive mood of harvest and vintage. For this they will be excluded from Yahweh's cult (v 5) and expelled from his realm (v 3). For a different understanding of *śmḥ,* see Greenfield (1959). On *gyl,* see Andersen (1976a:109).

peoples. In 8:12, Israel is associated with "foreigners." The rejoicing in 9:1 is condemned because it imitates "the nations."

been promiscuous. This is national, not personal. The *Qal* is usually used of females; here it is masculine for the sake of grammatical agreement with "Israel."

away from. Hosea uses other idioms with this verb: "from behind" (1:2); "from under" (4:12). This is the only place where the idiom *zny m'l* is found. *Zny min-* is used in Ps 73:27. The choice of the preposition seems to be influenced by some balancing phrase; *'al* recurs in the next line.

1b. *made love.* Since *'āhabtā* is parallel to *zānîtā* they are mutually defining; the second verb means "you made love," not simply "you loved." The motive was not avarice ("you loved the pay") but venery ("you made love, and were paid for it"); the charge of Ezek 16:33 may be involved. The intransitive use of *'āhab* is rare, but not impossible; cf. 4:18. In Jer 8:2, "love" is first in a series of verbs describing religious devotion to rival gods.

a fee. In 2:14 the children, probably, were called the *'etnâ,* the pay for services rendered. *'Etnān,* used here, seems to be a variant; it, unlike the other, is found elsewhere, to designate the fee paid to a prostitute. No difference in meaning has been established between them. In view of what follows here, it is worth noting that the *'etnān* could not be brought as an offering to Yahweh (Deut 23:19); cf. v 4bB.

threshing floor. The MT reads "every threshing floor of grain." We transfer the word "grain" to another line, holding the word in suspense until "and must" completes the common phrase. Although sexual activity is not described in what follows, it is possible that harvest festivities would be accompanied by promiscuous recreation at the work site itself. This is well-attested in the ancient world, and the Bible has examples of such customs at vintage (Judges 21, see Boling 1975:294) and harvest (Ruth 3). Both stories seem to have been whitewashed, but it does not take much imagination to work out what usually occurred on such occasions. If we believe the innocence of the sexual love in Ruth 3 (and there certainly must have been celebrations of harvest consistent with the moral standards of Yahwism), there was always the danger that the people would revert to the Canaanite norm. This is what seems to have happened on a grand scale in the time of Hosea. The use of both *kl,* "all, every," and the plural "threshing floors" supports this impression; cf. I Sam 23:1; Joel 2:24. The question arises whether threshing floors in the country became rustic shrines by their being dedicated to such activities, and whether statues or symbols of the gods were exhibited there.

2. There are several problems in this verse. There are both a masculine plural ("them," the object of the verb in v 2a), and feminine singular referent ("her/it" in v 2b); the latter is especially difficult, since the verbs

in v 1 are masculine. It has been explained as an effect of the word "Israel," or an anticipation of *'rṣ,* "land," in v 3.

2a. *Grain.* We transfer the last word of v 1 to v 2. "Grain and must and oil" are a conventional trio (2:10); sometimes the first two alone occur (2:11). For the sake of this pair we have linked "grain" to "must." "Threshing floor and wine vat" are also a pair (Deut 15:14; 16:13; II Kings 6:27), corresponding to freshly harvested grain and new vintage wine. In Deut 28:39 the threat is made that no wine will be made and this is evidently what v 2 is talking about; cf. Hos 2:11.

nourish. There does not seem to be any close connection between *yir'ēm* here and in 4:16, despite the identity of root. There is also a problem of number: in the traditional understanding the supposed subject, floor and vat, is plural and the verb is singular. This suggests that God is the subject of the verb in v 2 and the nouns are instrumental or "accusatives of specification." The subject is supplied.

them . . . it. Since 9:1 is addressed to Israel as "you," there is no immediate antecedent for "them" or "it/her." If c 9 picks up the themes of cc 1–3 (and the verb *zny* suggests this), then "she" and "they" could be the mother and the children once more, both standing for Israel. Some manuscripts and versions read "them" in both lines, but this is the result of leveling, and not the original reading. In the old orthography, the 3 m s suffix would have been written with a *he* (rather than *waw*); that reading would resolve the problem of *bh,* not *yr'm.*

2b. *fail. Khš* usually means "to deceive," but in Hab 3:17 a similar idea is met: *kiḥēš ma'ăśēh-zayit,* "The olive crop has failed." Elsewhere, *khš b* means "to act deceitfully against," not "to fail in/from." The *Pi'el* here is used causatively. The subject is supplied.

3. As already shown, this verse is a tricolon in which the first line states the general fact while the following bicolon spells out the particulars, giving the antithesis: the people of Israel will no longer dwell in Yahweh's land, but elsewhere.

3a. *Yahweh's land.* This is the only place where this phrase occurs in the Hebrew Bible and it is difficult to work out what Hosea meant by it. In Jeremiah, Yahweh calls the country "my land" (Jer 2:7; 16:18; cf. Ezek 38:16). In the Jeremiah examples, *'rṣy* is parallel to *naḥălātî,* "my estate." Even if the phrase is an innovation in Hosea, the idea is ancient. Exod 15:17 already speaks of Yahweh's *hr nḥltk* "(your) mountain property," a phrase which originally referred to the mythological abode of the god, so important in Canaanite theology, which was historicized in Mosaic Yahwism (Clifford 1972). Although restricted to Sinai at first, the phrase was extended or transferred to the land of Canaan, understood to be Yahweh's personal property, on which his people settled as tenants. A designation in Josh 22:19 could be transitional between **har naḥălat yhwh*

(Exod 15:17; cf. II Sam 20:19; 21:3) and *'ereṣ yhwh:* Cisjordan is there called *'ereṣ 'ăḥuzzat yhwh.* It contrasts with Transjordan, which is considered "unclean" (cf. v 3b) because it has no legitimate altar, and the tabernacle is not there. Furthermore, Joshua 22 resembles Hosea 8 in branding the construction of unauthorized altars as rebellion against Yahweh. The phrase "Yahweh's land" has deep historical meaning, and refers to the whole territory claimed by the deity and not to some specific political entity of Hosea's day. It would be strange if Hosea were restricting the term to one portion of Israelite territory. If the Exodus is to be reversed by expelling Israel from "Yahweh's land," the threat must include Judah as well as Ephraim, even though only Israel and Ephraim are mentioned in 9:1–9. The mention of Gibeah (v 9) brings in the notion of all Israel. The return to Egypt of Ephraim does not necessarily mean that Judah can now remain as the true Israel in the promised land.

3b. *return. Wšb* can be taken in either of two ways. According to the MT and in line with 8:13, it designates "returning to Egypt," a common note in Hosea. The parallel with *yēšĕbû* in v 3a suggests reading a form of *yšb:* "They will not live in Yahweh's land, but they will live in Egypt." So the LXX. Since there is no preposition in the MT, if *šb* means "return," *'el* must be understood (cf. 3:5); if *šb* means "dwell," then *b* in both phrases (*bĕ'ereṣ yhwh, bĕ'aššûr*) can be supplied by double duty. There is no morphological objection to translating *wšb* as "and he will dwell," and Ps 23:6 shows that no emendation is needed. However, the absence of a preposition after *šb* is no hindrance to the translation "return," as 8:13 shows.

Egypt. This has its parallel "Assyria" in the following line, but "Ephraim" has no parallel, and returning to Egypt resembles eating unclean food in Assyria only with regard to being in a foreign country. The use of the singular verb for "Ephraim" in v 3b raises the question of whether some other subject goes with the plural verbs in v 3a and v 3bB. It seems likely that we should associate Israel, mentioned in v 1, with Ephraim in the common experience of exile and life in a foreign country.

unclean food. The statement that Israel is defiled has already been made twice (5:3; 6:10), each time in connection with sexuality. Verses 3 and 4 are the only other places where Hosea uses the root *ṭm'*, and the connection with promiscuity may be made in v 1. Here there is a larger setting of cult practices; attention is given to the use of bread and wine, perhaps related to the flesh eating and the *zibḥê habhābay* of 8:13, which caused Yahweh displeasure. As punishment for defiling the land where they ate pleasant fruit (Jer 2:7), they will be compelled to eat unclean food in Assyria. What they have now eaten has defiled them (v 4aB); they have become indistinguishable from the heathen (8:12b). They might as well live with them and follow their ways of life in another land, not Yahweh's.

Amos 7:17 has a similar threat of expulsion to die (cf. v 6a) in a polluted land.

4. The first bicolon indicates that Israel will no longer worship Yahweh in the usual way, either because the cult is suspended (3:4) or because the people are excluded from it. The choice between these alternatives depends in part on whether "the house of Yahweh" in v 4bB means the country (parallel to v 3a) or the temple, as the cultic language would suggest. The difference is slight. The strong and repeated negations suggest something more drastic than Isa 1:12–17: religion there is active, but unacceptable, though amends can still be made by doing justice. Our text suggests an act of Yahweh, more positive than the withdrawal of 5:6. There they sought him, but he was not to be found. Here it is not that the offerings have ceased because people have neglected or deserted the cult; rather Yahweh has banned it.

4a. *pour out*. There is little in the Hebrew Bible about libations of wine, or, indeed, of liquids of any sort (see e.g. de Vaux 1967:291–302; cf. II Sam 23:16). The listing of wine before solid foods is unusual; "food and drink" is the usual sequence. The order here secures chiasm with "grain . . . and must" in v 2. The suffix "their" on "sacrifices" applies also to "must."

bring. The root *'rb,* "to enter," well attested in Ugaritic, is here used in the *Hipʻil,* as noted by van der Weiden (1966), Dahood (1970:47), and Kuhnigk (1974:114–115), who cites an offering scene in Keret in which *'rb* and *dbḥ* (= Hebrew *zbḥ*) are both used. (*UT* Krt 159–160). Jer 6:20 is similar to our text.

Indeed, the food. The MT has literally "like bread/food." The syntax of the clause is not clear, and the meaning of some parts is not certain. The MT "like food" is obscure and, in context, it is more likely that "food" is to be taken literally rather than in a simile. The problem can be resolved by reading asseverative *kî* for the preposition of the MT; this improves the parallelism with v 4bA. If food is part of the situation, it provides a good referent for the suffixed object of "those who eat *it*" in the next line.

idols. The interpretation of the line depends on the meaning of *'ônîm.* *'Ôn* means "vigor, wealth," and it has a masculine plural; the singular occurs in 12:4,9. This word does not make sense here. There is a root *'ny,* "to mourn," from which *'ônîm* may be derived. (It may occur in Deut 26:14 if the *mem* is to be read twice; it would balance "dead" in the verse, which also contains the word *ṭāmēʼ* and deals with the misuse of food dedicated to Yahweh.) If the word occurs here, the "food of mourners" would be food used in a mourning ritual (Pope 1977:210–229). The form here, however, is probably a plural of *'āwen,* "wickedness." The context makes it likely that another aspect of current Israelite religious practice is here condemned: idol feeding.

It is possible that *leḥem 'ônîm* is intended to parody *leḥem pānîm*, "the bread/food of (Yahweh's) presence," spread out in array before him. *'Ônîm* then may be the name of this rival god; and "their bread" in 4bA refers to the bread of such idols. We have identified *'āwen* as "idols" in, e.g., 12:12. *'Ônîm* may be another of Hosea's artificial plurals designed to imitate *'ĕlōhîm;* we may compare *leḥem hā'ăṣābîm* in Ps 127:2, reading Hosea's word for "idols" with Jerome and recently Dahood (1970:223). The food was offered to idols; this explains why it is defiled (cf. I Corinthians 8–10).

All who eat it. The connection with v 3bB has been pointed out. In Jer 2:3, all who eat Israel (Yahweh's holy thing) become guilty. Here, however, Israel forfeits its holiness (*qōdeš* and *ṭm'* are opposites) by eating what is forbidden.

4b. *for their life's preservation.* Since the lines before and after this one make good sense, the construction *kî-laḥmām lĕnapšām* is without obvious attachment. *Kî* cannot mean "because," since the line does not give a recognizable reason for either what precedes or what follows. The rhyme and the repetition suggest that the two lines about bread are parallel, but this does not clarify much. If the final *mem* in *lḥmm* were taken as enclitic, one troublesome pronoun could be eliminated. The phrase *lĕnapšām* means "for the preservation of their life" (Lam 1:19; 2:12). Verse 4 could mean that the only sustenance available is ritually unclean food, and to save their lives the people are forced to eat it (cf. Ps 78:18).

The most horrifying god-food is child sacrifice, and Hosea makes it clear that this practice had entered Israel in his time (see the NOTE on 5:2a and cf. 8:13 and Ps 106:34–40). Yahweh's anger against the people was aroused because they became *unclean* by their actions, and were promiscuous in their deeds. These deeds included sacrificing their sons and daughters "to the *idols* of Canaan" (Ps 106:38). "They poured out innocent blood" (Ps 106:38; cf. Hos 8:5), and "polluted the land with blood" (Ps 106:38; Hos 4:2).

There may be a connection between v 4bA and v 6bA. While *mḥmd,* "precious thing," can refer to the Israelite's supreme delight in the temple (Lam 1:7; Isa 64:10; II Chron 36:19), this seems to be a later development. Usually it refers to a wife (Ezek 24:16 — the term requires no further definition), lover (Cant 5:16), children (Ezek 24:21,25; Lam 1:11; 2:4; cf. Hos 9:16), or wife and children together (I Kings 20:6; cf. Joel 4:5). In I Kings 20 silver and gold are mentioned as well, which supports the collocation of "best" and "silver" in v 6bA; although our explanation is based on this collocation, we should present another line of argumentation. Eating ritually unclean food was not a major offense. The person was contaminated, but simple rituals of purification were available to rectify the fault. Eating blood was different. The exceptional attention paid to it arises from the sacral character of blood, a holy substance reserved for expiatory rites. The solemnity of Hosea's language shows that he has in mind a defilement of the utmost gravity, perhaps child sacrifice again.

Yahweh's house. Though there is no preposition, *byt* is often used for *bbyt;* the preposition may be lost by dissimilation to zero before labials. Of more interest is the sense of the word "house." The cultic language in the text suggests a temple, though not the temple of Solomon, since at this time there were many shrines to Yahweh. Nor is it likely that "house" is used collectively to refer to all the Yahweh shrines, since Hosea has no apparent interest in such structures.

Because of the parallelism with "Yahweh's land" in v 3a, it is possible that "Yahweh's house" refers to the promised land as Yahweh's abode or territory. This usage is not common, but is found elsewhere in the Bible.

This problem could be resolved if we knew who will not come into Yahweh's house. The nearest noun is "food," and if this is not to come into Yahweh's house, the statement parallels v 4a, and points to the exclusion of defiled offerings from worship. Persons, not things, however, are the usual subjects of "to come"; the *Hip'il* would be used for bringing things into the house. Since the usage in Hebrew is consistent — people enter, things are brought — the translation "it shall not come" (*RSV*) is erroneous. There are rules for banning persons, not things, from entering the *qĕhal-yhwh,* that is, from participating in the cult, in e.g. Deuteronomy 23, where unclean gentiles are banned from entering the assembly (cf. Lam 1:10). Since the Israelites have become foreigners (8:12b), they now come under this ban. In II Chron 23:6 the same idiom is used of the eligibility of priests to lead in worship; if this applies, Hosea is continuing his proscription of priests from cc 4–5. The passage seems, however, to refer to the nation as a whole. The singular number of the verb, which contrasts with the plural of *yēšĕbû* in v 3a, to which it is otherwise parallel, is a further problem. It does not allow the paraphrase "all who eat the bread of idols have defiled themselves (and so) (they) cannot enter the house of Yahweh," unless *kōl* is considered the singular subject of *yābô'.*

It is more likely that Ephraim is the singular subject, and the referent of the plurals in the rest of the verse is different (the people). This break in number, and the parallel to v 3a, also suggests that "house" here has the meaning of estate rather than shrine. Sacral associations are not necessarily excluded, since Yahweh's land is his dwelling. In the most general sense the cult will no longer be performed in Yahweh's "house." In Ps 68:13 *nĕwat-bayit* means "pasture lands," and, in Akkadian, temple lands in the open country are called *bīt-ilanī* (*CAD* B:287). That a territory rather than a shrine is meant is confirmed by the contrast between the *byt* of Yahweh and Assyria (v 3b), where unclean food will be eaten. Israel is not excluded from the worship of Yahweh simply because they have nothing to eat but taboo food; that could be remedied by bringing the right food. They are ejected from the land because they have themselves become polluted beyond remedy (Hos 5:3; 6:10). A person who takes part in the cult while in a state of *ṭāmē'*, "uncleanness," is excluded (Lev 7:20–21).

5. There is an abrupt change to second-person plural in this verse, the only occurrence of that person and number in vv 1–9. The questions here are rhetorical. There are other passages in which the interrogative *mh* is virtually negative. *Bammeh yiškāb* (Exod 22:26) is virtually a statement — "He will have nothing to sleep in." Hos 10:3b means, "The king can do nothing for us." Israel will have nothing to bring when the people assemble for Yahweh's festival. In spite of the involvement with paganism, there was still a desire to keep up the old Yahweh festivals as well, but this is now impossible. The reason must be sought in the surrounding text: either because their oblations are unclean and their land is devastated (v 6); or because they have been expelled (v 3).

If v 5 is actually negative, it is similar to v 1; the negative meaning of *mh* matches the prohibitive *'al*. Note also the three negations in v 4.

The reference to the *ḥag* in v 5 implies, at any rate, that the rejoicing banned in v 1 is the rejoicing that takes place in the festival; happiness in general is not meant. This exclusion from the Yahweh cult in all its aspects resembles 3:4.

5a. *festival*. The parallelism of *mô'ēd* and *ḥag* points to the seasonal festivals in which the round of the agricultural year was celebrated. The use of singular *ḥag* is odd since the word applies almost exclusively to the three great annual pilgrimage festivals: Unleavened Bread, Weeks, and Booths. There are few places (Exod 34:25 is the only explicit one) where Passover is called a *ḥag*. In Exod 12:14 and 13:6, it is called a *ḥag lyhwh*, because of its association with Unleavened Bread. If any of the three festivals deserves the title of *the* major *ḥag* of Yahweh, it is Booths, which is often called *ḥag lyhwh*, or, simply "the festival." In view of the reference to Gibeah in v 9, the designation of the festivities at Shiloh as *ḥag-yhwh* in Judg 21:19 could be significant.

6. In Lev 26:30 the Israelites were warned that their carcasses would be dumped on the carcasses of their idols. Hosea sees the fulfillment of such a curse when the people and their gods come to a common end.

6a. *flee*. The perfect verb can be used proleptically (the prophetic perfect) or as an imperative (the precative perfect); after *kî-hinnēh* it is generally past tense. A description of an accomplished fact seems out of place in this threatening speech; a future or present tense fits better. Recognizing the idiom *hlk mn*, "to perish from," Dahood renders "They shall perish from violence" (Dahood 1978:176).

devastation. Emendation to "Assyria" (e.g. *RSV*) is not needed and has no textual support. It cannot be justified as providing a parallel with "Egypt," since "Egypt" has its own parallel in "Memphis." The remainder of the verse completes the picture of ruin begun here. The word *šōd* is a favorite of eighth-century prophets (e.g. Isa 13:6; 16:4); and later Jeremiah often uses it. Cf. also Joel 1:15; Isa 51:19; Jer 48:3; Hos 10:14.

The notion of flight to escape the coming devastation is expressed by *nws* or *brḥ*. The idiom here may mean to flee *because* (*min* sometimes has this meaning) destruction has made the land uninhabitable (cf. v 6b). The ruin (*šōd*) pronounced against Israel in 7:13 means the devastation of the cities (8:14). That only "tents" remain (v 6b) may be meant literally, although in archaizing and romantic language (e.g. Deut 16:7), Israelite urban settlements were called "tents." At any rate, ruin is complete when briers and thistles take over.

To say the people will go off because of such desolation is related to v 3a. Unlike the patriarchs, who descended to Egypt because of famine, these latter-day Israelite migrants will flee from the horrors of war (10:14).

will collect. Egypt will afford no refuge; the people will die and be buried there. This could be the reason why Israel will never come into Yahweh's house (v 4b); there will be no survivors. This was the fate of Jehoahaz (Jer 22:10–12; cf. Jeremiah 52). A collocation of *'sp,* "to collect," and *qbr,* "to bury," occurs in Jer 8:2 and 25:33; there are two important differences from our text. The first is the use of *'sp,* as in Hos 4:3, rather than *qbṣ.* The second is that the threat is negative: the Israelite leaders will not be gathered and buried, but left like dung on the surface of the ground, a more ignominious sequel to death than burial by foreigners. Ezekiel 39 describes the cleansing of the land after the eschatological battle by collecting and burying innumerable corpses. These passages do not clarify the exact meaning of *qbṣ:* is it used as a euphemism for killing or as a synonym for *'sp?*

The reference to Egypt has a sinister note, and the feminine verbs show that Egypt and Memphis are the subjects of the activity, and not just the location. The Israelites will not conduct their own burial rites. Even the patriarchs, though living in Egypt, could be taken back to Canaan for burial in the family cemetery; Joseph's bones were brought back in due time. This privilege will be denied the Israelites of the present generation. It will be their final defilement to be buried in a pagan cemetery.

This is the only instance in which the name of Memphis is spelled *mp;* elsewhere the spelling is *np.* Both of these differ from other ancient transliterations. The reference here is to the city's vast burial grounds and enormous pyramids and tombs. Memphis could stand for the whole country, as a capital city often does.

6b. *their silver things*. The line is obscure. It is isolated by the well-formed bicola that precede and follow it. The main associations of silver in Hosea are with idol-making (2:10; 8:4; 13:2). The associations of "precious" are usually with beloved wives and children, as noted above. If it were not for the context, the words would suggest the offering of children to silver idols.

The root *ḥmd* describes things grievously mourned when they are lost (Amos 5:11; Isa 32:12). The root is often used of choice land or of Yahweh's favorite mountain. In some occurrences it is linked with precious metals. In Joel 4:5 "my silver and my gold" is paralleled by "my precious things."

LXX did not recognize *maḥmad lĕkaspām* as a phrase. It used clause boundaries which yield the translation: "Mop shall gather them; *mḥmd* shall bury them"; *kspm* then goes with the following words.

If *l* is referential, "a precious thing related to their silver" could mean a treasure bought with silver (cf. *miqnat-kesep*—Gen 17:12,27; Exod 12:44, referring to slaves). We follow *RSV*, which takes *lkspm* as attributive ("their precious things [*sic*] of silver"). The preposition could also be possessive.

The only firm point in all this seems to be that Hosea elsewhere associates silver with the idol; cf. Ps 135:15. "For their silver (idol)" here could contrast with "for Yahweh" in v 4. Note also the rhyme with *lĕnapšām* there.

We propose that the line goes with the opening of v 6a and refers to the flight from destruction. A fuller explanation may lie hidden in the difficult passage *UT* 51.v.77–80, which has the phrases *mid ksp, mḥmd ḫrṣ*, and *ksp wḫrṣ*.

dispossess. The bicolon about nettles and thorns balances the bicolon about Egypt and Memphis. *Yîrāšēm* rhymes with the last two verbs in v 6a, and all of them have the same object. People, rather than things, are the usual object of *yrš*, which most often describes taking over some nation's territory after conquest. This fits in with the general picture in this section of the expulsion of the Israelites from Yahweh's land.

The bicolon in v 6b has its own intricacy. It means, "Thorny weeds will dispossess them from their tents." *Qimmôš* and *ḥôaḥ*, variously translated, are probably synonyms; no exact botanical identification has been achieved. If, contrary to our reading, two distinct clauses are recognized, the second has no verb.

> Briers will take over their inheritance;
> Thistles (will be) in their encampments.

This verse confirms the authenticity of *šōd*, "devastation," in v 6a. When weeds grow freely, it is not because the land has been conquered and occupied by foreigners (but see 8:7bB) but because it has been rendered uninhabitable. There is a further nuance in the root *yrš*. The present owners will not hand on their heritage. It is like a fulfillment of the curse of Deut 28:42, that insects will take over (*yrš*) the farmlands. In Isa 34:11 various kinds of birds do this, and *qimmôš wāḥôaḥ* are mentioned in Isa 34:13.

7. The construction of this verse is complex, and needs to be viewed together with that of v 8.

7a *bā'û yĕmê happĕquddâ*
   bā'û yĕmê haššillūm

7b   *yēdĕ'û yiśrā'ēl*
   'ĕwîl hannābî'
   mĕšuggā' 'îš hārûaḥ
     'al rōb 'ăwōnĕkā
     wĕrabbâ maśṭēmâ

8a *ṣôpeh 'eprayim 'im-'ĕlōhāy nābî'*

8b *paḥ yāqôš 'al-kol-dĕrākāyw*
   maśṭēmâ bĕbêt 'ĕlōhāyw

The first three bicola set out above are marked by the usual devices of repetition and parallelism. The connections of the remaining lines are less clear; it is likely that references to Israel and Ephraim are related. The syntax of v 8 is particularly tortuous. The repetition of important words, like "prophet" and "hostility" suggests that there are linkages through the whole, but not necessarily between adjacent units. Two major themes are interwoven: the theme of sin and punishment, completed in v 9, and the theme of animosity toward a prophet.

7a. *have come.* This could be a prophetic perfect, especially in view of the imperfect verbs in v 9b, where *pqd* is used again.

days. The repetition of the plural in v 7 matches the repetition of the singular in v 5. The statements contrast. Instead of the joyful days of festival, there will be the terrifying days of judgment. For a related idiom, see Isa 7:17.

7b. *know.* What is Israel to know? What follows directly is not likely to be the answer: "Let Israel know (that) the prophet is a fool." A more remote connection, with v 9, seems likely. Israel will find out what is stated in vv 7a and 9b, where the inclusion with *pqd* makes the link; otherwise Israel will realize that they are defiled.'

prophet. The two clauses in parallel here are excellent examples of verbless clauses with a definite subject and an indefinite predicate. Who is "the prophet"? One individual is intended, and the only prophets we know about in the situation are Hosea himself and the prophet mentioned in passing in connection with the priest in 4:5. If it is the same prophet in both places, then some opponent of Hosea (perhaps a prophet of Baal) is being derided. It is more likely that here Hosea is recording his own experience of hostile rejection, like that in Amos 7. There is no reason to believe that the taunts were invented for Hosea; II Kings 9:11 suggests that they are old bywords.

iniquity. The syntax of the two bicola in v 7b is probably the same. The iniquity lines are clauses, continuing the denunciation of the prophet. Phrases such as those *RSV* translates ("your great iniquity"; "great hatred") would have the attributive adjectives after the nouns. The preposition *'al* must accordingly be recognized as a conjunction meaning "because." It, and the pronoun suffix, must both be recognized as doing double duty. Note the phrase *mērōb* '*ōnîm* in Isa 40:26.

8. The verse presents several difficult problems. Is the watchman Ephraim or the prophet? Does the word "prophet" belong with v 8a (*BH³*) or with v 8b (MT)? What is the difference between "my God" and "his god"? Is "the house of his god" intended to contrast with "the house of Yahweh" (v 4)? Does "house" mean "shrine" or "country"?

8a. *prophet*. The word "prophet" comes at the boundary between two clauses. The MT takes *ṣōpeh* as an absolute; thus, "Ephraim is a watchman"; the phrase "with my God" is a modifier of the predicate. Discontinuity in the predicate of a verbless clause is quite acceptable. The difficulty lies in the meaning: a watchman with God has no obvious function; and it is hard to see how Ephraim could be such. The MT places "prophet" at the beginning of the next clause, and either the prophet is the bird snare by all his (Ephraim's?) paths; or the prophet is a person who has a snare by all his own paths. The indefiniteness of the noun "prophet" is inexplicable, and makes it difficult to identify the word as the subject of either clause.

If *ṣph* is read as construct, a more reasonable clause is gained: "The prophet is a watchman of Ephraim with my God." If the participle were verbal, we would expect the subject of the verbless clause to precede the predicate; the point is slight. Since this is a positive assertion about the prophet's legitimate role, it could be a rejoinder to the slander of v 7b. In that case, who is speaking? Does "my God" indicate that Hosea is speaking?

This is not entirely satisfactory. While the prophet often figures as the people's guardian, he can also adopt a hostile role, looking after Yahweh's interests. The protective role of the prophet as sentinel is set out in Ezek 3:16–21 and 33:1–9: his task is to watch for approaching enemies, and blow the *šōpār* (cf. Hos 5:8 and 8:1). Note also Jer 6:17. MT's extraordinary phrase "with my God" places the prophet over against the people, and the rest of the verse seems to cast the prophet in a threatening posture. Compare the sarcastic use of "watchman" in Isa 56:10. The situation here is the reverse: in spite of the fact that the prophet is looking after Ephraim on behalf of God, he is in danger from the people whose welfare he seeks. He encounters animosity in the house of his God, a bird snare is beside all his (the prophet's) paths.

In Hos 5:1b the word *paḥ* is used in a way that is not obviously related to this passage despite the use of *'mq* and *šḥt/ṭ* in both following verses respectively.

my God. The only likely referent of the pronoun is the prophet. The name "Yahweh" is used several times in this speech, which, however, does not seem to be an oracle. The use of the phrase again in v 17 suggests that Yahweh is not their God (cf. 2:25). The idiom "with my (etc.) God" implies a relationship of influence, appropriate for a prophet.

8b. *trap.* In Ps 91:3 the phrase *paḥ yāqûš*, "the trap of a fowler," occurs (Dahood 1968:330). The metaphor has diverse associations. In Josh 23:13, the surviving Canaanites are said to be a *paḥ*. In Isa 8:14, Yahweh is a *paḥ* for the house of Israel. This diversity leaves undetermined the role of the prophet as victim or trap. Since animosity is parallel to iniquity in v 7b, and parallel to the trap in v 8b, the word is probably intended to describe hostility against the prophet.

hostility. The repetition of this rare word suggests that it occupies an important place in the argument. The hostility of the people toward the prophet is expressed in their slander that he is insane (v 7). The same root is used in Job 16:9 to describe what Job feels is God's implacable but groundless grudge against him.

Hos 9:7b–8 refers to the derogation of a true prophet of Yahweh, presumably Hosea himself. The experiences of other prophets show that their unpopular messages brought only obloquy (cf. Matt 23:29–37; Acts 7:51–53).

9a. *deeply defiled.* Another example of Hosea's use of two verbs in sequence without a coordinating conjunction to express one complex idea. A similar usage is met in Isa 31:6 ("they made deep apostasy"); cf. Isa 30:33. Here *he'mîqû* is used as a kind of auxiliary with *šiḥētû*. In Hos 5:2 the verb is preceded by the noun *šaḥăṭâ;* the two passages should not be normalized to each other, as *t* and *ṭ* are not readily confused in Hebrew.

Verse 9 sums up the whole speech. Israel is unchanged. The sins of the present recapitulate the worst sins of the past. They will bring the same kind of retribution.

Gibeah. Here an outrage was committed "the like of which had never been, and had never been seen, since the Israelites came up from the land of Egypt" (Judg 19:30); Hosea returns to this event in 10:9. After Gibeah one outrage led to another; a sexual crime led to a bloody civil war. In saying the days of Gibeah have come again, Hosea may have in mind the internecine strife of the last days of the Israelite monarchy. Although it is in the third person, the accusation of v 9a matches that in v 1 in the second person. The outcome of the atrocity at Gibeah was that one tribe was virtually liquidated. This suggests that the punishment threatened in v 9b will take the form of carnage on the same scale, just as Hosea threatens the house of Jeroboam with a bloodbath as thorough as the one his ancestor Jehu had meted out to Ahab's family (1:3). Yet the Gibeah incident as recorded in Judges 19–21 was not simply a disaster: it was one of the few occasions in the period of the judges when the tribes banded together to extirpate immorality, even though it meant destroying one of the tribes when the affair escalated into warfare.

9b. This bicolon is identical with one in 8:13b except for the conjunctions. Like that verse, it marks the end of a unit. It completes the unit of vv 7–9, which begins and ends with the root *pqd*, and the section of vv 1–9. This is no time for rejoicing; the time of retribution has come (v 7).

XVII. THE SPIRITUAL HISTORY OF ISRAEL: BAAL PEOR AND GILGAL
(9:10–17)

Past and present

9:10a O Israel, like grapes
>> I found in the wilderness
>> I discovered your forebears
>> like a fig tree's best yield in its first season.

10b They came to Baal Peor.
>> They dedicated themselves to Shame.
>> They became disgusting like the one who loved them.

11a O Ephraim, like a bird their Glory will fly away.

Curse and indictment

11b No childbirth. No gestation. No conception.

12a Even if they raise children,
>> I will bereave them before maturity.

12b Yes! Woe to them also, when I turn from them.

13a I saw Ephraim as in that place, by the Rival—
>> [a fig tree] planted in a meadow

13b —Ephraim indeed brought his children to the Slayer.

The Prophet's prayer

14a Give them, Yahweh! What will you give?

14b Give them miscarrying wombs and dry breasts!

Curse and indictment

15a Because of all their evil in Gilgal
>> indeed there I came to hate them.

15b Because of the wickedness of their deeds,
>> I will expel them from my house.
>> I will never love them again.
>> All their princes are rebels.

16a Ephraim is smitten.

Their root has dried up.
They will never produce fruit.
16b   Yet even if they do have children
I will murder the darlings of their womb.

The prophet's prediction and the final curse
17a   My God will cast them off
because they did not obey him.
17b   They will be wanderers among the nations.

NOTES

9:10–17. The bounds of this unit are more clearly marked externally than internally, i.e. the end of the preceding unit and the onset of the following one are clearer than the beginning and ending of vv 10–17 as a section. The name "Israel" is often present in the opening statement of a unit, as here (cf. 9:1; 10:1,9), and also at the end. While it does not occur in v 17, there is a note of finality in the closing words, and such a threat often ends a unit (cf. 8:13; 9:9).

Many of the ideas and much of the vocabulary in vv 10–17 are typical of Hosea, and continue themes already developed. Side by side with these are new words, such as *śûrî* (v 12b) and *ṣôr* (v 13a). Several threads of thought are interwoven. Sometimes they appear in fragmentary phrases, such as "planted in a meadow" in v 13a, which do not fit their immediate context, but which have links elsewhere: i.e. a pleasant description of a well-tended tree, related to the imagery of vv 10 and 16. In v 13, between these points, we have a fleeting glimpse of a tree, but otherwise vv 11–15 talk about other matters.

The unit talks about Israel (v 10) and Ephraim (vv 11,13,16). Both are nations of Hosea's time. The point made is that the national character, foreshadowed at the outset by the people's behavior at Baal Peor (v 10), persists in later times, and has more recently been expressed by something that happened at Gilgal (v 15a). A distinction between Israel and Ephraim is not clearly maintained throughout the unit.

According to Numbers 25, the evils committed at Baal Peor were cultic and sexual. They arose through joining in an idolatrous cult, ascribed to Moab and Midian. According to Ps 106:28, they ate human sacrifices (or sacrifices for the dead, if *mtym* is construed in that fashion). In a more general way Ps 106:34–39 discusses child sacrifices offered to "the idols of Canaan." It would seem, then, that around the memory of Baal Peor, which continued to trouble Israel's conscience (Josh 22:17), were gathered the worst aspects of the religion of Israel's neighbors. The crowning horror was when Ephraim brought his children to the Slayer (v 13b). There is no evidence that child sacrifice was performed at Peor. Psalm 106, Numbers 25, and Joshua 22 are alert to the dangers of the Transjordanian location, but say nothing about child sacrifice. Hosea does not tell us what he thought happened at Baal Peor, but v 10 expresses his great abhorrence of it.

The rationale of child sacrifice, in particular of the firstborn, is rooted in apotropaic rituals of dim antiquity, designed to ensure the production and survival of further offspring. This principle is found in biblical legislation assigning the firstborn to God, and laying on the parents the responsibility for the child's redemption. Such emphasis on the necessity of redeeming the life of the firstborn presupposed the practice of human sacrifice, which is confirmed by Ezekiel in an appalling statement about the law of God and its misapplication in the sacrifice of children (Ezek 20:26,31). It shows that the Israelites understood well the ultimate background of their treatment of the firstborn (cf. Genesis 22). Yahweh's punishment of such sacrifice has an effect opposed to the intended one: efforts to have children will be frustrated at every stage.

This is one of the most pervasive of the pseudo-sorites which dominate the section. Just as a flourishing tree can be smitten, withered at the root (v 16) and produce no fruit, so there will be no conception, no gestation, no childbirth (v 11b). Even if there is conception, there will be miscarrying wombs (v 14b). If children are born, they will be killed (v 16b). They will starve because the mothers will have dry breasts (v 14b). And even if they are raised, the parents will be bereaved of their children (v 12a). The references to these many aspects of childbearing are scattered through the unit in an order that does not correspond to actual events. Three of the moments are listed in reverse chronological order in v 11b, but the whole is not arranged in any simple pattern. The passage in which this theme occurs (vv 11b–16) is symmetrically organized around the central prayer of the prophet, which is a curse calling down such punishment. This prayer (v 14) is flanked by two passages of equal length (vv 11b–13 have sixty-five syllables; vv 15–16 have sixty-five syllables).

This section, vv 11b–16b, begins with a small unit (vv 11b–12a) in which Yahweh pronounces his curse; the speech has twenty-eight syllables. It ends with a similar speech by Yahweh (v 16) which has twenty-seven syllables. The grammar of v 12a is the same as that of v 16b (a conditional clause followed by the consequence, in a consecutive future construction). In v 16b, *gam kî* indicates clearly that what follows must be connected with something similar that comes earlier.

These preliminary observations are enough to indicate that there is some coherence and balance in the unit. In most of the preceding units the dominating speaker is Yahweh himself, although there are some verses, or even whole units, which belong in the mouth of the prophet. In 9:10–17 the main speaker is clearly Yahweh (vv 10,12,13,15,16). Verses 14 and 17a are the words of the prophet, the first a prayer addressed to Yahweh, the second a concluding statement about "my God." Verse 11b goes with v 12a. Verse 11a is part of the divine speech; like the other statements about Ephraim, it is made by Yahweh.

The overall structure of the unit can be traced.

A   Opening historical statement by Yahweh (v 10)
B   Ephraim's comparable conduct (v 11a)
C   Yahweh's curse (vv 11b–12a)
D   The indictment (vv 12b–13)
E   The prophet's prayer (v 14)
D′   The indictment (v 15)
C′   Yahweh's curse (v 16)
B′   The prophet's final statement (v 17a)
A′   Israel's historical destiny (v 17b)

A and A′, and B and B′ are not as close in theme or structure as C and C′, and D and D′, and A′ and D′ are related. The grouping around the prophet's prayer, however, shows that an introverted structure has been realized, and highlights the central position of the prayer, which would otherwise interrupt the flow of discourse.

Unlike other units in Hosea, this one has little poetic texture. Few of the lines can be arranged in pairs to secure parallelism of the usual kind. The opening of v 10a can be construed as two long lines (or four short ones) with some parallelism ("like grapes" // "like first-ripe figs"; "I found" // "I discovered"); but the second line is long (nineteen syllables; five words). Verse 10b reads like narrative prose, with normal use of the consecutive past construction. The repetition of *tēn-lāhem* in v 14 secures some rhythm, but beyond that the parallelism is not developed.

9:10a. *Israel.* The pronoun on "your fathers" shows that Israel is being addressed. The object of *mṣ'ty* is probably the same as that of *r'yty* and is delayed until a climax at the end of the half-verse. It is also possible that Israel is the object; the use of third-person forms along with second-person forms is common in elevated speech, and the omission of *'t* before Israel, if it were the direct object, would not be remarkable.

grapes. The opening words of the verse are sometimes treated as if Israel were being compared to "wilderness grapes," a rare phenomenon; if grapes did manage to grow in the wilderness, there is no reason to believe that they would be particularly delectable. This treatment is not grammatically warranted, although the position of the verb is unusual. The wilderness is not the usual starting point for Yahweh's historical relationship with Israel, although it is the locale cited in Deuteronomy 32. The wilderness reference prepares for the focus on Baal Peor.

I found. The verb implies, not so much discovery as a result of search, as seizure: I picked, or gathered. The mention of grapes suggests Yahweh's pleasure in Israel, which was full of delight in the young love that Jeremiah (Jer 2:2–3) and Ezekiel (Ezek 16:6–14) remember so ardently. So also was Hosea's marriage good at the start.

I discovered. Literally, "saw, watched." The verb is repeated in v 13. Since Hosea refers to the Exodus from Egypt several times, affirming the election of Israel at that early stage (11:1), and talks about the patriarchal period, the statement here should not be taken as showing ignorance of the pre-Mosaic era, or precluding the older traditions. The wilderness is the starting point for the present speech because it so quickly became the scene of the deterioration in the relationship described in v 10b.

best yield. The phrase *kĕbikkûrâ bit'ēnâ bĕrē'šîtāh,* with its sonorous triple rhyme, makes the second line long. Some scholars wish to remove the last prepositional phrase as a gloss, especially as it does not supply a direct parallel to "in the desert." The parallelism would be better if there were no suffix, i.e. *bĕrē'šît,* "at first," at the beginning of the (covenant) relationship. Jer 2:3 gives the title *rē'šît* to Israel in this period. The word *rē'šît* can mean the first productive season of a tree; the whole phrase means the first ripe figs of a tree's first bearing season. There is something virginal about the emphasis here. The *bikkûrâ* is always a fig, and reckoned a delicacy; *tĕ'ēnê habbikkûrôt* are the choicest figs, and in Isa 28:4 *bikkûrâ* designates a fig at the peak of ripeness, to be eaten at once.

The vine and the fig tree are associated in 2:14. The inequality of the parallels, "grapes" // "first yield of a fig tree in its first season," draws attention to a phrase floating free farther along in this speech. Grapes grow on a *gepen,* which can be described as *šĕtûlâ* (e.g. Ezek 19:10). The phrase *šĕtûlâ bĕnāweh* (v 13), "planted in a meadow," is generally rejected as corrupt, and it does not fit the context of v 13. If it completes the picture of v 10a, as part of the simile, we are seconded in our conclusion that the desert is the location of Yahweh's discovery of Israel, not the location of the grapes.

10b. *They.* The emphatic pronoun is used often by Hosea to contrast the perfidy of the people with Yahweh's goodness. There is, however, no contrasting use of "I" in this speech, nor is there a second *hēmmâ* to match this one, as in 8:9 and 13.

Baal Peor. A place, not a god, named "the House of Baal Peor"; it refers to a place sacred to the god. Just who Baal Peor, "the Lord of Peor," was is not altogether clear, but he is not simply to be equated with the great Canaanite Baal. Peor most likely is just a place name (Josh 22:17), but there may be an etymological meaning as well. Hosea does not extract any meaning from the name. This Baal must be the god of the Midianites, Yahweh of Midian. This may help to explain the overlapping use of the name Baal in reference both to Yahweh and Hadad.

dedicated. The verb *nzr* is rare. The institution of Nazirites seems to have been exclusively Yahwistic (de Vaux 1967:306–362). The verb, however, can describe a vow to idols (Ezek 14:7). Num 25:3,5 use *nṣmd,* "they yoked themselves." This difference in vocabulary suggests that Hosea is drawing on another tradition.

Shame. Bōšet is a derogatory name often substituted for Baal. Compare the discussion of *qālôn* at 4:7. The name is appropriate in view of the sexual acts involved in the Peor cult.

disgusting. Or "detestable." The usual interpretation, which we follow, makes this the complement of "your fathers." Compare Jeremiah's remark about the same development, when he says they went after "vanity" and became "vain" themselves (Jer 2:5). The contrast between *'ănābîm* and *šiqqûṣîm* is then like that between *śōrēq* and *bě'ušîm* in Isa 5:2.

Šiqqûṣîm may be another term for idols, the plural another imitation of *'ĕlōhîm.* Idols are to be treated with detestation (*šqṣ*—Deut 7:26). The statue of Zeus erected in the temple by Antiochus Epiphanes was called *šiqqûṣ měšōmēm* (and the like), "the abomination of desolation" (Dan 11:31; 12:11; cf. Dan 9:27; Hartman and Di Lella 1978:253, 299). In I Kings 11:5 Milkom (that is, Melek, "King," also called *mōlek* or *bōšet*) is called the *šiqqûṣ* of the Ammonites. Three gods are called *šiqqûṣ* in II Kings 23:3. Jeremiah (4:1; 7:30; 16:18; 32:34) calls the idols of his day *šiqqûṣîm.* It expresses the strongest revulsion. Hosea often omits prepositions; there is none with *bā'û,* for example. If the *l* of *labbōšet* does double duty, then vv 10bB and 10bC are synonymous parallels, and the latter means "and they came to belong to Disgusting."

the one who loved them. The placement of the word is uncertain. It may go with "Ephraim" which follows, in a simile, parallel to "like a bird," and rhyming with the next line. The form is difficult. It is neither the infinitive nor the participle; the reason for the MT pointing is unknown. The function of the suffix is ambiguous: it could be objective or subjective. Perhaps the best reading is the *nomen agentis* rendered here.

The MT may, however, indicate an infinitive: *le'ĕhōb* is found elsewhere only in Qoh 3:8, where it matches *liśnō'.* The thematic vowel in this m form (*o*) is different from that in the normal f (*a*). The stem *'uhb-* could be an abstract noun, attested only as the plural *'ŏhābîm,* "lovemaking" (Prov 7:18). This problem should be examined side by side with the unusual word *'ăhābîm,* "lovers," used with Ephraim in 8:9.

The preposition *k* makes its contribution to the ambiguity. It could be comparative, "like," or temporal, "when (they) loved them." *K* can also mark the complement in an equational clause. Hosea seems to be the only prophet who speaks of apostate Israelites as "loving" idols (cc 1–3) contrary to Deut 6:5. In this context "love" would mean religious allegiance, and to judge from Numbers 25, this could require sexual acts of devotion to the god.

11a. *bird*. In contrast to 7:11–12, there is no suggestion of silliness or being caught. Some interpreters understand '*ôp* to be collective — "birds." This is the only instance of the *Hitpolel* of '*wp,* and one would expect it to have an iterative meaning. Since this would not fit in with the usual interpretation of the Glory departing, which would be a decisive event, we leave the form of the stem unexplained.

Glory. In Hosea "Glory" can be a name for the pagan god that replaces Yahweh (4:7; 10:5). Here it seems to be Yahweh since it flies away under its own power. The departure of Yahweh ("their Glory" — I Sam 4:22) would be the supreme disaster (Ezekiel 8). Such a desertion may be described in v 12b; cf. 5:6b. However, since the context, e.g. v 11b, speaks of the loss of children, and the population is called "glory" in Isa 21:16, v 11a, if the imperfect verb is future, could be a preliminary threat (cf. v 17b).

Because of the singular verb, Ephraim could be the subject of "fly." In 8:9 Ephraim is a *pere' bôdēd*. A lonely bird is *ṣippôr bôdēd* (Ps 102:8). With a slight emendation we could read '*eprayim kā'ôp yit'ôpēp kĕbôdēd,* "Ephraim is like a bird; / he flies around like a solitary one." This, however, seems unnecessary.

11b. *No* (tris). We interpret *min* in these phrases as privative; cf. the Note on 6:6. It can hardly be spatial, unless the term "glory" refers to the population.

childbirth. The life process is traced backward here in another pseudo-sorites. Obviously, if there is no conception, there is no gestation or birth. Logic should not be given direct weight; see the discussion of 8:7. Working backward, the effect mounts to a climax: No birth / and no pregnancy / and no conception. The results of childbirth are dealt with further on in the speech. Verse 12a works the other way, through growth to bereavement; in v 16b bereavement follows birth before there is time for growth. If all these occasions were put together and spelled out fully, the curse would read as follows:

There will be no conception (v 11b).
Even if there is conception, there will be no gestation (v 11b).
　　　　　　　　　(Compare the miscarrying wombs of v 14b.)
Even if the women come to term, there will be no birth (v 11b).

Even if children are born, I will kill them (v 16b).
                    (Compare the dry breasts of v 14b.)
Even if they do survive and grow up, I will bereave their parents of
    them (v 12a).

Some scholars have tried to make the text more orderly by shuffling it
around. This ignores both the subtlety and the originality of the prophet.

gestation. Literally "belly"; the Hebrew term is often used as an equivalent of uterus to refer to the stage between conception and birth. Cf.
Job 3:10 and Hos 9:16b.

12a. *they*. The number changes to plural, perhaps to individualize the
fate of the people of Ephraim. The masculine shows that it is the whole
population, male as well as female.

before maturity. Literally "from man," here used to refer to adulthood.
A m form of the noun *'ădāmâ*, "land," is possible: "because of the land"
(Gen 5:29), "away from the land" (Hos 9:3–4), or "in the land" (Ezek
14:15). The phrase could also go with the three phrases in v 11b, to complete the series — "no human beings (at all)"; compare *RSV*, "till none is
left." This solution seems to be based on *mē'ādām* in Mic 2:12 and especially *mē'ên 'ādām*, "until there are no human beings left," a phrase often
used by Isaiah, Jeremiah, and Zephaniah (variant *mē'ên yôšēb*) to
describe total depopulation.

In I Sam 15:33 *škl min* is used comparatively: "Your mother will be
more bereaved than any other woman." Applied here this would mean
that Yahweh threatens to bereave the people more than any other people,
or even more than Adam himself, who lost two of his three sons.

Once more we must draw attention to the fact that it is Yahweh who
will do this. The verbs "to bereave" (v 12) and "to murder" (v 16) cannot be ameliorated. The theme of the ritual slaughter of children and its
reversal runs right through Hosea. According to Ezek 36:13, Israel gained
a reputation for bereaving the nation by devouring human beings; Yahweh
here binds himself to controlling that process.

12b. *Woe*. Compare 7:13.

when I turn from. No sure explanation of the unique form *bĕśûrî* is in
sight. The root *śwr* is probably an alternative spelling of *swr*, "to turn
aside." This phrase completes the idea of the departure of Yahweh as
Ephraim's glory (v 11). The form *wayyāśar* (Hos 12:5), which is associated with the etymology of "Israel," does not seem apposite here.
Wolff (1974:160) mentions several possibilities, preferring *śwr*, "to
depart." The expression *tāšûrî min*, "You shall come from" seems to occur in Cant 4:8, but its meaning there is much debated (Pope 1977:474).

13. Nearly every word in this verse constitutes a problem. All together,
they make translation and interpretation practically impossible.

13a. *as in that place*. The relative *'šr* here has its basic nominal sense, "place"; as often with *k*, the other preposition in a phrase (here *b*) is omitted. Ephraim now looks like the Israelites at Baal Peor.

by the Rival. That is, the current non-god, Baal. *Lĕṣôr* is usually emended, often to *ṣayid*, "food taken in the hunt," with LXX, with little increase in sense. The form could refer to the Baal of *ṣr*, "Tyre," slayer of children, or it could be read as *ṣûr*, "rock, deity." Note that "distress" (5:15) has this root; the root *ṣrr* describes an action done to an evil spirit in 4:19.

planted in a meadow. The meaning of this phrase is clear; the problem lies in its connection with the context. The epithet refers to vines or trees. Ps 128:3 compares children to planted olives; cf. Ps 92:14. This phrase goes back to v 10, and completes the description of the primordial grapes.

13b. *indeed brought*. Asseverative *l*, followed by a perfect verb, rather than an infinitive, which does not make a suitable predicate.

Slayer. Without an article, the participle seems to be a title. The word order allows for the rendering "Slayer of the children," which is not, however, appropriate. The direct object "his children" is probably delayed for climactic effect, since this is the end of the first part of Yahweh's speech.

14a. *Give them*. At this point the prophet interrupts the oracle with a prayer. It is not possible to reconstruct the dynamics of the situation, or even to identify the *Sitz-im-Leben*. At first Yahweh addressed Israel as "you," and then proceeded to talk *about* Ephraim and "they." The next part of Yahweh's address is indirect (vv 15,16), and the prophet speaks again in v 17. Here the prophet is not holding back the wrath of God by intercession as Amos (c 7) and Jeremiah (15:11) did. On the contrary, he is urging Yahweh to proceed with the extreme penalties, endorsing what Yahweh says in vv 12 and 16 about murdering the children.

The use of imperative verbs to issue peremptory commands to the deity is startling. The prayer is climactic: "Give them" is repeated after the vocative and a question, and only then is the horrifying object supplied. The petition for miscarrying wombs and dry breasts mocks and cancels the prayers for fecundity that went with the fertility rites.

What will you give. That Yahweh is the sole giver of all good was affirmed in 2:10,17. The question here can hardly be a pause in deliberation or a request for information. Purely rhetorical, it is more like the affirmation: "I know what you should give." Note the threefold repetition of "give." Since Ephraim gave his children to the Slayer (v 13b), Yahweh will no longer give them children to use in this way.

14b. *wombs*. The singular *reḥem*, "womb," and the dual *šādayim*, "breasts," are collective. These forms are used because the plurals could be interpreted as indefinite ("some wombs"). The *m* pronoun *lāhem* shows that the whole nation, and not just the females, are to be deprived of properly functioning reproductive organs.

15a. *all their evil.* The verb shows that Yahweh is speaking once more. The *'l* of the phrase after the main clause does double duty here. The phrase could also be handled as a verbless clause, "All their evil (is) in Gilgal." This is not likely; their evil was all over the country, not just in one spot. "I saw all their evil in Gilgal" contrasts with "I found (grapes) in the wilderness" (v 10). What began so beautifully now ends horribly. The testimony of Amos (4:4; 5:5) shows that Gilgal had become the center of wicked activities; and Hosea also refers to it in other passages (4:15; 12:12). In 7:2 Israel is accused of thinking that Yahweh had forgotten "all their evil," the same phrase as here. This is his reply: he has seen it. The word *rōa'*, "wickedness," repeats the root of *rā'ātām*, "evil." The word *m'llyhm*, "their doings," is the parallel of "their evil" in 7:2, just as here.

hate. The verb describes the hostility of a broken covenant relationship. Compare "enemy" in 8:3.

house. See the NOTES on "the house of Yahweh" at 9:4; here it is more likely to mean "domain" rather than shrine. The curses would suit a wife divorced for infidelity; hence a domestic setting is possible — "household" rather than estate.

15b. *love.* The antonym of "hate." It is more likely that it means "I will never love them again," rather than "I will no longer love them." Cf. 1:6.

princes. The term "princes" appears repeatedly through cc 5–8 and represents the royal court and party. This is the only mention of them in c 9. The phrase seems somewhat isolated in v 15. The attribute "stubborn, rebellious," echoes a point made in 4:16. The princes stand for the people as a whole, who are the principal subject of the whole speech, referred to everywhere as "they."

16a. *Ephraim.* Once more the verbs are singular. The verse returns to the image of the tree; the dry root is also a symbol of barrenness in child-bearing. The theme merges with that of the curses, and prepares for v 16b. The first two lines of v 16a are parallel and chiastic. The third line completes them, and also resembles the first line in v 16b. Note the rhyme of *ya'ăśûn* and *yēlēdûn,* with archaic durative endings.

smitten. The verb implies physical injury; cf. 6:1. The text may refer to the devastation described in v 6, where *maḥmad* also occurs.

never. Hosea is the only eighth-century minor prophet to use the negative *bl∼bly.* For the use of the verb "to make" to describe the production of crops, see the NOTES on 8:7.

fruit. This theme continues in 10:1.

16b. The similarity between v 16b and v 12a has been pointed out. The use of *gam,* "also," is a link.

darlings. See the discussion at 9:6.

womb. The same word as in v 11b. The masculine suffix, which at first seems strange, can be accounted for in three ways. (1) *Bṭn,* "womb," belly" can refer to the bodies of the fathers from whom children come. (2) The suffix may refer to the whole population, and "their" modifies "darlings" in the usual manner of a construct phrase. (3) The suffix may refer not to bearing wombs but to the wombs from which all are born, again referring to the whole population (cf. Job 3:10).

Mic 6:7 is the classic expression of the same idea: there is no reason to suppose that only women are included in the statement: "Shall I give my firstborn for my transgression / the fruit of my womb for the sin of my soul?" The context (cf. *'ādām* in v 8) shows that both sexes are intended.

17a. *My God.* This supports the authenticity of "my God" in 9:8. The position of the verb makes it possible that a jussive is intended, and that this is a curse, not just a prediction. On the verb, *m's,* "to cast off, reject," see the NOTES on 4:6.

obey. Literally "to hear, heed." It implies listening to the word and doing it. The accusation is thus like that in 8:1, so that 9:17 rounds off the discourse that began there.

17b. *wanderers.* Homeless as well as childless. The word has been used in 7:13, to describe willful wandering from Yahweh. This points to a connection between 9:12b and 17b. Further, just as they turned from Yahweh (7:14bB), he will turn from them (v 12b). They wandered from him; they will be wanderers.

nations. See 8:8 and 10.

Yahweh's gifts are misunderstood
10:1a　He made Israel, the vine, luxuriant.
　　　　　　He made it yield fruit for himself.
　　1b　The more Yahweh multiplied his fruit
　　　　　　the more Israel multiplied at their altars,
　　　　The richer Yahweh made his land
　　　　　　the more generous they were to the pillars.

Yahweh is repudiated
　　2a　Their heart became false.
　　　　　　Now let them be guilty.
　　2b　He will wreck their altars,
　　　　　　he will devastate their pillars.
　　3a　Now they say,
　　　　　　"We do not acknowledge a (divine) king.
　　3b　　　　Indeed, we do not fear Yahweh.
　　　　　　The (divine) king can do nothing to us."

Yahweh's covenant is violated
　　4a　They uttered promises.
　　　　　　They swore falsely.
　　　　　　They made a covenant.
　　4b　Judgment flourishes like poisonous weeds
　　　　　　on the furrows of the field.

The false god will go into exile
　　5a　About the heifers of Beth Awen they are excited
　　　　　　and about the Resident of Samaria.
　　5b　His people will indeed mourn over him,
　　　　　　his idol-priests, over him.
　　　　They will be in agony over His Glory
　　　　　　because he has gone into exile from it.
　　6a　He will be brought to Assyria,
　　　　　　a present for the Great King.

The false god will fail its followers
6b   Ephraim will receive shame.
            Israel will be ashamed of his image.
7a   The king of Samaria has been destroyed,
7b   divine wrath over the waters.
8a   The high places of Awen shall be destroyed,
            the Sin of Israel.
      He makes thorns and thistles grow around their altars.
8b   They will say to the mountains, "Cover us!"
            to the hills, "Fall on us!"

NOTES

10:1–8. The bounds of this unit are marked in several ways, notably change of subject: 9:10–17 deals with Gilgal, 10:1–8 with Samaria, and 10:9–15 with Gibeah. A prime clue to unit structure is the use of Israel in the first line of a unit (9:1; 9:10; 10:1; 10:9; 11:1). Sometimes the name Israel appears again at or near the end (8:8; 8:14; 10:8; 10:15, the last word in the chapter).

Unlike 9:10–17 and 10:9–15, in which the speaker is Yahweh, in 10:1–8 Yahweh is spoken about. Like cc 9 and 11, c 10 begins with reference to Israel, and talks about Ephraim in the body of the speech.

This unit is a further attack on the cult at Samaria and Bethel; cf. 7:1; 8:5,6. It is not certain that the king in v 7 is a human king of Israel; the Great King of v 6 is the king of Assyria. Verse 3 suggests that Israel had renounced the rule of Yahweh, abolishing the title of king for him; instead *šĕkan šōmĕrôn* (v 5) is used for another, ruling god. The abundant produce of the land, Yahweh's gift (v 1), is bestowed on this usurper god, who will go into exile (vv 5–6), and whose altars will be destroyed (vv 2, 8). Verse 5 may contain an indication that the gods in question were represented by animals. Perhaps the male was a bull. No personal names are given; the likely candidates, Baal, "Lord," Melqart, "King of the City," etc., have names which are derived from titles, and *šĕkan šōmĕrôn* is a similar formation. There is no proof of theriomorphism, in statuary or mythology: epithets such as "bull" could be honorifics (used for humans also), turned to derogation for polemical purposes by the Israelite prophet.

This unit displays a pattern of partly developed poetry, typical of Hosea. There are some well-formed poetic units, mainly bicola. These are interspersed with lines more prosaic in syntax. Other structural patterns based on long-range signals tie the unit together; repetition of key words and ideas is an additional integrating factor.

Verse 1a does not have much formal parallelism; the two lines develop a single idea, and are of equal length. Verse 2b is a classical bicolon, with synonymous parallelism, and rhyme. In v 6b Ephraim and Israel are parallel, and the root *bwš*, "shame," appears in both lines. In v 8b two lines have incomplete synonymous parallelism with rhythmic compensation.

More complex patterns are found. Verse 4a can be construed as three lines of two words each, with the parallelism of "promises" // "oaths" // "covenant." Verse 1b is a four-line unit with good rhythm, and A B A′ B′ rhyme, as well as general assonance. The adverb *'attâ* (v 2aB) followed by *kî 'attâ* (v 3aA) suggests that these two lines are parallel, as does the rhyme of the verbs. This bicolon is then wrapped around the well-formed v 2b, which interrupts the continuity and anticipates the judgment to be pronounced more fully later.

Verses 4b and 8aB are prose-like lines of similar length and syntax. Further, they develop the same imagery. The middle passage (vv 5–8aA), which they embrace, deals with the destruction and removal to Assyria of the idol of Samaria, the mourning of its devotees, and the shame of Israel. Verse 5bA seems to be a bicolon with parallelism, although the clause boundaries are not certain. (The bicolon may, with the next line, constitute a tricolon.) There is a similarity between vv 5a and 8a, with *'āwen* as a prominent link. In v 5a, the heifers are mentioned along with the Resident of Samaria, a title for the god, not a reference to "the inhabitants of Samaria" (*RSV*).

The noun "Israel" agrees with a singular verb (v 6bB); the plural verbs and pronouns refer throughout to the people of Israel, except in v 5b where the idol's people mourn, and his idol-priests wail. For this reason we suggest that the singular pronoun and verbs in v 1 refer to Yahweh, except for *hrbh*. When the speeches of the people are reported, the first-person plural is used (vv 3, 8b).

1a. *luxuriant*. The traditional rendering of *gepen bôqēq* as a phrase meaning "a luxuriant vine" may be questioned on several counts. First, there is a clash of gender: *gepen* is usually feminine. II Kings 4:39 is the only other place where it seems to be masculine, and there it is not a grapevine. The usage in 10:1 has been explained as masculine by attraction to Israel. Secondly, the root *bqq*, the apparent source of the form here, in nearly all its occurrences has to do with emptiness. It can describe a land laid waste (Isa 24:1,3; Nah 2:3; Jer 51:2), but never a vine. *Bôqēq* is traditionally identified here as the *Qal* participle of another geminate root, cognate with Arabic *baqqa*, "to grow profusely." LXX supports this, and it fits the context. A *Polel* perfect verb of a root *bwq* is also possible, and has the advantage of realizing the sequence of perfect // imperfect verbs in parallelism, both past tense. Thirdly, there are related problems in v 1aB: In agreement with most scholars we identify the pronoun *hû'* in v 2 as referring to Yahweh; and we note that in reference to the people of Israel plural verbs and pronouns are used in this unit. These factors suggest that the subject of the singular verbs in this opening verse is Yahweh. This presents a proper emphasis on Yahweh as the one who made Israel prosperous, a point which Hosea makes tirelessly. The poem about Israel as the vine in Psalm 80 (cf. Jer 2:21; Ezekiel 17) emphasizes the fact that it was Yahweh who planted it and made it fruitful; cf. Isaiah 5. We therefore read *bqq* as a factitive *Polel* parallel to *yĕšawweh;* its object is the discontinuous phrase *gepen . . . yiśrā'ēl,* "the vine, Israel."

The simile of 9:10 suggests a slightly different reading. As Israel there is compared to fruit trees, so the line here may mean: "He made Israel as luxuriant as a vine."

yield. The idiom is unusual, and the rare verb *šwy* seems to have a meaning here not attested in its other occurrences. Hence the text is often emended. The idea of adornment, illustrated by Ps 89:20, could be used here figuratively, however. The common expression for fruit-bearing is *'śy pry,* "to make fruit," as in 9:16; cf. 8:7; Gen 1:11–12. The Greek translators felt the difficulty, but since we cannot work out how they obtained *euthēnōn* from *yšwh,* we cannot be sure that this was their *Vorlage.* If *yšwh* is here a synonym of *y'śwn* in 9:16, it joins the common object "fruit," providing a domino-like link between the chapters.

for himself. It is not that Israel the vine produces fruit for himself; rather, Israel is supposed to produce fruit for Yahweh. The sustained complaint through this part of the prophecy is that the oblations, which were rightly Yahweh's, were wrongly donated to pagan gods or foreign rulers. A vine does not yield fruit for itself, but for its owner (Isa 5:2b). To translate "its fruit" (*RSV*) as if *pĕrî . . . lô* were a discontinuous phrase equivalent to *piryô* in the following line is banal. The four occurrences of *l,* "to," in the verse should be examined together; the pronouns in *lô . . . lĕpiryô . . . lĕ'arṣô* have the same referent throughout. Yahweh is the subject of *yšwh,* and *lô* is benefactive or ethical.

Such a parsing also suits the verb better, since it generally means to set things up in an orderly way. In this context, parallel to *bwqq,* it describes the work of a horticulturalist, making the fruit tree strong and excellent (v 1b). Yahweh is still talking about Israel as a source of first-rate fruit for his enjoyment (9:10).

1b. This is a four-line composition of a kind often used by Hosea. All explicit subjects in the translation have been supplied.

A	kĕrōb	lĕpiryô	5 syllables
B	hirbâ	lammizbĕḥôt	6
A'	kĕṭôb	lĕʾarṣô	5
B'	hêṭîbû	maṣṣēbôt	6

There is alternating rhyme. A and A' are almost completely assonant, and B and B' are also close (mzbḥt-mṣṣbt). Besides this, A and B are linked by repetition of the verbs, and so are A' and B'. By these means the utterly contrary ways of Yahweh and his people are put closely side by side. The symmetry fails only in the lack of a preposition with "pillars," and the difference in number of the two finite verbs. The whole is so compact that it is impossible to match the brevity without opacity. The text is dense because it is laconic; a paraphrase is inevitable: "According to Yahweh's great multiplication of the fruit of his [Yahweh's] land, Israel multiplied in gratitude the pillars by the altars."

A and A' speak of Yahweh's generosity in enriching Israel; B and B' describe the misuse of his gifts in pagan cults. The sequence of *Qal* infinitives (so we take *rōb* and *ṭôb*, both in construct with a following noun, both with a preposition within the construct chain), which describe Yahweh's actions, is followed by a sequence of corresponding *Hipʿil* verbs for Israel's actions; the verbs are probably elative in sense. The spareness of Hosea's language is seen in the omission of the particles often used in comparisons. The overall sense of the lines can be rendered thus:

> AA' The more he improved the produce of the land for himself,
> BB' The more they improved the pillars at their altars.

Yahweh multiplied. We take *rōb* as an infinitive used as a finite verb with the same subject as the preceding verbs.

his fruit. The suffix on *piryô* could be possessive, referring to Yahweh; or it could continue the benefactive *lô* in v 1a. Ps 80:9–12 emphasizes how large the vine became when Yahweh took good care of it.

Israel multiplied. MT *hirbâ* is a singular verb. In other parts of Hosea, singular and plural verbs are used with great precision to distinguish different subjects. This kind of distinction does not seem to obtain in the present unit, though most of the singular verbs and pronouns refer to Yahweh, the plurals to Israel. *Hirbâ* and *hêṭîbû* are parallels, and the first can pass as plural if it is read as an infinitive absolute — *harbēh*, with Israel (plural) as subject.

The usual interpretation of the line — "he built altars" — takes a noun with *l* as a direct object; this can hardly be an Aramaism. The other *l* nearby are referential or benefactive. Here, the *l* is locative: the concern is with the pillars by the altars.

richer. *Ṭôb* can refer to any aspect of fertility (rain, fat, wealth) or beauty. In 8:3 it is used as a name for God himself. The term is tied to intoxication in the Nabal story (I Samuel 25), and elsewhere to food (Gen 18:7; 27:9). The form here is a *Qal* infinitive.

the more generous. The verbs *hêṭîb* and *hirbâ,* in that sequence, occur in Deut 30:5. Hos 10:1 records the fulfillment of the promise made there. The good things intended for Yahweh's use (his gifts, in fact) were deflected, however, to standing stones near altars. The more bountiful Yahweh was, the more the people ignored him. This attitude resulted from, and reinforced, the basic theological errors denounced in c 2, especially v 10.

It is usual to interpret v 1b as a criticism of the opulence of worship in Israel in the time of Hosea. Some scholars would set the prophet over against the cult in disapproval of formal and ritualistic religion. Hos 6:6 is the favorite proof-text of this school. There was nothing intrinsically reprehensible about altars and standing stones. If, as we have tried to show, these things are the objects of a false cult, it is not their construction, but their use in connection with the worship of the wrong god, that leads to their condemnation.

2a. *false.* There are two roots *ḥlq:* "to be smooth" and "to apportion." LXX translated the latter here, as did the Targum and Vulgate, which further interpret the verb as passive. The root refers, however, to the division and allocation of property, which is different from the divided heart of split loyalties. Hosea, unlike Elijah, does not find in Israel indecision, a "limping between two different opinions" (I Kings 18:21). The people had quite made up their minds, as vv 3 and 4 show. They had formally renounced Yahweh, and given allegiance to another god. Hosea refers, here as elsewhere, to "heart" in the usual Hebrew sense as the central part of personality, divine or human, and the source of thought and will. Verse 2aA does not seem to have any parallel in this speech.

Now. This marks the transition to precatory discourse, the threatening response to the facts just stated. Hence *ye'šāmû* is jussive. The rendering "let them be guilty" is feeble: they are obviously guilty, and have been for some time. No other pre-exilic minor prophet uses this verb. Hosea uses it here and in 4:15; 5:15; 13:1; and 14:1. His meaning seems to be different from the standard established by its abundant use in Leviticus. In the present context it marks something decisive, and perhaps we should render "Now let them be adjudged (incorrigibly) guilty" or "Now let them be punished as guilty." The treatment demanded by their guilt follows in v 2b. Dahood (1966:35–36) suggests that both *'šm* and *ḥlq* mean "to die, perish." This goes too far; the judgment threatened here is not to destroy Israel, but its false religious system.

2b. *altars . . . pillars.* A bicolon of this kind often proclaims the impending doom (8:13b; 9:9b). Verse 2b thus completes v 1a. The catalogue of sins is not complete (more follow in vv 3 and 4) but the speech is not in disarray. As often, Hosea gives first a preliminary pronouncement of judgment, and then the details further along. The ruination of the altars is mentioned again in v 8a, and it is possible that the standing idols are referred to in v 6b. The actor here is Yahweh, although his name does not precede.

3a. *Now. Kî 'attâ* links v 3aA with v 2aB, though a jussive is less suitable here. If *kî* is resumptive, "for" is not a suitable translation; nor is "but" entirely suitable. The reason is that the logic works backward. Verse 3 shows why they are guilty or gives another aspect of their guilt. This fact of wrongdoing logically precedes the sentence pronounced in v 2.

We do not acknowledge a (divine) king. Literally "We have no king." This is not a simple negative existential statement. The line could mean "We have no king" as a matter of fact if the monarchy had disappeared, but kings are much in evidence throughout Hosea. The people, for example, are blamed for setting up kings, but not from Yahweh (8:4). All that is said here reveals contempt for Yahweh, and the following remark, "we do not fear Yahweh," shows that a radical renunciation of Yahweh has been made. Verse 3aB means that Yahweh is not the king for them, and the series *mlk-yhwh-mlk,* balancing the three 1 cg pl suffixes, leaves little doubt that Yahweh is the king they are talking about. Israel's rejection of Yahweh was not just neglect or forgetfulness (2:15; 8:14), but was willful apostasy. Verse 3 is an explicit negation (*'yn . . . l' . . . mh*) of the credal affirmation, "Yahweh is King," which was usually made with the verb *mālak,* rather than with the noun *melek* (but see Isa 33:22). Perhaps the latter usually was avoided because it was a title for Canaanite gods, just as the title *ba'al,* "lord," was not used for Yahweh in Israel's official creeds. In v 3 the word "king" occurs twice, flanking the word "Yahweh." The use of the definite article in v 3b, otherwise rare in Part II of Hosea, points to *the* king. For a human king we might expect the name to be supplied. *RSV* conceals this by translating "a king." The people did trust kings, both their own and those of the Assyrians; the remarks in v 3 show the opposite face of this misplaced trust. It was because they did not believe that Yahweh could cure them that they sent to the Great King (5:13). Israel's creed was *hû' yôšî'ēnû,* "He will save us." Hos 14:4 shows that Assyria was now cast in this role. This fact puts the unit 10:1–8 into international focus, notwithstanding the denunciation of apostasy in the local cultus. Despite the pressure to follow Assyrian ways, the Canaanite influence on the cult was dominant, no doubt because it was indigenous and familiar. The Resident of Samaria (10:5a) sounds Palestinian: paganized, syncretistic Yahwism. The sentiments expressed in 10:3 emerge from the attitude described in 5:13, with all the solemnity of an adjuration. There are three denials in parallel here, each using a different negation. The repeated *lānû* provides rhyme and balance.

3b. *fear*. The term "god-fearer" in the Hebrew Bible describes a genuinely religious person. The emphasis is on the attitude of reverence, not on a sentiment of dread. Here the verb points to an act of disavowal rather than to a psychological condition. The *kî* is asseverative, not a conjunction. Our emphasis on the formal and objective features of their response to Yahweh does not overlook the evidence that the people no longer felt regard for Yahweh; v 4 completes the picture by recording their oaths of allegiance to the new god.

nothing. The particle *mh*, "what?" is often, as here, negative in effect.

to us. Or, "for us." The plurals imply group or national rejection, as if a new national god had been officially proclaimed.

4. This verse is the opposite of v 3; Yahweh's covenant is replaced by another. The object of this anti-Yahwistic oath-taking may be named in v 5. The picture seems to reflect the establishment of a covenant relationship between Israel and Assyria (with the latter as suzerain) in which the oath is made and treaty ratified by invocation of the chief god of Assyria. This solemn action would be followed by the institution of rites and sacrifices dedicated to the superior deity.

4a. *promises*. *Dbr* is used technically.

swore. In 4:2 the normal infinitive absolute, *'ālōh*, is used; *'ālôt* could be the plural of *'ālâ* but we parse it as an eccentric infinitive, chosen to rhyme with *kārōt*. We distinguish the stages described in the first two lines of v 4a: a covenant involved both promises and oaths of autoimprecation. Because Israel is under oath to Yahweh, any further oaths would necessarily be false.

covenant. We have already seen in c 8 that the breaking of covenant with Yahweh took the form of making a foreign alliance that required swearing by alien gods. The third line of v 4a summarizes the two previous lines.

4b. *poisonous weeds*. The connection of this verse with the remainder of the speech is hard to find. "Judgment" is normally a good thing in the Bible, but its comparison with a rank growth suggests perverted justice. (The other sense of *mišpaṭ*, "custom," does not notably elucidate the line.) The meaning of *rō'š* is uncertain, and its position before the subject (if "judgment" is the subject) is a further difficulty. The common sense, "head," does not fit. The other, "poison," has been interpreted as "weeds" because of the association with "the furrows of the field." The description of "thorns and thistles" in v 8 might support this result. Perhaps *r'š mšpṭ* is a construct chain, or combination meaning "poisoned justice" or the like. Note also the parallel structures in vv 7 and 4: *kqṣp 'l pny mym*, "like divine wrath over the waters"; *kr'š . . . 'l tlmy śdy*, "like poison on the furrows of the field."

furrows. The same phrase occurs in 12:12. Noxious weeds in the farmlands are to be ruthlessly eradicated, and this would be a just thing to do for Israel. The sprouting of judgment like weeds seems an incongruous simile. If it were not for the word "judgment" this picture of weeds could characterize the growth of anti-Yahweh religion, instead of the fruitful cultivation of Israel as a vine (v 1).

field. The word *šādāy* is not a suffixed noun but an archaic form.

5. The difficulty of this verse stems largely from our uncertainty about the meaning of the verbs. It seems that the people and priests of the idol god are distressed because it has been captured.

5a. *heifers*. The *plurale majestatis* is another example of Hosea's use of plurals as the name of a deity, perhaps the female counterpart of the "calf of Samaria" (8:5,6), and consort of the "Resident of Samaria." In the following references to "his" people, "his" priests, this goddess seems to have receded from view. The feminine is unique here; elsewhere the object of idolatry is m s (Aaron's in Exodus 32), or m pl (Jeroboam's). Cf. the legend of Jupiter and Europa, parallel to Ugaritic Baal's consort. The Greek versions normalized the reference to Beth Awen's creatures to *'gl*, "calf" (or used a Hebrew text that had done so); this is followed by many modern translators and commentators. Since this emendation is generally accompanied by revocalization and pluralization of *škn šmrwn,* one must be dubious.

Beth Awen. In its other occurrences in Hosea (4:15; 5:8), this seems to be a derogatory name for Bethel. Since the remainder of the verse deals with the fate of an idol apparently in Samaria, another explanation may be needed. In 8:5,6 the idol in Samaria is called the "calf" (m). Samaria may be addressed as a "House of Idols" in v 5aA; the relevance of the "heifers," however, is hard to ascertain. Amos 4:1 may afford a clue. The prophet refers to "the cows of Bashan" on Mount Samaria. This f pl could be the counterpart of "his idol-priests" (m pl). We know from Hos 4:13–14 that the priests' daughters and daughters-in-law had been involved in the forbidden cult.

excited. It is possible that *yāgûrû* means "they will be resident aliens," and there is in the context reference to going into exile (v 5b); but the verb is best associated with *gwr* (~*gry*), "to stir up." Verses 5 and 6 strongly suggest that it was the idol that was to be carried away to Assyria as a resident alien. The plural is then out of place. The verb used here resembles a form used earlier in the book, *yitgôrārû* (7:14), which however required emendation.

It may be desirable to tie the verb here with *'ābal,* "to mourn." People, female priests (or consorts), and male priests would be distressed and frantic over the loss of their god, in actual mourning because of an exile, or in ritual mourning because the god has died and has yet to be raised from the dead. See NOTE on "exile" in v 5b.

Resident. The form *šĕkan* is unique, probably understood by the Masoretes, as the construct of *šākēn,* "inhabitant, neighbor." It has been taken as a collective, or altered to *šōkĕnê* (plural construct of the participle), "dwellers of." For this meaning it is hard to see why Hosea did not use a form of *yšb* (4:1,3). The plural verb suggests that *šĕkan šōmĕrôn* is not the subject, even if collective. In the following text there are six words which have a masculine singular referent ("over him" bis, "his people," "his idol-priests," "His Glory," "he has gone into exile"), and "Resident" is the eligible antecedent. This is the title for the god who had been acclaimed ruler in Samaria by the oaths in v 4, after the renunciation of Yahweh as king in v 3. It is equivalent to *'gl šmrwn.* The root *škn* has royal and cultic associations (Cross 1947). Num 35:34 illustrates its use in the theology of Yahweh's presence among his people, in the land which must not be defiled (Hos 5:3; 6:10). The original residence of Yahweh as *šōkēn* was Sinai (*šōkĕnî sĕneh/sînay,* Deut 33:16). This was transferred to Jerusalem, and Isaiah calls Yahweh Sebaoth *haššōkēn hĕhar ṣîyôn* (Isa 8:18); cf. *hr šmrwn* (Amos 4:1; 6:1). This title passed into the liturgy as "Shoken of Jerusalem" (Ps 135:21) and into apocalypse as "Shoken in Sion, my holy mountain" (Joel 4:17, cf. 21). For its royal associations see Job 29:25, where *škn, yšb, r'š,* and *mlk* all occur together (Andersen 1976a:234). The Masoretes evidently knew of a tradition in which a noun, rather than the participle, was used as a title. There are indications that this god was also called "Israel's Sin" (4:8; 10:8; cf. 13:12), unless that term refers to a goddess. In 10:8 the term occurs in conjunction with "the high places of Awen," and the double phrasing, "the high places of Awen, the sin of Israel," is like "the heifers of Beth Awen . . . the Shoken of Samaria." Both altars (vv 1 and 8) and idol (vv 6 and 7) are to be eliminated. Because of its royal connotations, "the Shoken of Samaria" can probably be equated with "Samaria, her king," in v 7a, indicating that the latter is divine, not human. This rival god had his own covenant (v 4), his own people (*'ammô,* an important word in Hosea — v 5), his own priests (*kĕmārāyw,* v 5), and even one of Yahweh's titles (*kĕbôdô,* "His Glory"— v 5). (This is not to deny that Akkadian *šakānu* has political uses which might be relevant; it can describe settlements such as the installation of a deputy or recognition of a vassal. The peculiar pointing of *škn* may be illuminating.)

5b. *mourn.* The two perfects, *'ābal* and *gālâ,* follow 3 m pl imperfect verbs, *yāgûrû* // *yāgîlû.*

be in agony. Yāgîlû has polar meanings. The meaning to "exult with joy" does not give a parallel for "to mourn." The meaning "to tremble," based on Ps 2:11, arises because the agitated movements of an excited dance can be produced by fear or grief (Dahood 1966:13). It is an irony that the same gyrations of the worshipers could express extreme delight or extreme distress. Dahood has suggested that the word *gyl* might not be present here at all; he repoints to *yigye lô*, "they will grieve (*ygy*) for him" (1978:178 n 11).

exile. There is wordplay between *yāgîlû* (root *gyl*) and *gālâ* (*gly*). Compare '*al-kĕbôdô kî-gālâ* with I Sam 4:21–22, where *kābôd* is the subject of *gālâ*. As in Amos 5:26–27, people and idol go into captivity together. In all likelihood, the idol is meant in v 6, which describes it as a "present" for the king of Assyria. If correct, the god in question is a local deity, of Canaanite extraction. The removal of the gods of subject peoples was a common practice in the ancient world.

from it. Or "from us." If "us" were correct, the clause would be a continuation of the quotation in v 3: "For it has departed from us." But it is more likely that the reference is to Israel as in the parallel passage, I Sam 4:21–22. Whereas in the latter passage the sadness relates to the capture of the ark, here it is the mourning of idolatrous priests over the captivity of their Glory. The reference, therefore, is to the place where the idol was installed, presumptively Israel (note the masculine form). That the Glory is something concrete is confirmed by the usual meaning of the verb *gālâ*, "to go into exile"; this statement has an exact parallel in v 6a, which describes physical removal, and not just the loss of splendor.

6a. *He.* The translation of '*ôtô* as "the thing itself" (*RSV*) is appropriate, since the emphasis is on the object. Placing the object in a prominent position, before the verb, together with the connective *gam*, links v 6a tightly to v 5, and shows that its theme continues. Going into exile and being taken to Assyria are the same. Amos 5:26 similarly hints at the removal of the idols. The prominent pronoun also stands in contrast with *hû'* in v 2: Yahweh versus the Resident of Samaria.

present. The use of *minḥâ*, "tribute," suggests that the idol will be taken to Assyria by Israel, not that it will be carried off as spoil.

Great King. See NOTE on 5:13a.

6b. The grammatical components of this bicolon stand in perfect introversion: Object / Subject / Verb // Verb / Subject / Object. While it appears to strike a note of finality, it lacks the usual marker of paragraph closing, placement of the verb at the end of the last clause. The bicolon is thus a contrastive intrusion into the continued theme of the destruction of the idol of Samaria. The "Glory" shall go to Assyria; Ephraim shall receive shame. The theme of shame is reiterated in the parallel line, but with the cognate verb rather than a noun. The verb *yiqqaḥ* implies acceptance of shame on Ephraim's part. The feminine form *bošnâ*, from the root *bwš*, is used only here; *-nâ* is not a regular noun afformative in Hebrew, but there is no root *bšn*. The word could be a Hosean coinage; cf. '*etnâ* (2:14), which is Hosea's alone. The meaning of *bošnâ* should be sought in the light of its parallel "his image," and in the context, which requires some connection with the idol of Samaria. Since both *bošnâ* and its parallel *'ēṣâ* are feminine, it is possible that this "Shame" is the female counterpart of the male *qālôn* (4:7,18).

image. In 4:12 the idol is called "a stick of wood." A feminine form of this occurs in Jer 6:6 (*'ēṣâ,* "tree"), and although the Masoretes may have misunderstood the reading, such a word may have existed. That it could be used for a female wooden idol is not unlikely. Such a meaning would fit *'ăṣātām* in Ps 106:43 quite well. There are two reasons for suspecting that *'ēṣâ* there means "idol" and not "advice": the latter does not suit the context at all, and special meanings have been devised with little textual or etymological support; the rebellion described in Psalm 106 is a provocation of Yahweh with idols.

7a. *king of Samaria*. Literally, "Samaria, her king"; the sequence, while unusual (perhaps unexampled), is grammatical and serves to emphasize the identification of the deity (— the bull of Samaria, or more precisely the deity elevated on the bull or whose symbol was the bull) with Samaria, its cult center. No human monarch was called "King of Samaria" (but cf. Jonah 3:6). In view of the rejection of Yahweh as king (v 3), we have supposed the accession of a pagan god in his place, with the formalities described in v 4 and the title in v 5. The idea that the god is king of the city is not uncommon in Canaanite religion.

destroyed. In 4:5 and 6 the priest's mother and Yahweh's people are "ruined," the root there as here being *dmy*. The resemblance between 10:7a and 10:15b suggests that intentional chiasm could explain the unusual word order in the former. Whether the parallelism requires the king of Israel in the latter to be equated with the king of Samaria here is an open question.

7b. *divine wrath*. Traditional, "like a chip," a colorful simile which could go with several nearby statements. It is doubtful that the picture of a chip on the water really illustrates the ruination of the king of Samaria, since a chip on the water does not "perish." It may be carried violently away, and a helpless person might feel like a chip tossed on floodwaters. If the emphasis is on the minuteness of a chip, then the king could be seen as of no account in the vast forces of the historical events of his times. Are the waters referred to by Hosea the forces of history? Is the term "chip" contemptuous? This is obviously fanciful and we are dubious.

This is the only place in the Bible where the meaning "chip" is invoked for the word *qeṣep,* which elsewhere always has the meaning of "divine wrath." It is the reference to water that requires some kind of congruency which eludes us. The association with "waters" must be ultimately mythological, as numerous passages in the Bible attest. There may have been links with the Canaanite mythic tradition of the repeated struggle between Baal and Yamm, the sea god, for supremacy. The nearest parallel to the present passage doubtless would be Ps 29:3, where the thunder of Yahweh is described as being upon the waters.

8a. *high places.* This is Hosea's only reference to the high places (Albright 1957; Ribar 1973). Cf. Amos 7:9; Mic 1:5. Hosea does, however, condemn ceremonies performed on the mountains (4:13). Whatever the cult at such places, the use of this word in the present chapter, especially in connection with Awen, shows that familiar and reprehensible practices are the target of the prophet's criticism. The verb *hšmd,* "to destroy," is generally used to describe the extermination of sinners, not the destruction of things. This makes an abstract "sin of Israel," which seems to stand in apposition with "the high places of Awen," improbable; it may be that Israel's "Sin" was an idol.

He makes . . . grow. The verb *y'lh* properly is *Hip'il* 3 m s — "he will make thorns and thistles grow up around the altars," i.e. they will be abandoned to the underbrush.

thorns and thistles. Cf. 9:6 and NOTE on "dispossess" there.

altars. This supports the conclusion reached earlier that it is the cult installations — altars and idols — that are to be demolished in the coming destruction.

8b. *They will say.* The cause of this dramatic cry is not explained. It contrasts with the bravado of v 3; the terror of Yahweh, which they treated with such disdain, overwhelms them inescapably. The references to hills and mountains give the bicolon an eschatological flavor. It is a climactic expression, appropriate at the juncture of major literary units.

XIX. THE SPIRITUAL HISTORY OF ISRAEL: GIBEAH AND BETH ARBEL
(10:9–15)

Gibeah: war

10:9a   Since the days of Gibeah, you have sinned, Israel.

  9b   There they stood —

      Indeed, war overtook them in Gibeah.

            — beside the Wicked Ones.

  10a   When I came, I chastened them.

  10b   Armies assembled against them,

      when I chastened them for their double iniquity.

Fieldwork: farming

  11a   Ephraim whom I love is a heifer trained to thresh.

      I placed upon her neck a fine yoke.

  11b   I harnessed Ephraim.

      Let Judah plow.

      Let Jacob harrow for himself.

  12a   Sow for yourselves for the sake of righteousness.

      Reap for the sake of mercy.

      Break up for yourselves virgin soil.

Trust and mistrust: farming

  12b   It is time to seek Yahweh

      until he comes and rains righteousness for you.

  13a   You have plowed iniquity

      Lawlessness you have reaped.

      You have eaten the fruit of lies.

Beth Arbel: war

  13b   For you trusted in your power

      and in the large numbers of your crack troops.

  14a   Tumult shall rise up from your army.

      All your fortresses will be devastated,

      the way Shalman devastated Beth Arbel.

14b　On the day of war, mothers were dashed to pulp
　　　　beside children.
15a　So may he do to you in Bethel because of your wicked
　　　　wickedness.
15b　When the sun rose, the king of Israel was utterly ruined.

NOTES

10:9–15. The coherence of this section as a literary unit is established externally and internally. Externally its boundaries are marked by the clear ending to the preceding unit and the clear beginning of the following one. Internally it is marked by use of Israel in the opening and closing lines (and nowhere in between), a device that we have met before. The unity and continuity of the passage is another matter, although there are indications of deliberate structuring. The text presents more than its share of problems. Any honest translation will reflect these difficulties. Neither the evidence of ancient versions nor the ingenuity of modern emendations has achieved much improvement.

The unit does not manifest a well-organized poetic scheme. Because of the difficulty of the text in places, there is uncertainty as to where one clause ends and another begins, and about the boundaries of the individual lines, assuming that there is some kind of poetic design. These are not quite the same thing; i.e. a poetic line is not necessarily a grammatical clause (cf. O'Connor 1980). Generally speaking, Hebrew does not often use a run-on line. When the line length is variable, the distinction between prose and poetry is hard to detect, and the effort to do so is probably misguided in the case of Hosea. In the present passage the lines, provisionally identified, vary greatly in length. The short lines in v 11b are undeniable; but some of the longer lines in the passage could be broken into smaller ones, quite apart from the possibility of assigning some of their opening or closing words to the previous or following lines.

A further complication is introduced by Hosea's fondness for anacolutha, although the term is not used in the strict sense. The apparent grammatical incompleteness is due to his use of ellipsis, often in idiomatic laconisms. In many instances we cannot retrieve the complete expressions by supplying the missing words. Another cause of apparent anacoluthon is the insertion of a piece of speech addressed in another direction, after which the preceding remarks are resumed at the point of interruption. The present passage has a good example of this in the material in the second

person, which alternates between singular and plural. Speech in the first
person constitutes another ingredient, and goes with third-person pronouns. There is also descriptive material, with third-person plural verbs
and pronouns. LXX already shows a tendency to normalize these changes.
This should be resisted. Many of Hosea's speeches are apparent agglom-
erations of pieces in various numbers and persons; time and again, we
have found system and balance in the interwoven patterns. The distinction
between singular and plural second-person pronouns is an important clue
to unraveling the strands in 10:9–15, especially as these passages (vv 9a,
12–14a, 15a) are among the clearest in the unit. If 6:4; 11:8, and other
passages may serve as a guide, either part of the divided kingdom may be
addressed in the singular; the plural is used when both are meant. Hos
6:4b is a good example of the latter usage, for it follows a singular passage. Hos 5:13b is equally convincing, for here the plural embraces both
kingdoms, each of which has an illness, referred to in the singular in
5:13a. In c 10 Ephraim, Judah, and Jacob are singular in v 11, which is
followed by a continuation of the agricultural figure in v 12, the states together being addressed in the plural. Israel as a whole or the people as
such are sometimes addressed in the plural, as distinct from a king or
priest.

In eliciting a clear picture from this text we are handicapped by the obscurity of some of the allusions. Shalman and Beth Arbel in v 14 remain
obscure; since the line cites a byword for destruction on an enormous
scale, and is used only as a simile, our ignorance is more irksome than restricting. It is hard even to be sure about "the days of Gibeah." The most
memorable Gibeah incident and the one probably meant here is the rape
of the concubine and the resulting civil war reported in Judges 19–21. It
was one of the greatest disasters in Israel's history, not only because one
of the more important tribes was almost wiped out, but more seriously because of the scars that such a war between the tribes left in national memory. It is, in fact, astonishing that consciousness of belonging to Israel as a
large reality persisted for centuries after the disruption following Solomon's death. Hosea shows a great concern for both kingdoms, and frequently talks about "Israel" as a whole. "The days of Gibeah" could stand
as a reminder of the awful consequences of civil war and as a condemnation of the wars between the kingdoms in the time of Hosea, and of the
wars within the northern kingdom itself as a result of the revolutions that
occurred during its last years. Since 10:9–15 speaks about "war"
(vv 9, 14), and condemns trust in military strength (v 13b), Hosea's
comparison of his times with "the days" of Gibeah is appropriate.

The smaller poetic units in this speech are of several kinds. There are
only a few bicola of familiar type. Verse 11b contains the best example:

yaḥărôš yĕhûdâ
yĕśadded-lô yaʿăqōb

The syntax is similar; the verbs have the same tense, and are semantically related; the parallelism of Judah and Jacob is unusual, and may reflect an older or different form of the common pairing, Judah and Israel. Verse 14a contains a bicolon with a beautiful chiasm; it will be described as part of a larger unit.

Verse 10, although full of problems, seems to be a tricolon of a type represented by at least three examples in this unit. The first and third lines resemble each other more closely than the line which they enclose. That we have a tricolon is shown by the consistent use of the 3 m pl pronoun. Even more unmistakable is the assonance of verb forms with the consonants ' and *s*.

Verse 11 contains a three-line unit clearly marked by the use of "Ephraim" at the beginning and end. This, and the contrast between the first- and third-person verbs, requires the separation of the last two lines of v 11b. These are usually kept together with the first line of v 11b because of the imagery of yoking and plowing, and the supposed series of Ephraim, Judah, and Jacob.

The eight lines in vv 12 and 13a constitute a symmetrical pattern. Two tricola of similar structure embrace v 12b, which is a long, prose-like statement. The tricolon in v 12a has short lines. Each begins with an imperative verb. The repeated *lākem* in the first and third lines contributes to the symmetry. At the same time *ṣdqh* and *ḥsd* are good parallels. Verse 13a has the same feature of short lines. Each line has the same syntax (verb and object), with the same sequence in the first and third, which again achieves symmetry. In the second line the sequence is inverted.

Verse 13b continues a second-person singular address that began with v 9a. Verse 14a, which we have already described as containing a bicolon, describes the consequences of this mistrust. The parallelism suggests that here the word *ʿam,* coming as it does between warriors and fortresses, means "army."

The remaining lines, in vv 9, 14b, and 15, are less amenable to poetic analysis. They do, nevertheless, contain some rhetorical touches worth observing. The agricultural imagery, which dominates vv 11–13a, is surrounded by military imagery in vv 9–10 and 13b–15. The word "war" occurs at the opening and at the close of the unit. The strange repetition *rʿt-rʿtkm,* "your wicked wickedness," in v 15 resembles "their double iniquity" in v 10.

The statements made about farming cover the sequence of activities from training draft animals to eating the produce. The moments come in bundles of two or three, with some repetition, although the sequence is not chronological. Compare the sequence of the various statements about childbearing in c 9. The moments are:

> Training the heifer for threshing (v 11a)
> Yoking (v 11a)
> Harnessing (v 11b)
> Plowing (ḥrš) (v 11b)
> Harrowing (v 11b)
>
> Sowing (v 12a)
> Reaping (qṣr) (v 12a)
> Tilling for the first time (v 12a)
>
> Plowing (ḥrš) (v 13a)
> Reaping (qṣr) (v 13a)
> Eating (v 13a)

Only the major tasks of plowing and reaping are mentioned twice. The purpose of it all, eating, is mentioned only once, and that at the end, where the last word is the dreadful product, "lies." The discourse switches abruptly after this point, and the number changes from plural to singular.

10:9a. *Gibeah.* From Hosea's four references to Gibeah (5:8; 9:9; and twice in v 9) it is clear that the place had a great present significance for him, derived from some past event. The people had sinned profoundly "in the days of Gibeah" (9:9), and have continued in sin since that time (10:9). These references to Gibeah are spread throughout the book; the first occurs at the end of a unit, the second at the beginning. This is typical of Hosea's habit of announcing a theme, and then going on with other matters before he returns to that theme to expound it more amply. Presumably the sin that persisted "from the days of Gibeah" was like the original sin there. In the Gibeah episode reported in Judges 19–21, there were two enormities. A crime of unexampled brutality (Judg 19:22–26) was followed by the refusal of the tribe of Benjamin to give up the few "base fellows" responsible in the city of Gibeah. The tribe was all but exterminated by the sustained onslaughts of the other tribes. It is not clear which aspect of the matter Hosea considers the "sin." We cannot assume, because our moral sensibilities are shocked by the bloodbath described in Judges 20, that Hosea regarded the punishment of the Benjaminites as cruel and unusual. Considering his strong views on sexual license, and the punishment he threatens against Israel in his own day for that kind of behavior, it is possible that he approved of such a thoroughgoing attempt to eradicate evil from Israel. In our NOTES on 1:4 we have argued that Hosea endorsed at least in part Jehu's liquidation of the house of Omri, and threatens the house of Jehu with the same fate, for a similar reason.

The remainder of the passage refers both to war and to fertility in the imagery of farming. There is no hint that 10:9–15 deals in particular with sexual activity. Hosea sees the internecine strife of his own day as a further example of the national characteristics displayed so early in history at Gibeah. Such a background of civil war is provided by the years after the death of Jeroboam II.

9b. *they stood.* Following MT, we take Israel as a vocative with the first clause. The change from second to third person shows that v 9a is an opening address, after which the focus changes to indirect description of past events. The initial theme (v 9a) is picked up in v 13b. Within v 9b, a new clause begins with *lō'*, and the verb usage changes from perfect to imperfect. Both verbs in such a sequence can have the same time reference; hence our translation "overtook" for the second verb. The statement "There they stood" is enigmatic as it stands, but should be linked with *'l bny 'lwh* forming an envelope around the intervening clause. The sense would be rendered as follows: "There they stood . . . beside the Wicked Ones. // Indeed war overtook them in Gibeah." The statement then is an allusion to the horrific episode described in Judges 19–21, highlighting the stubborn loyalty of the Benjaminites to the "base fellows" who precipitated the crisis, and the bloody carnage which followed.

Indeed. MT has a negation: "War did not/will not overtake them in Gibeah." As a statement of historical fact, if the verb is past tense, this is not true. As a prediction, if the verb is future tense, it is jejune, and contrary to the threat of war made at the end of the chapter. Because of such difficulties, translators and commentators prefer to find here a rhetorical question — "Shall not war overtake them . . . ?" However, the threats in this chapter are spoken directly to "you." Further, the reference to Bethel in v 15 shows that the location of the threatened punishment of Hosea's day is not specifically at Gibeah. Even in 5:8 Gibeah is listed with other places. It is likely that the Gibeah of v 9b is the Gibeah of Judges, and that the verb is past tense, in sequence with the perfect verb preceding it. We recognize the *l'* as asseverative with Gordis (1976:167) and Wolff (1974:178).

Wicked Ones. Literally "children of wickedness." The word *'alwâ* occurs only here. It is usually "corrected" to *'awlâ* (so Wolff 1974:178). Hosea's form could be from the root *'wl*, the result of metathesis in the living language, not a result of scribal error; or from a root *'ly*, not otherwise known (Koehler and Baumgartner 1958:707).

10a. *When I came.* Bĕ'awwātî is a difficult reading, although emendations which require extensive departure from the MT should be a last resort. The Masoretic tradition identifies a noun *'awwâ*, "desire"; the cognate verb is not uncommon. The conjunction before the next verb makes it difficult to establish the syntactic function of *b'wty,* but an infinitival construction would be within grammatical norms. The root used here is *'ty,* "to come." Its infinitive is not attested; by the usual rules it should be *ba'ătôtî* or the like. An objection against this identification is the fact that the root is chiefly Aramaic. However, *'ty* occurs over twenty times in Hebrew texts, with a wide distribution, and it exists also in Ugaritic; it was part of the general vocabulary of Northwest Semitic; it was a rare and poetic root in Hebrew. The use of a preposition followed by an infinitive is supported by the parallel *bě'osrām* in v 10b. The meaning "came" is supported by LXX, though this could also be explained by a Hebrew original *b'ty*, from *bw'*, which is more likely to be a correction of *b'wty* than the reverse.

I chastened. The line could be a threat of punishment, although this seems too big a break from the historical recital about Gibeah; and the remainder of the verse is a claim that Yahweh himself chastised them for their double iniquity. There seems to be repetitive parallelism in *w'srm* and *b'srm*, but the morphology of each is problematic. If the first means "I chastened," it comes from a secondary root *sr<ysr*, or the form is contracted from *w'ysrm;* the form in v 10b has the root *'sr* if it is an infinitive. The normal root for "to chasten" is *ysr;* see the discussion at 7:12. The similarities could lie entirely on the level of sound, especially since the other verb in the verse (*'spw*) also begins with the same two consonants.

10b. *Armies.* Literally "peoples." Since there was no gathering of other nations against Israel at Gibeah, the war being entirely internal, we take the reference to be to armies (of the tribes) against Benjamin. It is possible that foreign people are meant and that v 10 is a threat of Yahweh's intended punishment of Israel by means of foreign invaders.

when I chastened. If *bě'osrām* contains the root *'sr*, "to bind," there is a difficulty in the syntax. "When they bound" has no obvious object. A reflexive meaning ("when they bound themselves") seems unlikely for the *Qal.* If "them" is the object, then the subject must be Yahweh. We tie the form to the root *ysr*, "to chasten." The connection of the root *'sr* with the making of vows could be relevant, however.

iniquity. The Ketib *'yntm* may mean "their two eyes"; cf. "my two eyes" in Judg 16:28. Hosea uses the word *'āwōn* ten times, and it is the Qere here. In some of its occurrences, "iniquity" refers to the worship of idols, and almost becomes a name for the god, like "Sin" and "Shame." "Their two iniquities" could be two such idols. The *štayim rā'ôt*, "two iniquities," of Jer 2:13 suggest otherwise. The iniquities could also be the episode at Gibeah and the war between the tribes and Benjamin, or the episode and the consequent refusal to surrender the criminals which prompted the war; the latter was the worst violation of league solidarity. Verse 10 could reflect the action of Yahweh in chastising his people for their role in the Gibeah affair.

11. The introduction of the name Ephraim suggests that the focus has

changed from the past events at Gibeah to the present, yet the conjunction suggests continuity in the unfolding of the speech.

11a. *heifer*. There does not seem to be any connection between this word and the "heifers" of 10:5. Here it is a figure of speech, there it is literal. A "trained" heifer contrasts with an intractable cow (4:16). If this is intended to recapitulate historical development, it must go back to a time when Ephraim was docile; cf. 11:1. The figure is now developed in a way that presents Ephraim's later conduct as a reversion of a work animal to a wild condition. Cf. Jer 31:18. The comparison with 11:1 is apt and points the way to the correct interpretation of v 11a: *ldwš*, "to thresh," completes the meaning of *'glh mlmdh*, "a trained heifer" — i.e. "a heifer trained to thresh." The word *'hbty* is to be taken as the verb with a first-person subject (cf. *w'hbhw* in 11:1), Yahweh. Even the most docile and cooperative animal could hardly be described as "loving" to work, especially under the yoke. "Training" is another matter; besides, *'hbty* is more easily interpreted as the *Qal* perfect 1 cg s than as a participle. The Masoretic vocalization of *'hbty* as a participle is dispensable.

to thresh. The verb describes a trampling activity, presumably the treading out of grain. It can also be destructive: Babylon is denounced for trampling on Yahweh's estate *kĕ'eglâ dāšâ*, "like a threshing heifer" (Jer 50:11). Here, however, the animal has been trained for the task; cf. Judg 14:18, where reference is made to plowing with a heifer.

a fine yoke. The MT is unintelligible; literally "and I, I passed by upon goodness her neck."

The clearest clue is supplied by the word "neck." Verse 11a describes an animal trained to thresh; such a beast must be yoked to the plow. The word *'ōl*, "yoke," should be read for MT *'al* (Kuhnigk 1974:122). The yoke is a symbol of servitude (Gen 27:40). The phrase *'ōl 'al lĕḥêhem*, "a yoke on their jaws" (Hos 11:4) shows the sequence *'l 'l*, and it may be that a haplography should be recognized. An *'ōl-ṭûb* would then be either a handsome yoke or a well-fitting one, enabling good work, not burdensome and thus like that of Jesus (Matt 11:29–30; Albright and Mann, 1971:146–147). A difficulty in the way of this interpretation is the verb *'br*, not otherwise used with yoking. The verb is *nātan* for putting one on, and *sār* for taking off. In I Kings 6:21 the *Pi'el* of *'br* is used meaning "to cover," and we should read a *Pi'el* here, too (Kuhnigk 1974:122).

11b. *harnessed*. *'rkyb 'prym* apparently links what precedes with what follows; it may belong structurally with the two following clauses to form a tricolon as in v 13a. The past tense of our translation results from parallelism with "I covered." Since Hosea is concerned with the political relationships between north and south, we must ask if the picture is one in which Ephraim and Judah are yoked *together* in order to plow. The farming operations are more clearly indicated in the case of Judah and Jacob

than in the case of Ephraim. We must suppose that the role assigned to
Ephraim is connected with the activities of Judah and Jacob. Perhaps he is
on guard duty. *Rkb* has to do with mounting and riding, and in a derivative sense, with driving chariots. Heifers were not often used for such purposes (cf. Judg 14:18). Congruity of the metaphor and continuity with
what follows is secured by assigning the verb the unparalleled meaning "to
cause to draw a plow."

Ordinarily if "Ephraim" were the object of *'arkîb,* Ephraim would be
the rider, the mount or vehicle being marked by the preposition *'al.* The
usage here is unique.

plow . . . harrow. Isa 28:24 uses the same verbs in the same sequence.
Judah and Jacob occur in parallel again in Hos 12:3, in a way that suggests that the names are complementary. With Ephraim, they describe the
three components of greater Israel. In its other occurrence (12:13), Jacob
refers to the patriarch.

12a. The address changes to second-person plural, but the agricultural
imagery continues. The elements interact to produce a composite picture.
The three verbs describe related actions: plowing virgin soil, sowing seed,
reaping the harvest. All this is symbolic of life in the land characterized by
righteousness and loving-kindness. To do these things is to seek Yahweh
in repentance and renewed dedication.

for yourselves. The ethical datives here and in v 11b highlight the im-
mediacy of the direct address.

for the sake of mercy. Literally "to the mouth of mercy." *Lĕpî* is probably only a poetic variant of the referential preposition, and "for" may be a
sufficient translation.

Break up . . . virgin soil. It is typical of Hosea's poetry that the tilling
of virgin or fallow soil is not mentioned first, but only after sowing and
reaping. The previous verbs are used figuratively, as the prepositional objects show. The third verb, however, has a cognate direct object, *nîr.* Here,
and in its other occurrences (Jer 4:3, which is a quotation from this passage in Hosea, and Prov 13:23) *nîr* refers to soil tilled for the first time.

12b. *to seek.* This sums up the intention of the preceding injunctions.
The activity required is clearly some kind of repentance and intercession,
as a result of which Yahweh will arrive like rain.

rains. Reading with MT an imperfect verb *yoreh* in coordination with
the preceding. *Yôreh* is the name for the early rains (cf. 6:3). The full sequence of seasonal rains also includes *gešem* and *malqôš.* Jer 5:24 has the
three in the correct sequence. In Deut 11:14 *māṭār* is equivalent to *gešem.*

The figure of raining down righteousness is not found elsewhere. Joel
2:23 has *liṣdāqâ,* as in v 12aA, meaning rain in the right amount. A similar collocation of words is found in the Damascus Document 6:10–11: *'d
'md ywrh hṣdq b'ḥryt hymym.* The phrase has been explained as an alter-

native title for the familiar "Teacher of Righteousness" (Weingreen 1961). Gaster (1964:78) renders it, "until the true Expositor arises at the end of days." Many commentators prefer there the imagery of rain, especially in view of the theme of well-digging in the preceding text. Neither there nor in Hos 10:12 can it be simply a question of agricultural prosperity at the end time; "raining justice" is a metaphor. On the other hand, the association of rain and righteousness in Joel 2:23 does suggest that the seasonal blessings are a token of rightness with God. Worden (1953) has found in the language of 10:12 a background of Canaanite fertility myths.

for you. The chiastic sequence *lākem liṣdāqâ . . . ṣedeq lākem* at the beginning and end of the verse effects a closure.

13a. The past-tense verbs describe activities the opposite of those enjoined in v 12. The movement of thought is not clear. It could be that v 13 comes logically and temporally before v 12: it has been your practice to plow for wickedness, but now you must remedy this by plowing for righteousness. Verse 12 is then the remedy for v 13. However, second-person plural speech continues in v 15, after an intrusion with pronouns in the singular. Since v 15 is a threat of punishment, coherence can be secured if v 12 gives the original exhortation, v 13 records the contrary response, and v 15 announces the resultant punishment. Hosea's sparing use of conjunctions leaves such connections in doubt.

iniquity. The referential use of *l* in v 12a shows that the virtues are not the direct objects of the technical verbs. The same is true of the vices, which may rather characterize the manner of performing the activities. The reference to the wind in 8:7 was seen to have the same kind of grammatical function. This is the only Hosean use of *rešaʿ*. The noun *ʿawlātâ,* "lawlessness," seems to be a double feminine of the usual *ʿawlâ;* cf. *ʿalwâ* in v 9.

lies. *Kḥš* is a singular, used literally either of acts collectively, "lies," or of the action, "lying." The plural is used in 7:3, where it refers to political treachery. Here the fruit which is eaten at the end of all their efforts is not identified. It must refer to the outcome of their deceitful policies; but what form that took is not explained. The rest of v 13 cannot be directly drawn upon, because the change of number from plural to singular probably indicates a change in the point of reference. When the plurals are resumed in v 15, the consequences are described as a massive military disaster.

13b. *you trusted.* The singular resumes an address that began in v 9a, but was not developed.

power. In view of the multitude of troops, *drk* here, as in Ugaritic and in other biblical passages, probably means "dominion, power, authority" (cf. Wolff 1974:187). The great sin against which Israel is warned in Deuteronomy is arrogance, self-righteousness, and reliance on its own power.

crack troops. This is the only place where Hosea mentions this kind of soldier. The reproach of infatuation with prosperity is often made, using the root *rb* (10:1), which went with abundant material resources (2:10; 8:14), abundance of sin (9:7), and pride (8:11). The *gibbôr* was a proven hero. Not only the size of the army, but also the belief that it had an extraordinary number of outstanding fighters fostered the misplaced trust. If we are correct in joining v 13b to v 9a, it was precisely this self-confidence that constituted Israel's persistent sin. The verb "to trust," used only here in Hosea, describes a state of assurance that leads to complacency. This becomes ironical when we remember how helpless Israel was, for all such confidence, in the face of the Assyrian war machine.

14a. *Tumult. Šā'ôn* describes the uproar of the rampaging army or a lawless crowd, Jer 24:31; cf. Ps 40:3.

shall rise. The spelling *q'm* includes a vowel letter that has no basis in the etymology of the root. The use of *'alep* for an *a* vowel is rare in Biblical Hebrew, though common in late Aramaic texts. Its presence here can only be explained as a scribal inadvertence, although there are other signs of mixed orthography in Hosea, that is, the ' in 4:6, and the use of *w* in *yiqṭōl* forms (e.g. 8:12 Ketib and especially 9:9b *yzkwr* and *ypqwd,* cf. *yzkr* and *ypqd* in 8:13).

from. The preposition *b,* according to context, indicates not that hostilities rise against Israel's army, but that a tumult arises from the army in the revolutions and civil wars of Israel's last years. See the discussion of the motif of civil war in connection with Gibeah, in Note on 9a.

army. Literally "people," but *'am* often means troops, as in v 10b, and the present context requires it. "Your people" would mean Israel in relation to Yahweh, as the nation is never called "your people" in relation to a human king. Since the *'am* is the muster of all citizens obliged to bear arms, the use of this word here indicates a disaster on a national scale.

All . . . fortresses. The subject of the verb is considered to be *kl,* "all," singular (or collective) in spite of the plural "fortresses"; Hosea uses *mibṣār* only here; cf. 8:14.

devastated. A passive meaning for the verb form gains support from the passive verb at the end of the verse; *yûššad* presents some difficulties, notably the dagesh in *š*. The *Hip'il* is unattested, so the passive to be read is *Qal,* in spite of the orthography. There is a comparable play on the active and passive of *šdd* in Isa 33:1.

Shalman. Neither the person, nor the place Beth Arbel, nor the incident, has been identified with any confidence. It has been suggested (Astour 1971, 1976) that the Assyrian king Shalmaneser is called Shalman by abbreviating his name (cf. biblical "Pul" for the Assyrian king Tiglath Pileser); a contemporary Moabite king called Salamanu is another candidate (Wolff 1974:188). Though Beth Arbel has not been firmly identified, LXX transcribes the MT, confirming its correctness. The ancient city on the site of modern Irbid has been suggested (Wolff 1974:188); but no record of atrocities there is available.

14b. *the day of war.* The Masoretes connected this time phrase with the infinitive "devastated." Rhythmic balance associates it rather with what follows; the connection between vv 14b and 15 is secured by the parallelism between *bywm* and *bšḥr*. The plurals in v 15 show that this unit is to be separated from vv 13–14a. The war at the end of the unit matches the war at the beginning of the unit which overtook Israel. The connections could be settled with more certainty if we could determine the time reference of *ruṭṭāšâ*. If past, it could describe Shalman's cruelties; such atrocities are, however, routine even in modern war, and Shalman must have been excessive in cruelty for his name to become a byword.

dashed. Although here used of mothers, the verb can describe the hurling of children against solid rock (cf. Ps 137:9), the dropping of them from a height, or the smashing of their skulls. There is no particular emphasis on dashing them to pieces, as if their bodies had to be dismembered, as conventional translations have put it. An added cruelty consisted in murdering the children in front of their parents; cf. Isa 13:16; II Kings 25:7. The parents were slain thereafter. This could be the meaning of the idiom "mother beside (*or* upon) children." The same phrase in Gen 32:12 suggests total extermination. A similar construction in Exod 35:22 suggests that it means all the mothers and children. It does not describe the killing of a particular mother beside her children; the feminine singular verb agrees with "mother" rather than "children" in spite of the fact that the verb usually describes the smashing of infants.

It may be that this set phrase has been abbreviated from the full expression *'ēm ('al 'ēm, bānîm) 'al-bānîm,* as a description of wholesale slaughter. On similar expressions, see Greenfield (1965).

15a. *may he do.* The comparison with what Shalman did at Beth Arbel suggests that a similar event will occur at Bethel. As far back as LXX, the verb has been taken as future; Wolff (1974:181) thinks that the original Hebrew was *'e'ĕšeh,* "I will do," and that the MT is the result of a scribal error. Tense references can hardly be handled so cavalierly. If Shalman is Hosea's name for a contemporary Assyrian king, and the sacking of Beth Arbel was a recent event, Hosea could be saying that Bethel will share the same fate; Shalman would then be the subject of *'āšâ.* Given that Yahweh has done so much of the speaking and that Shalman is the most immediate antecedent, this is possible. Even if the speaker is the prophet and the actor Yahweh, the violence would be carried out through a human agent such as Shalman.

Bethel. The name of the city would be in apposition with *lākem,* "to you, O Bethel." It is more likely that the prophet is addressing the people, as in vv 12 and 13; and Bethel is the location of a major disaster that is looming. The preposition *b* is often omitted before a homorganic consonant, quite apart from Hosea's tendency to omit prepositions.

Because of the applicability of the entire speech to the whole nation, alteration of Bethel to "house of Israel," after LXX, is widely favored. Wolff (1974:181) argues in support of this emendation that Hosea usually calls Bethel "Beth Awen." Bethel occurs again, however, in 12:5. LXX reads *Beth-On* there, which only shows that the Greek translator (or the scribe of the manuscript used by him) realized the meaning of the alternate name for Bethel. Bethel is a better parallel to Beth Arbel, especially as the latter seems to be a city, not a state. It could, of course, be argued in general terms that the devastation of the whole country, and not just one town, would be a more fitting punishment for the sins described, in keeping with the ruin in v 15b. The text will stand if we remember the enormous symbolic importance of Bethel, not only as a shrine of antiquity, but also as a center of the calf cult and its royal patronage in the northern kingdom. Amos focused his prophecies on Bethel (Amos 7), even though from the political and military point of view it would not be a prime target for a foreign invader.

Other currents of thought are tied to the word Bethel. The "House of Yahweh" (8:1 and 9:4), compared with the unique "land of Yahweh" (9:3), seems to stand against "the house of his god" in 9:8. In each case it is not certain whether "house" means shrine or country. In 10:5 "Beth Awen" occurs alongside "Samaria," but whether as a twin city or as an alternate name (cf. *bāmôt 'āwen* in 10:8) for Samaria or part of it is again not clear. By the covenants described in vv 3 and 4 Israel renounced Yahweh and placed the country under the rule of another god. This god is not named; his name is not *'ēl,* which is here generic. The name Bethel, rather than Beth Awen, preserves the connection with the Jacob tradition, as in 12:5; cf. Gen 31:13; 35:7.

wicked wickedness. Literally "the wickedness of your wickedness."

15b. *the sun rose.* Literally "at the dawn." From 7:6 we concluded that the murder of a king took place in the early morning. For the meaning of *šaḥar* see the NOTE on 6:3. An attack just before sunrise has the advantage of surprise, with the whole day to follow through.

king. It may be that the kingdom (**mulk >mōlek*) is referred to here, although in view of the king's representational status the difference may be slight, and kingdom and king would share the same destiny. Nevertheless Hosea is more concerned with the fate of the nation than with individual kings.

ruined. The possible meanings of the root *dmy* have been discussed in the NOTES on 4:5 and 6. The meaning "to silence" is preferred here by some scholars, including Wolff (1974:181), who rather inconsistently translates "to destroy" in v 7. It is desirable to maintain the same meaning in both places.

XX. THE SPIRITUAL HISTORY OF ISRAEL: CHILDHOOD AND CONSUMMATION (11:1–11)

Childhood: out of slavery in Egypt

11:1a	When Israel was a youth, I loved him.
1b	From Egypt, I called him "My child."
2a	They called to them.
	They departed from me.
2b	They sacrificed to Baals.
	They burned incense to images.
3a	I was a guide for Ephraim.
	I took from his arms the bonds of men.
3b	They did not acknowledge that I had healed them,
4a	That I had drawn them with cords of love on their jaws,
4b	That I treated them like those who remove the yoke.
	I heeded (his plea) and made (him) prevail.

Consummation: back to slavery in Egypt and Assyria

5a	He will surely return to the land of Egypt,
	his own king, to Assyria,
5b	because they refused to return to me.
6a	The sword will damage his cities.
	It will finish off his strong men.
6b	It will consume their schemers.
7a	My people are bent on turning from me.
7b	They did not call on him as the Supreme God.
	He did not exalt him as the Only One.
8a	How can I give you up, Ephraim?
	How can I relinquish you, Israel?
	How can I make you like Admah?
	How can I deal with you like Zeboiim?
8b	My mind is turning over inside me.
	My emotions are agitated all together.
9a	I will certainly act out my burning anger.
	I will certainly come back to destroy Ephraim.

9b   For I am a god and not a human.
    I, the Holy One, will certainly come into the midst
      of your city.

10a   Behind Yahweh they will walk.
    Like a lion he will roar.

10b   Indeed he himself will roar.
    The children will come trembling from the west.

11a   They will come trembling like a bird from Egypt,
    like a dove from the land of Assyria.

11b   I will settle them on their estates.
    Oracle of Yahweh.

NOTES

11:1–11. The chapter divides into two principal parts (vv 1–4, and 5–11) although there are links between the parts, and interlocking elements. The human protagonists in both units are Israel (vv 1 and 8) and Ephraim (vv 3, 8–9), while Yahweh, the divine antagonist and respondent, speaks and acts in both first and third persons. The second part, vv 5–11, is bounded by references to Egypt and Assyria, a common pair in Hosea. The intricate pattern in vv 5 and 11 shows that the arrangement is deliberate:

    v 5: to the land of Egypt — Assyria
    v 11: from Egypt — from the land of Assyria

The shift in the word "land" in vv 5 and 11, along with the difference in motion ("to" in v 5, "from" in v 11) confirms the connections and the envelope construction. At the same time there are links with the first unit, especially in the repetition of the names Israel and Ephraim and the sequence of first- and third-person forms referring to Yahweh.

The first unit, vv 1–4, seems to be structured in similar fashion. Thus v 1 initiates the discourse which finds its concluding remark in v 4b to balance the bicola and complete the echo. We include v 3a in the framework:

1a   When Israel was a youth, I loved him.
    (A youth) from Egypt I called him, "My child."

3a   I was a guide for Ephraim.
    I took from his arms the bonds of men.

4bB   I heeded (his plea) and made (him) prevail.

The material in v 2, with third-person plural forms, is to be associated with vv 3b–4bA, which have similar grammatical features.

The formula "Oracle of Yahweh" is used sparingly by Hosea, in contrast, for example, to Amos, who uses it twenty-one times (Baumgärtel 1961). Three times in Hosea 2 it comes in the middle of a speech, almost parenthetically, although in 2:15 it may mark the end of a major section. This variable usage indicates that caution is needed in considering its occurrence in 11:11 as a sign that a major section ends there. Yet it is likely that this is so: v 11b seems climactic, and in c 12 the patriarchal traditions become prominent for the first time. At the same time there is continuity, at least into the opening verses of c 12. The dealings with Assyria have been a recurring theme in cc 5–11, and finally in 12:2 we have one of the plainest statements that the people have made a covenant with Assyria. There can be no doubt that a new section begins in 11:1. It recapitulates once more the story that has already been told in 9:10.

The speech is unified by the prominence of Yahweh; in no other passage are his personal feelings revealed more openly. Hos 6:4 discloses a similar anguish over inflicting the necessary punishment on Israel, but in c 11 the inner torment is made all the more painful by the conflicting demands of love.

There are several rhetorical signals which unify the discourse. There is repetition of key words in well-formed bicola, for example, *êk* in v 8, *lō'* in v 9 (in each instance without *wĕ*), *yiś'āg* in v 10. There is repetition of a catchword as a linkage between adjacent bicola, for example, *yeḥerdû* in vv 10b and 11a. A root is repeated to give balance to an extended structure, for example, the root *yḥd* is in the same structural position in vv 7b and 8b and the two bicola in which it occurs are in symmetrical positions in relation to the total structure. The similar uses of *hû'* in vv 5a and 10b also serve to unify the passage. Nevertheless there are serious structural dislocations in the chapter. This may be an authentic reflection of the turbulence of indecision, or the byproduct of varieties of textual disarray we cannot detect with certainty.

11:1a. *Israel.* Once more this name is prominent in the opening statement of a speech. Kuhnigk (1974:127) suggests that the patriarch is meant here, and his sons (reading the plural) are mentioned in v 1b. This is a premature anticipation of c 12.

youth. *N'r* means "lad, youth; servant, retainer." No precise designation of age is implied, but adolescence is the usual connotation. Kuhnigk renders "slave, servant" (1974:127).

loved. An act of election which makes Israel Yahweh's child. Adoption into a family may have been a relevant metaphor but it is more likely that the relationship was quasi-political, like that between a suzerain and a vassal. At Mari, loyalists are described as those whom the king loves, not, as we might have expected, those who love the king. The emphasis is on the favor shown by the king as benefactor (ARM 10:7 line 13, *ANET* 630).

The initiative in the relationship is taken by Yahweh who chooses Israel and confers the status of child on him. The first historical recognition of this is in Exod 4:22 where Yahweh says to Pharaoh, "Israel is my child, my firstborn." The latter term makes the relationship even clearer. Israel is not simply "a child of Yahweh." He is the senior, the privileged heir. The sentiment expressed here is echoed in the Book of Deuteronomy and often in the prophets, for example, Amos 3:2, "You alone have I acknowledged out of all the clans of the world."

1b. *From Egypt*. This line is quoted in Matt 2:15, on which see Brown (1977:202–230, esp. 204, 219–221). The time reference in the opening verse is to the most critical period in Israel's history, its childhood — when the people were delivered from bondage in Egypt and became a community in the wilderness. Although Hosea here begins the story of Israel in Egypt, he elsewhere refers to Jacob traditions unrelated to the Exodus; the link of patriarchal and Mosaic stories (whatever the historical realities) is full-blown in J, but seems rudimentary here. The verse is to be understood in combinatory fashion as follows: "When Israel was a youth in (*or* from) Egypt, I loved him and called him, 'My child.'"

The verbs are parallel and complementary in meaning: the 3 m s suffix with *w'hbhw* also serves the other verb, *qr'ty*. The idiom *qr' l* means both "to name" and "to summon." The expression *mmṣrym*, which is echoed and confirmed by *m'rṣ mṣrym* in 12:10, reflects the tradition of the deliverance, which is regularly described as being "from (the land of) Egypt." While the adoption of Israel as son and heir precedes the Exodus in the prose tradition (cf. Exod 4:22), the creation of Israel as a social entity took place in the wilderness, and this passage may identify the moment of adoption with the latter event. The phrase "from Egypt" may refer to the act of deliverance which was the climax of a series: I loved him, and called him "my child," and brought him out of Egypt.

LXX reads strangely "his sons," viz. "Israel's sons," apparently to avoid calling Israel "my son."

2a. *They called*. The change of number to plural means a change of subject; v 2 deals with a situation different from that in v 1, in spite of the repetition of the verb "to call." Neither subject nor object is identified. The object ("them") cannot be the Israel of v 1 (who is called "him"). As v 2 continues, it appears that this call had the opposite effect of Yahweh's call. Yahweh's call brought them into covenant relationship. This other call took them away from Yahweh, so that they sacrificed to Baal images (v 2b). The rather general statements of v 2 would fit a number of situations in the long history of Israel's repeated desertions of Yahweh to serve Baal. If v 1 describes the Exodus, something soon after would suit v 2, for example, the Baal-Peor incident. Hos 11:1 would parallel 9:10a quite closely; *māṣā'tî* // *rā'îtî* is an action like "I loved // I called." This result is supported by the language of Numbers 25. There the Moabite women "called the people to the sacrifices of their gods" (Num 25:2; similar language is used in Exod 34:15, including the key word "call"). Hos 11:2b describes involvement in such sacrifices. The sequence "called . . . sacrificed" is found also in Deut 33:19, where the sacrifices are apparently legitimate.

They departed. Literally, "they walked." Hosea has used this verb to describe the wife's desertion (2:7,15) and also the embassage to Assyria (7:11). The normal preposition for defection is *mē'aḥărê* (1:2); but Hosea varies his prepositions, and several have been used with the related word *zny*.

from me. The MT reads *mpnyhm*, "from their faces," which does not make sense. We follow the widely accepted emendation **mippānay hēm*, "from my face, they" after LXX (*ek prosōpou mou autoi*), cf. Wolff (1974:190–191), and Kuhnigk (1974:129). No change in the consonants is required. The use of *hēm* is typical of Hosea. "From my face" refers to the personal presence of Yahweh manifested in the cult. Participation in the cult is called "seeking the face of Yahweh" and walking away from his face means deserting his regular worship and seeking the "face" of rival gods in their shrines.

2b. *sacrificed.* Sacrificing and burning (incense) are not necessarily two distinct activities; they are two concomitant aspects of worship, as the frequent parallelism of *zbḥ* and *qṭr* indicates. The burning is generally of aromatic incense, not an oblation in its own right, but an accompaniment; the burning of flesh is the integral and essential part of the offering.

Baals . . . images. The nouns are complementary. Again it is not certain if the plural points to a multiplicity of pagan gods or is a variant of Baal (see the NOTE on 2:15). Historically it is not likely that Baal Peor (9:10) is the same as the great Canaanite storm god (Hadad), who was Yahweh's chief rival during the monarchical period, but Hosea may have thought so. This does not prove that 11:2 refers to Baal Peor, although its language resembles Numbers 25. The text is sufficiently general to describe many other similar incidents, such as Judg 2:11.

3a. *I.* The pronoun makes Yahweh prominent as agent. It serves to mark a new point of departure in the narrative and also, perhaps, a new phase in the history. At the same time the first-person usage serves as a link with v 1. The free form of the pronoun often serves to point up a contrast with some other agent and may require an adversative translation — "It was I, no one else . . ." or "It was I, not Baal. . . ." The act must, accordingly, have been one of great significance, yet one in which the role of Yahweh could be denied.

guide. The form *tirgaltî* is generally accepted as a *Tipʿel* verb, even though such a verb stem is a rarity in Hebrew. A -*t*- modifier in Northwest Semitic is often reflexive, but neither this sense nor a causative ("I made walk") seems appropriate here. The traditional "I taught to walk" has been influenced by the picture of parent and child given in v 1. This is simply wrong: a *naʿar* is not an infant that must be taught to walk. Further, the topic has changed from Israel to Ephraim, and we cannot assume that these are the same. If a causative is needed, we must ask why the *Hipʿil* was not used. The use of *l* with "Ephraim" makes it improbable that Ephraim is the direct object of the verb. In v 3 Yahweh is acting in some way beneficial "for Ephraim"; the *l* idiom is met in 7:1. The denominative of *rgl* is the *Piʿel,* which has the highly technical meaning "to spy, reconnoiter." The need for another denominative verb for a different kind of walking could have evoked the *Tipʿel,* meaning "to lead, walk in front of." The preformative is a morph which makes a quadriliteral root with a specialized meaning, here in a noun form. The action described is correlative with walking behind, the usual expression for loyal following of Yahweh. Such leadership was in evidence in the wilderness journey, and especially in entering the promised land.

Ephraim. The use of the name Ephraim makes it likely that we are now in a post-Exodus period. The terminology reflects, at the earliest, the situation in the time of the Judges, when Ephraim was a premier tribe, first in the league. As such Ephraim could represent the whole nation, or at least the northern coalition.

I took. The Hebrew text is problematical. The form *qāḥām* is unique. If it is not to be abandoned as a hopeless corruption, two solutions are available. The MT is literally imperative: "Take them upon his forearms." None of the pronoun references is evident, since Yahweh (first person) is speaking about Ephraim (normally singular). But "his" forearms, if not Ephraim's, would seem to be Yahweh's. What, then, is he doing with them? The "arm" is a symbol of strength, especially in fighting. The verb *lqḥ* is not employed to describe the use of the arms for lifting or carrying. Comparison with Isa 40:11 is out of order, even though such an interpretation has been imposed on v 3aB from earliest times. LXX translated "I took him up upon my arm"; either the translator took considerable liberties with the text, or else he was using a Hebrew text that had been simplified. Other ancient versions confirm that this is how the text was generally understood. The image of carrying an infant in one's arms does not seem to be congruent with the picture in v 3aA, whether the latter means leading or teaching to walk. This is not a fatal objection, because v 3b, assuming it is still talking about the same matter, has another image again, that of healing. The clearer passages, including vv 1 and 4, suggest that several aspects of Yahweh's beneficent activities are being recalled.

To secure the meaning "I took," a reading *'*eqqaḥ, rather than
*lāqaḥtî, is usually suggested. The former requires the restoration of only
one consonant. The text as it stands is possible, if qḥ is recognized as a
biconsonantal byform of lqḥ, a well-attested pattern. An infinitive absolute
would satisfy the requirements of grammar and the line would describe
the rescue of Israel from Egypt. If this is correct, the object for "took off"
must be bonds of some kind; in fact, the bonds mentioned in v 4 are the
object of the verb. The m of qḥm belongs with the preposition 'l to form
mē'al.

The imagery of ropes is met again in Isa 5:18:

> hôy mōšĕkê he'āwōn
> bĕḥablê haššāw'
> wĕka'ăbôt hā'ăgālâ ḥaṭṭā'â

> Woe to those who drag along iniquity
>   with cords of falsehood,
> and as with cart-ropes sin.

In its only other occurrence, ḥaṭṭā'â is parallel to 'āwōn (Exod 34:7); the
two words for "rope" are the same as in v 4, except that Isaiah uses the
singular, 'ăbôt. Isaiah's language is as enigmatic as Hosea's. "Ropes of a
cart" is without parallel; if we transfer -h (of 'glh) to the next word as the
article, we recover more of Hosea's language in the parallelism of šāw'
and *'ēgel, which may designate the false god to whom the people have
sworn covenant oaths. Ps 2:3 shows that "ropes" can describe covenant
obligations. Behind this vocabulary, there may be a ceremony of tying a
vassal as a bond servant to an overlord. The mention of the "rope of the
calf" as the bond with the false god may explain what Isaiah is talking
about. The people are loaded with 'āwōn (Isa 1:4), and hauling 'āwōn
(Isa 5:18), because they are bound to the false god, the calf. This suggests
that the bonds of love in v 4 are a true covenant with Yahweh, who set his
love on Israel (v 1). That ropes can symbolize an alliance is indicated by
the phrase "the rope of the wicked" (Ps 129:4; cf. Ps 119:61).

The meaning of the verb mšk in v 4a is an important part of the problem. It has a remarkably wide range of connotations. In Ps 10:9, for instance, it means "to capture, tie up in a net." To ensnare with ropes of
love would describe a new captivity within the covenant. In Gen 37:28
the verb mšk describes the rescue of Joseph from the pit, and Jer 38:13
has the same language, as well as the detail that ḥăbālîm, "ropes," were
used to haul the prisoner out. Deut 21:3 shows that mšk can describe the
work that a draft animal does using a yoke ('ōl, as in v 4aB); it probably
describes "a heifer which has never had a yoke tied onto her." 'Emšĕkēm,
then, resembles 'arkîb in 10:11: both may describe the harnessing of

Ephraim to do useful work for Yahweh, although in the Bible, ropes are more often used for tying than for pulling.

The verb in Judg 4:6,7; 20:37 probably means "to link up." That *'hb*, "to love," and *mšk* go together in the language of covenant-making is made clear by Jer 31:3:

> *wĕ'ahăbat 'ôlām 'ăhabtîk*
> *'al-kēn mĕšaktîk ḥāsed*

The parallelism, with chiasm, makes it clear that *ḥesed* is complementary to "love," and ought to have the same grammatical function; *ḥesed* is the object of *mšk*, and the pronoun suffix -*k*, "you," is not the indirect object, pace *RSV*, "I have continued my faithfulness to you" (Jer 31:3). In the poetic structure -*k* is the object of both verbs, and the verbs are synonyms. "I have drawn/bonded you with *ḥesed*" parallels "I have loved you with enduring love." The word-field is the same as that of Hos 11:1–4. The idiom may also be reflected in Hos 7:5 and Ps 109:12.

3b. *acknowledge.* Something more than "they knew" is needed for *yādĕ'û;* the people are blamed for rejecting knowledge gained by experience of Yahweh's healing, not for mere ignorance.

healed. A play on the name Ephraim is probably intended in the verb *rp'.* Hosea is protective of this attribute of Yahweh (5:13; 6:1). The title of Yahweh as "your Healer" goes back to the Exodus (Exod 15:26). More than one act of healing is attributed to the Wilderness period. Hosea's polemic against healers in rivalry with Yahweh makes us wonder if one of the unnamed gods was a god of healing. Hos 14:5 has the same association of loving and healing.

4b. *those who remove the yoke.* The difficulty of the word *'ōl,* "yoke," has been attacked wrongly by reading *'ūl,* "infant," which continues the picture of a parent caring tenderly for a little child. Wolff (1974:191) argues for the result "and I was to them as those who lift a small child to their cheek." But difficulties remain, the clash in number being very awkward; we would expect one person to be lifting a suckling "to *his* cheek." The "yoke" of the MT is an arched frame normally placed on the shoulders at the base of the neck (10:11).

If this is a simile, the use of the plural is strange. Why should Yahweh be compared with "those who lift up the yoke"? "Lifting a yoke" could mean to put it on a draft animal or to take it off. The yoke is a symbol of servitude, its removal a symbol of liberation (Gen 27:40). If v 4 records the most memorable act of liberation in Israel's history, the Exodus, we need to ask why that event is recounted at this point, and what its connection is with the statements before and after. This is not clear, since the rest of v 4 is obscure.

The picture is complex and confused. On the face of it, placing a yoke

on an animal's cheek, as described in the MT, seems impossible. Putting a
rope halter on the muzzle would make more sense. Two activities of Yahweh are described here.

> qḥ m'l-zrw'tyw . . . bḥbly 'dm   (vv 3aB . . . 4a)
> 'mškm b'btwt 'hbh . . . 'l lḥyhm   (vv 4a . . . 4a)

The parallelism of "his arms" // "their jaws," and "bonds of men" //
"cords of love," as well as the use of the same prepositions with the parallel nouns and the chiasm of the matching phrases, shows that a well-
formed bicolon is present. The pieces of the bicolon are here "reassembled" merely for the readers' convenience.

Each statement has a complete clause inserted at the point of discontinuity, and the insertions, which both have plural pronouns, are related.
The parallel statements contrast two moments in Yahweh's dealings with
this people. First he removed the ropes from Ephraim's arms, then he
harnessed the cords of love on their jaws. The full picture still eludes us:
what are cords of love, and what liberation and triumph are meant here?

heeded (*his plea*). The line remains cryptic. In the MT, 'aṭ is a *Hip'il*,
but has no object. This form of the verb occurs over seventy times and is
generally transitive. Here and Job 23:11 are the only places where it lacks
an explicit object and in Job the object understood is clearly "my ear."
The ear is the object of the verb in nearly half its occurrences, nearly always an act of God in listening to prayer. The preposition *'el* marks the
person who is listened to. Less common is the extension of the hand in an
act of destruction (Isa 31:3; Jer 6:12; 15:6; 51:25); then the preposition
is *'al*, "against," except in Ezek 30:25, where the MSS are divided between *'el* (MT) and *'al*. Otherwise the verb describes the perversion of
justice or the deflection of the mind into wrong thoughts. A laconic abbreviation is most likely to derive from a stock phrase, and thus we suppose
"I inclined (my ear) to him," which implies that Ephraim called on Yahweh out of distress, and was heard. It was the response of Yahweh to Israel's cries in Egypt that started the Exodus, and again and again after
that, Yahweh responded to his people's prayers in time of need. *'Ēlāyw*
then parallels *lĕ'eprayim* in v 3a.

made (*him*) *prevail*. When God answers a person's prayer, he enables
him to succeed. The root *ykl*, "to succeed," should be recognized in *'wkyl*,
rather than *'kl*, "to eat" (contrast Wolff 1974:191). The latter reading is
sometimes filled out by bringing in *lō'* from v 5, and reading *lô*, "to him."
RSV goes one step further and normalizes the whole to plural, a step already partly taken by the Syriac. The LXX, however, confirms the singular, but does read *lō'* as *autō*, "to him." Even so, *lô* hardly qualifies as the
object if *'wkyl* means "I fed." There is no evidence for a *Hip'il* of *ykl*, but
the status of *'wkyl* as a *Hip'il* of *'kl* is questionable. The *Hip'il* of *'kl* is

well attested, and its morphology is normal, preserving the *'alep*. Even if the first person is considered a special case, in which the root *'alep* dissimilates to zero, as in *'ōmar*, "I will say," the use of *w* to mark the vowel is almost without parallel and places the identification under suspicion. There is also a syntactic problem. The causative of *'kl* usually has two objects and even when only one is explicit the other is usually implied in the context. The absence of any object would be unique for the *Hip'il* of *'kl;* the inclusion of **lô* can hardly be considered satisfactory. The suggestion that *'wkyl* is a plene spelling of *'ōkel*, "food," is not much help, except as a further indication that "I fed" is not satisfactory.

Turning to the root *ykl*, we note the unique metaplasm of its stems, perfect *yākōl*, imperfect *yûkal*. The plene spelling of the *Qal* imperfect is almost universal, but the stem-vowel *-i-* can only be a sign of the *Hip'il*, whatever the root. The absence of an object is a feature strongly in favor of *ykl*, and the intransitive *Hip'il* could be elative. The lack of a conjunction between "I inclined" and "I enabled" is typical of Hosea.

The results of analyzing vv 3 and 4 can now be summarized.

1 I was a guide for Ephraim (v 3a).
6 I heeded (his plea) and made (him) prevail (v 4b).

2 I took from his arms . . . the bonds of men (vv 3a,4a).
4 I had drawn them with cords of love . . . on their jaws (v 4a).

3 They did not acknowledge that I had healed them (v 3b).
5 I treated them like those who remove the yoke (v 4b).

The six lines, two of which are broken, can thus be grouped into three pairs. In the last pair the sequence of verbs is perfect // imperfect, both past tense; in the others, the verbs of the second line are imperfect.

Verses 3aA and 4bB (⌗⌗1 and 6) surround the other statements; the lines refer to liberation from bondage (perhaps the original slavery in Egypt) and the provision for a relationship with Yahweh. ⌗⌗2–3 describe Israel's misunderstanding of these actions. This permits us to consider the grammatical connection between ⌗⌗3 and 5. It is possible that the latter are coordinated and that ⌗5 is equally governed by *kî* as a statement of what they did not realize. Since lifting the yoke is a beneficial act, similar to healing, this must describe the removal of the yoke of oppression, an act of Yahweh not acknowledged by Israel. The theme of vv 1–4 is the contrast between Yahweh's generosity and Israel's ingratitude.

5a. *surely*. Unless the Masoretic *lō'*, "not," at the beginning of v 5 is to be read as *lô*, "to him," and joined to the preceding verse, the apparent negation in v 5 cannot be accepted. Hosea threatens several times a removal or flight of the people to Egypt and v 11 below presupposes some such exile. The best solution is to recognize an asseverative *l'* with Gordis (1976:182; cf. Wolff 1974:192) and Kuhnigk (1974:133–134).

return. LXX reads "he settled." Confusion between forms of *šwb*, "to return," and *yšb*, "to dwell," often occurs in Hosea; sometimes there seems to be deliberate play on the contrast between the verbs (see 9:3). The LXX translation here would only be possible with defective spelling; this and other plene spellings in the MT must have been introduced late in transmission.

land of Egypt. The LXX reading "Ephraim" for *'l-'rṣ* of the MT is an error influenced by 9:3b, *wšb 'prym mṣrym.* That *'el-'ereṣ* is correct is scarcely to be doubted. The repetition of "land" in v 11, in a chiastic pattern already described above, would seem to be decisive. Hosea mentions "the land of Egypt" in four other places (2:17; 7:16; 12:10; 13:4).

his own king, to Assyria. Verse 5aB is not a close parallel to v 5aA, although "Assyria" balances "the land of Egypt," as often. The words *hw' mlkw* should be compared with *šmrwn mlkh* (10:7) and interpreted, "his own king," the suffix referring to Ephraim (or Israel). The translation of the passage as a whole would be: "His own king will surely go back to Egypt or/and Assyria." A statement about Israel's king going into exile fits here well, and 10:15 mentions the ruin of the king of Israel.

5b. *they refused.* Cf. Jer 5:3 where a similar statement is made. Once more there is a contrast between singular ("his own king") and plural ("they refused"). This is a guide to the structure of vv 5–7.

5a	*lō' yāšûb 'el-'ereṣ miṣrayim*	singular
	wĕ'aššûr hû' malkô	
5b	*kî mē'ănû lāšûb*	plural
6a	*wĕḥālâ ḥereb bĕ'ārāyw*	singular
	wĕkillĕtâ baddāyw	
6b	*wĕ'ākālâ mimmō'ăṣôtêhem*	plural
7a	*wĕ'ammî tĕlû'îm limšûbātî*	singular
7b	*wĕ'el-'al yiqrā'ūhû*	plural
	yaḥīd lō' yĕrômēm	singular

Verses 5 and 6 contain a bicolon with singular pronouns followed by a single line with plurals. Verse 7 begins with a line in which "my people" is plural, followed by a bicolon which probably has a singular referent.

The accusation of unrepentance in v 5b is general; no occasion is identified. It is important, nevertheless; following vv 1–4, it makes a completely new point. There the conduct of Israel was contrasted with Yahweh's. He was steadfast; they were fickle. Yet their willful and persistent violation of his covenant is not the ultimate, unpardonable sin. Even the idolatry described in v 2b, for which there would seem to be no excuse and forgiveness, need not mean the end of Yahweh's relationship with Israel. They could always change their mind again and turn back to Yahweh. Numerous incidents in their past history proved that. It was possible to restore the covenant. All they had to do was repent and mend their ways. Refusal to repent was the ultimate sin; it is being committed.

6a. *The sword.* Although v 5b may be the indictment for which v 6 states the punishment, we do not have the normal transition *'al kēn,* "therefore," but only the consecutive future. This lack makes it less certain that there is a logical transition between vv 5 and 6. In terms of chronological sequence, the destruction of the cities threatened in v 6 would precede removal to foreign countries, described in v 5a. We have met this reversal of time sequence before in Hosea. The bicolon in v 5a and the bicolon in v 6a encompass v 5b. If v 5b gives the reason for the disasters described in vv 5a and 6a, then *kî* must be translated "because." The noun "sword" is formally indefinite. This could be an archaism in Hosea's style; he uses the definite article sparingly except in cc 2 and 4. "Sword" could be the name for the agent of war, a member of Yahweh's heavenly army; cf. fire in 8:14. Even if Hosea has a human army, that of Assyria, in mind (v 5), this does not exclude the collateral participation of heavenly agencies.

damage. In *ḥlh* we meet once more a verb containing the consonants *ḥ-l* which offer so many possibilities. We read a form of *ḥly,* "to be weak," with the LXX and Vulgate. Others read forms of *ḥll,* "to begin," or *ḥll,* "to loose" (Kuhnigk 1974:135). This is the only place where any of these verbs is used with "sword." While "to writhe, dance" (root *ḥwl*) is possible (Wolff 1974:192, 200), this root normally describes the contortions of a person in extreme pain, especially a woman in childbirth. We read a *Pi'el* transitive form, notwithstanding the apparent gender clash.

A sword is used chiefly against people, and against cities only in a secondary sense. The noun phrases may form a combination: the sword will damage and finish off the strong men in his cities.

finish off. Since the verb is feminine, the subject must be "sword." This makes it improbable that *baddāyw* means "his bars," from *bad,* "separation." The etymological possibilities of *bd(d)* are quite numerous (Rabin 1973). Wolff (1974:192), assuming that "their schemes" in v 6b supplies the parallel, translates "his braggarts," invoking *bd,* "idle talk." There are a number of passages in which *baddāyw* means "his (proud) boastings," which will be proved groundless when Yahweh destroys an arrogant nation, particularly Moab (Isa 16:6; Jer 48:30).

The presence of the sword points to something more military. Jer 50:35–38 gives a long list of Babylonians whom the sword will decimate. The list includes "citizens," "princes," "wise men," and *baddîm,* "heroes," followed by *gibbôrîm,* "strong men." If the parallelism is any guide, the *baddîm* are functionaries, probably military. In Hos 10:13 Ephraim is accused of trusting in his *gibbôrîm*. Hos 10:14 predicts the devastation of the fortress towns, and 11:6 continues this theme. We conclude that *baddāyw* means "his warriors" or the like. (If, in Jer 50:36, *baddîm* is parallel to *ḥăkāmîm*, the connection with *bd* might stand: the "idle talk," the false wisdom of the advisers. In Hos 11:6 a parallel with *mō'ăṣôt* is then possible. Isa 44:25–26 lends support to this; for here *baddîm*, *qōsĕmîm*, "diviners," and *ḥăkāmîm* are all listed together as persons whose "signs" Yahweh confutes.)

Whatever the exact meaning, *baddîm* are evidently some influential class in the power structure. "Their schemes" (v 6b) refers to the work of these strategists.

6b. *consume*. There is some assonance among the three verbs in this verse. Each begins its clause in a *wāw*-consecutive construction. The feminine gender of the verb in v 6b suggests that it has the same subject as v 6a. The verb *'kl* describes the devouring activity of the sword in Deut 32:42. The sword is both "destroyer" and "devourer."

schemers. The word *mō'ēṣâ* can mean "advice" in a wholesome sense (Prov 22:20; cf. Job 29:21), and "evil plans" (Jer 7:24; Mic 6:16; Pss 5:11; 81:13; Prov 1:31). The preposition *min* is a further complication. A tie between *bdym* and *m'ṣwt* is possible. As so often in the Psalms, a feminine plural abstract is balanced with a masculine plural concrete noun. The meaning may be composite: the falsely wise or the "wise in their own conceit." The sword will devour them all. The shift from singular to plural shows the pattern in v 5; the 3 m pl suffix at the end of the verse anticipates *'ammî* at the beginning of v 7. If v 6 is not a tricolon, as the MT has it, but consists of a bicolon and a third, unrelated line, we could read **wa'ăkalleh*, "and I will bring to an end," using the preceding verb again.

7a. *bent on*. The verb *tālâ* normally describes the impaling of the body of an executed criminal, or the hanging of a utensil on a peg. The only way of sustaining such a meaning here would be if the phrase describes war atrocities such as those in Lam 5:12, accompanying the disasters of v 6. We follow Wolff (1974:192) in a more abstract sense. Kuhnigk (1974:136) ties the form to *l'y*, "to be strong."

turning. *Mĕšûbâ* means "turning back," often used of Israel's apostasy, with subjective suffixes. Here the suffix must have dative or ablative force: "their turning away from me."

7b. Literally "And unto *'al* they call him." The ancient versions point to a text considered unintelligible. Two clues enable some progress to be made. The preposition *'el* suggests that *'al* must be a noun. In association with the verb *qr'*, "to call," *'al* must designate the person invoked. *Yiqrā'û* has a direct object, so *'al* may be the name of a god to whom "they call." If the situation is like that in v 2, "to call" means "to invite," and *'al* is a rival god whom Israel is asked to worship, as in Exod 34:15 and Num 25:2. However, it is more likely to be the ascription of the title *'al* to the rival god which is described here, Israel's perverse response to Yahweh's naming Israel as "my son." This does justice to the literal meaning of v 7bA: "They call him Most High."

However, both LXX and Syriac, otherwise widely divergent, knew of a tradition that found the word "God" in this verse. This suggests that *'ēl 'al*, "Supreme God," is used here. That *'al* is a name of Yahweh is well known (Kuhnigk 1974:137–138). The title *'ēl 'al*, "Supreme God," is probably a variant of *'ēl 'elyôn*, an Old Canaanite appellative which some traditions attach to Yahweh. The negative of v 7bB does double duty; see below.

exalt. The *Polel* of *rwm* is often used to describe the exaltation of God. The word *yḥd* presents a major problem. In Ps 34:4, a *Polel* of *rwm* occurs in association with *yaḥdaw* to describe the united celebration of Yahweh's greatness. There the name of Yahweh is the object of *rōmēm;* this verb is commonly met with in the vocabulary of worship. In Ps 107:32, the parallelism of *yērōměmûhû // yěhalělûhû* suggests that the suffix *-hû* on *yiqrā'ūhû* does double duty with the verb *yěrômēm*. The parallelism in v 7b could be leveled if we keep the plural of v 7bA, since the alternation of singular and plural is constant in these verses. Finally, *yḥd* is parallel to *'l* and is a title, *yāḥîd*, for God as the Only One, or better, the first among gods (Kuhnigk 1974:138). *Yḥd* as a synonym of *'ḥd* would be close in meaning to *'al*, the first god being supreme over all the others; cf. Deut 6:4.

If v 7b describes allegiance to a god other than Yahweh, as often thought, then it expands on the apparent backsliding referred to in v 7a. A problem is the presence of *lō'*, "not," in v 7bB. This makes v 7bB negative, while v 7bA seems positive; otherwise we have close parallelism between them. There is one way of reconciling them, besides the one we have adopted; use of the double-duty negative. Assuming that v 7bA describes the apostate acclamation of Baal (v 2) as El Al, we can take v 7bB as adversative.

> And they call upon him as El Al
> (But) he does not exalt (Yahweh) as the Only One.

This preserves *Yḥd* as a title for Yahweh, a title not likely to be crucial in any rival religion. The previously proposed solution is simpler, however.

8. Verse 8 marks a new departure in the speech, though it grows out of v 7. Yahweh does not automatically relinquish his people, just because they have renounced him. His response to the denials recorded in vv 1–7, especially the repudiation of v 7, does not prevent him from continuing to refer to "my people." In v 8 we glimpse the agony in the mind of God as he

searches for some way of evading the response to which he has committed himself in the covenant curses (Leviticus 26, Deuteronomy 28).

The same incongruity explains the torment of Psalm 89. Here the
unqualified promise made to David applies to all his posterity, but the
hard fact of history is that some disaster overtook the royal house and
made the promise seem empty. Ps 89:31–32 makes provision for remedial
punishment, if any king should violate the covenant stipulations, but the
word to David is as unchangeable as the skies.

8a. The four lines of v 8a are intricately woven together. The interrogative *'êk,* which applies to them all, is used only with the first and third.
All the verbs are imperfect, and all have the same pronoun object, in the
singular, confirming our general hypothesis that Ephraim and Israel are
regarded as singular, whether here they are the same or different entities.
The verb *ntn* is used in the first line of each bicolon, but there is a
different verb in the following line. *Miggēn* is a rare verb, and, as a synonym of "to give" can mean "to donate" (Prov 4:9) or "to hand over"
(Gen 14:20). The comparison with the Cities of the Plain shows that
abandonment to destruction is in mind. *Sym* has been used in this sense already in 2:5,14.

It is strange that Yahweh is still undecided at this late stage, after so
many judgments have been mentioned as if his mind were already made
up firmly. The same kind of vacillation is revealed in all its pathos in 6:4,
which is embedded in a speech whose violence and wrath are as intense as
its sorrow. These expressions of the utmost reluctance to exercise the
fierce anger achieve two effects. They remove from the judgments all suggestion of vindictiveness. And, if the judgment is unleashed in spite of this
effort to restrain it — if, as the Psalmist says, Yahweh's nostrils are
stronger than his intestines (Ps 77:10) — it is because Israel's sin has
gone to the extreme, with no hope of renewal and no trace of contrition to
give grounds for compassion.

Admah — Zeboiim. These two places are usually mentioned along with
the better-known cities of Sodom and Gomorrah, whose fate they shared.
The cities became proverbial as the ultimate in wickedness and as a standing reminder of how devastating Yahweh's "wrath" and "anger" (v 9)
can be. The spelling of *ṣb'ym* for the usual *ṣb(w/y)ym* is unique.

8b. *turning over. Hpk* is the verb that is often used to describe the
"overthrow" of the Cities of the Plain. It is not certain whether the perfect
verb here is punctiliar or iterative, viz. whether it describes a decisive
change of heart — a reversal of the decision to destroy Israel — or a turbulence in which the mind is continually shifting.

inside me. 'Ālay could mean "against me," as if the contrary will to save
and will to destroy gave Yahweh a mind divided against itself, within

which the indecisive debate is raging. The use of the same idiom in Exod 14:5 and Ps 105:25 records a decisive change of policy, a reversal of sentiment from amity to hatred. I Sam 4:19, on the other hand, describes the pangs of childbirth, with '*al* meaning "inside." This is confirmed further by Lam 1:20 where *bĕqirbî*, "inside me," replaces '*ālay* in an expression otherwise identical to v 8b. Furthermore, Lam 1:20 shows that a tumult of emotions is occurring, not just a clash of ideas.

emotions. The word *niḥûmîm* occurs only here, in Isa 57:18, and in Zech 1:13. The emotion is one of compassion and pity; it describes the desire to bring consolation. As such it is close in meaning to *raḥămîm;* the proposed emendation to *raḥămāy* is fatuous.

agitated. Nikmar, always *Nip'al,* means "to become hot," as the comparison with the oven shows (Lam 5:10). In Gen 43:30 and I Kings 3:26, it describes the arousal of the most tender affection. The subject in both of these places is *raḥămîm,* and the feeling is one of pure love with no element of pity or compassion.

all together. The meaning of *yaḥad* in v 8b remains problematical. It should not be equated with *yḥd* in v 7 (where we read *yāḥîd*).

9a. *I . . . will certainly.* The use of *l'* here again is asseverative, registering the renewed determination of Yahweh to carry out his threatened judgments, in spite of the claims of sentiment expressed in v 8. A decision about this reading cannot be made with the help of grammar, because the contrastive-distinctive distributional syntax of asseverative *l'* and negative *l'* has not been discovered. The decision must be guided by the context. The best examples of asseverative *l'* have been established in this way; but this test does not work well here. The decision must arise from a theological expectation, and that depends on the meaning of v 9b.

When Yahweh reminds himself that he is a god, and not human, what aspect of the divine character resolves the dilemma for him? Is the execution of justice unswayed by sentiment a human characteristic, whereas God, by contrast, is more free to follow his emotions and act beyond the law? Or is Yahweh recognizing that it is typical of human beings to have their judgment clouded by their feelings, especially when it comes to showing favoritism?

Deut 1:17 contains a warning against this kind of partiality in either direction: there must be no leniency toward the poor out of pity; no severity against them because they are powerless. The rich too must be treated with strict equity; neither severely, because they are privileged, nor gently, because they are powerful. The reason given is that "the judgment appertains to God." People should judge as God judges, but they do not always do so; hence the admonition. If Yahweh were to give special consideration to Ephraim, he would be acting in a human way. This course he spurns.

The contrast between divine and human modes of action is drawn in similar language in other parts of scripture. Num 23:19 affirms that

> God is not a human (*lō' 'îš 'ēl*) that he should act deceitfully,
> not a mortal that he should change his mind.
> Did he ever say something and not do it?
> Promise something and not make it stand?

I Sam 15:29 similarly emphasizes that the Supervisor of Israel will neither deceive nor change his mind, "because he is not a human" (*kî lō' 'ādām*). (The opposite point is made in Isa 31:3 — the Egyptians are human, not divine.) If Yahweh were not to adhere to his pledged word, he would be a liar and an impostor, just like people, just like Israel.

His reason for following the course of strict justice is stated further by affirming his holiness. In some occurrences *qādôš* is a personal name for God (Ps 111:9; Job 6:10). If he were contemplating forgiveness, he would declare himself *'ēl raḥûm wĕḥannûn,* "a sensitive and gracious god" (Exod 34:6; Freedman 1955a). Yet even that supreme revelation cannot eliminate the ambivalence, for it makes the contrary assertion that "he will by no means clear the guilty." The effect of Moses' powerful intercession is not to cancel judgment, only to restrain it. Exod 34:6 emphasizes that Yahweh is long-suffering and slow to anger. Theoretically his wrath could be held in check indefinitely. Unlike Moses before him, and Jeremiah after, and unlike Amos in his own day, we do not see Hosea restraining Yahweh's anger with prayers. On the contrary, there are over a dozen places where punishment of the most violent kind is threatened, usually with explicit mention of death (2:5,14; 4:5; 5:12,14; 6:5; 7:12; 8:13; 9:6,9,12,16; 10:14; 11:6; 13:7–8). Only in 14:5 is there a promise of forgiveness, and there, as in 6:1–3, it is described as healing after injury, revival from death. That is, in Hosea's theology the divine compassion is expressed, not by deflecting or annulling just anger, but by restoration after the requirements of justice have been satisfied by inflicting the penalties for covenant violations. In v 9a Yahweh reaffirms his determination to carry out "the heat of his anger"; cf. 8:5.

We do not strain at this result in order to harmonize the text in a formal fashion, so that 11:9 will not contradict the long list of texts listed above. Hos 6:4 and 11:8 show that Yahweh has a mixed mind. His responses are not automatic. If a negative meaning is maintained for v 9a, this cannot be elevated into an absolute truth: to maintain that, in the final analysis, Yahweh cannot bring himself to carry out his anger at his people. At best, v 9a, if negative, declares a reluctance, not a permanent decision. The historical events evince wrath against Israel, not mercy for it; so all the later prophets interpreted the fate of the northern kingdom.

9b. *come.* This completes the series *l' 'e'ĕśeh — l' 'āšûb — wl' 'ābô'.* All the verbs are imperfect; all modified by *l'*. We line the third one up with the first two, with *l'* equally asseverative; the three lines form a tricolon. "Come" is a satisfactory parallel to "return." It is precisely because he is the Holy One in the midst of your city that he will exercise his fierce wrath. Dahood argues, in a personal communication, that the line means: "I will not depart from the city," but this is too vague.

into the midst of your city. MT reads the last word as "in a city," and LXX reproduces this; when combined with the phrase *bqrbk,* this yields good sense.

10. There is an abrupt change at this point. The situation is eschatological; the disasters of destruction and exile are presupposed. The dispersion to Egypt and Assyria (v 5) is the starting point of the new development. Wolff (1974:195), however, exaggerates the resemblance to Amos. Verse 10ab constitutes an envelope construction:

10a	*'hry yhwh ylkw*	7 syllables	12
	k'ryh yš'g	5	
10b	*ky-hw' yš'g*	4	12
	wyhrdw bnym mym	8	

The interior lines are repetitive, while the opening and closing lines are in chiastic sequence, with the verb ending the first and opening the last. Doubtless *bnym* provides the subject of both verbs, which can be combined neatly: "The children come trembling from the west after Yahweh." Verse 11, a tricolon, picks up the theme by repeating the key verb *yhrdw;* v 11b completes the thought and at the same time links up with and concludes the first-person actions initiated at the beginning of the chapter.

10a. In v 3 Yahweh was a guide for Ephraim. Walking behind Yahweh is a repetition of the trek from Egypt to the land of promise — a new exodus. It implies also a change of allegiance. Whenever the idiom "to walk behind" is used, the object is a god. Verse 10a is thus the reversal of v 2a.

There is a switch from the first to the third person in this part of Yahweh's speech, but there is no reason to suppose that there has been a change of speaker. The end of v 11 labels the whole passage as an oracle of Yahweh.

Like a lion. This roar of the lion is a reversal of the usual effects of the voice of Yahweh. In Amos 1:2 the lion's roar declares an oracle, and it causes fear in Amos 3:8. This summons will bring children from three points of the compass: from the (north)west, from the north(east), and from the south(west); none will emerge from the south(east)ern wilderness and desert.

10b. *The children.* The noun leaves the returning ones unidentified. Presumably they are Yahweh's covenant offspring (Isa 1:2). They may be the children of the nation, i.e. the present generation of Israelites will die in exile (9:6) and their descendants will return, after "many days" (3:4). *Bānîm* is used in the same way in Jer 31:17.

trembling. The verb *ḥrd* describes persons in a highly agitated emotional condition, usually as a result of shock (Gen 27:33; Ruth 3:8; I Kings 1:49). It is often a state of fright (Exod 19:16), in a time of disaster (Isa 32:11) or panic (I Sam 14:15). In most of these instances a common factor is dread at a sudden noise, the meaning of which is not understood, but which probably indicates that something is wrong (Gen 42:28). Job 37:1–4 shows that such quaking can be a response to the majestic voice of God when he "roars," more in wonder than in terror (Andersen 1976a:264–265). This is the only passage containing the verb where the meaning approaches one that seems suitable for 11:10–11. Joy rather than fear should mark the return, but *ḥrd* nowhere has such a connotation. In the second exodus they will be completely subdued, and will journey in constant fear of offending Yahweh in any way. The comparison with the birds portrays such timidity.

the west. Literally "from sea." The inclusion of this third location is strange, since Hosea's attention is entirely on Egypt and Assyria. In Amos 8:12 the seas mark the east-west extremities of the known world. The other points of the compass are the Euphrates and the Nile (cf. Zech 9:10; Ps 72:8). A similar eschatological perspective is found in Mic 7:12.

11a. *the land of Assyria.* This completes the pattern that commenced in v 5, where the land of Egypt is parallel to Assyria.

11b. *settle.* Cf. 2:20. The orthography points to derivation from *yšb*, not *šwb*, *pace* Wolff (1974:193), Kuhnigk (1974:141) and LXX.

estates. Literally "upon their houses," but it is not likely that residences are intended. Resettlement in the land means a return to the farms. *Bêt* often has the meaning of property or real estate in a wider sense.

Oracle of Yahweh. This formula clearly marks the end of the unit. A new section begins with 12:1.

Parents and children: Bethel, Egypt, and Assyria

12:1a Ephraim has surrounded me with deception,
  the House of Israel with treachery.

  1b Judah still wanders with the holy gods.
  He is faithful to the holy gods.

  2a Ephraim shepherds in the wind.
  He pursues in the east wind.
  All day he multiplies lies and destruction.

  2b They made a covenant with Assyria.
  Oil is conveyed to Egypt.

  3a Yahweh has a dispute with Judah.

  3b He will certainly punish Jacob for his ways.
  For his deeds he will requite him.

  4a In the womb he grabbed his brother's heel.

  4b   In his vigor he contended with God.

  5a He contended with God.
  He overcame the angel.
  He wept and implored him.

  5b At Bethel he met him.
  There he spoke to him.

  6a Yahweh is God of the Armies.

  6b Yahweh is his name.

Children and parents: wealth, prophecy, and idolatry

  7a You should return to your God.

  7b Keep loyalty and judgment.
  Wait for your God continually.

  8a Canaan: in his hands are treacherous scales.

  8b   He even defrauds an ally.

  9a Ephraim said, "How rich have I become!
  I have acquired wealth for myself!

9b   None of my crimes will ever catch up with me,
      my iniquity which I have wrongfully
      committed."

10a   I am Yahweh your God, from the land of Egypt.

10b   I will make you live once more in tents,
      as in the days of the Tabernacle.

11a   I speak through the prophets.
      I make visions numerous.

11b   Through the prophets I create parables.

12a   They were in Gilead with idols,
      indeed, with false gods in Gilgal.
      They sacrificed to bulls.

12b   Their altars were indeed like stone heaps
      beside furrows of the fields.

13a   Jacob fled to the land of Aram.

13b   Israel worked for one wife.
      For another wife he kept sheep.

14a   By one prophet Yahweh brought Israel
      up from Egypt.

14b   By another prophet he was watched.

15a   Ephraim has caused bitter provocation.

15b   He will hold him responsible for his murders.
      His Lord will return his disgrace upon him.

NOTES

12:1–15. The fluidity of Hosea's thought is particularly evident in this chapter. Centuries of history are compressed into a single sketch. Fragmentary glimpses of decisive moments in Israel's past are linked with the nation's present predicament. The comparisons are implied; there is no systematic development. Once more the ideas are juxtaposed in an artistic manner, and some statements seem to have more than one level of meaning, particularly when the familiar names, Israel, Jacob, Ephraim, and Judah, are involved. Judah is the only term that refers exclusively to a political state of Hosea's own day. There is no hint that the prophet has in mind either the eponymous ancestor of the Genesis traditions, or even the ideal kingdom of David's time, although a close connection between Judah and Jacob is apparently made in v 3. It may be that the parallelism is synonymous, and "Jacob" is associated with the southern kingdom, "Israel" with the north. Each link reflects a pairing of father and son. This is worked out more clearly in the case of Ephraim, whose conduct, especially in vv 1 and 9, is strikingly like that of his ancestor Israel. There is no talk of twelve tribes. The descendants of Jacob/Israel are Judah and Ephraim. Together they represent the whole people. Since Ephraim was not even a son of Jacob originally, except by adoption (Genesis 48), we see in this terminology the later political realities. The foreshortened historical perspective, or rather, the prophet's vivid historical memory which sees long-past events as if they happened yesterday, permits one picture to pass into another to make a composite in which the passage of time is swift. The leap from the earliest memories of national identity in Jacob/Israel to the present touches along the way on the period of the Judges, just as elsewhere the Exodus is used as a bridge.

The strife between siblings in the time of Judges (in the days of Gibeah, cf. 10:9) comes midway between the Jacob-Esau competition (12:4) and the civil wars of Hosea's own day. The name "Israel" provides the basic continuity, just as its etymology provides the theological momentum. In this chapter Israel is the patriarch (vv 4,5,13); the people brought up from Egypt (v 14); and the nation of Hosea's day (more precisely, "the House of Israel" — v 1).

The sequence in which the four names used here to refer to Yahweh's people are arranged shows a unifying pattern, although it does not attain complete symmetry. Such connections as can be perceived are useful, for they enable related passages to be interpreted together. A chart of the names brings out the structural patterns, and the inherent pairings.

1a	Ephraim	Ephraim	15a
	Israel	Israel	14a
1b	Judah	Israel	13b
2a	Ephraim	Jacob	13a
3a	Judah	Ephraim	9a
3b	Jacob	Canaan	8a

The patriarch, per se, is identified in v 13 as Jacob/Israel, and this is confirmed by the verb-play in vv 4–5aA. Ephraim is the key term in this section, forming the envelope around the whole chapter, and also being paired with almost all of the protagonists: Israel, Judah, Canaan (v 8a); Jacob is linked with Judah more directly (v 3).

As is typical in Hosea's literary compositions, each verse here is connected in some way with something else in the chapter. Often the clue is supplied by the repetition of the same word, or of a synonym. The action of Ephraim in surrounding God with *mirmâ*, "treachery" (v 1a), is echoed in the *tmrwrym*, the "bitter provocation" in v 15a; *mirmâ* reappears in the "treacherous scales" (v 8a). The multiplication of lies and destruction (v 2) matches the increase of wealth (v 9). The preposition *'im*, "with," is used in both vv 2 and 3 when talking about covenant relationships. It is not clear that the "brother" in v 4a turns up again but we suspect that the oppression in v 8 represents a similar betrayal of a close relationship. The fact that the word *'ôn*, "wealth, vigor," turns up in vv 4 and 9 is a further link. There is a play on the word *mṣ'*, "to find," in vv 5 and 9. The name "Yahweh" is prominent in this chapter, occurring five times. Statements of credal solemnity (vv 6 and 10a) stand in contrast to the sordid tale of Ephraim's crimes. The word "your God" (vv 7 bis, 10) is a similar link. The motif of observance (*šmr*) runs through vv 7,13, and 14. The chapter has no fewer than fifteen words to refer to sins or sinful attitudes of various kinds, though *mirmâ* is the only one that occurs twice. We have already pointed out the juxtaposition of the two reports on ancestor Jacob in vv 4–5 and v 13; the Exodus is similarly alluded to twice (vv 10 and 14).

These observations should correct an impression of incoherence or discontinuity in the development of the chapter. When each verse is linked with the one to which it has the closest correspondence, or to which it stands in contrast, the related pairs do not make a symmetrical introversion. The closest pairs are vv 1 and 8–9; vv 2 and 12; vv 3 and 15; vv 4–5 and 13; vv 6 and 10; and vv 11 and 14. The invitation to repent (v 7) is the only statement that has no counterpart in the rest of the chapter, and is significantly near the center.

The poetic features of c 12 are well developed. It contains a number of well-formed bicola. Even when the rhythms are quite unequal, as in vv 13b and 14, the poetic devices of parallel words are used. There is a bicolon with complete parallelism in v 2b, with balance and correspondence, though without synonymy; the parallelism suggests that the oil is tribute to an overlord, and, by that token, defines the covenant as one of submission. Verse 4 contains a similar juxtaposition of different relationships in words which match each other in detail. It is not certain that the two lines in v 5b are synonymous, but it is likely that they are. The use of *šām*, "there," shows that "Bethel" is the location of both activities; each line could be an aspect of the same event. There are some bicola which have complete parallelism with chiasm or inversion of some kind, e.g. v 3b:

He will certainly punish Jacob   for his ways
For his deeds   he will requite him.

The first and last lines of v 11 constitute a chiastic bicolon:

I speak   through the prophets
Through the prophets   I create parables.

Some bicola have incomplete synonymous parallelism, e.g. v 1a:

> He has surrounded me   with deception   Ephraim
>   with treachery   the house of Israel.

The four verbs in v 5a cover three lines; both the syntax and grammatical structure are quite intricate, in spite of the brevity of the passage. Verses 6,13b, and 14 have parallelism between lines of unequal length. Verse 1b shows inversion with incomplete parallelism.

The chiasm in Ephraim's speech in v 9a is not well developed, since the first verb does not have an object to parallel the object of the second verb. Verse 15b is also an incompletely developed bicolon with some inversion.

Verse 2a contains one bicolon. The parallelism of "shepherding" and "pursuing" points in that direction; the correlatives "wind" and "east" constitute a well-known phrase. The remainder of the verse is less clear, and uncertainty about the position of "all day" compounds the difficulty.

Verse 3a seems to be an isolated line. The position of "Ephraim" at the beginning of v 2a and of "Judah" at the end of v 3a suggests that the lines might be related. But parallelism between "Judah" in v 3a and "Jacob" in v 3b is also possible; in which case v 3 is a tricolon with v 3a as the introductory line followed by an expository bicolon. Verse 15a also seems to be an unmatched line, which contains "Ephraim," a good parallel to "Judah." Furthermore, v 15a seems to be reproachful, like v 3a, and v 15b expounds v 15a just as v 3b expounds v 3a. The presence of the expression *yāšîb lô* in vv 3b and 15b is a further link, and *'ădōnāyw* (v 15b) is a good parallel for "Yahweh" in v 3a.

Verses 3,11, and 15 are probably tricola. Verse 7 is another, unified by various poetic devices, although the transition from the imperfect verb *tāšûb* to the two imperatives is strange. The repetition of "your God" brings the first and third lines together, with chiasm in the verbs. The middle line resembles the others only in a general way.

Verse 10 is more prose-like than the rest of the chapter. It should not be inferred from this, or from the general failure of the poetic units in this chapter to rise to the level of the classical *parallelismus membrorum,* that this prophetic discourse is written in prose with only a touch of the poetic. As with the rest of Hosea, it is neither poetry nor prose. It is balanced, rhythmic discourse, unified by interwoven themes. It is almost completely lacking in logical connectives.

The chapter is a single literary unit in which comments on Israel's current disloyalty to Yahweh are intermingled with recollections of events in the life of Jacob-Israel, the ancestor. Unfortunately, it is not immediately clear what Hosea is doing with those patriarchal traditions, which are mingled further with references to the Exodus and subsequent events. Commentators cannot even agree that Hosea's attitude to Jacob is uniformly favorable, or the opposite. If it is favorable, Hosea contrasts Jacob's original good standing with God with Israel's present decline from this primeval high rank. If, on the other hand, Jacob is represented as a rogue, Hosea's point would be that his present-day descendants are the same.

That the latter is Hosea's belief is indicated by several general considerations. Since the introduction of the wilderness themes in 9:10, the prophet's argument has been that Israel has proved to be incorrigible. The same is shown by reminiscences drawn from the age of the judges (10:9). Israel has always been the same. It is true that the incidents selected from the Jacob tradition as we know it from the Book of Genesis do not include the more dramatic occasions on which the eponym thoroughly earned the name of "Cheat." On the contrary, the glimpses given seem to highlight his legitimate achievements, such as working for a wife. His more reprehensible deeds — cheating Esau of his birthright and blessing, and perhaps cheating Laban of his property — are not reported. Perhaps Hosea thought it was enough to report briefly on his struggle with his brother "in the belly" (Gen 25:19–26); this is apparently recounted as a matter of fact, with no value judgment. If synonymous parallelism is implied, the corresponding adult dealings with God must be due for the same blame or praise. But which? Prominence is given to encounters with God at Bethel (Gen 28:10–22) and Penuel (Gen 32:23–33). The accounts in Genesis preserve many details which gloss over the equivocal aspects of Jacob's human character, but the moral balance is not against him. The stories have a vivid realism and an astonishing honesty. Jacob turns out all right in the end; and from the point of view of biblical narration, that is all important. Hosea does not give us the glimpses of Jacob's broken but ennobled spirit supplied in the closing pages of Genesis. His cryptic references to earlier events contain few hints that he finds in Jacob the things that he is criticizing in the Israel of his day, notably, disloyalty to Yahweh, dishonest business practices, foreign alliances, attachment to rival deities. A note of censure could, however, be implied by quoting Ephraim's boastful words about his wealth ('ôn) in v 9. This is just what Jacob might have said. The implied comparison depends in part on 'ôn in v 4. Boasting about one's power to become rich is prohibited in Deut 8:17, since it is claiming credit for the gifts of God. Jacob certainly made a great show of his property to impress Esau (Genesis 32), but his own attitude attributed it all to the grace of God, according to Gen 33:5, where the verb ḥānan is the nearest that the extant patriarchal traditions come to matching yitḥannen in v 5. Jacob's activities, as reported by Hosea, are not treacherous; but Israel's "lies," which already have been exposed, are referred to by three different words in 12:1–2.

The use of the Jacob traditions in c 12 has aroused a great deal of discussion, and agreement has yet to be reached on many questions. It is not certain whether Hosea had access to the traditions now found in Genesis. A provisional answer to this question is needed before we can make use of the Genesis traditions to fill out the extremely terse statements in Hosea. There are remarks about Jacob in c 12 which touch on Genesis stories at several points. Hosea's silences, as we indicated above, are even more startling; but we do not know if this indicates ignorance of certain matters, or a refusal to make use of them. By way of comparison, Jeremiah, who also uses the association of Judah and Jacob (Jer 5:20), knows the Deuteronomic idea of Jacob as Yahweh's "inheritance" (Jer 10:16; 51:19), and the gift of the land to "the forebears." (Hosea mentions forebears only in 9:10, and they are not the patriarchs.) Jeremiah calls the people of the end time "Jacob." The verbal links with Genesis material are certain in Hos 12:5aA, but hard to prove elsewhere. The rest of v 5 is particularly puzzling in this regard.

If Hosea is simply trying to tell the story of Jacob, he uses a sequence of events quite different from that in Genesis. The arrangement seems haphazard. But it would be rash to infer that, because Hosea does not trace Jacob's biography in a chronological way, there is no system in his treatment, or he did not know the story. We suspect that the arrangement is intended to make sense, although we have not always succeeded in discovering what Hosea intends. In v 3 he introduces Jacob (apparently in parallel with Judah), announcing that Yahweh will punish him for his deeds. It seems to be implied that the doings of this latter-day "Jacob" (whether "Israel" as a whole or "Judah") can be illustrated from the life of the national ancestor, in whom the character of the people was already expressed, not merely latent. (There is no trace of a doctrine that the ancestor's sins are, at long last, to be paid for by his descendants.)

If Hosea's intention were to demonstrate unity between Father Jacob and eighth-century Israel, we might expect a catalogue of the Father's deceptions (v 1) drawn from the traditions, which are free of whitewash, lined up with Israel's current conduct. Yet such a procedure could be superficial; and what would it prove? Even Genesis, for all its honesty, does not represent Jacob as an arch-sinner. Although it is surprisingly candid in telling of Jacob's trickery, the story is told in such a way as to finish up with a positive treatment of Jacob/Israel as a man who, after all, is in covenant with God. This undercurrent gives the stories their strange twist, and leaves Jacob himself an enigma. The double name preserves this ambivalence. Yet even the implied reversal in the name "Israel" is not sufficiently clear, for neither the meaning of the word nor the implications of what happened at Penuel is clear; and this opacity remains in 12:5a. Genesis does not offer the suggestion (present in the Abraham traditions, at least in the E recension) that Jacob's status with God was grounded in piety, or in some great expression of covenant-loyalty after testing, like

that in Genesis 22. Jacob is destined before birth for such privileges; the
point is made in the way the story is told that his covenant status is always
a gift, never a reward for his virtue, and is in no way neutralized by his
personality traits as a "cheat." So deft is the editor of Genesis, so detached, that it is not clear to the reader whether the clever stratagems by
which Jacob defrauds first Esau and then Laban are recorded in Genesis
simply to be condemned. Jacob is an admirable, even lovable person, who
could never be described simply as a sinner. He is convincingly human,
and this is important in the realistic storytelling of Genesis. The narrator
refrains from moralizing and Jacob remains enigmatic from the moral
point of view; this is true also of Hosea's allusions. We cannot tell whether
he is applauding or deploring his subject. He gives no evaluation, and he
does not develop the comparison between Jacob and the Israel of his day.

Hosea's allusions to the Jacob tradition are as follows:

1) He seized his brother's heel in the womb (v 4a), Gen 25:26.
2) He went to Aram (v 13a), Gen 28:5.
3) He met God at Bethel (v 5b), Gen 28:13.
4) He served for two wives (v 13b), Gen 29:15–30.
5) He struggled with an angel of God at the Jabbok (vv 4b, 5a), Gen
   32:23–33.
6) There was weeping and praying in the contest with the angel or in
   the meeting with Esau (v 5aB), Gen 32:27 or 33:4.

In the struggle with the angel of God at the Jabbok, the divine being
sought his release from Jacob. In that sense Jacob prevailed. The story is
not exactly the same in Genesis and Hosea, but the connections seem in-
disputable. The same verbs are used in both passages (śry and ykl in Gen
32:29 and Hos 12:5). Further, the change of name from Jacob to Israel
is attested in Genesis and assumed in Hosea (with plays on the verbs 'qb
and śry); both names, Jacob/Israel, appear in the account of the patriarch
in 12:13.

12:1a. *surrounded me.* It is possible that the imagery of binding with
ropes, already used in 11:4, is being used here once more. Sarcasm appears
in this chapter more than once; but sarcasm is notoriously difficult to be
certain about in a text. The sustained theme of cc 8–11 is the rupture of the
covenant relationship with God and its replacement by a covenant relationship with foreigners and their gods. The relationship with Yahweh is
inverted. The use of the verb "to surround, encircle" gives a strange picture of Yahweh besieged with hostility. In the Psalter this verb, with the
suffix, is used seven times in laments to describe the predicament of a
terrified person whose enemies prowl around him like wild animals. The
spelling there is always *plene,* so that 12:1, with defective spelling, leaves

the plural in some doubt, especially since "Ephraim" usually has singular verbs and referential pronouns. The plural may be acceptable, since Ephraim and the House of Israel constitute the coordinated subject, and the House of Israel is not the same as Ephraim.

There are many statements about Yahweh in the third person in this chapter; he is the speaker in v 10. It is not likely that the "I" in v 1 is the prophet, referring to Israel's hostility to him (cf. 9:7; Wolff 1974:208–209). The charge of treachery against God has been made several times.

1b. Most translations of v 1b place Judah in a favorable light, influenced by a general expectation that all references to Judah in Hosea contrast with his disapproval of the north. In the present context the adjective ne'ĕmān, "reliable," which refers to one of God's great attributes, is taken to set the tone for the whole. The meaning of its apparent parallel rād is unknown, but it is assumed to be a synonym equally laudatory. When rād is emended, the result is usually positive. Thus RSV "Judah is still known (yd') by God" (11:12) draws support from LXX. The Hebrew text that can be glimpsed though this attempt of the Greek translator is close enough to what we now have to generate suspicion that the translator has done his best with a text that presented the same difficulties to him as it does to us.

Looking first at Hosea's general attitude to Judah and accepting the references to Judah as authentic, we are influenced from the outset by the traditional interpretation of the first occurrence of Judah, at 1:7. Here Yahweh's supposed compassion toward Judah stands in contrast with his rejection of Israel. The same contrast has been imposed on 12:1. Ephraim-House of Israel's relationship with Yahweh is characterized by lies and deception, whereas Judah is rād and ne'ĕmān with God. We have expressed doubts about the traditional interpretation of 1:7 and linked Judah with Israel in the same condemnation. There are numerous other places in Hosea where Judah and Ephraim are treated in the same way (5:5,12,13; 6:4,10–11; 8:14; 10:11). The hypothesis that Hosea is anti-Ephraim and pro-Judah would never have gained a footing had 1:7 not come so early in the book.

So far as 12:1 is concerned, a statement congratulating Judah on loyalty to God is difficult, since v 3 asserts that Yahweh has a lawsuit against Judah. To get rid of this evidence by reading "Israel" instead of "Judah" in v 3a is a desperate, if popular, step. We have only to remember the gravity of the charge against Judah in 5:10.

In analyzing a bicolon like v 1b, it is a common grammatical principle that a two-word phrase can be distributed over the two cola in the parallelismus membrorum. While matching words are often synonyms, it is also possible to have a lead noun in the first colon and an attributive ad-

jective or modifier in the second (O'Connor 1980). The phrase *'ēl* . . .
qĕdôšîm affords a good example in this bicolon, although the discord
in number is a problem, and *rād* . . . *ne'ĕmān* may be another. Perhaps
Judah is a trustworthy *rād* with the "holy god(s)." This does not prove
that *rād* is a virtue, unless we already know that Judah's trustworthiness is
with Yahweh, i.e. Yahweh is the "holy god." To make this identification
we must suppose that v 1b contrasts Judah's loyalty with Ephraim's
perfidy, and we see no reason to do so.

still. Of ten occurrences of the word *'ōd* in Hosea, only two (here and
in v 10) are defective. Indeed the defective spelling of *'ōd* is rare.

In the context of covenant-making, the possibility of reading *'ēd* should
be taken seriously. It is remarkable that so many of the adjectives and
nouns that Hosea uses to describe Israel's attitude to Yahweh are used as
attributes of *'ēd*, "witness (to an agreement)," good or bad. The bad:
kĕzābîm, mirmâ, šeqer, ḥāmās, šāw', bĕlîya'al. The good: *'ĕmet, 'ĕmûnîm,
ne'ĕmān.* In Prov 14:5 and 25 an *'ēd 'ĕmûnîm* or *'ĕmet* contrasts with
a speaker of *kĕzābîm* and *mirmâ.* Yahweh is the "reliable testator" (*'ēd
'ĕmet wĕne'ĕmān*) par excellence (Jer 42:5).

wanders. A biconsonantal form like *rād* could have several different
roots. The root *rwd*, "to wander," is attested in Hebrew and can be compared with an Arabic cognate meaning "to roam." This, or some other
verb of motion, such as *yrd*, "to go down" (cf. Vulgate *descendit*), can
form the basis of a statement that Judah "follows" a god (*yrd;* Wolff
1974:205); we accept this solution reluctantly, and with a twist.

There are other verbs containing *r-d*, which, although attested meagerly,
could fit the situation in c 12 as well as the verbs of motion (Wolff
1974:210). In Jer 2:31, when Yahweh's people renounce their allegiance
to him, they say, *radnû*, "We are *rad*," a statement explained by the words
— "We won't come to you any more!" This could be a form of another
root *rwd* or of another root altogether. In a similar prediction of independence for Esau in Gen 27:40, *tārîd*, "You will *rd*," is explained "You
will tear off his yoke from upon your neck." This verb is usually derived
from the root *rdd*, "to subdue," and hence, in Esau's case, to win the mas-
tery. But throwing off the yoke is not the same as subjugating the former
lord; and such an idea is out of the question at Jer 2:31. A similar
misfit is found in the root *rdy*, "to tread down, dominate." (There is another root *rdy* in Judg 14:9 and Jer 5:31.) If this root *rdy* is identified
here in Hosea, a passive ("ruled by God") or at the least an intransitive
meaning would be required. The preposition *'im* would then have to be interpreted as "ruling with (the help of) God." Those scholars who would
find here a pro-Judean gloss see a contrast between Judah's political survival and Ephraim's conquest by Assyria; but why put the matter so ob-
scurely? Rather we believe that the evidence of Gen 27:40 and Jer 2:31,

although slender, may support the existence of a root *rdy,* "to renounce," which would reverse our present understanding.

holy gods. Yahweh is not meant. The Canaanite pantheon is rather the object of Judah's fidelity. Both *'ēl* and *qādôš* are used in 11:9, where it is Yahweh who is called "a god," and "the Holy One"; cf. "Living God" in 2:1. The plural "holy ones" is appropriate for the gods of the religion in which Israel has become involved (7:8). There is no need to secure concord by emending to *'ēlîm,* as proposed by Reines (1950); *'ēl* could be collective. There is ample evidence that (*bn*) *qdšm* means "gods" in Ugaritic, Phoenician, and biblical texts (Pss 16:3; 89:6,8; Job 5:1; 15:15; and cf. Dahood 1966:87–88, Kuhnigk 1974:143–144). Job 15:15 is close to Hos 12:1 in saying that God has no confidence in "the holy ones." The use of *ne'ĕmān* with *'ēl* (Ps 78:8; cf. Ps 78:37) is also in line with Hos 12:1.

The use of the preposition *'im* here is comparable to the phrase *'im 'ēl* in II Sam 23:5. Hosea's words could almost be a parody of that great affirmation. The word *ne'ĕmān* describes David's standing "with" Yahweh in covenant; cf. Isa 55:3. David says that his house is "certainly legitimate (*l' kēn*) with God" (II Sam 23:5). As an attribute of royalty, *kēn* connotes reliability as well as validity.

faithful. Hosea's use of *ne'ĕmān* to describe Judah's engagement with "holy ones" is unique, and twists the word away from its standard use in the Bible to describe trust in Yahweh, by persons of conspicuous constancy in their adherence to the covenant — Abraham (Neh 9:8); Moses (Num 12:7); the high priest (I Sam 2:35); Samuel (I Sam 3:20); David (I Sam 22:14; 25:28). Best of all, it is Yahweh's attribute in keeping steadfastly to his promise (Deut 7:9; Ps 89:29). The preposition is important: making a covenant "with" (*'im*) Assyria (v 2b) may have required loyalty "with" (*'im*) their "holy ones" (v 1b).

2a. *shepherds.* Like Wisdom writers, Hosea draws similes and metaphors from nature. Animals, birds, and plants supply comparisons. The purpose of the shepherd image here, however, is not clear. The holism of the bicolon unites "wind" and "east" in a familiar phrase; and this suggests a similar linkage of the two participles of the MT, "grazer (shepherd)" and "pursuer." The relationship between shepherding and wind is, however, not obvious. Dahood (1972:392–393) suggests that "Ephraim grazes on the wind," i.e. he feeds on it, in a "description of unsatisfying activity." This does not solve the main difficulty; it is sheep that graze, not the shepherd. Traditional translations make "wind" the object of the verb "shepherd," representing the flock ("Ephraim herds the wind" — 12:1 *RSV*); the problem is the sense.

Remembering that Hosea often omits prepositions, we concluded at 8:7 that the difficulty of "wind" as the object of "sow" can be obviated by rec-

ognizing that the noun is adverbial. The same applies here. The east wind
creates the worst weather in Palestine, causing the land to mourn when the
pastures dry up (Hos 4:3; cf. Amos 1:2).

pursues. Elsewhere Hosea uses *rdp* to describe the search for God, false
(2:9) or true (6:3). More commonly it describes hostile pursuit, and this
idea is found in 8:3, where Israel is pursued as an "enemy." Here, however, it describes the shepherd out after his flock. Given that Ephraim
shepherds and pursues (the flock) in the east wind (under bad conditions),
we must try to link this with the next unit which charges him with lying.
Is this the common prophetic charge leveled by prophets against false
shepherds?

All day. It is not clear whether this phrase goes with what precedes or
what follows. In view of the variable length of the lines in this discourse,
scansion does not settle the point.

he multiplies. There is no basis for *RSV*'s "they multiply" (12:1); the
verb is singular, and should not be normalized to v 2b. While the subject
could be Ephraim, continuing from v 2aA, Judah may be intended, to
make a statement that balances what was said about Ephraim in v 1a. In
5:13aA Ephraim and Judah appear as parallels in a bicolon. In 5:13aA
Ephraim appears in the first line of the bicolon, and we have argued that
Judah is the implied subject of the second. The same may be true here.
Verse 1a is a bicolon about Ephraim; v 1b is a bicolon about Judah.
Verse 3 is a tricolon about Judah, and v 15 is a matching tricolon about
Ephraim. In 5:13 the statements about Ephraim and Judah singly are followed by a statement about both together, and the pronouns switch to plu-
ral. The change to the plural verb in 12:2b has the same effect here: v 2b
is about Ephraim and Judah together. So v 2a may be about Ephraim and
Judah individually, and v 2aB about Judah, although we cannot claim certainty in this. The suggestion receives further support from the fact that
Judah is paralleled by Jacob in v 3. Verse 1 accuses Ephraim of lies and
treachery, and in v 9 Ephraim boasts as Jacob might have. The pattern is
complete if v 2a accuses Judah of lies and violence.

lies and destruction. The two nouns balance "deception" and "treachery" in v 1a. Kuhnigk's emendation (1974:145) of *šōd* to *šēd* in the hendiadys *kāzāb wāšēd*, "lying demons," is unnecessary.

2b. *They made.* Literally "they cut." This is the clearest identification of
the covenant that Hosea has been complaining about as contrary to Yahweh's (10:4). We suggest that this is the covenant negotiated in c 7; note
the roots *sbb* (7:2) and *khš* (7:3), both used in 12:1. Alliances with foreign powers were intended to secure safety. In the end it will prove a false
hope (14:4). Worse than any political disaster, Israel has lost its relationship with Yahweh. We take the plural form of the verb here seriously.
Except for *sĕbābūnî*, whose spelling is ambiguous in this respect, the verbs

and adjectives in vv 1–2a are singular, referring to Ephraim and Judah individually. In v 2b they are spoken of together. Both countries are guilty
of entering non-Yahwistic covenants. This does not mean that they acted
in concert, in a joint alliance. We cannot recover the historical occasion,
and Hosea's accusation may be general, especially when we notice that
Egypt is included in the picture. The north and south tried to curry favor
with Assyria at each other's expense. There are also indications that they
played Egypt off against Assyria. There were pro-Assyrian and pro-Egyp-
tian parties in both countries, and the balances swung. All such thinking
and scheming was condemned by the prophets.

Oil. The parallelism suggests that the taking of oil to Egypt had something to do with a covenant in that quarter also. As such, it could be a
present taken by negotiators, a part of the covenant-making ceremony, or
the tribute paid as the result of a covenant. If the last, it would show that
Israel had become a vassal of Egypt in one treaty or another. It is likely
that some kind of submission would be the price for Egyptian protection
against Assyria. From Assyrian texts, McCarthy (1964) has argued that
oil could be used in covenant-making (cf. Wolff 1974:211). It would be a
mistake to link the covenant exclusively with Assyria, and the oil with
Egypt. Both are tied to both, and we must suppose that the oil ceremony
is a part or consequence of making a covenant. As noted, both Ephraim
and Judah were intriguing with both Assyria and Egypt.

3a. *a dispute.* With the word *rîb* we return to the opening words of the
prophetic discourse that began in 4:1. That charge was couched in general
but comprehensive terms. It seemed, however, to concentrate on infringements of the covenant in Israel's social and civil life. Now the setting
has expanded, and the scope is international. Nevertheless the singular
pronouns used in v 3b restrict the charge to Judah. The parallel "Jacob"
in this context could refer either to Ephraim, as a counterpart to Judah, or
to the nation as a whole. The balancing charge against Ephraim, also in
the singular, is given in v 15. The gravamen of the charge is not specified;
we can only assume that it has to do with the covenant referred to in v 2b.

3b. *punish.* In 8:13 and 9:9 *pqd* and *zkr* are parallel. Comparison of
two nearly identical bicola with the parallels *pqd // hšyb,* in v 3b and 4:9b
indicates what variations can be introduced. Many of the same verbs,
nouns, and prepositions are used, and each line in the bicolon has the
same elements in the same sequence. The parallelism of *'al* and *l* is noteworthy, although allowance must be made for the limits of the verb
correlatives. Apart from the change from first to third person, the omission of "and," and the reading "upon Jacob" instead of "upon him," the
most striking differences in the 12:3b form of the bicolon are the introduction of *k* before each noun, the asseverative, and the use of what seems to
be an infinitive *lipqōd,* which can hardly be correct. The *l,* too, is assevera-

tive, though between a *waw* and a perfect verb the construction is unique, so far as we know.

In vv 1–3 there are separate statements about Judah (vv 1b, 3a) and Ephraim (v 2a), both in the singular. There are some statements in the plural (vv 1a, perhaps, and 2b). No subject is identified in v 2b, but it is reasonable to apply the statement to the two countries. Since Ephraim is clearly singular in v 2a, the plural "they surrounded me" of v 1a suggests that the subject is "Ephraim . . . and the House of Israel," two distinct entities in coordination. This, in turn, suggests that "Ephraim" and "the House of Israel" are not identical in this text, but does not identify "the House of Israel." It is not likely that "House of Israel" means Judah, but if it means "all Israel" (as against Ephraim), it could include Judah. Each part of the country is equally guilty of treachery against the covenant. The disloyalty takes the form of foreign alliances (v 2b). Giving v 2b its fullest meaning, both countries have resorted to diplomatic negotiations with both Assyria and Egypt. This included the making of formal compacts, and the payment of tribute. The treaties involved the recognition of foreign gods.

Beyond such general inferences, the text does not yield precise historical information. Nor does our knowledge of the times permit these statements to be attached to recognizable historical situations. Ephraim and Judah were caught between two great powers. Within each kingdom counsels were divided. Whether v 2b means that they oscillated between the two (cf. 7:11b) or entered deceptively into simultaneous, conflicting, agreements with both, we cannot tell. We can only surmise that any realistic politician would have considered the prophetic policy of trust in Yahweh alone, with a total ban on treaties with any outside powers, to be visionary. Little wonder that the people thought the prophets were lunatics (9:7b).

4. This bicolon does not trace Jacob's life from beginning to end, but only from birth to Penuel. Perhaps the latter was the last decisive event in his life. The verse reports that at the very beginning Jacob dared to supplant his superior, his older brother Esau; and that in adulthood he tried to overcome the God who is his lord. The verbs here in v 4 have no explicit noun subjects. The nearest antecedent is Jacob in v 3, and he is obviously meant, even though there Jacob is parallel to Judah. Verse 3 says that God will punish "Jacob" for "his/its ways," and vv 4–5 and 13 recount some of the ways of the original Jacob. It seems, then, as if these ways are considered reprehensible The names Jacob // Israel appear in v 13, in the order of their historical development. The names are concealed in the verbs *'qb* and *śry* in v 4. The correspondence between vv 4 and 13 in this respect shows that they are part of a single treatment of the theme,

in spite of their separation, although it can hardly be said that working for his wives (v 13) is a deed for which Jacob should be punished.

4a. *In the womb.* Literally "in the belly." In Gen 25:22 the expression is *bĕqirbāh,* "inside her." That account uses a different verb for the intra-uterine struggle, *ytrṣṣw.* Perhaps a different stream of tradition flowed to Hosea. Little of Genesis 25 is attributed to E, generally supposed to be the northern recension. *Bbṭnk* does occur in Gen 25:23, the oracle, where the parallelism with *mimmē'ayik* suggests that it may mean "(they will be separated) from your belly." If Hos 12:4 uses the same idiom, then *babbeṭen* means "from the belly," that is, after birth; cf. Job 3:11. According to Gen 25:26, Jacob was born after Esau, with "his hand seizing (*'ḥzt*) Esau's heel (*'qb*)." While this seizing could describe his first observed action after birth, which those present would watch as a significant omen, the impression is given that he came out that way; having clutched Esau's heel in the womb before birth, he would not let go. His tenacity was manifested from the beginning, and his refusal to let go of the person at Penuel so long afterward was entirely in character.

4b. *vigor.* The word *'ôn,* "vigor, wealth," has more than one side; confusion with *'āwen,* "wickedness," is also possible. Since the meaning "wealth" is required in v 9a, it may be that the same meaning should prevail here. But there are passages where it refers to fully developed power, often, more precisely, to sexual potency (Deut 21:17; Ps 78:51). "Manhood" (so *RSV* 12:3) then would balance the natal condition of v 4a. Furthermore, in spite of v 9a, it is Jacob's native strength, not anything acquired, that is displayed in the bout at Penuel, and celebrated in his new name "Israel."

contended. The meaning of the verb *śry* is quite uncertain (Wolff 1974:212). It occurs only here and in Gen 32:29, in connection with the name Israel, although for all we know the verb may be derived from the name. The original meaning of "Israel" may be a separate question, without a clear answer. Attempts to link the name or the root *śry* with a verb developed from the noun *śar,* "ruler," have been unsuccessful. Search further afield into roots like *'šr,* "to be happy," or *yšr,* "to be just," is more venturesome, though it derives a little encouragement from the mysterious name Jeshurun (Deut 32:15; 33:5,26; Isa 44:2). Such names, which would be the opposite of Jacob, perhaps "Cheat," would suit Israel in his reformed character — assuming that that is the meaning of the Penuel experience, an assumption easier to maintain in Haggadah than in exegesis! In spite of the confluence of *śin* and *šin* in some areas, the certainty of the pronunciation of *yśr'l* is a further restraint on such equations. All we can say is that the verb *śry* describes something that Jacob did "with God" at Penuel.

The conclusion that *śyr* (or *śrr*) means something like "to contend" rests on evidence from the report of a person who "wrestled" with Jacob. This person did not overcome Jacob at first (Gen 32:36), but it is not certain that Jacob could have overcome him. It is only an inference that this person is God. However, *'yš*, "person," is a generic term, covering both human and divine beings who have the same appearance; thus the Genesis account, which intends to be mysterious, does not contradict Hosea, who identifies the "person" as an "angel of God." The contest itself seems to have been inconclusive: Jacob was injured, but the other person could not free himself. Whether we think Jacob prevailed or not, the author (and the "person") thought so.

Jacob received a permanent injury and had to disclose his name, although his request to learn the name of his opponent was not granted. This latter feature is indirect evidence that the person was God, or at least "a messenger of Yahweh"; cf. Judg 13:6. Although the account does not clearly say so, Jacob's incredible resistance could be interpreted as fighting back against his assailant, and "struggling with God." Further, the story and the naming of the place clearly imply that Jacob was dealing with God or his angel, face to face. The verb *ykl*, "to succeed," the strongest verbal link between Hosea and Genesis, describes success after effort. If we go to the story to inquire into Jacob's ultimate "success" at Penuel, we discover that he acquired three things — a new name, an injured thigh, and a blessing. (The giving of the name seems to be the form of the blessing, or at least part of it; the words of the blessing are not reported.) The person, in giving a new name to Jacob, says "You struggled with gods and men and you have prevailed." That is all that counts; the meaning of *ykl* is not in doubt.

5. The MT reads the first two lines of v 5a as one, "He contended unto (*'el*) an angel and he overcame." The use of *'l* here is suspicious, but the usual emendation to *'t* is not necessary. The text can be retained with only a slight change in the vowel if *'ēl*, "God," is read (Wolff 1974:206). This draws support from the occurrence of the word *'ēl* in v 1, and from the fact that the Penuel tradition is part of the cycle of stories of El, God of the Fathers, from patriarchal times. There is no article with *ml'k*, "angel," in the MT, but it is more likely that a particular individual is intended, the person of Genesis 32, than that the word is used generically.

In the story of Jacob told in Genesis, there are two great climaxes in God's dealings with the patriarch. They are arranged symmetrically at the beginning and end of his sojourn in Paddan-Aram (reported here in v 13). Genesis 28 records the flight of Jacob because of Esau's resolution to kill him. At Bethel he meets Yahweh, and makes vows. On his return he meets "a person" at the ford of the Jabbok. Hosea's fragmentary remarks refer to at least these two incidents, even if the language he uses does not altogether correspond to that of Genesis. In v 5, the sequence of Bethel (v 5b) and Jabbok (v 5aA) is the reverse of the biblical tradition; Hosea seems to have reversed it deliberately. The reference of v 5aB may be to the encounter at Penuel or the meeting with Esau directly after.

The poetry in vv 4 and 5 is well developed. In spite of the variable length of the lines, there is good parallelism; there are seven lines and eight verbs. In the middle (v 5aB) is the line that is hardest to connect with any other Jacob tradition we now have. Since the first four lines (vv 4 and 5aA) deal largely with Penuel, it is tempting to attach v 5aB to v 5b to make a tricolon dealing with Bethel; poetic symmetry, however, cannot alone decide this question.

In vv 5aB and 5b, the subjects and objects of the verbs are unidentified. While Jacob is the most obvious subject of the verbs, we cannot assume this uncritically. There is no report of Jacob weeping and imploring in either the Bethel or Penuel encounters. There are a few occasions in Genesis on which Jacob wept: when he first met Rachel (Gen 29:11); and with his brother when they were reconciled (Gen 33:4). It would be difficult to find weeping and beseeching in Jacob's request for a blessing (Gen 32:27), for there he is laying down a condition, as the one who has the upper hand. For a more desperate prayer we have to turn to Gen 32:10–13, a reference to the reunion with Esau.

We approach this problem cautiously by making a few more observations on the structure of vv 4 and 5. In spite of the repetition of the forms of *śyr~śrr,* v 4b and the first line of v 5aA are not poetic parallels. It could be that the first two lines in v 5 are an exposition of v 4b, and this leads us to look for a similar expansion of v 4a. This could be, as we have noted, v 5aB, if it refers to Esau. It is more likely, however, that in v 5aB the angel is begging Jacob to let him go before the day dawns. He is eager to conceal his identity from Jacob, as his refusal to reveal his name shows; he must be gone while it is still dark.

Verse 5b seems to deal with one incident, because *bêt-'ēl // šām* indicates one location. The operative verbs of v 5b do not occur in Gen 28:11–22, but no better identification presents itself, and the two accounts can be squared with each other if God met Jacob there, and if *dbr,* "spoke," refers to Jacob's vows. The divergent vocabulary hints that Hosea is drawing on Jacob traditions no longer extant. And, if different in language, why not different in material details as well?

Verse 4, in spite of its excellent parallelism, links two moments widely separated in Jacob's life. These are the episodes which provided him with his two names, the beginning of two lives. Verse 4 embraces the theme of Jacob's triumphs over both man and God, a double achievement made explicit in Gen 32:29[28E]: "You have striven with God and with people and have prevailed." Verse 4a deals with a person, Esau; v 4b deals with God. By using the plural, however, Gen 32:29 seems to commemorate more than Jacob's struggle for supremacy over his brother Esau (v 4a); the obvious other individual is Laban (v 13b). Verse 5 is largely restricted to Jacob's encounters with God; his dealings with people, which receive so much attention in Genesis, seem not to receive further development in c 12.

Gen 32:27[26E] records Jacob's demand for a "blessing," his condition for releasing the person over whom he has the upper hand. The upshot of this incident is that Jacob "prevailed" (*ykl*). The emphasis is on strength, the meaning of *'ôn* in v 4b. The verb *ykl* is used twice in Genesis 32, and is built into the pronouncement on the name "Israel." In 12:5a the conclusion of the whole matter is *wayyūkāl;* used in this way, the verb refers back to an activity previously described, not to some further activity about to be described.

The weeping is probably a continuation of the Penuel story, without taking away the climactic effect of "He overcame." The lack of a conjunction at the beginning of v 5aB is curious in Hebrew.

The rivalry between Rachel and Leah offers an analogy to the struggles of v 5 (Andersen 1969a). Rachel saw her struggle for children as competition with Leah, and even such an achievement as having children through her slave Bilhah she took as a triumph over her sister. Both these sons, Dan and Naphtali, she sees as tokens that God had responded to her prayers. She "prevailed" over her sister by means of twisting or wrestling (root *ptl*, cf. Naphtali) with God, as she says in Gen 30:8:

> naptûlê 'ĕlōhîm niptaltî
> 'im-'ăḥōtî gam-yākōltî

> Wrestling (with) God I wrestled.
> With my sister I succeeded also.

Gen 32:29[28E] has a similar parallelism:

> kî-śārîtā 'im-'ĕlōhîm
> wĕ'im-'ănāšîm wattûkāl

> For you have contended with God
> and with people you have prevailed.

The structural similarity to Gen 30:8 invites recognition of the clause boundaries shown, in spite of the conjunctions in the second clauses. This leads to a translation in which God and the person are in different clauses, as in v 4. It may also place some doubt on the association of both nouns with both verbs — "You struggled with both God and men, and you overcame both!" Taking a lead from Gen 30:8, we could rather say that

Jacob, like Rachel, who overcame her sister by prayer, overcame people because of the action with God.

wayyāśar 'ēl
mal'āk wayyūkāl

In each instance there is a postpositive conjunction in the second line. The two statements may, then, be distinct and *'ēl* and *mal'āk* not the same, since the "angel" in 12:5aA occupies a structural position the same as the sister and the brother in Genesis.

If the parallelism is not synonymous and the two verbs do not have the same objects, then the arguments that led to the belief that the verb means "to strive" are weakened. This would be a suitable conative verb before "succeeded," but neither verb tells us what precisely the subject strove for and succeeded in doing. Our investigation falls short of demonstrating that Rachel and Jacob overcame their sibling rivals because of their relationship with God.

The meaning "to wrestle" for the root *ptl* in Gen 30:8 rests on flimsy foundations. The root describes devious conduct, and only by a fancy is this kind of twisting connected with twisting oneself around an opponent in a wrestling match. It would fit Rachel's conduct to say that she outwitted her sister. In such matters she and Jacob were well matched. The role of God as the object of this activity needs to be made clearer before we can equate *nptl* and *śry*. In the MT, *naptûlê* in Gen 30:8 could be a construct noun (hapax legomenon), before the word "god," used as an attributive, viz. "mighty wrestlings" (so *RSV*). We do not so interpret it, in part because no such interpretation of the word "God" is possible in Gen 32:29.

The belief that Jacob strove with God at Penuel rests on two inferences — first, that struggle precedes success; and second, that the person is God. We do not intend to reject these inferences, only to be cautious in resting too much weight on them. Let us compare the four relevant passages once more:

A′ . . . Jacob contended (*śry*) with (*'et*) *'ĕlōhîm*   Hos 12:4
B   . . . Rachel wrestled (*nptl*) with (no preposition) *'ĕlōhîm*   Gen 30:8
C   Jacob contended (*śry*) with (*'im*) *'ĕlōhîm*   Gen 32:29
D   Jacob contended (*śry*) with (no preposition) **'ēl*   Hos 12:5

A   . . . Jacob seized (*'qb*) his brother   Hos 12:4
B′ Rachel prevailed (*ykl*) with (*'im*) her sister   Gen 30:8
C′ Jacob prevailed (*ykl*) with (*'im*) people   Gen 32:29
D′ Jacob prevailed (*ykl*) with (no preposition) an angel   Hos 12:5

These four bicola should not be forced into congruency. Among the matters in common is conflict between siblings (A, B′). The verb *śry* is always used to describe something that Jacob did "with God" (A', C, D). The only difference lies in the use of the preposition *'et* in A' and the apparent lack of a preposition in D. If our interpretation is correct, there is an omission of the preposition in B also, although it is present in the parallel (B') and we can suppose that it does retroactive double duty. The collocation of *śry* with God (A', C) supports the emendation of *'el* to *'ēl* in D.

The person who wrestled with Jacob is called simply *'îš* (Gen 32:25). Since this might mean simply "somebody," we should not attach too much importance to the word as attesting the humanoid form of the wrestler. Nowhere is the word *mal'āk* used in Gen 32:23–33 but its use in Gen 48:16, where it is parallel to *'ĕlōhîm*, should not be overlooked. Because the word *'ĕlōhîm* is used in some of the passages, it is a ready inference that the "angel" in Hos 12:5 also represents God. This word must have been derived from some form of the Jacob tradition no longer extant. This observation receives strength from the fact that there are few references to "the angel of Yahweh/God" in prophetic writing until the post-Exilic apocalypses. The word *'ĕlōhîm* in v 4b must also be derived from the tradition, since Hosea does not elsewhere use it as a name for God.

The verb *ykl* is an authentic part of the tradition, especially as it is unmotivated by aetiological considerations. It is always in the second colon (B', C', D'). What is less clear in Hos 12:5 is the object of this verb: *wayyūkāl* usually follows a conative verb — he tried to do something, "and he succeeded" in doing it. Negation is common, and indicates failure to achieve what is referred to by the preceding verb. Jer 20:7 is a good example of a more absolute use: "You overcame me, because you are stronger (than me)." But Jer 20:9 means "I exhausted myself trying to suppress it, and I failed (to do so)." To judge from the other passages which say that Jacob succeeded, his struggles had two interfaces. He struggled with people and with God. It is more likely that these struggles are integral and related than merely parallel and comparable. Since the circumstances of Rachel's struggle are most fully known, it would seem that her triumph over her sister is the result of "twisting" God (perhaps in prayer). This at least is implied by the use of the word "God" in the etymologizing comment on the name of Naphtali (Gen 30:8), and also by Jacob's earlier expostulation that he cannot usurp the role of God and so satisfy her demand for children (Gen 30:2[1E]).

This brings us back to the problem of why "God and people" and not simply "God" seems to be the object of the verb *śry* in Gen 32:29[28E]. At first the mysterious wrestler is called simply *'îš* (Gen 32:25[24E]), but in the end Jacob says he has seen "God" — *'ĕlōhîm* is used in v 31, not *'ēl*, because this is the work of E; the original name *'ēl* is embedded in the aetiology of Penuel and in the play on the name "Israel." The encounter at Penuel affords no grounds for supplying the word "people" as a second object. That must reflect the stories of Jacob's "successes" in his dealings with Esau and Laban.

The emendation of *'el,* "unto," to *'ēl* can be supported by another consideration in addition to the grammatical, poetic, and historical arguments already developed. The name "Israel" is scarcely concealed in the first two words of v 5. The play on the name was probably much closer in Hosea's time than in the pronunciations which have become standardized in the MT. It would, however, be going too far to take the consonants *wyśr 'l* as an invitation to read the name "Israel" as such. This would create fresh difficulties in grammar and history. As a typical Middle Bronze Age name, Israel was probably at first an affirmation about El, in which the name of the God was the subject of the verb. Our ignorance of the meaning of the verb prevents us from recovering the original meaning. The vocalization of MT *yiśrā'ēl* has been confirmed most recently by the reading of the name *iš-ra-il* in an Ebla tablet (Pettinato 1976:48).

5a. *angel.* Jacob came into contact with angels on several occasions. In the dream at Bethel there were "angels of God" going up and down the staircase (Gen 28:12). They do not do anything else in that story; it is Yahweh who addresses Jacob. In a later dream, however, the God (of) Bethel (*hā'ēl bêt-'ēl*) is introduced as "the angel of God" (Gen 31:11). On Jacob's return there was a brief encounter with "God's angels" (Gen 32:2) at Mahanaim. Jacob's reference to "the angel, the redeemer" in the blessing of Joseph (Gen 48:15–16) could be more germane, for here the title "the angel" is used absolutely, in series with God. Gen 48:16 thus provides a close analogy to Hos 12:5. No angel is mentioned in the Genesis accounts of the incidents that Hosea is talking about. The phrase *'ēl/ mal'āk,* "god, angel," is a unity, split up over two parallel lines. The base is "the Angel of God," representing the deity himself, though the phrase **mal'ak 'el* is unattested. It is probable that the *mal'ak yhwh,* who would never have been called that in patriarchal times, was *mal'ak 'ēl* in the preliterate traditions, and Hosea's material could go right back to such terminology. Ps 2:2 contains a construction which clarifies the relationship between El and dependencies. Rebellion against "the anointed of Yahweh," whom Yahweh calls "my king" in v 6, is rebellion "against Yahweh and against his anointed."

wept. Either the "angel," in fear of losing his anonymity, begs Jacob for release; or Esau and Jacob weep in their reconciliation. The weeping in either case is not an expression of outrage or grief, but a plea for grace.

implored. This verb can be used to describe an act of supplication toward God or people; the prepositions *'el* or *l* are used with the object. The idiom in Esth 8:3 shows that we have an example of hendiadys: weeping and imploring are a single act, the act of a desperate person who beseeches with weeping. This is probably Hosea's imaginative embellishment of the Penuel incident, although it may reflect an ingredient in the tradition, not given in Genesis, which reached Hosea.

5b. *Bethel*. The other occurrence of the name in Hosea is at 10:15. Unlike Amos, who refers to the city by its proper name seven times, Hosea generally uses Beth Awen (4:15; 5:8; 10:5). It seems certain that Bethel in v 5b comes from the Jacob traditions. Jacob had two significant encounters with God at Bethel, reported in Gen 28:11–22 and 35:6–15. The latter account is rather overshadowed by the Penuel tradition, and also apparently contaminated by it in places. None of this material throws any light on Hosea's use of the verb *mṣ'*; we do not know who "met" whom at Bethel. Hosea uses *mṣ'* to describe the meeting of a worshiper with God in the cult (5:6). In this sense, at Bethel Jacob found God, and Jacob made a promise to God. Jacob's success in this matter then contrasts with Israel's later failure, a failure made more poignant if the same location is the center of the pilgrimages of Hosea's day. We recall also that *mṣ'* often means "to overtake, apprehend," not merely find, whether accidentally or by search. This important nuance is evident in 9:10, which, like 11:1, describes the initiative of Yahweh in securing Israel as his people. Hos 12:5 records an earlier stage in this election: it was Yahweh, whose name is proclaimed in v 6, and again in v 10, who "found" Jacob at Bethel. Bethel was the original location of Yahweh's formative dealings with Jacob, in judgment and promise.

There is another motif in the Jacob story that matches Hosea's analysis of what Yahweh is doing with his people in his own day. Jacob fled to Paddan-Aram (v 13). He returned chastened, as Israel will return when the lion roars (11:11). It was one of Jacob's requests at Bethel that God should bring him back safely to his land (Gen 28:21). After all the years in which Jacob lived in exile, without his "standing stone" (Hos 3:4; Gen 28:18,22), he was directed by another vision from "the God of Bethel" (Gen 31:13) to return home. A recapitulation of Jacob's experiences in his later descendants would then include a promise of restoration.

spoke. Jacob's response to the first theophany at Bethel was to make a vow (Gen 28:20). In the account of the second appearance at Bethel (Genesis 35), it is repeatedly called "the place where God spoke (*dbr*) with him." The action meant goes beyond speaking; the covenant was reaffirmed. This makes it almost certain that God, not Jacob, is the subject of the verb *yĕdabbēr*.

to him. MT *'immānû* usually means "with us." This can be made to fit here on the theory of the identity of Israel with its ancestor, a corporate personality, but gracelessly. Continuity of reference should be maintained; there is, however, no need to emend to *'immô* (contra Wolff 1974:207,

213). The 3 m s form of the preposition *'m, 'immānnû,* is attested (Kuhnigk 1974:146).

6a. *God of the Armies.* The formula *yhwh 'lhy ṣb'wt* is a late version, the word *'lhy* being inserted since *yhwh ṣb'wt* was no longer understood as a sentence and *yhwh* was not treated as a verb. This formula serves as a boundary marker, and closes the first large unit of the chapter. Yahweh is not part of the Jacob traditions. On the phrase and its antecedents, see Freedman and O'Connor (forthcoming).

6b. *his name.* The use of *zikrô* rather than the usual *šĕmô,* as in Exod 15:3, is notable. Hos 12:6 is the only place where *zikrô* substitutes outright for *šĕmô* in credal hymns of this kind. The words are, however, interchangeable, as comparison with Exod 3:15 shows.

7. This verse is a good example of a characteristic phenomenon in Hosea: it reads like an isolated oracle whose connections with the surrounding text are dubious. Verse 6 is a liturgical affirmation that stands alone, and v 8 moves on to a new theme. Narrative form is clearly resumed in v 9. Verse 7 is an address in second-person singular, a mode which reappears in v 10. This recurrence of similar material points to more than a loose editorial stringing together of small pieces, and suggests more deliberate and coherent authorship. The balance of *wĕ'attâ* (v 7) and *wĕ'ānōkî* (v 10) as well as the repetition of "your God" links the two verses. Furthermore the content of v 10 shows that the "you" being addressed in both verses is Israel as a whole.

7a. *return.* The form is indicative. The use of an imperfect given imperative force by following imperatives is unusual, as is the placement of *tāšûb* and *šĕmōr* at clause ends. The third verb seems more normal in this regard; its placement serves the interests of chiasm.

to your God. The preposition *b* is not usual with the verb *šwb,* except in the idiom *šwb bĕšālôm,* "to return safely," or *šwb bĕrō'š,* "to return (something) on (somone's) head." *Šwb* in the sense of "to go back" is rarely used without a preposition, which is usually *'el.* If *b* is *essentiae,* as in Hos 1:7, the line means "Return (to me) *as* your God."

7b. *Wait.* This is the only place where Hosea uses the verb *qwy.* Hos 2:17 speaks of "a door of hope." The verb usually has *l* as its preposition; *'el,* which appears here, occurs only a few times. Since Hosea often omits idiomatic prepositions, the name El might be read as the object of the verb; this would support the identification of El in v 5a.

8a. *Canaan.* The usual word for "Canaanite" is *kĕna'ănî,* which, in later texts, comes to mean "Phoenician" (II Sam 24:7) or "merchant" (Prov 31:24). The word used here is *kĕna'an.* Aside from expressions like "the land of Canaan," "daughters of Canaan," "rulers of Canaan" (Exod 15:15; cf. Judg 5:19), and "kings of Canaan," the word is rarely used. It occurs here and in Isa 23:11, in the genealogies of Genesis 10 and in I Chronicles 1, and in the story of the eponymous ancestor in Genesis 9. The land is always "the land of Canaan," a phrase used consistently and abundantly in the Torah and Joshua. "The land of the Canaanite" is an infrequent variant.

Practically no mention of a social group of Canaanites is met after the conquest. We need only point out that (the land of) Canaan is never mentioned in the books of Samuel and Kings, and that "the Canaanite" is referred to only once in each (II Sam 24:7; I Kings 9:16), to underscore this remarkable fact. The Song of Deborah reflects the disappearance of Canaan from history as a social and political entity.

On the other hand, the meaning of "merchant" occurs in prophetic literature beginning at least with Zephaniah (Zeph 2:5), who exemplifies the transition. There is reason to suppose that this usage was already current in the time of Hosea, especially since the context (i.e. deceptive scales) suggests the meaning "merchant." That the term applies to Israel or one or more of its component parts need not be doubted for the period in question.

treacherous scales. For a similar comment on Israelite merchants, see Amos 8. Verse 9 follows v 8 in uncovering the dishonest business practices by which Ephraim became rich. This is comparable to Jacob's reputation, and the reference to scales is symbolic of crooked dealing. Ephraim's sin has two aspects; he is greedy *and* dishonest. He acquired wealth by fraudulent means. Verses 8 and 9 explain what is meant by v 1, as the repetition of the word *mirmâ* shows. This is his moral-ethical failure. Verse 12 explains his religio-cultic failure. Between these two accusations comes a reminder of Yahweh's kindly dealings from the Exodus down through a long line of prophets. The juxtaposition of the ethical and the religious is typical of Israelite prophecy, and so is a concrete expression like "treacherous scales," which identifies a physical instrument of human wickedness, focusing on sin as act and not just disposition. The opposite is the "balances of *ṣedeq,*" accurate scales (Lev 19:36; Ezek 45:10; Job 31:6). The use of such expressions in Wisdom literature, for example, Prov 11:1; 20:23, can make them a symbol of any kind of dishonesty. Amos's use of the same phrase (Amos 8:5) points to business practices; it is not just a general symbol.

8b. *defrauds.* The meanings "to oppress, extort" are usually given to the root 'šq. The context of Amos 3:9; 4:1; and of Jer 7:6; 22:3, suggests that advantage is taken of the weaker members of a community. The cognates emphasize that the oppression is rough and strong. Such oppression occurs in the economic areas of life (Lev 19:13; Deut 24:14), in the matter of wages and prices, with dishonesty as well as cruelty involved (Mic

2:2). The word has already been associated with Ephraim in 5:11. The *l* is emphatic with a perfect verb.

an ally. The traditional translation "He loves to oppress" is open to several objections. (1) The use of the verb "to love" as an auxiliary completed by an infinitive is almost unknown (but cf. Hos 10:11; Jer 14:10). (2) The placement of the infinitive before the auxiliary makes such a construction even harder to accept. (3) Further, the traditional translation achieves a wrong focus if *'āhēb,* "he loves," describes as a character trait the enjoyment of crime. It is wealth Ephraim loves, not dishonesty. The root *'hb,* "to love," has to be given a strange meaning to arrive at this result, since it does not mean "to enjoy." It refers to interpersonal relations, notably covenant relationships, cf. 11:1. A "lover," as we take *'hb* here, is a partner in a compact; *'ōhēb* has the same meaning in Jer 20:6. (Too much importance should not be attached to the Masoretic pointing of the form as stative rather than participle; it serves to make it easier to have a clause without an explicit subject.) To mistreat such an ally violates sacred obligations; cf. Jacob's defrauding of his brother (v 4a). *'hb* is the object of the verb. Exploitation, carried out by dishonest business practices, has made Ephraim rich.

9a. *How rich.* In some of its occurrences, *'ak* has an intensifying function. An adversative conjunction is not needed.

acquired. Literally *mṣ'ty,* "I have found." See the discussion of *mṣ'* in v 5b.

wealth. See *'ôn* in v 4.

for myself. Or "by myself."

9b. *my crimes.* Words derived from the root *yg'* have in common the idea of toil, weariness, even distress, but not dishonor. It is the words *'āwōn,* "iniquity," and *ḥēṭ',* "sin," in this line that confer on *yĕgîa'* the connotations of wickedness. This word occurs in Gen 31:42, where Jacob uses it in chiding Laban to describe the exertions by which he acquired his property in Aram.

my iniquity which I have wrongfully committed. Verse 9bB in the MT apparently consists of two nouns in apposition with the relative *'ăšer.* We read *ḥṭ'* as an infinitive absolute. We further suppose that the -*y* of v 9bA also applies to *'wn,* which combines with *ygy'y* to produce "my iniquitous exertions." We take *'wn 'šr ḥṭ'* as a modifier for *ygy'y:* "My iniquitous and sinful exertions."

10a. *I.* This liturgical assertion (cf. v 6) is repeated in 13:4.

from. A temporal meaning of *min-,* "from," is possible. The term may be geographical, if the expression is a condensation of the full formula: "I am Yahweh your God who brought you up from the land of Egypt" (cf. Exod 20:2).

10b. *live*. Or "dwell"; the same verb as in 11:11b. This invites comparison of "houses" and "tents."

tents. In 9:6, "their tents" become a scene of desolation and neglect. Here the picture is that of a desert encampment, as the reference to Egypt indicates. If *'ōd* means "again," there is to be a second exodus (cf. 11:11), and a promise of redemption, not judgment, is made.

as in the days of the Tabernacle. Literally "as in the days of the assembly," a religious gathering (2:13), not a season of the year (2:11). The plural "days," in contrast to the singular in 9:5, points not to one festival, but to an epoch. In the context of the wilderness, when the people lived in tents, we suggest that *mô'ēd* is short for *'ōhel mô'ēd,* "the tent of meeting."

11. Verse 11 is a tricolon. The first verb may be future tense, continuing the prediction of v 10b. If there is continuity, v 11aA predicts an activity of the prophets after the new exodus. The next verb, "multiplied," however, is a normal perfect, past tense. The last verb, imperfect, while neutral in the matter of tense, probably follows its predecessor. The repeated plural "prophets" (cf. 6:5) brings us down into the monarchical period.

11a. *through the prophets*. Literally "upon the prophets," *'l-hnby'ym;* LXX translates *pros* as if it read *'el,* "unto." The idiom is hard to account for. In a speech of rebuke, the accountability of the people depends on the messages from God *through* (*b*) the prophets. The preposition *'l* seems odd and is the more remarkable because the agential *b* is used nearby (v 14; cf. 6:5).

11b. *I create parables*. The roots in *dmy* form a complex group; see 4:5–6. We prefer the meaning "to ruin" there. The parallelism here suggests that Yahweh spoke to the prophets, and multiplied visions for them, and through them he brought messages, which combine vision and word in unique verbal pictures, parables, or similitudes (cf. Wolff 1974:207). To cause ruin at this stage is premature. The chiasm of vv 11aA and 11b suggests that the meaning, too, is equivalent: *dbrty // 'dmh,* "I spoke // I made figures of speech," i.e. "I spoke in figures of speech." The alternation of perfect and imperfect is also appropriate.

12a. In this verse there is additional evidence that Israel's capitulation to the incursions of foreign religion was not a limited, nominal recognition for political purposes, restricted to court circles in the capital. This is the context of Deut 32:16 re-created after several centuries. Quite apart from the centers mentioned in other places in Hosea, such ancient sites as Gilead and Gilgal were the scenes of illegal sacrifices. The parallelism of the first two lines is close:

> *'im-gil'ād 'āwen*
> *'ak-šāw' hāyû baggilgāl*

Gilead and Gilgal are obvious parallels, as the alliteration and assonance show. So are *'āwen* and *šāw',* especially in view of Hosea's use of both these terms to designate false gods; cf. Jer 18:15. The parallelism further invites the application of the preposition *b* to both Gilead and Gilgal. *Hāyû* serves as copula for both statements, and is plural because of the two subjects. Finally *'ak* is a resumptive parallel to emphatic *'im*. A conditional meaning for *'im // 'ak* is not evident, since *hāyû* seems to convey a statement of fact, and even gives the impression that it happened long ago.

Our analysis differs from the Masoretic punctuation, which has *zāqēp qāṭōn* on *hāyû*. But *šĕwārîm* is a good complement to *zibbēḥû*, in spite of the shortness of the line.

Gilead. There is no reason to doubt that the Gilead of Hosea's day deserved the accusation, but the possibility that he is referring to some notorious past failure cannot be ruled out. A contemporary reference would be more appropriate if this region was still part of Israelite territory when this remark was made. Unlike other place names used by Hosea, Gilead was not a city; Ramoth in Gilead could be intended. The prosperity of which Ephraim boasts in v 9, as well as the possession of Transjordan, would suit Jeroboam II's reign; but the alliances with Assyria and intrigues with Egypt which are the main subject matter for cc 7–11 may be political developments after Jeroboam's death. Gilead could have been singled out for special mention because of the association of the place with Jacob (Genesis 31), although the materials from the Jacob tradition used by Hosea do not include any allusions to his treaty with Laban.

bulls. The hapax *šĕwārîm* is the only occurrence of the plural of *šôr*, "bull." The Masoretic vocalization could be bookish. Nouns originally of form **ṭawru* tend to become *šôr* with an invariant stem, but other such plurals of a regular segolate type are known.

Two ways of removing the troublesome word are available. One is to emend to *laššēdîm*, conforming the text to Deut 32:17 and Ps 106:37; the emendation, however, requires considerable alteration of the text, and even if the event is the same as that in Ps 106:37, this is no reason why the vocabulary should be made uniform. With these other texts to serve as a control, it is hard to see how the present reading could have arisen. LXX points to another solution: its *archontes* is from Hebrew *śārîm*, a word common enough in Hosea. Such a reading would come from a stage when the word was defectively spelled, an original *śrm*. The scribes went too far with the *plene* spelling, leaving the Masoretes no choice but to admit a plural. Such a plural form is otherwise unknown. In relation to the verb "to sacrifice," a noun could be the subject ("princes" as in LXX), the direct object ("they sacrifice bulls" — *RSV*), or an indirect object (the emended reading "to demons"). "Princes" does not suit well, since there does not seem to have been an issue of civil officers usurping sacerdotal functions (I Kings 13:4; II Chron 26:16–21). There is nothing wrong with the sacrificing of bulls as such (*pace* Grimm 1973). It is the focus of the sacrifices which makes them evil. Since Hosea uses no preposition, the grammatical function of šĕwārîm remains undefined. The rest of the verse suggests that šwrym is a god rather than a sacrifice. Perhaps a l should be restored before šwrym, which was lost by haplography or scriptio continua (Kuhnigk 1974:148).

12b. *indeed*. Hosea's use of *gam* is not always in line with classical Hebrew norms. We would expect "their altars" to be linked to some similar word nearby about which something similar is said.

stone heaps. The image of the stone heaps beside the furrows is to be compared with the use of the phrase "furrows of the field" in 10:4. There the poisonous weeds along the furrows of the fields present a picture of the rank and evil growth of injustice, and the comparison with stone heaps seems rather far-fetched; the common feature seems to be abundance. In 12:12, also, the impression emerges that their altars became like the numerous stone heaps in the farmlands.

There is a punning assonance in the words gil'ād, gilgāl, and gallîm. Memorial cairns had been erected at the former places at great moments in Israel's history (Gen 31:45–54; Joshua 4–5). The earlier monuments seem to have been approved of because of the acts they commemorated; however, the comparison of the later altars with heaps of stones could be a contemptuous way of referring to them. Verse 12b is a verbless clause. It could be a simple comparison — "Their altars are like heaps of stones," or, since the destruction of altars is threatened several times in Hosea (e.g. 10:2,8), it may predict that "their altars will be like stone heaps. . . ." The reference to "furrows of the field" is part of the description of the stone heaps, not information about the location of the altars.

13b. *one wife . . . another wife*. The quantifiers are supplied; it is possible that there is only one wife, but it is dubious. Cf. v 14. Jacob served two distinct terms for his two wives (Gen 29:30; 31:41). Both wives are meant here, but Hosea does not extract any particular point from this fact.

The structure of the tricolon in v 13 is intricate. The parallelism of "Jacob" and "Israel" links the first two lines, even though fleeing to the field of Aram and serving for a wife afford no parallelism. The final, short line, "For another wife he kept (sheep)," with its chiasm with the second line, is parallel to it.

for one wife. The language could have been taken directly from Gen 29:18,20. This use of *b* is marginal to its common meaning; it is not even the so-called *beth* of price. He worked "for," that is, in order to gain, a wife, his work taking the place of the customary bride-price.

kept sheep. Literally "watched." The verb is found in the Jacob story (Gen 30:31), though not in direct connection with working for the two wives. Nevertheless, it provides the appropriate context in which we find the implied object, "sheep."

14b. *one prophet . . . another prophet*. Again, the quantifiers are supplied and the two lines are disproportionate in length. It has been suspected that the second line of v 14 is incomplete. The similarity of the lines

$$13bB \quad \hat{u}b\check{e}'i\check{s}\check{s}\hat{a} \; \check{s}\bar{a}m\bar{a}r$$
$$14b \quad \hat{u}b\check{e}n\bar{a}b\hat{i}' \; ni\check{s}m\bar{a}r$$

supports the integrity of the present text. This shows, furthermore, that vv 13 and 14 have to be interpreted together as far as possible. In fact, the resemblance between them is largely formal. The meaning of b is hardly the same in each verse. The relationship of Jacob to his wives is quite different from that of Yahweh and his prophets. What Jacob did in Aram "for a wife" does not resemble what Yahweh did in Egypt "with a prophet." Hosea may have put these two verses together because formal resemblance aids memory.

Only a general inference can be made from the comparison. Verse 13 refers to two wives of Jacob, and v 14 thus probably speaks of two preeminent prophets. Wolff's contention (1974:216) that only Moses is meant is insupportable. "By (one) prophet Yahweh brought Israel up from Egypt" (cf. Hos 12:10; 13:4): this is Moses (Deut 18:15; 34:10). The second prophet of comparable eminence is more likely to be Samuel than Elijah, although the latter is not altogether to be ruled out. Samuel is more likely because he was earlier than Elijah and already a legendary figure in Hosea's day (as in Jeremiah's), while Elijah was probably still a controversial figure to be canonized and sanctified later. Samuel was a prophet for all Israel, and his leadership was not yet complicated by the emergence of a strong monarchy. In Elijah's time the nation was divided. Elijah's career might, however, have had more significance for Hosea than Samuel's, because it was more recent in memory, because of his interest in the house of Jehu (1:4), and because of Elijah's achievement in the conflict with Baalism. Samuel's problems were different. Furthermore, Elijah's courageous opposition to kings might have appealed to Hosea more than Samuel's inauguration of the monarchy (Hos 8:4; 13:11). Albright (1961:9) identified the second prophet as "probably Samuel." He refers in particular to Jer 15:1, which links Samuel and Moses together, precisely in their reputation for interceding effectively with Yahweh for the preservation of Israel.

Albright also felt that the stylistic features of Hos 12:13–14, notably the repetitive parallelism, pointed to a date as early as the eleventh century. The poem would then be a fragment of an ancient piece intended to elevate Samuel to the same rank as Moses. Such results cannot be considered firm. The poem is too small to permit dating by style. There is a certain Wisdom touch in its arrangement of wives and prophets in pairs; and a certain historical perspective was probably needed for such a reflection.

The formalism of vv 13 and 14 does, however, suggest that the difficulty we experience in working out what Hosea is doing with these lines is probably to be explained by the fact that they came to him ready-made. He is simply quoting them. They contain particulars which did not all apply to his purpose, but which he left unchanged. The wives are part of the Jacob story, but not themselves of central interest. The two prophets fit into the picture because their successors have been mentioned in v 11. If Hosea had wished to talk about Israel's continual hostility to the prophets, as in 9:7, Moses and Samuel could have supplied him with good material to show that Israel's behavior had been of a piece all along. As it is, v 14 seems to be tangential to the chapter.

14a. *By.* Agential *b* is rarely used with an active verb. In occurrences like Hos 1:7 we have recognized *beth essentiae.* The *b* in Hos 12:7, 13:9, etc. is more puzzling.

14b. *was watched.* The use of the passive *nišmār* could have been influenced by the fact that agential *b* is more commonly used with a passive verb; see Deut 33:29; Isa 45:17; Pss 18:30; 44:6; 56:5,11; 60:14.

Its use is such a departure from the otherwise close imitation of v 13, where the *Qal šāmar* was used, that it must have been intended to secure an important distinction, the more so, since the other resemblances are formal, not semantic. The passive could also have been chosen to avoid repeating either the subject or the object (Israel); yet pronouns would have sufficed for that. A middle meaning seems insipid.

15. A strong indication of the unity of c 12 is the correspondence between vv 3 and 15. The design of the tricola is similar; an opening statement is followed by a bicolon, with parallelism, which explains the opening statement in more detail. There is some repetition of vocabulary; *yāšîb lô,* "he will return/requite (to) him," is quite striking. Even when the same words are not used, related ideas are expressed. Thus the provocation (*hikʿîs*) is matter for a *rîb,* and contributes to the emotional tone of the *rîb.* The final *ʾǎdōnāyw* (the only occurrence of this title in Hosea, as contrasted, say, with twenty-six times in Amos) supplements the name Yahweh in v 3, the breakup of the expression "His Lord Yahweh." The sequence of prepositions *ʿal // l* is used several times in Hosea, notably in both vv 3 and 15.

Fixed pairs are not always used in the recurring threats of judgment. The parallels *zkr // pqd* have already been used twice (8:13; 9:9), and they have the same objects in each place. The parallels *pqd // ʾāšîb, yāšîb* are used in 4:9 and 12:3, with the same noun object in each place. Hos 12:15 has the same prepositions for the indirect objects as 4:9 and 12:3, and one of the same verbs. But the noun objects are different, and the rare verb *nṭš* is used. This is the more striking because the object of *yiṭṭôš*, "blood," is compatible with the verb *pqd* (Hos 1:4).

The structural correspondence between vv 3 and 15 is seen in the fact that the former is followed by the first installment of the Jacob material (vv 4–5), while the latter follows the second installment (vv 13–14).

15a. *caused . . . provocation*. *Hikʿîs* is normally used with God as the object; Ephraim must be the subject. Yahweh is the subject of v 15b, but we have to wait to the very end for "His Lord." The cause of the provocation is not revealed. In proximity to the reminders of Yahweh's great acts of redemption (vv 6,10,14), "they forgot me" (Hos 13:6; cf. 2:15) sums it up. Arrogance in success (12:9; 13:6a) and resorting to pagan cults (12:12a; 13:2) were provocations; but in these matters we have moved to themes for which the biography of Jacob the patriarch affords no comparison.

bitter. The word *tamrûrîm* occurs again in Jer 6:26; 31:15. Bitterness, expressed in words based on the root *mrr*, is a human emotion. It seems that Ephraim provoked a state of bitterness in Yahweh; this may be incorrect. Remembering Hosea's propensity for reduplication in roots, there could be a connection with *mĕrî*, "rebellion," a word which figures particularly in the wilderness traditions. Whether its use here is tied to the "bitterness" sense or the "rebellion" sense, it combines with *mirmâ* in v 1, so that these two words frame the entire chapter.

Dahood (personal communication) suggests that *tmrwrym* is a divine title, which with *'dnyw* forms a composite name whose elements can be in the Ugaritic personal name (*bn*) *mr adn*. The relevant sense of *mrr* is not bitter but strong, a sense well attested in Northwest Semitic. The plural abstract form is analogous to *qĕdôšîm* in 12:1, which Dahood takes as a reference to Yahweh; thus he proposes an inclusion around the chapter of the composite divine names *'l-qdwšym* and *tmrwrym-'dnyw;* the inclusion is chiastic with abstract elements in opposed positions in the names.

15b. *hold him reponsible*. *Yiṭṭôš* usually describes an act of God (I Sam 12:22; Ps 94:14). The verb has the central meaning "to abandon," but Ps 78:60 shows that more positive action can be involved. The "abandonment" of the tabernacle of Shiloh was the consequence of provocation (Ps 78:58, the same verb as in Hos 12:15).

murders. The "bloods" of 4:2. For the idiom *hšyb dm 'l* (*rō'š*) see I Kings 2:32.

disgrace. *Ḥerpâ* commonly describes some ignominy for which someone endures reproach. Honor can be restored by revenge (I Sam 17:26) and the "disgrace" is "removed." Here the situation is different. The disgrace that Ephraim has brought upon God through murders will be returned to Ephraim. Jeremiah frequently says that in the judgment Yahweh will make Israel a *ḥerpâ*.

XXII. RETROSPECT AND PROSPECT: THE END OF EPHRAIM
(13:1–14:1)

The sin of idolatry and human sacrifice
13:1a Truly He had spoken terrifyingly against Ephraim.
　　　　　　He had lifted up (his voice) against Israel.
　1b He became guilty at Baal and died.
　2a Now they continue to sin.
　　　　They made a cast image for themselves.
　　　　From their silver they made images
　　　　　　according to their skill.
　2b The whole thing is the work of artisans.
　　　　Those who sacrifice people speak to them.
　　　　　　They kiss the calves.
　3a Therefore they will be like morning mist
　　　　　　and like dew that goes away early,
　3b Like chaff that is whirled from a threshing floor
　　　　　　and like smoke from a chimney.

The origins of the sin
　4a I am Yahweh your God, from the land of Egypt.
　4b You have never known any god but me.
　　　　　　There is no deliverer except me.
　5a I knew you in the desert,
　5b 　　in the land of drought.
　6a When I fed them they became self-satisfied.
　　　　When they were self-satisfied, their heart became
　　　　　　arrogant.
　6b Therefore they forgot me.

The punishment for the sin
　7a I will be to them like a lion.
　7b 　　Like a leopard by the road I will watch.

8a   I will fall upon them like a bereaved she-bear.
        I will rip the lining of their heart.
8b   I will devour them there like a lion,
        like wild animals that tear them apart.

The inevitability of the punishment
9a   I will destroy you, Israel,
9b   for (you rebelled) against me, against your helper.
10a Where is your king, who would bring you victory,
        in all your cities, where are your judges
10b Of whom you said,
        "Give me a king and princes"?
11a I gave you a king in my anger.
11b   I took him away in my wrath.

The avoidance of the inevitability
12a Ephraim's iniquity is wrapped up.
12b   His sin is hidden away.
13a The pangs of a woman in childbirth came for him.
        He was an unwise child.
13b At the time when children are born, he would not have
        survived.
14a From the grasp of Sheol I ransomed them.
        From Death I redeemed them.
14b Where are your plagues, O Death?
        Where are your ravages, O Sheol?
     The cause of sorrow is hidden from my eyes.
15a He became the wild one among his brothers.

The punishment for the sin
15b The east wind, Yahweh's wind, comes.
        It rises from the wilderness.
     His spring will dry up.
        His fountain will become dry ground.
     He shall plunder the treasure,
        all the attractive objects.

14:1a^a   Samaria has become guilty,
         for she rebelled against her God.
  1b   They will fall by the sword.
     Their infants will be smashed.
     His pregnant women will be torn open.

NOTES

13:1 – 14:1. This unit of prophetic discourse rounds off the proclamation that has been made in cc 4–12. It reiterates the main accusations: "they forgot me" (v 6; cf. 2:15); they made idols out of silver (v 2; cf. 2:10; 8:4). These are no more than human artifacts (v 2; cf. 8:6). This idolatry concerns Baal or Baal Peor (v 1; cf. 2:10,18–19), and v 2 hints at dark practices connected with this. There is a return to the theme of kings (vv 10–11; cf. 7:3–7). Terrifying threats of punishment (vv 7–8; 14:1; cf. 5:14) are accompanied by moving references to redemption (v 14) and reminders of ancient favors (vv 4–5). As in the rest of the prophecy, lavish use is made of multiple similes (vv 3,8).

Yet, in spite of all this recognizable material, there are several passages which are obscure, and the total impression is one of incoherence. The relationships among these diverse materials within the discourse are hard to find. It is no wonder that many scholars have concluded that Hosea is no more than a congeries of unconnected fragments. Yet some progress can be made in finding a pathway through the tangle. The method of composition is the same as in the rest of the book. The smaller units range from well-formed poetic bicola or tricola of standard types to sentences which are simply prose to all intents. All find their place in a well-woven fabric of words and clauses, because themes are developed, and corresponding materials are placed in balance in the total structure. Although the Hebrew text begins a new chapter with 14:1, the Jewish reading tradition included 14:1 with c 13. Rightly so; for 14:2 begins a new, more hopeful exhortation, while 14:1 matches 13:1, making a frame for the whole. The name "Ephraim" marks a beginning in 13:1, and "Samaria" balances it in 14:1. Ephraim is "he"; Samaria is "she." Ephraim and Israel are parallel in v 1, and each name is used once more later on (vv 9, 12). The two uses of '*šm,* in 13:1 and 14:1, constitute an echo and unite the chapter. The names are contemporary, but references to Egypt and the

---

^a Some English translations remove the chapter division from this point to the next verse. Thus MT 14:1 = English 13:16; MT 14:2 = English 14:1, etc.

desert (vv 4–5) give the passage a time-depth we have found elsewhere. The fragment of Exodus tradition in vv 4–5 may balance v 13, an apparent fragment of patriarchal tradition. The Israel of Hosea's day is reminded that it gained its identity and character through the formative events of the Exodus.

The recurring themes are not developed and related systematically. There is rather an alternation of light and dark shades. The discourse is complicated by the variety of referential pronouns used in relation to the several protagonists. Statements about God are interleaved with statements evidently made by God, without the usual introductory formulas. Ephraim is "he" in vv 1, 12, 15(?). Israel is "they" in vv 2, 3, 6, 7, 8. Israel is "you" (m s)in vv 4, 5, 9. Yahweh is "he" in vv 1, 15. Yahweh is "I" in vv 4–11, 14. The unglossed "he" of vv 13 and 15 could be Jacob. "You" (m s) refers to Death and Sheol in v 14. The "she" in 14:1a is Samaria, but "they" and "he" in 14:1b are not identified. All this is consistent with the style used elsewhere. Most of the discourse, possibly all of vv 4–14 (or 15a), is a speech made by Yahweh spoken either to Israel (the north), or about the whole nation, or about Jacob. This is framed by statements about Yahweh as "he." The combination of statements in utmost contrast — savage threats and the most ardent assurances of rescue from death — is like the combination in Hos 5:12 – 6:6.

The prosody does not achieve a high level from a formal point of view. The best examples of poetry are supplied by the clusters of similes in vv 3 and 7–8. Both use the same device of saying "They are/I am like X" followed by "like Y" with attributive phrases. In each case k is used four times in comparisons. In v 3 they come in pairs. The arrangement in vv 7–8 is more elaborate: two words for "lion" begin and end the series, with leopard and bear in between; there is a further, more general, reference to wild animals which is a fifth simile, although k is not used.

Verses 11 and 12 contain bicola with fairly conventional, incomplete synonymous parallelism. The description of the desiccating effect of the east wind in v 15 is developed in four lines (two bicola). More elegant is the opening tetracolon in v 14. In addition to the parallelism in each of the bicola, there are two elaborate chiastic patterns.

14a	Sheol	First-person verb
	Death	First-person verb
14b	Particle + object	Death
	Particle + object	Sheol

The arrangement of the Underworld references in pairs constitutes one chiasm; the arrangement of the rest of the clauses constitutes another.

Other parts of the discourse read like narrative prose, especially when the verb with waw-consecutive is the form used for past tense. No descriptive material is attached to the discourse itself, in order, for example, to identify the speaker; that has to be inferred. In one or two places the inner logical connections are shown by conjunctions. Thus *wĕ'attâ* provides a link between the original sin at Baal Peor (v 1) and the current repetition of the same sin (v 2). In v 6 *'al-kēn,* "therefore," traces Israel's forgetfulness to arrogance. Similarly, *lākēn,* "therefore," in v 3 argues that Israel's precarious hold on existence is the consequence of idolatry.

The similar placement of the two connectives in vv 3 and 6 is a guide to the organization of ideas in vv 1–8. At the center (vv 4–5) is an affirmation of Yahweh's primal relationship to his people. These lines have their own organization. A line describing God's activity in Egypt (v 4a) and a bicolon about the desert (v 5) flank a double assertion that Yahweh is the only god and savior (v 4b). Israel's behavior contrasts with this. One example is given in vv 1–3, the other in vv 6–8. Because of idolatry (vv 1–2), they will fade away (v 3). Because of pride (v 6), they will be torn to pieces (vv 7–8).

A further example of Israel's willfulness is given in vv 10–11, the insistence on having a king. Verses 9, 15b and 14:1 could be a response to this; they threaten destruction in a variety of conventional vocabularies. Verses 13–15a seem to tell the story of a previous redemption. Verse 12 is obscure in its connection with the rest of the chapter.

13:1–3. These verses have a certain coherence, and belong with the following material as well. A more refined description might be attainable if we knew better how the conjunctions serve both to link and to separate. We would also be more sure of our results if we understood how the verb system worked. The two systems — verbs and conjunctions — work together in a single syntax. In approaching the problem we have to make up our minds whether we feel entitled to revise the MT, and to what extent. If, for the time being, we are reluctant to alter a single vowel, let alone consonant, it is not because the MT is sacrosanct, but because we cannot pretend to know better. The present unit illustrates the problem.

Mays (pp. 171–173) divides it into the past (v 1), the present (v 2), and the future (v 3). This analysis derives some support from the use of conjunctions. *Lākēn,* without "and," introduces the predictive threat (v 3); elsewhere in Hosea this particle is used, in 2:8,11,16 (Wolff 1974:224), in a section which balances this one in the book's overall structure. The preceding diagnosis (vv 1–2) is divided into past and present by "(and) now." Mays takes *wĕ'attâ* simply as an adverb, but it often marks a transition from indicative to precative moods, from description to prediction. The text could be better described if we were more confident about the meanings of the verb forms, or rather, knew which of their possible meanings fitted with the various conjunctions. To gain the flexibility he needs, the interpreter must suppose that the tense system is loose, not to say labile. So, to secure Mays's result, we must assume that "he became guilty" in v 1b is past tense, while "they made" in v 2a (the same form category) is present. We must further assume that "they continue" in v 2a is present tense, while "they will be" (the same form category) in v 3a is future. Mays's scheme has the advantage of simplicity, in the progression from past to present to future, but his scheme splits up the time referents of verbs which are identical in form, cutting a Gordian knot.

1a. Literally, MT opens with "like-to-speak Ephraim," an infinitival construction in which Ephraim seems to be the subject. The tightly packed construction is usually expanded and emended to make the next word "terror" a complete clause, modified by the infinitive. Hence *RSV*, "When Ephraim spoke, men trembled." This is unlikely: Ephraim has no reputation for inspiring terror by speech. So far as the Bible is concerned, the utterance that causes fear is the word of Yahweh. By the principle of complementary parallelism, each line can complete what is lacking in the other. The speaking here may refer to an oath to enact vengeance. The verb *nāśā'* as a parallel would then be short for *nāśā' qôlô* or *nāśā' yādô*. The first line would refer to the act of God in uttering a decree, the second to an oath confirming it. The *k* here is asseverative and the verb is a finite *Pi'el* form.

The parallel for "Ephraim" is "Israel," and the preposition *b* does double duty with both nouns. In the common interpretation, "He (Ephraim) was exalted in Israel" (*RSV*), *nś'* is read as *Qal* passive or *Nip'al* (middle). It is simpler to suppose the verb's object has been elided. *Hû'*, "he," is a suitable way of referring to Yahweh, the subject of both verbs.

> k dbr   'prym rtt
> nś' hû'   byśr'l

The bicolon has the character of an opening formula or heading, announcing an oracle of terror proclaimed by Yahweh himself against Ephraim // Israel. The historical narrative, which begins in v 1b, has no direct logical connection with v 1a.

terrifyingly. Until the discovery of the Dead Sea scrolls, this was the only known occurrence of the word *rĕtēt*. The meaning "terror" is evident in *1QH* 4.33 (Mansoor 1961:130; Wolff 1974:219). *Rĕtēt* is not necessarily Aramaic. In any case *reṭeṭ* (Jer 49:24) can hardly be a cognate, although it is similar in meaning, since *t* and *ṭ* do not interchange.

In view of the word *mārĕtâ* in 14:1 (cf. Jer 50:21), we could read (*'pry*)*m* twice to obtain the verbs *mrt* // *tnś'*. This is unnecessary.

had lifted up. See the discussion of *nś'* at 1:6. The traditional "he was exalted," reading a *Nip'al* participle (Wolff 1974:219), has been justified by referring to other cases in which *nāśā'* is allegedly intransitive. Of these, the forms in Ps 89:10 (render, "When he [Yam] lifts up his waves") and Hab 1:3 are probably transitive. Nah 1:5 could be a parallel.

Another possibility is *nāšā'*, "to deceive, beguile." As a parallel to a putative *mrt*, "you rebelled," **tinnāšā'*, "you were beguiled," would refer to Ephraim's seduction by the worshipers of other gods. See Isa 19:13; cf. Job 34:31. We rather suppose that the verb is parallel to *dbr*, with God as the implied subject; the expression is elliptical for "he lifted up (his voice)."

1b. *He became guilty*. There is no logical connection between vv 1a and 1b, in spite of the conjunction *w*. Verse 1b takes up a narrative. If v 1a introduces an oracular utterance of Yahweh, then vv 4 and 5 are the self-affirmation that frequently goes with such a speech. In this speech Yahweh tells the story of his experiences with Israel, but not consecutively. A declaration of guilt leading to death should come at the end of the story, but we do not have the account of Yahweh's onslaught until vv 7–8. Verse 1b anticipates the consequences of the sins listed in vv 2,6,10. Verse 12 contains another pronouncement of Ephraim's guilt.

at Baal. The preposition *b* is never used with the root *'šm* to identify an accomplice in sin, *pace* Wolff (1974:219). Ezek 22:4 approaches the idiom used here:

> *bĕdāmēk 'ăšer-šāpakt 'āšamt*
> *ûbĕgillûlayik 'ăšer-'āśît ṭāmē't*

> You are guilty with your blood which you shed.
> You are defiled with your idols which you made.

Cf. Lev 5:26. It is more likely that *b* is locative, and that "Baal" is short for "Baal Peor" (9:10). This would fit the desert setting of v 5. As elsewhere in Hosea, the behavior of Israel in the present is linked with similar behavior in the early days. The use of "Ephraim" in such a connection would be an anachronism, but not a serious one. In connecting Ephraim's idolatry with Baal Peor, Hosea has a different historical perspective from the editors of Exodus 32 and I Kings 12, who connect the golden calves (see v 2) with Horeb.

and died. According to Numbers 25, the Baal-Peor apostasy occasioned many deaths. To say that Ephraim "died," in this simple and final way, when the nation still existed, could mean that they received the death sentence. But the following "(and) now" suggests that v 1b records some past event from which Ephraim did not learn, since the people committed the same sin all over again.

2a. *Now they continue to sin*. *Yôsīpû* here can describe the continuation, repetition, or escalation of sin. The making of an idol was nothing new. If this is the sin which led to death (v 1), and which is now repeated (v 2a), then *yôsīpû* means "they persisted" in making images, heedless of warnings from the past. If, on the other hand, v 2b describes the introduction of human sacrifice into the cult, it refers to a depravity far worse than what happened at Baal Peor, perhaps a reversion to long abandoned practices.

Verse 2aA interrupts the continuity in the narrative that uses *waw*-consecutive verbs, which begins in v 1b. The imperfect *yôsīpû* does not fit well with the following clause, and thus v 2aA might be parenthetical, a general comment: they keep on sinning in the same manner, beginning at Baal Peor. This means that "(and) now" does not have its usual function of marking transition to precative speech; it is simply an adverb of time.

a cast image. The cult object at Horeb was *'ēgel massēkâ* (Exod 32:4,8). Verse 2b has the singular "work of artisans," and *klh,* "the whole thing," also suggests that one particular idol is meant. The plural *'ăṣabbîm,* which is parallel to *massēkâ,* joins with it to make a phrase — "a casting of idols." As elsewhere in Hosea, the plural "idols" (4:17; 8:4; 14:9) does not point to the multiplicity of images, but is an imitation of *'ĕlōhîm* to describe the rival god, Baal. By the same token the plural "calves" in v 2b refers to the image of Baal as a young bull.

for themselves. As in Exod 32:8. At Baal Peor the Israelites joined an available cultus. At Horeb they made an image for themselves. The Decalogue prohibits making images "for yourselves" (Exod 20:4, cf. 23; Deut 4:16; cf. Hos 8:4).

their silver. Since Exodus 32 mentions only gold, this detail makes connection with the Horeb incident somewhat less likely. Hosea mentions silver more often than gold in connection with idol-making, and never gold without silver (2:10; 8:4; 9:6). Silver and gold are made into *'ăṣabbîm* in 8:4 and into Baal in 2:10.

according to their skill. The authenticity of MT's *kitbûnām* is in doubt, because the masculine form is unique. It can be normalized in either of two ways. The word *tabnît* is a possible alternative (so Wolff 1974:219), because of its associations with idol-making. It means something built (from the root *bny*); in Exod 25:9; Deut 4:16–18; and II Kings 16:10, it means a *replica,* and the standard translation, "model," is not appropriate. The thing made is the *tabnît* of what it is copied from; the original is not the pattern of the manufactured object. In Exod 25:9, what Moses saw on the mountain was not a plan of the tabernacle, but an actual tabernacle, the real or original one. What he made was an exact reproduction, so that the glory of God could be housed on earth in a manner comparable to God's dwelling in heaven. Such a procedure does not suit Hos 13:2. Further, emendation from *ktbwnm* to *ktbnyt* (*BHS,* following LXX) requires considerable alteration of the consonants.

Wolff's stricture (1974:219) that the f form *tĕbûnâ,* "understanding," would have to be read instead of the m *těbûn* to preserve the sense of MT is too rigid, although this solution departs less from the text than reading *tabnît*. Both forms are from the root *byn*, "to discern"; cf. 4:14, and v 13. The emendation is not absolutely required. It is true that nouns made from hollow roots using preformative *t-* are usually feminine; but a masculine form is not impossible. The reference is to the stupidity of the people. In view of the parallelism of *těmûnâ* and *tabnît* in Deut 4:16–18, it is also possible that *těbûn* is a coined word which fuses features of these two words, and the ideas they express. This could have given rise to the reading of LXX.

2b. *The whole thing*. Literally "all of it." The masculine suffix is in agreement with *ma'ăśeh*.

artisans. Hos 8:6 also mentions artisans in deriding the worship of artifacts. Cf. "the work of artisans" with "the work of our hands" in 14:4.

Those who sacrifice people. The plain meaning of the phrase *zōběḥê 'ādām* can scarcely be evaded (so Wolff 1974:219). Once more we meet the horror of human sacrifice. The sacrifice of "calves" to Yahweh was part of Israel's religion. Here the calves receive religious homage, and human sacrifice is offered to a casting in the shape of a calf! Examination of *zibḥê mētîm* in Ps 106:28 shows that the noun governed by *zibḥê* in construct can be neither possessive (the party making the sacrifice) nor appositive (the sacrifices consisting of what the *nomen rectum* refers to), if *mētîm* means "the dead." Dead persons do not offer sacrifices, and since *zbḥ* means "to slay" it is impossible for the victims to be "dead men." Taking *mētîm* as indirect object ("sacrifices to the dead") or benefactive object ("sacrifices for the sake of the dead") is not much better. The simplest and best solution is to read *mětîm*, "human beings," so that *zibḥê 'ādām* and *zibḥê mětîm* are synonyms. This phrase is in apposition with *hēm*.

speak. The participle suggests an habitual utterance, repeated in the cult. The chiastic structure also shows that *'ādām* and *'ăgālîm* are in opposition. This underscores the complete inversion of values. Kuhnigk's emendation *'immarê-m zibḥî*, "sacrificial lambs" (1974:149), reading an enclitic *m* and an archaic genitive ending, is euphemistic and apologetic.

to them. That is, to the idols; cf. 4:12 and Hab 2:19. Wolff (1974:219) renders, "they say to themselves," but this should be *blbm* in Hebrew.

They kiss the calves. Ritual kissing is not well attested in the ancient world. I Kings 19:18 suggests that worshipers might have kissed the idol of Baal directly. This is close to 13:2 if, as we have suggested, "calves" is majestic plural for Baal. Cf. Ps 2:12; I Kings 19:18.

3a. *Therefore*. A simple statement of fact does not follow from such a conjunction. If the following imperfect verb is future, a curse of some kind would fit. The clause-initial position of the verb *yihyû* suits such a precative function. The string of comparisons is part of the stock-in-trade of curses. There are four comparisons, one to each line; cf. 11:8 (Wolff 1974:224). They come in two natural pairs — "mist" and "dew"; "chaff" and "smoke." The first two have already been used in Hos 6:4, with the same words; there it was Israel's *ḥesed* that was transitory. There is only one verb for each pair of lines in 13:3. In v 3a, since *bōqer* and *maškîm* are correlatives, it is possible that *hlk* is the verb parallel to *yihyû,* the two verbs opening and closing the bicolon. *Hlk* would then have to be revocalized as an infinitive. It is more likely, however, that the participles *maškîm hōlēk* constitute a phrase, rightly translated "going away early."

3b. *whirled.* The sense of the *Po'el* is passive and the text need not be emended to a *Pu'al,* contra Wolff 1974:219. Because the verb is singular, it modifies "chaff" in a relative clause, rather than being parallel to *yihyû,* which carries all four similes. "Let them be like (1) mist, (2) dew, (3) chaff, and (4) smoke." The verb "(which is) whirled" goes with both "chaff" and "smoke." The similes are congruent. All bring out the speed with which these four things disappear; they leave no trace. The destructive power of the wind is mentioned again in v 15. Comparison of the wicked with chaff is almost a cliché (Pss 1:4; 35:5; Isa 17:13; 41:15–16). The image of smoke is found also in Pss 37:20; 68:3; Isa 51:6.

What is unusual in these similes is the lack of clear connection between the sin and its punishment. Perhaps the logic is that since idols are nothing at all, those who worship them will be like the most insubstantial and impermanent things.

chimney. The vent was not necessarily in the roof. It could have been a lattice in the wall.

4–8. This passage, or vv 4–6, is sometimes recognized as a distinct oracle. The usual criteria of form criticism have to be stretched to make this an oracle of judgment. The central accusation, "they forgot me," cannot be joined simply with vv 4–5, because the address changes from second to third person after v 5. We would expect that the recapitulation of salvation-history (vv 4–5) would involve the remote "them," and the indictment of present conduct (v 6) would be aimed at the more immediate "you." The alleged oracle is, then, not internally consistent. Further, some of its contents are close to other material in the chapter. The threat of punishment in vv 7–8 is similar to v 3. The second-person address of vv 4–5 is resumed in vv 9–10. It is better to preserve these connections by regarding the whole chapter as a single assemblage of related materials.

4. This verse has been considerably amplified in LXX.

And I am the Lord your God
establisher of the sky
and creator of earth
whose hands created all the host of heaven
and I did not show you them
so that you might walk behind them.
And I led you out of the land of Egypt.

This achieves a certain biblical effect. The opening phrases, using participles, resemble the credal hymns; they are not self-affirmations like those in
MT. The homiletical remark about worshiping the host of heaven attacks
a form of idolatry not met elsewhere in Hosea.

Verse 4 makes the identity of the speaker clear. It is Yahweh and his
speech goes back at least to the beginning of v 2. There is no antecedent
for the 2 m s "you." Verses 2–3 are plural and third person. We have to go
back to v 1 for a singular (Ephraim); but a quotation like this does not
need a tight connection with its context.

The affirmation of v 4 is traditional. The interpretation of *min-* as
"since" in v 4a present difficulties. Cf. 11:1. It would be possible to restore "who brought you out," as in LXX. This is a common idiom; and it
would improve the poetry. The missing participle *môṣî'* would then parallel *môšia'*. The formula may, however, be a deliberate abbreviation, as in
12:10.

4b. *known.* In speaking of their idolatry, there is no concession that
they have come to know any other gods. Yahweh alone is real. In turning
to rival, imaginary deities, they have not denied but forgotten Yahweh (v
6b). Since the perfect of *yāda'* is generally used for present knowledge,
acquired in the past and retained, the imperfect used here is more likely to
be pluperfect than future.

5a. *I knew you.* Once again the first-person pronoun is prominent, as in
v 4. Hos 11:1 speaks of calling Israel as a child "from Egypt." Here no
kinship term is used to indicate the relationship in the verb "I came to
know you." To judge from 2:16, it is marriage, and in sequence with
Egypt this suggests the wilderness wanderings as the historical moment.

5b. *drought.* This is the only occurrence of this root in Hebrew. Its
equivalent is *'ereṣ ṣîyâ;* see the NOTE on 2:5. The Akkadian *la'ābu,* "to
exhaust," as with a fever, shows a different semantic development (*CAD*
L:6).

6a. *When I fed them.* This verse traces Israel's deterioration step by
step. It is a common story; cf. Deut 8:11–20. LXX begins it in v 5 by
reading: "I pastured them [i.e. *r'y* not *yd'*] in the desert." This appears to
be an intrusion from the next line. The emphasis on the barrenness of the
land highlights the incredible feat of Yahweh in providing food so miracu-

lously. The story properly begins in v 6 with *kĕmô rĕ'îtūm*, "when I fed them," rather than MT's "in accord with their pasture" (cf. Wolff 1974:220).

they were self-satisfied. In the step-by-step development, there is no need to remove the second form of *śb'* as a dittograph. The argument that prosperity (due entirely to Yahweh's bounty) leads to complacency and forgetfulness is made in Hos 4:7, Deuteronomy 32, and Deuteronomy generally; it is developed in Jeremiah 2.

6b. *they forgot.* Cf. Hos 2:15.

7a. *I will be.* The use of the form *'ĕhî* may pun on the divine name *'ehyeh* both here, and in vv 10 and 14, in which it seems to be an interrogative particle.

like a lion. The image of Yahweh ripping his people to pieces like an enraged beast has already been used in 5:14. The list of animals here makes the passage quite terrifying. It is hard to tell whether vv 7–8 are a threat or a description of punishment already inflicted. The lion-bear sequence occurs in Amos 5:19.

7b. *watch.* See Jer 5:26.

8a. *she-bear.* The simile is hackneyed (I Sam 17:34–37; II Sam 17:8; Prov 17:12; 28:15; cf. Dan 7:5), but there is theology in it. The bear takes god-like vengeance by tearing to pieces the children of those who snatched her cubs from her; her rage is blind. The imagery is used to stress a particular quality in an animal in which it exceeds or surpasses humans.

8b. *lion.* Kuhnigk (1974:150) emends to read *w'klm šm kl b',* "All who come eat them," a remarkably euphemistic change, without textual support.

wild animals. On wild animals as the instruments of God's judgment, see the NOTES on 2:14,20.

tear. The same verb as in 14:1.

9–11. The form-critical character of vv 9–11, whether a speech or a fragment, cannot be established. The passage is unified by its form of address, second person throughout, and by the discussion of Yahweh as helper and leader, in contrast to human kings and princes. To call it a disputation does not provide a basis for firm interpretation; the situation of use cannot be recovered. The taunting question in v 10 could serve rhetorical purposes.

As a record of history, the passage continues the recital that began in v 2. The most notable example of a single king, given in anger, and taken away in wrath, is Saul. If, as seems likely, two kings are involved, then the order is reversed. The new king is given after the former king has been removed: both were the objects of divine wrath. The best candidates would seem to be Zechariah, Shallum, and Menahem.

9a. *I will destroy you.* The interpretation of MT's *šḥtk* can hardly be separated from the use of the same root elsewhere in Hosea. In 11:9 (in connection with Ephraim again!), the *Pi'el* describes Yahweh's destructive action. In 9:9 it describes the nation's self-destruction. Here MT reads "he has ruined you," i.e. Yahweh has ruined Israel. In the surrounding text, Yahweh speaks in the first person; hence our reading *šiḥattîkā*, "I will destroy you," is best (so Wolff 1974:220, after the Syriac). The line sums up the statements made about God's destructive punishments. The same verb is used to describe the work of the Flood and the fall of the Cities of the Plain. In Exod 32:7 it describes idolatry as self-destruction; cf. Deut 9:12.

9b. MT seems to mean "in/with me, in/with your help," or "although/ for your help is in me." LXX points to *'ōzĕrêkā*, "your helpers." The helpers, accomplices, would share Israel's fate. The contrast, however, seems to be between Yahweh's role as "helper" and his role as destroyer. It is this conflict of roles that causes the anguish in Yahweh's mind (11:8). Although apparently abstract, "help" is a common epithet of God (Exod 18:4; Ps 146:5). The sense of the line only emerges if an ellipsis of *pš'*, "to rebel," is recognized.

10–11. These verses belong together. They deal once more with the appointment of a king at Israel's request (v 10b) and his removal in divine anger (v 11). The tradition that kingship was forced from Yahweh derives from I Samuel 8, on which see McCarter (1980); cf. Judges 9. If an individual monarch is referred to by the singular noun, the classic case is Saul. There are several other cases of dynastic termination in the northern kingdom which would qualify, for example, the dynasties of Jeroboam I, Baasha, Omri, and finally Jehu. The imperfect verbs in v 11 are past tense; v 11b does not seem to be forecasting the eventual cessation of the monarchy. The phrase "king and princes" takes us back to c 7 (cf. 3:4), suggesting that more recent kings are meant. Verse 11a may contain the one-sided statement that even the original concession was an act of divine wrath; the acquiescence in I Sam 8:22 is bland by comparison. The reason for Yahweh's anger is stated in v 10a, an overreliance on human rulers, though the verse is not entirely clear. "Your judges" probably corresponds to "princes" (as in c 7) and the one who saves you or brings victory may be a designation of the king. This long phrase then serves as antecedent to *'ăšer.*

10a. With Wolff (1974:221) and Kuhnigk (1974:150) we render *'hy* (cf. *'ayyēh, 'ay*) "where." The sense of the lines is combinatory: "Where are your king and judges who were to bring you victory in all your cities?" Kuhnigk's suggestion (1974:150–151) to read *'ryh* as a word for "rulers," cf. Ugaritic *ġyr*, "to protect," is attractive but the need to refer to the *beth essentiae* and the resultant simplification of the syntax do not recommend the solution.

12–13. The discourse switches to the third person. The connections are hard to find here: "Ephraim" in v 12 may balance "Israel" in v 9; cf. both in v 1. In v 13, the birth pangs are those of the mother, which affect the unborn child; the child, being foolish, does not even go about getting born properly. If v 14 continues this narrative, it is not clear what event it describes.

12. The connection of 13:12 with its context is not easy to trace; neither of the adjacent verses seems to throw light on it; perhaps it is a completely self-contained oracle. The only clue gleaned from the context is that the prophet's tone is disapproving. It may describe the great heavenly book mentioned by Moses in Exod 32:32, or the burden put on the head of the goat of the demon Azazel in the Day of Atonement ritual (Lev 16:21). Wolff associates *ṣrwr* with a legal document (1974:221, 227) and *ṣpwnh* with a treasure, but the split is questionable.

Vuillenmier-Bessard (1958) has sugested that the imagery is derived from the practice of wrapping up precious manuscripts and putting them in storage. The MSS found at Qumran afford the best-known example, but opinions differ as to the reason why these documents were placed in the caves, some carefully protected by sealed earthenware jars. There are three theories. (1) The caves were used as a library annex, and the scrolls were kept there as a normal practice of the community. (2) The caves were used as a Genizah, the last resting place of MSS no longer in use, put in a safe place to protect them from profanation. (3) The MSS were hidden in the caves in an emergency when the community was in danger, with the intention of retrieving them once the danger was past; it is assumed that the community was wiped out by the Romans and the MSS were never recovered. Vuillenmier-Bessard's theory is that *ṣrr* describes the wrapping of a scroll in fabric and sealing in a jar, while *ṣpn* refers to concealment in an inaccessible place, such as a cave.

Jeremiah stored the title deed to his family estate in an earthenware jar, to keep it safe "for a long time" (Jer 32:14). The intention was to retrieve it in the future, when it would be needed to establish ownership.

The metaphor of wrapping up and putting in storage is applied, not to a scroll but to "iniquity // sin." If these nouns have their usual abstract meaning, what does it mean to pack up iniquity, and to hide sin away? It could mean simply to leave sin concealed, that is, not to admit it. Something more deliberate seems intended. The iniquity, like a scroll, is something precious to be stored away safely for future use. Vuilleumier-Bessard says that fourteen out of eighteen occurrences of *ṣpn* in the Bible refer to the hiding of something valuable for safekeeping, so that *ṣāpûn* comes to mean precisely "hidden treasure" (= *maṣpūnîm* in Obad 6).

If, as we have already seen elsewhere, '*āwôn* and *ḥaṭṭā't* are used concretely for "idols," then what is described here is the removal of idols to safe storage, with the intention of retrieving them again in the future. Cf. Hosea's references to precious treasure in 9:6; 13:15.

We are handicapped by not knowing who is the implied subject of the passive verbs. In Isa 65:16 sin is forgiven when God hides it from his sight. Cf. the last line of v 14 here.

13. This verse may be a fragment of the Jacob traditions; perhaps the first line of v 15 belongs with it. The incident that comes to mind is Gen 25:22–26; cf. Gen 38:27–30. In other passages referring to the patriarch, Hosea makes the point that the present conduct of Israel the nation was already manifest in the character of Jacob the ancestor. Yet the allusions of v 13 are obscure in relation to the story of Jacob; obscure as an example of the nation's behavior; and obscure in relation to its context, since little connection can be found with either v 12 or v 15. The childbirth tradition in Jeremiah 6 and 22, and in the apocalypses refer to the woman rather than the child.

The verse shows signs of careful internal organization although the lines are quite uneven in length. Verses 13aA and 13b have references to labor in childbirth. Verses 13aB and 13b both have "not"; the "not standing" is a sign of "unwisdom." The impetuosity of the child is disapproved.

13a. *childbirth.* The word *ḥēbel,* "pain" (generally plural), is nearly always used of the pains of childbirth. The focus is on the plight of the mother, but as a metaphor it can be applied to a man (cf. Jer 30:6). Verse 13a says literally "The pains of a woman in childbirth have come to/for him." It may be that the metaphor is used in the same fashion as Jer 30:6, though the remainder of the verse finds evidence of unwisdom in the behavior of the child being born. Verse 13a thus means that labor pains "for him" have come (to his mother); the time is called "the breaking out of children." The latter expression is not entirely clear. In the plural *mišbĕrê-yām* means breaking waves of the sea; II Kings 19:3 (= Isa 37:3) suggests that the *mašbēr* is the cervix itself, "the place where children break out," rather than a time. Here, the temporal use is clear, however: the second stage of delivery is perilous, and when there is no strength for giving birth the agony is prolonged. The blessings of a speedy delivery are celebrated in Isa 66:7–11 (Isa 66:7 contains the same idiom as Hos 13:13a, with *lāh* instead of *lô*). If the second stage is protracted, it can be fatal for the mother (Gen 35:16–19), injurious or fatal for the child. The child here endangers his mother. The use of '*et* is unusual; it is more often followed by an infinitive (Hos 10:12; cf. '*et yôlēdâ* in Mic 5:2; cf. Qoh 3:2; Job 39:1–2; Gen 38:27).

unwise child. With *bēn lō' ḥākām,* compare '*ām lō'-yābîn* (4:14) and note the discontinuous construction, *bēn . . . lō' ya'ămōd,* a closer parallel. The motif of unwisdom continues from references in early chapters to rejection of the knowledge of God.

14. In Israelite monotheism Yahweh's powers are comprehensive. He is not just a god of one thing; he embraces the functions of the rival gods he eliminates. He absorbs the attributes of other gods, and sometimes takes on their names. The name of Yahweh was not consistently supplemented by the names of superseded gods whose attributes he absorbed. Thus Yahweh acquired all the attributes of Mot (Death), but he is never called this name. He could take on the name El safely, but sparingly. The title Adon was similarly compatible with his place as supreme deity. Other Canaanite appellatives, such as Baal ("master") and Milk ("king") were more dubious, and in due time the former was banned (see 2:18) and the latter used only as a common noun, not as one of God's names.

This conflict of ideas can still be glimpsed in v 14. Mot is a power from whose grasp people must be rescued. Sheol and Death are at base aspects of the same divine being and his place. Mot reigns in Sheol, and either or both may represent both god and realm; *myd* would seem to go with both terms. There is no trace of the myth in which Mot overcomes the god who claims supreme power, as in the case of Baal at Ugarit. Yahweh is the living god (Hos 2:1) who never dies (Hab 1:12). Plague and pestilence are his servants (Hab 3:5), not in Mot's retinue. Now, in fact, the death of Death is brought about by *Deber* and *Qeṭeb,* instruments of Yahweh.

14a. *ransomed . . . redeemed.* This positive assertion is the answer to the death threatened in v 13. Both Kuhnigk (1974:152) and Wolff (1974:221) read v 14a as interrogative. Compare, rather, the relationship of the resurrection passage in Hos 6:1–3 to its context (preceding and following). For the language of redemption, see Exodus 15 and Psalm 78 (vv 35,42). Yahweh's role as Redeemer arises from a kin relationship and the duty of kinsfolk is to rescue. The figure of ransom is not developed in the detail of a payment made to a captor (or slave owner) for the release of a relative. The emphasis of v 14 is on the destruction of death by force.

14b. *Where are.* The form *'ĕhî* is difficult. It can be taken as (1) an interrogative, reading *'ayyēh* for MT; (2) a *Qal* verb form, with the later Greek versions and the Vulgate (cf. Wolff 1974:221) ("I am your plagues"); (3) a *Hip'il* verb form ("I bring about your plagues"); (4) a proper name, a variant of Yahweh, as elsewhere in Hosea ("Ehî/Ehyeh is your plagues"); (5) an exclamatory particle ("Alas for your plagues!"), in which case v 14b would be an expansion of v 14a, a listing of the dangers from which God delivers his people. The third possibility is morphologically unlikely; the first and fifth can hardly be distinguished from each other. The fourth can be set aside because the form does not occur in clear contexts. The choice among the alternatives is hard to make. The allusions in I Cor 15:55 and Rev 6:8 are of little help.

your. Both the suffixes can also be read as emphatic *k*'s (Andersen 1969b) within construct chains: "the plagues of Death," "the destruction of Sheol."

plagues . . . ravages. Deber and *qeṭeb* occur in parallel in Ps 91:6, and the association with demons is palpable in the context. *Qeṭeb* is parallel to *rešep* in Deut 32:24, and *rešep* and *deber* are parallel in Hab 3:5. *Deber* is one of the traditional destroyers, and is the most widespread of the three terms. The vocalization here points to *Qōṭeb*, a collective in parallel with the plural "plagues." This language is thus somewhat removed from the demonology of the singular forms.

Qeṭeb does not occur often enough for its denotation to be determined. The attribute *mĕrîrî* in Deut 32:24 is found again only in Sir 11:4. It seems to be related to *mĕrîrût* (Ezek 21:11), with connotations of bitterness. One of Yahweh's destroyers in Isa 28:2 is *śaʿar qāṭeb,* "a storm of stings." Perhaps wind-borne biting insects (mosquitoes) are meant. Kuhnigk (1974:152–153) in rendering *dbr* as "goads," and Wolff (1974:221) with "thorns" and "stings" underestimate the numinous realm.

The cause of sorrow. Nōḥam is a hapax legomenon. The meaning of the last line of v 14 and its connection with the rest of the discourse are unclear. *Nōḥam* probably denotes the grief of repentance, or its source. To be hidden from the face of God is to be excluded from his presence and favor (Gen 4:14). Why should God banish regret, unless it is the eschatological abolition of all sorrow promised in Isa 25:8, a hope of joy that will reach a crescendo in Hosea 14? But the line may describe the suppression of God's own compassion (cf. 11:8) in a severe mood harmonious with v 11 or v 15. The *Nipʿal* verb may be reflexive and *nḥm* some sort of agent: "The one who repented concealed himself from my eyes." Cf. the Genesis accounts of Adam and Cain.

15. This verse can be construed as seven short lines. The devastating effect of the east wind is described in four lines of poetry. A connection between v 15a and v 15bB might be suspected because of the reiterated *hûʾ*. Cf. v 13 as well.

15a. *wild.* The traditional interpretation "fruitful" (*KJV*) supposes a misspelling of the root *pry.* Ephraim has been called *pereʾ*, "ass," in Hos 8:9, with a play on the sound of the name, and the root here is *prʾ*, "to be wild," an elative *Hipʿil* denominative of *pereʾ*. In the patriarchal traditions this notion refers to Ishmael (Gen 16:12), or to Joseph (Gen 49:22); here it is linked to a descendant group.

among his brothers. MT reads "a son of brothers." LXX reads "between brothers." *Bn* would be the correct spelling for the preposition "between" in northern orthography. The emendation of '*hym* to a form of *'hw,* "reed,'" is unnecessary (Wolff 1974:222).

15b. *The east wind.* The line describes the terrible rising of sirocco, the east wind. The parsing by Wolff (1974:228–229), "The East Wind will come as Yahweh's wind," is defensible but the result is bland.

will dry up. MT apparently, "he will be ashamed." We can read *ybš* with a Qumran text (Testuz 1955; Wolff 1974:222; Kuhnigk 1974:152–153), or more simply take *ybwš* as derived from a byform of the root *ybš,* rather than from *bwš,* "to be ashamed."

treasure. In Jeremiah the three common destroyers are plague, drought, and sword. Here, vv 15b and 14:1 complete the trio begun earlier in the chapter, and describe devastation wrought by war. The subject of "plunder" cannot be Ephraim (the victim). It could be Yahweh, indirectly; no human invader is identified here. When Jeremiah and Ezekiel have a fourth destroyer, it is wild animals; cf. vv 7–8.

attractive objects. The same phrase occurs in Nah 2:10; Jer 25:34; I Chron 32:27; 36:10; and Dan 11:8 in a variety of contexts which suggest the treasures of palace or temple looted by a conqueror. The use of the root *hmd* in 9:6 suggests that these valuable utensils are the images of silver and gold. This provides a connection with 13:2. In 9:6 the spoiler is Egypt; in 10:6 the image is taken as tribute to Assyria. Here there is no hint as to which of these is the plunderer; but note Assyria in 14:4.

14:1a. *guilty.* Cf. 13:1. Wolff's rendering (1974:222–223), "Samaria must bear her guilt," is tendentious. This last reference to Samaria completes the series in 7:1; 8:5,6; and 10:5,7. Kuhnigk's use (1974:153) of supposed *'šm,* "to be ruined" (cf. *šmm*), eliminates the 13:1 – 14:1 link.

rebelled. The verb *mry* has associations with the wilderness rebellions.

1b. *They will fall.* The kings; see 7:7. The pronouns change throughout this verse — "her God" (Samaria's); "their infants"; "his pregnant women." If, as usual, "his" refers to Ephraim, "their" refers to the whole nation. There is no indication why such a distinction should be made at this point.

His pregnant women. The subject is f pl, but the verb is m pl. The inconsistency is jarring, especially in that the passive here matches the passive *yrtšw,* "they will be smashed." Reading *ybq'w* as an active form would introduce a new subject. The temptation to correct the text should be resisted since MT is more likely correct (so also Wolff 1974:222) and we simply are not interpreting it correctly. Perhaps *'llyhm* is the controlling subject of both verbs: both infants and pregnant women will be smashed and ripped open, though this seems unlikely.

XXIII. RETROSPECT AND PROSPECT: RETURN, RENUNCIATION, AND RESTORATION
(14:2–10)

The people are implored to address Yahweh

14:2a   Return, O Israel, to Yahweh your God,

2b   although you have stumbled in your iniquity.

3a   Bring vows with you.
      Return to Yahweh.

3b   Say to him: "You will forgive all iniquity—
      accept all that is good.
      Let us pay in full the promises we have made.

4a   Assyria will not rescue us.
      We will not ride on horses.

4b   We will never again say 'Our god' to the work of our
      hands.
  —for the orphan is pitied by you."

Yahweh's reply is sketched out

5a   I will heal their apostasy,
      I will love them generously,

5b   for my anger has turned back from him.

6a   I will be like the dew for Israel.

6b   He will prosper like the crocus
      and will strike his roots like the Lebanon crocus.

7a   His suckers will spread everywhere.

7b   His Glory will be like the olive tree
      and his fragrance like the Lebanon olive.

8a   Once again those who live in his shadow will flourish.
      Like grain they will prosper.

8b   Like the vine is his remembrance
      and the wine of Lebanon.

9a   Ephraim, I won't deal with idols any more.
      I have answered and have watched him.

9b   I am like a luxuriant fir tree.
       Your fruit is obtained from me.

* *Coda*

10a Whoever is wise
       let him understand these things.
      Whoever is intelligent
       let him learn them.
10b The paths of Yahweh are upright.
      The righteous will walk in them.
      Sinners will stumble in them.

NOTES

14:2–10. This discourse is a fitting conclusion to the entire prophecy. Its note is entirely positive: the repentance of Israel is matched by the forgiveness of Yahweh. The restoration of the nation is described in extravagant terms. As a recapitulation, most of its vocabulary can be found in earlier parts of the prophecy. Similar techniques of composition are used, and help to explain many apparent inconcinnities.

As elsewhere, the nation is addressed as singular (v 2) or plural (v 3); it responds "we" (vv 3b–4).

The most prominent feature is a marvelous speech made by God (vv 5–9). It contains the kinds of alternations used elsewhere. First Yahweh speaks about his attitude to "them" (v 5a), then about "him" (vv 5b–7), and about "them" (v 8). Note the chiasm. Verse 9 opens and closes with a second-person address which encloses third-person usage.

The exhortation to "you" (pl) (v 3a) finds its response in vv 3b–4a. The opening exhortation to "you" (s) in v 2 finds its response in v 9. "Israel" in v 2 and "Ephraim" in v 9 (both singular passages) constitute an important inclusion. This leaves the referent of the plural passages to be identified. Unless this variation between singular and plural is immaterial, which is unlikely, usage in other parts of the prophecy suggests that plural passages refer to the nation as a whole — Israel and Ephraim or Judah together.

Hosea 14 is thus an elaborate dialogue between Yahweh and Israel. The *verbum dicendi* is not used, except in v 3b, but the identity of the speakers is seldom in doubt. Here, as elsewhere, it is impossible to separate the prophet from his God and vv 2–4 may be an exhortation by Hosea or one he attributes to Yahweh. Verse 9 is difficult in this regard. We prefer to take it as a continuation of Yahweh's speech, but it is possible to regard it as alternating dialogue. The opening of the verse would be address to God by Ephraim. The nation would be saying, "What have I to do with idols any more?" and the first word would identify the speaker. Like "Israel" in v 2, a name, standing alone at such a point, would normally be vocative.' A careful study of the biblical practice of reporting dialogue without identifying the *dramatis personae* or using verbs of speaking has been made by Gordis (1971:104–159). He has identified an example similar to Hos 14:9 in Jer 50:7, where the word "Yahweh" at the end of the verse fits neither rhythm nor sense, and has accordingly been excised by LXX and some critics. Gordis (1971:115) links it to Jer 50:8 as *dramatis persona* of the ensuing speech; as such it could be a gloss. That *'ănî* has an introductory function (= "I say") in Qoh 8:2 is commonly recognized, and the same could be true in v 9aB here, since the pronoun is redundant with a finite verb.

It may be that the whole discourse is uttered by God. He issues a twofold invitation (vv 2–3a), and prescribes the speeches to be made in response (vv 3b–4). Finally he predicts what he will say in reply (vv 5–9).

The invitations to "you" (s) and "you" (pl) and the responses "we" (Israel) and "I" (Yahweh) are arranged chiastically, with the speech of promise between the last two. This antiphonal chorus, with its eschatological setting, reminds us of 2:23–25. The verb *'ānâ* is used in both places. The reference to grain, (olive) oil, and wine in vv 7–8 matches the participation of these crops in the eschatological chorus of c 2. There all the parties have something to say, as new relationships are declared.

This discourse has not been developed far in the direction of poetry. Verse 4a is a bicolon. Otherwise the best art is reserved for the rhapsody in vv 5–8. The discourse is all of a piece, and is not easily broken into constituent passages. The lines from v 6b to v 7 have a certain symmetry, with two bicola of similar structure, vv 6b and 7b, around the central line, v 7a. The most striking thing about this poem of promise is its use of similes. The multiplication of similes is characteristic of Hosea; they are numerous, and often come in clusters. Here there are eight similes in ten lines (vv 6–8): the dew, the crocus, Lebanon, the olive, Lebanon, grain, the vine, the wine of Lebanon. The second and sixth of these use the verb *prḥ*. To this list should be added "like a fir tree," in v 9b. Lebanon enters into these comparisons three times. Although chiefly renowned for its cedars, the comparisons here seem to be restricted to agricultural produce. We have the crocus of Lebanon, the olive of Lebanon, and the wine of Lebanon. These are also a few of the links between c 14 and the Song of Songs, treated by Wolff (1974:234) and by Pope (1977). The impression is given that Lebanon is fabulous, an eschatological paradise (Wolff 1974:236).

14:2a. *Return*. Repentance, of which return from political exile is a symbol, is meant; *šwb* is a common word in Hosea. The command in the singular to the nation is restricted to v 2, since it is unlikely that "accept all that is good" in v 3b is another such. *Šûbâ* in v 2a parallels *šûbû* in v 3a. Different prepositions are used. For *'ad* see Amos 4:6,8,9,10,11; Isa 9:12. On repentance, see the NOTE on 11:8.

3b. *Say*. The third of three imperative verbs.

forgive. The final answer to God's opening statement that never again would he forgive them; see the NOTE on 1:6.

all iniquity. A parade example of a discontinuous construct chain. Wolff (1974:231), on the supposed basis of LXX, emends *kl* to *bl,* but the result is unconvincing. Others (e.g. Harper, p. 411) interpret *kl* adverbially, but it belongs with the noun *'wn*. MT, properly understood, has the correct reading. This prayer is completed by the otherwise isolated statement at the end of v 4b — "the orphan is pitied by you" — so that this speech is enclosed by an appeal to God's mercy. The prayer has seven lines, three positive, three negative, and the conclusion.

accept. This is another command embedded in the prayer. In 8:3 Yahweh is called "Good," and in 3:5 the people return to Yahweh's "goodness." Those confessing sin here ask God to accept their goodness, specifically their good words (*dbrym*), as in v 3a (similarly Wolff 1974:231). As a parallel to the petition, "Forgive all sin," *qaḥ ṭôb* could be taken as "Accept (us), O Good One," with Kuhnigk (1974:154–155).

Let us pay. The cohortative shows that this is the consequence of acceptance, not the grounds of acceptance.

promises. MT reads *prym,* "steers." LXX renders "fruit," as if reading *pry*. There is no need to delete the *mem* of MT; it is an unassailable example of the enclitic particle, as Wolff (1974:231) and Kuhnigk (1974:154–156) allow; the latter also allows for a bovine pun in a bit of bet-hedging. The writer to the Hebrews identified the "fruit of the lips" as "the sacrifice of praise to God" (13:15; Buchanan 1972:236–237). There is nothing in this that a prophet would have disagreed with; but Hosea also intended a return to the proper offerings of real fruit. Fruit of lips must mean the vows and promises made, including not only offerings but commitment in worship and service.

4a. *Assyria*. As throughout the prophecy political and religious declension go hand in hand, so in repentance alien gods and alien overlords are renounced.

rescue. The same verb as in 13:10; cf. 1:7.

horses. This seems to refer to battle and alliances, but the situation is not clear.

4b. *Our god*. Cf. Deut 6:4. Contrast 13:2.

pitied. The same root as in 1:6. This prayer has *six* vocabulary connections with the second birth oracle — *again, forgive, pity, rescue, horses,
our God*. This is impressive evidence that c 14 is not a makeshift addition
by a later scribe (so Wolff 1974:231–232); it is woven into the fabric of
the whole work. The line also links with v 3: Yahweh will forgive because
he is kind to orphans. This must be an allusion to the fatherlessness of Israel and Ephraim. The "you" (s) passages form an envelope around "we"
passages.

5–8. All the horror of the preceding judgments is canceled by the ardor
of this promise. It is Yahweh's last word, and it is a word of life. The criticism that concludes that everything optimistic in Hosea is a scribal addition reasons in a circle; there is no proof that Hosea was a prophet of un-
mitigated doom. On the contrary, his own passion revealed a power in love
which many waters could not quench. It could not be less so with God,
whose final word is "I will love them generously" (v 5a).

5a. *heal*. Cf. the hope expressed in 6:1.

them. The two lines in v 5a has "their" and "them"; the next has "him,"
Israel.

love. As in 3:1.

5b. *anger*. See 11:9; 13:11. There is no explanation of how God's anger
is appeased, except that his ultimate nature is compassion. Yet Hosea's
apparent illustration, pity for the orphan, does not reach the extreme of
pardon for the guilty sinner; it must be taken literally: Ephraim/Israel is
the orphan.

6a. *dew*. In 6:4; 13:3 this provides an illustration of Ephraim's ephemeral loyalty; here an illustration of Yahweh's loyalty, benign and healing.
Cf. Deut 32:2.

6b. *strike*. Hosea has several times used forms morphologically jussive
as indicatives, including this word in 6:1, where it is past. Here the verb
has no connotations of injury.

Lebanon. Wolff (1974:232, 235) silently expands the first occurrences
of Lebanon to refer to the forest, which may be correct but requires some
notice. We prefer to think of the crocus and olive tree of Lebanon, rather
than the cedars.

7a. *suckers*. *Ynqt* is a general term for runners or tendrils, applicable to
vine (Ps 80:12) or cedar (Ezek 17:22). The language applies to a tree,
not the crocus. The image is not a new one for Israel, although the elaborate treatment in Psalm 80 and Ezekiel 17 is later.

Since the word *ynqt* is feminine, the subject (primary) of verb *ylkw*
should be *šršyw*. Perhaps Lebanon throughout stands for "cedars" with
their shade and roots, and the like.

spread. Literally "walk." For another verb of motion, *yṣ'*, see Job 8:16. This resuscitation is rather like the figure developed in Job 14:7–9 (Andersen 1976a:171–172).

7b. *fragrance.* See Cant 4:11 (Pope 1977:486–487). The word here may form a combination with *hwd,* "his splendid fragrance."

8a. *Once again.* Literally, "they (re)turn." The verb *šwb* here is an auxiliary with *yĕḥayyû* and not a direct description of a return from exile. Cf. Wolff (1974:232). The emendation to "my shadow" simplifies the dialogue but again without due warrant; cf. Lam 4:20 on the shadow-figure.

Like grain. The preposition *k* in the following line does double duty. Those who dwell in the shade of the great tree, presumably God or at God's behest, will again prosper like grain, a sign of settlement and renewed prosperity.

8b. *vine.* This may belong with Lebanon in the next line, in the implied phrase *gepen hayyayin* (Num 6:4; Judg 13:14).

9. This verse is replete with echoes of the preceding material which it recapitulates and climaxes.

9a. *idols.* The choice of the noun is significant. This is the final act of renouncing Baal. We agree with both Wolff (1974:233) and Kuhnigk (1974:156) in crediting this renunciation to Yahweh; Kuhnigk takes *ly* as a third-person form and Wolff emends to *lw* with LXX. On the idiom see Wolff (1974:237) and Brown (1966:99).

any more. '*Ôd* here matches '*ôd* in v 4.

have watched. Kuhnigk's rendering (1974:156–157), "I have appeared to him," is attractive, but the supposed Ugaritic cognate involved and the action it describes are both difficult.

9b. *luxuriant.* The emphasis is not on the color, but on the abundance of foliage. Yahweh is like a leafy tree under which the returnees find shade and shelter; or there may be a reference to a tree of life (Wolff 1974:251).

Your fruit. The fruit to be offered in worship is, in fact, God's gift. Part of the intention of worship is to acknowledge this fact. This is what Israel had forgotten (2:10). "Fruit" thus occurs in vv 3 and 9.

10. The final verse is evidently a piece of advice to the reader. It seems to imply that the prophecy has already become an object of study and a guide to life. Although somewhat intellectual (it emphasizes wisdom, understanding, and knowledge), it is in keeping with the concerns of the prophecy. The author, whether Hosea or another, characterizes idolatry as ignorance and folly (4:6,14). His concern is for knowledge of God (4:1,6; 6:3). Most recently Israel has been called an unwise son (13:13). The distinctively Hosean vocabulary includes *kšl* and *pš'* (Wolff 1974:239). The overall pattern of the forms of *kšl* is noteworthy.

4:5	*kāšaltā*	A
	kāšal	B
5:5	*yikkāšĕlû*	C
	kāšal	B
14:2	*kāšaltā*	A
14:10	*yikkāšĕlû*	C

The overall alternation in cc 4 and 5 gives the patterns AB and CB, which are bridged by the elimination of the common term in c 14.

The contrast between wisdom and folly, which correspond to righteousness and wickedness, is a Wisdom theme (Psalm 1). The good person walks "in the ways of the Lord," an activity essentially ethical.

Verse 10 is a complete poem in itself, and is neatly made. The opening injunctions (in which *mî* does double duty) are characteristic of Wisdom discourse. The concluding tricolon is linked by the three plural nouns — "upright," "righteous," "Sinners." The first two lines have two positive words. The last two have "in them." The matching verbs contrast.

If we take "upright" and "righteous" as synonyms, we leave the prevailing interpretation of v 10bA as a verbless clause, and suppose that its grammar is the same as the following parallel; in the phrases "in them" // "(in) the Lord's paths," the preposition would do retroactive double duty. The verb "walk" would be understood as operating equally in both lines. We would translate then "The upright walk in the paths of Yahweh."

APPENDIX: HOSEA'S REFERENCES
TO PAGAN GODS

The pagan practices attacked by Hosea are not easy to identify. The components of sexual license and magic were present, along with idolatry; human sacrifice, primarily and perhaps exclusively that of infants, was also involved. Only one god is named — Baal. But many other words are used to refer, with degrees of transparency, to rival gods. Some of these are feminine, suggesting that at least one goddess is also present. The most obvious candidate is Baal's (or Yahweh's) consort. Our ignorance of Canaanite religion during this period, from its own sources, prevents us from naming this goddess. We cannot confidently bring in evidence from other times and places, such as Late Bronze Age Ugarit, or even contemporary adjacent Phoenicia.

The number of terms used by Hosea to designate pagan deities is remarkable. We cannot insist that they all denote specific gods. In fact, we cannot prove that any except the generally recognized ones do, but these establish the usage, and encourage the search for more. Some of the suspected titles listed are epithets rather than names; it is difficult to distinguish these.

1. *Words already recognized as designating pagan gods*
   habba'al (2:10, [18])
Ba'al in 13:1 is probably the place Baal Peor (9:10). The plural form, habbĕ'ālîm (2:15,19; 11:2) could refer to the multiplicity of Baals, but more likely it imitates 'ĕlōhîm. The several plural nouns in the following inventory should be interpreted in the same way, and reflect prevailing usage.

2. *Technical words used specifically for idols*
   massēkâ (13:2) — a cast image
   'ăṣabbîm (4:17; 8:4; 13:2) — idols
   pĕsīlîm (11:2) — images
Cf. the familiar Deuteronomic 'ĕlōhîm 'ăḥērîm, "other gods" (3:1).

3. *Concrete nouns in the plural, which probably designate "Baal"*
   'ăhābîm (8:9) — lovers
   mĕ'ahăbîm (2:7,9,12,14,15) — lovers
   'ăgālîm (13:2) — calves
   šĕwārîm (12:12) — bulls

Some of these may refer to humans, and a double reference may also be intended. The unusual *'ohŏbām* (9:10) may refer to the god as the "lover."

4. *Abstract nouns used to refer to the god(s)*
    'āwen (12:12) — idols
    'ônîm (9:4) — idols
    bōšet (9:10) — shame
    ṣāw (5:11) — filth
    qālôn (4:7; cf. 4:18) — ignominy
    šāw' (12:12) — false gods
    šeqer (7:1) — idol
Note also *bĕnê 'alwâ*, "wicked ones" (10:9).

5. *Concrete terms for the god as a material object*
    ma'ăśēh ḥărāšîm (13:2; cf. 8:6) — the work of artisans
    ma'ăśēh yādênû (14:4) — the work of our hands
    maqqēl (4:12) — staff

6. *Parodies of traditional epithets*
    kābôd (9:11; 10:5) — glory
    lō' 'āl (7:16) — no-god (*'āl* is Yahweh in 11:7)
    ṣôr (9:13) — rival (cf. *ṣûr*, "Rock"; esp. in Deut 32:31)
    qĕdôšîm (12:1) — holy gods (Yahweh is *qādôš* in 11:9)

7. *Other titles*
    hōrēg (9:13) — the slayer
    rûaḥ zĕnûnîm (4:12; 5:4) — a promiscuous spirit

8. *Titles of the god who rules in Samaria*
    'ēgel šōmĕrôn (8:5,6) — the calf of Samaria
    šĕkan šōmĕrôn (10:5) — the resident of Samaria
    šōmĕrôn malkāh (10:7) — the king of Samaria
In the *'ēgel* passages it is clear that the title refers to an idol.

9. *Feminine nouns used as titles of the goddess*
    ḥṭ't (10:8), cf. *ḥṭ'* — sin
    'eglôt bêt 'āwen (10:5), cf. *'ēgel* — the heifers of Beth Awen
    'ēṣ (4:12), cf. *maqqēl* — wood
    'ēṣâ (10:6) — image
    qālôn (4:18) — ignominy
    rûaḥ 'wth (4:19) — her lustful spirit
Most of these have masculine counterparts, and some look like artificial feminine derivatives. On the plural formations, see the comment under No. 1.

10. It is less certain that words like *zimmâ*, "enormities" (6:9), and *ša'ărûrîyâ*, "disgusting things" (6:10), refer to deities.

INDEX OF AUTHORS
Including Modern Translations

INDEX OF SUBJECTS

INDEX OF WORDS

1. Hebrew

' unvocalized

'wn 442
'ḥr 170, 307, 406–7
'ḥryk 407
'l 156, 359, 477, 608
'ly 336–37, 554
'm 371
'sr 470, 566
'ph 451
'py 451, 455
'šr 465, 469, 607
'šrth 49, 326

' vocalized

'ābal 339, 555, 556
'abnê 282
'ādām 438, 439, 546
'ădāmâ 286, 438, 543
'admâ 588
'ădōn 597
'ahab 506
'ăhābîm 135, 541, 649
'āhēb 135, 157, 169, 295–96, 323, 375,
    379, 505, 510, 523, 541, 545, 567, 577,
    581, 617
'āwen 372, 526, 607, 618, 650
'āwôn 637–638
'awwâ 565
'awwātāh 376
'āḥaz 607
'aḥar 303
'aḥărît 308
'aṭ 582
'ay 636
'ayyēh 636, 639
'ak 345, 422, 617, 619
'ākal 362, 387, 395, 467, 510, 582–83,
    586, 635
'ākēn 395
'al 322, 522, 529
'almĕnût ḥayyût 304
'āmal 340
'āmar 115, 135, 137, 155–56, 204, 210,
    212, 227, 230, 239, 253, 488, 559
——— 'l 187
——— l 187
'ănaḥnû 417, 553, 557, 646
'ănî/'ānokî 122, 134, 197, 198–99, 228,
    241–42, 245, 271, 278, 282–83, 288, 290,
    304, 305, 319, 348, 382, 390, 413, 429,

437, 472, 491, 516, 578, 615, 617, 644,
    647
'anšê (had)dāmîm 338
'āsap 530
'ap 408, 494
'ăraḥēm 133
'ărām 438
'āraś 133, 156, 280, 282–83, 299
'ărî 415
'armĕnôt 511
'aryeh 414–15
'āšam 391, 416, 552, 626–27, 641
'ăšēr 60–66, 132, 203, 240–41, 252, 254,
    469, 487, 544, 617, 636
'ăššûr 463
'attâ/'at 134, 205, 237, 288, 294, 319,
    320, 322, 348, 370, 483, 516, 565–66,
    581, 615, 646
'attem 134, 197, 198–99, 212–13, 516
'eben 366
'ĕhab 133
'ĕhî 635, 639
'ehyeh 197, 198, 639
'eḥād/'aḥat 208, 587
'êk 576, 588
'el 151, 219, 304, 305, 308, 473, 477,
    582, 613, 615
'el-'al 477
'ēl 172–73, 572, 602, 603, 611, 612, 613
'ēl zār 397, 509
'ēl ḥay 205
'ēl nēkār 509
'ēl 'al 587
'ēl 'elyôn 587
'ēlîm 603
'ĕlōhāy 138, 490
'ĕlōhê hannēkār 298
'ĕlōhîm 230, 257, 258, 324, 378, 397,
    527, 541, 612, 631, 649
'ĕlōhîm 'ăḥērîm 397, 649
'ĕlōhîm ḥayyîm 205–6
'ēm 228
'ĕmet 336, 602
'ĕmûnîm 602
'ên 190, 305, 553
'ēpôd 306
'eprayim 171, 505
'ereṣ 124, 209, 226, 282, 286, 287, 290,
    335, 339, 425, 524, 584
'ereṣ 'ăḥuzzat yhwh 525
'ereṣ yhwh 525–26
'ēšet bĕrît 159
'ēšet zĕnûnîm 116, 159, 162, 325
'ēšet-ḥayil 229

INDEX OF SCRIPTURAL REFERENCES

* Sections of the commentary and chapters of the book appear in bold face.

KEY TO THE TEXT

Chapter	Verses	Section	Chapter	Verses	Section
1	1–9	I	7	3–7	XII
2	1–3	I	7	8–16	XIII
2	4–25	II	8	1–8	XIV
3	1–5	III	8	9–14	XV
4	1–3	IV	9	1–9	XVI
4	4–19	V	9	10–17	XVII
5	1–7	VI	10	1–8	XVIII
5	8–11	VII	10	9–15	XIX
5	12–15	VIII	11	1–11	XX
6	1–3	IX	12	1–15	XXI
6	4–6	X	13	1–15	XXII
6	7–11	XI	14	1	XXII
7	1–2	XI	14	2–10	XXIII